Daniel R. Fesenmaier
Stefan Klein
Dimitrios Buhalis (eds.)

Information and
Communication Technologies
in Tourism 2000

Proceedings of the International Conference
in Barcelona, Spain,
2000

Springer-Verlag Wien GmbH

Dr. Daniel R. Fesenmaier
Tourism Research Laboratory
University of Illinois at Urbana-Champaign, U.S.A.

Dr. Stefan Klein
Institut für Wirtschaftsinformatik
Westfälische Wilhelms-Universität Münster
Münster, Federal Republic of Germany

Dr. Dimitrios Buhalis
Department of Tourism
University of Westminster, London, U.K.

Graphic design: Ecke Bonk
Printed on acid-free and chlorine-free bleached paper
SPIN 10760694

With 101 Figures

ISBN 978-3-211-83483-1   ISBN 978-3-7091-6291-0 (eBook)
DOI 10.1007/978-3-7091-6291-0

Preface

ENTER has now met for six years, providing a valuable forum for researchers and practitioners to discuss and debate their ideas and perspectives regarding the nature and role of tourism and information technology in global society. Over the years, the nature and rate of change in the tourism industry has been overwhelming. The internet and related technologies are now dominant agents of change and have created a "new economy" which requires new processes and strategies to replace those developed for the "old economy". The theme of ENTER 2000, "Keeping Pace with Change – New Frontiers for IT and Tourism", captures the challenges that we face at the beginning of the new millennium. The papers included in this volume illustrate the incredible growth in research and development in this area and reflect its youth, vitality and at the same time, maturation. Perhaps most important, these papers document how this new technology has changed and, in turn, how the industry has responded. The series of proceedings of which this volume is a part is creating a unique body of knowledge about the intertwined emergence of tourism and technology.

There are, perhaps, three overriding themes of this congress.

First is the focus on the tourist. Professor Stock's keynote address "Intelligent Interfaces for the Tourist" is a good representative of a series of papers discussing how information systems, electronic markets, and user interfaces have been or can be developed to enhance the tourist experience.

A second theme focuses attention on small to medium tourism enterprises (SMTEs). In this time of change when emerging information technology offers empowerment and poses threats, SMTEs could/should be the vanguard in the evolution of the industry. However, as discussed in these papers there are many factors affecting the ability of SMTEs to respond to these forces of change. Today, it appears they are at the crossroads and a number of authors propose strategies that enable SMTEs to respond positively to these challenges.

A third focus is on evaluating and benchmarking IT and the change it has created. While some papers provide a solid foundation for understanding IT-related research, other papers elaborate on this theme and offer exciting new perspectives that should provide the foundation for building systems (both human and electronic) that facilitate growth in this sector of the tourism industry.

We would like to thank all the authors for contributing to the success of ENTER 2000. The forty-eight papers represent new, innovative and vital areas of inquiry in IT and tourism. They also enable us to look to the very exciting future of this emerging field. We also want to thank the Scientific Track Committee for their help in organizing and reviewing the papers. Last, we want to thank the organizers of ENTER and IFITT for this opportunity to once again come together to share our experiences and insights with the goal of contributing to the knowledge economy.

Daniel Fesenmaier, Dimitrios Buhalis, and Stefan Klein

Contents

Index of Authors

Programme Committee

Seventh International Conference on
Information and Communication Technologies in Tourism,
Barcelona, Spain, April 26–28, 2000

Intelligent Interfaces For The Tourist

Oliviero Stock
ITC-IRST
38050 Povo, Trento, Italy
email: stock@itc.it
URL: http://www.itc.it/enITCirst/

1 Introduction

Artificial intelligence techniques can provide support in many areas relevant for tourism: e.g. support for the tourism resources decision maker, support for automatic negotiation or transaction management and so on [Werthner and Klein, 1999]. In this paper we shall concentrate on interfaces for the tourist.

Intelligent interfaces may open new scenarios for tourism and for helping in the fruition of *real* (not only virtual) cultural sites. The main prospect made possible by the adoption of these technologies is to move from the current mass-oriented approach to an approach oriented toward the individual. This has at least two facets: on the one side systems will have to take into account the specificity of the user with his own interests, idiosyncracies, and so on - and accordingly take action; on the other side the user will be the main agent in his exploration, he will take the initiative and exploit the high level of interactivity that will be available in intelligent interfaces.

In principle I would schematise the overall phases of the individual tourist activity in this way:
- exposure to promotion, idea and curiosity formation
- information access
- decisions and actions
- preparation for the visit
- visit
- after the visit

Access to online information and some systems for resource reservation and commercial transaction management for the tourist's side are the first level of service that current commercial technology is beginning to provide. I believe the main needs go much beyond this.

They start from providing information of the appropriate quality. The shortest resource for society in the next century will be people's time and attention. This will require a technology able to provide adequate instruments for the interaction with the individual, in order to reach an objective of information, persuasion or more in general of communication (in all sectors – cultural, educational, social – but also in product promotion or in documentation and explanation).

Information access will require true availability of information, possibly in different languages and formats and a high-level modality of interaction so that information can be accessed by content. Tools may help negotiating and performing the right decision so that actions can be taken: booking, performing commercial transactions. Only then the probably richest part of the interaction begins: the one that is really oriented toward the individual experience, the visit and its consequences. I believe the intelligent, language-based interfaces will contribute to the development a new level of tourism, especially in the case of cultural tourism.

2 Scenarios

Hypermedia systems for tourism (or for museum exploration) are rather common at present. They exploit multimedia and virtual reality technologies, but in general provide rather limited possibilities.

The principal weakness of these systems lies partly in the difficulty of making precise, complex requests in the information space and partly in the impossibility to pursue specific aims through communication with the system. Interest for a destination and its culture grows slowly and autonomously and imposing more data or experiences than a person is prepared to cope with has no positive effect at all. It becomes essential to provide the user with the possibility to "drive the game" and to explore culture according to his interest.

2.1 Before the visit: exploring the information space

A cultural visit often begins before the departure for the chosen destination. The visitor might have read an article about an exhibition, might have read books and touristic guides about a town, might have seen some videos or sought the advice of friends or experts. All these activities have nowadays a technological counterpart in the digital libraries made accessible through Internet, in the videos on-demand, in the newsgroups in the Web etc... Nevertheless the advantages offered by these technologies are often made useless by the vastity of the information space. The need of the user is to have different integrated ways for access to information: goal-oriented and exploration-oriented interactions.

2.2 During the visit: physical space and augmented reality

The experience of a visit to a museum or an art city typically consists of moving in a physical space and acquiring information on the objects one has met. Modern technologies, such as palmtop computers and wireless networks can help innovate substantially the way information is made accessible to the visitor: right at the moment it is more necessary, presented through the most adequate channel (e.g. audio or video) and in the form that better suits the user's interests and knowledge. The visitor, equipped with a wearable computer supplied with localisation devices (e.g. infrared sensors in a closed environment, GPS in the open) moves freely in a museum or in a city. In this new scenario the computer allows integration between real physical space and information space: the visitor is at the centre of the physical/virtual space exploration and his movements and interactions provide an indication to the system for dynamically producing appropriate and personalised presentations. The system exploits and increases the model of the visitor's knowledge and interests it had begun to build during the user's interaction before the visit.

2.3 After the visit: taking home what one has seen

Most often tourists like to buy catalogues, videocassettes or cd-rom's about what they have seen. An advanced use of the new technologies can produce a new type of personalised catalogues built before and during the visit and completed at home, connected to the multimedia Internet sites of the museum or of the town. In addition, the visitor model built during the visit will allow the user to interact and go deeper into what he has been exposed to, once he is back home. The home system knows what he saw and what is interesting for him, it will keep him "connected" in order to envisage new developments, including the "relationship" with the physical place he visited.

In addition to this the whole sector of "community" opens: community of visitors, relationship between visitors and residents in view of a cultural exchange and of a deeper awareness in the cultural experience. Technology can play a completely innovative role in this.

3 Some technology needs

With the rapid advancement of the web world, what was evident to some specialists is becoming obvious: some natural language processing capabilities are essential, if we want to deal seriously with information for all people. Most information is in linguistic form and we need tools for accessing it, systems that filter only what is interesting for the specific user, extract the relevant essential information, provide a translation in our language and so on. But language processing is essential also for communicating with a system and for receiving personalised information from the system. Language processing (especially dialogue processing) is a very difficult task and complete language understanding is not a realistic task, but the good news is that in interacting with a computer some combination of language and other communicative resources may be exploited.

3.1 Multimodal dialogue

Often the user does not know what information is available, or may not have a clear idea of what he is searching for. The need arises for systems that integrate a mediated information access paradigm and a navigational paradigm, where the user may use different modalities to explore the material in a way possible only with a computer. All this is becoming apparent with the current diffusion of the web and its various browsers. There is a necessity for systems that integrate the capability of accessing information through goal-oriented dialogue (based on natural language), and through browsing, in a seamless fashion. Systems will have to integrate graphics-based interaction modalities with the natural language-based one.

A key element of flexibility lies in the possibility of a system of having a model of the user, including his interests, idiosyncrasies and the dynamic aspects inferred during the interaction. This is instrumental for making sense of partial or not detailed requests (or other acts) by the user, and for determining the system's actions.

Multimodality means also entertaining a dialogue with one system and the same information source through different available media, so that the characteristics of the user interaction are affected: if you interact through a phone, perhaps with a small additional display, things are different from when you interact with a computer through keyboard, mouse and a large screen. You perceive, memorise and act differently.

Multimodal dialogue will be an important element for the development of all edutainment systems – systems that combine entertainment and education.

3.2 Flexible information presentation

Presentation of information constitutes an area that will be increasingly important. There are many reasons for this:

a) the growth of information quantity has to be matched by appropriate ways of presenting it at the appropriate level of detail and with the best chances of conveying the message to the audience;

b) attention is becoming precious goods, therefore presentations must match the challenge;

c) cultural and linguistic specificities need to be addressed; market globalisation has product localisation on the other side of the coin;

d) tailoring information to the individual is often desirable and it is equally desirable that the form of the presentation is adapted to the specific user characteristics (competence, previous information etc.);

e) integration of various media, including language, graphics and video opens new perspectives.

If information is to be presented in a flexible way, it is essential that an automatic processor does the job. In particular, for text presentations, a natural language generation system is a fundamental resource. A Natural Language Generation system is a computational tool that automatically "builds" a text (a sequence of sentences) starting from abstract (non-linguistic) specifications.

Given the internal representation of the knowledge sources, the system decides what is the relevant information to be communicated, it organizes a coherent text structure and produces the most appropriate linguistic expressions to convey the message.

Multilingual generation is also a possibility: in principle this is not more complex than monolingual generation (of course it needs language resources such as lexica and grammars for all the involved languages).

Multimodal flexible presentations exploit synergistically the advantages that different media can provide in conveying the message to the user. In this case all processors must start from an internal representation and the problems include media allocation and media coordination.

4 Prototypes

Any intelligent multimedia and multimodal system [Maybury 1993; Maybury 1997] requires components that exploits the context to make presentation decisions (media selection, co-ordination, allocation, etc.) or to interpret multi-channel input [Maybury and Wahlster, 1998]. In particular, given information that needs to be displayed to the user, a multimedia co-ordinator automatically builds a coherent and co-ordinated presentation using a combination of available media. [see for instance Wahlster et al, 1992].

Following [Arens, 1993] any complex multimedia co-ordinator needs to be built around a collection of models: a model of virtual devices, a model of the characteristics of information to be displayed, a model of the discourse and the communicative context, a model of the interaction participants' beliefs, goals, attitudes, capabilities and interests. Input and output processes interact with the dialogue manager that maintains the discourse structure and ensures a coherent interaction between the participants.

Along these lines at IRST we have worked for several years at developing and integrating advanced research concepts in some prototypical intelligent multimedia systems.

4.1 AlFresco

Let me now summarise a system called AlFresco. AlFresco [Stock, 1991] is an interactive, natural-language centred system for a user interested in Fourteenth Century Italian frescoes. It has the aim of providing information, and also of promoting other masterpieces that may attract the user. Hypermedia is integrated both in input and output. The user can interact with the system by typing sentences, navigating in an underlying hypertext, and using the touch screen in a coherent multimodal discourse setting. In output, images and generated text offer entry points for further hypertextual exploration. The result is that the user communicates linguistically and by manipulating various entities, images, and text itself. The system builds a simple model of the user as the dialogue proceeds and uses it for output decisions, while allowing the user to browse around freely.

A higher-level, pragmatic component decides how to react in the given dialogic situation, considering the type of utterance by the user, the context, the model of the user's interest, the things already shown or said to the user and so on. The dialogue may cause zooming into details or changing the focus of attention onto other frescoes.

We have proposed a level of multimodal acts representation [Stock *et al*, 1997] that, starting from communicative intentions, allows to process all acts and conditions for performing them in a uniform way.

Let us follow an example of an actual interaction with AlFresco. The user asks: "Speak to me about Ambrogio Lorenzetti" (see Figure 1). answers producing a generated text with buttons in a hypertextual card. A generated text with buttons can be seen as an implicit negotiation. The system proposes the responsibility to

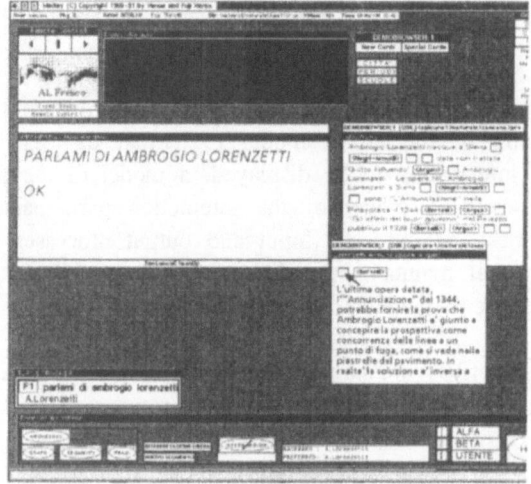

Fig. 1

the user, but the final decision is left to the user herself: she can choose whether to shift from a mediated to a navigational browsing or not. Let us suppose the user wants to see a comment by Argan (a famous art critic) about the "Annunciation" (a fresco by Lorenzetti) and she clicks on the <Argan> button. The user starts a hypertextual navigation.

Once the user has chosen to follow a hypertextual link she takes the responsibility of giving structure to information on her own. The system mantains awareness of the changes in the context of the communication: so the user is free to give back the responsibility to the system whenever she wants. In Fig. 2, the system displays Argan's comment about the "Annunciation". After having read it, the user may want to see the fresco and clicks on the first button of the card. The touchscreen now is displaying the "Annunciation" by Ambrogio Lorenzetti.

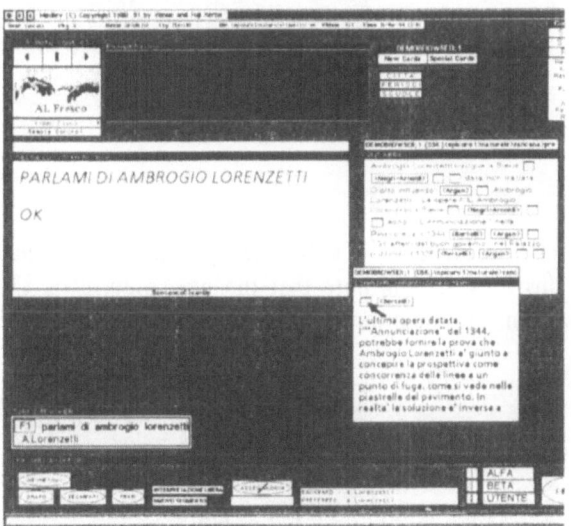

Fig. 2

A complex nonlinguistic exchange, starting with a clicking act on a hypertextual button has taken place, which links the subsequent linguistic question to the preceding one. In Fig. 3 the user switches from hypertextual navigation to an NL query and asks: "Who is this person?" touching a character of the fresco (on the touch-screen, not represented in this picture). The system answers 'Madonna'. By adopting NL the user is giving the responsibility back to the system. The system is aware that on the touch-screen the Annunciation is now shown, even if its displaying was not under its responsibility. Then the user comes back to the generated hypertext, claiming the responsibility for herself once again, and clicks a button to see "Gli Effetti del Buon Governo" (The Effects of Good

8

Government), another fresco painted by Lorenzetti. The latter fresco is now displayed on the touch-screen.

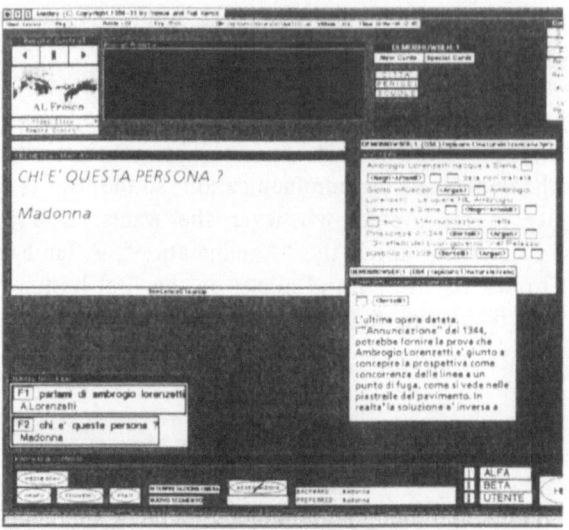

Fig. 3

Finally, the user comes back to a NL query and asks: "What is the town?". 'Siena' is the answer. Let us note that the new picture on the touchscreen is essential to give sense to the question (the Annunciation does not include a town).

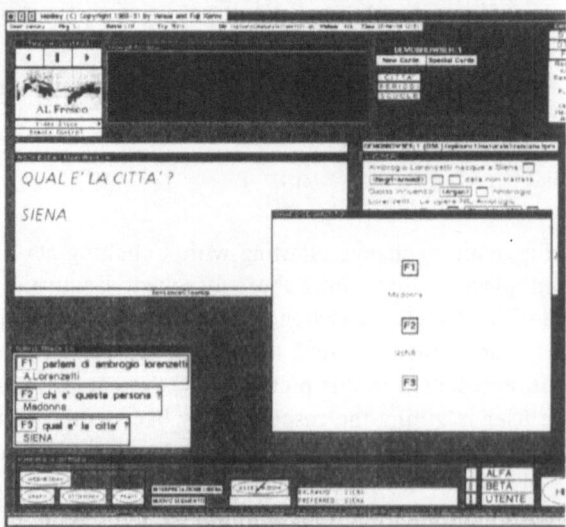

Fig. 4

The dialogue cohesion management module [Zancanaro *et al*, 1997] provides also a graphical feedback of the dialogue cohesion status to the user. This visual representation: (a) reassures the user at a glance on the system's interpretation (as such it takes the place of a paraphraser), and (b) allows co-operative recovery from discourse misconceptions by means of a series of "intuitive actions" when this interpretation is not the one the user meant.

In general a tighter integration of different modes of exploration, language-oriented and navigational, has been accomplished. I think this is a very fruitful concept that can lead to various applications. The study of the involved cognitive aspects is of great importance and lab experiments with implemented prototypes and simulated systems will make all of us understand better this kind of amplification of human communicative capabilities.

4.2 Presentations in the physical location

One further element for advancing in the direction of personalisation and context-sensitivity is offered by ubiquitous information access, made possible by hardware technologies such as portable devices and wireless networking. A museum is a privileged environment for introducing adaptive information with ubiquitous access. In fact, the experience of visiting a museum typically consists of moving in a physical space and acquiring information about the objects shown (and of course in becoming interested and moved by what is displayed!). In the new interaction scenario, the computer (a hand-held device including spoken output) allows the integration between the physical space (through a positioning system) and the related information space, yielding a new way of exploring cultural heritage. The individual visitor is at the centre of the physical-virtual space exploration and his movements and interactions provide input to the system to tailor appropriate presentations.

The approach presented here was developed inside a project at IRST called HyperAudio [Not *et al*, 1998]. The results are at the basis of the development of an even richer interaction scenario that is being explored jointly with other partners in HIPS, a European project of the Esprit I^3 program[1].
The problem of adapting content for information presentations in physical hypernavigation shares many features with the problem of producing adaptive and dynamic hypermedia for virtual museums [e.g. ILEX, Mellish *et al* 1997] or dynamic encyclopaedias [e.g. PEBA-II, Milosavljevic *et al*, 1996].

Content adaptation in a physical environment poses some problems that are related to the fact that the visitor is experiencing a "real" situation: the cognitive

---

[1] The[HIPS] consortium includes: University of Siena (Italy, coordinating partner), CB&J (France), GMD (Germany), IRST (Italy), SIETTE-Alcatel (Italy), SINTEF (Norway), University of Dublin and University of Edinburgh.

problems that may arise when a person is moving in a virtual information space, are different when the user is seeking concrete objects, moving in a real environment that provides stimuli, attention grasping and feedback. Information is presented in different situational contexts, determined mainly by: (i) user position and movements; (ii) the structure of the surrounding physical space (e.g., whether objects are close or not); (iii) whether other people are examining the same item or not; (iv) whether the user came alone or not.

HyperAudio (and HIPS) integrates the individual, dynamic modelling of the user with a general model of the environment, of the user's movements and of the discourse history to best tailor information presentations. Different forms of adaptation are introduced by the system, both in the information provided and in the further steps suggested. In general the approach points to a realistic and evolutionary adoption of generation techniques; at present it yields a rhetorically coherent dynamic combination of small existing fragments of speech.

The architecture abstracts away from specific implementation solutions. It can be implemented on a single mobile platform (as in HyperAudio) or with some modules running on a standing platform and communicating with the mobile computer via a wireless connection (this solution is investigated within the HIPS project).

When deciding what information to include in the presentation and the most suitable discourse structure, the system takes into account various knowledge sources about the user and the interaction. The user model is accessed to exploit: a) the user's interests (which are inferred from her behaviour), to include in the new message information that can stimulate the hearer's attention, possibly proposing information about other objects/sites strictly related to what the user is seeing, to increase curiosity and desire to explore; b) the user's background knowledge, in order to relate the new information presented to what she already knows (therefore reinforcing learning) and to decide whether additional clarification or exemplification of new concepts is required to help her understand. As the interaction proceeds, the system refines its assumptions about the user's interests and knowledge by observing the user's behaviour and by keeping track of the information she has been exposed to. Another knowledge source is the history of previous interaction. An important role in content selection is also played by discourse strategies that the system exploits to guarantee that topics are presented in a coherent order and the various discourse chunks are linked by rhetorical relations that reinforce the understanding of discourse flow. The system consistently limits the length of audio messages, deciding to realise part of the content as clickable links on the screen to avoid overwhelming the visitor with information.

The language style adopted for each single user is selected according to the user type. According to information contained in the current context of interaction (e.g. position in relation to displayed objects, to the more extended environment) and in the discourse history (e.g. the topic of the previous sentence or presentation), the system selects an appropriate linguistic realisation for referring expressions and spatial references. Other cohesion devices (like anaphora, conjunctions, lexical cohesion) are properly introduced to guarantee the fluency of the message and enhance understanding.

The system includes also a graphical interface that helps to orient the visitor and is useful for complementing linguistic instructions. Besides, clickable elements in the oral presentations appear on the screen.

Input provided by the user to the system can be both implicit, corresponding to movements in the physical space, and explicit, corresponding to interaction with the palmtop screen. Input is first analysed to decide the most suitable type of processing required (e.g., plan a new presentation, stop the current presentation, plan a navigation support message, etc.) and for refining the user model.

An overall presentation is then planned that integrates (where appropriate): object descriptions, images supporting descriptions, buttons and menus for follow-up information requests, directions for navigation support and maps.

Many of the issues presented for the museum setting apply to any physical hypernavigation setting in which individual, dynamic guides would be appropriate: for example historical cities, archaeological sites or natural settings such as gardens, parks or mountains. It is obvious that wide open spaces introduce additional options from the technological point of view (for example the adoption of a GPS as the localisation system) and suggest more ambitious scenarios (for example: new functions to support groups of visitors, access to on-line services such as meteo forecasts). All that is subject to investigation inside the European I^3 Project HIPS. Another element being explored in HIPS is the adoption of global strategies for presenting information and promoting items, making sure the visitor does not miss them. The simplest strategy is a gravity-driven one: there is a basic path where the visitor, through presentations and suggestions is attracted, whatever deviations she performs; distances from a position to the next position tend to be minimised. Another one brings into the picture the dimension of play: for instance a dynamic treasure hunt, where typically physical distances tend to be maximised.

Yet another innovative feature is the introduction of collective memories. The visit trace is kept. The data can be used by the visitor: when she is back home she will be able to go deeper into the domain she has been exposed to, with a system (for instance AlFresco) that knows about her visit and will support her in her successive exploration.

Other possibilities are there for treasuring some specific itinerary (for instance one made by an art critic or by a public person) so that it can be followed with minor deviations by another visitor. Yet another opportunity is to build models of the behaviour of classes of visitors and , for instance in the case of a museum, on that basis influence the curators' choices.

4.3 Spoken Language Technology

Speech processing is a key element for natural interaction systems. I believe that synthesis in particular will prove even more important than recognition. Often the user's input can be very simple (as in HIPS) but output, as it may depend on other implicit input or on a user profile, may require a lot of sophisticated processing for achieving a good presentation level. With personalised output often you want information to be presented as a coherent text, prepared for you and presented orally. Concept-to-speech (integration of generation and synthesis) is yielding good results, but even synthesis per se has improved tremendously.

Coming to spoken input, there has been a lot of progress in spontaneous speech recognition, albeit in highly constrained dialogic settings. For instance within the C-STAR II consortium IRST and its partners have built a prototype aimed at making possible that two persons physically remote and each speaking her own language [Cettolo et al, 1999], entertain a conversation oriented to book a hotel room. Again the application is relevant for the tourism domain and translation is the most apparent result, but probably the really important technological progress in input is in the ability to treat natural speech phenomena, such as false starts, hesitations and so on.

5 Conclusions

Intelligent interfaces can help realise individual-oriented tourism, yielding a more active role for the tourist. I believe this is an essential element for any leisure situation. Cultural tourism in particular is a situation that certainly requires qualitatively rich interaction; the prototypes described in this paper emphasise the role of natural language integrated with other means of communication. There are other intelligent technologies and a set of applied contexts that look promising for a combination of what presented here with other Artificial Intelligence techniques: for instance case-based reasoning, for adapting solutions that have been successful for a "similar" tourist combined with dynamic information presentations; or planning and temporal and spatial reasoning combined with advise about where to go during a visit, given a set of constraints (weather, crowd or traffic, terrain, interests, physical conditions, available time etc.) or for organising the visit as a an interactive game.

In the future the tourist will enjoy a visit more and more because it is a culturally fulfilling experience, one in which he or she will have learnt a lot, and that is leading to further interests. A personal intelligent interface will be an important element for making this possible for all individuals.

Acknowledgments

I wish to acknowledge the contribution of all the people at IRST who have worked at the projects described in this paper.

References

[Arens *et al*, 1993] Y. Arens, E. Hovy and M. Vosser. On the Knowledge Underlying Multimedia Presentations. In M.T. Maybury (ed.) *Intelligent Multimodal Interfaces*. AAAIPress/MIT Press, Menlo Park CA/Cambridge MA, 1993.

[Cettolo *et al*, 1999] M. Cettolo, A. Corazza, G. Lazzari, F. Pianesi, E. Pianta, L. M. Tovena. A Speech-to-Speech Translation-Based Interface for Tourism. In D. Buhalis, W. Schertler (eds.), *Information and Communication Technologies in Tourism 1999. Proceedings of ENTER '99*, Springer Verlag, Vienna, 1999.

[HIPS] HIPS Project, WWW home page:
http://www.ing.unisi.it/lab_tel/hips/hips.html.

[Maybury, 1993] M.T. Maybury (ed.) *Intelligent Multimedia Interfaces*, AAAI Press, Menlo Park, Ca./MIT Press, Cambridge, Mass., 1993.

[Maybury, 1997] M.T. Maybury (ed.) *Intelligent Mutimodal Information Retrieval*, AAAI Press, Menlo Park, Ca./MIT Press, Cambridge, Mass., 1997.

[Maybury and Wahlster, 1998] M.T. Maybury and W. Wahlster (eds.) *Readings in Intelligent User Interfaces*, Morgan-Kaufmann Press, San Francisco, 1998.

[Mellish *et al*, 1997] C. Mellish, J. Oberlander, M. O'Donnell and A. Knott. Exploring a Gallery with Intelligent Labels. *Proceedings of the Fourth International Conference on Hypermedia and Interactivity in Museums (ICHIM97)*, Paris, 1997.

[Milosavljevic *et al*, 1996] M. Milosavljevic, A. Tulloch and R. Dale. Text Generation in a Dynamic Hypertext Environment. *Proceedings of the Nineteenth Australasian Computer Science Conference*, Melbourne, 1996.

[Not *et al*, 1998] E. Not, D. Petrelli, M. Sarini, O. Stock, C. Strapparava, M. Zancanaro. Hypernavigation in the Physical Space: Adapting Presentations to the User and to the Situational Context. *The New Review of Hypermedia and Multimudia,* Vol. 4, pp. 33-45, Taylor Graham Publishing, London, 1998

[Stock, 1991] O. Stock. Natural Language and Exploration of an Information Space: the AlFresco Interactive System. *Proceedings of IJCAI-91, the Twelfth International Joint Conference on Artificial Intelligence*, Sydney, 1991. Also in M.T. Maybury and W. Wahlster (eds.) *Readings in Intelligent User Interfaces.*, Morgan-Kaufmann Press, San Francisco, 1998.

[Stock, 1995] O. Stock. A Third Modality of Natural Language? *Artificial Intelligence Review,* 9, Kluwer Academic Publishers, Dordrecht, 1995.

[Stock, 1995] O. Stock. Was the Title of this Talk Generated Automatically? Prospects on Intelligent Interfaces and Language Invited talk in *Proceedings of IJCAI 99, the Sixrteenth International Joint Conference on Artificial Intelligence,* pp. 1412-1419. Stockholm, 1999.

[Stock *et al*, 1997] O. Stock, C. Strapparava and M. Zancanaro. Explorations in an Environment for Natural Language Multimodal Information Access. In M. Maybury (ed.) *Intelligent Mutimodal Information Retrieval.* AAAI Press, Menlo Park, Ca./MIT Press, Cambridge, Mass., 1997.

[Wahlster *et al*, 1992] W. Wahlster, E. Andrè, S. Bandyopadyay, W. Graf and T. Rist. Wip: The Coordinated Generation of Multimodal Presentations from a Common Representation. In A. Ortony, J. Slack, and O.Stock (eds.), *Communication from Artificial Intelligence Perspective: Theoretical and Applied Issues*, Springer Verlag, Berlin,1992.

[Werthner and Klein, 1999] H. Werthner and S. Klein, *Information Technology and Tourism – A Challenging Relationship*. Springer Verlag, Vienna, 1999.

[Zancanaro *et al*, 1997] M. Zancanaro, O. Stock and C. Strapparava. Multimodal Interaction for Information Access: Exploiting Cohesion. *Computational Intelligence*, 13(4), 1997.

DEEP MAP: Challenging IT Research In The Framework Of A Tourist Information System

Rainer Malaka and Alexander Zipf
European Media Laboratory - EML
Schloss-Wolfsbrunnenweg 33
69118 Heidelberg, Germany
<firstname>.<lastname>@eml.villa-bosch.de

Abstract

Deep Map is a research framework that aims at building the prototype of an intelligent next generation spatial information system. Deep Map realizes the vision of a future tourist guidance system that works as a mobile guide and as a web-based planning tool. This long term research project addresses several challenging research aspects covering intelligent integration of information from different data sources and services including geographical information systems, multi-media databases, and interactive internet data sources such as reservation systems. On the basis of this complex information system the European Media Laboratory plans to build user interfaces that allow intuitive and easy access to information. Such a user interface including visual and natural language processing will be included into a mobile device that navigates the user through a city. Also virtual tours in a 3D-reconstructed city will be possible. In this paper, we present the current system that already covers a number of these aspects and demonstrates how tourists may be guided in the future.

1. Introduction

Information technology (IT) is one of the driving forces in the information society. Current trends indicate that computers will soon be integrated into many devices and that there is virtually no limit of inter-networking all kinds of computers and services. These advances in computer science are basically quantitative and in many applications, a lack of qualitative improvements yields systems that are not better but even worse in terms of their usability. In spite of finding more information there is a tradeoff leading to spending more time searching for information. This effect also happens to many tourism applications of IT. The number of tourism-related services in the Web grows every day offering hotels, flights, tickets and information of all sorts. Since every service provider has a proprietary interface and a unique selection of services, it becomes hard for a tourist to effectively plan a trip to an unknown city and to collect the right information in advance. Moreover, when the tourist reached the destination, he or she will miss some information and be cut off from these information sources..

Even though, information as such can easily be carried around, it is still not really accessible for tourists for mobile use. A CD-ROM, for instance, may have all the useful information on a city such as a list of hotels, recommendations for restaurants, or knowledge on the architecture of a castle. But unless equipped with a laptop, it is quite useless when the user leaves the home PC. Therefore, most projects that aimed at bringing out tourists guides on CD-ROM more or less failed. The classical book is still a very powerful hardware that contains a lot of useful information, never runs into battery problems and is quite robust for rough conditions that occur in outdoor use.

A survey that was conducted by EML and the University of Heidelberg, recently showed that many tourists are very much reserved against IT assistance for their trip. Interestingly, however, the same amount of people would like to have some IT in form of a mobile computer. Thus, the question if people would like to use computers as a replacement of the traditional books and maps as tourist guides, splits the tourists into two groups: traditionalists who want to stick with classical paperwork and experimentalists who would like to try out new technologies. The question remains, why the second group still does not use mobile computers. The answer is simple, there are not yet the right IT systems available. PDAs are not powerful enough, Laptops not practical, networking is too slow, the systems do not know where they are and there are just not the services available that could compete with the information in a book.

In Deep Map, we aim at building information systems that overcome these problems. This imposes research challenges in a wide range of fields of IT research. In particular, the main research areas of Deep Map are geo-information systems, data bases, natural language processing, intelligent user interfaces, knowledge representation, 3D-modeling and visualization. The goal is to develop information technologies that can handle huge heterogeneous data collections, complex functionality and a variety of technologies, but are still accessible for untrained users.

2. Components and Design of Deep Map

In the long run, Deep Map will be a mobile system able to generate personal guided walks for tourists through the city of Heidelberg and to aid tourists in navigating through the city. Such a tour shall consider personal interests and needs, social and cultural backgrounds (age, education, gender) as well as other circumstances (from season, weather, traffic conditions to time and financial resources). Even though Deep Map is a long term research project, the current prototype already provides a good impression of the tourist guide for the future. In the following, we present an outline of the components of the current system and discuss how they are embedded in the whole Deep Map system.

2.1. GIS and Databases

The core of Deep Map is a geographical information system (GIS). It can handle spatial and topological queries, allows navigation and route finding. Touristical information is location-dependent by nature. Each sight, building, hotel, restaurant, etc. does

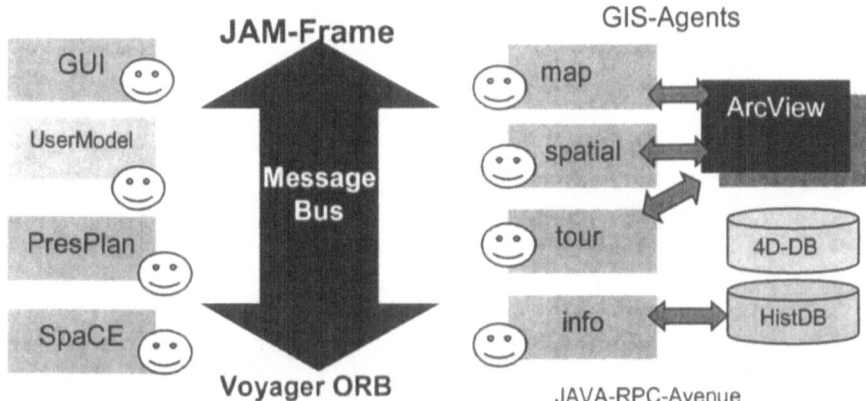

Fig. 1. Overview of the architecture of the GIS-agents. The four DB/GIS agents on the right realize access to the GIS and the DBs. They interact (also with the other agents on the left) via a message bus.

have a spatial location. Moreover, during mobile use, the tourist has a location and one important task is to relate the tourist's location to attractions in reach, the tour she wants to take and to the goal she wants to reach. This leads to a range of geography-related questions a tourist is likely to ask, such as:

- Where am I?
- How do I get from A to B?
- What attractions can I reach?
- Where can I find a hotel/restaurant/...?
- How do I get there in the fastest/cheapest/nicest manner?
- What was here before?
- Why does the area look like this?
- How did this part of the area evolve? (Why?)
- Which areas of the city are interesting for me or especially dangerous/ugly?

All of these questions need geographical knowledge that has to be managed by a GIS. Some questions take the position of the user into account and for their answer, we need to know the user's location. Some of the questions will also have to relate information from databases and other resources such as restaurant guides to the GIS. Of particular interest for tourist applications are questions that relate to historical and temporal changes. Here we also need temporal databases. And in many queries, the system has to handle fuzzy and user-specific measures such as "interesting", "ugly", or "in reach". In the following, the GIS and the databases of Deep Map are presented. Together, they form the core knowledge repository.

2.1.1. An Agent-Based GIS

Albeit Object-Orientation is a natural choice for development, object-orientation alone

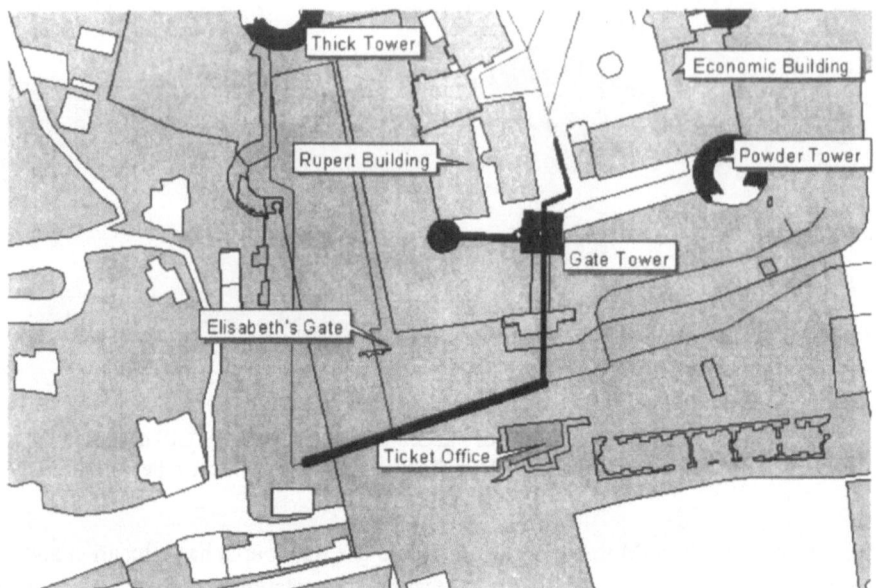

Fig. 2. Example of a map produced by the first version of the Map Agent with a tour and its active tour segment highlighted.

is too little for such an ambitious project such as Deep Map. Therefore we decided to take a step further and make use of the so-called agent-oriented software paradigm. Agents form a higher level of abstraction in software design. Moreover, the agent-based approach allows an easy re-use of components in different systems that may consist of a different set of agents and thus providing another range of services. This is especially important in our scenario where we have two quite different application platforms: a Web-based system for home-users (Zipf and Malaka 1999a) and the mobile system for a tourist on site (Zipf et al. 2000).

The GIS and databases are accessed through the following agents (Fig. 1):
- the *database agent* retrieves non-spatial information from the database,
- the *geo-spatial agent* retrieves spatial information from the GIS and performs a range of geo-spatial computations on that information,
- the *route agent* computes and manages routes and their segments,
- the *map agent* generates and handles maps and their visualization.

First prototypes of these agents have been developed using the ArcView GIS as server platform. The agents themselves communicate via a message bus (Java Agent Management framework - JAMFrame (Chandrasekhara in prep.). Fig. 1 shows an overview of the System. The GIS-agents are implemented using Java wrappers that communicate with the ArcView GIS running on a specified server via RPC (Remote Procedure Call). Since on the one side, only string messages can be passed via RPC and on the other side, messages on the bus are represented as Java objects, these objects must be converted from/to text. For this reason an XML notation is used that allows the automatic conversion of Java objects from/to XML using the Java reflection API.

As an example we present one of these agents in more detail: The task of the Map-Agent is to render maps of specified areas. After receiving an appropriate request it figures out the suitable area and requests the geo-spatial data from one or more specified servers. Other options include the possibility to specify which data has to be shown explicitly and which have to be highlighted. In particular it is possible to visualize previously calculated tours as well as highlighting particular (actual) sections of these routes by specifying their identifier (Fig. 2).

A first version of the Map-Agent creates a map as a raster image on server side and returns this image to the requesting agent. The new Java based version gets the geometric data of the spatial features, that have to be displayed from a geo-server, and renders this vector data on client side. These two approaches will be evaluated against each other. Both belong to the three possibilities the OpenGIS Consortium identified in their recent Web Map Server Specification draft (OpenGIS 1999). The first one is the so-called picture case and the second the feature case. Similarly, the other agents allow flexible access to the data and can be parameterized in various ways in order to suit the user's needs.

2.1.2. The Tourist Database

Most of the knowledge and data about our tourist destination is stored within the GIS and a database we developed to capture all the information about the history, geography and cultural items o Heidelberg. We want to offer the most flexible ways to browse through the knowledge within our database on geographical and historical information on Heidelberg to the different users of Deep Map. Therefore we needed to develop a data model capable of integrating very different kinds of information in a very flexible way. This resulted in an "event" based data model for historical geo-referenced data. This relational data model consists of relations of different types between locations (several types of spatial objects and their respective subclasses) - persons (historic, real and legal persons) and (historic) events of different granularities. As it supports different media types from text images, video, sound to 3D and VR models, and all the links and relationships between these multimedia documents and literature, persons, places and events and as it is geo-referenced through the coupling of the locations in the database with the GIS, the data base has the power to act as a prototype of a digital library for Heidelberg. This is being realized within a conventional relational database, resulting in a quite complex data model with over 120 tables in spite of our struggle to keep it as simple as possible.

For easy data maintenance, an user interface for data input has been developed, that supports sophisticated access and maintenance for different kinds of users (Häußler

1999). All information in the database can be given a time period for which it is valid. This period can be specified with different granularity and also supports the specification of the accuracy of the data entry to allow fuzzy time specifications, what is often necessary for historic data. Even though, the data collection is only done for the city of Heidelberg, the database is developed in a general way such that it could easily be used for any other city.

2.1.3. From 2D to 3D Information Systems

Normal maps just contain 2D information. For many aspects in our application, however, 3D information is needed. For instance, the natural language interface described below, needs 3D information in order to direct a person to a city. The reason for this is that we attempt to generate route instructions that do not sound as:

go 205.4 meters straight, turn 30 degrees to the right and go 67.9 meters straight,

but rather like:

follow the street and turn right after the big red building and head towards the church.

In order to do so, we need knowledge on the visibility of objects from each location and we need the 3D information for the selection of good landmarks that are both prominent and visible. 3D-information can also be used for resolving queries such as "What is under the Karlstor?" that impose three-dimensional topological questions. Such questions may also occur when tourists ask for architectural details of complex tourists sights such as the famous Heidelberg castle. A third aspect is of course the usage of 3D as a means for visualization. The use of 3D-models is always a very attractive means for visualizing virtual sights of a city.

In the current version of Deep Map, we have extended 3D knowledge for the area of the old town of Heidelberg. Here we have 3D reconstructions of buildings with textures from photographs. For the rest of the city we only have the surface information and can generate simple block-based 3D models.

2.1.4. From 3D to 4D Information Systems

Many types of data are not only spatial but also temporal, e.g., environmental, climate, or city development data (Meusburger and Zipf 1998). In the domain of Deep Map, the need to handle 4D data comes naturally facing questions of tourists standing in front of a historical place like a ruin of a castle asking *how did that look like when it was not destroyed?* In this case we would like to turn back the time and allow a virtual time travel displaying a reconstruction of that place as a VR model. At the moment, we included a 3D reconstruction of the Heidelberg castle into Deep Map, where destroyed parts can be re-built on the user's mouse click.

We also aim at reconstructing less spectacular buildings in order to be able to allow the virtual view back into history at other locations. For this purpose, a collection of architectural elements (windows, roofs, doors etc.) that have been used during the centuries is being initiated. This database serves as a repertoire of building blocks for reconstructing buildings at different locations and epochs (Weinmann et al. 2000) where old maps and images (photos, paintings, engravings) are used for identifying shape and type.

2.2. Personalized and Integrated Services

The vision of Deep Map wants to allow the user to get personalized and easy access to a variety of information. We already described how geographical information, a tourist database and even 3D and 4D information is integrated within the databases of Deep Map. We now want to outline aspects on how these data can be used for personalized services and how a user can access multiple data sources without complex queries.

2.2.1. Proposing personalized tours to tourists

For Deep Map, we develop a tour planning system that is capable of generating individual tour proposals through a city based on the personal preferences and interests of a tourist. In order to achieve this, several problems have to be solved. These include recognizing of the individual interests. For building such user models, we plan to integrate user model components that are built together with colleagues from GMD[1].

If the user interests are known, there are several possibilities how to include them into a tour planning or tour proposing algorithm. First of all the range of possible attributes that may influence the choice for a particular section of a route have to be identified and modeled. Appropriate variables have to be included into the database and attached to the street network within the GIS. Such attributes include both „hard" restrictions, or physically given attributes (like height, steepness, turn rules, legal rules, etc.) as well as a range of more dynamic and „soft" parameters, which importance can vary extremely from person to person or time to time. Such parameters could include esthetic aspects, the social milieu of the area, dislike of motorized traffic or preferences for areas with high degree of architectural interesting buildings or just a high rate of nice viewpoints.

Right now we have developed two planning algorithms that take into account a range of hard and soft parameters for each street section. They are implemented using the Network Analyst extension for ArcView GIS. One is based on interpolating so called service areas on the street network, the second is based on buffering the street network algorithms (Roether 1999, Roether and Zipf 2000). The maps shown in Fig.3 the results of the first algorithm when varying the degree of importance for particular soft

---

[1] German National Research Center for Information Technology, Bonn.

22

Fig. 3. Calculated tours for passenger with high preferences against noise and smoke versus high preferences for attractive areas.

parameters are displayed. The first is the result, when there is a high dislike of smoke and noise and the second shows the route with a preference for attractive areas in general. Thematic interests such as interest in particular architectural epochs or for particular persons are not taken into account within this examples. Right now the tourist can choose between several modes of transportation (car, foot, bike and wheelchair).

2.2.2. Information Integration

Apart from the core databases, additional data sources are necessary for online data that has to be updated frequently, e.g., hotel reservation services. The user, however, should not be bothered with a variety of different interfaces for these systems. Moreover, the user should have seamless access to those systems without even realizing that not only one database but a whole set of integrated databases and services are connected within Deep Map. Therefore, the system must provide standardized means for the integration of these additional sources that are independent of the core system. This is also essential for continuous automated database maintenance.

There are several possibilities for technical solutions for that problem that have to be combined on multiple levels of abstraction. In our framework, we employ an agent-based approach (Fig. 1 and 4) where agents communication complies with the FIPA standard (FIPA 1997, 1999). The underlying communication system of the agent platform for sending and receiving messages uses the middleware technologies CORBA or RMI. This allows a flexible distribution of the components on a network and also the integration of service agents that reside on remote servers.

The message content is modeled using an object-oriented ontology that is represented in a class hierarchy. This allows an agent communication where agents can communicate on a higher semantically level. Moreover, this ontological approach allows a unified representation and translation of concepts for all sub-systems.

2.3. Human-Computer Interaction

Usability is one of the most important aspect for the future success of tourist information systems such as Deep Map. The tourist as a user who wants to use the system for entertainment and on vacation won't bother with an extended tutorial or with complex interface languages. The system needs to be intuitively usable and it should be comfortable to carry and to use it. Fig. 4 shows the architecture of Deep Map in a view that shows how the layout of the system provide means of easy access.

The interface layer provides multiple modalities for input and output. For mobile use, natural language is one important modality that allows hands-free operation which is important for a user that moves as a pedestrian or car driver. Here, visual information is not adequate. In other situations, a visual/graphical user interface (GUI) can be useful when complex information has to be visualized, e.g., in maps. An additional 3D interface allows interaction with 3D VRML models. Note that not each modality is used at every time. In particular, the 3D interface is currently only used for the stationary PC version due to computational performance restrictions on the mobile device.

The cognitive layer aims at translating human concepts into system queries and system responses back into human-adequate presentations. The query and answer translator (QUATRA) and the presentation planner are doing this for either direction.

On the knowledge layer, the GIS and databases presented above, external services and other systems provide the knowledge on the contents and on how to solve problems like tour planning.

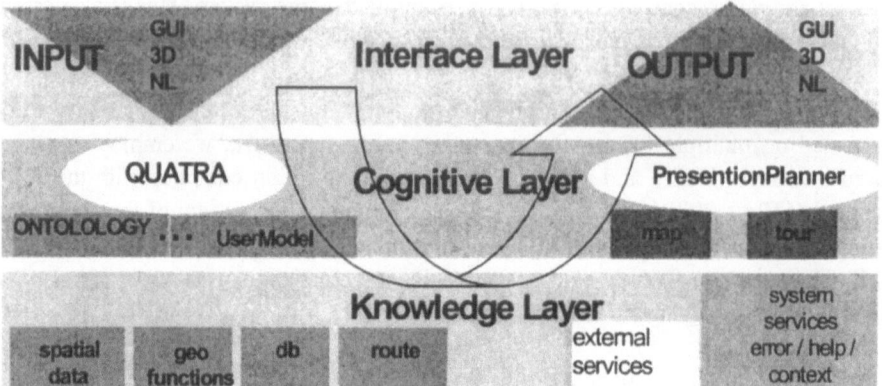

Fig. 4. Deep Map Architecture.

2.3.1.　Natural Language Processing

A natural language interface for a system like Deep Map that is not a command-word driven interface but that allows free speech and real dialogs, is a quite ambitious research project. The focus of research at the EML lies in building components for NLP systems that allow a deeper understanding of utterances beyond their word-by-word meaning. Another focus is the multi-modal integration of NLP with gestures on the input and graphics on the output side.

Currently, the system uses a recognizer and parser for English provided by the Interactive Systems Labs (Woszczyna 1997). For language understanding, we also employ modules of DFKI that deal with spatial relations (Kray and Blocher 1999). A special focus in language generation lies on natural route instructions that are similar to those used by humans (Porzel et al. 2000). Next to the English version, a German and a Japanese version are in preparation. The scientifically most challenging question is the translation of queries like: "How do I get from here to the castle?", "Is there a bakery?", "What is this?", "What was here before?" Such sentences have to be disambiguated and translated into database queries. The user's context and previous experience may help the system and if necessary, the system has to ask qualifying questions like "Did you mean the big red building on your left?" Language understanding also requires an intermediate representation (knowledge representation, formal ontology) that represents the concepts within the Deep Map database.

2.3.2.　Virtual City

Next to NLP, graphical interface techniques are of high importance. Graphical information is very useful when complex spatial data has to be given to the user. Maps as a two-dimensional representation are widely used for this purposes (Fig. 2). We also use the 3D modeling and 3D reconstruction in various ways. If, for instance, a tour has to be visualized, we can display the tour in a 2D map, but we can also give a 3D relief picture that can help the user to identify landmarks and thus make it easier to grab the spatial information. Advanced techniques could also visualize a tour in a video sequence where the user is taken on a virtual flight through the 3D model of Heidelberg (Zipf and Malaka 1999a, b). Moreover, the three-dimensional Virtual Heidelberg allows users to take virtual walks through today's and yesterday's Heidelberg. In a prototype of our Web-based system, the tourist will have the possibility to go on a virtual tour through Heidelberg.

Fig. 5. Tourist with Mobile Deep Map System based on a wearable computer.

2.4. Mobile System

Deep Map appears as a system with different faces. One version is be a Web-based planning and exploring tool for virtual visits and pre-trip planning. The mobile version uses a wearable computer that allows hands-free usage. The current prototype is based on a wearable computer (Xybernaut MA IV) with a handheld color LCD display and a light weight headset with microphone and earphones (Fig. 5). For instant access to services in the net and for server access, the system is equipped with wireless LAN that allows data communication with stationary computers. The current mobile version is realized as a prototype that can be used for a limited area around Heidelberg castle.

3. Current State and Future Directions

Deep Map is not a product but rather a framework that poses a long term challenge to our research. Nevertheless, a first prototype already demonstrates the concepts of Deep Map in a real world scenario. This first prototype includes natural language processing, GIS, databases, VR simulations, combined multimedia presentations on tourist sights, all available on a mobile "wearable" computer. Thus this proof of concept demonstrates the new possibilities for IT-based tourism guidance.

Next to the mobile system, a Web-based interfaces allows to use Deep Map components from a home PC. This scenario employing two faces of one system makes a perfect tourist assistant that can help the user at home and on her visit. In the next stages, we plan to extend the system such that we can work on usability studies. Meanwhile, further research is done on all areas of Deep Map: GIS, databases, agent systems, VR modeling, user interfaces. In particular for the mobile use of Deep Map, performance issues concerning the quality of service, location awareness and networking are of importance.

4. Conclusions

Tourism and IT are two areas that fit well together. On the one hand, IT has continuously influenced tourism and the use of advanced IT products in Tourism is still growing. On the other hand, tourism makes a perfect application domain for IT research on new interactive user systems that allow easy access to complex information systems. Both aspects are covered by Deep Map. It represents a vision for future tourism assistance systems and it incorporates challenging IT research. Even though a product with Deep Map technology will need another five years of development, some of the demonstrated features could soon be integrated in simpler but still useful systems.

There are a number of lessons that can be learned from Deep Map. Each single field of research brought further insight into new and challenging aspects of IT research. On the level of the whole system, the main message from this project is that real progress in building ambitious new IT applications for the future, require a whole set of intelligent technologies rather than just one new idea. The integration of various techniques such as databases, artificial intelligence, natural language understanding and more is a very hard task but it sets the stage for those new and easy-to-use systems we will take for granted once they are available. Deep Map already outlines how such a system can be used in the tourism domain.

Acknowledgements

Deep Map is a research project funded by the Klaus Tschira Foundation. The research presented here is conducted in collaboration with Interactive Systems Labs (Karlsruhe and Pittsburgh), DFKI (Saarbrücken), FhG-IGD (Darmstadt) and the Universities of Heidelberg and Stuttgart.

References:

Chandrasekhara, V. (in prep.): *Jam Frame. The Deep Map Java agent management framework.*
Foundation for Physical Agents (FIPA) (1997) *Agent Communication Language ACL / Agent management (Specification version 2.0)*, http://www.fipa.org
Foundation for Physical Agents (FIPA) (1998) *Specification version 1.0*, http://www.fipa.org/spec/fipa98.html
Häußler, J. (1999) *Prototyp eines GIS-gestützten historisch-geographischen Städtführers für das WWW*, Diplomarbeit, Geogr. Institut der Universtät Heidelberg.
Kray, C. and Blocher, A. (1999) *Modeling the Basic Meanings of Path Relations*, Proc. of the 16th IJCAI, Morgan Kaufmann: San Francisco, CA, 1999

27

Meusburger, P. und Zipf, A (1998) *Auf dem Weg zu einem 4D-Geoinformationssystem - das Projekt Deep Map*, HGG-Journal, Heft 12.

Open GIS Consortium (OpenGIS) (1999) *The Web Map Server specification* (draft), http://www.opengis.org.

Porzel, R. Klabunde, R. and Jansche, M. (2000) *Generating spatial descriptions from a cognitive point of view*. In: Olivier, Spatial Language, Kluwer, Dortecht, to appear.

Roether, S. (1999) *GIS-basierte Routenfindung mit individuellen Streckenpräferenzen*, Diplomarbeit, Geographisches Institut der Universtät Heidelberg.

Weinmann, R., Häußler, J. Zipf, A., Malaka, R. (2000) *Die Besucher Heidelbergs informieren: Die multimediale Deep Map Datenbank*, In: HGG-Journal 1/2000, to appear.

Woszczyna, M. (1997) *Fast speaker independent large vocabulary continuous speek recognition*, Ph.D. Thesis, University of Karlsruhe.

Zipf, A. und Malaka, R. (1999a) *3D und 4D - Deep Map - das historische Touristeninformationssystem für Heidelberg*, In: GeoBit 07/99.

Zipf, A. und Malaka, R. (1999b) *Web-basierte Planung und animierte Visualisierung von 3D Besichtigungstouren im Rahmen des Touristeninformationssystems Deep Map*, In: AGIT 99. Salzburg.

Zipf, A., Chandrasekhara, V., Häußler, J. and Malaka, R. (2000) *GIS hilft Touristen bei der Navigation – ein erster Prototyp des mobilen Deep Map Systems für das Heidelberger Schloß*, In: HGG-Journal. 1/2000, to appear.

Zipf, A and Roether, S. (2000) *Tourenvorschläge für Stadttouristen mit dem ArcView Network Analyst*, In: Liebig: ArcView Arbeitsbuch, Huethig Verlag, to appear.

Meta-level Programming for Legacy TIS Integration

Thomas Steiner
HEC, University of Lausanne
thomas.steiner@hec.unil.ch

Abstract

The current pace for software revolutions is driving a key problem into the field of Tourism Information Systems (TISs): many TISs are or become legacy systems. The common view of legacy systems associates operational TISs to obsolete, old-fashioned systems. In contrast to this broad opinion, we discuss legacy TISs as a treasure for wider implementations. We focus on TIS interfaces and demonstrate, how Meta-level Programming (MlP) can be used to integrate them within new functional environments. Recent studies have pointed out that real-world IS processes can be extended with a meta-layer, which alleviates the masking of underlying interface complexity. Our paper concretely discusses the relevance of MlP for legacy TIS integration. We illustrate the problem of a legacy TIS with the migration of a traditional, large TIS towards ubiquitous access and its integration into modern environments (1). In the following, we shortly outline the power of MlP for TIS integration (2). The relevance of cognitive architectures for such knowledge based integration is the object of the subsequent section (3). We then undermine our propositions with a completed, fielded sample application in the domain of distributed TIS software agents (4). Our ongoing research (5) is finally outlined with early trends in the context of the World Hospitality Interface Standard (WHIS) and XML for the tourism industry. The general focus is on the strategic relevance of MlP for legacy TISs rather than on technical considerations.

1 Introduction

The current pace for software revolutions is driving a key problem into the field of Tourism Information Systems (TISs): many TISs are or become *legacy systems*. As IT-literate intermediaries - even without having prior tourism specific knowledge - enter the market and drive new economic issues like switching costs, network externalities and value based pricing [12] into the industry, the traditional key players often feel overwhelmed by the new trends. This is all the more true because many of their IT investments from the 1980s are not yet fully amortized. Legacy TISs represent therefore a major strategic challenge at the beginning of the new millennium. A majority of Small and Medium-sized Tourism Enterprises (SMTEs) [3] report in fact severe problems with the accelerated pace of *IT changes*. Although comparable industries seem to be able to reinvest periodically in new IT equipment and software, SMTEs are often forced by financial constraints to run their IT equipment for a longer period than the average of information intensive industries.

An *integration gap* consequently arises between IT equipment that must be used for longer periods and the current trends towards ubiquitous, personalized and integrated information systems.

It is therefore not surprising that recent *scientific discussions* specifically address TIS interoperation and integration issues. The KNITE forums [11] are for example directly concerned with these topics.

In this paper, we will discuss the relevance of Meta-level Programming (MlP) for legacy TIS integration. Some parts of the paper refer to accomplished, fielded work. Others position new application areas and outline the state of our current research. The focus will be on strategy rather than on technical details. Readers interested in technical details are invited to refer to our recent publications [18], as well as to our presence in the WWW [19].

2 Legacy TIS Integration

Today, the TIS field paints a very *complex and heterogeneous* panorama, with database-systems of different providers, specific individual data models, multimedia objects, linguistic disparities, etc. [5] It is undeniably true: we are living in a world where Information Technologies (ITs) in general and Tourism Information Systems (TISs) in particular are permanently changing.

A majority of TISs can not keep pace with these changes - they are becoming obsolete, old-fashioned, out-dated. It is for example a well-known fact that many older ("legacy") TISs still use raw TCP/IP sockets to pass information between two systems. But the tourism industry is fortunately not the first industry to face such integration issues. Blueprints for their (partial) solution are available in the form of *standards*.[22]

Interoperation standards allow us today to live quite well with these legacy systems. The latter have first been identified as "obsolete, old-fashioned, out-of-date systems". A more recent point of view sees legacy systems as *a treasure of information* and tries to integrate them as much as possible into the constantly changing business logic.

According to a survey of the Gartner Group, by the year 2000, organizations will integrate and/or transition 85 percent of *mainframe-based functionality*, at one-fifth the cost of new development, in the implementation of client/server applications. In 1995 already, 84 percent of the businesses answering to the survey said to have a *legacy transition strategy*.

The most illustrative case of a legacy TIS transition strategy is probably the opening of traditional CRSs/GDSs to the Internet. In the 1970s, these systems focused on information *access*: intermediaries (travel agencies) were allowed to access for example SABRE in order to realize transactions. In the 1990s followed a period, during which the engineers focused on *globalization*: the Internet provided the technological basis for global, personalized, ubiquitous access. The result of this trend is the Travelocity (www.travelocity.com) Internet site - basically a modern interface over the SABRE system that responds to the new business requirements.

The current focus of TIS engineering is no longer on access or globalization, but on complete *integration* of these systems within one customized solution, be it for service providers (Swiss service providers maintain availability information in a national Web-engine implemented by Switzerland Tourism), tourists (customers gain control in diverse Web-based TISs [15]), or intermediaries (Imholz Salt-'n'-Pepper integrates basic selling processes into their last-minute auction [8]).

The importance of direct and all-inclusive information and services has been significantly leveraged in the last few years. *Tourists* acquire new IT knowledge much faster than most SMTEs, and they are no longer interested in collecting decisive information from a variety of sources. [2] The demand clearly points into the direction of all-inclusive, *one-stop shopping* experiences.

Existing TISs are today more than ever seen as *components* that must be integrated into such customized, all-inclusive environments if they have to keep pace with the IT evolution. They *ideally* expose their services through *well-defined interfaces* (the API in programmers' terms) and are collectable by any user-centric application to come.

This ideal view of TISs as interoperating components is unfortunately still a dream for the moment. *TIS software migration* is a very complex task due to the fact that tourism information itself is highly dynamic, heterogeneous and not at all standardized yet. To make things worse, the implied SMTEs have often limited IT infrastructures and financial power. [21]

It is no secret that *interface standards* to legacy systems are urgently needed in the tourism industry. The absence of such standards has been one of the most expensive technology-related problems for years. Interface and interoperation standards are a relatively new topic in the field of TISs. Some authors even claim that a few months ago, interface standards were little more than a dream.

Today, in Switzerland as well as in other countries, a typical tourism service provider runs up to a dozen of *TIS subsystems*. The providers constantly try to integrate all these applications. For a long time, the only solution to this dilemma has been to buy a custom interface solution. The cost of such interfaces has been estimated $1'500 to $3'000 each [22], an investment that tourism SMTEs simply couldn't afford with each new IT trend. They remain therefore often in a "waiting position" and resist acquiring more powerful solutions.

Big IT players have recently manifested a strategic interest in TIS interoperation issues[e.g. 22]. Some of them started working on an open set of interface and interoperation standards. The Hospitality Industry Technology Interface Standards (HITIS) body, formed by the American Hotel & Motel Association, is currently working on a *Windows Hospitality Interface Standard* (WHIS) [22]. Other important efforts consider the application of XML to TISs.

The prime focus of these standards is of course *platform-independence* and *vendor-neutrality*. Efforts to support heterogeneous TISs in distributed environments (e.g. CORBA, RMI and DCOM) are underway. The interfaces to legacy systems can potentially be implemented using any programming language (sample data descriptions and demos already exist in Java, C++ and VB).

Recent efforts in meta-system theory now try to reconcile current legacy TIS environments with new business requirements and identify several techniques "to fill the gaps". Some legacy engineers prefer to *extend existing systems* (1) with the functionality required by the new environments. Others prefer to *extract the data logic* that underlies the legacy system (2 - e.g. [20],[13],[5]). Yet others adopt a *data warehousing* approach (3 - e.g. [10]). The most difficult approach is the attempt to extract the legacy system's *process logic* in order to assist the development of new systems (4 - e.g. [14]). *Wrappers* (5 - e.g. [18]) finally build an envelope around the existing system, which maps the services offered by the legacy application to the services required by the new business environment.

The explicit representation of tourism and TIS knowledge is not new. Sample applications have already been exposed at ENTER conferences, which apply the philosophy of *the knowledge creating company* to TISs. The ITIMES system [6] provides for example the basis for "learning and knowledge sharing". According to [6], the *key to knowledge creation lies in the mobilization and conversion of tacit knowledge and interaction with explicit knowledge*. IT change management furthermore invites us to focus on *human thinking* rather than exclusively on processes and technology. [2]

The rest of this paper discusses *Meta-level Programming* (MlP) with *declarative, logic languages* (i.e. Prolog) in the context of legacy TIS integration. Think of meta-level programming as of programming about programming. The utility of such a meta-level does of course not lie in functions that call functions, but in *(integration) knowledge that operates on (legacy) knowledge*.

3 Extending Legacy TISs with a Meta-layer

The achievement of widespread reuse for complex, legacy TISs requires in fact a focus on fundamental *design patterns*, which underlie the legacy software systems. The structure and collaboration of the individual components must be identified on a higher level than source code or object-oriented models. This calls for an additional *level of abstraction*, on which the knowledge about the real-world legacy components can be expressed.

Most interestingly, legacy TIS components can be seen as systems associated with a *meta-level* allowing the representation of this specific high-level knowledge [1]. This level is concretely implemented by a logic programming engine, which then hooks into the real-world, legacy processes (figure 1). It is this knowledge about the real-world legacy knowledge that we call *meta*. We specify this meta-knowledge in a Prolog program, which explicitly states the integration intentions for the use of the legacy systems.

The integration of legacy TISs will not begin at the code level: it starts with planning and the "human thinking" - a *legacy transition strategy* will formalize the intentions of the management towards the existing applications. Such intentions (the *intentional stance* [4] towards the legacy TIS) are hard to translate directly into low-level code, especially because the management's top-down view (compile intentions into code) and the TIS engineer's bottom-up view (translate available/feasible code into management intentions - a *design stance*) are not easy to link. An intermediate, meta-level of logic programming fits well with these management knowledge representation issues. And modern logic programming environments - such as Amzi!Prolog (www.amzi.com) allow engineers to write language extensions (i.e. extended predicates) in host languages, which let the knowledge level hook into the real-world application.

The implementation of any legacy TIS integration is therefore a *compromise* between theoretical feasibility (the engineer's view) and pragmatic realization (the new business requirements).

The AI community has forwarded much research on how to *represent knowledge* (knowledge based systems), belief, desire, intention, etc. ("intelligent agents") with logic programming. Early applications to TISs exist, but the essence of MIP for legacy TIS integration is still in its infancy.

To summarize the conceptual split between the meta- and the realworld-level, consider the following statement: *".. the designer has made the intelligent part when he or she worked at the metalevel, defining an efficient method to solve a particular problem. It only remains for the system to do the stupid part: to apply this method."* [16].

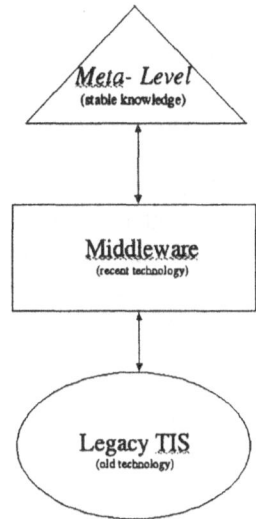

Fig. 1 - Extending legacy TISs with a meta-level

4 Real World TIS Processes and Meta-level Functionality

The goal of combining real-world TIS processes with logic is to provide a support for allowing traditional objects to define and use a *meta-knowledge representation*. The knowledge representation in legacy TISs might be straightforward, if appropriate declarative environments can be found.

It is interesting to see that the discussion of early TIS knowledge prototypes has many parallels with the current discussion about "intelligent agents" and their use in the tourism industry. Whenever the legacy question is debated with specialists of the tourism industry, the experts are convinced that there is a need for much more *human-like interfaces* in the TIS field.

According to these discussions, the *ideal tourism software agent* would interact much more personally with the end-user. It would be able to recognize on its own a search profile, and operate on knowledge in diverse information contexts in order to solve the problems of the tourist's decision making process. The ideal agent would also negotiate on its user's behalf, perform electronic transactions, and keep useless messages out of reach.

It has been underlined that the tourist's *decision making process* is very complex. In order to better approach the needs of TIS end-users, future interfaces to legacy systems will need to implement at least some cognitive functionality. As tourist information on the WWW is dynamic and constantly changing, it would for example be very tempting to introduce *believable aspects* into legacy TIS interfaces. The latter could be used to deal with the uncertainty of the existing system within its new context. Another issue for TIS interoperation is the heterogeneity of information. Smarter TIS interfaces could represent and use the end-user's needs in different *information contexts*.

Such integration dreams call for new knowledge representation and coding techniques in the TIS field. To match the client's high expectations, modern legacy TIS interfaces will need to represent *B*eliefs, *D*esires and maybe also *I*ntentions. In the domain of "intelligent" agents, such interfaces are called *BDI-agents*. The implementation of such smart interfaces is very hard - not to say nearly impossible - with traditional programming environments. The meta-level approach with declarative languages - as it is suggested in this paper - is one possible way to implement smart, higher-level interfaces to legacy and not-yet-legacy TISs.

5 Software Agents for WWW-TISs : A Sample Application

The prospects for higher-level software agents in TISs are in fact very promising. Besides the "intelligent" user interface agents that have earlier been suggested in the TIS field, context-aware and believable agents could be used in diverse sub-domains of TISs. We claim that the best market opportunity for such implementations will be *interoperation agents* that alleviate the integration of legacy TISs within modern environments. [18]

We base this statement on the results of a prototype agent system in the context of Swiss destinations. The problem with WWW-based destination ISs is that much of the information quickly becomes obsolete. Such legacy information overloads the underlying communication medium and increases the research complexity. Our first (fielded) application of MIP to TISs consisted of *distributed software agents* that wrapped around constantly changing WWW-based TISs and integrated them within a meta-architecture in order to fit new business needs.

The DATIS [18] meta-architecture promoted the distribution of indexing knowledge as an alternative to traditional, central index-based WWW-search architectures. The suggested meta-architecture was essentially conceptual. Our distributed software agents *replaced* the traditional bots and indexes. The most elegant result has been that the indexing services did no longer depend on the WWW's hierarchical structure but essentially on the communication services between the DATIS agents.

On one hand, the results obtained from the prototype clearly show that MIP for TISs is both *feasible and effecient* for an integration of quickly changing, heterogeneous tourism information within an evolving information research behavior in customer decision processes. On another hand, it became also clear that traditional low-level software objects as well as the DATIS-like mid-level software agents would hardly ever fully address the problems of legacy tourism information. The *market opportunity* for yet higher-level (BDI?) agents remains very promising: PhocusWright estimates travel and tourism related on-line sales of $5 billion for the year 2000 (www.phocusWright.com). As the tourism industry is extremely information-based, and as most of these information is still stored in legacy TISs, the latter will provide an excellent testbed for the most extravagant agent theories to come.

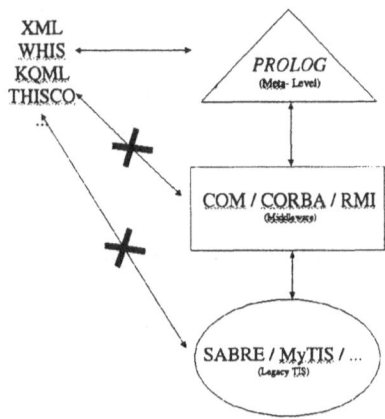

Fig. 2 - Sample applications: Distributing and Integrating TIS knowledge

The *main lesson* that can be learnt from early MIP in the field of TISs so far is that although the business requirements to TIS interfaces will always require compliance with the most recent trends (be it XML, WHIS, THISCO or whatever), the engineers of existing TISs are not forced to constantly adapt their interfaces: if they arrive at stating their legacy system's knowledge on an intermediate meta-level, the latter quickly adapts to the new interface intentions. The hooks into the real-world processes basically remain the same. No more coding at the middleware- or object-level should be necessary (Fig. 2).

The advantage of a Prolog meta-layer over traditional functional languages clearly appears, when we once again consider the heterogeneity and distribution of TIS solutions: The three current *middleware architectures* (CORBA, RMI and DCOM) for example all address the needs of software integration. However, data representation, method invocation and object distribution are differently solved in each of these architectures. Once the TIS engineer's integration intention has been explicitly stated on the meta-level, the Prolog engine can hook into CORBA, RMI and DCOM architectures.

6 WHIS / XML Parsing : An Outlook

Fortunately enough, only a few number of data elements are in fact needed to be represented within a TIS. But unfortunately, there have been no standards so far stating how to represent this service data in a *neutral form*.

Recent standardization efforts (WHIS but also XML for the tourism sector) try to analyze all these data access functions that every TIS device must accomplish, instead of writing a new specification for each new device class. The approach clearly aims at a certain *universality and openness* for TIS interoperation. The data and functions used by all the interfaces are identified and standardized.

WHIS compliant interfaces are for example based on a new, *common data dictionary* with clear syntax and semantics. In the future, the situation where one TIS component represents dates as strings and another one as integers, should consequently no longer be a problem for TIS interoperation. Syntax diagram - literate TIS engineers will be able to recognize the common data definition, and to map it to their legacy TISs. One of our current research directions aims at providing a specific *parser for WHIS compliance*. The parser actually distinguishes from early code templates that are provided as illustration code by the WHIS body: we aim at writing a WHIS parser in Prolog *on a meta-level*, which then easily hooks into the Java language on the real-world level [18].

The interest in meta-level TIS-standard parsers goes of course further than WHIS: Standardized General Markup Languages (SGML) have heavily been deployed across legacy systems for a variety of applications (finance, defense, government, etc.) A "light" form of SGML technology is widely used today in the form of HTML. A more recent daughter is the *eXtensible Markup Language* (XML). This new form of representing data is the parent for state-of-the-art TIS porting projects.

Recently, new devices have also been suggested (Palm Pilot, Tour Advisors, Mobile Phones, etc.), which do not fall into the *traditional application categories of TISs*. The new tourism & hospitality based data representation standards are supposed to alleviate interoperation between any compliant device. However, whether your legacy TIS data takes the form of WHIS, XML or any other standard to come and is exploited by a Palm Pilot, a Mobile Phone or whatever trendy facility: the approach of interpreting the interoperation language and of linking to the existent systems basically remains the same. Engineers essentially agree on a common language to express their intentions. On another hand, the design of your low-level legacy interface will not significantly change.

7 Conclusions

Legacy TISs *are* a major challenge for the tourism industry. New Information and Communication Technology trends are at the roots of a constant need to adapt established structures and processes in the tourism industry. [17] Many existing TISs can not cope with these rapid changes. They become legacy systems.

The folk opinion about such legacy systems (obsolete, old-fashioned, out-dated) is wrong. Legacy systems can be treasures for wider system implementations, if effective integration and interoperation methods can be found.

Hence, keeping pace with software revolutions does not mean running after the newest development tools. New strategic behavior - towards legacy TIS transition - is beginning to *replace the traditional reactive thinking*. [17] Concentration on the modelization of strategic business knowledge is needed in order to integrate legacy TISs in wider functional environments.

Traditional hard-coding integration methods are definitely inappropriate for legacy TIS integration. In this paper, we have identified *Meta-level Programming* (MlP) to address interoperation issues between heterogeneous new and existing TIS components.

Sample applications have illustrated that legacy TIS interfaces can effectively be extended with a *meta-level*, which declaratively expresses the new business requirements. Potential applications to WHIS / XML compliance for TISs (our ongoing research) are very promising.

However, for any organization attempting to integrate and transition legacy TISs to modern architectures, the key to success will be first *understanding* those legacy TISs. Much further work will be required to bring the implicit knowledge hidden behind such an understanding into an explicit form.

To give knowledge is like giving a fish to a starving man, to give meta-knowledge is like teaching him how to fish. It is a colossal task to provide various systems with the knowledge they need. Let us rather give a general system meta-knowledge to find knowledge useful for each particular problem. [16]

References

[1]-AMANDI, A. & PRICE, A.: *Towards Object-Oriented Agent Programming: The Brainstorm Meta-level Architecture.* Proceedings of the AGENTS97 conference, ACM Press 1997.
[2] - BIEGER, T.: *Discussion Paper: Rengineering Destination Marketing Organisations - The Case of Switzerland*, and *Call-Center - Lösungen im Incoming Tourismus: Konzept, Stand der Umsetzung, Erfolgsfaktoren.* http://www.idt.unisg.ch/publi/online.htm
[3] - BUHALIS, D.: *Information Technology For Small and Medium-Sized Tourism Enterprises: Adaptation and Benefits.* Information Technology & Tourism. Vol. 2, pp. 79-95, 1999.
[4]-DENNETT, D.: *Kinds of Minds*, Weidenfeld & Nicholson 1996.

[5]-DUNZENDORFER, A.; KUENG, J. & WAGNER, R. R.: *Data Access to Heterogeneous*

38

Tourism Information Systems. Proceedings of the ENTER98 conference in Istanbul.

[6]-FESENMAIER, D.R.; FESENMAIER, J. & PARKS, D.: ITIMES - *A Knowledge-based System for the Tourism Industry*. Proceedings of the ENTER98 conference in Istanbul, Springer 1998.

[7]-Hospitality Industry Technology Integration Standards (HITIS): *White papers on Legacy Systems & Technology Independence*. http://www.hitis.org/

[8] - www.imholz.ch

[9]-INKPEN, G.: *Information Technology for Travel and Tourism*, Addison Wesley Longman 1998.

[10]-KIRKGOEZE, R.; KURZ, A.; REITERER, H. & TJOA, A M.: *The Relevance of Meta Modeling and Data Warehouses for Executive Information Systems*, Proceedings of the ENTER97 conference in Edinburgh, Springer 1997.

[11]-Knowledge Network for IT and Tourism in Europe (KNITE): *Discussion Paper for the first stage of the KNITE project & IFITT White Paper on Open Issues and Challenges in IT and Tourism*. 1999, http://knite.lii.unitn.it/

[12]-KOCH, K.: *Der Tourismus als Informationsgeschäft - Die ökonomische Perspektive*. To appear.

[13]-KUENG, J.; DUNZENDORFER, A. & WAGNER, R.R.: *A General Datamodel for Tourism Information Systems*. Proceedings of the ENTER99 conference in Innsbruck.

[14]-MAZUMDAR, S.: *Realizing Travel Malls: A Logic Programming Based Approach*. Proceedings of the ENTER97 conference in Edinburgh, Springer 1997.

[15] - O'CONNOR, P.: *Electronic Information Distribution in Tourism and Hospitality*. CABI Publishing 1999.

[16]-PITRAT, J.: *AI Systems Are Dumb Because AI Researchers Are Too Clever*, ACM Computing Surveys, 27/3, September 1995.

[17]-SCHERTLER, W.: *Einsatz von neuen Technologien im Marketingmanagement von Tourismusorganisationen*, Publication of the AIEST, Vol. 40, 1998.

[18]-STEINER, T.: *Distributed Software Agents for WWW-based Destination Information Systems*, PhD Thesis, University of Lausanne 1999.

[19] - www.hec.unil.ch/people/tsteiner

[20] - TJOA, A M. & WERTNER, H.: *Interfacing WWW with Distributed Database Applications*. Proceedings of the ENTER96 conference in Innsbruck.

[21]-WERTHNER, H.: *Design Principles of Tourist Information Systems*, Proceedings of the ENTER96 conference in Innsbruck, Springer 1996.

[22]- *Windows Hospitality Interface Specification (WHIS)*.

http://www.microsoft.com/industry/hospitality/developers/initiatives/whis/default.stm

A Critical Analysis of Tourism Information Technology Research

Andrew J Frew
Director, ITR
Napier University, Craighouse Campus
Edinburgh, EH10 5LG
Tel: 0131 455 6123   Fax: 0131 455 6190
a.frew@napier.ac.uk

Abstract

This work represented here is an attempt to bring together the tourism information technology research literature and provide an initial critical analysis. Sources were restricted to reviewed research work in the domain from which significant themes, trends and issues were derived. Within the identified contextual boundaries, definitions and resource constraints some preliminary analyses and interpretation are offered. The findings illustrate that the last six years have witnessed a sustained high level of research activity with the principal sources being the UK, Germany, Austria and the USA. Significant efforts have been focused on tourism information systems, electronic distribution and commerce and a variety of web-based initiatives. However, research gap areas would appear to include quality assurance, mobile access and the training domain.

1. Introduction

The aim here was primarily to assist those working at the interface of tourism and information technology and provide both a basis and a stimulus for further discussion and research. Original impetus for the work came from 'State of the Art' research work undertaken on behalf of the DG XIII KNITE* project for which a searchable database was constructed. The objectives were to identify *research* articles in tourism information technology (principally drawn from the journal and conference literature but as a qualifying criterion must have undergone a refereeing or peer review process), and to subsequently draw out significant themes, trends and issues. The analyses and interpretation presented should be viewed in the context of the boundaries, definitions and general resource constraints of the research.

2. Methodology

The work was undertaken in several iterative phases with boundaries and definitions established to delineate the broad area under investigation. As stated, only sources potentially capable of yielding refereed or reviewed *research* work were examined and thus often excluded from coverage were areas of market intelligence and specific business application. A second boundary to some extent arising from the overall resource constraint was that only English-language publications were considered for inclusion. The debatable assumption here is that although much original material does indeed often first appear in other languages (notably German), in almost all instances the works are either contemporaneously or subsequently reproduced or re-worked in an English-language format. The definitional issues were somewhat less tractable e.g. that a work has a significant element of Information Technology (in its broad definition) may be relatively easy to ascertain, although, at the extremes includes work which may be more appropriate to the publication domains of computer science, information science, knowledge management etc. Equally, the boundaries between tourism and hospitality or between tourism and leisure are often indistinct. An inclusive approach has been adopted whereby papers featuring hospitality or leisure to be classified as being in the area of Information Technology in Tourism (ITT), must exhibit a clear link into mainstream tourism. All work encompassed by the literature search produced a superset from which, ultimately a qualified subset of ITT references emerged.

Secondary sources were 'cascaded' from these initial core sources:

- The proceedings of the ENTER conferences 1994 – 1999
- The proceedings of the HITA conferences 1994 – 1999
- Texts in Hospitality and Tourism Information Technology
- The Information Technology and Tourism Journal

A database was then constructed from a wide range of publication types with an extended keyword field added to permit flexible searching and detailed analysis. Keyword allocation was a particularly iterative process with keywords being extended and 'cleansed' regularly throughout to provide as far as possible comprehensive coverage and consistency of use. Electronic communication with peer researchers represented the final stage in this process. A wide variety of *keywords* was applied to the articles under consideration. The selection and application of keywords is fundamental to the ultimate validity of the database and it should be recognised that while numerous keywords are widely accepted and arise naturally in many of the works cited, a number have been necessarily subjectively allocated by the author. Unlike the keyword approach adopted by research journals and other research forums, the intention here was to provide much broader accessibility to the database contents and so while the usual summary and conventionally accepted keywords have been applied, these have been supplemented by more inclusive terms. These keywords serve two purposes, firstly to provide an indication of the most significant aspects of the work in terms of topic and so forth and it is these which give an indication of the themes and trends in research, and secondly a wider range of keywords which, while of lesser significance, should facilitate more productive searching of the overall database.

3. Preliminary Results

Fig. 1   Tourism IT Articles by Year

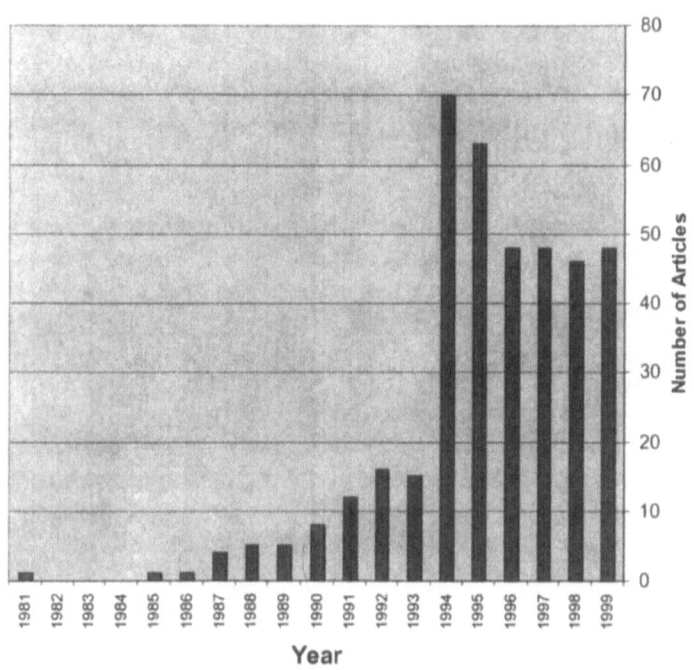

Of 750 references 391 remained when reports, books, newspaper articles and electronic sources were removed. An indication of the chronological trend for ITT articles etc. can be seen in Fig. 1. Caution should be attached to any interpretation - it is derived from a restricted sample of the tourism IT research literature and in addition, there are undoubtedly many factors at work. The trend reflects the fact that the ENTER conferences commencing 1994 provided a hitherto unavailable forum for publication of tourism IT research. Possibly it is reflecting a genuine underlying upsurge in development and in interest in the field of tourism IT (one of the drivers for conferences such as ENTER and HITA in the first place). Note that 1994 was when the Web first began to generally impact tourism, in fact there is no mention of the Internet prior to 1994 in any of the work covered by this paper. In any event there currently seems to be a much higher but stable level of activity. Much of the analysis will look at the past 6 years as this has produced the substantial majority of the output and an initial attempt at breaking these articles down into key research areas is, presented in Table 1 by illustrating the 15 most frequent citations for all years.

Table 1
Topic Frequency

Keyword	Frequency	%
Marketing	61	9.9
Tourism Information System	61	9.9
DMS	55	8.9
Internet	51	8.2
CRS	45	7.3
Web	42	6.8
Electronic Distribution	40	6.5
Reservations	36	5.8
GDS	35	5.7
SME	35	5.7
Destination	34	5.5
Multimedia	34	5.5
Computing	32	5.2
Hotel	32	5.2
Electronic Commerce	26	4.2

Fig. 2.
Research by Country

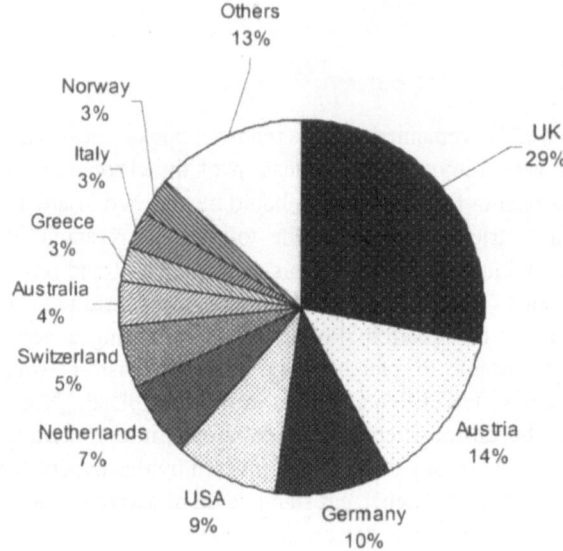

It will come as no real surprise to see the predominance of Internet/Web related work, nor to see information/reservation systems, especially those predicated upon a destination orientation, having such a predominant position. Another interesting global illustration is to look at where research work originates and this is depicted in Fig. 2. These are of course very unsophisticated indicators and may undoubtedly be further refined as the database is extended and developed, however even as interim results it is interesting to see such a prolific output from the UK, especially in view of the generally acknowledged weaknesses in a number of the key application areas, especially destination/internet/information systems. On the other hand, it is not at all surprising to see the significance of Austria much of which must reflect the success of TIScover/TIS and associated research. A puzzling contrast with this is the dearth of Irish work when one considers the Gulliver counterpart. Of course there is a degree of bias here since four ENTER conferences have been held in Austria. Some of the major topics of the last six years are presented in Fig. 3.

Fig. 3
Cumulative Topic Frequency 1994-1999

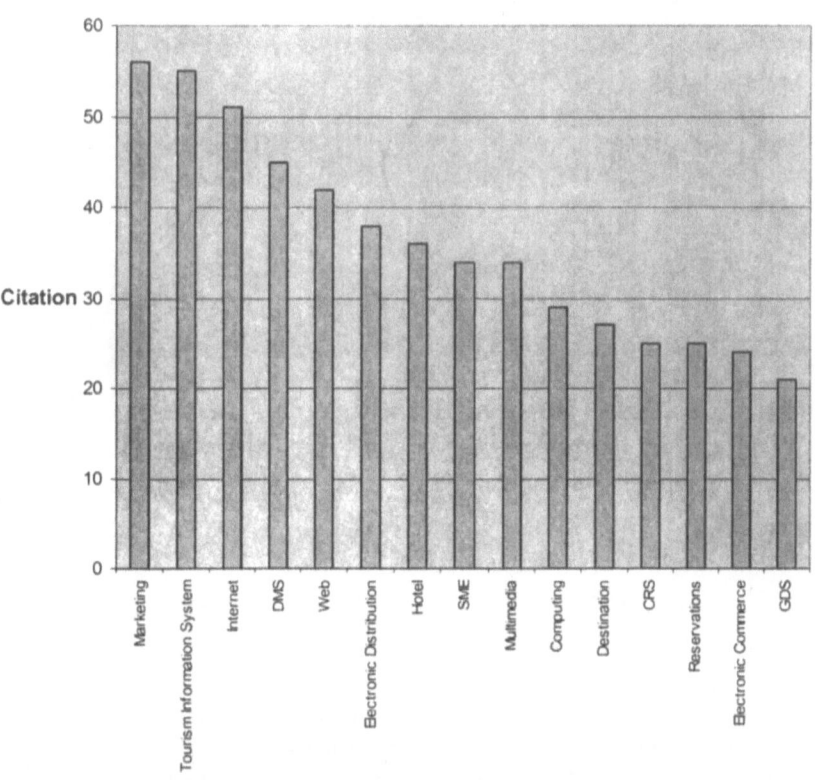

This profile of topics is not markedly different from the cumulative picture produced by querying all references from all years. There are a few rearrangements of relative position but the main research themes and trends are still readily evident. This is a *cumulative* picture whereas Fig. 4 illustrates the *changing* level of interest in each of these themes over the same six-year period, in other words their *relative* contribution.

Fig. 4
Annual Topic Frequency 1994-1999

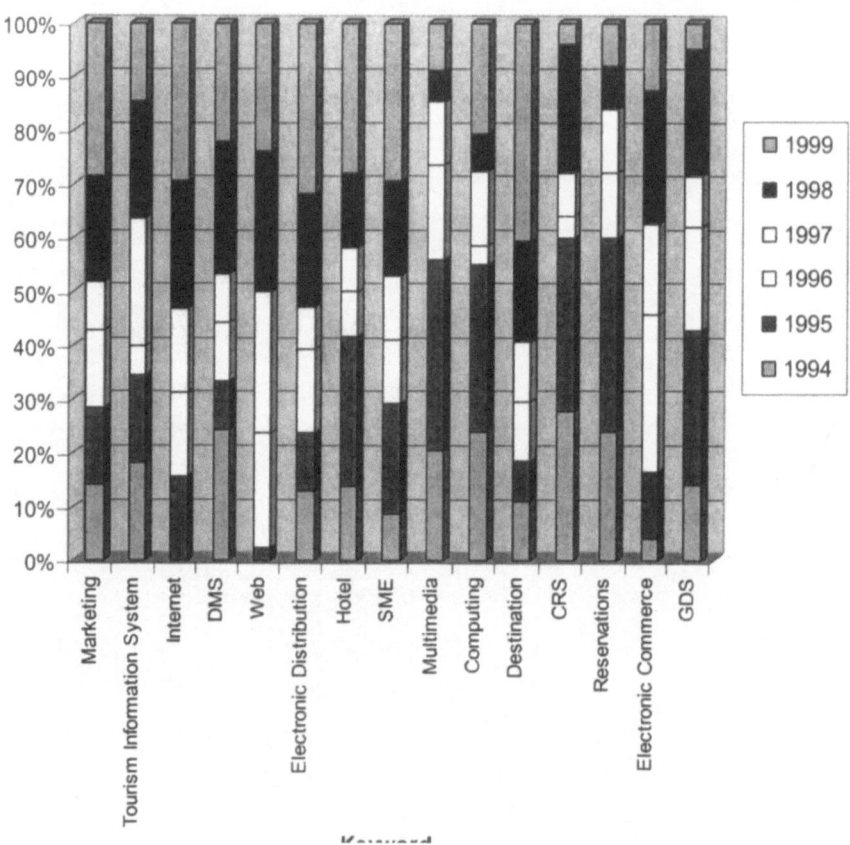

In trying to adopt the inclusive approach to keywords described earlier, there are a number of difficulties, which arise (even supposing agreement with the allocation of the keyword descriptors). Firstly having multiple terms applied to each article, while assisting the database search process, may give rise to an apparent over-reporting of interest e.g. the terms electronic distribution and electronic marketing may apply to one piece of work and the *frequencies* therefore increased in two allied areas.

Secondly, there are many specific terms which accurately reflect work in a niche area and which may disappear from view (and thus not contribute to the main field) through infrequent citation. Thirdly, and an interesting exercise to consider perhaps, no *weighting* has been given to any individual pieces of research, i.e. all are assumed to be of equal merit. This is open to debate and while the report has largely focused on work that has gone through double blind peer review, the robustness of this process is at best uneven. Following on from this point, it must be recognised that value judgements may have to be made regarding the significance of contribution to the body of knowledge, from any piece of work. An excellent range of review pieces may well be useful to many peer researchers, while a single paper describing fundamental empirical work could have a profound effect on an individual area.

These issues have largely been side-stepped for future research being deemed more appropriate for broader consideration at this stage, rather than the presumption of a single individual. And finally, it is evident that a number of authors are perhaps over enthusiastic in recycling perhaps one or two empirical pieces of work through a large number of publications in journals, conferences and so forth. No attempt has been made to moderate this and thus all identified citations have been included. In effect, only the first two of this non-exhaustive list of potential criticisms have been tackled with the research works being re-coded with, where possible, the single or at most the two keywords, which best described the overall focus or theme of each work. The reader should always bear in mind the caveat that the purpose of the report is largely to make qualitative observations - the frequency of occurrence of topics should consequently be interpreted very broadly.

All ITT records were re-classified against a more restricted keyword set, where allied themes were 'clustered' to facilitate the coding. Even so, it could still be argued that such a reduction in keywords sacrifices discrimination and it is a challenge to strike a balance along this spectrum of information loss versus information overload.

4. Results Re-visited

In the event, the database was then re-treated and for comparison with Table 1 the fifteen most frequently cited terms have been listed in Table 2. It can readily be seen from this that the previously predominant themes are still coming through.

While it may be reassuring to many to see strong representation of the perceived crucial areas of electronic commerce in its broadest applications and destination-oriented work, especially related to SMEs, it is perhaps of concern to see so little attention devoted to service quality research or to training and education research or IT skills for example.

Table 2.
Topic Frequency - restricted keyword set

Keyword	%
Tourism Information System	13.8
Web	10.9
Electronic Distribution	8.7
Marketing	7.9
DMS	7.7
Electronic Commerce	6.6
GDS	6.0
Computing	5.5
Multimedia	5.3
Expert System	4.0
SME	3.8
Travel Agent	3.4
Strategy	2.1
Decision-Support System	1.9
Hotel	1.7
Service Quality	1.7
Virtual reality	1.7

Tourism Information Systems have clearly been widely researched, indeed of the 65 references in the database, 51 had a different primary author and 26 were produced in the past three years. A sample of such work [1-8] illustrates its diversity. It should be remembered that much research will span two or more keyword categories and in particular both marketing and tourism information systems research will have substantial overlap with the closely related area of destination management and destination marketing systems (DMS). Turning to work where the principle focus was the *Web* (which was used in this instance as a term incorporating most Internet references) we have a combined total of 89 references, more than half of which have appeared in the last two years, again with wide authorship, however, of note is the significant level of Scandinavian work as evidenced among others, in the work of Aanonsen, Marcussen and Tjostheim, [9-11]. *Electronic Distribution* has been a consistently significant area over the past five years and a total of 41 research references have been included in the database, a sample of which include [12-26]. Around 25% of authors in the field have published twice or more in the past five years. *Marketing* oriented research has been conducted by a range of authors with for example Main and Wober separately producing several works on Marketing Information Systems, closely allied to the Tourism Information Systems above. A selection is appended [8,11,39-47] with work ranging from cybermarketing and travel marketing through to the marketing of strategic alliances. *DMS* research as noted, obviously overlaps considerably with other topic areas - in fact all of the above, however, this category was derived from those papers which very clearly emphasised the destination in Destination Marketing (or Management) Systems. This area too has produced a wide range of activity [1,27,28-38].

5. Research Domains

The 1997 report of the 'think tank' (the strategic advisory group on the 5th framework program on information society applications for transport and associated services) on Information Society Technologies (IST) for tourism, which underpinned initiation of the KNITE project, sought to foster the identification of research domains. The domains postulated within this programme (italics) have been taken as a reference point in the context of the current work and it is perhaps useful to tentatively map the nature and level of research activity onto these thus:

Quality assurance in tourism -very little work has been identified, only 10 citations referring to quality in any way and this appears to constitute a significant research gap. *The organisation of information systems for tourism* is quite evidently one of the most vigorous research areas with work of increasing sophistication emerging from many authors in many countries while *value added brokerage,* despite the level of interest in electronic commerce, has yet to be examined by tourism IT researchers and would again constitute a research gap. *Information processing in the value chain* - once again, a well-researched and vital area with distributed databases and architectures producing significant efforts in the last few years. *Information presentation/user interfaces*- this is a very exciting and growing research area with much work being undertaken and much to addressed across the spectrum from multimedia/hypermedia to user interfaces generally. Substantial research work will be needed to explore the burgeoning fields of usability and natural language.

New marketing technologies and techniques, again, as can be seen from even a cursory analysis of the outcomes above, this is currently one of the most fertile territories for research and will undoubtedly drive and cross-fertilise with most other research domains. *Management Information and Decision Support* - the depth and quality of work emerging in DMS, Expert Systems and DSS among others gives this potential domain a solid foundation and a rigorous framework perhaps only equalled in one or two other areas. The evidence points strongly towards increasing use of public and private web-based resources being constructed, queried and applied in alliance with intelligent software. Continued and strong activity in this area would be deemed necessary to take full advantage of the proliferation of potentially useful (to management decision-making) sources. *Information Access and Distribution* - except insofar as work has been undertaken on electronic distribution and applied computing in support of this area, very little work has been undertaken that specifically supports e.g. the mobile user; technologies, architectures and channels must command more attention for future research activity if this is to be profitably exploited. *Multimedia content* - if production and delivery systems of multimedia materials in support of tourism are to be coherently developed then substantial work is necessary in this domain. While there is a significant body of work that has examined the production of multimedia materials, little research has actually been brought to maturity on the delivery mechanisms. Digital media and communications channels provide a great challenge for the future of tourism and with many authors arguing that rich media will provide a crucial competitive advantage for destinations in the upcoming electronic distribution battleground, research in this domain may well be viewed as a priority area. *Training Systems* - as far as tourism IT research is concerned, this domain has been almost neglected with the current study revealing only a handful of authors even touching on the area e.g. [48-50]. Much of the vitality, quality and efficiency of the tourism infrastructure is governed by the scope and standard of education and training support systems and materials from formal education and training through flexible and lifelong learning and expansion of research activity here would surely reap dividends.

6. Limitations

It is envisaged that this database will undergo further update through ongoing literature search and feedback via the KNITE network, the ENTER conference and beyond and this will be reflected in further reporting and analysis along with the establishment of a dynamically updated source for general research use. The author is neither a librarian nor an information scientist and makes claims regarding neither the rigour of nomenclature nor the classifications used in this report except inasmuch as they should be useful to the researcher and practitioner. The report does not purport to be a comprehensive coverage of all tourism IT literature and indeed it is anticipated that there will be many missing references – in the time-scale it was not a viable proposition to offer a total coverage of all literature. Instead the position adopted was to presume that any research work of significance would appear in the proceedings of one of the major research conferences or cited therein.

*KNITE, DGXIII Project Number : 25292; Activation the Community of Actors as a Networked Dynamic Knowledge Base on Information Society Technologies for Tourism within Europe

References

1. Archdale, G., *Destination Databases: Issues and Priorities*, in *Tourism - The State of the Art*, A.V. Seaton, Editor. 1994. p. 246-253.
2. Ebner, A., *TIS Tourism Information System for the Tyrol*, in *Information and Communications Technologies in Tourism*, W. Schertler, *et al.*, Editors. 1994, Springer-Verlag: Vienna, Austria. p. 35-42.
3. Pollock, A., *The Impact of Information Technology on Destination Marketing*. EIU Travel and Tourism Analyst, 1995. **No 3**.
4. Marcussen, C. and P. Morthorst, *Public Tourist Information Offices as Booking-Centres for Accommodation*, in *Information and Communications Technologies in Tourism*, S. Klein, *et al.*, Editors. 1996, Springer-Verlag: Vienna, Austria. p. 168-179.

5.   Burger, F., *et al.*, *TIS@WEB - Database Supported Tourist Information on the Web*, in *Information and Communications Technologies in Tourism*, A.M. Tjoa, Editor. 1997, Springer-Verlag: Vienna, Austria. p. 180-189.

6.   Tjostheim, I., *The New Network in the Norwegian Tourism Industry*, in *Information and Communications Technologies in Tourism*, A.M. Tjoa, Editor. 1997, Springer-Verlag: Vienna, Austria. p. 110-118.

7.   Frew, A.J. and P. O'Connor, *A Comparative Examination of the Implementation of Destination Marketing System Strategies: Scotland and Ireland*, in *Information and Communications Technologies in Tourism*, D. Buhalis, A.M. Tjoa, and J. Jafari, Editors. 1998, Springer-Verlag: Vienna, Austria. p. 258-267.

8.   Fesenmaier, D., A.W. Leppers, and J.T. O'Leary, *Developing a Knowledge-based Tourism Marketing Information System.* Information Technology and Tourism, 1999. **2**(1): p. 31-44.

9.   Marcussen, C.H. and D. Skoldager, *Extranets of National Tourist Organisations*, in *Information and Communications Technologies in Tourism*, D. Buhalis, A.M. Tjoa, and J. Jafari, Editors. 1998, Springer-Verlag: Vienna, Austria. p. 103-119.

10.   Tjostheim, I. and J.-O. Eide, *A Case Study of an On-line Auction for the World Wide Web*, in *Information and Communications Technologies in Tourism*, D. Buhalis, A.M. Tjoa, and J. Jafari, Editors. 1998, Springer-Verlag: Vienna. p. 149-161.

11.   Aanonsen, K., Y. Lindsjorn, and G. Kamfjord, *International Marketing via Broadband Networks - Building the Local Network in a Norwegian Region*, in *Information and Communications Technologies in Tourism*, W. Schertler, *et al.*, Editors. 1995, Springer-Verlag: Vienna, Austria. p. 308-317.

12.   Buhalis, D., *The Impact of Information Communication Technologies on Tourism Distribution Channels: Implications for Small and Medium sized Tourism Enterprises' Strategic Marketing and Management*, . 1995, Surrey: Guildford.

13.   Geyer, G., C. Kuhn, and B. Schmid, *An Electronic Product Catalog for Distributed Environments*, in *Information and Communications Technologies in Tourism*, S. Klein, *et al.*, Editors. 1996, Springer: Innsbruck, Austria. p. 60-69.

14.   Karcher, K., *The Four Global Distribution Systems in the Travel and Tourism Industry.* Electronic Markets - International Journal of Electronic Commerce, 1996. **6**(2).

15.   Lyle, C. *The Changing Economics of Travel Distribution.* in *Seminar on Tourism and New Technologies: Global Distribution Systems.* 1996. Cote D'Ivoire: WTO.

16.   Marcussen, C., *Marketing European Tourism Products via the Internet.* Journal of Travel and Tourism Marketing, 1996. **6**(3/4).

17.   Frew, A.J. and C. Dorren, *A Qualitative Analysis of Hotel List Providers on the World Wide Web*, in *Information and Communications Technologies in*

50

Tourism, A.M. Tjoa, Editor. 1997, Springer-Verlag: Vienna, Austria. p. 221-230.

18. Marcussen, C., *Electronic Distribution of Holiday and Business Hotels*, in *Information and Communications Technologies in Tourism*, A.M. Tjoa, Editor. 1997, Springer-Verlag: Vienna, Austria. p. 190-198.

19. O'Connor, P. and J. Rafferty, *Lessons in Distributing Small Hotels Electronically*, in *Hospitality Information Technology*, K.P. Brewer, Editor. 1997, HITA: Las Vegas. p. 30-39.

20. Daniele, R., *An Overview of the Evolution of Electronic Distribution of Travel and Tourism in Australia*, in *Information and Communications Technologies in Tourism*, D. Buhalis, J. Jafari, and A.M. Tjoa, Editors. 1998, Springer-Verlag: Vienna, Austria. p. 328-337.

21. Schuster, A.G., *A Delphi Survey on Electronic Distribution Channels for Intermediaries in the Tourism Industry - The Situation in German Speaking Countries*, in *Information and Communications Technologies in Tourism*, D. Buhalis, A.M. Tjoa, and D. Buhalis, Editors. 1998, Springer-Verlag: Vienna, Austria. p. 224-234.

22. Buhalis, D. and S. Keeling, *Distributing B&B Accommodation in York, UK: Advantages and Developments Emerging through the Internet*, in *Information and Communications Technologies in Tourism*, D. Buhalis and W. Schertler, Editors. 1999, Springer-Verlag: Vienna, Austria. p. 228-237.

23. Frew, A.J. and P. O'Connor, *Destination Marketing System Strategiesin Scotland and Ireland: An Approach to Assessment.* Information Technology and Tourism, 1999. **2**(1): p. 2-13.

24. Hopken, W., *Modelling of an Electronic Tourism Market*, in *Information and Communications Technologies in Tourism*, D. Buhalis and W. Schertler, Editors. 1999, Springer-Verlag: Vienna, Austria. p. 161-171.

25. O'Brien, P., *An Architecture for a Distributed Travel Reservations System*, in *Information and Communications Technologies in Tourism*, D. Buhalis and W. Schertler, Editors. 1999, Springer-Verlag: Vienna, Austria. p. 172-178.

26. Tjostheim, I., M. Bergan, and J. Lous, *The New Extranet for the Norwegian Tourism Industry*, in *Information and Communications Technologies in Tourism*, D. Buhalis and W. Schertler, Editors. 1999, Springer-Verlag: Vienna, Austria. p. 357-364.

27. Buhalis, D., *Regional Integrated Computer Information Reservation Mangement Systems as a Strategic Tool for the Small and Medium Tourism Enterprises.* Tourism Management, 1994. **14**(5): p. 366-378.

28. Haines, P., *Destination Marketing Systems*, in *Information and Communications Technologies in Tourism*, W. Schertler, *et al.*, Editors. 1994, Springer-Verlag: Vienna, Austria. p. 50-55.

29. Buhalis, D., *Information and Telecommunication Technologies as a Strategic Tool for Tourism Enhancement at Destination Regions*, in *Information and Communications Technologies in Tourism*, S. Klein, *et al.*, Editors. 1996, Springer-Verlag: Vienna, Austria. p. 131-142.

30. Sussman, S., *The Impact of New Technological Developments on Destination Management Systems*, in *Progress in Tourism, Recreation and Hospitality Management*, C.P. Cooper and A. Lockwood, Editors. 1994, Belhaven Press: London. p. 289-296. 90.

31. Wober, K., *Strategic Planning Tools Inside the Marketing Information System in Use by the Austrian National Tourist Office*, in *Information and Communications Technologies in Tourism*, W. Schertler, *et al.*, Editors. 1994, Springer-Verlag: Vienna, Austria`. p. 201-208. 31.

32. Gerdes, *A National Destination Management System (DMS) based on the examples of Germany and Switzerland*, in *Information and Communications Technologies in Tourism*, D. Buhalis, A.M. Tjoa, and J. Jafari, Editors. 1998, Springer-Verlag: Vienna, Austria. p. 248-257.

33. Mutch, A., *The English Tourist Network Automation Project: A Case Study in Inter-organisational Failure.* Tourism Management, 1996. **17**(8): p. 603-609.

34. O'Connor, P. and J. Rafferty, *Gulliver - Distributing Irish Tourism Electronically.* Electronic Markets - International Journal of Electronic Commerce, 1996. **7**(2).

35. Fesenmaier, D., *Traveler Use of Visitor Information Centers: Implications for Development in Illinois.* Journal of Travel Research, 1994(Summer): p. 44-50.

36. Sheldon, P.J., *Information Technology and Computer Reservation Systems*, in *Tourism Marketing and Management Handbook*, Witt and Moutinho, Editors. 1994, Prentice Hall: Hemel Hempstead. p. 126-130.

37. Sussman, S. and M. Baker, *Responding to the Electronic Marketplace: Lessons From Destination Management Systems.* International Journal of Hospitality Management, 1996. **15**(2): p. 99-112.

38. Pringle, S. and A.J. Frew, *Hi-Line - Destined to Fail?*, in *Tourism State of the Art*, A. Seaton, Editor. 1994, John Wiley and Sons inc.: Strathclyde, Glasgow. p. 500-509.

39. Wober, K.W., *Tourism Marketing Information System.* Annals of Tourism Research, 1994. **21**(2): p. 396-398.

40. Desinano, P. and C. Vigo, *Marketing and Information Technology in the Hospitality Industry. A Strategic Approach*, in *Information and Communications Technologies in Tourism*, W. Schertler, *et al.*, Editors. 1995, Springer-Verlag: Vienna, Austria. p. 65-75.

41. Frew, A.J., E. Crichton, and G. McKenzie, *Multi-media Marketing across ATM Broadband Networks - A Hospitality and Tourism Perspective (Part II - Global DMS?)*, in *Hospitality Information Technology*, M. Kasavana, Editor. 1995, HITA: Edinburgh. p. 47-64.

42. Froeschl, K., *Macrodata Integration Support for Electronic Tourism Marketing*, in *Information and Communications Technologies in Tourism*, W. Schertler, *et al.*, Editors. 1995, Springer-Verlag: Vienna, Austria. p. 318-327.

52

43.   Karcher, K., *The Emergence of Electronic Market Systems in the European Tour Operator Business.* Electronic Markets, 1995. **4**(13/14): p. 11.

44.   Hawkins, D.E., M. Leventhal, and W. Oden, *The Virtual Tourism Environment - Utilisation of Information Technology to Enhance Strategic Travel Marketing.* Progress in Tourism and Hospitality Research, 1996. **2**: p. 223-238.

45.   Walle, A.H., *Tourism and the Internet: Opportunities for Direct Marketing.* Journal of Travel Research, 1996. **35**(1): p. 72-77.

46.   Marcussen, C., *Marketing European Tourism Products via Internet/WWW.* Geography and Tourism Marketing, 1997: p. 23-34.

47.   Main, H., *Emerging Technologies and their Role in Developing a Marketing Information System (MkIS) for Tourism and Hospitality Products*, in *Information and Communications Technologies in Tourism*, D. Buhalis and W. Schertler, Editors. 1999, Springer-Verlag: Vienna, Austria. p. 345-356.

48.   O'Connor, P. and D. Buhalis, *IT in the Curriculum*, in *Hospitality Information Technology*, A.J. Frew, Editor. 1999, HITA: Edinburgh. p. 1-8.

49.   Buhalis, D., *Information Technologies in Tourism: Implications for the Tourism Curriculum*, in *Information and Communications Technologies in Tourism*, D. Buhalis, A.M. Tjoa, and J. Jafari, Editors. 1998, Springer-Verlag: Vienna, Austria. p. 289-297.

50.   Daniele, R. and N. Mistilis, Information Technology and Tourism Education in Australia: An Industry View of Skills and Qualities Required in Graduates, in Information and Communications Technologies in Tourism, D. Buhalis and W. Schertler, Editors. 1999, Springer-Verlag: Vienna, Austria. p. 140-150.

The Failure Of The New Discipline: Information Technology, Business Process, And The Control Of Tourism Operatives

Martin Peacock
Business School
University of North London
Holloway Road, London N7 8DB, England.
Email: m.peacock@unl.ac.uk

1 Introduction

Information technology within tourism presents us with a conundrum. While clearly reshaping the tools of communication and the technological landscape, what is questionable is the impact IT has on overall business performance. The 'productivity paradox' which contrasts the investment on IT against the lack of significant improvements in productivity has become one of the key questions for the new Millennium. This paper explores the relationship between corporate culture, the motivations behind the development of information systems and real working experiences. It suggests that a key reason for the lack of success for information systems is an inadequate assessment of the role of information systems and their impact on working practices.

Claims of overall increases in productivity caused by increasing use of information technology are difficult to justify empirically both at the local and the global level. US improvements in productivity can be linked directly to computer *manufacturing* (Anonymous, 1999) with productivity growth in other sectors stalled or falling. Landauer (1995) reported Roach's findings that information workers in the US (1960-87) had seen no increase in productivity.

Although there are clearly specific installations where technological innovation can be linked to increases in productivity, there are also installations where systems do not generate enough additional revenue or reduced costs to cover their purchase and installation. Moules (1996) reported that IT projects tend to run late and/or significantly over budget. Baker *et al* (1998) quoted Clegg who claimed that 90 percent of IT projects fail to meet their performance goals. There is no evidence linking the revolution in technology and working practices to significant overall improvements in productivity within the tourist and hospitality industry (Peacock, 1998).

Pilot studies suggested the hypothesis that there is a wide divergence between the system developers and the users. What the innovators were wanting to happen simply wasn't happening, or if it was, not in the expected manner. It was this 'gap' between the vision of the initiators and industry realities, which was felt to be significant in perhaps explaining what underlay the 'productivity paradox'.

While most industry practitioners have adopted a crude technological determinism, where the system is seen as a logical product of the technological possibilities, the research decided to focus on the philosophies underpinning the innovations. It could be argued that information technology within tourism is less a blank screen awaiting the creativity of the developer and user, but more a new tool for imposing the mind-sets and preconceptions of these same developers. In the same way in which the first steam powered factories and workshops were modelled on water-powered ones and the initial development of the motorcar leaned on experiences with horse-drawn carriages, technological innovation can take on the inappropriate characteristics of a previous age.

This paper suggests that there is a link between the limited commercial impact of information technology within tourism and the continuation of attitudes and practices more appropriate to a previous level of technology. Specifically this paper examines the relationship between technological innovation and attempts to 'discipline' and control operatives within the tourism and hospitality industries.

2 'Discipline'

Technology has often been used as an instrument of control and the term itself has a link with the use of tools to control inanimate objects. Possibly the best illustration of the use of technology to control people is Zuboff's (1988) example of Bentham's *Panopticon*. Here a prison is designed with glass walls and corridors radiating out like spokes from a wheel. The concept is that these corridors can be controlled by one guard situated at the centre of the wheel. The technology (in this case glass walls, a rotating chair and innovative design) is used to control the inmates. This is not an image totally distant from modern information systems within tourism and hospitality.

There is an aspect of modern computing that emphasises the collection and dissemination of data, even when it is at odds with the personal experiences of operatives and managers. After all: "Brabbage's idea for a programmable computing machine arose within a society that was entering upon an obsessive affair with data" (Beardon, 1994). Lyotard (1984) argues that the computer is closely allied to positivist thinking and promotes only the formal scientific aspects of knowledge.

Using the computer and its data manipulation as a source of control appears to be a key issue for the tourism and hospitality industries. Kasavana (1994) claims that "the new elements of success appear to be controls, controls and controls". Ritzer identifies the 'Fordism' of technological applications, as they are used to improve 'efficiency', 'calculability', 'predictability' and 'control'. "Thus over the long term we have seen a shift away from control by people and toward control by technologies" (Ritzer, 1993). He illustrates these themes with an exploration of how McDonald's operates. Collins and

Bicknell (1997) suggest that computers' potential effectiveness is exaggerated because of the popular belief that computers are synonymous with efficiency.

Suggested reasons for the link between technological innovation and the *panopticon*, could include the link between the computer and positivism, illustrated by the power of the spreadsheet. But other reasons could include accountancy driven system development (illustrated by an emphasis on timely profit and loss statements) or simple management distrust of operatives particularly prevalent in cash based sectors of the tourism industries. Product X "spots the fiddles, management's greatest problem" (sales literature).

Modern information systems privilege a vision of technology which has close links with Bentham's glass prison. In the NEDC working party report on competitiveness in tourism (1992), TGI Friday's use of technology to provide "control and monitoring systems", is listed under Case Studies Best Practices. The same report also praises McDonald's use of systems. Baker *et al* (1998) suggested that the EPOS system developed for Bass Taverns removed the "uncertainties" of operative fraud and the "black economy" for public house managers.

3 Methodology

There is a tendency for central management to perceive the development of their systems as operator driven, even when there is no evidence to support any claims of consultation (e.g. Rocco Forte in Teare & Boer, 1991). For the purpose of this research it was decided to focus on the actual users of the information systems: line managers and operatives.

A pilot study indicated considerable variation between the perspectives of system developers and actual users. To illustrate this it was decided to use a case study approach where the emphasis was on developing relationships of trust. Rather than use the (now oddly traditional) method of postal questionnaire, it was decided to select two tourism and hospitality operations and use observation and interview. The impact of new technology has been studied in these two organisations for the last year. The confidentiality of these organisations and our informants has been preserved.

The focus of this research was the divergence between the information generated by the technological system and reality. Areas studied included cash handling procedures, payment fraud, system manipulation (specifically in relation to performance targets), unit management financial fraud and the degree of tolerance for fraud. Different perspectives ("dual culture" - interviewed manager) on system data were critically examined and related to external factors, such as labour shortages. Automation of customers and company use of 'mystery customers' was also explored.

The degree of tolerance for fraud and system manipulation was related to the inability to recruit or retain competent line management. 'Operational flexibility' has become a key concept which defines the parameters of 'acceptable' fraud and misuse of the management information system. It was investigated in some detail.

4 The Delivering Company

Our first focus was a unit for a company specialising in delivering, highly perishable cooked foods principally to tourists in hotels in the central London area. This was a company which has recently completed a huge investment in information technology, including a sophisticated computer telephony integration (CTI). Customers ring a central number with their order. If the number is recognised it is transferred to the local outlet and customer details (e.g. delivery address) appear with the call. The company (a market leader) puts considerable faith in it's sophisticated information systems.

The company has a bonus system for managers which is tied into two main measures of performance: sales and efficiency. Efficiency is defined as the percentage of consumers who receive their order within 30 minutes (called the "under 30s", in the company colloquialism). Managers perceive the sales figures as outside their control, so they tend to emphasise the 'efficiency' figures: "who gives a damn about sales as long as my service ['under 30s'] is above 95% each day - so what!!" (interviewed manager).

The 'efficiency' figure is manipulated at the point of order. If the operative left the order on the screen (without pressing the button to have the order transmitted to the kitchen) then the beginning of the thirty minute count could be delayed. Orders could still be taken on other lines. Head office countered this manipulation by recording how long the orders were kept on screen. This device is now being countered by pressing the 'edit' button for the order. This means that the order is not on screen, the clock is not running, but the kitchen is processing the order as the order has been passed verbally.

The second method of manipulating the time of the order is to put through the order as if it is required in the future. Successful manipulation of the information system to maximise bonus needs skilful professional practice. After all, "people bad at their legitimate jobs, are unlikely to be any better at coping with fiddling" (Mars, 1994). An example of the manipulation failing is the customer who received their product before the order had technically been placed by the system. Bonuses are regulated by the successful use of this manipulation.

Apart from using bonuses in an attempt to influence employee behaviour the company also uses technology to make employee behaviour more predictable. Modern information systems often come complete with a 'scripting' of operatives to make sure that predictability is maintained: modern property management systems can remind the receptionist whether it is 'good morning' or 'good evening'. This company, with it's eight step telephone guide, is no exception. Unfortunately the rigidity of the system creates it's own problems, apart from operative fatigue. There are now websites available detailing questions that can disrupt the script, but simply an enquiry followed by an order will create sufficient problems.

One area where information systems were expected to cut back on fraud was the move away from cash to cards. Observation would tend to suggest that this is not the case. Firstly phone card checks can enable the criminal consumer to check if his or her stolen credit card is still usable. Secondly, even with an authorisation check the volume of business subsequently found to be through stolen credit cards was thousands of pounds a year. Tolerance for use of these cards seemed surprisingly high, even when their users were known to staff at the unit. Pressure of business led to these losses being written off. One managers said that prosecuting known offenders might have the effect of publicising the ease of the crime.

The high proportion of stolen credit card business could be down to the consumer offering a different card to the one mentioned (and authorised) on the phone. However a significant proportion was internal fraud. One unit manager (not in the surveyed unit) was recently dismissed after hidden video cameras caught him replacing cash orders with stolen credit card ones (and pocketing the cash). The amounts here were highly significant and it seems likely that a general level of this type of fraud is endemic. It was observed that stolen card numbers were used to place bogus orders, which then subsequently became staff food. Normal staff meals can impact on performance bonuses but stolen credit card orders, subsequently eaten as staff food, do not.

Use of information systems for internal fraud is not unusual, even when the computer systems is designed to stop precisely this type of abuse. Thompson (1997), in an interesting study of computer crime in Australia, noted that 90 per cent of those that had experienced computer-related incidents had been subjected to sources internal to their own organisation. To some extent, the distancing effect of technology (the move away from face-to-face communication) can assist those with knowledge of the weaknesses and loopholes of the system.

Computer fraud can be seen as part of a struggle between the centre and local units. One duty manager specifically related her manipulation of the bonus system to the head office's recent decision to stop funding taxis home for managers working beyond one in the morning. She was confident that increasing technological monitoring (including video surveillance) could be matched by increasing sophistication on the part of local unit personnel.

In part, head office tolerance for widespread (and often obvious) manipulation of the systems, was the product of problems recruiting and retaining staff. As their 'Operational Effectiveness Survey' (a difficult to obtain document) noted: "We do not feel that we retain the right people needed to maintain long term success." Those committing fraud were often the most skilful and hardworking employees (particularly duty managers), which the company needed. With a limited loyalty and low morale from local managers, senior management need care to retain key staff.

Unit managers believed that fraud was often known about and accepted (within limits) by area managers, but not known about and accepted by head office. Line managers saw head office as out of touch in more ways than one. Head office's technological solution to communication problems (a highly sophisticated voicemail system) was universally derided. Frequently, researchers were provided with the story of the head office ice cream promotion, where considerable quantity of ice cream was supplied to local units, but no additional freezer space.

Interestingly, head office has become increasingly committed to a language of empowerment and local control, at the same time as its information systems have moved further away from these principles. Head office was renamed 'Restaurant Support Centre' and the management structure was made flatter. Considerable effort was put into obtaining the views of local managers. What is interesting is how this contrasts with a local management perspective which sees itself as (in one manager's words) "cogs in a wheel". They would dispute the Restaurant Support Centre's view that it is empowering the local units, as the question of "who gains remains largely mute" (Burdett, 1999). If unit managers experience a declining work experience, then changes of terminology, or delayering have less impact than an automating information system.

5 The Sustenance Company

The second establishment is public house within a large brewery chain. It's situated in a large central London Square and has recently completed a major programme of refurbishment costing hundreds of thousands of pounds. "State of the art" (interviewed manager) information systems were installed, costing tens of thousands of pounds. The establishment was selected partly to build on the work of Baker *et al* (1998) in their study of EPOS systems in public houses, but also because it's high proportion of tourist business is unusual, even for Central London. Like the company in the case study above, the brewery also believed that it was "flattening the organisation, empowering the staff and providing significantly enhanced communication ability".

In the first month of trading in it's newly refurbished format the public house 'lost' £30,000. There is an acceptance that Public houses are closely involved with processes of 'fiddling', as Mars (1994) noted "drink is often used as the medium of exchange in personal dealings" and this has traditionally meant that there is an association between public houses and 'fiddling'. What was unusual about this case was the shear scale of the theft, combined with the sophistication of the system designed to stop it occurring. Managers watched video footage, patched through directly to their computers in the offices downstairs, mystery customers from the company visited everyday and spreadsheets were pored over with increasing anxiety. Apart from the information that the losses tended to be concentrated on those areas where the mathematics were simpler (when the pint cost £2.50, for example), the cause of the problem was impossible to determine.

At the end of the first months trading, when the 'fiddling' had cost almost as much as the systems designed to prevent it, the problem simply disappeared and fiddling dropped to an "acceptable" (interviewed manager) level of £1000 a month. There were a large number of (voluntary) staff changes, which have been linked to the improved figures, but the method and detail of the fiddle has still escaped management detection.

What makes the scale of the theft even more impressive was the depth of information which the system was able to provide. Detailed performance statistics could be provided on each member of staff and this could be related, for example, to the current promotions which the brewery was operating. Operatives found this system alienating and they also objected to name badges and the ability of the EPOS system to display the names of the operative. The ability for customers to use the first names of serving staff was found to be intrusive by most operatives. Operatives also felt that on occasion managers were "hiding behind" their computer screens and avoiding more difficult confrontations with customers. The sophistication of the new system took managers way from their more traditional 'front-line' role and shifted them towards a 'back-office' one. One experienced operative commented with resentment what she felt was an increasing trend for managers not to serve customers themselves.

In the Baker *et al* paper (1998), jointly written with the brewery head office, the studied installation is claimed to "belong to the 10-20 per cent of successful IT projects". When the brewery for the studied public house above, was contacted for it comments on the installation of the information system, it described it as a "complete success". In both cases, possible reasons for this claim were missing. It is possible that the advanced EPOS system improved the speed of service, though operatives claimed that additional keying slowed down service. It is possible that detailed examination of consumer behaviour enabled breweries to restructure prices more profitably, though again operatives felt that it was the drinks that were most sensitive to prices changes, which were increased the most. It is possible that managers were empowered by the additional information available to them, but no data was found to support this.

In the minds of brewery managers, one of the key motivators behind the development of their information system was the control and prevention of operative 'fiddles'. In the case above this intention clearly failed. It is possible that the sophisticated system was used to facilitate the scale of the theft, but, at the least, it did not deter the theft, hinder it or discover the method. A system designed to impose predictability and transparency of the actions of operatives had precisely the opposite effect - and at great expense.

6 Conclusions

The case studies indicate significant problems with information systems in what are generally considered technologically sophisticated and successful companies. These systems can be seen as a battleground between the intentions of the developers/installers and the actions of their users. Failures in implementation cannot be seen as a software or training problem, but as a part of a continuing tension between different levels of authority, fought out through the application of the information system. While central management and system developers tended to think in terms of 'technological fixes' line management and operatives were able to use their knowledge skills to circumvent (to varying extents) the intentions of senior management.

Both the selected companies have previously been used by writers in this area, as examples of good practice, but it seems that claims made from head offices are more difficult to substantiate at the local level. Our data would tend to suggest that our chosen examples are not completely untypical. Modern writing on information technology in tourism (even when using the jargon of 'empowerment') has "an emphasis on the role of management, and top management in particular, as defining and constructing systems of control in their organisation" (Mars, 1994). It is the ignoring of the role of the base level of this structure (especially the workgroup), which lies at the heart of explaining the 'productivity paradox'.

References

Anonymous, *Cost and Manpower Productivity in UK Hotels*, NEDC Working Party on Competitiveness in Tourism and Leisure, 1992.

Anonymous, 'Leader: How real is the new Economy?' *The Economist*, 24th July, 1999.

Baker, M., Wild, M. & Sussman, S., 'Introducing EPOS in Bass Taverns', *International Journal of Contemporary Hospitality Management*, Vol. 10, No. 1, 1998.

Beardon, C., 'Computers, Postmodernism and the Culture of the Artificial', *AI & Society*, Vol. 8, pp. 1-16, 1994.

Collins, A. & Bicknell, D., *Crash: Ten Easy Ways to Avoid Computer Disaster*, Simon & Schuster, London, 1997.

Kasavana, M., 'Computers and multiunit food service operators', *Cornell HRA Quarterly*, pp. 72-80, June, 1994.

Landauer, T., *The Trouble with Computers*, The MIT Press, Cambridge, MA., 1995.

Lyotard, J., *The Postmodern Condition*, Manchester University Press, Manchester, 1984.

Mars, G., *Cheats at Work*, Dartmouth, Aldershot, (revised edition,) 1994.

Moules, J., UK tops project failure league, *Computing*, 8th February, 1996.

Peacock, M., *Management Information Systems in the Hospitality Industry*, Brunel, Uxbridge, 1998.

Ritzer, G., *The McDonaldization of Society*, Pine Forge Press, California, 1993.

Teare, R. & Boer, A., *Strategic Hospitality Management*, Cassell, 1991.

Thompson, D., 'Computer Crime and Security Survey', *Information Management and Computer Security*, Vol. 6, No. 2, pp. 78-101, 1998.

Zuboff, S., *In the Age of the Smart Machine: The Future of Work and Power*, Heinemann, Oxford, 1988.

Vague Queries in Tourism Information Systems

J. Palkoska, A. Dunzendorfer and J. Küng
Institute for Applied Knowledge Processing (FAW), University of Linz
Altenberger Str. 69, A-4040 Linz, Austria
e-mail: {jp, ad, jk}@faw.uni-linz.ac.at

Abstract

The vague Query System (VQS) allows to efficiently carry out rankings for user defined queries according to the semantic meta-information of attributes. It can easily be added to existing relational database systems. In this article we demonstrate the applicability of the system on Tourism Information Systems (TI-systems). We will show that for cases where the structure of the existing database is not directly suited for the use with VQS, we can achieve compatibility by using views. Furthermore we will show a concept for integrating VQS into the query language TIS-QL, in order to achieve an even tighter integration into TI-systems.

1. Introduction

Relational databases represent the de facto standard in many application areas. They provide standardized query languages (e.g. SQL) for retrieving records and manipulating data. However, this type of databases is mainly designed for crisp query processing. That means, that for a given query only records complying exactly with the query conditions will be returned. In many application scenarios this is desirable and the only way for fulfilling the user needs. If, for instance, a manager looks for the salary of the project member *Miller*, he wants to know the facts for that, and only for that employee.

With new evolving types of information systems like Internet based Tourism Information Systems (TI-systems), the crisp query feature of relational databases can lead to drawbacks. If a tourist looks for instance for a hotel room in the city of *Salzburg*, but all rooms are booked up, he would be happy to get at least a room in a neighbor city of Salzburg.

Unfortunately, relational databases do not support vague query results and so we need advanced retrieving techniques in order to provide *best match searches*. The best solution would be to realize modules that can easily be added to existing database applications to provide semantic based similarity search functionality.

At the Institute for Applied Knowledge Processing (FAW) a prototype with the name *VQS* (*Vague Query System*) has been developed, providing the capability to enhance relational database systems with vague query facilities [1]. The main intention was to realize concepts and methodologies for providing a framework for modeling semantic meta-information of abstract database objects. This information should then be used for semantic based similarity searches. In this article we will outline the main features of VQS and stress their applicability for TI-systems. We think that especially in this application area vague query facilities will become more and more important in order to fulfill the needs of the consumers.

This article is organized as follows: In section 2 we take a look at some interesting approaches which try to provide semantic based similarity queries. In section 3 we resume the main features of VQS, which are exemplary applied on a simple TI-system in section 4. In section 5 we introduce an approach for the integration of VQS into TIS-QL, a concept developed to access heterogeneous TI-systems [6]. As a conclusion we will summarize our work in section 6 and we will show our further plans.

2. Related Research

Since semantic based similarity searches are essential for many application areas, a lot of research activities exist to develop effective storage and retrieval procedures. The application domains reach from multimedia and geometric databases over time sequence and stock databases to biological applications like DNA sequence databases. Most of these approaches have in common that they store the semantics of the objects by means of feature vectors which represent the objects in a kind of multidimensional space. The drawback of these attempts is that they are in most cases specialized for specific applications and they even use specific structures for the storage of the objects.

For many systems traditionally working with relational databases the need for similarity searches increases, too. Especially new media like the World Wide Web change the way of accessing the services dramatically. Only very few approaches exist, that try to augment relational database systems with the general capability to realize semantic based similarity searches. Ichikawa et. al. presented for instance the *Associative Information Retrieval System (ARES)* which is able to get fuzzy results for exactly formulated queries. In ARES the semantic meta-information is stored in so called *similarity relations*. They hold numerical similarity values for pairs of numerical and non-numerical attribute values [2].

VAGUE, proposed by Motro, is another very interesting approach that enhances the facilities of relational databases. The implementation bases on the idea of four types of *data metrics*, that can be mapped to attributes: *computational, tabular, referential* and *standard metrics* [3].

Another interesting work is *Preference SQL 1.2*, where standard SQL is combined with the possibility of giving preferences to desirable criteria. This concept provides the base for building electronic sales interfaces that behave like natural salespersons. It is useful for database applications where customer wishes are modeled more naturally by preferences than exclusively by conditions [4].

3. Basic Functionality of the Vague Query System (VQS)

Within a previous project of the FAW a system with the name *VQS* (*Vague Query System*) has been developed, providing the facility to enhance relational database systems with vague retrieval capabilities [1]. The main features of the system can be summarized as follows:

-   *semantic based similarity searches*: In the case of failing to find an exact match for the query, the system is able to provide at least the best match. Retrieving the best match is realized by regarding semantic meta-information of the query-attributes.
-   *integration into existing database systems*: Applying VQS does not require special database management systems. It is possible for the system to work "on-top" of existing database systems.
-   *application independence*: Adding the system to existing applications does not require the underlying databases to be changed.
-   *transparent query facilities*: The query-language of VQS is very similar to SQL.

3.1 Semantic Modeling in Dimensions

We decided to use multidimensional concepts to carry out similarity searches: VQS uses numeric coordinates in a feature space as representation for non numeric attribute values like the solutions in numeric classification. For this purpose we introduced so-called *NCR-Tables* (*Numeric-Coordinate-Representation-Tables*). They are used to represent the numeric coordinates of the attributes in the feature space. The attribute itself is the key of the NCR-Table (*NCR-Key*). Furthermore an NCR-Table contains several numeric *NCR-Columns*, which represent the dimensions of the feature space. NCR-Tables can be mapped to corresponding attributes of existing relations. Attributes for which a mapping exists, are called *FuzzyFields*.

3.2 Searching for Similar Records

VQS represents similarity of attribute values as the Euclidean distance between the coordinates stored in the associated NCR-Tables. If the query spans more than one attribute, the system has to find the record, which is the nearest over all criteria. The special capability of VQS is to build a "combined" semantic distance over all query conditions. The result of this computation is called *Total Distance (TD)*. Furthermore VQS allows to define individual weights for the single criteria.

A special feature of VQS is the facility to associate more than one NCR-Table with one single attribute. In this way complex semantic configurations can be defined. With this method the semantics of cities could, for instance, be expressed through a combined measurement regarding location, sea level and the number of inhabitants.

Similar to the computation of the *Total Distance* the system computes a kind of averaged distance to express the similarity of attribute values.

3.3 Representing Query Results

Because the user gets vague results for exact queries, VQS has to provide information about the relevance of the retrieved records for the query. Therefore the system represents the results as a ranked list of all relevant records together with an additional attribute *TD*. The user can judge about the single records' relevance for his needs by means of the TD-values.

3.4 Query Language

VQS is intended to enhance arbitrary relational database systems, where the users need the possibility to tell the system what conditions should be vaguely interpreted. Therefore we have defined a specialized query language: *VQL (Vague Query Language)*, which is close to the SQL-syntax. Since the user does not need to be concerned about the semantics behind the single attributes, VQL is very useful for carrying out ad hoc queries. A formal definition of the query language can be found in [1].

4. VQS in the Application Domain of Tourism

In the previous section we have shown that within VQS semantics are represented in multidimensional space. Of course we can not find suitable representations for all kinds of data, but we have seen that at least for a great set of data objects mappings to a multidimensional semantic space can be found.

In this section we show an example how VQS works at a fictive tourism database that holds available offers for short holidays in Austrian cities. This database contains for instance the relations *Hotels* and *Short_Holidays* shown in Fig. 1. Here we can see that the main facts of interest are the name of the hotel, the name of the city and facts concerning category and available dates for booking.

Hotels				Short_Holidays			
@Hotel	City	Category		@ID	Hotel	From	To
Royal	Filzmoos	economy		1	Royal	Jul-31-99	Aug-03-99
Kingston	Salzburg	standard		2	Kingston	Jul-31-99	Aug-07-99
Imperial	Salzburg	comfort		3	Imperial	Aug-07-99	Aug-10-99
Rose	Linz	standard		4	Rose	Jul-31-99	Aug-03-99
CityView	Salzburg	standard		5	CityView	Aug-15-99	Aug-22-99
Harriot	Salzburg	comfort		6	Harriot	Aug-02-99	Aug-05-99

Fig. 1. Part of an exemplary Tourism Database

Now let assume that the system administrator of the database wants to provide vague query facilities for users, who can access the TI-system through the World Wide Web. For this purpose he can simply plug VQS into the existing database system. Afterwards he has to define the relevant semantic meta-information for attributes that could be affected by vague query conditions.

Since most queries in this database are defined by location, category and time criteria, VQS has to be configured to regard the semantic meta-information of these attributes. As semantics for the location criteria the geographical longitude and latitude of the hotel's city should be used. The time criterion is affected by two main features: Start date of the offer and duration. The categories' semantics can be represented by a mapping of the categories' names to a scale from 1 to 5. For these purposes the structure of the tables in Fig. 1 can, however, not be used directly.

Therefore a special feature of VQS is used, and the meta-information is defined on view level. On the basis of the needs for our example we can define the view *Short_Holidays_ViewVQS* (Fig. 2). The tables *Hotels* and *Short_Holidays* were joined in order to have direct access to the cities where the hotels are located and to the categories of the hotels. Furthermore we have prepared the time attributes for the direct treatment by VQS: The attribute *From_Day* holds for each date of the underlying table the number of the day calculated from the beginning of the year. *Duration* holds the number of days the single offers span. The conversion of the two date attributes can be realized by applying functions within the view definition.

Short_Holidays_ViewVQS						
ID	Hotel	City	Category	From_Day	From_WDay	Duration
1	Royal	Filzmoos	Economy	212	SAT	4
2	Kingston	Salzburg	Standard	212	SAT	8
3	Imperial	Salzburg	comfort	219	SAT	4
4	Rose	Linz	Standard	212	SAT	4
5	CityView	Salzburg	Standard	227	SUN	8
6	Harriot	Salzburg	comfort	214	MON	4

Fig. 2. Prepared View Providing the Structure for the Application of VQS

4.1 Defining the Semantic Meta-Information

Now we have to define the semantic meta-information for the affected attributes by mapping them to suitable NCR-Tables. Since the location of the hotels should be represented by geographical coordinates, we can use the table *City* of Fig. 3. Accordingly we can use the table *HotelCategory* as NCR-Table for the FuzzyField *Category*. Fig. 4 shows the graphical visualization of the NCR mapping. *From_Day* and *Duration* do not need explicit NCR mappings, because they are numerical attributes, of which the domains can be used for similarity calculations directly.

City		
@Name	X	Y
Salzburg	2500	2000
Filzmoos	3500	3000
Munich	500	2500
Linz	6500	4500

HotelCategory	
@Category	Category_Number
Basic	1
Economy	2
Standard	3
Comfort Line	4
S_Class	5

Fig. 3. Tables used as NCR-Tables within the Exemplary Tourism Database

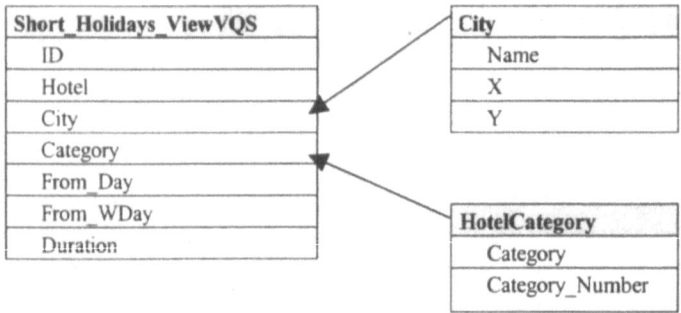

Fig. 4. Visualization of the NCR-Tables' Mappings to the Associated FuzzyFields

4.2 Executing Vague Queries

Having defined the semantic meta-information, the system can very easily be accessed through VQL-statements. The client application can transmit the statements to the *Vague Query Execution Module* (*VQEM*). Regard for instance a tourist, who searches for a short holiday in the city of Salzburg, beginning on Jul-31-99 and ending on Aug-03-99. Despite we have shown that a semantic meta-definition exists for *Category*, we neglect this attribute in the exemplary query, in order to keep the simplicity. As we can see in Fig. 2, in Salzburg no arrangements are available for this time period. A crisp query would therefore produce an empty resultset. Because the database is prepared for VQS, the client application can, however, very easily produce a VQL-statement of the following form:

```
SELECT FROM Short_Holidays_ViewVQS WHERE
City IS 'Salzburg' AND
FROM_DAY IS 212 AND
DURATION IS 4
INTO ResultTable1;
```

On the basis of the semantic definitions VQS is able to calculate the relevance for each record according to this query. For each object we can very easily calculate the deviation from the query value *Salzburg* on the basis of the associated NCR-Table. Furthermore the deviations from the *From_Day* and *Duration* values can be calculated and a normalization can be carried out on the basis of the attributes' feature spaces. Finally we get the Total Distance of the records by combining the single normalized distances. Fig. 5 shows the result set that has been ranked according to TD. We can see that arrangement 6 (hotel Harriot) seems to be the best choice, because this hotel fulfills the location criterion and the date differs only 2 days.

ResultTable1	ID	Hotel	TD
	6	Harriot	0.043
	1	Royal	0.075
	3	Imperial	0.157
	4	Rose	0.249
	2	Kingston	0.333
	5	CityView	0.667

Fig. 5. Ranked Result Set of the Exemplary Query

Attributes for which no meta-information exists, can nevertheless be referenced by VQL-statements. In these cases the *standard distance* capabilities of VQS become applied (compare [1]).

4. 2 Additional Conditions

The result of the above query suggests to the user to book an arrangement in Salzburg that starts a few days after the date that he has defined. But what, if the tourist wants to start his journey in any case on a weekend, caused for instance by the available flight connections? For such needs, VQS can regard crisp query conditions too. If the arrival should be in any case on a Saturday, the following VQL-statement could be formulated:

```
SELECT FROM (
SELECT * FROM ShortHolidays_ViewVQS WHERE
FROM_WDAY = 'SAT') WHERE
City IS 'Salzburg' AND
FROM_DAY IS 212 AND
DURATION IS 4
INTO ResultTable2;
```

The crisp query condition FROM_WDAY = 'SAT' is formulated within a standard SQL statement that is used as data source of the query, and it filters away all arrangements with weekdays others than Saturdays. The execution of the query leads to the ranked result set represented in Fig. 6. As we can see, the system now recommends an arrangement in a neighbor city of Salzburg beginning at the desired date.

ResultTable2	ID	Hotel	TD
	1	Royal	0.075
	3	Imperial	0.157
	4	Rose	0.249
	2	Kingston	0.333

Fig. 6 Ranked Result Set of a Query with Additional Crisp Conditions

In this way the best matching record for the query "*short holiday with a duration of about 4 days, preferably in Salzburg, beginning on a Saturday, ideally on Jul-31-99*" was found.

4.4 Performance Aspects

VQS has been designed for carrying out a ranking of all records in the affected relations according to the specified query conditions. In large databases, however, calculating TD for every single record can lead to performance problems, because the computation has to be carried out for every potential match of the result set. However this feature of VQS is not really a drawback for our purposes: The crisp part of the queries can in most cases be processed very efficiently by means of conventional indices. Since even in very large TI-systems the number of potential matches can be extremely cut down by crisp query conditions, the time consuming calculations of TD have in most cases to be carried out only for a small subset of the records.

Furthermore we have developed a concept, that enhances the search capabilities of VQS for the ability to optionally carry out an efficient *nearest neighbor-search* [5], instead of a ranking for all records. The concept works on the basis of an incremental extension of the search intervals around the query values, which is repeated until the best match is proven to be found. If large recordsets have to be processed, these search abilities could then be used to achieve performance improvements.

5. Embedding VQS into the TIS-QL Concept

Integrating vague query facilities into TI-systems seems to be very useful in many cases and a highly efficient feature for modern applications. We have seen that an even higher degree of effectiveness could be achieved through the integration of VQS capabilities into tourism specific database concepts. In this section we will therefore introduce an approach for the modular integration into a query architecture, that allows access to heterogeneous TI-systems.

In [6] we have introduced an architecture that allows transparent access to arbitrary TI-systems, without the necessity to learn different user interfaces and functional structures. For TIS-QL, so called *server adapters* are used to access the different TI-systems and to offer a unified interface to the clients. The logical integration is realized by means of a general datamodel, into that every specific data model is transformed [7]. On the basis of this architecture the clients are able to access the system by a specific query language with the name *TIS-QL* [6].

Since the adapters transform the TIS-QL statements into system specific SQL-statements, we have an ideal framework for integrating vague query facilities. Due to the application area independent concept of VQS and its modular design it is possible to fully integrate vague query facilities into TIS-QL. For this purpose the system specific TIS-QL adapters are extended with VQS modules (see Fig. 7), which operate as an additional layer between the adapter and the database system.

For the purpose of integrating VQS into the heterogeneous framework we had to extend the syntax of TIS-QL. This results in the TIS-VQL (Tourism Information System – Vague Query Language) and its server adapter.

Fig. 7. TIS-VQL Adapter with Vague Query Facilities

Through this extension the server adapter provides a crisp as well as a vague working mode. The crisp interpretation is done like described in [6]. In the vague working mode, the server adapter gets a fuzzy TIS-VQL statement. This has to be transformed into database specific VQL-syntax (described in [1]) as input for the VQS-module of the ·server adapter. Then the VQS-module generates the system specific SQL statement fitting for the underlying database.

6. Conclusions

By means of the vague query facilities given by VQS, tourism information systems can be enhanced significantly. Due to the architecture of VQS which is designed as an "add-on" to existing database systems, the value of already existing TI-systems using a database in the background can be increased.

We have shown the capabilities of VQS to find the best matching records for ad-hoc formulated queries. The practical applicability of the system in the area of TI-systems has been demonstrated, and in form of an example the possibilities for preparing existing database systems for VQS were introduced. Furthermore we have shown an architectural concept for the integration of VQS into TIS-QL, an approach that allows to transparently access heterogeneous TI-systems. The tight integration has been achieved by an extension of the query language TIS-QL with concepts of VQL.

In our further work we will concentrate especially on VQS-functionality for adapter-adapter communication within TIS-VQL. In this context we will have to find methods to integrate heterogeneous NCR definitions. Furthermore it is planned to implement the TIS-VQL concept in form of a prototype and to carry out tests in real world environments.

References

1. J. Küng, J. Palkoska: "VQS - A Vague Query System Prototype", *Proceedings of the Eight International Workshop on Database and Expert Systems Applications, DEXA 97*, Toulouse, France, September 1-2, IEEE Computer Society Press, 1997, pp. 614-618

2. T. Ichikawa, M. Hirakawa: "ARES: A Relational Database with the Capability of Performing Flexible Interpretation of Queries", *IEEE Transactions on Software Engineering*, Vol. 12, No. 5, 1986, pp. 624-634

3. A. Motro: "VAGUE: A User Interface to Relational Databases that Permits Vague Queries", *ACM Transactions on Office Information Systems*, Vol. 6, No. 3, 1988, pp. 187-214

4. Database Preference Software GmbH; Preference SQL 1.2 technical white paper: http://www.preference.de/docs/technical_white_paper.pdf, 1999

5. J. Küng, J. Palkoska: "An Incremental Hypercube Approach for Finding Best Matches for Vague Queries", *Tenth International Conference on Database and Expert Systems Applications*, DEXA 99, Florence, Italy, August 30 – September 1, Springer 1999, pp. 238-249

6. Josef Küng, Anton Dunzendorfer, Roland Wagner: "TIS-QL - A Unified Query Language for Tourism Information Systems"; in Werthner H. (Ed.): *Information Technology & Tourism, Applications, Methodologies, Techniques*; Cognizant Communication Corp., Vol. 1., ISSN 1098-3058, New York – Sydney – Tokyo 1998, pp. 73-82

7. J. Küng, A. Dunzendorfer, R. R. Wagner: "A General Datamodel for Tourism Information Systems"; in Buhalis D., Schertler W.(ads): *Information and Communication Technologies in Tourism 1999*, Springer Computer Science, Wien 1999, pp. 151-160

Integrating Heterogeneous Tourism Information in TIScover – The MIRO-Web Approach

M. Haller†, B. Pröll†, W. Retschitzegger‡, A M. Tjoa†, R.R. Wagner†

† Institute for Applied Knowledge Processing (FAW)
University of Linz, AUSTRIA
email: {mhaller, bproell, amt, rwagner}@faw.uni-linz.ac.at
‡ Institute of Applied Computer Science, Department of Information Systems (IFS)
University of Linz, AUSTRIA
email: werner@ifs.uni-linz.ac.at

Abstract

A broad spectrum of tourism information is already distributed over various web sites. However, a major problem for the tourist is to find these web sites and to deal with the differences concerning information presentation and information access. At the same time, it is not feasible to store every kind of information a tourist might be interested in at one web site neither in terms of storage costs and even more important in terms of maintenance overhead. Therefore, in the course of the *ESPRIT project MIRO-Web* the official Austrian tourism information and booking system TIScover is extended in order to federate multiple structured and semi-structured tourism information sources on the web. In particular, MIRO-Web supports a homogeneous view on these heterogeneous sources which can be either materialized or defined as virtual. On the basis of this view, appropriate query mechanisms as well as a web-based interface provide the user with a single point of access.

1 Introduction

With the tremendous growth of the web, accessing information on the Internet has become less a question of determining whether the information is out there, but rather, in what form, and how to find it [5]. This situation is especially true for the tourism industry where a broad spectrum of tourism information is already distributed over various web sites and stored using heterogeneous formats. It is obvious that this situation is very undesirable since the tourist is burdened with finding and visiting various web sites in order to gather all the desired tourism information and products. The situation gets even worse since web sites usually differ very much especially concerning information presentation and information access. What is therefore required is that the tourist is enabled to collect all desired tourism information and tourism products at one place, e.g., information about weather and traffic conditions, schedules of trains, planes and buses, or information about actual events like movies at the local cinema including movie reviews as published in different online newspapers are required.

To fulfill this requirement it is of course not feasible to store every kind of information a tourist might be interested in at one web site neither in terms of storage costs and even more important in terms of maintenance overhead. A more promising idea would be to take advantage of the huge amount of other relevant tourism information that is already distributed all over the web. In the course of the *ESPRIT project MIRO-Web* [4] which was started at the end of 1997, the official Austrian tourism information and booking system TIScover is extended in order to federate multiple structured and semi-structured tourism information sources on the web. These sources comprise different in-house databases employed in the various tourism offices, Excel files used for managerial purposes, and finally and most important HTML-pages of other web sites [3].

The rest of the paper is organized as follows: After a short overview about TIScover in Section 2, the basic concepts and technologies of MIRO-Web used in order to integrate heterogeneous information sources are presented in Section 3. Section 4 demonstrates the applicability of MIRO-Web to TIScover by presenting two different application scenarios comprising an *Event Agent* and a *Golf Agent*. Section 5 concludes the paper by discussing lessons learned and pointing to future work.

2   An Overview of TIScover

The development of TIScover has been started in 1996 based on the experiences made with the pioneering system TIS@WEB [1]. The aim of TIScover is twofold [11, 12, 13]: first, tourists should be *supplied with comprehensive, accurate and up-to-date tourism information* on countries, regions, villages and all destination facilities they offer like hotels, museums or other places worth seeing. Second, it aims to *attract the tourist to buy certain tourism products* either offline or even more important to allow the tourist to buy them *online*. Originally, TIScover was realized to market the facilities of a certain region of Austria, namely Tyrol, only. Meanwhile, four other Austrian regions have joined TIScover [15]. Besides that, TIScover has been employed in Asia, presenting tourism information about Thailand [16][1], it is used by the German company START Media Plus, a major player in the area of online reservation systems, to present tourism information about Germany [17], and it is online in Switzerland as KISSswiss, employed by the companies Kümmerly+Frey and Basler Versicherungen [18].

The functionality provided by TIScover can roughly be categorized into three different components, the *public Internet* component, the *Extranet* and the *Intranet* [12]. The *public Internet* component comprises that functionality of the system that is accessible to the public, whereby the most important modules are *Atlas* and *Booking*. The module Atlas allows the customer to browse through all kinds of tourism information by navigating through a geographical hierarchy and to use a *full text search*. The module Booking allows for a *precise structured search* based on a subset of the tourism information presented by Atlas, like villages, hotels, available rooms,

---

[1] Note, that due to the economical crisis in asia, TIScoverasia is currently not operating.

events and camping sites along the geographical hierarchy as well as *online booking* of these tourism products. Furthermore, TIScover provides an *Extranet* allowing authorized tourism information providers, no matter being a small guesthouse or a large local tourist office to update and extend their tourism information and products directly. Finally, the *Intranet* component of TIScover which is accessible at the system provider's side only allows to configure the whole system in various ways. It is, for example, possible to extend the geographical hierarchy, to specify expiration dates for reports and to define the default language for all system components.

Currently, TIScover stores all tourism information and tourism products within a central relational database. The common database schema of TIScover Austria consists of about 300 database tables and has been constructed on the basis of a domain data model which incorporates all conceptual entities gathered during the process of requirements definition with numerous tourism information providers and from the experiences with the predecessor system TIS@WEB [1]. The database of TIScover Austria comprises about two gigabyte of data. To facilitate performant access, web pages are automatically generated out of the database every time one of the 7.000 tourism information providers ranging from hotels to local tourism offices maintains the content covering among others around 2.000 towns and villages and nearly 40.000 accommodations [14]. As a result, there exist more than 400.000 web pages stored in some million files. Per month, the system has to handle up to 8,6 million pageviews, 2 million visits as well as up to 40.000 requests for information on booking and online bookings.

Although, these figures illustrate that TIScover manages a fairly huge amount of tourism information, it is of course far from being complete. To be able to satisfy also requests for certain information which is not part of the TIScover database, but already available at other web sites, the MIRO-Web project was intended to provide a proper technical basis.

3 Basic Concepts and Technlogies of MIRO-Web

The integration of heterogeneous data is a challenging problem when trying to utilize existing information on the web. Many of the problems encountered in building such systems are similar to those addressed in building heterogeneous database systems [5, 8]. However, the integration of information sources on the web poses some fundamentally new challenges:

Heterogeneity of Sources. Web information is stored within distinct heterogeneous sources, whereas the important kind of heterogeneity in our context is *structural heterogeneity* [2, 5]. As an extreme we find *fully structured data* coming, e.g., from databases having a rigid and explicit schema. At another extreme, there is data which is *fully unstructured* having no schema, such as images, sounds, and raw text. But most of the data falls somewhere in between these two extremes, called *semi-*

structured data (e.g., HTML-files), where the schema can be implicit and does not have to be rigid.

Evolution of Sources. Information sources at the Internet *evolve at a much higher pace than databases* in a controlled business setting and therefore increase the maintenance overhead of the integration schema.

Autonomy of Sources. Many sources are characterized by a high degree of autonomy, allowing a partial integration only.

Lack of Source Meta Data. Commonly, there is little meta data available about the characteristics of the sources which further complicates their integration.

Most of current web sites do not fully cope with these challenges and do not allow for the integration of multiple data sources beyond simple links between them. The MIRO-Web project [4] focuses on the development of a set of middleware components providing integrated and transparent access from standard web browsers to multiple data sources, ranging from databases to more or less structured files, located on different web sites.

3.1 The Architecture of MIRO-Web

MIRO-Web builds on the technology developed and the knowledge acquired in the course of the ESPRIT project IRO-DB, aiming at the integration of heterogeneous databases [8]. In the spirit of IRO-DB, MIRO-Web is based on a *three-tier architecture*, consisting of a *Data Source Adapter Layer*, a *Mediation Layer* and a *Client Layer* (cf. Fig. 1).

Data Source Adapter Layer. The Data Source Adapter Layer consists of a number of adapters, also known as wrappers, which are needed to mask the heterogeneity of data sources and to transform source data into a structured format [7]. Data source adapters have two main functions: they first translate a query to the underlying query system used by the source and then they translate the results sent by the source after evaluation of the translated query. MIRO-Web adapters can be used in conjunction with a mediator (cf. below) or independently by an application. In the first case they provide an API well suited for the interaction between the mediator and the adapter. In the latter case they provide a JDBC [9] interface through which they support a subset of SQL depending on the query management capabilities of the data source and on those implemented in the adapter itself. MIRO-Web supports several kinds of adapters depending on the nature of the data source, such as relational adapters as well as structured and semi-structured file adapters. To facilitate both, building and maintenance of data source adapters a Java toolkit called *Adapter Development Kit* has been developed.

Mediation Layer. According to [20], mediators "simplify, abstract, reduce, merge and explain data". The Mediation Layer of MIRO-Web provides the means to combine and integrate these heterogeneous sources into a homogeneous view and supports query possibilities on this view in terms of a single point of access. For a more detailed discussion it is referred to Section 3.2.

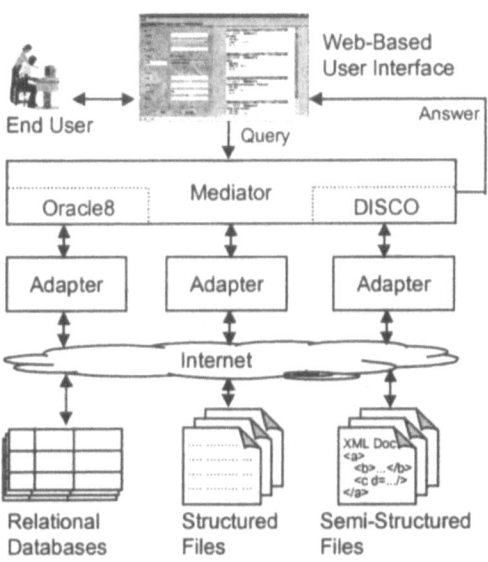

Fig. 1. Overall Architecture of MIRO-Web

Client Layer. The Client Layer provides web-based user interfaces, allowing both, to express queries to the underlying heterogeneous sources and to present the results of these queries in a uniform way. Section 4 presents the user interfaces, which were realized for the application of MIRO-Web to TIScover.

3.2 Materialized Mediation versus Virtual Mediation

An important distinction in building web data integration systems is whether to take a *materialized approach* or a *virtual approach* for mediation. MIRO-Web supports both approaches in order to combine the advantages of each of them. It is the responsibility of the database administrator to decide which approach is suitable for a certain data source.

Materialized Mediation. In the materialized approach, data from multiple web sources is loaded into a warehouse, and all queries are applied to the warehoused data. In particular, a materialized mediator stores data received from the adapters, and provides for integrated views on these imported data. The materialized mediator of MIRO-Web is built on the basis of the object-relational data model of Oracle8 [10], which can represent multi-valued attributes by means of nested tables as well as object references. Appropriate tools are provided for the database administrator to integrate necessary data and to query them through Oracle views.

Where data volume, timeliness, security considerations and frequent changes of the remote data source do not prevent materialization, this approach has the following advantages. First, autonomous sources need not be available all the time and adequate performance can be guaranteed at query time. Second, adapters can concentrate on data mapping and enrichment, and can be limited to rather restricted query capabilities. Finally, queries combining information from multiple sources can be processed locally, and dedicated indices and representation schemes can be used for improving efficiency.

Virtual Mediation. In the virtual approach, the data remains in the web sources and is not replicated at the mediation layer. To manage query processing in this scenario, the mediator proceeds in several steps at runtime. First the query is decomposed and optimized into sub-queries and a composition query. Each sub-query extracts the necessary information from an adapter. The composition query combines the sub-answers from the sub-queries into the final answer, which is returned to the user through the mediator. Virtual mediation is performed in MIRO-Web by DISCO (Distributed Information Search COmponents) a distributed extensible query engine which provides a uniform query language and data model for declarative access to a heterogeneous collection of data sources [19].

Virtual mediation provides several advantages. First, it is not limited by the storage capacity of the materialized mediator. Thus, arbitrarily large collections of data can be combined. Second, no *a priori* decision must be made by the database administrator *which* data must reside in the materialized mediator. All data is equally available to a mediator using virtual views. Third, data returned through virtual views is topical since data sources are accessed at query time. A materialized mediator must consider the issue of the materialized data becoming out of date with respect to the data sources. Finally, an additional advantage involves security, i.e., each query can be considered independently from a security point of view.

4 Applying MIRO-Web to TIScover

To demonstrate the applicability of MIRO-Web to TIScover in the following two different scenarios are presented, where some kind of *agent* assists the tourist in querying heterogeneous tourism information sources in a transparent way. These agents comprise an Event Agent and a Golf Agent and correspond to the Client Layer of MIRO-Web as described in Section 3.1.

4.1 The Event Agent

A common case is that a tourist wants to find a hotel, which should be near some event locations, such as an exhibition, a sporting event or a cultural event, e.g., a musical or a movie. Furthermore, the weather forecast should be fine and the hotel should cost less than a certain amount of money, issued in an arbitrary currency. To specify such a request, the Event Agent provides a uniform graphical interface in terms of a Java applet (cf. Fig. 2).

The Adapter Layer of MIRO-Web extracts the answer for this request out of different heterogeneous data sources. First, information about hotels is extracted directly out of the TIScover database. Second, information about actual events can be found on different already existing web sites (cf., e.g., www.austria-tourism.at or www.film.at or www.events.at). Third, the weather information is gathered via file transfer protocol in form of a structured file and finally the exchange rates for calculating the requested currency is available in a semi-structured format, namely as an email.

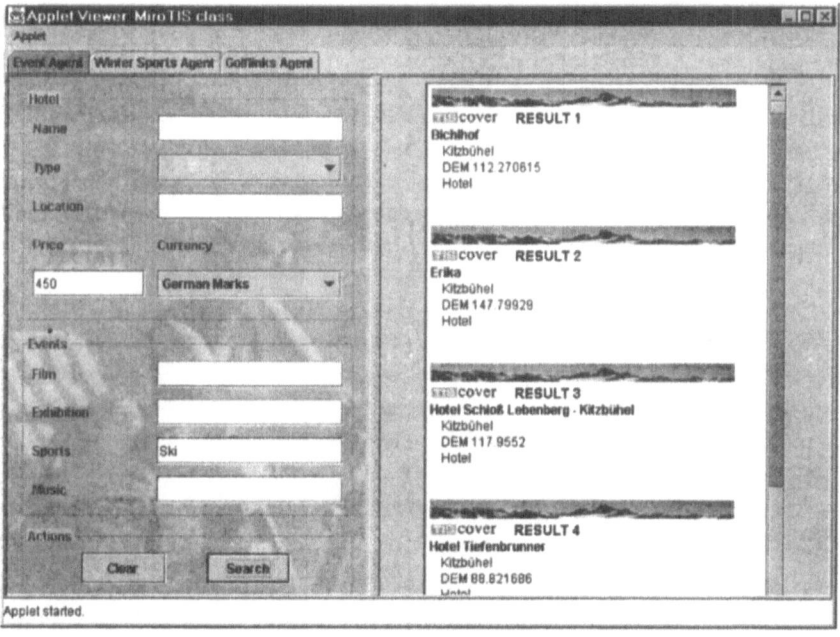

Fig. 2. Event Agent User Interface

The basic join criteria for the query which is used by the Mediation Layer to satisfy an information request is the name of the location. On the basis of this join attribute information about the events can be joined with weather information and hotel information. Finally the price can be calculated and converted by means of the exchange rates and joined with the hotel information. Finally, the Client Layer, i.e., the Java applet presents the result of the information request in a uniform way at the right side of the panel (cf. Fig. 2).

4.2 The Golf Agent

The Golf Agent represents a scenario, where among others, the services of a geographical information system in terms of a route planner are integrated. In particular, the Golf Agent allows a tourist to specify the kind of desired golf courses in a detailed way as well as to define the maximal driving distance to the course (cf. Fig. 3).

As result, the user gets a list of all golf courses taken from a web site providing all golf courses in upper Austria (www.golfweb.at), as well as map, containing the driving directions to each of the proposed golf courses. The latter information is extracted from a German web site, providing online route plans.

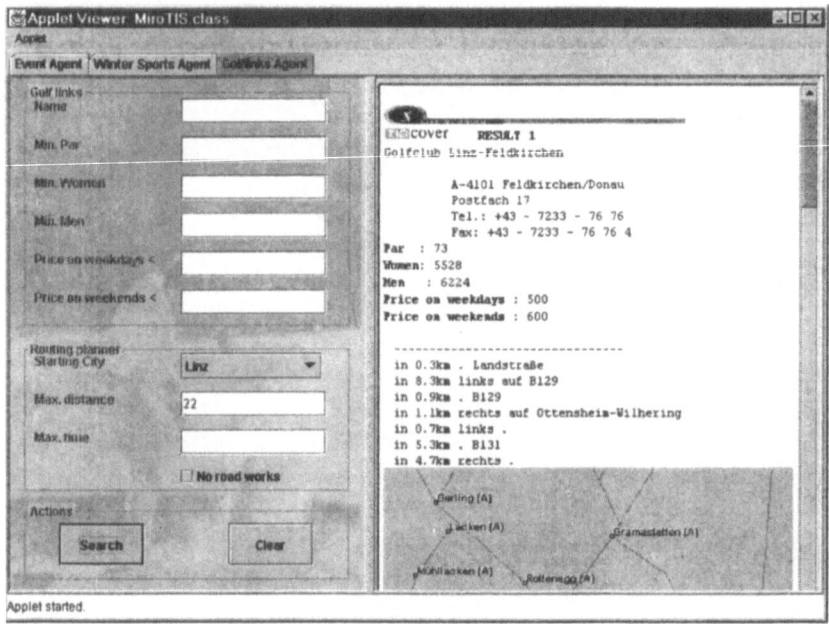

Fig. 3. Golf Agent User Interface

As in the case of the Event Agent, the join criteria for golf courses a driving directions is again the location.

5   Lessons Learned and Future Work

This paper has illustrated the MIRO-Web approach and its application to TIScover. In the course of applying MIRO-Web to TIScover, several interesting issues have been encountered. It has been shown for example, that a lot of web server providers are interested that their data is published not only on their own web sites, but also on other web sites, thus facilitating the federation of web sources. However, a major problem concerning the integration of the various sources is to find a common join criteria for all of the sources. In most of our prototypical realizations, the location or the zip code of a location has been used. One of the most severe problems is the dependency on the web sources to be integrated. If the network is down or slow or if the servers of the provider are even shut down the integration of the data sources is in case of virtual mediation not possible. Furthermore, every time the structure of a data source changes, the corresponding adapter has to be modified too, constituting a maintenance effort which should not be underestimated.

Future work will be done primarily in the course of the follow up ESPRIT project of MIRO-Web called XML-KM (XML-based Mediator for Knowledge Extraction and Brokering). The goal of XML-KM which is strongly based on XML [21] is to enhance the components and tools developed in the course of MIRO-Web in order to be able to collect and disseminate *knowledge* instead of just data. Through a rule-based XML-wrapper, information from corporate databases, HTML files and office applications will be collected in data warehouses [6]. Using classical data mining tools, knowledge will be extracted out of the warehouses in the form of derived information and rules. Through XML-based query tools, users will be able to subscribe and receive personalized information in an appropriate format on various devices including computers, mobile phones and faxes.

References

1. F. Burger, P. Kroiss, B. Proell, R. Richtsfeld, H. Sighart, H. Starck, *TIS@WEB - Database Supported Tourist Information on the Web*, Proc. of the Int. Conf. on Information and Communication Technologies in Tourism (ENTER'97), A Min Tjoa (ed.), Springer, Edinburgh, 1997.
2. R. Domenig, K.R. Dittrich, *An Overview and Classification of Mediated Query Systems*, SIGMOD Record, Vol. 28, No. 3, Sept. 1999.
3. A. Ebner, M. Haller, K. Plankensteiner, P. Starzacher, E. Stauder, and A M. Tjoa, *Tourism Application Requirements Definition (D7B-1/1)*, MIROWEB (EP 25208), April 1998.
4. P. Fankhauser, G. Gardarin, M. Lopez, J. Munoz, A. Tomasic, *Experiences in Federating Databases: From IRO-DB to MIRO-Web*, Proc. of the 24th Int. Conference on Very Large Data Bases (VLDB'98), A. Gupta et al. (eds.), New York City, USA, Morgan Kaufmann, Aug. 1998.
5. D. Florescu, A. Levy, A. Mendelzon, *Database Techniques for the World Wide Web: A Survey*, ACM SIGMOD Record, Vol. 27, No. 3, Sept. 1998.
6. G. Gardarin, F. Sha, T.D. Ngoc, *XML-based Components for Federating Multiple Heterogeneous Data Sources*, Proc. of the 18th Int. Conf. On Conceptual Modeling, LNCS 1728, Paris, France, Nov. 1999.
7. G. Huck, P. Fankhauser, K. Aberer, E. Neuhold, *Jedi: Extracting and Synthesizing Information from the Web*, Proc. of CoopIS'98, IEEE Computer Society Press, 1998.
8. E. Kapsammer, W. Retschitzegger, R. R. Wagner, *Meta Data-Based Middleware for Integrating Information Systems: A Case Study*, Proc. of the 4th Int. Conf. on Information Systems Analysis and Synthesis (ISAS'98), Orlando, July 12-16, 1998.

9. The JDBC Database Access API, http://java.sun.com/products/jdbc, 1999.

10. Oracle Corpration, http://www.oracle.com/, 1999.

11. B. Proell, W. Retschitzegger, R.R. Wagner, A. Ebner, *Beyond Traditional Tourism Information Systems - TIScover*, Journal of Information Technology in Tourism (ITT), Vol.1, Inaugural Volume, Cognizant Corp., USA, 1998.

12. B. Proell, W. Retschitzegger, R.R. Wagner, *TIScover - A Tourism Information System Based on Extranet and Intranet Technology*, Proc. of the 4th Americas Conf. on Information Systems (AIS'98), Baltimore, Maryland, 1998.

13. B. Proell, W. Retschitzegger, R.R. Wagner, *Holiday Packages on the Web*, Proc. of the Int. Conf. on Information and Communication Technologies in Tourism (ENTER'99), D. Buhalis et al. (eds.), Springer, Innsbruck, 1999.

14. B. Proell, W. Retschitzegger, H. Sighart, H. Starck, *Ready for Prime Time - Pre-Generation of Web Pages in TIScover*, Proc. of the 8th Int. ACM Conference on Information and Knowledge Management (CIKM), Kansas City, Missouri, Nov. 2-6, 1999.

15. Homepage of TIScover, *http://www.tiscover.com*, TIS Innsbruck, FAW Hagenberg, 1999.

16. Homepage of TIScover ASIA, *http://www.tiscoverasia.com*, GoThailand, 1998.

17. Homepage of TIScover Germany, *http://www.deutschlandreise.de*, START Media Plus, 1999.

18. Homepage of TIScover Switzerland, *http://www.kissswiss.com*, Kümmerly+Frey, Basler Versicherungen, 1999.

19. A. Tomasic, L. Raschid, P. Valduriez, *Scaling heterogeneous databases and the design of DISCO*, Proc. of the 16th Int. Conf. On Distributed Computing Systems, Hong Kong, May 1996.

20. G. Wiederhold, *Mediators in the architecture of future information systems*, Computer, Vol. 25, No. 3, March 1992.

21. The World Wide Web Consortium (W3C), http://www.w3.org/XML/, 1999.

Integration of Heterogeneous Information Sources

Marion Kaukal and Hannes Werthner
Department of Information Systems
Vienna University of Economics and Business Administration
{marion.kaukal, hannes.werthner}@wu-wien.ac.at

Abstract

The description of tourism products and services can be characterized by heterogeneity. Suppliers use – in most of the cases – very different concepts and vocabularies to describe their products and services. Even within a specific domain such as hospitality, varying terms as well as structures refer to the same concepts. Obviously, this represents a barrier to automated communication on the WWW. In the following, we present a solution to that problem. It is based on a mediated architecture assuring interoperability on a tourism market – without forcing individual suppliers to agree on a common standard data model. It is shown how semantic modeling - using the Resource Description Framework (RDF) - provides new possibilities for unifying distributed heterogeneous data models.

1 Electronic Business Communication

In comparison to human communication, electronic communication requires a more structured approach to allow the automated processing of messages and their content. Communication partners have to agree on the structure of a message as well as on the vocabulary used to articulate specific information. In order to prevent the definition of new communication formats for each communication process, Electronic Data Interchange (EDI) standards appeared in the 1980s. Those standards set the rules for the composition of specific message types like orders or invoices. The standards most commonly used are UN/EDIFACT and ANSI X.12. Within those exist industry-specific specializations like Unicorn, Rescon and AVLABL for tourism messages. Within EDIFACT, the message development group EEG 8 is responsible for Travel, Tourism and Leisure (TTL). Member Airlines of the International Air Transport Association (IATA) are deploying UN/EDIFACT conform message types and to date, 62 message types are adopted. In EDI, small and medium sized tourism suppliers are lagging behind [1].

The shortcomings of most of these EDI systems are mainly the expensive set up and maintenance efforts. For each trading partner that uses a different EDI standard, costly configurations have to be carried out. Especially small and medium sized enterprises (SMEs) are often forced to adopt the standard of their more powerful business partners. Communication between the EDI systems is mainly conducted over expensive and proprietary value added networks (VANs). Further limitations of EDI are the complex syntax and the lack of human readability.

The EDI standard message types are merely not suitable for ad-hoc contacts. Configurations have to be done in several face-to-face meetings between the partners in order to agree on concrete message formats. In most of the cases the messages refer to pre-defined products by a product-ID. New product types or suppliers call for reconfigurations. Requests comprising detailed or uncommon product or service preferences are not supported. Consequently, traditional EDI is too inflexible for the new requirements of global dynamic trading relationships. But with the advent of the Internet, especially the WWW, EDI has a new potential. Internet access is much cheaper than VANs and business data interchange may be handled by the use of a simple Web browser on the client side. On the server side most standard database management systems offer suitable and easy to configure Web interfaces. This allows also SMEs to take part in the EDI world at small costs.

2   Assuring Semantic Interoperability within Web based Communication

On the WWW, the Hypertext Markup Language (HTML) is still the predominant way for encoding information. But HTML is not suitable for content structuring that allows machine-readable information as it only supports a predefined and fixed structuring of document parts like headings <h1> or tables <table>. These shortcomings may be avoided by the eXtensible Markup Language (XML) [2], that provides a mechanism for information structuring by the use of individually definable tags. Those tags may refer to some domain-dependent meaning, e.g., a price of a hotelroom may be described by a new tag <roomprice>. The naming, structure and integrity constraints for specific elements can be defined by a XML Document Type Definition (DTD) or – more advanced – by a XML Schema [3]. Thus, XML enables the definition of domain specific own business languages and the according syntax requirements.

In that context the term XML/EDI refers to initiatives that try to bring traditional EDI messages to the Web by the use of XML. Therefore, the standard EDI message components are translated to XML tags as well as new message elements may be defined. XML/EDI is easier to configure and adaptable to specific domains. In addition, due to the use of DTD new or reconfigured XML structures can be processed by any XML/EDI enabled machine without human intervention.

However, XML/EDI alone doesn't solve the problem of semantic ambiguity or mapping, respectively. As on the Web with its many different information suppliers, rigid standardization doesn't work, another approach that allows the integration of heterogeneous data models – with appropriate semantic mappings – has to be followed.

A suitable concept are abstraction mechanisms that are based on metadata definitions.

Metadata are used to describe specific information, i.e., it is information about information. For example, libraries are using metadata for a long time to describe location or publisher of their book inventory. On the Web, metadata can be defined as "machine-understandable descriptions of Web resources" [4]. Metadata is suitable for providing information to manage and retrieve resources requiring more structure than is inherent in the data itself. Also the relationship between specific Web pages can be described. For communication purposes metadata may be used to describe the language, message types and the syntax requirements needed.

3 The Resource Description Framework (RDF) Providing Descriptive Information

The Resource Description Framework (RDF) [5] was developed by the W3C Metadata Activity [6]. It provides mechanisms to describe the syntax as well as the semantics of Web resources. RDF offers a model for representing named properties and property values for describing resources and the relationships between resources. A specific resource together with one or more named properties plus the values of these properties constitute a *RDF Description*. The framework is based on a directed labeled graph where the nodes are referring to a resource, each resource is described by a set of properties represented by graph arcs. Fig. 1 shows a part of an example hotel RDF description. The hotel Web Site (the resource) is represented by a node in a graph. The arcs are delineating properties (`messageformat` and `schema`), property values can be either other resources (the schema identified by its Web address `http://www.hotelA.com/schema.dtd`) or literals that are shown as rectangles (the message format `XML`). Each resource that is identifiable by a Uniform Resource Identifier (URI) [7] can be described by RDF.

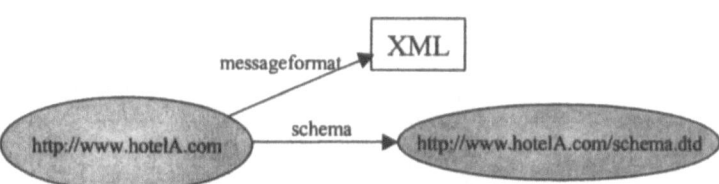

Fig. 1. Hotel RDF Model

```
<rdf:RDF
    xmlns:rdf=„http://www.w3.org/1999/02/22-rdf-syntax-ns#"
    xmlns:hotel=„http://www.hotelmarket.org/rdf-ns#">
<rdf:Description about=„http://www.hotelA.com/">
  <hotel:messageformat>XML</hotel:messageformat>
  <hotel:schema
        rdf:resource=„http://www.hotelA.com/schema.dtd" />
</rdf:Description>
</rdf:RDF>
```

Fig. 2. Hotel RDF XML Representation

In addition, the *RDF Schema* Specification offers an extensible object-oriented typing system for the resources and properties used in the RDF data model and defines concepts such as classes, subclasses, properties or sub-properties [8]. It also allows the expression of integrity constraints. Both, the RDF Data Model and RDF Schema propose XML as a serialization syntax. Fig. 2 shows the XML representation of the RDF model of figure 1. At the beginning, the XML Namespace facility [9], labeled xmlns:, refers to the respective vocabularies. Element and attribute names used in the document are associated with namespaces for the belonging data schemes that are identified by a URI reference. In the example there are two namespaces in use, each identified by a prefix. rdf: denotes the prefix for the core RDF namespace, hotel: denotes the prefix for the vocabulary provided by the RDF schema of the specific domain.

One important feature of RDF is the possibility to define containers to refer to a collection of resources or literals. RDF therefore defines *bags* (unordered lists), *sequences* (ordered lists) and *alternatives*. Fig. 3 shows a RDF bag of hotels in a city. The city is represented as Web resource and described by the property hotels. The according property value is itself another resource that is further described by the property rdf:type. This identifies the specific collection, here rdf:bag, comprising an unordered list of hotels, themselves represented as Web resources. The membership relation between this container resource and the resources that belong in the collection is defined by a set of properties named "_1", "_2", "_3", etc.
In the following, a mediator is presented, that applies RDF for assuring semantic interoperability between heterogeneous and distributed hotel supplier applications.

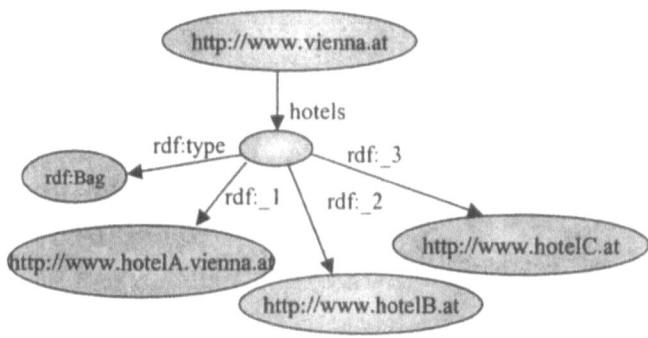

Fig. 3. RDF Bag

4 A Mediation Server and its Ontology Specification

Mediated architectures represent a solution for markets with heterogeneous information sources. They allow the interoperation between distinct data models. Mediators
allocate information from diverse sources and are responsible for providing integrated
information that is automatically composed without physically integrating the base
data sources. They are responsible for accessing and retrieving relevant data from
multiple heterogeneous sources, for abstracting and transforming retrieved data into a
common representation [10]. A mediator is based on an *ontology* for assuring
interoperability of multiple distributed systems. An ontology provides a common and
unambiguous vocabulary used for describing the objects and relationships in a specific domain of interest. Therewith it serves as interlingua for the translation between
different languages and representations.

The degree of formality by which the vocabulary of an ontology is built and the
meaning of terms are specified, varies from informal definitions expressed in natural
language over a taxonomy of terms that are arranged into a generalization-
specialization hierarchy to definitions stated in a formal language based on first-order
logic with a rigorously defined syntax and semantics [11]. For the mediator proposed
here, a highly formal ontology is applicable. While traditional first order predicate
calculus languages like KIF [12], CYCL [13] and LOOM [14] are appropriate, RDF
is simpler to implement and especially suitable for distributed Web resources.

For this purpose, RDF offers the possibility to describe the semantics of the message
content delivered to and received from different suppliers. Thereby the domain is divided into different concepts, and for each concept, the respective vocabularies, data
types, relationships and structures are explicitly defined in the ontology. For example,
by the use of RDF, any tourism hotel supplier registered at a mediation server can be
contacted for price offers concerning specific hotel room preferences. The messages
are composed by rules available in the mediator's RDF model that describes the do-
main-vocabulary of the individual suppliers. Likewise, the incoming offers may be

retranslated in a unified model in order to provide a homogeneous result view for the customer.

Obviously, the mediation task of providing semantic interoperation is highly domain dependent. The concerning domain should be limited by its ability to define and maintain internal consistency [10], i.e., identical semantics for the terms used. Even in the domain of tourism we can expect a set of different mediators, since many applications will need to cover different topics [1].

One such topic is the hotel supply side which will be described in the following tourism mediation facility. It makes use of metadata for describing the heterogeneous domain models of *hotel market suppliers*. In the following, the main message type is a Request For Information (RFI) that allows a customer to state his preferences and to ask for appropriate product or service information. The suppliers respond by the use of the message type Response to Request For Information (RRFI). It is assumed, that the suppliers use XML as transfer language and the appropriate data schema is available as XML DTD. This is feasible as most of today's standard database software packages provide according XML interfaces.

4.1 A Hotel Market Mediator

Fig. 4 shows the communication processes between the mediator and a customer as well as between the mediator and different suppliers representing a hotel information query and the according result. The customer fills in an online form (1) where he can state his preferences for location, price, date and other hotel attributes like room view etc. The mediator receives the form data and composes RFI messages for the appropriate suppliers (2). Afterwards, it receives the RRFI answers, i.e. the query results (3), and presents them to the customer in a uniform view (4).

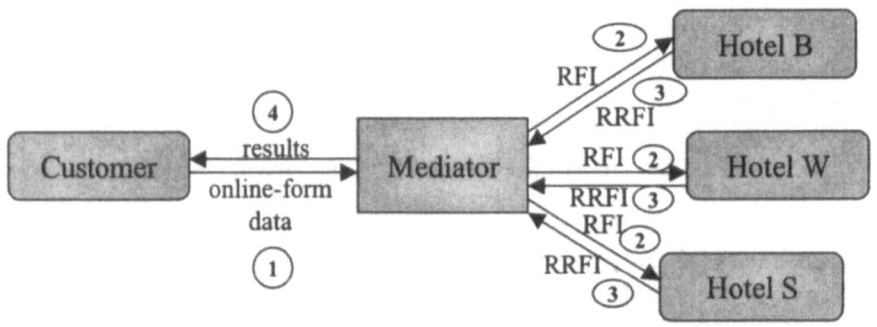

Fig. 4. The Hotel Market

Thus, a mediator offers the following services:

- *Message management*

On customer request, the mediator selects the appropriate suppliers and composes RFI messages according to the suppliers' data schemes. Likewise, it receives the reply RRFI and is responsible for providing a uniform result view to the requesting customer.

- *Translation mechanisms for the used terms*

Suppliers may require different terms. The mediator must be able to "translate" between the central terminology managed by the mediator and the individual vocabulary of the suppliers.

- *Calculation and mapping mechanisms for individual data types and structured values*

The suppliers may also expect varying data values following different data types and structure. The mediator must be able to provide according calculation and mapping mechanisms. For example, a currency conversion or string pattern format mapping may be provided.

- *Addition of a new hotel supplier*

New suppliers may be included in the market at any time. Their vocabularies – data structures – may be added either as new alternatives (within existing properties) or as new concepts. It is assumed that this process is controlled by the human generator of the mediator service.

- *Keeping a list of hotels and according sub RDF models*

The mediator keeps a list of hotels represented as WWW resources. Each supplier data schema refers to a subsets of the ontology components.

4.2 The Message Management

A tourism customer may use the mediator's system by online selecting some predefined options such as country or city and then fills out some input fields where he states his preferences for a hotelroom. Attributes like preferred price range, arrival and departure date, roomtype etc. are typed in. These values are then transferred to the mediation server.

The mediation server identifies the appropriate hotels, for example, by general metadata for location etc. Only relevant hotels should be contacted with the request for information. For each hotel, additional metadata are required, like the URI location of the data schema for syntax requirements and the target address for the RFI.

Assuming, that the hotels are all sending and receiving XML formatted messages, the suppliers' individual XML DTDs are accessed by the mediator. Based on these individual DTDs, the mediator composes the required messages for the RFI. The mediator has to translate the information to be included in the RFI to the terms required for the respective local XML elements or attributes. Also for providing the data values themselves, the mediator has to follow the requirements of the suppliers. Either the form values can be taken directly or the data types and structures have to be adjusted. In addition, calculations like currency adjustments etc. are done by the mediation server.

In the following, an according and prototypical RDF model is presented.

4.3   The core RDF Model of the Hotel Mediator

Fig. 5 shows a part of the hotel domain RDF model. Therein the alternative terms and relations for the hotel domain concept *"bednumber"* in a room are included. bed-Number itself is only one property in the RDF Model and may refer to a Web resource, as for example the online form presented to the customer. Bednumbers may have different labels depending on the individual data model. In the example, there are three alternative labels: beds, roomType and bed_in_room. Therefore a RDF property label is available which may take alternative values, presented by the RDF container RDF:Alt.

In addition, a property values is specified, which is described by alternative representations. Each one represents a new resource (identified by one_bed, two_bed, three_bed) and is again described by its own alternatives for according property values (e.g., concept one_bed – alternative labels: single, one).

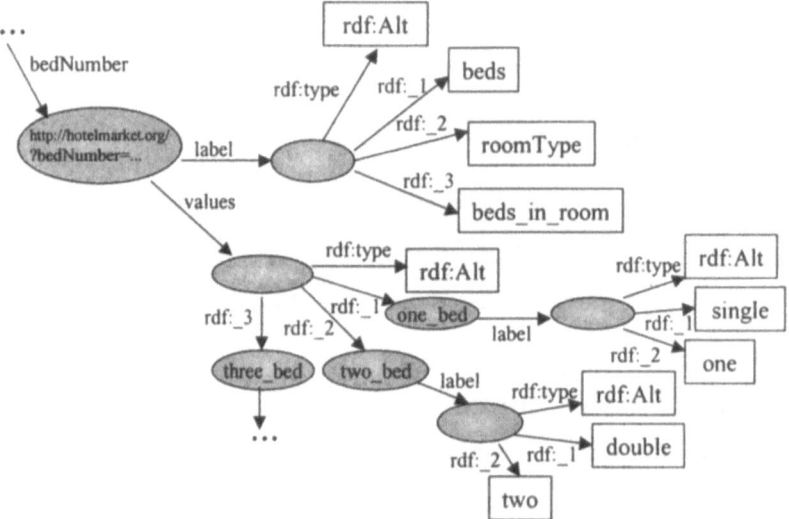

Fig. 5. Bednumber Translation

Fig. 6 shows another feature of the mediation RDF model, the *hotelprice* concept. Price is a term used to refer to different concepts, either price per night and person or price per night and apartment. This is considered by the property "deployedFor" and an RDF alternative container of appropriate literals. Additionally, the structure of a price may differ. Some applications may require a combination of price and currency, others may have different attributes for each of them. currency may be an extern resource that describes the currency data type. The property values again refers to suitable data types. Some alternative literals define the format requirements for hotelPrice as string patterns, another resource provides a further description as an integer data type.

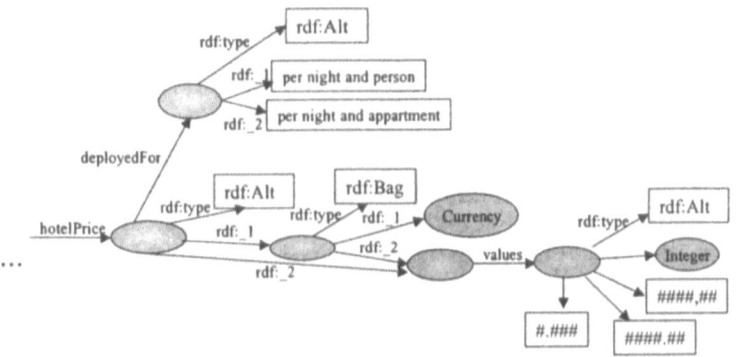

Fig. 6. Price Translation

4.4 Adding a new Supplier Node to the RDF Model

Each supplier to be included in the core RDF model, has to provide his data schemes by means of XML DTDs, required for the different message types. For each element the position in the core data model has to be defined.

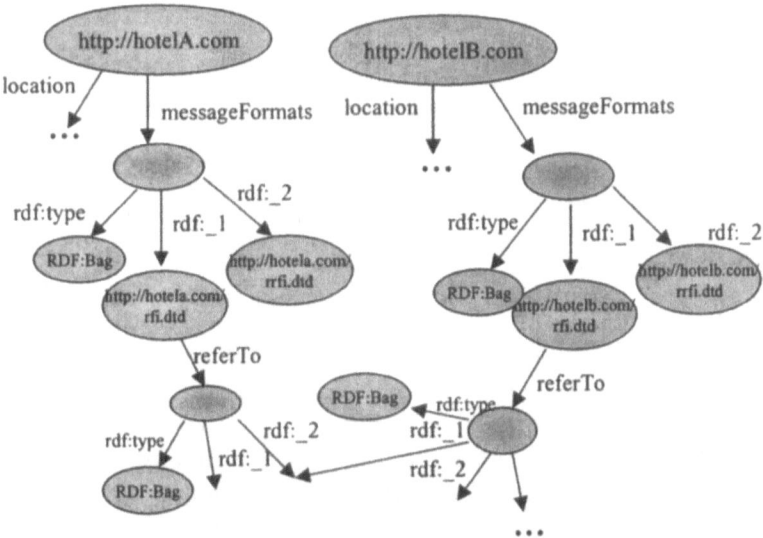

Fig. 7. Hotel Supplier Integration

Fig. 7 shows the section of the RDF model with the description of two hotels. The model contains message formats as well as additional information for each hotel. The message formats are represented as RDF:Bag of possible messageFormats. In our example, the message types RFI and RRFI are presented as membership properties. The belonging values are Web resources where the according data schemes are accessible. The schema itself, i.e. its elements and attributes, are described by the referTo property values that are integrated in a RDF bag. For example, Hotel A may refer to the bedNumber concept by referencing the label beds, while Hotel B may reference the label roomType. Of course, different hotels may refer to the same values and resources. Each hotel, in addition to its data schema, is described by some information such as its IP address or geographical location, which serves two purposes: it supports the communication process with and the identification of hotels.

The proposed mediator approach doesn't force the individual businesses to conduct complex adaptations to standard formats or to define formal semantics on their own. They may continue to use their legacy system or standard software and only have to provide an open interface for the mediator where the desired data can be requested. Most of the standard database management systems are able to provide a XML tranlation of query results and tables and therefore can be applied for data access on the supplier side.

4.5 The Communication Process

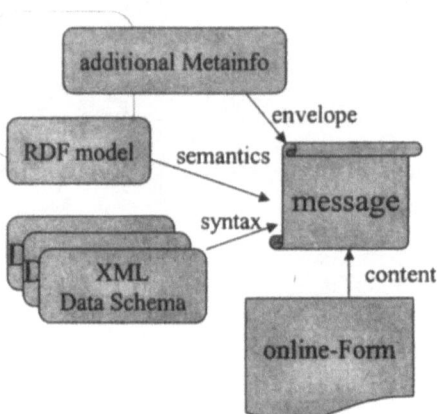

Fig. 8. Message Composition

Fig. 8 shows the constituent parts for message composition. First, the hotel customer request is delivered by an online-form and defines the information *content* of the message. For the message itself, the *syntax* is delivered by the individual data schemes of the suppliers. *Semantics* for the terms required as well as additional metainformation (such as the supplier's IP address or geographical location) are provided by the mediator's RDF model. The IP address is part of the message's envelope needed for the electronic communication.

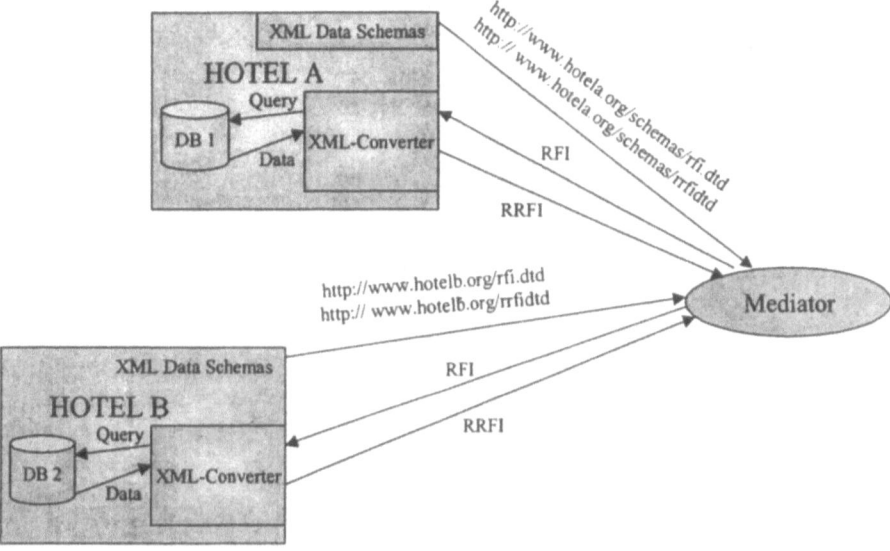

Fig. 9.
The Communication Process

Fig. 9 summarizes the communication process between the mediator and the suppliers. The mediator collects the XML data schemes from the suppliers appropriate for the customer query and composes the corresponding RFIs. These are sent to the specified supplier interface. The receiving supplier application activates the according database query. Their database management system collects the data and generates XML coded results. These are included in the reply message which is also based on an appropriate data schema and is sent back to the mediator.

At the mediator, the supplier specific RRFI formats have to be retranslated again to a mediator internal format in order to provide a comparable and unique query result view for the customers.

Additional information, that is not part of the core RDF model and specific to each supplier may be provided individually. These information cannot be interpreted by the mediator and the according descriptive information may be provided directly by the supplier. Therefore, the suppliers put this type of information in the RRFI together with a URI for the specific descriptions. The mediator adds this reference to the result page.

5   Conclusions

We presented a mediation facility responsible for integrating heterogeneous data models. It supports language- and context independent communication between different hotel suppliers and the mediator. We concentrated on the pre-contract business transaction interaction where mainly personal preferences and product information are exchanged between supplier and customer.

While suppliers are providing syntax requirements, the mediator is responsible for semantic integration within the market place. This is based on RDF as a promising concept to define semantics for distributed data models. In our future work we will focus on the definition of such a RDF metamodel with the related translation and integration functions, including the implementation of a prototype.

6 References

1. Werthner, H., Klein, S.: Information Technology and Tourism - A Challenging Relationship. Springer. Vienna. 1999.

2. Bray, T., Paoli, J., Sperberg-Mc Queen, C.M.: Extensible Markup Language (XML) 1.0, W3C Recommendation. http://www.w3.org/TR/1998/REC-xml-19980210, 1998-02-10

3. Malhotra, A., Maloney, M.: XML Schema Requirements. W3C Note, http://www.w3.org/TR/NOTE-xml-schema-req, 1999-02-15.

4. Lassila, O.: Web Metadata: A Matter of Semantics. IEEE Computer. July/August 1998. pp 30-37.

5. Lassila, O., Swick, R. R.: Resource Description Framework (RDF) Model and Syntax Specification. W3C Recommendation, http://www.w3.org/TR/REC-rdf-syntax/, 1999-02-22

6. The W3C Metadata Activity: http://www.w3.org/Metadata/

7. Berners-Lee, T., Fielding, R., Irvine, U.C., Masinter, L.: Uniform Resource Identifiers (URI): Generic Syntax. Internet Engineering Task Force Network Working Group. RFC 2396.. http://www.ics.uci.edu/pub/ietf/uri/rfc2396.txt, August 1998.

8. Brickley, D., Guha, R. V.: Resource Description Framework (RDF) Schema Specification. W3C Proposed Recommendation, http://www.w3.org/TR/PR-rdf-schema/, 1999-03-03

9. Bray, T., Hollander, D., Layman, A.: Namespaces in XML, W3C Recommendation. http://www.w3.org/TR/1999/REC-xml-names-19990114

10. Wiederhold, G., Genesereth, M.: The Conceptual Basis for Mediation Services. IEEE Expert Intelligent Systems 12/5, 38 - 47, 1997.

11. Uschold, M., Gruninger, M.: 1996, Ontologies: Principles, Methods and Applications, Knowledge Engineering Review, 11/2.

12. The Knowledge Interchange Format (KIF); http://logic.stanford.edu/kif/kif.html

13. CycL: The CYC Representation Language; http://www.cyc.com/tech.html#cycl

14. The LOOM Project: http://www.isi.edu/isd/LOOM/LOOM-HOME.html

Virtual Tourist Destinations:
Assessing Their Communication Effectiveness With And Through Foreign Intermediaries

Robert Govers

Centre for Tourism Management, Rotterdam School of Management, Erasmus University, P.O. Box 1738, 3000 DR Rotterdam, The Netherlands, RGovers@DubaiPolytechnic.com

Myriam Jansen-Verbeke

Institute for Social and Economic Geography, Catholic University Leuven, De Croylaan 42, B-3001 Heverlee, Belgium, Myriam.Verbeke@geo.kuleuven.ac.be

Frank M. Go

Centre for Tourism Management, Rotterdam School of Management, Erasmus University, P.O. Box 1738, 3000 DR Rotterdam, The Netherlands, FGo@fbk.eur.nl

Abstract

Travel and tourism is by now generally perceived to be the market with the biggest online potential for e-commerce. The success of major online travel agents and the growth numbers in online tourist expenditure are proof of that. As this was also recognised by the Flemish government, a research study into the effectiveness of the online communication of Flemish' tourist destinations was commissioned. This paper reports on the findings resulting from a focus group session with twelve tour operators held in the Netherlands, the first foreign market for tourism in Flanders. It discusses issues such as dis-intermediation, use of the Internet by intermediaries themselves, and roles they play in the new market situation. It shows that, although traditional players are increasingly online, they are still a long way from understanding the new economy.

1. Introduction

Because of the tremendous speed at which the Internet is still growing, the potentials of e-commerce are by now generally accepted. US studies, for instance that of the Commerce Department named "The Emerging Digital Economy" found that "information technology, including business on the Internet, is growing twice as fast as the rest of the economy... Internet traffic has doubled every (90 to) 100 days." One of the fastest (when not THE fastest) growing online market is travel and tourism. According to predictions in early 1998 by (amongst others) Jupiter Communications, the online travel expenditures would reach up to 5 billion dollars by the year 2000, even surpassing the sales of PC hard- and software, entertainment and books and CD's. [2, 8: p.73] At that time it was also estimated that the 'big travel sites' had approximately US$ 2-4 million worth of selling per week and between 2 and 4 million subscribers. [20: p.8]

But, in October 1998 Forrester Research [18] announced that, "the explosive growth in the online travel industry had caused the research company to overhaul its predictions...". The online market is now expected to grow from US$ 3.1 billion in leisure travel bookings in 1998, to over US$ 29 billion in 2003, accounting for 12 % of the overall travel market. By 1998 there are already four Internet travel agencies ranked in the top fifty US travel agents [11]. These are:

- Microsoft's Expedia, with a record online travel industry sale of US$ 16 million in the first week of April 1999 and over 4.2 million visitors each month during the second quarter of this same year; [6: a]
- Preview Travel, that recently announced its millionth transaction since its start in May 1996 and counting over eight million registered members; [6: b]
- ITN (Internet Travel Network), the first site that developed Web-based online travel reservation technology and recently changed its name to GETTHERE.COM, [6: c] and;
- Travelocity, reporting a gross sale of over US$128 million for the first quarter of 1999, a growth of 156 % compared to the same period a year earlier. The site also registered an impressive 1.2 million new members during those months. [6: d]

McKinsey [1: p.156] has underpinned the high potential for travel services in the electronic marketplace based on two factors (see Figure 1): the sophistication of buyers and the inefficiency of current transactions. The latter is for instantly illustrated by the fact that, as part of the SABRE Group [3: p.134] the biggest travel site, Travelocity, offers the opportunity to gain access to 420 airlines (representing 95 percent of all available airline seats), 40,000 hotels, and 50 car rental companies. It also has the most online seat-selection maps of any online booking site (no more

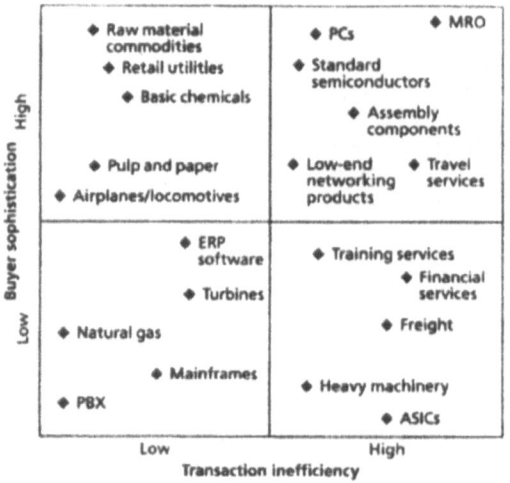

Fig. 1: Opportunities for electronic marketplaces

middle seat over the wing for you). [6: e, 7] Latest news is that SABRE HOLDINGS Corporation has acquired Preview Travel Inc., creating the clear leader in online travel. The new company will also benefit from a new, five-year US$200 million contract with America Online Inc. in which Travelocity.com will process all travel reservations booked through AOL's sites (No.1 site with 36.8 million unique visitors in August 1999 [12]).

In addition, Yahoo! Inc. (No.2 site with 33.6 million visitors in August 1999 [12]) has extended its existing contract with Travelocity.com and has agreed to invest in the new entity. Pierre Kleinhans, CEO of leisureplanet.com, has offered the following comment on the merger of Travelocity and Preview Travel. "The merger of these two major US online travel services providers reinforces the fact that online travel is one of the fastest growing and most dynamic segments in e-commerce. It also validates our assumption that online travel will be dominated by two or three major players in each market." [6: f]

As far as Europe is concerned, the online sales of travel products, amounting to just $7.7 million in 1997, will be worth $1.7 billion by 2002, according to market analysis firm Datamonitor. [9] And also in the Netherlands the travel industry is reconsidering their initial reservations about the potential of the Internet. The last survey with the continuous national travel panel resulted in an estimate of 1.4 million (appr. 10% o the adult population) Dutch traveller using the Internet to plan their trips.[15].

2. Background

The trend is clear, although there might still be more lookers than bookers, the use of Internet for planning, reservation, booking, and payment of travel products and services displays the highest growth numbers when compared to any other industry, only tailed by the 'entertainment' industry. Vigilantly, the Flemish government and the Flemish Tourist Board have recognised this trend and have therefore commissioned the Institute for Social and Economic Geography (ISEG) of the Catholic University Leuven (KU-Leuven), to conduct a research study into the effectiveness of Internet communication regarding tourist destinations in Flanders. The objective of the study is to develop innovative strategies in destination and database marketing, using strategically 'new' information technologies. The study includes two complementary approaches as also illustrated in Figure 2. First, an analysis on the tourism supply side in Flanders is conducted, in order to evaluate the contents of destinations' Internet sites and the organisational context in which initiatives are launched and managed (Top block Figure 2). Secondly, an analysis on the demand side, both in the domestic and the foreign market is carried out. In the Dutch origin-market, being of primary interest for Flanders, the focus is on the intermediaries and end consumers (Other blocks in Figure 2). In order to study the Dutch market segment for tourism in Flanders, co-operation was established with the Centre for Tourism Management (CTM) of the Erasmus University Rotterdam (EUR). This paper will discuss the results of the latter part of the project, and the research among intermediaries in particular.

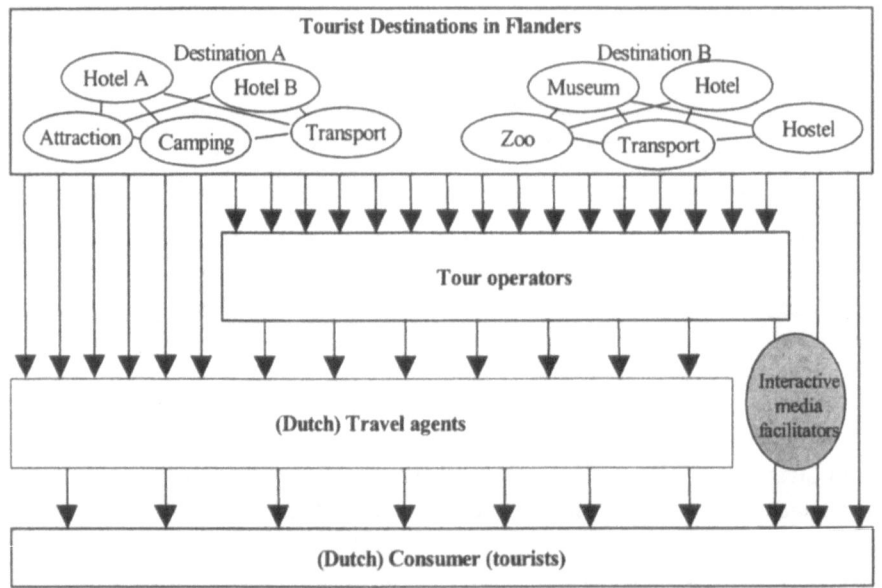

Fig. 2: Distribution Chain Tourism Industry

3. Problem definition

It is generally asserted that traditional intermediaries, such as travel agents and tour operators, will loose market share if they do not reconsider their role, adjust their services to specific consumer preferences and add value.[14] Traditionally the core business of travel agents consists of information provision, booking/reservation, and added value creation (professional advise, insurance, guaranties, safety & security). It is expected that the first two tasks will loose importance the more consumers find their way online, not only to gather information but also to book and pay. The use of credit cards, ticketless travel, e-tickets and e-cash transactions will only speed up this process.

As a result, cybermediaries are rapidly gaining ground, as was discussed in the introduction. Many large travel principles (airlines, hotel chains) are also successful in exploiting the WWW to make a direct sale. This eliminates the need to pay agents a commission, and also reduces customer service outlay. [11] In addition, it has been asserted that "the transaction costs of bookings made online can be up to 10 times lower than those made through call centres" let alone physical outlets. [9] In fact, in the first half of October 1999, as a direct result of booming online sales, all major US and their partner European Airlines dropped commission rates from 8 to 5 % on ticket sales in the US and Canada [5: a]. Major questions arising from that are: "How will this effect the traditional travel agents and tour operators, will it unavoidably lead to complete dis-intermediation? And if so, what will that mean for the virtual representation of physical tourist destinations? How will (virtual) tourist destinations best be able to influence the decision making process of consumers considering their next business meeting, holiday or conference destination?

Adding customer value that is not provided by the travel principles themselves will be one of the few competencies that will make a difference in the competitive arena. Earlier studies by the Centre for Tourism Management support the notion that travel agents should drastically re-positioning themselves, no longer being distributors of tourist products on behalf of the supplier, but acting as competent service advisers to the customer, matching consumer preferences and customised demand with appropriate supply at the bast value for money. [16]

Issues to be investigated within this part of the study are:
- "Direct marketing", which as Walle [19: p.72] points out, "is a viable option when a significant segment of the market is willing to forgo whatever benefits the traditional intermediaries provide in order to gain resulting convenience and/or savings", then what are the opportunities for direct marketing and direct selling, as the travel principles are now able, maybe with the help of interactive media facilitators (amongst which Cybermediaries [17]) to communicate directly and interactively with their customers at low cost, despite of any physical distances, national borders, traditional players or rules and regulations? [10] and what are then the dangers of dis-intermediation as a result of the growth of the Internet?
- Benefits the Internet might provide intermediaries, when they will be able to better serve their customers and maybe sustain a competitive advantage?
- The emerging e-commerce link is characterised by operational dispersement and institutional concentration, in that dispersed actors (being various actors in one single destination, or actors in different destinations combining their efforts) are brought together by virtual means. Therefore, Virtual Tourism Destinations (amongst which Cybermediaries) may be defined as tourist locations on the Web that allow electronic interaction and thus dynamic communications, between consumers, suppliers, destinations and possibly intermediaries. They provide an important means to bridge the heterogeneous and fragmented nature of tourism, through the promotion of a brand name that represents and is linked to the separate identities of the various destinations' actors, both public and private. A third important issue is therefore what the chances are for such Virtual Tourist Destinations within the current tourism industry, and how can such 'bridges' be virtually organised?

4. Research method

On September 17, 1999, a focus group session on 'The Internet in the Travel Industry' was held in Rotterdam, The Netherlands. Twelve senior managers from various travel businesses were present. Eleven tour operators (TO's) were represented, of which two poses their own travel agencies and three are pure direct sellers. Two of the eleven TO's are generalists, offering a wide range of destinations and products. The other nine are specialists, with specific programmes and destinations. Four of the participating companies actually offer Flanders in their travel programme, but all of them have a company web-site, and seven of them even provide online booking pacilities, or are planning to do so in the near future.

Three major issues were discussed in the session in the following way. First, the participants were confronted with the examples of online travel providers as discussed in the introduction: Expadia, Travelocity, Sabene (the national carrier) offering direct booking facilities through the Internet, etc. Then the respondents were asked: "do you feel threatened by this?" and "will this lead to dis-intermediation?.

In a second stage, respondents were presented with examples of TO's offering their products and services through the Net. Also other examples were provided, such as sites offering information on travel and tourism in Flanders, like Tourism Flanders (the National Tourist Board) with their event-database, or the VanDyck-site, created to promote the special event in Antwerp during the summer of 1999, with a major exhibition on this classical painter and other related activities. Then participants were asked if they themselves offer their products and services online, if they use information from third parties (for instance the various destinations' public sites) or utilise other services offered by outside players on the Internet.

Third, participants were asked if they think their roles will change as a result of their technological transformations. A starting point for this is provided by Sarkar et al. [17] who have studies the future role of intermediary organisations in the electronic marketplace. They distinguish four services an intermediary can provide towards consumers and six towards producers, or within the context of this paper, travel principles (TP's).

Consumer services	Producer services
• search and evaluation	• Product information dissemination
• needs assessment and product matching	• Purchase influence
• customer risk management	• Provision of customer information
• product distribution	• Producer risk management
	• Transaction economies of scale
	• Integrating consumer & producer needs.

The question posted was: "to what extent intermediaries are convinced that these tasks and recommendations are valid and important and if they are of the opinion that they are providing such services to the Flemish destinations and TP's and the tourists visiting them?"

5. Results

Some of the results coming out of the discussions arising form the aforementioned issues and questions will be presented below, after which recapitulating recommendations will be listed briefly, before concluding the paper in more strategic terms.

5.1 Dis-intermediation

The participants identified various opportunities and threats for travel agents (TA's) and TO's that originate from the current developments in e-commerce and online customer service. They are listed in Table 1.

Table 1. Opportunities and threats of e-commerce for the travel industry

Threats for TA's	*Threats for TO's*
• Decreasing turnover because of increased direct sales of TP's and TO's • Lower margins because of reduced commission rates from TO's and TP's, for whom TA's are of less strategic importance	• Losing buying power discounts with TP's that increase their direct market share through -commerce • Many TO's' strong ties with TA's makes them reluctant to start direct marketing, which might harm them in the end
Opprtunities for TA's	*Opportunities for TO's*
• Use Internet as tool, to compare products • Be a reliable objective source to customers • Offer a social role, personal contact • More advisory role as specialist in certain specific areas or travel and tourism • Form buying groups or franchises to create buying power • A 'natural' equilibrium might be recreated when the big TO's dispose of their own TA's in future. Smaller, specialist, customer oriented TA's should then be able to survive • Start-up of the badly needed quality impetus	• No commissions leads to cost reduction • Equal competition on the Net, while TA's are often biased towards bigger TO's • Better customer service because TO knows the own product better than the TA does • Strong competitive edge compared to direct sales op TP's because of buying power. The question is where the breakpoint will be • Learning by doing, start with basic TO- products and gradually increase complexity • Small niche players can now easily access low density markets world-wide

5.2 Internet for intermediaries

Regarding the second issue of the use of Internet by the travel industry, a discussion took place whether or not TO's should offer additional information online, supplementary to that provided in the brochures and guides. Two arguments were used in favour of such added online information service:
- to create added value and service to the customer;
- to answer any questions consumers might have, in order to stimulate direct sales.

Others advocated that it should be sufficient to just copy the prospectus onto Internet, because:
- Internet users themselves should be able to find any information needed online;

- TO's are on the Net to get people to book, information provision is a task that others should provide, as for instance national tourist boards (NTB's).

The latter viewpoint seems to be very consumer unfriendly and completely ignores the roles TA's traditionally fulfilled regarding product information dissemination, purchase influence and integration of producer and consumer needs. Therefore, in the end, most of the participants seemed to agree that additional information services should be offered in an online marketplace. Table 2 lists how that might be done.

Table 2: Advantages and drawbacks of ways to provide online information

Links to third parties, advantages:	All the information on own site, advantages:
• Others do all the work • Reciprocal links, better 'searchability' • (Ostensible) objectivity, info. not provided by the actor that has the commercial interests • Provides added value to consumers	• Visitors do not leave the site • Everything is kept in-house, governed and verifiable by company management • Others might refer and virtually link to me, while I don't have to refer visitors to others
Drawbacks:	Drawbacks:
• It leads visitors away from the own site • Possibly bad quality of the external sites	• A lot of work, one would almost have to keep an encyclopaedia

Table 2 illustrates that many actors in the travel business are not very networking oriented. Many like to see others refer consumers to them, but prefer not to do that in reverse. They are afraid visitors will be led away from the site and that others do not provide the level of service they expect. Internet logic is not well understood, external links or not, there is never any guarantee that a visitor will ever stay on any site, it is not like television. In fact, server log-file analysis on the Van Dyck and City of Brugge-sites showed that between 10 to 20% of visitors immediately leave the site after viewing the homepage, depending on the purposefulness of the site search. An alternative to linking the site to third parties or DIY is to get NTB's to make information downloadable for TO's to use the content in their own sites.

5.3 Intermediary roles

As far as Sarkar's intermediary roles is concerned, the only role identified by the participants is 'providing customer information'. However, it was explained as TP's or tourist offices forwarding client data to the TO's in order for them to follow up, instead of the TO providing background information on its client database to his suppliers, in order to improve customer service, as it was meant by Sarkar. The latter situation, and the TO's' opportunity to create added value in this way, is not recognised and is perceived to be undesirable, as it might lead to misuse of data and indirect competition in the eyes of the participants, when TP's and tourist offices could use this information to create their own direct market. Again, there seems to be a lot of distrust and a lack of co-operative attitude. Whenever there are customer complaints, the participants clarify, they are forwarded to the supplier or destination concerned, but there is no question of any mutual exchange of information or co-operation of any kind. Bringing in bookings and creating economies of scale, buying power and therefore competitive pricing is what the industry seems to be blinded by.

5.4 Recommendations

In summary, Table 3 provides terms and suggestions for virtual tourist destinations.

Table 3: Opportunities and threats of e-commerce for the travel industry

Conditions that linked sites should meet	Tips to stimulate the use of NTB-sites
• Up-to-date information • Orderly • Easy to link (fixed pages & addresses) • Reciprocal links • Objective information • Find what your searching for in 3 clicks • Downloadable information	• Centralised tree-structure with detailed information at the leaves • Standard navigation structure on national, regional and local level • Answer consumers' FAQ's • Quality NTB-sites should be able to get links from portal sites • Internal search engine with annotations

6 Conclusions

Our study can not repudiate that there are still more lookers than bookers, but instead of using this as a false pretence and plea ignorance, the industry should concentrate its efforts on surfacing consumers' motivation for this behaviour. Some of the reasons are widely known [4, 10, 13]: consumers' inexperience, allegedly unsafe payment procedures, lack of trust towards online brands, and concerns regarding after sales and services. Undoubtedly, all these factors will be neutralised as the Internet will become as established as telephones or ATM's (other technological innovations that sceptics regarded as science fiction, because of a lack of human interaction). What is more is that the tourism industry is far too much focused and grafted onto the actual booking of the customer. Obviously, this has always been the point at which tourism enterprises were able to sustain their very existence, but some actors have to become aware of the effects that the 'new economy' will have on their business. Why?

Whereas the industrially-based enterprises depend on scale economies of supply, virtual tourist destinations depend on developing scale economies of demand. Specifically, as the virtual demand increases the marginal costs of production tend to decline. Put differently, networks and co-operation in the new economy reverse the economic logic 180 degrees. The latter observation is underscored by the actions of astute actors in terms of their pricing strategy. They 'give services away' for free so as to accumulate critical mass on the demand side, quicker than their competitors. They seem to understand that the real value in the emerging networks is that economic worth resides in the number of interacting clients. The real question would be what attracts 'lookers' on the Web in the first place; and what appeals to them. Booking a trip is but only one phase in the actual decision making process. The appeal of online search can play a different role in the different stages of the decision making process, the use of the internet for information and planning is probably more advanced than for actual booking and payment. The interesting issue for further research would then be how to match and integrate online consumer demand for information, entertainment and other facilities, related to the specific phase within the decision making process, with the communication objectives of the virtual tourist destination(s). Obviously, these objectives should be closely related to the interests of the participating physical destinations, because in the end we still want the same thing: to get the consumer to physically visit 'our' destination.

From such observations arises the major problem, namely, virtual tourist destinations, especially the actors in its means-end chain, must realise that their fortune is closely tied to their ability to successfully compete for the attention of large numbers of potential bookers. Same implies that such virtual destinations must be able to: first, identify potential bookers in the vast virtual market; second, develop a clear profile and; third, match both of the former variables to the identity of the physical tourist destination(s). In short, the challenge is to become the actor in the chain who is able to attract the attention of an ever growing number of potential bookers thereby stimulating a self perpetuating cycle, that is based on a strong attraction, turned into reputation, brand name, trust and repeat customers. Amazon.com is but one well-known example of such a cycle at work in the new economy. There are many other actors that are following suit.

References

1.   Berryman, K., L. Harrington, D. Layton-Rodin, and V. Rerolle, 'Electronic Commerce: Three emerging strategies', *The McKinsey Quarterly* (1), 1998, 152-159.

2.   CNN, 'Internet airline reservations begin to take off', Published by CNN, www.cnn.com, April 17, 1998.

3.   Dombey, A., 'Separating the emotion form the fact', in: D. Buhalis, A.M. Tjoa, and J.Jafari (eds.) *Proceedings of the International Conference on Information and Communication Technologies in Tourism* (ENTER'98), Istanbul, Turkey, 1998, Wien-New York: Springer Verlag, 129-138.

4.   Forrester Research Inc., in *The virtual mall gets real*, H. Green, Editor, 1998, 48-49, (Refernced in *Business Week*, January 26, 1998).

5.   Freesun News, 'Airinfo', Published by Freesun, www.freesun.be, 1999, respective no. **(a)** 228(October 8), 230(October 12) & 231(October 13).

6.   Freesun News, 'Travelinfo', Published by Freesun, www.freesun.be, 1999, respective no. **(a)** 135(15 April) & 204(23 July) **(b)** 107(26 February) & 187(29 June) **(c)** 200(16 July) **(d)** 170(4 June) **(e)** 138(21 April) **(f)** 236(5 October).

7.   Hospitality Net Editorial, 'Travelocity Receives People's Voice Award For Best Travel Web Site', Published by Verdonk Otten Dirk & Wiegerink, www.vodw.nl/clsonly/tourist/, March 30, 1998.

8.   Lobal, S.R., 'Designing Effective Documents for Destination Information Systems', in: D. Buhalis, A.M. Tjoa, and J.Jafari (eds.) *Proceedings of the International Conference on Information and Communication Technologies in Tourism* (ENTER'98), Istanbul, Turkey, 1998, Wien-New York: Springer Verlag, 73-83.

9.   Milburn, R., 'Online sales of travel products in Europe set to reach $1.7 billion in 2002', *Press Release*, Published by Datamonitor, www.datamonitor.com, 24 May, 1999.

10.   NBT, *Digitale Revolutie in de Reisbranche*, Voorschoten, 1997.

11.   New York Post, 'Online Travel Business Exploding', Published by NUA Limited, www.nua.ie/surveys, October 2, 1998.

12.   Nielsen Net Ratings, *AOL Retains Top Web Property Slot*, Nua Internet Surveys News-Series No. 4 (38), Sorcha Ni hEilidhe (ed.): Nua Limited, www.nua.ie/surveys, September 27, 1999.

13.   Pro-Active, *Effecten van Internet op de Reisbranche*, Diemen, februari, 1998.

14.   Raaij, W.F.v., 'Interactive Communication: Consumer power and initiative', *Journal of Marketing Communications*, 4, 1998, 1-8.

15.   Reisrevue, 'NIPO: Steeds meer vakantiegangers schakelen reiswereld in', 25 november, 1998, 7.

16.   Rekom, J.v., W. Teunissen, and F. Go, 'Improving the Position of Business Travel Agencies: Coping with the information challenge', *Information Technology & Tourism*, 2, 1999, 15-29.

17.   Sarkar, M.B., B. Butler, and C. Stienfield, 'Intermediaries and Cybermediaries: A Continuing Role for Mediating Players in the Electronic Marketplace', *JCMC*, 1 (3), 1997, http://shum.huji.ac.il/jcmc/vol1/issue3.

18.   Shirer, M., 'Yahoo!, Travelocity, And Expedia Receive Top Rating For On-line Travel Sites From Forrester', *Press Releases*, Published by Forrester Research Inc., www.forrester.com, July 1, 1999.

19.   Walle, A.H., 'Tourism and the Internet: Opportunities for Direct Marketing', *Journal of Travel Research*, summer, 1996, 72-77.

20.   Werthner, H., 'Editor's Introduction', *Information Technology and Tourism*, 1 Inaugural, 1998, 1-12.

Putting the Tourist into Tourist Information

J. C. Bullock and C.A. Goble
Department of Computer Science, University of Manchester, U.K.
joe.bullock@virgin.net, carole@cs.man.ac.uk

Abstract

This paper introduces TourisT, a prototype hypermedia tourism information system, which was developed at the University of Manchester. A key theme of the TourisT project was that the system must address the real needs of tourists, and this was investigated using the following approach. The project used ethnographic studies [1, 2] to determine how tourists ask for information, and how tourist information advisers respond; the findings were used to inspire the design of the prototype. The prototype uses a conceptual hypermedia architecture [3, 4, 5], which is able to capture the diverse interaction styles suggested by the studies.

This paper discusses the findings of the ethnographic studies, and describes how the principles suggested by these are realised in the TourisT prototype; it then discusses the wider implications of TourisT for the structuring and presentation of content in public-facing systems.

1. Introduction

With the growth of the WWW and other interactive media, there is a proliferation of public-facing tourism information systems [6, 7, 8]. Superficially, these are impeccably presented; however, they are typically based on a rather simplistic information model:

- Information is organised into strict categories, and the category structure is quite shallow: beneath a couple of hierarchical layers, information is typically organised in alphabetical lists.
- Information is associated by direct links, with limited cross-referencing; search facilities are typically based on keywords or limited database fields.

The premise of this project was that such systems are likely to be inadequate: their rigid categorisations will not accommodate the true diversity of searchers' needs, and their unprincipled linking will make it hard to pursue lines of interest. Essentially, it may be difficult for the searcher to locate appropriate information.

The TourisT project thus took a step back. It used ethnographic studies, performed in tourist information centres, to determine how tourists ask for information, and how tourist advisers respond; the findings were used to inspire the design of the prototype.

2. Inspiring the System Design: Ethnography

The ethnographic studies were conducted in the main tourist information centres of Manchester and Chester, which are both busy, city-centre offices, handling a large number of enquiries from both locals and visitors. The studies observed the interactions at the counter between advisers and customers asking for information; over the course of the studies, eight advisers were observed. Since the aim of the studies was to scope the system design rather than to provide a definitive account, a "quick and dirty" ethnographic style [1] was adopted, involving intense bursts of observation over a relatively short period; in total, the studies lasted for four weeks. Following the studies, interviews were conducted with two members of the Manchester centre staff to clarify details.

2.1 Providing Tourist Information

In principle, the provision of tourist information is a classic intermediary encounter: the customer requests some information, which the adviser tries to provide using available information sources. In practice, customer requests are diverse, ranging from simple requests that the adviser can respond to directly, to complex requests that involve a lengthy discussion between the customer and the adviser. Furthermore the role of the adviser goes far beyond simple "question-answer" activities: they take a proactive role, which is fundamental to a successful outcome, aiming to raise the customer's awareness and provide an answer that is helpful and agreeable to them. For clarity, this section concentrates on one particularly common request that illustrates many typical features of customer-adviser interactions; a full discussion of the ethnographic findings, and their relation to other studies is presented in [9].

2.2 An Example: Places to Visit

Customers often want to find out about places to visit. Sometimes they already know of places that they are interested in. Often, however, they are unsure of what is available and do not have specific places in mind; they describe what they would like and want the adviser to suggest suitable places. Customers have different backgrounds, interests and priorities, and may be uncertain about what they want; their descriptions thus vary in form and clarity. Typical examples are: (1) Simple "kind of" categories, e.g. "art galleries"; (2) Categories defined in terms of another activity e.g. "places to take the children", "places for lunch"; (3) Abstract categories, e.g. "the main sights", "days out", "places to do with crafts"; (4) Complex descriptions where the customer "paints a narrative picture" of what they would like.

It is not always possible for the adviser to reconcile what the customer asks for with what is available, and there is a discussion between the two to clarify what is required. A typical example (based on the Manchester studies) is that the customer wants to know about the sights and places of interest; typically, however, they simply ask "What should I see", or "What are the main sights". As it stands, such a request is ambiguous: Manchester has many places of interest, and it would be impractical to describe all of them. The adviser needs a clearer picture of what the customer is looking for; for example, what interests do they have when they are looking for a particular kind of place. The customer's circumstances are also an important factor: how much time do they have, are they using private or public transport etc.

For some details, the adviser can ask the customer directly. However, for others, such as the customer's interests, direct questioning may not be the most productive course: the customer may be unsure of exactly what they want or what is available. The adviser thus adopts a more proactive role and prompts the customer with suggestions. For example, they can suggest themes of interest, such as art, architecture, shopping etc., often using "formative" questions ("do you like"). If the suggestions appeal, the adviser can go on to identify suitable places; if the customer is unsure, or just has a general interest, the adviser can identify a selection of places.

To identify places, the adviser uses pre-printed maps, which they annotate; this helps to make the information more coherent, since they can highlight particular areas and link sites into a "tour", and the customer can take the map away with them. For each place, the adviser marks its location and describes it to the customer. However, it is rarely the case that they simply present a set of places in one go; rather they involve the customer, and allow the topic of interest to evolve. If the customer seems particularly taken with a place, the adviser can identify similar or related ones; or the customer may become clearer about what they would like, something "like this but...". As with their request, the customer may have varied perspectives on what is "similar", so the adviser offers a variety of possibilities. The adviser remains proactive, and can introduce items of interest throughout the discussion. For example, if the customer likes the sound of Affleck's Palace, a craft centre, the adviser can include not only the nearby craft market, but also the "cafe-culture" area where it is situated; this may in turn lead to other topics.

There are other important ways in which the adviser helps to raise the customer's awareness. They can address the customer's uncertainty by offering items that almost match what they ask for, and they present information in a useful format, in particular indicating how well items match the customer's requirements, and the distinctions between them. Furthermore, they can provide the customer with related information that they are likely to need, effectively preempting "what about" requests; for example, if the customer is visiting for a day, the adviser can include places to eat or drink in the map tour.

The key factor underlying the adviser's approach is that the customer's perceptions of what is available may be incomplete or incorrect, so they may not know what to ask for; by prompting them, the adviser aims to raise their awareness and inspire their interest. There is also an important affective dimension to the adviser's approach: the information that they give may shape the customer's impression of the area, so if the customer cannot find things of interest or feel that they have missed out, they will be disappointed.

2.3 Inspiring the TourisT Design

The studies thus found the provision of tourism information to be a diverse, dynamic, inherently human process; the aim of TourisT was to use these findings to inspire the design of an information system capturing the spirit of the real-life situations. TourisT has concentrated on the "places to visit" scenario, and identified three major characteristics of the interactions:

- **Diversity**. Customers have varied interests and may be uncertain about what they want, so their requests can vary widely in topic and detail. Significantly, they may consider their requirements from a number of perspectives: there are many kinds of "kind of", depending on the customer's point of view.
- **Spontaneity**. The topic of discussion between customer and adviser evolves freely, as items catch the customer's interest; significantly, this allows their interest to evolve into areas that they may not initially consider. In effect, the customer asks for something "like the current item"; as with requests, they may consider "like" from a number of perspectives.
- **Lucidity**. The role of the adviser is crucial: they are proactive, making suggestions to help raise the customer's awareness, and to inspire their interest. This promotes the spontaneity of the discussion, and is also important for providing alternatives when what the customer asks for is unavailable, and they may be disappointed.

These findings led to the following design principles for the prototype:

- It must provide diverse information structuring. It must be possible to identify items from varied viewpoints, and associate items that are similar in various ways.
- It must provide a supportive interface. This must help the searcher to formulate their requirements, providing lucid, conceptual support to make them aware of the scope of available information.

3. Supporting Diverse Interaction: Conceptual Hypermedia

These principles are realised through a conceptual hypermedia architecture (Figure 1). This has two components: a set of documents, and an index space that maintains concepts (terms) used to describe them. Each document is tagged with a **descriptor**, composed of concepts from the index space. Rather than being directly linked, documents are associated through queries:

- The searcher can browse the index space to identify concepts that describe what they require; the system then retrieves the documents whose descriptors match.

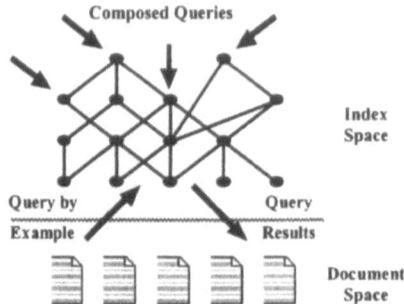

Fig. 1: Schematic of Conceptual Hypermedia Interaction

- The searcher can move between documents by using the descriptor of the current document as the starting point of their query for others with similar descriptors (query by example).

In essence, the approach associates documents with similar descriptors. The key factor determining how documents are associated is the richness of the index space: a richer index space can capture more diverse distinctions between descriptors, and hence more diverse associations between documents. To provide diverse document association that captures a range of perspectives, the TourisT index space is represented using the GRAIL description logic [10], a knowledge representation that allows complex concept models to be readily created and maintained.

3.1 Description Logics

There are two basic components of a description logic (DL): (1) A set of elementary concepts, organised into an isa hierarchy; (2) A set of roles that can apply between concepts; these may also be organised into an isa hierarchy. Complex concepts can be composed from simpler ones using roles. Consider a model with the following concepts and roles:

Concepts: Place, Artefact, Art, PaintedArt (PaintedArt isa Art)
Roles: displays, hasType, hasTypeWell (hasTypeWell isa hasType)

The concepts **Artefact** and **Art** can be combined using the **hasType** role to give **Artefact-hasType-Art** ("Artwork"); this can then form part of the more complex concept **Place-displays-[Artefact-hasType-Art]** ("Art-Museum"). In this respect, a DL is like any frame-based knowledge representation. However, the key benefit of a DL is that as new complex concepts are added to the concept model, they are automatically categorised with respect to existing ones; e.g., if the model already contains the concept **Place-displays-Artefact** ("Museum"), **Place-displays-**

[Artefact-hasType-Art] is automatically categorised as a kind of this. If a more specific concept is added, it is positioned as a parent of any more general concepts.

Categorisation of a complex concept takes account of its constituent elementary concepts, and the roles between them. So since **PaintedArt** is a kind of **Art**, **Place-displays-[Artefact-hasType-PaintedArt]** ("Picture-Museum") is a kind of **Place-displays-(Artefact-hasType-Art)**; since **hasTypeWell** is a kind of **hasType**, then **Place-displays-(Artefact-hasTypeWell-PaintedArt)** ("Fine Art Museum") is a kind of **Place-displays-(Artefact-hasType-PaintedArt)**. Concepts may be categorised under many parents; e.g., in the Tourist model, the "Art-Museum" concept is concurrently categorised as a "Museum", "Building", and "Arts-Venue".

3.2 Description Logics and Applications

The GRAIL DL is realised in three parts. (1) Concepts are specified using the GRAIL modelling language. (2) Models are constructed using the development environment, which provides a set of modelling tools; concept definitions can be entered interactively, or read from files. (3) The application interacts with the model through the Terminology Server (TeS). This maintains the model and offers a well-defined API that allows the application to inspect the model and execute queries. It also provides services to make the model more usable in applications; in particular concepts can be given natural language labels (e.g. "Art Museum"), so that they can be presented clearly in an interface.

3.3 Description Logics and Conceptual Hypermedia

The DL thus allows complex, diverse concept models to be built, and TourisT uses such a concept model as its index space. Each document is described by a (complex) concept, and the dynamic categorisation of the DL is used to underlie document retrieval. Identifying a set of descriptors (hence documents) involves the following steps. (1) The searcher composes a query concept describing their requirements. (2) The DL categorises this, so it is now a parent of any more specific concepts. (3) The application searches its child concepts to locate those with associated documents. (4) The documents are returned to the searcher.

This approach allows the ethnographic design principles to be met:

- The searcher can express their needs from various perspectives; e.g. a document described by "Art-Museum" can be found by queries featuring any of the concepts categorising it. The searcher can also browse from a document to find others that are similar from various perspectives (i.e. categorised by one or more of the same category concepts).
- Multiple categorisation of concepts respects the searcher's uncertainty, since it is less likely that they will miss information by looking in the "wrong" category.

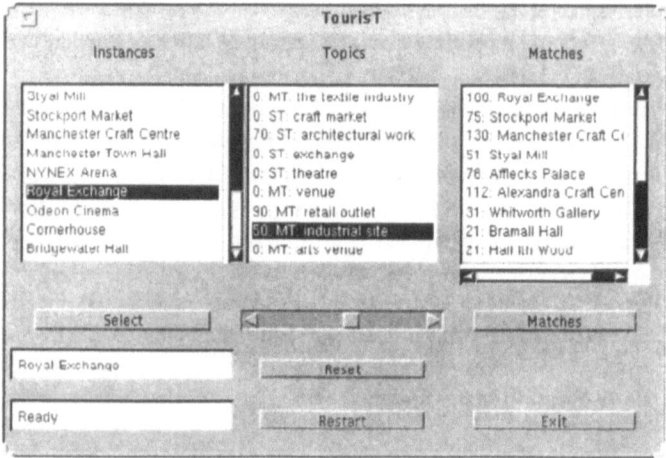

Fig. 2: The TourisT Interface

Furthermore, the index space contains concepts of varying detail (e.g. "Venue" is a kind of "Public Place"), allowing the searcher to pose general or specific queries.

- The index space is open to the searcher, allowing them to explore it and discover the range of topics available.

4. The TourisT Prototype

The TourisT prototype provides an interface that allows the searcher to explore a sample document set, which describes industrial heritage sites around Greater Manchester. The interface allows the searcher to:

- Compose a query: the searcher explores the index space to select concepts.
- Query by example: the interface presents the concepts that categorise the current document, and the searcher selects from these.

4.1 Interacting with TourisT

An illustration of query by example is shown in Figure 2. Interaction takes place using the three panes (from left to right: Instances, Topics and Matches), as follows:

1. The Instances pane shows the set of available documents.
2. The searcher selects a document (The Royal Exchange in the example).
3. The Topics pane shows the concepts that categorise its descriptor.
4. The searcher selects from these to compose their query. Note that they can "score" query concepts to indicate their relative significance.
5. The Matches pane shows the documents whose descriptors are retrieved by the

query. Each descriptor is scored according to how well it matches the query.

6. The searcher selects a document from the result set; the Instances pane now shows this as the current document.

It is thus possible for the searcher to perform a browsing sequence, comprising multiple iterations through the above steps; they can backtrack to previous iterations with the Reset button. Note that: (a) The searcher is not restricted to the category concepts presented in step (3): they can explore the index space to include other concepts of interest, effectively asking for documents "like this, but also". (b) Stage (5) retrieves descriptors that partially match the query, i.e. are not categorised by all of the query concepts.

4.2 Presenting Information

The TourisT interface was designed primarily as a proof of concept of underlying technical issues. Whilst it is simple and aesthetically poor, it does illustrate some important principles derived from the ethnographic studies:

1. The searcher does not have to explore the index space excessively, since the interface presents categorising concepts at varying levels of detail. This allows the searcher to change the scope of their search quickly.
2. The interface guides the searcher by highlighting significant categories as Major and Sub Topics (MT, ST in Figure 2).
3. The searcher chooses which aspects are important to them, and can indicate how important these are (what kind of "like" they would like).
4. Partial match retrieval respects the searcher's uncertainty: the searcher does not miss suitable items because they pose a slightly "wrong" query, and if nothing exactly matches, they can choose from items that almost match.

The key principle is to compensate for the searcher's uncertainty by shifting effort from them to the application (i.e. the application explores the index space, and tries multiple, partial queries).

5. Future Work

Whilst TourisT is a small-scale prototype, developed during a PhD project, it raises important questions about the deployment of conceptual hypermedia:

1. **Scaling**. So far, the TourisT approach has been applied only to a small document set (<50 documents); in practice, it must apply to much larger, more diverse document sets (e.g. a city guide WWW site). The approach has also assumed that each document is described by a single descriptor; in practice, a document may require several descriptors, reflecting different aspects of its content. Current work at the University of Manchester is investigating such scaling issues [11].

2. **Integration**. The TourisT project investigated DL-based conceptual hypermedia in isolation. In practice, it is likely that the approach would be applied in conjunction with other indexing and linking schemes. For example, the searcher might start with a statically-linked guided tour, then use conceptual linking to "escape" from this to follow up specific items. Current work at the University of Manchester is considering how DL-based conceptual hypermedia can be applied as part of a general hypermedia framework [9, 11].

3. **Evaluation**. The TourisT project primarily evaluated the technical feasibility of DL-based conceptual hypermedia. If the approach is applied to a live public-facing system, user-centred evaluation should be conducted to determine how the interface should be presented, and how the index space should be structured to address searchers' needs best. These issues are discussed further in [9].

6. The Significance of TourisT

TourisT raises important issues about the implementation of public-facing tourist information systems. The ethnographic studies found the needs and perceptions of tourists to be diverse, uncertain and dynamic. An information system that is rigidly categorised or poorly linked is unlikely to satisfy this diversity: even if suitable information is available, the searcher may not find it. This is bad for the searcher, and for the information provider:

*   An ineffective system will disappoint the searcher and create a poor impression of the place it aims to promote.
*   Content is expensive to produce, yet if the searcher cannot find it, it is worthless. For example, the Boston CitySearch Visitor's Guide [7] features a large number of high quality documents, some of which are linked into hypertext guidebooks. However the limited querying and indexing facilities waste the potential of such extensive content. Query results are presented in uncategorised lists that the searcher must page through; having found an item they like, either via a query or a guidebook, the facilities for finding similar items are very restricted.

By offering diverse access, the TourisT approach aims to add value to an information system. From the searcher's perspective, it is easier to locate content in a manner that matches their perceptions, and to follow up lines of interest; in essence, it is easier to discover what is available. From the provider's perspective, it is more likely that the searcher will explore the site, and there is thus more scope to promote items to them.

The ethnographic studies showed that tourism advisers try hard to avoid disappointing their customers. As information systems are increasingly used as tourism "advisers" they must do the same: accommodating searcher diversity and uncertainty is thus likely to become a defining factor of their success.

References

1. Hughes, J., King, V., Rodden, T. and Andersen, H. (1994) Moving Out From the Control Room: Ethnography in System Design. In: Proceedings of CSCW '94, the ACM conference on on Computer supported cooperative work (Chapel Hill, NC):429-439. ACM Press, New York.

2. Martin, D., Wastell, D. and Bowers, J. (1998). Ethnographically Informed System Design: The Development and Evaluation of an Internet-Based Electronic Banking Application. In: Baets, W.R.J. (Ed.), Proceedings of ECIS '98, the Sixth European Conference on Information Systems, Vol. II:513-527. Euro-Arab Management School, Granada.

3. Bruza, P.D. and van der Weide, T.P. (1990) Two Level Hypermedia - An Improved Architecture for Hypertext. In: Proceedings of DEXA '90, the International Conference on Database and Expert Systems Applications, (Vienna, Austria):76-83. Springer Verlag.

4. Cunliffe, D., Taylor, C. and Tudhope, D. (1997). Query-based Navigation in Semantically Indexed Hypermedia. In: Proceedings of Hypertext '97, the 8th ACM Conference on Hypertext, (Southampton, UK):87-95, 245-246. ACM Press, New York.

5. Nanard, J. and Nanard, M. (1995). Adding Macroscopic Semantics to Anchors in Knowledge-Based Hypertext. International Journal of Human-Computer Studies, 43(3):363-382.

6. Associated New Media Ltd. (1998). This Is London. http://www.thisislondon.com.

7. CitySearch.com (2000). Boston CitySearch. http://boston.citysearch.com.

8. International Conference on Information and Communications Technologies in Tourism. http://www.tis.co.at/enter.

9. Bullock, J.C. (1999). Informed Navigation: Description Logic Based Hypermedia Linking. PhD Thesis. University of Manchester. Contact author for further information.

10. Rector, A.L., Bechhofer, S., Goble, C.A., Horrocks, I., Nowlan, W.A. and Solomon, W.D. (1997). The GRAIL Concept Modelling Language for Medical Terminology. Artificial Intelligence in Medicine, 9:139-171.

11. University of Manchester Information Management Group. http://potato.cs.man.ac.uk/starch.

'Intelligent' Museum As Value Creator On The Tourism Market: Towards A New Business Model

Valeria Minghetti[+], Andrea Moretti[#] and Stefano Micelli[*]
[+] CISET- Ca' Foscari University, Venice
[#]Department of Economics and Business - University of Udine, Udine
[*]TEDIS-Venice International University, Venice

Abstract

The educational mandate of museums is being transformed as marketing strategies play an increasingly crucial role in promoting cultural products. The electronic management of contents, reference communities and distribution channels represents a challenge for cultural institutions that wish to gain a competitive advantage on the global market. This paper outlines the competitive responses that can be adopted by on-line museums, discusses the re-engineering of their role on the tourism market and proposes a prototype of a multimedia portal aimed at creating valuable synergies between cultural and tourist services.

1 Introduction

In Italy and continental Europe, the exploitation and organisation of cultural heritage are living a dramatic evolution. Museums and other cultural institutions can no longer confine themselves to performing a mere conservation function [1, 2, 3, 4]. The tightening of public sector financial support is forcing them to develop new management and marketing strategies so as to promote an innovative supply, tailored on specific needs of different users (whether researchers/curators and tourists) and then to attract increasing audience and sponsors [5, 6, 7, 8, 9].

The introduction of Information and Telecommunications Technologies is a key-factor in streamlining such transformation [10, 11]. The use of multimedia information systems and the Internet enable cultural organisations to re-design traditional products and create new contents, by involving a worldwide community of potential visitors, who participate in the production of the cultural service. Furthermore, through the Web the museum 'breaks' the traditional value chain and enhances its role on the tourism market. From being a 'passive' attraction marketed by travel agencies, hotel operators and other intermediaries (e.g. ticket offices), it has the opportunity to gain competitive advantage and become the node of a new distribution channel developed around the cultural event.

Until some years ago the spread of ITTs has merely involved the automation of recording and cataloguing procedures, while it has hardly influenced the marketing and distribution of cultural services as well as the relationships between the museum and the operating environment. A number of European projects [see, for example, 12,

13, 14, 15] have been launched to support the digitisation and storage of collections for education and dissemination purposes. However, very few of them have analysed the relationships between cultural heritage, multimedia and tourism industry and then the power the Web can have in promoting not only large museums, but also cluster of small isolate institutions, which can join forces and improve their 'visibility' on the tourism market.

The aim of the paper is firstly to discuss the mechanisms that lead the technology transformation of museum as a cultural business and, specifically, to give an insight on the re-engineering of its role on the tourism market. Secondly, to propose a first reference model for the setting up of a multimedia cultural portal. After an overview on the changing trends in museum management and marketing induced by ITTs (Section 2), in Section 3 the processes that 'legitimate' and leverage the cultural organisation as a value creator on the tourism market are analysed. A short description of the Promemoria case study is included in Section 4. Concluding remarks and outline of future research are given in Section 5.

2 From traditional to virtual marketing and management of cultural services

Culture and heritage are a constituent part of the tourism industry. In urban centres museums, especially the most famous institutions, have been used as the main attractions drawing tourism into the city. The promotion of permanent and temporary exhibitions enables cities to 'market' themselves as cultural centres that both "delight residents and tourists and appeal to professionals and investors" [5]. The evocative nature of heritage becomes a potential instrument for combining local consumption activities with personal, lived experience.

Under this viewpoint, DMOs, incoming agents and hotel operators have generally 'managed' the role of the museum within the tourism value chain. They have 'brought' demand to cultural institutions, the visit being only a component of a global tourism product [16], where key-elements are represented by travel, accommodation and other facilities.

The changing operating environment and then the need to adopt economy-oriented management schemes, so as to self-finance cultural events, are compelling museums to acquire consciousness of their central role in the tourism market. The paradigm shift from museum as a mere 'container' of works of art to a museum as a proactive cultural business — to which the principles of the service management theory can be applied [7] —, requires the definition of a new product and marketing approach as well as the implementation of new positioning strategies [17, 18].

Technologies contribute to accelerate such change. The dramatic development of on-line and off-line tools, and particularly of Internet-based platforms, leads to huge opportunities of a commercial nature for museums and galleries, as well as for their traditional non profit-oriented activities, such as for public access, dissemination and education.

ITTs enable museums to transform in 'liquidity' their fixed capital invested in heritage knowledge and cultural goods. Through the digitisation of images, sounds and words they have the opportunity to build up interactive infrastructures in which (real and virtual) visitors can live a valuable cultural experience.

The marketing orientation through ITTs transforms the production, exchange and consumption of the cultural service. The separation between producer and consumer becomes less clear and relevant, the value created by the cultural experience resulting from increasing interactions between different partners, in which users are principal actors. The radical growth in connectivity enabled by the Internet and the WWW gives rise to new communication and co-ordination mechanisms both across museums and visitors, and also within groups of visitors themselves.

Under this viewpoint, the definition of the reference market derives from the identification of communities of interest (researchers, curators, tourists, etc.) in which the museum invests its effort to become an attractive element. Far from being a major perspective of museum managers yet, the evolution pattern from traditional to virtual marketing and management should follow three integrated steps:
• *attracting visitors*, through 'appealing' contents, suitable marketing strategies and customisation of cultural supply;
• *promoting the participation of visitors* and other actors to the production of the cultural experience, by enriching and updating contents also through the storage of those produced by the users themselves;
• *building visitors' loyalty*, through a wide typology of forums and membership programs in which the information flow from the museum to the visitors is a crucial tool to develop a new co-makership with customers.

In Italy, the websites of many cultural institutions are generally poor, both in terms of information provided and interactive mechanisms applied. Apart from outstanding cases (e.g. the Museum of Science History in Florence), in most cases the WWW represents no more than a virtual window where traditional brochures are displayed in digital format [1, 19]. There is the need to develop advanced Web platforms, whose setting up can be managed within the museum boundaries or through a cultural network, controlled by the museum itself. This network, which can be shared with other cultural institutions, acts as a sort of 'service centre' that supports the animation of communities of interest and the distribution of common information services, thus favouring the achievement of economies of scale and scope [20].

3 Virtual museum in the marketspace

The willingness of a museum to evolve from an embryonic presence on the WWW to the setting up of an advanced website generally derives from the awareness of being a primary attraction and then from the need to profitably manage its product and distribution channels. The question arising is whether the museum is able to face the challenge Internet is bringing forth and, consequently, to empower its role even becoming the pivot of a new value chain, through the electronic management of contents, reference communities and markets. In the following paragraph, two alternative processes that lead the museum to implement an evolved Web platform are schematised. The re-engineering of the role the museum has on the tourism market, which is induced by such processes, is discussed in paragraph 3.2, where two possible scenarios are drawn.

3.1 Development paths of a virtual museum

The value of an on-line museum that aims at aggregating large communities of potential users, providers and sponsors is based on the development and combination of two different elements:
- *contents*, meant as the creation of a large and updated database of data, texts and images that can be easily accessed from any computer with an Internet connection and a Web browser. The attractiveness of the museum site, and then the visitor's loyalty to the community, depends on a cost-benefit evaluation and is measured in terms of ease of navigation, browsing speed and exhaustiveness of information tracked;
- *interaction*, meant as the development of a continuous and meaningful communication flow between the museum and the user and between each member of the community and other participants. In this case, the decision to join the community is not motivated by an economic assessment, but by the opportunity to share interests, experiences and information.

The evolution from a virtual window to a multimedia platform requires the museum to enhance and balance communication needs and quality of information provided. Moving from bottom left to top right (Fig. 1), the different combination and intensity of these two elements generate two alternative development paths.

The first path (shown by the thick arrow) is more likely when the museum has large archives, whose digitisation and storage represent the main service offered to the reference community. The generation of a virtual counterpart of the real museum attracts the attention of a number of users who, on their turn, can determine an increase in the level of site interaction (e.g. newsgroups, on-line booking, merchandising, etc.). Here, the cultural mandate of the institution maintains a crucial role in relation to business-oriented goals. The growth of virtual users generally stimulates an increase of real visitors: the information provided on the Web induces many people to visit the museum or the exhibition [6].

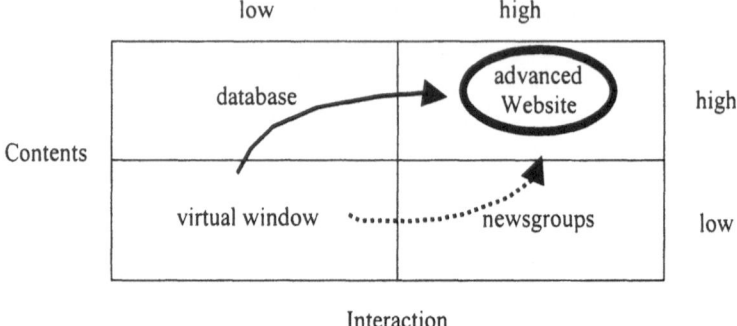

Fig. 1. Development paths of a virtual museum

The second path (shown by the dotted arrow) focuses, on the contrary, on an advanced communication strategy. Through newsgroups, guestbooks and memberships programs the museum site becomes a meeting space where actual and potential visitors share opinions, suggest new themes for exhibitions and events and build up their cultural experience. The interactions between the museum and the users and between the same users produce a huge amount of information that can be stored within the site. Growing interaction generally implies the enlarging of information made available and then the research of new material to be collected.

The attitude of a museum to create an advanced site, and then to evolve according to a mandate-driven or a market-driven model, is generally determined by a number of exogenous and endogenous factors (Fig. 2).
Among exogenous variables, we can mention:
• the *state legislation*, i.e. rules and restrictions to exploitation of collections;
• the *museum-business relationships*: from total state funding, to public-private partnership, to total private funding.
As for endogenous variables, the most important ones are as follows:
• the *geographical location*: in a city (an important tourist attraction) or in an isolated area;
• the *structure* and *organisation* of the museum: type of institution (science museum, ethnographic museum, university museum, etc.), supply size (number of collections exhibited and events organised), type of services offered (pre-visit, on site, post-visit, etc.);
• the *volume and characteristics of visitors*: number of visitors by typology (curators, critics, professionals, tourists, etc.);
• the *marketing strategies* already adopted and *brand identity*;
• the *actual ITT equipment* and the functions/services in which new technologies are spread;

- the *business culture* and the *attitude of management towards innovation and new technologies.*

In continental Europe exogenous factors still affect museums' autonomy and, consequently, the implementation of innovative IT management models. The incidence of government restrictions is impressive especially in countries that export cultural assets and have a rich heritage, like Italy and Greece. Whether in the UK and in the USA the approach generally followed is based on economic considerations in reproduction and exploitation, in those countries they are founded on Author's moral rights.

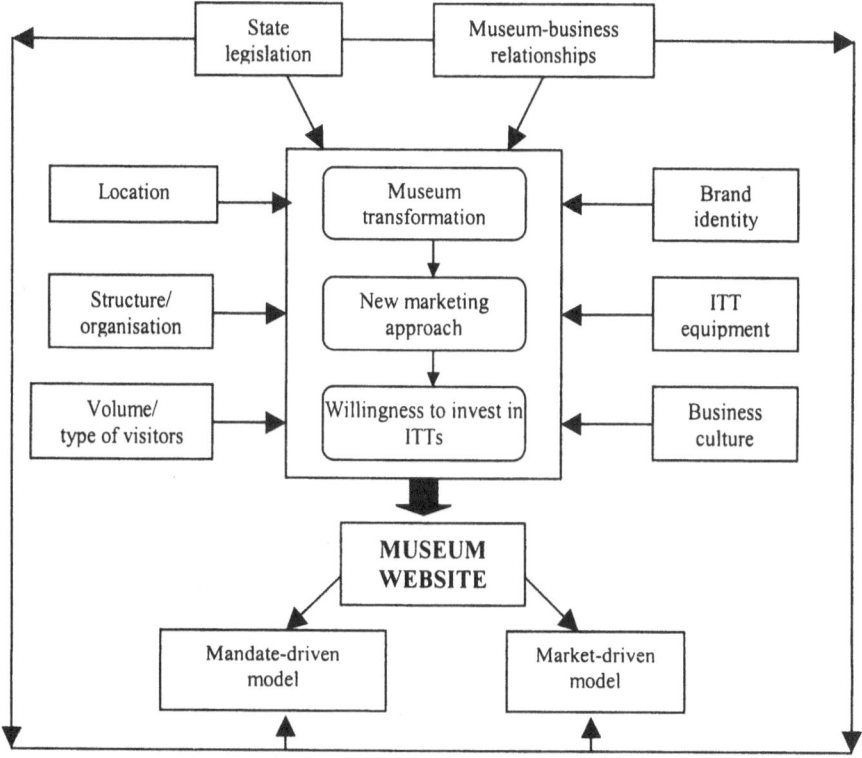

Fig. 2. The process of setting up a museum Website. Influencing factors

Exogenous factors being equal, large museums located in famous art cities, with consistent visitor flows and a good brand identity are expected to be keener on investing on Internet than small and medium-sized institutions. But the propensity also relies on the typology of museum (e.g. a science museum vs. a generic art museum) — which affects the kind of reference community involved, the standardisation of the site components and the interactivity level — and on the actual use of ITTs. For example, the probability to invest in an advanced Website would be higher in a cultural organisation where multimedia representations are an important part of the service offered, than in one where automation only concerns administrative functions. In the latter case, the technology culture of management may be an important stimulus to introduce expert systems.

The setting up of an innovative virtual museum depends on an accurate definition of the development process and influencing factors. Through a survey to be carried out among a sample of museums in Italy and abroad, these preliminary assumptions should be checked.

3.2 The re-engineering of the museum' role in the tourism value chain

The decision to implement a mandate-driven or a market-driven model has also important implications on the role of museums on the tourism market.
Two scenarios can be drawn, the second representing an evolution of the first one.

Scenario 1: Museum as active player in the tourism system

Thanks to ITT penetration, the institution improves its 'visibility' and enjoys higher negotiating power with local tourism operators (incoming agents, hotel operators, tourist boards, etc.) and with other real or virtual intermediaries (T.O., GDSs, etc.) involved in the distribution of the global tourism product (Fig. 3). Through the Web, the museum is able to manage accessibility and bookings and to segment clients according to purpose of visit (tourists, schools, professionals, etc.), travel organisation (independent vs. package visitors) and attitudes (highly motivated visitors vs. passing tourists). It is now the cultural product that 'propose itself' to demand: the application of database marketing techniques and the building of client profiles allow the museum to develop an in-depth understanding of users' evolving needs, expectations and requirements and then to customise cultural supply.

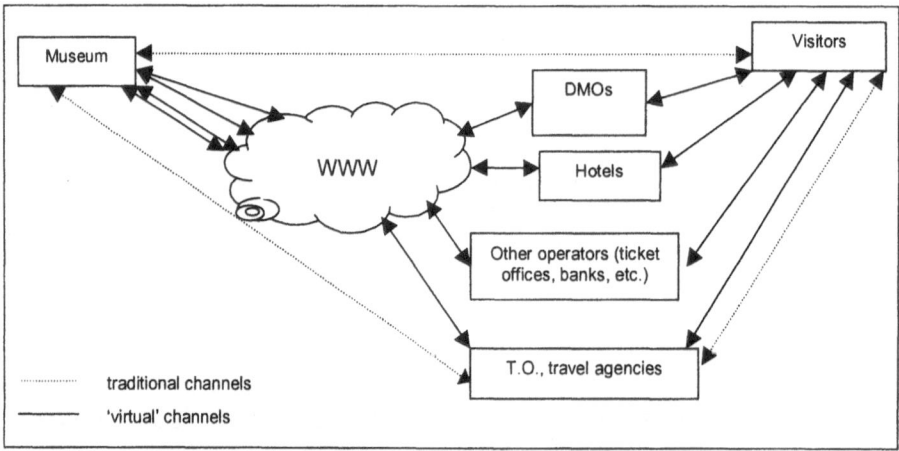

Fig .3. The museum marketspace. Traditional and virtual distribution channels

Scenario 2: Museum as pivot of an innovative niche supply

The enhanced management autonomy enabled by ITTs opens further commercial opportunities to museums. Not only can the institution manage demand and supply, but technology flexibility also allows it to evolve as catalyst of a local tourism network, developed around the cultural event (Fig. 4). Permanent/temporary exhibitions become the core of an innovative package tour that includes a number of tourist services (accommodation, transport, catering, etc.) that complement the visit to the attraction. The museum negotiates with local tourism principals and aggregates a niche supply that can be marketed through its Website directly to final consumers, by-passing traditional intermediaries.

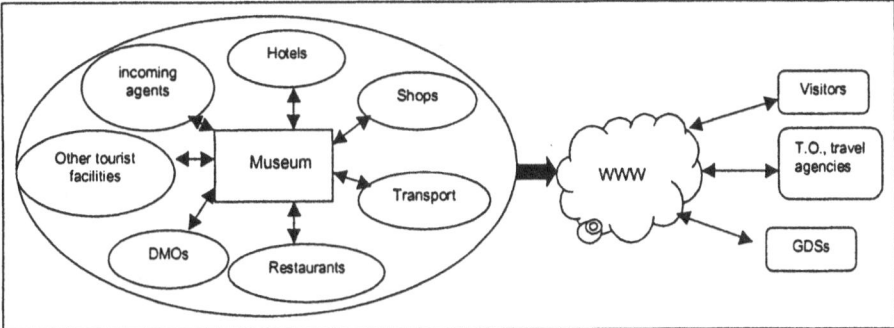

Fig. 4. The museum as pivot of a local tourism network

The aggregating role of the museum can also develop outside the boundaries of local tourism market. Through a dedicated travel office displayed on the Web, the institution can organise and promote tours for selected group of travellers to the regions/countries where the collections exhibited in the museum originate. First examples in this field are given by the National History Museum of the Los Angeles County and by the British Museum.

The risks inherent in such a scenario are to alter the cultural mission of the museum and to distort its image/identity as perceived by visitors. The first outcome generally results from a repeated process of mission redefinition, in which enlarging audience and acquiring new financial resources, also through the selling of holiday packages, are put on top of the museum's goals. The second outcome can be a consequence of the first one and derives from a diversification of exhibition activities in relation to museum's specialisation. For example, an ethnographic institution that organises an important archaeological exhibition with an impressive success tends to change its positioning in visitors' mind. Both results have to be monitored by museum managers to balance cultural mission with profit-oriented goals.

4 A prototype multimedia portal for the distribution of innovative cultural services

In paragraph 3.1 we have singled out two alternative paths leading to the creation of a museum portal which should be characterised by both rich contents and strong interaction between the institution and the reference community. The two paths require a different focus on business development, different organisational competence, and a different set of alliances and partnerships with players from other industries. Furthermore, the alternative patterns reflect two distinct business models that should be carefully taken into account to implement a viable strategy.

Apart from the model adopted, the link between tourism-related activities and the museum virtual offering represents a key-element in the construction of the portal: the economic sustainability of the project largely depends on the museums' ability to create a synergy between innovative cultural and tourist services.

Promemoria - Multimedia cultural village

The Promemoria case study (*www.promemoria.net*) represents an interesting experience to analyse and discuss the implementation of these alternative strategies. The project has been conceived and launched in 1998 by the Telecom Italia company and the Venice City Council in 1998 to promote the diffusion of technological innovation in the culture industry. Prototype of a cultural portal, Promemoria gathers four important cultural institutions (Querini Stampalia Foundation, Peggy Guggenheim Collection, Giorgio Cini Foundation and Municipal Venetian Museums) to create a virtual community opened to professional operators, researchers and visitors in the fine arts field.

The Promemoria initiative has been based on two strategic assumptions. Firstly, innovative solutions have to be designed and developed in co-operation between technologists, intermediate and end-users. Secondly, supply and demand of technology services have to engage themselves into a common learning process aimed at discovering and implementing innovative applications coherent with the needs and the requirements emerging in the actual use of services and tools. The basic idea is to experiment and distribute a wide range of innovative cultural services to a population of potential users, as well as to favour access to the databases of different cultural organisations in Venice and in Italy.

The system consists of four basic modules:
- *Art metasearch*, a multimedia tool for automatic cataloguing of cultural heritage and simultaneous customised query and extraction of information, images and pictures from different databases;
- *Emporium*, a system designed to offer tools and services for the promotion of culture to tourists and professional users through the WWW;

- *Laboratory*, the Web interface of a training laboratory promoted by Promemoria, which organises seminars for cultural professionals and operators;
- *Agorà*, an on-line information service through which a number of experts reply on questions relating to cataloguing, network architecture, multimedia and management.

Promemoria also includes a multimedia information and booking centre, *Teleart*, through which Web users can buy tickets for museums, galleries and temporary exhibitions in Venice and in Italy.

Not differently from other important portals, Promemoria relies on the functionality of a powerful search engine based on the Z39.50 protocol to capture audience and visitors (Fig. 5). The most interesting feature of Promemoria search engine is its capacity to simultaneously explore several databases (adopting the same protocol) belonging to different cultural institutions, starting from a single query. In the beginning, the search engine has represented the most relevant feature of the portal, attracting mostly professional and researchers interested in optimising research procedures in large and differentiated databases. At the same time, a rich training program concerning relevant technological issues has been launched to support local operators in modernising traditional back-office and front-office activities with on-line tools. All teaching materials have been collected and translated into distance learning programs accessible to all registered members of the community.

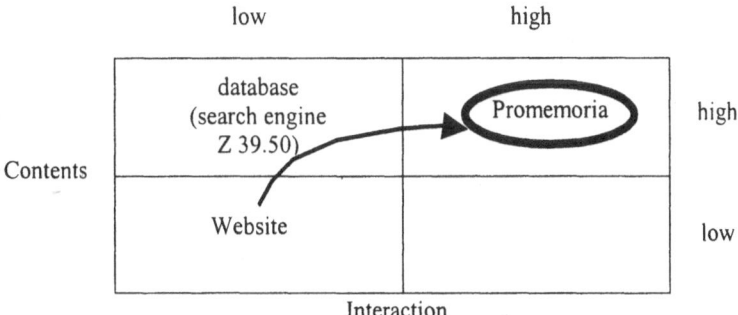

Fig. 5. Promemoria portal. Development pattern

At the beginning of 1999 Telecom Italia proposed the integration of Promemoria whithin *Tin.it* horizontal portal. The integration aimed at enlarging traditional Promemoria audience, acquiring new visitors outside the boundaries of the cultural and artistic community. The increase of site visitors would represent the first step in developing a strategy more focused on commercial services (mainly tourist services) and on interaction among community members. The expertise achieved by *Tin.it* in managing on-line and off-line community communication flows and its competence in selling advertising could represent fundamental resources in promoting a second phase in Promemoria strategy. Contacts with important tourism operators have been started to design 'bundles' the cultural operators could certify and promote in the next future. Up to now, an evaluation of such initiatives is still premature.

5 Concluding remarks and future work

This paper has proposed a logical framework to analyse the development paths of an on-line museum and the implications that such a process has on the role played by the institution on the tourism market. Then a prototype of a multimedia portal for the distribution of innovative cultural services has been presented.

The results of a comparative in-depth investigation in Italy and continental Europe will provide the elements to test the mechanisms governing the technology transformation of museums, to analyse the tools currently used and to check the variables that mostly influence the adoption of alternative business models. Such information will support the completion of the Promemoria architecture.

Concerning the Promemoria case study, it emphasises important aspects that should be carefully considered to successfully launch a cultural portal; some of them are related to Italian institutional context, some others are more industry specific.

Firstly, the design and implementation should consider the impact of innovative communication tools in an organisational environment focused more on conservation rather than dissemination. Most Italian museums and cultural institutions have little or no experience in managing contacts and relationships with regular and occasional visitors and still show a limited interest in adopting a more marketing-oriented perspective. A new strategic attitude, shaped after having redefined the institutional mandate (more communication and dissemination-oriented) and increased awareness of economic constraints, should be developed through innovative training programs.

Secondly, portal strategy should carefully analyse patterns to enlarge the community without losing its cultural identity. The cultural community, based on the contribution of experts, researchers and operators, is reluctant to accept newcomers (e.g. tourism operators) with no scientific or artistic background. The mix of two different worlds should be managed in order to maintain cultural legitimacy and to develop, at the same time, economic opportunities.

References

1.   Moretti, A., Micelli, S., 1997, Il Museo virtuale: dalle esperienze ai modelli, Rapporto di Ricerca, Consorzio Venezia Ricerche.
2.   Frey, B., Pommerehne, W.W., 1989, Muse e mercati. Indagini sull'economia dell'arte, Bologna, Il Mulino.
3.   Lumley, R. (ed.), 1988, L'industria del museo. Nuovi contenuti, gestione, consumo di massa, Genova, Edizioni Costa & Nolan.
4.   Spranzi, A., 1996, Un nuovo approccio all'economia dell'arte, in Commercio, 57, pp. 5-54.
5.   Tufts, S., Milne, S., 1999, Museums. A supply-side perspective, Annals of Tourism Research, Vol. 26, No. 3, pp. 613-631.

6. Galluzzi, P., 1997, Nuove tecnologie e funzione culturale dei musei. Opportunità e scenari per il terzo millennio, in I formati della memoria. Beni culturali e nuove tecnologie alle soglie del terzo millennio, Firenze, Giunti editore, pp. 3-39.

7. Bagdadli, S., 1997, Il museo come azienda. Management e organizzazione al servizio della cultura, Bologna, ETAS Libri.

8. Bernardi, B., 1996, Economicità e gestione del museo in Roncaccioli, A. (ed.) L'azienda museo, Padova, CEDAM.

9. Roncaccioli, A. (ed.), 1996, L'azienda museo, Padova, CEDAM.

10. Fahey, A., 1995, New Technologies for Museum Communication, in Hooper-Greenhill, E. (ed.), Museum, Media, Message, London, Routledge, pp. 82-96.

11. Kavanagh, G., 1995, Museum in partnership, in Hooper-Greenhill, E. (ed.), Museum, Media, Message, London, Routledge, pp. 124-134.

12. AQUARELLE - Sharing Cultural Heritage Through Multimedia Telematics, http:// ://ww2.echo.lu/libraries/en/projects/aquarelle.html

13. MAGNETS - Museums And Galleries NEw Technology Study, http://www.brameur.co.uk/vasari/magnets/VGMA1.html .

14. VAN EYCK-Visual Arts Network for the Exchange of Cultural Knowledge, http://ww2.echo.lu/libraries/en/projects/vaneyck.html

15. MEDICI - Multimedia for EDucation and employment through Integrated Cultural Initiative, http://www.medicif.org.

16. Rispoli, M., Tamma, M., 1995, Risposte strategiche alla complessità: le forme di offerta dei prodotti alberghieri, Torino, Giappichelli Editore.

17. Solima, L. 1998, La gestione imprenditoriale dei musei, Padova, CEDAM.

18. Kotler, N., Kotler, P., 1998, Museum Strategy and Marketing, San Francisco, Jossey-Bass.

19. Moretti, A., 1999, La produzione museale, Torino, Giappichelli Editore.

20. Valentino, P., 1997, Criteri e metodi per la scelta delle tecnologie informatiche applicabili ai beni culturali, in I formati della memoria. Beni culturali e nuove tecnologie alle soglie del terzo millennio, Firenze, Giunti Editore, pp. 167-201.

DATATUR:
Tourism Statistics Information System –
The Experience of Spain

Jorge Rubio Navarro
Subdirector Adj. Instituto de Estudios Turísticos. Ministerio de Economía y Hacienda
España (Economics and Finance Ministry)

Jesús Quereda Rubio
Jefe de Análisis Sectoriales. Instituto de Estudios Turísticos. Ministerio
de Economía y Hacienda España (Economics and Finance Ministry)

Abstract

This article describes the project carried out by the Instituto de Estudios Turísticos for setting up a Tourism Statistics Information System (hereinafter called DATATUR). The Instituto de Estudios Turísticos has a wealth of information proceeding mainly from its own two surveys Frontur and Familitur plus the reprocessing of secondary sources from other national, regional or international bodies. All this information, whether in-house or brought in from elsewhere, is dispersed throughout the whole organisation in various formats: digital, texts, documents, graphs or images. It is therefore essential to set up a common platform capable of pooling all available information as a great "data warehouse for the tourism sector". This would then serve as the starting point for " a new use of the information, geared towards information and decision taking". The project involves the creation of a statistical databank using the so-called Business Intelligence techniques, thus setting up, in the terminology of said technique, a Data Warehouse in all its phases. Among other things DATATUR will enable us to use information from the Economic Indicators System for the analysis of tourism, as defined by the Instituto de Estudios Turísticos.

1 Introduction

The Tourism Statistics Information System *DATATUR*, is set up as a great *Statistical Data Warehouse* primarily designed for reference and for extraction of said data for analysis with tools especially designed for that purpose. This warehouse or databank has to give due consideration not only to the statistical information itself but also all document registers including notes necessary for the correct understanding thereof.

The final aim of the project is thus to build and set up a Tourism Statistics Information System (hereinafter DATATUR) that harmoniously pools statistical data and documents. It has to cover the following functions:

- Conserve and keep up to date all statistical data, complemented with the corresponding document-type information for the correct use thereof
- Facilitate a quick, error-free updating system
- Meet external demands for information on tourism trends
- Automatically fuel the periodical publications and reports drawn up by IET
- Permit access to the information, the tabulation and graphic representation thereof, browsing, plus subsequent processing by means of final analysis tools.
- Define and develop the system input processes so that they are integrated into the current data-generation processes of the IET.

The statistical databank will be built up by means of the so-called Business Intelligence techniques, so setting up, in the terminology of said technology a Data Warehouse in all its phases.

The initial aim is to incorporate the host of statistical tables deriving from IET's own surveys, plus all the aforementioned statistical products, to be able to draw up the Economic Indicators System specified by IET.

The information system must also allow for access to the various databases (primary data and aggregate data), with a clearly differentiated definition of the access rights, once all reference to the owners has been eliminated to safeguard statistical secrecy.

The IET currently has a document database with more than 65,000 references and a Geographical Information System (GIS) for the analysis of tourism. As the main object of the project is to design a Tourism Statistics Information System, the aim is to integrate the above into the information system and amplify it.

This new statistical development strategy in the tourism sector includes not only a policy of methodological transparency but also a open-door attitude to the wealth of information it is possible to supply.

The Tourism Statistics Information System should therefore allow dissemination of the information (reports and periodical publications) built up from its databases on the internet, intranet and extranet systems of the IET, with a due definition of access levels in each case.

2 Administrative And Functional Environment

The Instituto de Estudios Turísticos (IET) depends directly on the Secretaria de Estado de Comercio Turismo y de la Pequeña y Mediana Empresa (State Department for Trade, Tourism and Small- and Medium-Sized Enterprises) of the Ministerio de Economía y Hacienda (Economics and Finance Ministry). Its main mission, within the central government, is research into, analysis and dissemination of the economic and sociological factors of tourism.

128

The Instituto de Estudios Turísticos (IET), besides being a data-production body, includes amongst its functions that of disseminating tourism information among the public and private tourism sector, other government departments of Spain, the regional bodies in each of the 19 Autonomous Communities, the network of 27 Spanish Tourism Offices abroad, the European Union and other international bodies.

In terms of statistical matters the IET has designed and been running since 1996 two basic statistical surveys on tourism demand ("Movimientos Turísticos en Frontera" ((Border Tourism Movements)) and "Movimientos Turísticos de los Españoles" ((Tourism Movements of the Spanish)) ***FRONTUR[1]*** *and* ***FAMILITUR,[2]*** respectively). These give a monthly quantification of the flows of both national and international journeys and journey makers and analyse their behaviour. The institute also carries out a monthly reprocessing and analysis of secondary sources: EOH (Hotel Occupation Survey) and CPI of the INE (National Statistics Institute), tourism payments and revenue of the Balance of Payments, to keep up to date with the main tourism trends on a macroeconomic level. A Working Programme has also been designed for setting up a National Indicators System for analysing the tourism economy with a view to drawing up the Tourism Satellite Accounts of Spain[3] (TSA-S).

The importance of tourism in Spain's economy and the growth forecasts for this activity on a world level and especially in Spain have boosted the demand for statistical information that would allow a thoroughgoing measurement of the impact of tourism on the economy and enable trends to be monitored in the interests of designing business and political strategies.

The Instituto de Estudios Turísticos disseminates its statistical data in the form of its official publications and through the web server of information on tourism studies and statistics. In its first 20 months of existence, since October 1997 it has received about 70,000 visits. The web server allows on-line consultations of the Centro de Documentación Turística de España (Tourism Document Centre of Spain) and access to other similar information centres.

3 Technological Environment

In the last two years IET has developed a system capable of managing and disseminating its information. This system has three clear objectives:

---

[1] Statistical Survey of "Movimientos Turísticos en Fronteras". Working document drawn up by the Instituto de Estudios Turísticos
[2] Statistical Survey of "Movimientos Turísticos de los Españoles". Working document drawn up by the Instituto de Estudios Turísticos
[3] Tourism Satellite Account. Conceptual Framework. World Tourism Organisation (WTO). 1999.

Manage a large volume of information. The two statistical surveys run by the IET have, in their time, generated a vast amount of data, such as primary-data files, non-IET secondary data files, files containing the results of statistical operations, etc.

Integrate the various sources of in-house and external information. It has been necessary to set up suitable mechanisms for transforming the various data files so that they can be used by the research personnel, with computing standards defined in IET

Facilitate rapid dissemination of results. It is essential nowadays to be in possession of suitable tools for the dissemination of the data using the new information technologies. IET has therefore set up Web servers of internet, intranet and extranet, which it directly runs and inputs.

IET's computer system is made up by four great subsystems:

TURSET. Management and reference system for tourism statistics. This is a system considered to be of internal management by IET. Its main purpose is to serve as repository for all statistical tables generated month by month in FRONTUR. It makes it possible to find any table or set of tables corresponding to FRONTUR's operation plan.

SIGTUR[4]. Geographical Information System for the Analysis of Tourism.

DOCUMENT SYSTEM OF THE CDTE (Tourism Document Centre of Spain). Database of bibliographical references. It contains over 65,000 references computerised in nine catalogues and more than 400 titles of specialised magazines, from which articles can be extracted.

INTERNET SERVICES. System for the dissemination of tourism statistics and studies.

IET has set up the network infrastructures necessary, on the one hand, for internal management and research work and, on the other, for liaison with other bodies and companies it has relationships with.

IET has a private network with its own servers, which back up the applications and files used by management and research personnel. Particularly worthy of mention are the following: the email server used for internal mail and for internet mail, the server for the document database SABINI and the Web servers for intranet/extranet and internet.

---

[4] Methodology for developing the Geographical Information System for the Analysis of Tourism. Technical note drawn up by the Instituto de Estudios Turísticos

IET is in turn integrated into the private data network of the Secretaría de Estado de Comercio Turismo y de la Pyme (SECTYP), and through this network it has access to the Spanish Tourism Offices (Oficinas Españolas de Turismo: OETS) abroad, to the Trade Offices (Oficinas de Comercio: (OFCOME) and the various organisations of SECTYP (ICEX, Central Services, etc). The whole SECTYP network shares the same email system[5] (almost 2000 internal mailboxes), plus an in-house IP network addressing plan (designed in accordance with MAP specifications). The SECTYP network has its own intranet, of which the reports and data furnished by IET form an important part. This network is considered to be the biggest international private network possessed by the Spanish government.

Besides being an active part of the SECTYP network, the network of the TURESPAÑA building has a permanent high-speed (2 Mb Frame Relay) link with infovía-plus for entering and leaving internet.

To avoid any security problems bound up with internet access, a Firewall server has been set up; this establishes three different network zones: the private network, containing the main servers and workstations, the DMZ network or demilitarised zone, containing the internet services accessible by outside users and the internet zone. This buffer system means that users of the internet zone are allowed access only to the DMZ zone, thereby avoiding forbidden access from the internet zone to the private network.

4 Functional Description Of The System

The core of the Tourism Statistics Information System will be made up by the following: the data and indicators produced in IET's studies and research area in its two statistical surveys FRONTUR and FAMILITUR, the data currently managed by the application TUR_SET , the data of the statistical sources identified in the IET and the necessary document data for the correct use of DATATUR. Constructon of the Tourism Statistics Information System (DATATUR) involves taking into account the following:

1. Clear differentiation of two types of data: Primary data, referring to individual units generated from the statistical surveys FRONTUR and FAMILITUR, and aggregate data, generated from the former and presented in the form of statistical tables. The great difference between these two types lies mainly in their degree of confidentiality, their structure, operational flexibility needs, computing tools for their management and the logical views presented to their users.

2. The identification of two sets of information so disparate makes it recommendable in principle to separate them logically into three different databases within

---

[5] Strategic plan for setting up an MS Exchange in SECTYP. 1998

DATATUR: *Primary-data* base, *aggregate-data* base and a *Metadata Repository* (information on multiple sources inside and outside IET necessary for the analysis of tourism)

The first two databases will be relational in type, providing for the efficient capture and debugging of primary data and the storing of the tables of aggregate data defined in the operation plans of IET's statistical surveys. Analysis of these databases will enable the following: the definition of filters, the carrying out of aggregation and partitioning operations and the use of statistical tools for analysis of series and multivariables.

Primary-data base or microdata. The basic information stored corresponds to the final file of sample data where registers have been rendered anonymous to guarantee statistical secrecy. The primary-data base will allow the end user to:

- Carry out the necessary operations for aggregating data according to the desired criteria
- Select register blocks that meet given conditions
- Carry out calculations on the selected register blocks

To avoid problems of confidentiality and other errors deriving from use of the primary-data base the following measures will be taken:

- Control of operations that select a small number of registers (to safeguard confidentiality to the utmost)
- Announce sampling errors of aggregate information obtained by use of microdata
- Generation of all necessary documentation for the user to find out all methodological and technical aspects of the statistical operation in question

Use of the primary-data base will be restricted to the technical personnel of IET. Only occasionally, and by one-off concession, may it be used by technicians of other institutions, duly bound to maintain statistical secrecy

Aggregate-Data Base. The basic information stored will correspond to the aggregate-data file obtained by statistical use of microdata and other sources. Problems of confidentiality and sampling errors do not arise in this database. Only the information that IET deems fit for dissemination will be stored.

The ultimate objective is to incorporate into DATATUR any type of existing statistical information conducive to a better knowledge of tourism trends and their relation to other socio-economic activities.
3. The third to be considered is the *Metadata Repository*, a database developed with *Data Warehouse* (*DW*) technology, designed for multidimensional analysis. It will be loaded mainly from the two above-mentioned databases, from the existing

documentation in IET (studies and research projects of other bodies), from non-IET data sources in various formats. It manages n-dimensional information in an efficient and flexible way, allowing for its suitable analysis and dissemination. This object of this low-confidentiality Metadata repository will be:

- Analysis and dissemination of data to end users
- Furnish users with an integrated information source
- Speed up information-obtaining processes
- Furnish users with the necessary data-analysis tools to make them self-sufficient

4. The content of DATATUR is structured into the following major subsystems:

- That generated by the fieldwork of the various statistical surveys (interview data)

- That generated by direct use of IET surveys.

- That generated by direct use of original data of surveys not run by IET (in this case it is necessary to have original primary data)

- That made up by statistical data from publications or computer files catalogued in the IET's document database (statistical data of the autonomous communities or other bodies of interest to tourism analysis)

- The subsystem of economic indicators defined in IET's SINTUR[6] project

- The subsystem corresponding to the Employment[7] operation.

- The subsystem of secondary sources necessary for analysis of the Economic Indicators System and for the GIS analysis of tourism and territory

- The subset of demands made by users which, in the opinion of the DATATUR administrator, should be kept for future use.

---

[6] System of Statistical Indicators for Analysis of the Tourism Economy (Sistema de Indicadores Estadísticos para el Análisis de la Economía del Turismo: SINTUR). A work programme of the Instituto de Estudios Turísticos for the period 1998-2000. Working document drawn up by IET
[7] Although employment is included as one of the economic indicators of SINTUR, the importance of this study justifies the creation of an exclusive subsystem for it.

5 Conceptual Schema: DATATUR

Once a definition has been made of the information products required by the sector and the administrations, all integrated around the core of the System of Indicators for Analysis of Tourism, the next step is to develop the information systems making it up. The main one is the *data warehouse for the tourism sector* which will integrate the different types of data coming from both internal and external sources and their various formats (digital, texts, graphics, images, documents etc.). This *data warehouse* will mark the start of a *new use of the information geared towards knowledge and decision taking.*
DSS (decision level), designed for expert users of medium/high level. It would offer a complex analysis of the research data and business lines.

EIS (executive level), designed for executive users. It would offer access to strategic information for decision taking, with debugged, summarised data and a historical perspective that would allow for a predictive analysis.

QUERY (reference and reports), designed with the non-expert user in mind. It would offer a minimum level of information with ad hoc queries and predefined reports.

5.1 Necessary Data Sources For Constructing The Datatur Information System.

As has already been pointed out, the following data will make up the core of DATATUR: primary data, the aggregate data, the data managed by the application TUR_SET , the data from sources outside IET and the necessary document-type data. An account is given below of these data sources:

Data Managed by the Application TUR_SET: This is an in-house IET application to allow non computer buffs to obtain and use periodical statistical information from the survey Movimientos Turísticos en Fronteras (FRONTUR), directly run by IET itself.

Apart from the above, the application creates an environment for managing and consulting all the statistical tables linked to the FRONTUR survey, to facilitate the tasks of inexperienced users.

To carry out the necessary and at times complex statistical processing of the information, this application uses the well-known statistical package SPSS, which automatically executes the processes defined above.

The current functionality of the TUR_SET application has to be included in the Tourism Statistics Information System, in what we call primary-data bases and aggregate-data bases. The following table shows the current volume of tables managed by TUR_SET:

Fig. 1. Conceptual Schema DATATUR

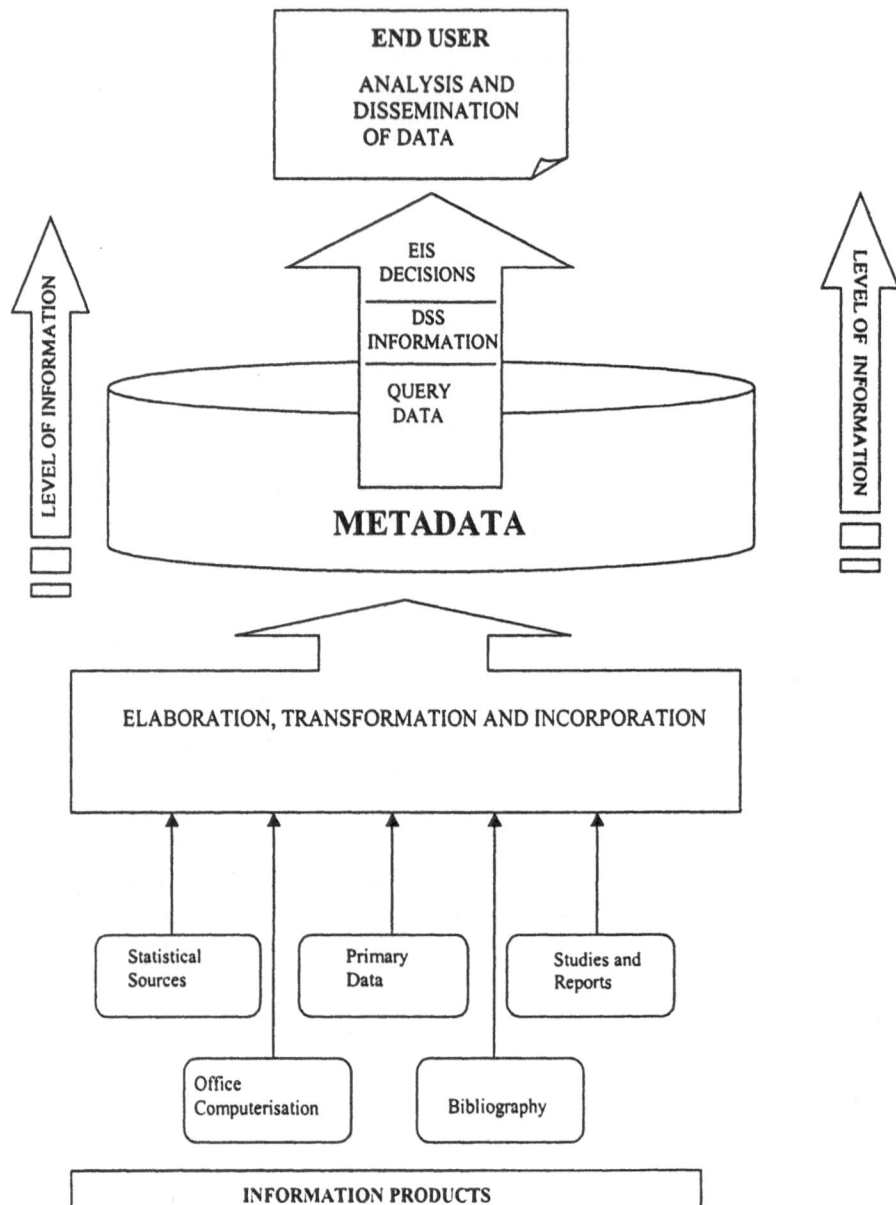

Table 1.

PROCEDURE	NUMBER OF TABLES	FREQUENCY	CURRENT TOTAL
Incoming visitors (elevated) Advanced data	35	Monthly	2,100
Incoming visitors (elevated) Definitive data	35	Monthly	2,100
Incoming visitors (samples)	15	Monthly	900
D.G.T. use– Survey capacities	14	Monthly	840
Behaviour of visitors Outbound survey	55	Three-monthly	1,100
Summer season	62	Annual	310
Winter season	62	Annual	310
Annual total	62	Annual	310
Distribution of results	31	Monthly	1.860
Analysis tables	-	-	720
Total	-	-	**10,550**
Total Registers (approx. 40 per table)			**422,000**

Data from Statistical Sources: Compilation[8] of government and private statistical sources considered to be of most relevance for keeping track of socio-economic trends in the tourism economy and analysing same, to which users have free access. These statistical sources include those operations that result in the capture and/or organisation of a set of structured data with a precise aim, and which meet minimum conditions of rigour in the capturing and processing thereof. A distinction is made of the following types:

- Publications with a statistical content
- Statistics from administrative registers / processes
- Survey statistics
- Statistics deriving from demands for tourism information
- Census or directory

---

[8] Guide to Statistical Sources for the Tourism Economy and Regional Sources of Quantitative Information on Tourism, published by IET

136

- Statistical summary
- Databases with a statistical content

The source guides produced in IET include 320 descriptions of statistical sources. The sources have to be accessible from the Tourism Statistics Information System, firstly as pure reference and secondly as extraction of their content in the information system with the same frequency as each source itself, so that the information contained therein can be found and used.

Volume of data contained in the statistical sources:

- Number of sources: 320
- Number of tables / source (average): 200
- Number of registers per table (average): 40
- Frequency: Monthly at least
- Available registers (regardless of frequency) : 2,560,000

- EMPLOYMENT[9]: The study of employment in the tourism sector initiated in IET as part of the SINTUR programme; it includes three lines of action designed to give more information on employment in the tourism industry:

- Estimate the number of people employed in the year as a whole
- Assess the number and type of contracts produced throughout the year
- Give the personnel characteristics of the workers employed: skill level and remuneration

Not only will the study of employment allow the corresponding table to be drawn up in the future Tourism Satellite Account, but it also has the enormous potential of serving as a base for analysing the job market of a series of activities that until very recently has lacked the statistical framework that would allow the tourism industry to be dealt with on a par with farming, manufacturing or construction.

In its first stage this project involves drawing up 20 tables with data from DATATUR and statistical sources drawn up by the INE, Ministry of Employment and Social Affairs and the Instituto de Estudios Fiscales (Fiscal Studies Institute).

The information to be used will be fed into the Tourism Statistics Information System DATATUR and serve as reference for taking on subsequent studies on the business population of the tourism sector, the qualification levels of the labour force associated with tourism, the territorial specialisation of these workers, their working conditions and a whole set of studies that IET will promote once DATATUR is up and running.

---

[9] Employment and Tourism: Research project with a view to the tourism satellite account. Working document drawn up by IET

Given their importance, a list is given below of the 10 sources used in the Employment operation:

F1. Encuesta de Población Activa (Active Population Survey)

F2. Encuesta de Coyuntura Laboral (Labour Trends Survey)

F3. Afiliación de Trabajadores al Sistema de Seguridad Social (Workers' Membership of the Social Security Scheme)

F4. Encuesta de Salarios en la Industria y los Servicios (Survey on salaries in Industry and Services)

F5. Empleo, Salarios y Pensiones en las Fuentes Tributarias (Employment, Wages and Pensions in Taxation Sources)

F6. Empresas inscritas en la Seguridad Social (Companies Registered in the Social Security Scheme)

F7. Directorio Central de Empresas (Central Directory of Companies)

F8. Estadística de Contratos Registrados (Statistical Survey of Registered Contracts)

F9. Empresas de Trabajo Temporal (Temping Firms)

Document Database produced in IET by the Tourism Document Centre of Spain, CDTE. The CDTE has 65,000 computerised references in nine catalogues and more than 400 titles of specialised magazines from which articles can be taken. The documents are computerised by the Library Computerisation System SABINI.

CDTE's document database has to be integrated into the Tourism Statistics Information System in such a way that it is possible to find any document reference relative to the data analysis being carried out by the users.

5.2 Areas Of Identified Analysis

DATATUR has to satisfy the following identified analyses, which constitute IET's strategic plan for the next three years.

ECONOMIC INDICATORS[10]: The information system has to include the nineteen tasks that the Instituto de Estudios Turísticos considers necessary for the creation, in the medium term, of a System of Indicators for the Analysis of Tourism. This is a field in which the IET has been working for the last two years, either defining or implementing same.

---

[10] A system of indicators for the analysis of tourism: Working Project. Instituto de Estudios Turísticos. Feb. 1999

Table 2.

Description of the Indicator	Related Source Systems
Demand	FRONTUR
Incoming non-residents	FRONTUR
Behaviour of the visitors	FRONTUR
Journeys and tourism behaviour of the Spanish	FAMILITUR
Journey makers lodging in collective establishments and hotels	INE, FRONTUR, FAMILITUR
Employment in tourism activities	INE data, Ministry of Employment, IEF
Tourism price trends	CPI (INE)
Forecasts for tourism seasons	Aena, Reports of the OETs
Business Structure and Activity	
Trading results of tourism establishments and firms	INE, IEF, Surveys
Business characterisation	
Strategic actions	
Tourism Infrastructures	
Register of collective tourist accommodation (hotels, camping sites, statistical directories, apartments, rural accommodation)	Statistical directories INE, Auton. Commmunities
Non-collective accommodation (second dwellings of tourist use, timeshare)	Auton. Communities, INE and other surveys
Other facilities of tourism use (marinas, golf courses, theme parks, …)	Business associations, government registers
Tourism-related residential construction	Ministry of Public Works
Source Markets	
Reports on tourism in source markets	IET, Turespaña
Study of potential mkets/ preferences of consumers	New surveys
Destinations and Tourism Products	
Evaluation of the efficiency of the corresponding promotion campaign	External sources
Est. increase of demand in destinations or products	
Tourism and Territory	
Population indicators	Diverse sources of the INE, Ministry of Public Works and other organisations
Accommodation structure	
Second dwelling	
Facilities	

It will therefore be necessary to define the calculations of the analysis indicators already defined by the IET, for quantifying and assessing the economic impact of tourism on the national economy, working from the data fed into the system. The initial indicators to be considered are summed up in the above table[11].

Given the importance of the study of employment in the tourism sector, and of the analysis of tourism and territory, these two points are dealt with apart:

TOURISM AND TERRITORY. Furnish the necessary broken-down data for studying tourism at the level of autonomous community, province or tourism zones. The aim is to make an analysis of:

Supply. The basic information sources will be the censuses or directories of the INE (used for the Hotel Occupation Survey) and Turespaña, such as the guide to hotels, camping sites, apartments, travel agencies, etc.

Occupation: The main source will be INE's Hotel Occupation Survey

Expenditure: Sources to use FRONTUR, FAMILITUR, survey data of family expenditure of INE

Indicators: Indicators in the territorial sphere will be developed, for an ongoing, precise study of trends.

Other Exploitations: As a general principle, any indicator or operation prone to be linked to the territory will be dealt with by GIS tools. Consideration will therefore be given to any methodological and technical aspect referring to the geo-spatial analysis of multidimensional databases.

5.3 System Access Profiles

There are basically two broad groups of DATATUR users, whose attitudes towards the form of use thereof differ:

- Business users. All users who access DATATUR to extract and analyse strategic information on the tourism sector.

- Technical users. All users who construct, manage and maintain DATATUR information.

We will now analyse access profiles in terms of these two types of users:

---

[11] System of Economic Indicators. Executive Report. Instituto de Estudios Turísticos. Sept. 1999

Business Users. The following types of information access and use have been identified

- They will *not* have access to the Primary-Data base
- *Free Queries.* Users responding to this profile analyse the existent information on DATATUR combining dynamically different perspectives or variables influencing the value of any given data that is object of analysis. Among other operations the following will be permitted:

  - Display data
  - Aggregate in rows, columns or heads:
  - States of the same characteristic, naming the new state and summing the states making up the aggregation.
  - Characteristics generated by mathematical formulae or by combination of states
  - Erase states or characteristics in rows, columns or heads
  - Reorder in rows, columns or heads
  - Partition in rows, columns or heads
  - Transfer between rows, columns and heads
  - Basic calculation on variables contained in a table
  - In relation to two statistical tables:
  - Basic calculation on variables contained in two tables
  - Insert, merge between two tables, add states
  - Concatenate, juxtapose between two tables, adding characteristics
  - Pseudo-matrix or tabular calculation

- *Reporting System and Predetermined Reports.* Reports with a fixed structure and given frequency. They serve for monitoring the trends of the set of indicators at set intervals.
- *Predetermined Analysis.* This is a type of analysis whose general structure can be previously defined but allows browsing through the data to investigate in greater detail any particularly important detail or aberrant results.
- *Simulations or "what if" analysis.* With this type of analysis situations are simulated by varying a given variable to see how it would affect the rest of the variables under consideration.
- *Predictive Analysis.* Analytical modelling techniques are used to predict results of the various actions included in DATATUR.

Technical Users. The following types of information access and use have been identified

- Generation of direct database queries. This profile includes all users who construct and execute SQL sentences directly on the databases; either for the creation of predetermined reports, for the preparation of complex queries or the manual optimisation of queries of high cost for the database.

- Construction, loading and updating of DATATUR. Users who effect the loading and periodic updating of the data.
- Administration and management of DATATUR. Users who carry out the tasks of administration and management of DATATUR, back-up procedures, monitoring of performance, creation and maintenance of user profiles and security levels and development of maintenance process utilities.
- Reference and extraction of data from the Primary-Data Base. Technical users with statistical functions within IET.

Provision has been made for a link procedure to generate the necessary information for the use of standard type SPSS tools or others to facilitate the statistical analysis of the information contained in the *Tourism Statistics Information System.*

The data of the Tourism Statistics Information System will be updated by semi-automatic data-importation methods, using internal sources (FRONTUR and FAMILITUR) or external sources (those defined for each indicator). Procedures and interfaces will be designed for extraction, transformation and loading of this data in the various databases of DATATUR. Based on the above, user interfaces will also be created for the manual input of data where automatic loading is not viable.

6 Proposed Development Architecture: Data Warehousing

From the computing technology point of view the objective of data warehousing[12] is the distribution of the precise information as and when needed to the suitable persons of the organisation. This is always an ongoing process, not a one-off solution, and calls for a different approach to the development of transactional systems.

A data warehouse is a compilation of data to support decision-taking by company management; it is *business centred, integrated, time variable and non-volatile*[13]. This means that the data warehouse focuses on a business concept (for example sales) rather than a business process (for example invoicing) and that it contains the necessary information on the concept, which comes from several processing systems. This information is collected and presented at set intervals and does not change rapidly.

A data warehouse integrates operative data, with name conventions, measurements, physical attributes and coherent semantics. The first step in generating the data

---

[12] Joan Tort. The Data Warehousing Architecture. An overall vision. Novática Mar./Apr. 1999 n° 138

[13] W.H. Inmon. Building the Data Warehouse 1992

warehouse is a management process: determining the areas that should be included and developing a set of agreed definitions.

This involves interviewing end users, business analysts and executives for finding out and documenting the scope of information requirements. Only after an in-depth knowledge has been gained of the business aspects can the logical aspects be translated to a physical data warehouse.

After the physical design, the systems are available for continuously building[14] the data warehouse from the operative systems. Data representation in the operative systems and in the data warehousing are different, so building the data warehouse requires a previous transformation of the data: summarising, translating, decoding same, eliminating invalid data, etc. These processes must be automated so that they can be performed continuously: extracting, transforming and migrating the original data with the necessary frequency for satisfying the business requirements of the data warehousing.

The data in a data warehouse represent information over a long period of time and the aim is for the information to be faithful at any given moment. In fact the data warehouse contains a long series of views (multidimensional analysis) of the most important business areas.

Finally, the information is made available to analysts and executives of the company for browsing, analysing and writing reports. Several tools can be used as an aid in the analysis stage; ranging from simple report generators to advanced data-mining tools[15] (based on artificial intelligence techniques, statistical algorithms, etc). But the analysis tasks lead to the final iterations of the data warehousing process: modifying the design of the data warehouse to contain new information, improving system performance or allowing new types of analysis. With these changes the process starts anew and continues throughout the whole life of the data warehousing.

A data warehouse always includes several components[16], including the following:

- Sources of operative data

- Design/development tools

- Data-extraction and -transformation tools

- Database management system

---

[14] Gill H.S, Rao P.C. Data Warehousing. The integration of information for better decision taking. Prentice Hall, 1996.
[15] D.E. Goldberg. Genetic Algorithms in search, Optimization, and machine Learning. Addison Wesley, Reading, MA. 1989
[16] J. Celko. Don't warehouse dirty data. Datamation, 10, 1995.

- Data-access and -analysis tools

- System management tools

For the development of the Tourism Statistics Information System DATATUR, the Instituto de Estudios Turísticos has chosen the Microsoft Data Warehousing Framework[17], based on its own database SQL Server 7.0 and OLAP Services, as an open development platform containing all necessary technology for integrating products of diverse manufacturers.

Fig. 2. Microsoft Data Warehousing Framework

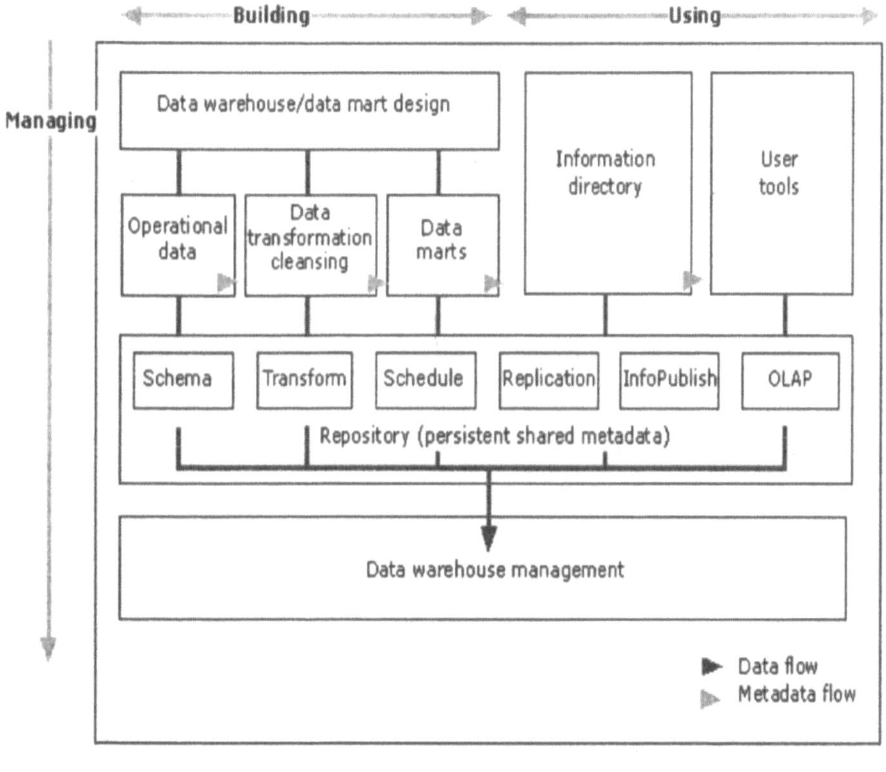

The development techniques of Data Warehousing will be applied to the construction of a statistical database (DATATUR).

Multidimensional data are used for the creation of data warehouses. Dimensional databases store facts on the business activity, such as sales in pesetas and units, in a context of dimensions such as time, geographical area, client demography and

---

[17] Microsoft Data Warehousing Framework: A platform for improving decision-taking by means of data access and an easier analysis. Microsoft 1999.

products. Describing and storing data in this way means that high-performance ad hoc queries of the data can be made.

7 Data Access Technologies, Multidimensional Analysis: the three OLAPs

Multidimensional analysis[18] could be summed up as an analysis of economic facts, or facts of another type, from the point of view of their components or dimensions, also taking into account the different levels that these dimensions may have. It must be possible for the analysis to be either joint or individualised. This means that the analysis can be made on the basis of one component or a set thereof.

For an optimum analysis the multidimensional schema has to be based on specific databases called multidimensional BBDDs. These BBDDs store the data in matrices or hyperdimensional cubes. The engines of these databases build up the totals or aggregations of the upper levels of each dimension. This is done both in the interests of speed and also because multilevel accumulations are not usually possible in SQL groups by operations.

The main feature of multidimensional analysis is the possibility of browsing through the data by moving up and down through a dimension into higher or lower levels and also by moving horizontally from one dimension to another to obtain new views. The terms used for this process are drilling down and drilling across respectively.

The OLAP[19] technology (On Line Analytical Process) is used for data storage in multidimensional format and to facilitate rapid access thereto.

There are three types of dimensional data storage: multidimensional OLAP (MOLAP), relational OLAP (ROLAP) and hybrid OLAP (HOLAP).

MOLAP uses compressed indices and a search engine optimised for the storage format in question. MOLAP stores aggregations for a rapid access to the data.

---

[18] R. Duro. Multidimensional Analysis. Novática Mar. / Apr. 1999 n° 138
[19] Chaudhuri, S. Y Dayal, U. An overview of Data Warehousing and OLAP Technology. ACM SIGMOD Record 26.

Fig. 3. Microsoft. OLAP Services Architecture

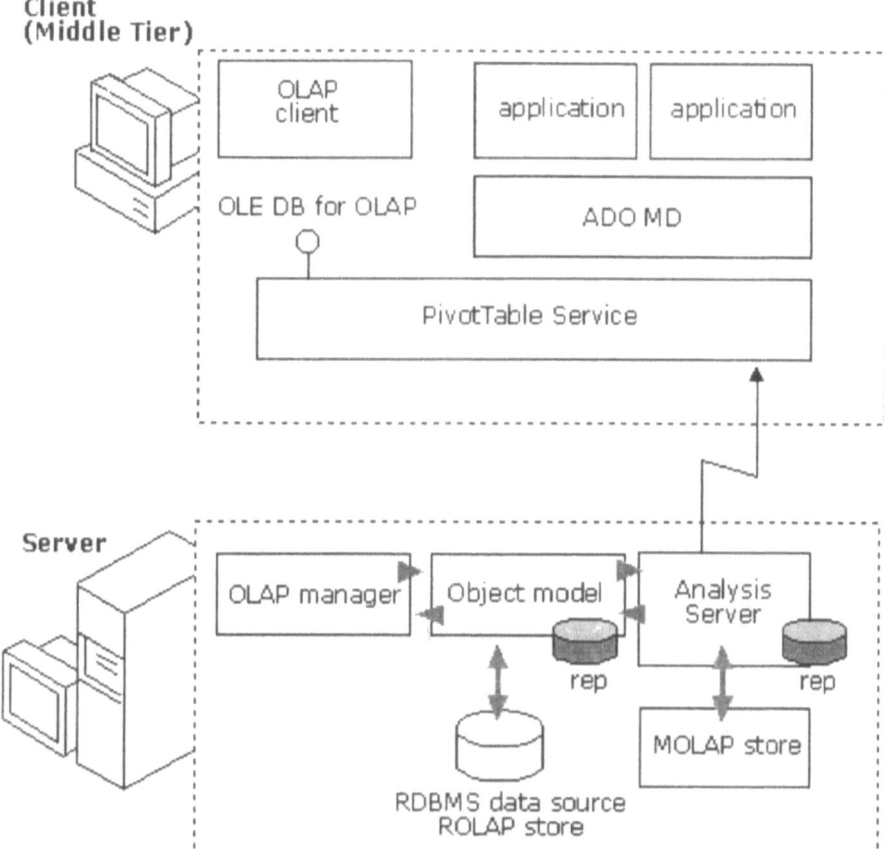

ROLAP stores aggregations in a relational operative database in summary tables to speed up data access. This technique might imply the use of a large amount of disc space and is not usually as quick as MOLAP.

HOLAP conserves the fact tables in the origin database and stores aggregations along the lines of the MOLAP model. Some experts claim that this solution combines the best characteristics of MOLAP and ROLAP. Nonetheless, if all necessary aggregations are not stored in the Data Warehouse, queries of the origin database at detail level will be slower.

The platform chosen for developing DATATUR (Microsoft OLAP server + SQL*Server 7.0) can work with the three types of OLAP.

The client applications are developed with internet technology and will be accessible via a browser or explorer. These applications will access the OLAP server functions through the PivotTable service with the specification OLE DB for OLAP and the data model ActiveX Data Objets Multidimensional (ADO MD).

Fig. 4. Microsoft Development Architecture based on an OLAP server.

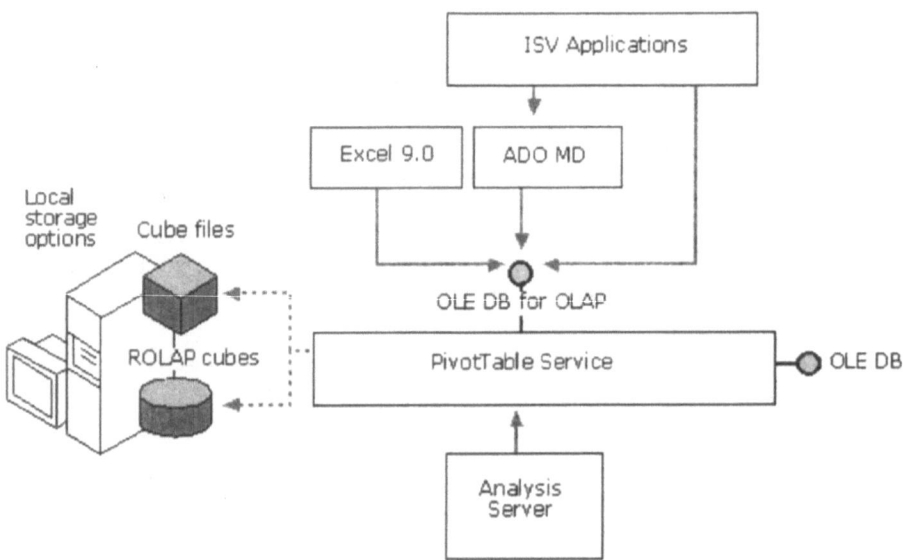

Developing A Business Information Data Warehouse For The Australian Tourism Industry – A Strategic Response

P. Sharma, D. Carson and T. DeLacy

IT R&D Program, Cooperative Research Centre For Sustainable Tourism,
University of Queensland, QLD 4072, AUSTRALIA
P.Sharma@mailbox.uq.edu.au

Abstract

To meet various competitive challenges and to take advantage of recent developments in information technology a business information data warehouse is being developed to supply business intelligence and related products and services for the Australian tourism industry. This paper outlines the concept and reports on the research issues and the current state of the project to build the prototype data warehouse.

1 Introduction

The broad characteristics of the Australian tourism industry are similar to those of many other countries and conform to the "generic" characterisation (Werthner 1996, p70). These are:

- Tourism and leisure industry in general are of major importance for the local, regional and national development. Economic and infrastructure entry barriers for new entrants are low – therefore product standards are difficult to implement.
- The industry has essentially a two-tiered structure: Tier 1 consists of a small number of large often global players (eg. the airlines, hotel chains and tour operators) who are generally well versed in current management practices including IT applications; and Tier 2: a much larger collection of small and medium enterprises (SMEs). These SMEs have mostly limited technological infrastructure and financial power; level of marketing know how is generally low; direct access facilities to the market and the final consumer (particularly, in the online mode) are rather limited.
- Impact of the changing world market: Marketing of products increasingly organised at the global scale; changing consumer behaviour (shorter vacations etc).

To these "generic" characteristics we must add some specific Australian characteristics:

- It may not be in the interests of some of the bigger players in the Australian tourism industry to market the Australian product generally. By not doing so, they reduce competition for their own products, but also contribute to low international awareness of Australian product.

- Existing marketing arrangements in international markets may prevent the Australian industry from benefiting from recent (technological) developments eg. direct selling in target markets.
- Distance from some key markets (e.g. over 15 hours travel time from continental USA and European countries) – this factor further accentuates the market dominance by the larger players.
- Despite the importance of domestic tourism (accounting for around 75% of a $60b market) much of the industry emphasis is on the more volatile international component of the market
- The industry does not have a strong track record on research (Delacy & Boyd, 1998).
- There is a strong involvement of governments (both at national and state levels) in the tourism industry – "commercial" operations are excluded by statutory provisions or by political lobbying by the industry.

It can be seen that the Australian tourism industry is facing many challenges to which many responses are possible. A key strategic response to many of these challenges is to make the industry "information smart" - with high quality, readily available information, the tourism industry would be in a better position to assess the effectiveness of measures to meet the challenges it faces.

Many types of tourism information systems have been proposed and developed in Australia and elsewhere (for some recent state-of-the-industry reviews see [7,6,10,11,4]. These systems typically focus on products and destination marketing – in Australia at the national level the Australian Tourist Commission (ATC) and the state level the various State tourism organisations (such as Tourism Victoria and Tourism Queensland) have a well earned reputation for being early adopters and developers of destination marketing systems (or similar products).

The research reported in this paper focuses on meeting the information needs of the industry rather than those of consumers. Developments with similar objectives have been reported from Austria and Canada [11] – the Canadian CTX system, in particular, appears to be driven by similar objectives. The Tourism Business Information Facility (TBIF) includes research into the requirements for and the development of a data warehouse prototype which meets the information needs of the Australian Tourism industry in the following areas: market intelligence; compliance information; training and education resources; information about industry assistance; and business information about destinations and products to assist in making investment decisions. It is expected that this "one stop shop" will make a significant contribution to the reduction of costs associated with starting and running a tourism business in Australia.

2 The Data Warehouse Project

TBIF was proposed as a strategic response to various developments both within and outside the Australian tourism industry. This project has been facilitated by a AUD1m grant from the Australian Government

2.1 Data Warehouses – a brief introduction

Data warehouses represent a logical development of database technology over the last decade or so [5]. Operational data bases have been developed and optimised to support day to day transactions relating to the business of the firm; in contrast, the data in data warehouses has often been integrated with data from other sources and some of it may be stored in summarised form. The main idea is to apply various tools and analyse the data to identify patterns and relationships which may be hidden in the data - hence the term data mining. The term data mart is applied when large data warehouses support specialised subject content areas (please refer to Section 4 for the Twin Share website as a data mart example).

Data warehouses have greater utility when recent developments in communications technology are used to create extranet and Internet based applications. In these situations, users can access information servers and provide public information world-wide thereby significantly reducing (if not eliminating) long-standing barriers to collaboration and teamwork [5]. It should also be noted that while data warehouses trace their lineage to DSS, MIS and EIS concepts they are primarily aimed at producing integration and consolidation of data from various sources and producing consistent data of high quality. Indeed, their success will assist in the development of systems which help in the making of better decisions – DSSs can be one of the many applications that a data warehouse may support

2.2 The TBIF Concept

There is considerable tourism (and tourism related) data that is in existence in Australia – some of it (like those held by the Australian Bureau of Statistics ABS) is well documented and readily available while little can be said about the existence and availability of others. There are also many gaps. TBIF is designed to provide varying levels of access to all tourism data. Conceptually, the TBIF model is relatively simple – the facility aims to provide a "one stop shop" for tourism data and related services.
- It will have at its core a Web based data warehouse which will provide access to various data repositories. Considerable effort will be expended on developing the metadata as this will be the main attraction that will drive the 'one stop shop' concept.
- From the outset, it is the intention to avoid data storage within TBIF where ever possible. (This avoids any conflicts – commercial or political - with data providers and also avoids the perennial data update problem by leaving

the update responsibility with the data providers). It was considered that the significant technical problem of providing access links to various data providers was solvable by appropriate "middleware" – the EC funded ESPRIT Program's MIRO-Web project is along similar lines [1]. Like MIRO-Web TBIF will develop "adapters" for key data suppliers.

- TBIF will support a variety of interfaces and services: for the expert user a data mining capacity will be available; for others, reports (both 'hard-wired' and customisable) will be available. Query options will also take account of different user expertise levels and are to include map based options. Other services such as news services and employment exchange will follow existing Web design best practices. Consultancy services may also be available in the final suite of products and services. The common guiding principle for all products and services is that they support key business processes of Australian tourism enterprises.
- Training services are being developed with twin objectives: (i) using the TBIF system, (ii) conducting research in tourism (including using TBIF) – this is to increase the level of research in tourism and, hopefully, expand the overall demand for TBIF
- The service will be run on a commercial basis but will include a significant 'free-to-air' component. Apart from the usual 'freebies' that many sites have, free use of the full TBIF metadata, as a reference source, may have to be used to attract paying users.

2.3 Research Issues

In theory, developing a data warehouse is a relatively simple task as it is based on one of several well known and proven systems development methodologies. However, the reality is much more complex. The traditional approach is: Requirements Analysis and Functional Requirements Specification, Conceptual Design, Physical Design, Build and, Test and release of the system.

The typical data warehouses is developed at the enterprise/organization level. In the present project the data warehouse is at the industry level – and that for an industry which is noted for the variety in its data requirements (eg. information required for a resort development vs. information required to assess the effectiveness of a marketing promotion). Thus, an industry type warehouse faces more complex issues relating to interfaces for data access and communications generally; to these *technical issues* we must add a layer of operational complexity of *administrative issues* (eg. update and financial arrangements with many suppliers regarding sale of data).

These issues indicate several areas in which research is required. These include:

- user requirements analysis - types of activities which make up the universe of business processes in the Australian tourism industry

- current data availability and ways of filling data gaps (development of a high level data model for the Australian tourism industry; development of metadata – what data exist, where it is located, and how it can be retrieved)
- data extraction and cleansing issues
- architecture of the proposed system (especially with regard to the extraction and structuring of data from many suppliers)
- types of users and interfaces required
- storage and retrieval of geographic/map data (query and visualisation issues, in particular)
- what data brokering/charging model is appropriate
- how can the data warehouse be commercialised ?

3 Building the data warehouse – progress to date

As indicated earlier, TBIF will include only business intelligence information. Product and destination marketing information will not be a part of the facility. A successful prototype TBIF will demonstrate the capacity to manage the various suppliers; information packets; information topics; upload and maintenance arrangements; and financial arrangements. The many technical issues (ranging from user interfaces to system architecture) are important but are considered to be less difficult i.e. solved relatively easily by IT specialists.

3.1 Scope of Information – a data model

The first step in the requirements analysis phase was to develop a preliminary high level data model for the Australian Tourism industry (National Tourism Information Model NTIM). This model provides the basis for (a) cataloguing what data is available, (b) identifying gaps in data availability and (c) developing strategies for collecting data that is currently not available. It provides a strong rationale for developing industry data standards. Without a data model it is both inefficient and difficult to extract, clean and integrate data from various sources and to develop metadata.

The key features of NTIM are summarised in Table 1. The NTIM will be the basis for developing a data structure for TBIF, and for designing data mining engines.

Approximately 3,000 data suppliers (with 11,500 potential sources of information) have been identified. Data suppliers will come from public sector (Government, Government agencies), university/research sector (universities, research organisations), and private sector (Industry Organisations, Businesses, Consultancy Firms, Small Area Specialists) . There is a preponderance of public sector suppliers because information from these is generally more accessible and broad based, whereas private sector organisations tend to have data that is more specific (in time, scope or geographic coverage), proprietary, and collected for specific rather than broad purposes.

Table 1. The National Tourism Information Model NTIM

Feature	Description/comment
Entities	Entities are the units which are described by information in the Facility. The NTIM identifies five core entities: Person, Activity, Product, Organisation and Location. Each entity has sub-entities eg. information may be collected about a person in their role as a visitor, resident, or employee.
Domains	NTIM identifies a range of domains - the broad classifications information - for each entity. Domains for person include: demography; socio-culture; and economy. Other common domain names are : environment; legal/regulatory; and description.
Subjects	Each domain includes a number of subjects, which are more specific descriptions of information for the entity. Subjects are aspects of the domain to which they belong. The model continues to sub-subject levels to identify specific fields for inclusion in a data structure (eg. male and female are fields for the sex subject in demography domain for the person entity). CRC Tourism has collected commonly used fields for each subject, and is developing standards for those subjects for which fields do not currently exist.

3.2 Data Suppliers and Data Access Issues

From the initial data inventory several key suppliers have been identified, and are forming the core of the development of the *Guide to Getting Data on TBIF*. Our intention is to develop a system which is appropriate for including information packets from these 'high yield' suppliers, and then encourage other suppliers where possible to meet the standards that are set through this system. While technically feasible, it is far too unwieldy to develop unique systems ('adapter' software) for each potential supplier (about 3,000 as noted above), so the decision was made to develop a system which suits key suppliers, and make this an agent of change for other suppliers whose standards and processes do not meet TBIF specifications. As new key suppliers emerge, the base system may need to be altered.

There is likely to be a range of other types of data suppliers who will have information included in TBIF, but not as part of the standard product suite. These would include organisations who provide electronic publications for sale through TBIF's online bookshop, and organisations who provide customisable information that is selected and configured by each user eg. news services; weather information; stock information services; travel advice services and so on.

3.3 Typology of Information Packets and TBIF Products

TBIF products are built from information packets. An information packet is a discrete item which comes from a single supplier and is a component of a TBIF product. We have developed and are continuing to develop the National Tourism Information Model which identifies the range of topics for information packets of relevance to the tourism industry. Information packets may have a number of purposes: Quantitative measurement, Qualitative analysis, 'announcement' type, educational/ instructional material, information gathering (eg. Forms), and compliance type. Information packets may, of course, represent a combination of these, as they may represent a combination of topics.

We have also developed a typology of data formats, identifying information packets which are: Statistical collections (unit record files URFs); Numerical tables (summaries of URFs etc.); Charts, maps, and other manipulable images (i.e. change appearance on manipulation of underlying data, or can be added to); Static images; Unpublished reports/papers (i.e. with flexible formatting); published reports/papers; Newsletter/brochure/interpretation type; Multimedia formats. Each of these formats will require separate consideration in terms of: file formats (.pdf, .gif etc); how they are uploaded; how data is maintained on the system; and the processes required for including information packets in specific TBIF products.

3.4 Metadata creation - Data Inventory

Metadata will be crucial to the technical and commercial success of TBIF. Metadata creation has commenced with a data inventory being developed from the catalogue of 11,500 information packets so far identified in the supplier research. The data inventory will be available to users through TBIF to encourage the use of industry standard classifications systems for collection and dissemination of information packets. The data inventory in Microsoft ACCESS will consist of at least the following fields: name of information packet, name of supplier, type of supplier, date of collection, date of publication, retail price, data purpose, data format, relevant model fields, upload and maintenance mechanism, and maintenance/update schedule

3.5 Data Upload and Maintenance Models

TBIF will not be responsible for maintenance of content. Table 2 indicates the range of upload and maintenance options that are available in TBIF.

To reduce administrative overheads with management and updates an automated management system based on "use by dates" will be instituted. Each information packet will have a "use by" date which will trigger a query (electronic or otherwise) back to supplier for updated information. Regular "use by" dates will be applied to:

Table 2. TBIF Data Upload and Maintenance Options

Data Upload and Maintenance Option
Upload via API
Electronic lodgement directly by supplier of existing packet
Electronic lodgement by supplier using forms
Electronic lodgement by TBIF management of existing packet (provided to TBIF by supplier in a range of formats)
Electronic lodgement by TBIF using forms
User entered information

contact details; data with set time spans (eg. news and events announcements); regularly updated collections and items; pricing information. URF Information that is older than three years from date of collection will be accordingly flagged in the system, with an archive maintained allowing use of older information. Some data sources (eg. Census data) will have longer flag periods. Reports will have a default flag time of five years.

TBIF will have to have a system for identifying new suppliers, new information packets, and negotiating lodgement practices. The data inventory will identify which packets are updated and how regularly - currently, tests are being conducted on a small number of test data collections. Various access methods (including 'generic' APIs) are also currently being investigated with the Australian Bureau of Statistics – a key data supplier.

3.6 Financial Arrangements – pricing and charging

TBIF has been proposed as a commercial project from the outset – thus research into pricing and charging for its services are necessary if TBIF is to have a life beyond the prototype phase.

There are a range of cost structures involved in the enormous variety of information identified so far. It is vital that the data inventory includes information on how data is currently distributed (price, regularity and format). Main pricing regimes include the following :
- Set price at point of sale for discrete data products (especially publications)
- Price per data set (for URF)
- Price per query generated from URF
- A proportion of the data considered important is provided free of charge
- Subscription arrangements

The most appropriate model appears to involve royalty payments based on secondary distribution arrangements. We are in the process of establishing working systems for ABS and BTR which will be precedent for URF type data. What is clear is that a final system will need to accurately identify: source of each information packet, recording system for when information packet is distributed to a client, price of that information packet, method for distributing income via secondary distribution arrangements.

Without an accurate assessment of what information packets are required (i.e. an accurate description of what products clients are after) it is impossible to start calculating price structures at this stage. The basic system, however, will be based on negotiated price per packet with suppliers and price per TBIF product; this will have to be supported by an income distribution process to ensure that packet suppliers receive appropriate remuneration.

4 A Data Mart case study: Twin Share website

The Twin Share Web site (http://twinshare.crctourism.com.au) which will be included within the TBIF warehouse is an excellent example of a data mart. The purpose of Twin Share (Tourism Accommodation and the Environment) is to assist the development of environmentally sensitive accommodation for tourists. It attempts to achieve this by providing advice, information, procedural assistance and benchmarks for developers of tourism accommodation. Local Governments, developers, environmental agencies, and tourism promoters can use the site to identify the standards that should be met in developing environmentally sensitive accommodation for the tourism industry. The database includes a directory of establishments which meet industry benchmarks. As this directory is compiled, tourists can use the site to identify environmentally friendly accommodation options for their travel experiences.

Currently, the site provides information about the importance of environmental management issues in developing tourism accommodation. This information comes in the form of short papers written by academics and commissioned by the Office of National Tourism. These papers are supplemented by case studies of accommodation establishments which have applied the principles outlined in the essays in unique and successful ways.

Plans are underway to expand the database to include access to:
- Local Government planning regulations and Development approval processes (including building codes)
- Environmental Impacts Statement requirements
- Guidelines from environmental organizations (such as Green Globe)
- Information about training courses etc. (including a bookshop)
- Information about useful contacts in the tourism industry and elsewhere who may assist in developing environmentally friendly accommodation

5 Summary

Tourist information systems are generally designed to cover products/destination marketing. The prototype TBIF data warehouse being developed in this project is national in scope (but covers all industry relevant geographic units) and is focussed to serve the business information needs of the industry rather than those of consumers. As such it is in a very select group of such initiatives in the tourism industry world-wide. Research conducted in the project shows that while there are significant technical issues in creating such data warehouses it is the non-technical issues (mainly financial and organisational) that pose major hurdles.

References

[1] BullSoft: Access and Integration of Distributed, Heterogeneous Information, 5pp, http://dyade.inrialpes.fr/mediation/pub/white_paper.html (1999)

[2] De Lacy. T., Boyd. M.: An Australian Research Partnership Between Industry, Universities And Government: The Cooperative Research Centre For Sustainable Tourism. CRC for Sustainable Tourism, Gold Coast, 8pp (1998)

[3] Dunzendorfer, A., Kung, J., Wagner, R. R.: Data Access to Heterogenous Tourism Information Systems. In: Buhalis, D., Tjoa, A.M., Jafari, J. (eds) Information and Communication Technologies in Tourism 1998, Springer, Vienna, pp 46-54 (1998)

[4] Fesenmaier, D.R., Fesenmaier, J., Parks, D.: ITIMES: a knowledge-based system for the tourism industry. In: Buhalis, D., Tjoa, A.M., Jafari, J. (eds) Information and Communication Technologies in Tourism 1998, Springer, Vienna, pp 162-169 (1998)

[5] Kirkgoze, R., Toja, A.M.: The use of data warehouses as a basis for strategic decision in tourism. In: Buhalis, D., Tjoa, A.M., Jafari, J. (eds) Information and Communication Technologies in Tourism 1998, Springer, Vienna, pp 162-169. (1998)

[6] O'Connor, P.: Electronic Information Distribution in Tourism and Hospitality, CABI Publishing, New York, 173pp (1999)

[7] Sheldon, P.J.: Tourism Information Technology, CABI Publishing, New York, 224pp (1997)

[8] Tunnard, C.R., Haines, P.: Destination Marketing Systems – a new role for tourist board marketing in the information age. Journal of Vacation Marketing, Vol 1, No 4 [at http://www.infocentre.com/news/DMS.htm] (1999)

[9] Werthner, H.: Design Principles of Tourist Information Systems. In: Klein, S. et.al. (eds) Information and Communication Technologies in Tourism 1996, Springer, Vienna, pp 70-77 (1996)

[10] Werthner, H., Klein, S.: Information and Technology – A Challenging Relationship. Springer, Vienna, 323pp (1999)

[11] World Tourism Organisation: Marketing Tourism Destinations Online: Strategies for the Information Age, World Tourism Organisation Business Council, Madrid, 168pp (1999)

Data Management in Tourism: Chaotic and Quixotic

Joseph T. O'Leary
Purdue University
Dept. of Forestry and Natural Resources
W.Lafayette, IN 47907-1200

Abstract

Large quantities of data continue to be collected describing many facets of travel and tourism. These new data are layered on top of extensive collection efforts of the past causing claims of data overload and information and knowledge underload. Using travel demand data and examples from throughout the world, this paper discusses issues and problems encountered at various levels in utilizing data. Further, it points out alternative ways in which these data might be managed to create a knowledge management framework.

Introduction

In the mid-80's, a colleague and I sat in an office of a large government organization to discuss a natural resource project that included using international tourism data. The person indicated a willingness to let us use the longitudinal data, except the organization had gotten into a flap with their provider and were fighting to get their data back. They had never been provided with copies of the data they had paid for, were even concerned that the provider would "lose" the data out of spite, and already knew that some of the original data tapes had been lost or misplaced. These were the data that established estimates for inbound and outbound visitation for a nation, and were used to estimate tourism expenditures and exports. But she did have some copies of the reports and would certainly be willing to share those with us to meet our data needs.

Although my interest in data and secondary analysis had begun in the early 1970's, experiences of having people take data out of desk drawers with little or no documentation has continued to this day. The question that has persisted in my mind has always been why, having spent so much money to collect the data, is there such disregard even in large tourism organizations for the analysis, management and utilization of the data material?

Attempts to address this issue have been quixotic. Looks of concern, terror or indifference cross people's brow as the challenge of addressing the chaos of large quantities of data is considered. But if the argument that knowledge is power and the new currency of the 21st Century is accepted, the mission must be how do we move forward on this need in the tourism industry?

Down the Road Demands

Werthner and Carter (1999:64) have identified an important list of issues and challenges related to IT applications for the next five years:

*Companies have to manage knowledge, which is seen as a primary competitive resource. The permanent development of the work force needs new approaches and methods...
*Adaptive cooperation tools are needed where all different stakeholders can participate at an equal level. These are needed for providing feedback about market behavior, strategic planning, information distribution, product creation and decision making.

The opening observation that some agencies may not be as sensitive as they could be to managing information underscores the importance of the first point above. But collecting or knowing what drawer the data are stored in is not management. It is much more likely that management will be enhanced by changes in organization culture as well as knowledge of and improvement of tools. So it is much more of an IT solution.

Change is a driving force. Important changes in the way in which consumers are involved in travel are taking place. These could be observed in traveler and trip characteristics, expenditures, use of information and technology, and basic changes in behavior. For example, in research being done on eight years of the U.S. International Inflight Survey, Japanese average travel expenditures have ranged from a high of about $3000 in 1990 to a low of around $900 in 1997. There are a broad array of potential reasons for this change, including the Asian economic crisis, rise of the FIT market, and a fundamental change in the nature of the travel experience. For many countries, the Japanese market was viewed as being extremely important and very active marketing programs were put in place to capture a "fair" share. But while we are interested in understanding the change, we are also anxious to assess how the changes contribute to a new strategic view for the future. How do we position travel marketing activities to take into account market change? How do we address the data to move us in that direction?

Tourism Data and Data Fragments

Fesenmaier et. al (1999) presented a knowledge based tourism management framework. With the tremendous growth in data, this was an organized way to present a WEB based knowledge system that incorporated Industry Intelligence, Strategic Market Data, Tools, Collaboration, and Development and Training. While this was a helpful way to outline how a system could be put together, an earlier version of this material identified and discussed the issue of "data fragments," pieces of data that tourism organizations encounter in and outside the organization but which actually and potentially define the information and knowledge environment.

But a larger issue is that the tourism industry is dominated by small and medium size enterprises (SME) (Buhalis 1993; Sheldon 1997) often with limited expertise in analysis and management of data much less the inclusion of sophisticated technology applications for information and knowledge management (KM). In fact, the display of the array of data fragments would be imposing and perhaps overwhelming for most of these organizations.

Sheldon (1997: 205) looked at one piece of this puzzle when she suggested that as technology became less expensive, additional smaller firms would acquire and have it available. Training programs through a variety of public and private providers would improve awareness about the use of software. Gates (1999) has argued that small firms have been placed in a more competitive position because of the availability of software that makes business activity easier and more efficient. But if this addresses the technology and software, it still leaves the emphasis on KM unclear.

Many of the models and discussions about improvements in KM have been presented using large firms as examples of change. In Tom Peters' (1992) discussions about the *nature of change in organizations*, he devoted a number of chapters to the idea of knowledge management, information technology and concepts of networking, pointing out how different firms have increased their adeptness in taking advantage of data and information. A persistent theme in these examples are that some person takes or is given the responsibility of being a "champion," acting as a facilitator between units within the organization, and looking for opportunities to improve utilization through feedback and experience. For a large organization there is the likelihood that a critical mass of personnel will provide an opportunity to lead this agenda. But in the SME environment found in tourism this resource is unlikely to be available. What are the alternatives for the SME?

The Role of Networks

One of the important discussions in the literature related to organizational change has been the growing attention given to networks. Miles (1998) argues that the change from a traditional organization moves us toward network issues that have three dominant themes:

1. the central or host firm that forms the core of the "network" because it usually plays a dominant role as the designer of the product

2. the set of other organizations—usually suppliers, distributors, and customers—that fill out and connect the network in action at any given time
3. the population of organizations from which they may draw their next set of partners (Miles 1998:115)

This description of a network in some ways is consistent with the organizational description provided by Peters that we noted above. In his example we have a person inside a firm who has the responsibility (either self chosen or organizationally tasked) to seek out and make connections for data, information and knowledge development. The products that are developed might initially come from that central person, but ultimately develop from different parts of the organization. However, points 2 and 3 raise other questions for tourism SME's. The network of organizations is represented by many players oriented toward some particular goal or objective. However, that network of players is dynamic, shifting depending on the issue, agenda and passage of time.

Managers have to learn to build teams across organizations that are partnering. They have to manage an effort to pull together a customer, distributor, supplier, and designer into a working partnership that may last only for one major delivery of a product or service. This means learning to collaborate across organizations. (Miles 1998: 116)

The "network firm" that emerges in Miles model takes on "spherical" characteristics. This means it can rotate its' resources to meet the needs of the variety of partners, opportunities, problems and questions that are engaged.

Lipnack and Stamps (1998:126-136) discuss another example where a "teamnet" concept develops for a firm(s). While there are a number of examples, the underlying features for this to work include:

1. Unifying purpose—shared commitment to the same goal, not legalisms, hold the firms together; (*The Purpose of Purpose—Purpose is the glue and driver*)
2. Independent members—each company is different. Each retains its independence while it cooperates with others on specific projects; (*Declaration of Independence: each member has a healthy independence*)
3. Voluntary Links—they communicate extensively and meet often. No one is forced to participate. There are many criss-crossing relationships; (*Link City, Planet Earth: teamnets have many links—expansive relationships among people and extensive connections through technology*)
4. Multiple leaders—Different people and companies lead depending on what needs doing. During any given process, more than one person leads; (*Climbing Through the Teamnet Vines: Fewer bosses, more leaders*)
5. Integrated Levels—people work at many levels within (...) and other partner companies in the teamnet. This network itself is part of the ____business,

which is embedded in the _____ County economy, which contributes to the U.S. industrial base. *(The Hierarchy and the Lower-archy: Teamnets are naturally clumpy and clustered)*

These examples and discussion of networks are important. Although the model works for a large organization, the examples also point toward a mechanism to bring together smaller organizations for collaborations and partnerships that are fleeting or long standing. Also the concept material points out important ingredients or elements that need to be considered to make these network relationships more likely to be successful.

The KM Organization

The network theme can be further developed in at least one other conceptual way. Nonaka and Takeuchi (1995) discuss the challenges of "the knowledge creating company." Of interest to this discussion is the outline of the hypertext organization and the basic framework link to tacit and explicit knowledge (Fig. 1).

Let us review briefly these two concepts. Explicit knowledge represents most of the

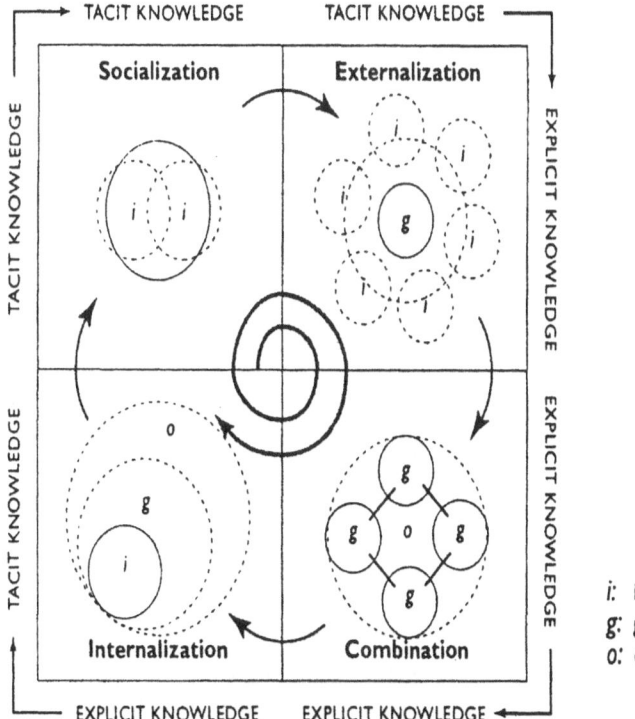

Figure 1. Nonaka and Konno (1998:43)-Sprial Evolution of Knowledge Conversion.

material generally presented as words and numbers that show up in data, reports, manuals or which can be created through the use of formulae (Nonaka and Takeuchi 1995; Nonaka and Konno 1998). On the other hand, tacit knowledge is more personal and difficult to formalize, often residing in the minds and experience of the individual. Nonaka and Konno (1998) point out that there are two dimensions to tacit knowledge. The first is the "know how" often associated with technical knowledge of a subject or area; the second is composed of beliefs, values, norms, etc., that frame the manner in which we look at the world.

In tourism, the material we have experience working with includes both explicit (travel statistics, expenditures, seasonal patterns, etc.) as well as tacit knowledge ("based on my experience..."). However the model presented in Fig. 1 begins to point out issues related to process and the challenge for any organization: how do we bring together the two dimensions to improve what we can know and do within and between groups and individuals? For SME's in tourism it is particularly challenging. Where there are few people in the individual organization, much of the tacit/explicit process must occur across organizations of different shapes and sizes.

The Hypertext Organization

The simplest way to describe the hypertext organization concept outlined by Nonaka and Takeuchi (1995) is to divide the pieces into three layers or pieces (Fig. 2). The first part relates directly to organizing explicit knowledge. It's the place where data is stored and organized. It represents that place where examples like the Tourism Management System or the data fragments discussed above are located. It provides a basis for access as well as synthesizing the data resources. The second or middle layer incorporates the day to day business system activity and parts of the company that carry out those responsibilities. The third layer represents the special project arena where resources and people are brought together using both tacit and explicit knowledge to deal with short term issues and development.

In the three level model, there are several important observations we might make. First, the knowledge base layer contains all the data elements that would normally be described by a data management or marketing information system. It is consistent with the model outlined by Fesenmaier et. al (1999). It is likely the various elements contained are linked and searchable. Second the material on this layer is likely to contain the universe or inventory of all explicit and tacit defining information available to organization members.

Second, there is a high level of permeability between the layers to facilitate knowledge building for various organization dimensions. Day to day, business level

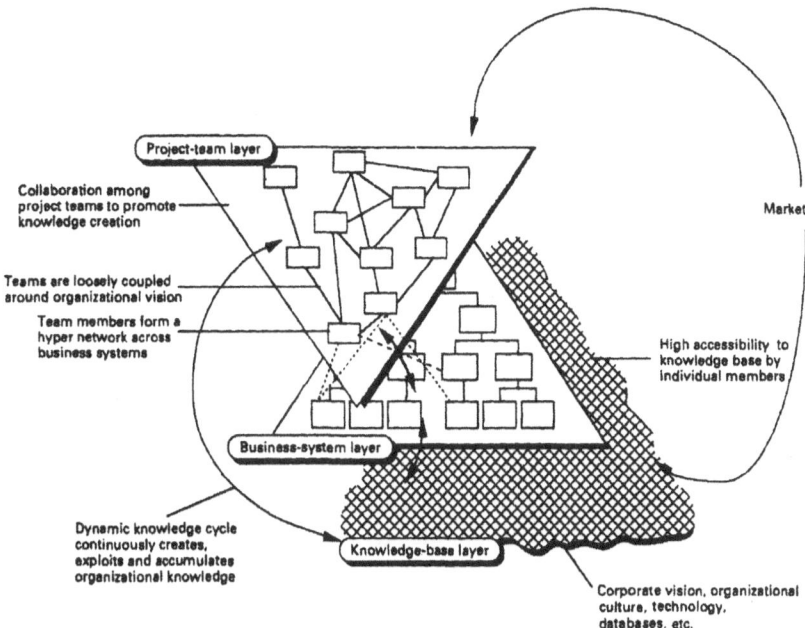

Figure 2. Nonaka and Takeuchi (1995:169)- The Hypertext Organization

activity will readily use the knowledge base layer resources within and between nodes, but use is also reflected in new inputs to the knowledge layer.

Third, Nonaka and Takeuchi (1995) and Nonaka and Konno (1998) paint an important role for the project team layer. Conceptually and in the examples they provide, projects tend to be unique events that last for finite periods. Ideally, a project team member works in this activity for a short, finite period and is removed from other business layer system activities during this time. Issues, problems, new product development, etc. are addressed by bringing together the explicit and tacit knowledge of the team along with what is contained on the knowledge base layer, ultimately creating new explicit and tacit knowledge that is carried away by team members and relayed back to the knowledge base layer. Then referring back to Figure 1, the movement of project team members back to the business layer level allows for the evolution of knowledge to evolve through the spiral process—individual to individual or group; inside/outside the organization.

It should be apparent that the spiraling that goes onto link tacit and explicit knowledge and which links inside/outside, individuals, groups and organizations is consistent with the network structure discussed earlier. But what is so important for the SME structure is that it provides a framework (e.g. "teamnet") in which multiple groups can come together to address some elements of the knowledge development and management agenda.

Discussion and Conclusion

Jalal (1998) in discussing information as an "infinite resource" suggests:

> It is now possible to combine high performing information networks and
> dynamic organization structures to produce an unusual capacity to amass
> raw information from diverse sources, store it in common data bases, distill
> the data into valuable knowledge, and allow units to retrieve it from any
> part of the network (Jalal 1998:19)

But Jalal (1998) also argues that three revolutions are underway that affect
knowledge.

> Exploding complexity is relentlessly decentralizing institutional controls,
> the benefits of collaboration are attracting diverse parties into pockets of
> corporate community, and knowledge invariably leads to a search for
> meaning and purpose (Jalal 1998:253).

These two issues are very important for looking at tourism SME's. On the one hand
we know what is technically possible, but it unlikely that an individual SME will
have the technical skills to take advantage of the potential. There are at least three
options that would address the discussion of network resources above.

One option could be to introduce the public agency as a central cog that initiates
operation of a network. In some places this could be the National Tourism
Organization (NTO) or a state, provincial or regional tourism agency that takes the
responsibility for facilitating the development of the knowledge base layer and then
works with various organizations to maintain and grow the explicit and tacit base.

Another alternative would be to take advantage of university resources and organize
a structure similar to that noted above in that environment. Since most public
tourism agencies are not organized to actually maintain or build a knowledge layer, it
is possible that option one and this second alternative could be blended. But the tacit
nature of the two types of organizations must become a central issue needing
attention. The mission, values, beliefs and norms of the university are not the same
as the NTO. So to make this work, attempts at harmonization must take place.

A third option could be more closely in tune with the plumbing example noted
above. There could be firms that do maintain data bases and where product
development and planning brings them together for short periods of time to address
some particular issue. This is something that already occurs in areas like building
package travel arrangements, but it suggests the need for a knowledge layer that is
dynamic and some vision on the part of the participants on how to make this occur.

There are several very persistent themes in the literature that we should note. In exploring ingredients for this paper, I informally asked a number of people in organizations who were either current or former research directors of tourism or tourism related organizations what they thought was the key to achieving a successful knowledge management program. Every person indicated that it was necessary for the leader to believe in it, to help solicit the resources for the activity, and to regularly share that vision with the organization. This might be the same theme as having a Chief Knowledge Officer (CKO) or Knowledge Champion in the organization. However, it is more challenging with the SME network framework, and perhaps even more so because of the spiral theme we noted earlier where issues and resources change the nature of the partnerships. But some form must still be present to champion the knowledge layer dynamic.

In discussing and comparing differences between organizations that are better able to turn knowledge into action, Pfeffer and Sutton (1999:104) note:

> The difference is in the systems and day-to-day management practices that create and embody a culture that values the building and transfer of knowledge and , most important acting on that knowledge. Leaders of companies that experience smaller gaps between what they know and what they do understand that their most important task is not necessarily to make strategic decisions or, for that matter, any decisions at all. Their task is to build systems of practice that produce a more reliable transformation of knowledge into action.

Building the approaches we are describing means that we have to try things, experiment and recognize that on the way we will make mistakes. SME's are often in a fragile economic position and how mistakes on the way are addressed must be an important concern.

Finally, to do some of the things being discussed there must be aggressive educational and learning programs that show networks in place and show and teach about the WHY and the HOW of hypertext arrangements.

References

Buhalis, Dimitrios. RICIRMS as a strategic tool for small and medium tourism enterprises. Tourism Management (October): 366-378. (1993)

Fesenmaier, D. R.,Leppers, A.W., & J.T. O'Leary. Developing a Knowledge-Based Tourism Marketing Information System. Information, Technology & Tourism. 2(1): 31-44 (1999)

Gates, Bill and Collins Hemingway. Business @ the Speed of Thought: Using a Digital Nervous System. Warner Books. 470pp. (1999)

Halal W.E. Through the Eye of a Needle: The Coming Three Revolutions. In W.E. Halal (ed.) The Infinite Resource: Creating and Managing the Knowledge Enterprise. San Francisco: Jossey-Bass, Inc.) pp. 223-258 (1998)

Lipnack, J. and J. Stamps. The Age of the Network. In W.E. Halal (ed.) The Infinite Resource: Creating and Managing the Knowledge Enterprise. San Francisco: Jossey-Bass, Inc.) pp. 123-138. (1998)

Miles, R.E. The Spherical Network Organization. In W.E. Halal (ed.) The Infinite Resource: Creating and Managing the Knowledge Enterprise. San Francisco: Jossey-Bass, Inc.) pp.111-122. (1998)

Nonaka, Ikujiro and Hirotaka Takeuchi. The Knowledge Creating Company. New York: Oxford University Press. 284pp. (1995)

Nonaka, Ikujiro and Noboru Konno. The concept of "Ba": Building a Foundation for Knowledge Creation. California Management Review. 40(3): 40-54 (1998)

Peters, Tom.. Liberation Management. New York: Alfred A. Knopf. 834pp. (1992)

Pfeffer, J. and R.I. Sutton. Knowing "What" to Do is Not Enough: Turning Knowledge Into Action. California management Review 42(1):83-108 (1999)

Senge, Peter. The Fifth Discipline: the Art and Paractice of the Learning Organization. New York: Doubleday. 423pp. (1994)

Sheldon, Pauline. Tourism Information Technology. New York: CAB INTERNATIONAL. 224pp. (1997)

Tourist Satisfaction Based
Multilevel Intelligent Decision Support System

Bozidar Klicek
Faculty of Organization and Informatics
University of Zagreb
Pavlinska 2, 42000 Varazdin, Croatia
e-mail: bklicek@foi.hr

1 Introduction

In the coming years the quantity of information will grow exponentially, creating real labyrinths where tourists and tourist professionals will have to solve complex problems quickly. In the most far-sighted visions intelligent systems will have an important role [4, 18]. They will be imperatively used as research tools in tourism, but also as integrators of existing technologies and performers of such tasks that until now have only been executed by people. The article illustrates some achievements in the application of intelligent systems in tourism obtained with the project "Intelligent decision support systems in management of complex systems". The aim of the project is to research and create the methodology of developing the second generation of intelligent systems [9, 10]. Next, second generation of intelligent systems, according to F. Hayes-Roth, should overcome the limitations of today's intelligent systems, introducing some new characteristics: "context reusable building blocks, reusable knowledge, high value component functions, composite architecture for multi-task systems, architecture for semantic interoperability, and a small number of domains, which should be attacked persistently [2]".

In the project the emphasis has been put on research as well as creating characteristics above. The goal is to accumulate a great amount of multiproblem domain knowledge, focusing on acquisition of knowledge and its adaptation to the environment. The research covers several overlapping areas. One of the directions is the innovative approach to using knowledge on tourist satisfaction, based on their own experience on visiting a destination, and obtained through a survey.

The following hypotheses are basic to our research in the area of tourism:

1. The knowledge about tourist satisfaction is complex and not entirely researched.
2. The initial knowledge can be efficiently aquired from existing databases and previously done research through knowledge discovery in databases (KDD). The acquired knowledge on tourist satisfaction should have enough reliability to be used on different levels of decision-making, compensating the tourist profesional's lack of knowledge. Thus it will drastically accelerate many tasks where this knowledge is frequently applied.

3. An intelligent system should have features recognizing individual characteristics of particular users.
4. Special searching strategies have to offer a solution created to satisfy individual users. A tourist-advisory intelligent system should be accomodated to local environment and temporal changes. This is achieved through acquistion of additional knowledge in interaction with users and the ability of self-improvement of the existing knowledge.

2 Theoretical background

2.1 Models of satisfaction

Customer satisfaction is the feeling that a product has met or exceeded the customer's expectations [12]. As Otto and Ritchie stated, service quality measures may be insufficient to understand the tourist satisfaction [16]. Subjective, affective and experiential factors comprise a substantial portion of consumer satisfaction with services [12]. To completely understand the satisfaction in the tourist industry many perspectives should be involved [3,6,15,16]. Krulwich demonstrated the applicability of artificial intelligence technology in predicting the life style of customers [11]. Many indirect variables could be sufficient indicators of some other characteristics and could be efficiently used for the purpose of customers classification. The usage of indirect variables, among other features, enables avoiding invasion of privacy. More complex situations are expected in tourism: millions are traveling to temporarily change their life styles. Interaction of different life styles with a new environment does not necessarily have to be efficient. The purpose is to understand this interaction, achieve the maximum satisfaction of tourists offering a firm footing to management in tourist industry.

Although many different aspects of tourist satisfaction has already been researched, our approach was determined with a need for artificial intelligence-oriented research and the availability of knowledge sources. The initial knowledge is acquired through the techniques of KDD from TOMAS research projects on attitudes and consumption of tourists [17]. According to the definition given by Fayyad, knowledge discovery in databases (KDD) is a non-trivial process of identifying valid, novel, potentially useful, and ultimately understandable patterns in data (widely popular term *data mining* denotes a step of the KDD process) [5]. The TOMAS project has its role model in a similar project in Switzerland called *Touristisches Marktforschungsystem Schweiz* [17]. The institute for Tourism in Zagreb has been conducting the project in Croatia from 1986, engaging in it periodically every few years. In our project the results from 1994 were used.

In the TOMAS project the attitudes and expenditure of tourists in Croatia were processed on a sample of 1999 tourists (a slightly larger sample was reduced from technical reasons). In that research various data on tourists and different circumstances in which they spent their holidays in Croatia were acquired. The tourists were asked to express satisfaction with different features of their holiday. Survey data initially contained 123 basic variables that were transformed to new variables to make them more suitable for further research. Variables are divided in eight groups: socio-demographic data d_i, descriptions of destination and its contents p_i, descriptions of the travel and sojourn f_i, experience with former travel in Croatia b_i, organization of travel o_i, expenditures e_i, comparison with other destinations c_i, pair (s_i, ps_i) incorporate degree of satisfaction with some features s_i and importance of this feature for the tourist ps_i, and finally degree of satisfaction with the overall travel in Croatia s_T. Survey data have the following form:

$$d_1, ..., d_{n_1}; p_1, ..., p_{n_2}; f_1, ..., f_{n_3}; b_1, ..., b_{n_4}; o_1, ..., o_{n_5}; e_1, ..., e_{n_6};$$
$$c_1, ..., c_{n_7}; (s_1, ps_1), ..., (s_{n_8}, ps_{n_8}); s_T \qquad (1)$$

Index n_i describes the number of variables in a group. Degrees of satisfaction are expressed numerically with grades ranging from 1 (poor) to 4 (excellent), and the importance of individual features with grades 1 (important) and 0 (unimportant). Variables that are not numerical in type are transformed in numerical ones by translating in the sets $\{0,1\}$ using standard techniques. Besides, after the data mining processing, all numerical variables have been changed from discrete to continuous.

A linear model of total satisfaction was created with several widely used theoretical models as template (linear regression and analytical hierarchy process AHP). The total degree of satisfaction s_T of a tourist is defined as a sum of degrees of satisfaction with an individual feature s_i, multiplied with the degree of importance of the feature ps_i, according to formula:

$$s_T = \sum_{i=1}^{n_8} s_i \cdot ps_i \qquad (2)$$

Example 1. Degrees of satisfaction and degrees of importance with a feature are given for a tourist: $s_1 = 3.2$, $ps_1 = 0.6$ for comfort in accommodation; $s_2 = 2.9$, $ps_2 = 0.7$ for quality of service; $s_3 = 3.8$, $ps_3 = 0.4$ for attractiveness of natural landscape; $s_4 = 2.9$, $ps_4 = 0.3$ for quality of restaurants. Total degree of satisfaction s_T is:

$$s_T = 3.2 * 0.6 + 2.9 * 0.7 + 3.8 * 0.4 + 2.9 * 0.3 = 6.34.$$

The degrees of satisfaction s_i, are defined through functions dependant on several attributes (input variables x_i) that define the holidays, according to the formula:

$$s_j = f_j(x_1, ..., x_n), \text{ where } j = 1, ..., m. \qquad (3)$$

These functions can be exercised through intelligent models with the application of decision trees, rules and neural networks. These functions represent the approximations that describe the data.

In the process of decision support of tourists, their degrees of importance have to be corrected, according to their reaction to the offered temporal solutions. The corrections are made according to the formula:

$$ps_i(k+1) = ps_i(k) + \Delta ps_i(k) \qquad (4)$$

The degree of importance $ps_i(k)$ marks the preference of feature s_i at step k, and $\Delta ps_i(k)$ marks the correction for the preference. Correction $\Delta ps_i(k)$ is defined empirically in an intelligent module.

2.2 Application of intelligent systems

All the previous articles in this field have not looked into specificity of decision-making process in tourism. Likewise, little is known about the process of concealing tourist agents [8]. That is why the process of decision making is modeled like general models. A general expert systems model called UNIK-SES, is used to advise clothes buyers and very thoroughly encompasses all decision-making steps [14]. Moreover, several examples are related to the application of neural networks designed to foresee the travel of tourists from Japan to Hong Kong [13]. Genetic algorithms are applied to the allocation of tourist resources [7].

A system with such features in unlikely to have its ideal in only one of the few already-existing examples. Creating the architecture of one such system and its physical prototype means a peculiar contribution. The basic principles of the system are described in the article already presented at the ENTER 98 conference [10]).

3 Research methods

The research process is carried out in the following way:

1. Execution of the KDD in data concerning the degree of tourist satisfaction.
2. The developed knowledge is analyzed through the application of several techniques and the accuracy of the created models is assessed.
3. Intelligent models are used in an experimental simulation of increasing the tourist degree of satisfaction.
4. The creation of experimental decisions support systems on different hierarchy levels that use the created intelligent models.

On a sample of N=1999, described with 215 variables, KDD is executed. This sample covers typical tourists in Croatia, surveyed in 26 tourist destinations and 93 facilities from July to August 1994 [17]. Program tools that were used are a family of commercial products of Attar Company [1]. These are tools for data mining, lined-up in evolutionary order: Analyzer (neural networks and decision trees), Profiler (decision trees) and Miner (decision trees). The more recent tools have more advanced features, but are also more complicated to use. To model intelligent systems XpertRule (also by Attar) was used. That has advanced features of decision tree integration with rules, fuzzy logic, genetic algorithms and procedural programming.

Three techniques of data mining are used with working parameters:

a) Decision tree induction towards an optimized algorithm (Profiler), and the parameter with a minimum of 60 examples in a leaf. All samples are for learning.
b) Decision tree induction with the use of entropy measure (Analyzer), with a minimum of 40 examples in a leaf, 70% of data for learning (b_1), and 30% for testing (b_2).
c) Neural network learning with the model of backpropagation (Analyzer), learning coefficient 0.6, momentum 0, stopping at RMS 0.001, or average deviation 5%, or at 50 learning cycles. The number of hidden layers is 1, and the number of neurons in each layer is set by an algorithm. Transfer function is sigmoid.

Seventy-three models are created. 32 pairs of models are related to a) degree of satisfaction with a feature, and b) importance of that feature. The next 11 models are related to expenditure. The models for variables s_i are created: (accommodation features) 1 - equipment of facility; 2 - comfort in accommodation; 3 - quality of service; 4 - quality of catering in facility; 5 - attractiveness of immediate facility surroundings; 6 - value for money (facility); (destination features) 7 - attractiveness of natural landscape; 8 - climate and weather; 9 - picturesquesness of town; 10 - personal safety; 11 – value for money (destination); 12 - accessibility of town; 13 - service along roads; 14 - local transportation; 15 - postal and telephone services; 16 - attractiveness of micro-environment; 17 - cultural events; 18 - signs marking attractions; 19 - catering in restaurants; 20 - diversity of restaurants; 21 – entertainment; 22 - sports facilities; 23 – excursions; 24 - walking and hiking; 25 – shopping; 26 - suitability for conferences; 27 - family holidays; 28 - short break; 29 – information; 30 - friendliness of population; 31 - knowledge of foreign languages. Variables 32 – 62 are importance of features 1-31 ps_i, respectively. Further variables are expenditure: 63 - cost of package tour; 64 - cost of package tour per person per day; 65 - round trip travel (not included in package); 66 - accommodation; 67 - accommodation per person per day; 68 - trip travel; 69 - local transportation; 70 - food; 71 - shopping; 72 - cultural events, sport, entertainment; 73 – other. (The numbered identifications of variables are used in figure 2 for category assignment on the x-axis.)

172

All models are verified on the data set for learning (cases a, b_1 and c_1), as well as on the set of data for verification (cases b_2 and c_2). Verification of accuracy is realized through the function of average deviation [1, 5]).

The created models serve for judging whether or not it is justified to build an intelligent system for holiday recommendation. Our ambitious was to establish how accurately the tourists have chosen the holiday destination and facilities. Simulation made it possible to determine satisfaction as if the tourists had sojourned **in the same way** in any other of 93 tourist facilities. The ratio of satisfaction improvement I_r was monitored as $s_{Tbest}/s_{Tchosen}$: the ratio of the best possible holidays and the ones chosen.

Tourist satisfaction intelligent models are the basis of decision support on different levels, three examples of which are described here:

1. Individual: recommendation at the intelligent tourist agency [9, 10]
2. Local: destination management
3. National: optimal allocation of tourists and promotional activities.

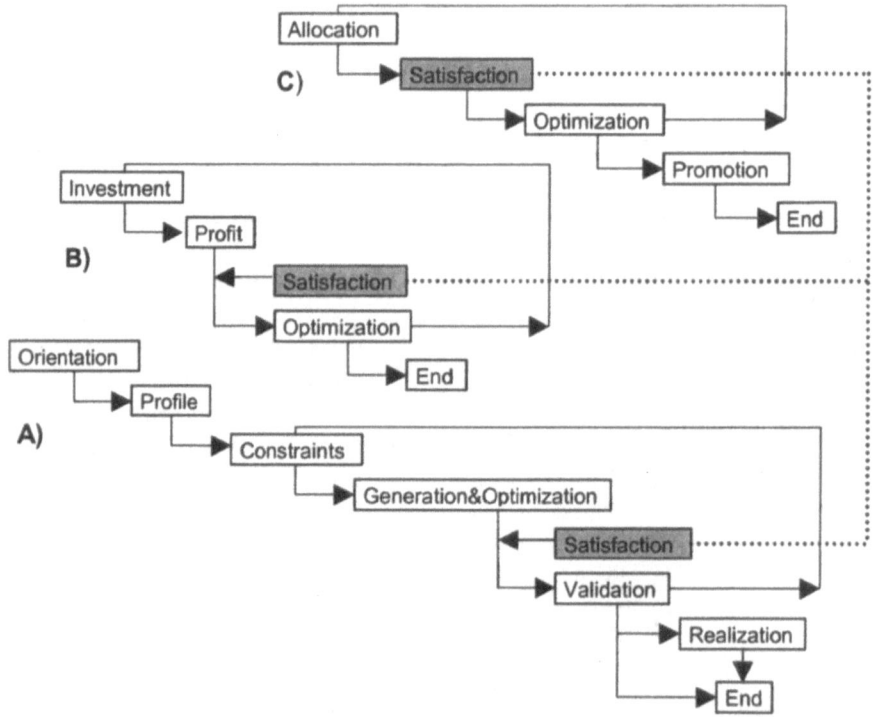

Fig. 1. Architecture of multilevel intelligent decision support on: a) intelligent tourist agency level, b) destination level, c) national level. Knowledge base *Satisfaction* is common.

The architecture of that multilevel system contains a unique knowledge base *Satisfaction* (logical or physical), and different applications that use this knowledge base (figure 1). For the purpose of research the knowledge base is realized as an module in XpertRule tool, but also as a dynamic link library. The basic knowledge base can also contain supplements and variations of the basic knowledge.

Application in the intelligent tourist agency

Generic architecture of the intelligent tourist agency consists of a subsystem for problem-solving and a subsystem for communication with the user (an intelligent multimedia system [9, 10]). Subsystem for problem-solving consists of knowledge from domain of tourism, partially acquired from survey data through data mining techniques. Problem-solving subsystem consists of databases on characteristics of destinations and their contents. Intelligent multimedia subsystems for communication consist of intelligent modules with knowledge of multimedia presentation creation and multimedia databases.

A tourist picks the destination with the aid of Intelligent Tourist Agency, a PC intelligent multimedia application [9]. A virtual agent represents a user friendly interface, obtaining socio-demographic data from tourists, helping them to express their attitude and constraints concerning the offered destinations. The temporal solutions are created, optimized in accordance with the user's total satisfaction. The temporal solutions are presented as multimedia presentations.

1. *Orientation.* Setting the preferences for communication (language, etc.).
2. *Demography.* Obtaining demographic data from users and their basic wishes.
3. *Constraints.* Identification of user's constraints.
4. *Generation/optimization.* Creation of the degree of satisfaction for every destination from its characteristics and preferences profile. The most suitable potential solutions are chosen.
5. *Validation.* The most suitable solutions are presented with the aid of personally created multimedia presentations. The presentation emphasizes general characteristics and significant differences of the solution. The user validates the offered solutions. In case of acceptance the phase of realization follows. In case of non-satisfaction, phase 3 follows, in which preferences are corrected and new demands obtained. In case of failure phase 7 follows.
6. *Realization.* Phase of realization of the chosen variant. Phase 7 follows.
7. *End.* Saving the data of the decision process and finish.

The described model is static and simple (picking a destination and one of several hotels there with a variation in the way holidays are spent). However, this research also considers the more complex and dynamic models. The data of the decision processes are data mined and the obtained knowledge is used to improve the system.

Application on the destination level

The model of satisfaction is used to define the priority of investment with a view to improving some characteristics of destination that will obtain both high profit and high satisfaction of tourists. We also used the function of dependency of the change of features of facilities on investments. Genetic algorithms are used for optimization.

Application on the national level

One question is how a tourist from a typical market should be optimally allocated to national tourist resources to be maximally satisfied and to obtain full capacity. The other question is what kind of promotion should be applied to obtain this goal. We use the models of the satisfaction of users, databases of tourist capacities, database of tourists from the market, and tourists' promotion preferences. Different profiles of tourists are informed on different features redirecting them to different locations.

4 Results

As a result 73 different models with variations (trees, neural networks) are created. Knowledge obtained is also remarkable – it consists of 1737 leaves, equivalent to the same number of rules. The obtained knowledge is a new direction for a complete understanding of satisfaction in tourism.

The degree of satisfaction during holidays is dependent on tourist socio-demographic characteristics, characteristics of destination and their configuration (arrangement). The degree of importance is also variable and changes according to the feature of destinations. While neural networks represent knowledge without easy understandability, the explicitness of decision trees is their advantage. To completely understand the knowledge in a decision tree, certain effort is necessary.

Table 1. Summary of accuracy of different models.

Average deviation %	a_1) Profiler	b_1) Tree Training	b_2) Tree Verify	c_1) Neural Net Training	c_2) Neural Net Verify	The best models
Minimum	0.7	2.7	2.7	1.2	1.2	0.7
Maximum	10.19	10.19	19.36	13.3	20.4	10.19
Mean	6.12	10.04	11.07	6.65	8.65	5.90

The accuracy of different models is highly acceptable. Survey data could be very efficiently used in creating intelligent models of tourist satisfaction. The summary of accuracy of different models is given in Table 1 and Fig. 2. Empirical research of the accuracy of different methods in data mining and making theoretical explanation based on that research is a great challenge. Inaccuracy of models is a consequence of a) granularity of satisfaction degrees (only grades 1, 2, 3, and 4 for satisfaction, and grades 0 and 1 for importance), b) inaccuracy of models, and c) variations of individual tourists. The inaccuracy of models has consequences for the recommendation strategy. The intelligent tourist advisor can not immediately offer a ready-made solution, but, in interaction with the user, gradually needs to recognize their individual differences and offer improved solutions. Our first findings, that still need to be confirmed, show that if the average deviation of the model is less than 2%, there is no need for interaction – the solution is (almost) optimal. If the average deviation is greater than 2% and smaller than 10%, the interaction is small. If the deviation is greater than 10% and smaller than 20%, the interaction will be high. If the average deviation is greater than 20%, intelligent advisor is not appropriate. The proper solution is a system with ordinal menus.

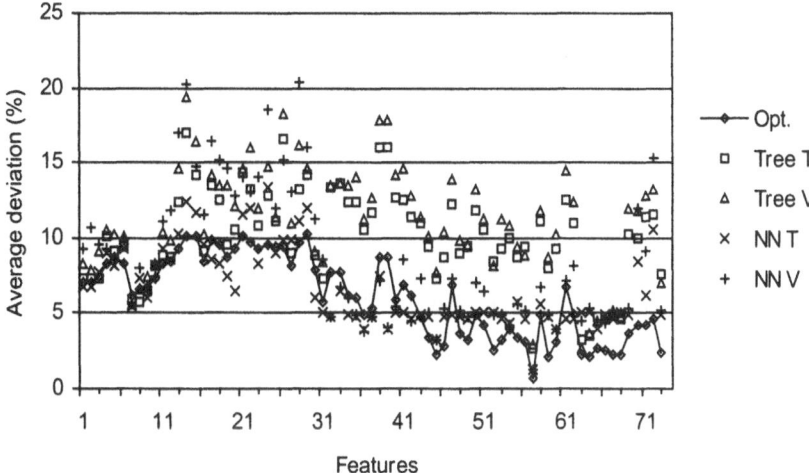

Fig. 2. Accuracy of feature models presented with different techniques. (Opt. - optimized decision tree, Profiler; Tree T and V – decision tree, training and verification; NN T and V – neural network, training and verification.

The models are applied in order to find the best holiday solution for 234 tourists choosing from 93 facilities in 26 destinations. The possible improvement of their satisfaction in comparison with the already chosen holidays is remarkable (figure 3). Only 10% of tourists pick their holidays quite well (part of curve to point A on figure 3). Therefore, the improvement of their satisfaction can not exceed 25%. For the other 60% of tourists the possible improvement of satisfaction ranges from 25% to 60% (curve A-B). The greatest improvement for 30% of tourists is expected from 60 to 160%.

Further research will encompass validation *in vivo* of an intelligent tourist agency and application of decision support system in concrete problem solving and decision making.

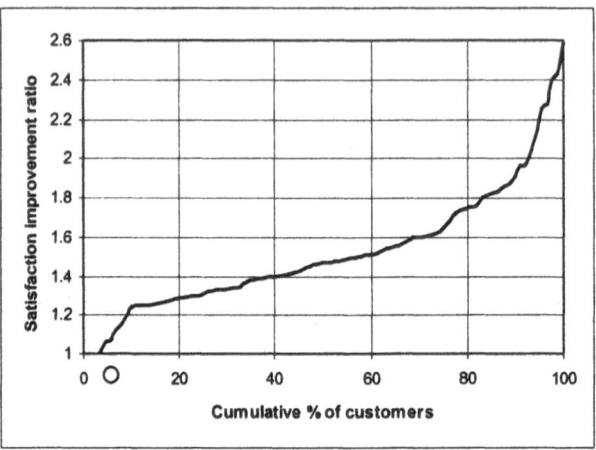

Fig. 3. Satisfaction improvement

The models are applied in order to find the best holiday solution for 234 tourists choosing from 93 facilities in 26 destinations. The possible improvement of their satisfaction in comparison with the already chosen holidays is remarkable (figure 3). Only 10% of tourists pick their holidays quite well (part of curve to point A on figure 3). Therefore, the improvement of their satisfaction can not exceed 25%. For the other 60% of tourists the possible improvement of satisfaction ranges from 25% to 60% (curve A-B). The greatest improvement for 30% of tourists is expected from 60 to 160%.

Further research will encompass validation *in vivo* of an intelligent tourist agency and application of decision support system in concrete problem solving and decision making.

5 Conclusion

The approach offered has made contributions in two areas:

Information technology (artificial intelligence). The application of intelligent systems in tourism shows great potential. We demonstrated ability for achieving systems of high performance applying a relatively small number of artificial intelligence techniques. The secret lies in correct modeling of desired features with a well-thought-out combination of artificial intelligence techniques and not in the techniques themselves.

Tourism. Techniques of knowledge discovery represent a strong research tool which is capable of achieving very precise models of the degree of tourist satisfaction and developing knowledge that until now has not been accessible through standard statistical research methodologies. Creation of computing models and their application in tourist recommendation in destination choosing could achieve significant improvement in their satisfaction with the product. By simply applying this knowledge, according to the simulation, the degree of satisfaction with the holiday could be improved by 25% to 160% for 90% of tourists. That is a significant challenge for tourist industry and offers very optimistic promising prospects to information technology.

Naturally, a full confirmation of ideas and results would require additional research, like: validation of the approach on a larger amount of data, testing the models in real conditions, system optimizing, development of primary explicit knowledge on satisfaction and achieving flexibility of the system.

References

1. <URL:http://www.attar.com/>
2. Blanchard, D.: *AI looks to the future: AAAI '96, Portland, 4-8 August 1996.* Expert Systems, 13 (4), 306-308 (1996).
3. Chadee, D. D., Mattsson J.: An empirical assessment of customer satisfaction in tourism. Service Industries Journal, 16 (3), 305-320 (1996).
4. Doyle, J., Dean, T.: Strategic Directions in Artificial Intelligence. AI Magazine, 18 (1), 87-101 (1997).
5. Fayyad, U.M., Piatetsky-Shapiro, G., Smyth, P., Uthurusamy, R.: Advances in Knowledge Discovery and Data Mining. MIT Press (1996).
6. Gnoth, J.: Tourism and motivation and expectation formation. Annals of Tourism Research, 24 (2), 283-304 (1997).
7. Hurley, S., Moutinho, L., Witt, S. F.: Genetic algorithms for tourism marketing. Annals of Tourism Research, 25 (2), 498-514 (1998).
8. Klenosky, D.B., Gitelson, R. E.: Travel agents destination recommendations. Annals of Tourism Research, 25 (3), 661-674 (1998).
9. Klicek, B.: *"Intelligent System Models and Procedures for Personalised Multimedia Presentation".* Media Reasearch, 4 (2), 173-198 (in Croatian) (1999).
10. Klicek, B.; Vidovic, S.: "Complex intelligent systems: Case study of intelligent tourist agency". In: Buhalis D. et al. *Information and Communication Technologies in Tourism.* Springer, Wien, New York (1998).
11. Krulwich, B.: Lifestyle Finder. AI Magazine, 18 (2), 37-46 (1997).
12. Lamb, C., Hair, J., McDaniel, C.: Marketing. South-Western College Publishing, Cincinnati (1998).
13. Law, R., Au, N.: A neural network model to forecast Japanese demand for travel to Hong Kong. Tourism Management, 20 (1), 89-97 (1999).
14. Lee, S.-K., Lee, J.-K.: Expert Systems for Marketing. From Decision Aid to Interactive Marketing. In: Liebowitz, J. (ed.).: The Handbook of Applied Expert Systems. CRC Press, pp. 29.1-29.15 (1998).
15. Lounsbury, J.W., Polik, J. R.: Leisure Needs and Vacation Satisfaction. Leisure Sciences, 14 (2), 105-119 (1992).
16. Otto, J. E., Ritchie, J. R. B.: The service experience in tourism. Tourism Management, 17 (3), 165-174 (1996).
17. Weber S., Mikacic, V., Radnic, A.., Vrdoljak-Salamon, B.: Attitudes and Consumption of Tourists in Croatia TOMAS '94. Institute for Tourism, Zagreb (in Croatian) (1994).
18. Weld, D. S., (ed.): The Role of Intelligent Systems in the National Information Infrastructure. AI Magazine, 16 (3): 45-64 (1995).

Cooperative Techniques And Tools To Increase The Quality Of The Software In Tourist Companies

S. Gálvez, A. Guevara, J.L. Caro and A. Aguayo
{galvez,guevara,jlcaro,aguayo}@lcc.uma.es
Dpt. Lenguajes y Ciencias de la Computación
Escuela Universitaria de Turismo
University of Málaga, Spain

Abstract

In this article we present methods for the analysis and design of Cooperative Object-oriented Information Systems. These methods enable companies to achieve competitive advantages, as well as increase the quality of software development. In addition, they involve users much more in the development of Tourist Information Systems. In order to accomplish the foregoing, it would be necessary to re-examine business organisational structure as well as the methods used in the development of Information Systems (IS).

We introduce a set of cooperative tools, based on a powerful and user-friendly graphic interface that facilitates user participation in new stages of system construction and in re-engineering processes.

In order to illustrate the characteristics of these tools, we will especially focus on the database definition tool: CDB (Cooperative Database). We show the need for cooperation between users and, with an example applied to the management of a Golf Club, the user-friendly character of the interface. This example will also enable us to see the power of this tool for the automatic generation of relational databases, and its radically different philosophy when compared to most database assisted design tools.

1 Introduction

One of the aims of any company in the tourism sector (travel agencies, accommodation, guide agencies, etc.) is to have available high quality software for the management of their Information Systems, i.e., they have to make sure the automated processes efficiently manage the different tasks they are supposed to carry out. This is mandatory in order to offer top quality service oriented to satisfying the client.

Currently, most small and medium-sized companies are not satisfied with the results obtained with the software programs they work with, for several reasons [15]. Among these the following may be highlighted: i) the system requirements of the business have not been fully implemented; ii) the standard programs installed do not 100% cover the specific requirements of the company's system; and iii) the interface is not user-friendly and so users do not feel comfortable working with it.

The SICUMA research group (Cooperative Information Systems of the University of Málaga) is currently developing a project whose objective is to change the approach to the development of Inform tion Systems (IS) for tourist sector companies and organisations. Our fundamental objective is to apply CSCW methods (Computer Supported Cooperative Work) to the development of IS to increase the quality and reliability of business information systems. In order to accomplish this, the aim is to fully engage the users themselves in the design and construction of the information system they will later work with, in order to diminish long-term costs and increase the competitiveness of the companies in the sector. The present work is geared in this direction.

Section 2 presents the basic characteristics of the Cooperative Methodology and Tools needed to implement the foregoing in practice, create higher quality software, and be more user-friendly for the final user. Section 3 focuses on the most important of these tools: the CDB (Cooperative Database), whose function is to provide the necessary mechanisms for users to cooperate with each other regarding the decisions about what data they want to have stored in the IS. Simultaneously, an operational database is automatically created, which can then be fine-tuned by IT engineers, should this be required. Section 4 shows a real example of managing the administration of a Golf Club (the case has been simplified for reasons of space), and illustrates how this can be done in a direct and simple way by use of our methodology, and by applying the basic knowledge any user has who is familiar with this kind of business. Finally, Section 5 deals with the conclusions and the relevance of our methodology for the development of software applications.

2 Co-operative methodology: Cooperative and Object-Oriented C.A.S.E. Tools

In order to produce applications with a minimum degree of quality, the IS department of any tourist company has to apply a Software Engineering Methodology. Our work considers the evolution from Structured Methodology to Cooperative Methodology [7,8,16], emphasising at each point how data can be created in a cooperative way.

The philosophy behind Cooperative Methodology differs from any other currently applied in business IS. In most current methods, the development of an IS is carried out entirely by specialist personnel from the IS department, and is based on eliciting the needs of managers and users, as well as on viability studies. Our methodology seeks the participation of all the members of the company: managers, users, IS engineers, and consultants.

All these people have to agree about the best way to split the IS into several subsystems that can be handled more easily. The interrelationships existing between such subsystems requires that the development methods are applied cooperatively. The cooperative tools [9] that will be described further on, will be used in each subsystem and then the outcome will be integrated to set up the global system.

Equally, we propose a radical change in the analysis and design of the system: up to now IS departments have been in charge of carrying out the design, whereas in our proposal, the users do this in a cooperative way. This is achieved by implementing cooperative and object-oriented tools which assist users in analysing and designing their system while maintaining control over the entire process. Such tools should have powerful but friendly user interfaces capable of handling the transfer of information between the different subsystems of the final IS.

Finally, constructing and testing the system will be done simultaneously with the cooperative creation of a set of instructions that will allow the final user the optimum use of the system. This means that code will be generated, databases implemented, and integration tests carried out. Therefore, this stage has to be done co-operatively by all the agents involved in the analysis process, and will be assisted to a great extent by automated computer processes.

This entire methodology should be supported by tools that should embrace two important features: on the one hand, they should be user-friendly, because it will be a tool for final users; and on the other hand, they should have powerful development potential.

The SICUMA group is developing a coordinating and cooperative module [10,11] based on this methodology. The key element in this module is the Cooperative Data Dictionary [9] which allows us to carry out the entire process in a cooperative way, and handle all the information about the objects described in the system. The functions carried out by this module are:
- Controlling the user's work.
- Use of the object-oriented paradigm to determine user requirements.
- Cooperative consolidation of the data introduced by users.
- Automatic consistency control during all the design processes.
- Integration of the different sub-IS designed by users.
- Generation of a relational model based on the user's data needs.
- Coordination between data models and process models.
- Code generation from the merging and description of primitive processes.

In order to manage all these tasks, the coordinating module is made up of a set of strongly interconnected tools, all of which make use of the Cooperative Data Dictionary. These tools are:
- CDFD; a cooperative data flow diagram tool.
- CDB; a tool for cooperatively designing the database.
- CSCR; a tool for designing the visual appearance of the application.
- CREP; a tool for generating reports.
- CDD; the cooperative data dictionary.
- CGT; a code generator.

The purpose of our work is to develop the set of tools that make up the cooperative, coordinating, object-oriented module. We also focus part of our attention on the workflow methods needed to facilitate the distribution of tasks in the cooperative design of the IS [2,3]. At present, we have a graphic interface prototype as well as the CDFD and CDB prototypes which allow the user to specify elements and later classify and group them by areas of interest. In the following section we describe the basic characteristics of the CDB.

3 Cooperative Tool for Database Design

One of the main elements of any Tourism Information System (TIS) is the database. The role of the database is not only to store information regarding the different elements of the system (clients, items consumed, expenses, etc.), but to establish relationships between them which will enable obtaining useful reports [12]: statistics on the months with more clients, departments with a deficit, control of resource availability, etc.

Therefore, among the tools mentioned in the previous section, the CDB -- a cooperative tool for the definition of the database -- has the greatest significance.
The CDB follows the Cooperative Methodology philosophy, as it promotes the shared participation of users who, after all, are the ones who know best what data they need and how it should be related. Once achieved, the aim is to automatically create a useful, high quality database. The CDB is based on three main ideas [6]:
- It should be easy to use for designing the necessary data elements.
- Elements used by multiple users have to be designed in cooperation.
- The engineering aspects of the database are transparent to the user.

The way the CDB works is based on the Forms Semantic Data Model (FSM) that handles all the operations carried out on the CDB, and converts them into direct actions on the working database. Tools like Oracle Developer/2000 forms [14], Form Tool 97 and GeneXus [1] also enable the creation of applications and prototypes based on forms, taking as a starting point *previously* and directly built databases [5]. By contrast, CDB, with the support of FSM, builds up the database automatically, and indirectly, as the forms are being designed. With this philosophy, CDB proves to be such a simple tool that any user of the TIS can manage it and, at the same time, is so powerful that it can be used to create the entire design of the database. Figure 1 compares both paradigms. The choice of the form concept as a means to express data needs is in consonance with the current trends in data exchange, such as the one proposed in [13] and [17].

The CDB tool simulates the production of forms on the computer, which will be filled in later and stored in a file, taking advantage of computing power at each stage to avoid insertion of redundant data, and speed up data access. The users interact with the CDB and design forms electronically, in a way that is not so very different to what they do when they have to design them to order them from the printers. The definition of a form by a given user generates part of the database in an automatic and transparent way, so that when another user fills in a form with specific data (in the system validation stage), such data will be stored in the database created. With this method, we can make it easy for users to describe the information they need for their work without having to know anything about databases.

According to the working methodology we propose, the people defining the forms are the final users, who are responsible for the subsystems created during the first stage (customer service, invoicing, payrolls, personnel, accounting, marketing and publicity, etc.). The final users can contribute much valuable knowledge regarding how to attain important competitive advantages in the sector. Given that the data needs of each user have points in common, the definitions of forms cannot be done in an totally independent way, but rather team-work is necessary so that the forms created are consistent with each other. Thus, the need for cooperation appears, which is based on the following points:

- Use of a single database common to all designs.
- All information referring to the same entity, but appearing in two different forms, has to be consistent.
- The CDB has to maintain this data consistency when changes are made in data shared by several forms.
- Each user has his/her own view of the data, regarding structure as well as the amount of data.

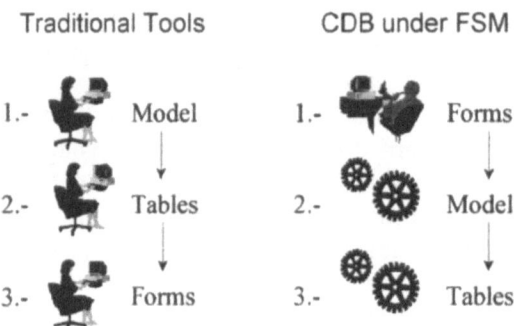

Fig. 1. With CDB, the users themselves define the forms and thanks to FSM the database is automatically generated.

In this working method, the analysis and design stages are closely related, because users can use the forms they have created to introduce data. This means that the actual structure of the form is a preliminary design or prototype which can be used to validate the system before proceeding to its final construction.

Among the most interesting characteristics of the forms users would be able to design, we can mention:

- The possibility of including multimedia elements, mainly digitised pictures, which would ensure handling tasks such as making customised electronic cards in hotels, attaching digitised photocopies, etc.
- The possibility of arranging all the forms belonging to a certain type according to different criteria, in this way speeding up searches and statistics.
- The possibility of including all types of control mechanisms in the data introduced: correct VAT values, non-empty ID/Passport fields, etc.
- Transferring data from one form to another.
- Inserting repetition lines to show, for example, invoices with several service lists, multiple work reports, etc.

The FSM automates the conversion of forms into a relational database, which enables making use of powerful Database Management Systems, such as Oracle, Informix, Ingres, etc.; or even others for home use such as Access, Paradox, Xbase, etc. This conversion is carried out based on:

- The specification of data shared between forms.
- The relationship between a form and the repetition lines (sets of fields that can appear more than once in a given form. For example, the tasks to be carried out by a given employee) that it contains.
- The association of attributes with such relationships.

In the following section we will see a practical example of how to apply these techniques to the creation of a database for a Golf Club. In the example, it is worth paying particular attention to the fact that the database (which follows a relational model) is automatically generated from the forms, and not the other way around.

4 Use of CDB in a Golf Club

In this section we will show the great versatility of our model to generate a database. We will focus on the database needed for the management of a Golf Club. We want to store information about players, game tickets issued for each player, as well as to keep a record of the Agencies the Club has made special deals with to offer discounts to clients coming to the club via such Agencies [4].

The only task the user has to do is to define the forms that would allow him/her to manage and handle the information he/she wants. For example, the user can begin by designing a form to record basic data about the Club members and the more regular clients. This form would look like the one in Figure 2.

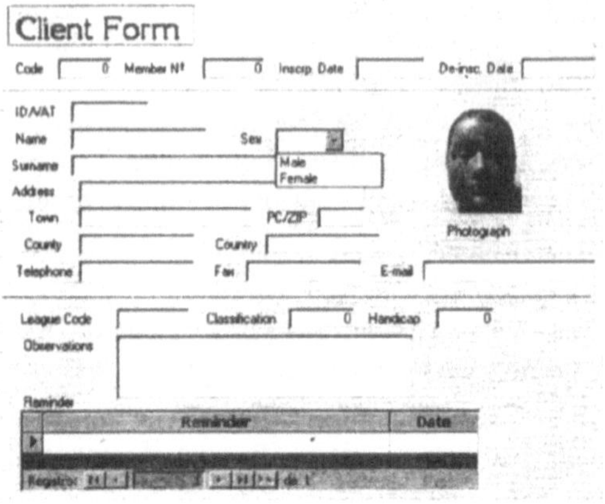

Fig. 2. Example of Client's form showing the different elements making up a form.

By default, the fields are considered as text, so that the size of the box defined by the user will determine the maximum number of characters that can be included in the field. Also, all types of basic data are accepted, such as date, Yes/No values, and numbers with or without decimals. On the other hand, in our example, the list called Reminder has the role of centralizing information regarding expiry dates for membership fees, prize-giving dates, lost objects, etc. When creating the fields that constitute the form, it is possible to associate data validation rules with them. In this example, the field Sex can only contain the value "Male" or "Female". The rules can be as complex as one wants them to be, although only the simpler ones can be specified graphically, as in the case of Sex.

In a similar way, agency data will be stored in another form which, once designed by the user, will look like the one in Figure 3. The Agencies are companies (hotels mainly) that send those clients who want to play golf to our Club. Such clients are directly billed by the Agency and, at the end of the month, the Golf Club bills the Agency for all such clients, but applying a special rate. The tariff applied depends on the particular agreement reached with the Agency. The higher the number of clients sent by the Agency, the higher the discount our Club will apply which will be reflected in the invoice. The list entitled Range indicates how much will be billed to the Agency for each client sent, and these are established depending on the number of clients the Agency sent.

These two forms are independent of each other. A different procedure is applied to Tickets issued at the moment a Client demands a service. The Tickets form has some basic data that includes: the name of the Ticket holder, who will be a Client of the Club, which therefore should have an entry in the Clients form with the structure that we saw in Figure 2. Similarly, the Tickets include some service lists where we can

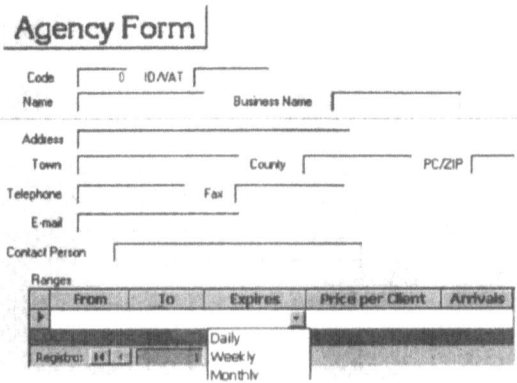

Fig. 3. Example of Form.

specify the Agency that issued the service (it is quite normal for several Clients to come from the same Agency to play golf together, and it is necessary to record each of them separately and correctly bill the Agency). This Agency must necessarily be in the Agencies Form. Those situations in which data from other forms appears in a current form is marked with a different colour, because forms are designed in such a way that a different colour is assigned to each type which helps to identify the exact data source. Thus, the Ticket would look something like the one in Figure 4.

We can see that the Ticket holder is a Client who must exist, as such, in the Clients form. The CDB makes this situation explicit by highlighting the Client's data with a box in a dark colour. It is also possible to create a new Client entry by directly filling in his/her data in the Ticket form. Equally, each service list contains a data sequence which includes Client and Agency. Again, a dark colour in the heading indicates that

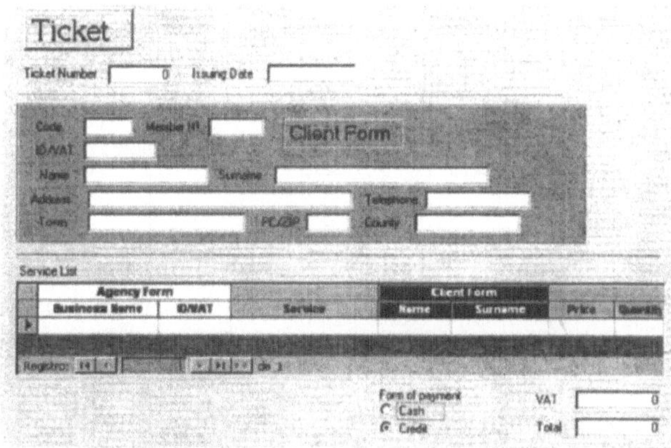

Fig. 4. Example of a Tickets' form.

186

the data is coming from an already existing entry, either in Clients or Agencies. The user indicates the type of form generated by each data block by means of the toolbar provided in the CDB. Also, the different colours allocated to data about the Client in the Ticket and in the service lists, indicate that, although both come from some entries in Clients, they are probably different.

In this way, when a user wants to fill in data in the Ticket form, the Management System of the Database will help him/her select those entries from Clients and Agencies from which data could be taken, so preventing inserting inconsistant or irrelevant information. Also, via an relational process, it is possible to automatically update the discount range to be applied to a given Agency.

From the cooperative point of view, each of these forms could have been designed by different users, and so new forms can be created based on the designs already made by these other users.

In this way, once all the forms have been designed, a database will be created automatically that will reflect the structure chosen by the user to interrelate the different data blocks. By means of this FSM model technology, a relational scheme like that shown in Figure 5 is created automatically.

These forms can also be used to introduce new data into the already created database. This allows us to view the form from two different perspectives: one oriented to the design of the form itself, and another oriented to filling in the form.

The CDB makes the creation of reports an easy, intuitive and flexible process, because the FSM model supporting it makes it possible to automatically rearrange the data introduced in the forms.

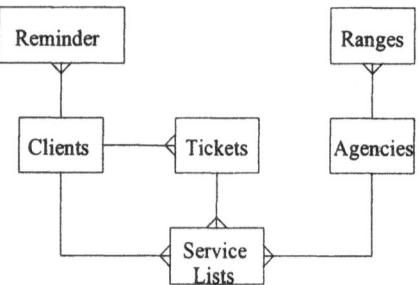

Fig. 5. ER Diagram automatically generated by the FSM from the forms in figures 2, 3 and 4.

The creation of a report that lets us know all the service lists in which an agency appears is as simple as shown in Fig. 6. The key to this report resides in the use of the sentence "Service list" of the Ticket, which allows the CDB to recognise that the data we want to visualise is that which appears in each ticket. Note that this sentence coincides with the sentence appearing in the Ticket in Fig. 4. We see that it is possible to introduce information regarding the Ticket itself in each Service list (number and issuing date), because the FSM establishes the relationships to access such data.

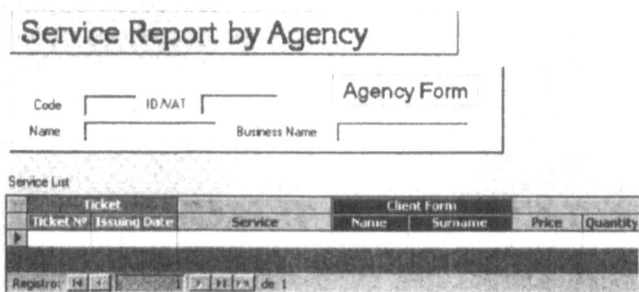

Fig. 6. The information included in the different forms can be automatically restructured.

5. Conclusions

The research project that we are developing in the School of Tourism's SICUMA group at the University of Málaga, is novel in the sense that it turns the way Information Systems are designed in tourist companies and organisations upside down. This new approach increases the quality of the software developed and so in the mid-term its implementation will considerably reduce service and maintenance costs, which currently are very expensive.

The model has been validated by its practical application with non-specialist user groups who are merely familiar with the use of computers. After receiving minimum training on the creation of forms and how to interrelate data proceeding from several forms, 65% of users were able to accurately model their work environment and their data needs, compared to only 15% of users who were given more complex models.

One of the main reasons for this success resides in the fact that the methodology as well as the tools used reverse the current working methods applied with other tools: the CDB automatically generates a relational database from a form instead of permitting the creation of forms only after the database has already been created, so the users are not fully involved in the direct manipulation of the tables. The latter is the case with most other software products at the present time.

References

1. ARTech Cons: Tutorial GeneXus, (1997).
2. Caro, J.L., Guevara, A. Aguayo, A. González, L.: In: A Min Tjoa Ed. Fourth International

Conference on Information and Communications Technology in Tourism - ENTER '97, pp. 307-317 (1997).

3. Caro, J.L., Guevara, A., Aguayo, A., Galvez, S., Tecnología workflow aplicada a los sistemas informáticos de gestión hotelera. In 1st Congreso Nacional Turismo y Tecnologías de la Información y las comunicaciones: Nuevas tecnologías y calidad pp. 145-158, (1999)

4. Club Soft. Club manual del usuario (1998).

5. Gálvez, S., Guevara, A., Aguayo, A., Caro, J.L.: Forms Management System. In 3rd East European Conf. On Advances Databases and Information Systems. Maribor, Slovenia. September, (1999).

6. Gálvez, S.: Participación del usuario en el diseño cooperativo de bases de datos. Metodología y herramientas. Ph.D. dissertation. Dept. of Lang. y Computing Sciences. Univ. Of Málaga. Spain. (2000).

7. Guevara A.: Planning Methodology of Information Systems Based on Bottom-up and Top-down Strategies Under Cooperative Design. In: 12th World Computer Congress IFIP-92, Madrid-Spain (1992).

8. Guevara A.: Planning Methodology of Information Systems under Cooperative Design. Computer Science 2, Ed. Ricardo Baeza Yates, Plenum Press, New York (1993).

9. Guevara, A., Aguayo, A. Falgueras, J.: Intelligent and Cooperative Data Dictionary. 13th World Computer Congress, IFIP'94, Hamburg-Germany, (1994).

10. Guevara, A., Aguayo, A. Gálvez, S, Falgueras, J., Gomez, I.: Tools for Development in Participative Design, AoM's 13th Annual International Conference, (1995).

11. Guevara, A., Aguayo, A. Gomez, I. Galvez, S., Falgueras, J.: Intelligent and Cooperative CASE Tool Kit for Development of Information Systems. Proceedings of ISD'94. Bled-Slovenia. pp 609-703 (1994).

12. Hull, R., King, R. : Semantic Database Modeling: Survey, Applications, and Research Issues". ACM Computing Surveys, vol. 19, n°. 3. (1987).

13. Kinetic Information: Public Use E-Forms: Web Solutions for Self-Service Government (1999).

14. Lulushi, A. : "Oracle Developer/2000 forms". Ed. Prentice-Hall. (1999).

15. Piattini, M. Villalba,J., Ruiz,F., Fernández, I., Polo, M. , Bastanchury, T. , Martínez,M.A.: Mantenimiento del software: conceptos métodos, herramientas y outsourcing. Ed Ra-ma. (1998).

16. Triguero, F., Guevara, A.: User Participation in Information Systems Development. Techniques and Tools. ACM SIGOIS Bulletin. August, (1995).

17. USA. Office of Management and Budget: "Proposed Implementation of the Government Paperwork Elimination Act". Federal Register. (1999).

Desktop: How Culture In An International Multi-Locational Travel Organisation Affects The Successful Implementation Of Technology Solutions-Two Years On

Anna MacVicar
Department of Hospitality, Tourism & Leisure
Glasgow Caledonian University, Glasgow, G3 6LP. Tel 0141-337-4000

Hilary Main
Swansea Business School
Mount Pleasant, Swansea, SA1 6ED. Tel 01792-481151

Abstract

This paper is a follow-up on a multi-site travel organisation (Company X) which, two years ago, was moving from traditional hierarchical functional departments ("silos") to an empowered, "delayered" enterprise business culture. This was precipitated by the desire to add value and implement cultural change in tandem with the acquisition of a new computer system at the cost of forty two million pounds. Given the increasing costs, both in terms of money and time to design and implement new information systems in large organisations, it was seen as crucial to attain high acceptability and internal customer satisfaction, particularly within a company with significant powerful stakeholders. The initial process of selection of technology solution was examined in a previous paper and this work looks at a case study of the implementation of DESKTOP, an EDS/ORACLE based management information system within Company X where a platform had been developed for their legacy system. Initially a seamless transformation was anticipated with high levels of user satisfaction. This paper follows up on the last two years of implementation ENTERPRISE, the successor to DESKTOP, with a focus on the impact of the internal cultural diversities of management on the implementation process. Various methodologies are used to gather the required data including a literature review and in depth interviews with a sample of key decision makers within the company. This research concludes that a cultural shift and change management programme is required to handle successful implementation of the chosen technology solution.

1 The Development of Culture

Every organisation develops a culture of its own. Although members of the organisation may not be consciously aware of culture it still has a pervasive influence over their attitudes, behaviour and actions. Culture clearly does affect organisational behaviour and performance [1] .Culture helps to account for variations among organisations and managers, nationally and internationally. Culture can help reduce complexity and uncertainty. It provides a consistency in outlook and values, and makes possible the processes of decision making, co-ordination and control. Culture, then is clearly an important ingredient of effective organisational performance[2].The culture of an organisation is shaped in response to a complex set of factors. We can, however, identify a number of key influences that are likely to play an important role in its development. These include: history; primary function and technology; goals and objectives; size; location; management and staffing; and the environment. The notion that organisations as mini societies can be considered as having a culture, has its theoretical origins in sociology and anthropology, where the concept is fundamental to the understanding of any society or societal group. Schein [3] offers the following definition of organisational culture as being:

> *"A pattern of basic assumptions - invented, discovered or development by a given group as it learns to cope with its problems of external adaptation and internal integration that has worked well enough to be considered valid and therefore to be taught to new members as the correct way to perceive, think and feel in relation to those problems".(Schein ,1995, pp 15)*

Whilst there are many other definitions of organisational culture within the management literature, they all tend to reflect the classic sociological/ anthropological understanding of the concept. In that, culture concerns the internalisation of a set of values, feelings, attitudes and expectations which provide meaning, order and stability to its members lives and exert a powerful, enduring and pervasive influence on their behaviour. Business culture is reflected in many ways: the way in which people ritually interact, and the language and technical *"jargon"* which they use even the way in which they dress; the norms which govern the way in which work is organised and conducted ; the organisational climate; as conveyed by its physical layout and its general atmosphere (i.e. warm friendliness v cold efficiency).

1.1 Types of Organisational Culture

Previous research [4,5] stressed the importance of cultural strength and coherence. They argued that strong cultures, in clearly communicating corporate objectives and thus creating *'super-ordinate'* goals, are likely to be powerful in increasing motivation and internal cohesiveness. Organisations with a strong culture are generally considered to be inherently resistant to change in rapidly changing market climes and they therefore run the risk of obsolescence. When organisations combine in circumstances of merger, acquisitions or other collaborative activities like joint ventures, *strong highly resistant cultures become an obstacle to integration.* Therefore, the type of culture an organisation has, and the willingness of its members to abandon or change it if required, is as important as its coherence.

Organisational cultures are influenced by a variety of factors and differ between organisations and sometimes within the same organisation in that sub-cultures develop in particular departments or divisions. History, ownership, size, technology, the external environment and organisational members, particularly company founders and leaders, all contribute to shape the culture and structure of an organisation.

Organisational culture can be usefully considered as falling into four main types - *Power, Role, Task/Achievement and Person/Support*. A *power culture* is the centralisation of power and is the most important feature of this type of culture. It is frequently encountered in small entrepreneurial organisations, where power rests with a single individual, usually the founder or a small nucleus of key individuals. *The role culture* epitomises the Weberian concept of a bureaucracy, as its guiding principles are logic, rationality and the achievement of maximum efficiency. The salient feature of a *task culture* is the emphasis which it places on accomplishing the task, and the energy which it directs toward securing the task related resources and skills. A task culture is a team culture and are characterised by their flexibility and high levels of worker autonomy, making them potentially creative and satisfying environments in which to work. However the lack of formality means that control is problematic to task cultures. The main characteristic of the *person/ support* culture is egalitarianism. It exists and functions solely to nurture the personal growth and development of its individual members.

Within that person/ support culture there is focus currently on *"knowledge management"* and the effect it has on culture. Knowledge management can be defined as the need to understand and manage the process by which knowledge and innovation is created, shared, transferred and exploited. Knowledge management can be seen as soft or hard. Hard approaches include intranets, knowledge databases and staff appointed to manage knowledge. Soft approaches include the actual environment which is required to support knowledge processes. There are two types of knowledge within an organisation. These are tacit and explicit knowledge and have to be dealt with in different ways with explicit knowledge being that which is easily stored and tacit being that learned by observation and behaviour where *trust* is frequently the key. Technology obviously lends itself well to explicit knowledge and its processing and managers who begin to see the value of knowledge assets also begin to realise that they need new processes, roles and Information Technology (IT) tools to facilitate the flow of knowledge across their organisation. This will obviously have an impact on the culture of an organisation[6]:

> *"knowledge management success = technology + culture + economics + politics"* and *"knowledge management is one third technology and two thirds change management". (Rock, 1998,p53)*

1.2 Influences on Culture and Technology

Government intervention can profoundly influence an organisations culture often playing a dominant role on the strategic business direction adopted. Particularly pertinent to this research is the anti-monopolies legislation policed by the Competition Commission and the stranglehold this has on the main profit generating activity of this case of Company X. This demanded innovative income generating alternatives to be incorporated by the new CEO and Board into business strategy. A second factor was the plethora of anti-Trade Union legislation pushed through parliament in the early eighties to stifle Trade Union power and therefore liberating businesses to adopt more competitive human resource management /change management strategies than were previously possible. Having *the government as a major customer* profoundly affects a company's internal culture, [7]. Government agencies in general are large organisations with complex procurement processes backed up by detailed regulations, specifications and audits.

Another influence on a company's culture is the strength of *personal networks* extending across the enterprise, at least across the Business Units. This company followed a 'technology leader' approach because this strategy continued what the company knew best fitted the inclinations and personal values of the engineers leading the company and led to programmes that required and could afford retention of the company's large and expensive population of highly skilled technology engineers

Individual entrepreneurship and bottom-up leadership also influenced culture and technology. Moreover, the most successful of these new businesses were initiated from the bottom up, not from the corporate office. Both the enterprise and its leadership the value of wide-spread individual entrepreneurship and such behaviour continued to be encouraged and rewarded. Alliances with other companies and *business partners* are of increasing importance because of the need to acquire additional competencies, diversify and globalise.

The Chief Executive Officer (CEO) can play an important part in culture and technology decisions. The CEO is normally an entrepreneurial figure who is crucial in determining the innovative attitude in an organisation [8]. CEOs who are more knowledgeable about IT are more likely to adopt IT and champion it particularly if it is going to add value to the business through resource efficiencies and for example the production of accurate business information to allow effective decisions to be made. This applies to culture individually, organisationally and nationally. The larger the business the more it is able to hire or contract people with specialised skills and this too affects technology decisions.

The *competitiveness of the environment* is also a crucial factor, a company in a less competitive environment would not be faced with a push to be innovative to drive down costs. Market power is generally thought to be a positive purchase influence. There are claims [9] that the best gross indicator of competitiveness may be simply the amount of resources committed to information infrastructure Also businesses that are more information intensive, such as in the travel and transport sectors, are subject to greater pressures when purchasing technology.

Operating new technology is essential to success, applying in an inappropriate culture and to a "chimney, vertical or silo" structure is a disaster. Toffler [10] states,

" no nation can operate a 21st century economy without a 21st century infrastructure, embracing computers, data communication and the other new media. This requires a population as familiar with informational infrastructure as it is with cars, roads, highways, trains and the transportation infrastructure of the smokestack period" (Toffler, 1990, p369)

Recent research [11,12] maintains that culture creates barriers to business process reengineering and that *three levels of culture* must be recognised in process redesign-*national, corporate and work group culture.* Baba [11] maintains that national culture has the most profound impact and it permeates all levels of management as individualism and autonomy are key features of American culture that work against the logic of process integration by rewarding individuals for pursuing their own self interests. This tendency also generates a lack of trust which in turn creates barriers for sharing data. Trust is an essential ingredient in an enterprise/ knowledge sharing environment.

2 From Desktop to Enterprise (Company X)

This organisation has at least 8 functional *silos* at numerous business locations where the management are wary and suspicious of non-home based IT solutions. Additionally the organisation, with 8,000 employees, operates a matrix management structure where managers can report, for example to the Managing Director vertically and laterally to the Group Financial Controller and *staff have to juggle* their superiors priorities (leading to major status issues). A serious concern throughout this process (implementation of an integrated business solution) is how can Company X facilitate these corporate managers to devolve their power throughout the organisation and share knowledge.

Once the level platform was created with project Desktop the next phase was project Enterprise. This is a business change programme with the aim of providing simplified consistent business support processes across the organisation supported by an integrated business solution (IBS). An IBS is a suite of IT applications that are closely coupled such that they use the same information and have the "same look and feel". The IBS will include the following applications: General ledger; accounts payable; accounts receivable; cash management; purchasing; inventory; fixed assets; project accounting; human resources; training administration and payroll. The implication of this is that data is entered once and only once. The whole business will be affected by Enterprise - the four main areas of focus are:
- Resource, Develop and Motivate People (RMDP) - the mechanisms by which staff are managed to ensure that they can give their best
- Acquire and maintain Assets (AMA) - How the business buys or constructs their assets and consumables and look after them once we have them
- Plan and Develop the Business (PDP) - the establishment of business aspirations and plans

- Fulfil Customer Demand (FCD) - provision of profitable customer service

> *"Most of the benchmark organisations introduce new IT systems and then re-engineer their processes or vice-versa but not both together. The change is enormous and they are all likely to hit the business units at the same time. Four change processes have four teams mainly with the same people on them so by default implementation will be planned." (Anon, Co X,1999)*

The phase the business is currently in is called - Stage 0 - "Getting Fit for Enterprise": this is achieving the behavioural change before the systems are dropped in Stage 1 - "Implementation of Enterprise". Much of the behavioural change is non-IT dependant. For example if line managers have to deal with more aspects of employment law themselves referring to online information - it is essential that the business ensures that they have a gained an understanding of some key principles. However *no budget* was originally allocated for implementation locally and the management of change/training that would be required. Bids for funding are being submitted from each operational centre to cover their estimated change management costs.

The budget overall for Enterprise to date has ranged from 20 million to 90 million depending on the key stakeholder addressed. Company X are trying to move toward an Enterprise system and have partnered with IBM on this project and are currently 18 months into an anticipated 3 year relationship with them . It is expected that they will move towards a knowledge based/ empowered structure through the implementation of this chosen software strategy. The company mission statement states that we will "encourage clear leadership which creates innovation". The key element in Desktop and subsequently Enterprise is to *chart workflows* in the organisation and hence become more knowledge and project based rather than the functional/ hierarchical structure that it was.

3 Methodology

Semi-structured in depth interviews were selected as an appropriate data collection mechanism. In this research many of the concepts had to be explained and therefore face to face interviews were crucial for in depth responses and to facilitate a flexible approach. This method also gave an opportunity to further probe as prompts were included in the format to encourage elaboration on some sensitive, key areas. The questionnaire was in 5 key sections, their background, culture, knowledge management, human resource management issues and technology. The focus for this paper is on the aspects on culture that have an impact on technology. Most questions were of a qualitative nature which should provide insight into the perception and attitudes of the respondents. Five key personnel were interviewed individually. These were all senior managers and middle managers who were directly involved with technology , two were the key people that were involved in the purchase of Desktop, three years ago, and remain key to the implementation of the Enterprise solution which is in the process of being rolled out into the organisation. The usage of technology among these interviewees varied, with some stating that it was high, over 60%, and essential to job performance and execution, those who used it mostly to cascade information and those managers who used it minimally, less than 10% of their work time. This usage in some cases reflects the nature of their roles within the organisation. All interviews were conducted at their place of work, recorded and transcribed in full detail. All respondents were very candid and anonymity was guaranteed. Access was also given to company policies, background and details on Desktop and Enterprise. Interviews were executed in November 1999.

4 Analysis of Interviews

To examine in more detail the effects of culture on the post desk top phase the following 4 areas (national, organisational, work group and business partner cultures) that proved to be of most conflict were considered. At a *national level* the organisation aims to move from a from a hierarchical/bureaucratic culture towards a web entrepreneurial, culture. It appeared Scotland was further down the path of the preferred behaviour than other UK parts of the business :

> *"it is your contribution that counts rather than your rank or place in the hierarchy, where it is your role that counts rather than your status - where innovation is encouraged and where we recognise and celebrate achievement - Scotland is renowned for flexibility, responsiveness and lack of bureaucracy it is therefore further down the continuum and whilst still having to follow the company processes and procedures."(Anon, CoX,1999)*

To some therefore the organisation is in transition from a 'role-based' culture, in the form of functional 'silos' to a 'power-based'/'task-based' culture. The role-based culture has historically influenced IT purchasing at all levels where individuals bought in piecemeal approach. The majority felt the culture within the operational business areas had not yet shifted:

> *" difficult to initiate at Edinburgh". "Trade unions are not well trained. They adopt a 1970's approach rather than a working in partnership approach" "it all comes from down South" (Anon, Co X,1999)*

At an international level, they have several overseas locations but there they make every effort to adapt to cultural diversity within these regions, including legal and political imperatives, and not impose Company X culture.

Organisational culture has an impact in terms of CEO support, with a new CEO and board of Directors who are from the private sector this IT initiative is one of the strategic imperatives because it will help to drive down organisational costs. Most interviewees felt the rationale for Enterprise was "spot on". Achievement and progression towards the Enterprise goal is highly valued in the organisation and employees did view it as a way they might personally progress in the organisation. However some found in practice that:

> *"there was still very little decision making power in practice at line manager level because of: the nature of the individuals at the top; the impossibility of getting valid information ... so you can't be sure decisions are good and there was currently a lack of capability in the management teams." (Anon, Co X,1999)*

Work culture has been influenced by the use of established performance indicators (approximately 5 years ago) and targets linked to team objectives where the emphasis is on employee participation, managing anti-champions and recognising the differences between sub-groups. Approximately half of the respondents felt that the immediate work groups they were in did now work on a team based culture

The majority of employees are not yet aware of what Enterprise means to them and how it will impact on individual work cultures, apart from a few areas of the business such as Finance where 9 finance units will shortly become one. Many staff in this area have doubled there skills in one year (becoming multi-skilled) and the company as an employer has recently one a national training award for achievements in this area.
At this level Enterprise is very hard work - re-engineering the processes in "incredibly plodding" This is a staged project and the organisation has only recently started to communicate/action the fuller picture - with bulletin sheets to employees. Enterprise is an information technology based change programme.

"The company are developing new systems to enable us to change our behaviours". (Anon, Co X,1999)

One initiative established to achieve workplace behavioural change is that if you try to use non-compliant software the company system will wipe off the offending software regardless of your status in the organisation. In the recent past there has been as many as 50 very similar but often non transferable IT initiatives occurring and developing within the company at the one time - shortly this will be a thing of the past and a culture shock for employees who are used to autonomy in technology purchasing.

The IT *partner* for Desktop in the first IT initiative was chosen for IT compatibility. The Enterprise partner on the other hand was chosen on the basis of Enterprise expertise and the support of global expansion. The current relationship with the IT partner (IBM) is very contractual and customer /supplier orientated

> *"they struggle to see that some of the things that are happening may be mutually beneficial..if they have to do more for us they want more*

money.....in 18 months.. 4 new project managers it is therefore difficult to build up trust".(Anon, Co X,1999)

The key business partner here is IBM which have own the standard Enterprise solution. The above comments highlight the distinct cultural difference between the two organisations with IBM operating at a more formal level than Co X.

It is clear that all interviewees have different perceptions of what, exactly, the overall business culture is within Company X. The senior managers already perceive that the culture has changed (perhaps only because they are trying to drive the business forward and have a more strategic view) and the less senior management are looking still towards a cultural change, not viewing it as something that is occurring at their level. Certainly the focus here is on the influence of technology and again different viewpoints were reflected. Most did perceive that the culture had changed in the last 5- 10 years , but that it was a gradual change. Senior managers saw this facilitated by removal of long serving, stagnant staff members through enhanced retirement packages. The low turnover of all staff, less than 5%, does not facilitate culture change. All saw that there was also an "attempt" at a shift in culture with regards to IT but most felt that they were "not there yet". The size of the organisation itself impedes the rapidity of change. It has a history also as a nationalised industry (and some doctrines prevail) and that influence is still very clear in terms of culture and resistance to change. These senior managers describes the dominant culture in diverse terms such as " team Based", "events-driven" and "customer focused", reflecting the variety of cultures that exist within Company X.

One manager was keen to point out that he felt that technology was enabling change and that there were several initiatives that were key to this e.g. e-mail, the "X files"(shared files) , information technology groups and continuous improvement groups. However, in contrast, there are still half of the employees , some 5000 , that were not on e-mail and had no real access to technology and those below senior level also stated that their access to the company's intranet was poor and unreliable. If a move towards a knowledge based environment is expected then these issues need to be addressed.

In term of success and how they viewed the Enterprise roll out it is clear that perceptions here vary widely again, with some managers championing the Enterprise solution and declaring it already to be a success while others comply with company policy and agree on implementation but are more guarded in their evaluation of the success. Others feel that management have over estimated the extent of cultural changes in place and predict that they are much further away from being "fit for Enterprise " than the predicted 18 months. There remains a preference for traditional methods of communicating e.g. bulletin boards as opposed to e-mail. Though management see the "Continuous Improvement Groups" as a way of communication up and down various channels, from experience these are not always effective tools.

This company have always had to be technologically advanced, due to the nature of their industry, but the pervading disparate cultures within the organisation has hampered a standardisation of technology and culture has not changed symbiotically as anticipated by senior management.

5 Discussion

Managers must fully appreciate the sensitivity of the process, *different cultures affecting the organisation must be acknowledged and respected.* particularly in the final phase where employee relations issues are inevitable. Cultural boundaries generate negative stereotypes and cultural discontinuities between *work groups* inhibit the flow of electronic information just as surely as technological incompatibility.

Enterprise, it is hoped, will make the business much more efficient and effective, eventually releasing managers from routine work as key process workflows are streamlined and releases their time to be innovative in their roles. This rationale is sound but implementation will prove "challenging" and it is vital that the culture change is achieved in the "Getting fit for Enterprise" stage before the technology is dropped in. Key competencies of line managers must be considered and any performance gaps must be addressed speedily prior to Enterprise implementation. Those managers identified as unable to match the required change must be directed to a voluntary severance package or redeployment to a more suitable position. It is clear that staff within this organisation have guarantees of employment, not job security.

One concern about Enterprise is that it could stifle innovation .The business has and should consider numerous initiatives to encourage innovation which are highlighted here: innovation must be adopted as an organisational value; emergent strategic agenda issues should be tackled by carefully selected cross functional teams and not senior hand down; managers should be encouraged not to be stagnant (hopefully reducing the propensity for the creation of functional silos); learning must be recognised by the business as an essential ingredient of innovation. Investment in "learning techniques" is essential to generate open-mindedness and acceptance of change as a way of life. Additionally, techniques of knowledge management must be developed in order to share information.

The business has a considerable distance to go before it will be fit for Enterprise Implementation but this research reveals that every effort is being made to ensure that implementation is a success with the organisation recognising what a massive change management process this is, conducting regular audits of the organisational culture and climate, establishing implementation teams and adopting suitable approaches to managing this process. Change management facilitators locally and nationally have been appointed. It is disappointing however how little thought has been given to the 5,000 non-IT users within this company and how, if at all, Enterprise may impact on them.

References

1. Depres, C (1997) Information technology and culture, Technovation, Vol 16, No 1, pp.1-20

2. Mullins L et al (1996) Developing culture in short-life organisations, International Journal of Contemporary Hospitality Management, Vol 5 , No 4, pp. 15-19

3. Schein EH (1985) Organisational culture and leadership, San Francisco, Jossey Bass

4. Peters T (1993) Liberation Management, Pan books Ltd., London

5. Peters T & Waterman R (1982) In search of excellence, New York, Harper & Row

6. Rodgers, EM (1983) Diffusion of innovation,3rd ed, The Free Press, New York

7. Rock F (1998) Knowledge Management-A Real Business Guide, CBI, IBM, Caspian

8. Davis S & Davidson B (1991) 2020 Vision: Transform your business Today to succeed in tomorrow's economy, New York, Simon & Schuster

9.. Royle, T (1995) Corporate culture vs societal culture: a comparative study of human resource strategies in two European countries, Germany and the UK, Labour Process Conference, April

10. Toffler A (1990) Power Shift:knowledge wealth and violence at the end of the 21st century, New York, Bantam

11. Baba M et al (1996) Technology management and American culture: implications for business process re-design, Research methodology Management, Vol 39, No 6, pp. 44-54

12. Baba, M et al (1996) American Culture and technology: historically grounded biases, Research Technology Management, Vol 39, No 6, pp. 46

Service Dimensions Of Travel Distribution: An Indian Case Study

Martin Friel
School of Business, University of Buckingham, England
martin.friel@buck.ac.uk

Angelika Sombert
Independent researcher

Brandon Crimes
School of Economics, Social Sciences and Tourism,
University of Hertfordshire, England

1. Introduction

For the tourism service provider the use of technology can serve a number of ends: to lower costs, increase productivity, improve the way the service is delivered, customise the service, collect data on customer needs, add value for the customer, allow for differentiation of the service and build relationships with customers [1]. Perhaps the chief aim of techology in a service context is to provide some extra benefit to the customer in the form of more convenience, increased reliability, greater control, lower prices or some other value-adding property [2]. It could be argued that the Internet is one technological medium that has the potential to provide this extra benefit in the following ways: the better travel web sites allow the on-line customers to search for information and to make bookings at times that suit them (more convenience); information is timely and updated regularly, and more powerful and capacious servers and greater bandwidth entail fewer down-times and broken connections (greater reliability); the customers are not limited to a narrow range of service providers and products as might be proffered by the local travel agent and customers undertake the pre-trip consultancy themselves (greater control) and there is a wider range of prices on offer including some below high street levels (lower prices) [3]. The Internet then can help to offset some of the criticisms levelled at travel agents, namely that travel agents are reactive and not proactive in terms of adding value for the customer; that 24-hour access to the travel agent is usually not possible; that commissions make products bought through travel agents more costly and so on [3].

Key to competitive advantage is adding value for the customer [4] and this applies equally to the Internet as to travel agents. In order to add value for the customer it is necessary to understand on an ongoing basis what it is that the customer needs, wants and values by way of product/service solutions. This necessarily entails building a rapport with the customer and facilitating 'the creation of a marketplace where a segment of one is the norm' [5]. It is through its personalised, customised interface that the Internet can contribute to building rapport. Indeed, it is precisely in the area of acting small [2], that is, delivering personalised treatment on a large scale that new technologies such as the Internet come into their own. Collier [6] suggests that the independent traveller needs a broader range of information at the point-of-sale and here again the Internet has the capability to deliver.

This would seem to constitute a bleak prognosis for the long-term survival of the travel agent who is increasingly being bypassed [7] by a consumer growing in sophistication on the one hand and who is seeing commissions squeezed by travel principals, particularly the airlines, on the other hand. But the outlook is not necessarily sombre. Dombey [8] argues that more and more travel agents are taking advantage of the Internet to offer interactive services and that travel agents are seeing Web sites as another travel booking opportunity. Walle [7] contends that the Internet will augment travel agents not compete with them. For some travel agents however one short-term solution to a fall in business has been to introduce service fees [9, 10]. But this is simply likely to be a retrograde and ultimately self-defeating route for travel agents since the more that their margins are squeezed the greater the temptation will be to charge service fees and this in turn is likely to discourage customers from using travel agents. This will have the effect of squeezing margins and so the vicious circle spirals. Hamill and Gregory [11] argue that in order to survive in an environment where the end-user and the producer are connected by the Internet intermediaries will need to begin offering a different range of services and that their value-added will lie in the collection, collation, interpretation and dissemination of vast amounts of information [7]. Whilst many changes are already taking place in the travel distribution arena and in the role and services of the travel agent [8] Inkpen [3] suggests that travel agents need to make a number of changes that will allow them to compete more successfully. These changes include:

- Focussing not on short-term gain but on how to add value for the customer by way of providing quality consultancy advice that the customer *would* be prepared to pay for;

- Building their own Internet-based business, effectively embracing the emerging technology rather than seeing it as a threat.

For many travel agents this is now one way forward that is being increasingly adopted and no less so in less-developed countries such as India.

2. The study

Until fairly recently India, like many other less-developed (and even more developed) countries, had a very small Internet community, but numbers of on-line users have grown exponentially in the last two or so years. India, South America and parts of

Africa have seen their Internet user numbers grow at least three-fold in the previous two years while China has posted an eight-fold growth in Internet users, although a note of caution must be sounded on the accuracy of these figures. Even so, even using conservative estimates the general trend is upwards (apart from certain parts of Africa which have seen a decrease over the previous two years). It was only in November 1998 that the Indian government relinquished its Internet Service Provider (ISP) industry monopoly and there are now (January 2000) in excess of seventy ISP licenses issued. There are an estimated 250 000 Internet subscribers in India accessed by between 500 to 800 000 individual users. As a result of the deregulation of the ISP market the number of Internet users is expected to surge, with one million active by the end of the year 2000 [12].

Such growth has prompted travel companies to reassess the value of the Internet to their business and to consider adding the Internet to their distribution arsenal. One such company is Thomas Cook India Limited (TCIL) who in 1998 commissioned research to enable them to become more customer-focussed. The main aim of this research was to establish how to turn TCIL into a fully customer-driven organisation. From this research TCIL was able to identify a set of eight service dimensions that appertained to customers when making travel arrangements. The research also identified the need to establish a customer-oriented Web site. To this end the present study was undertaken. The key objectives of the study were:

1)   to investigate and identify current usage of the Internet in accessing travel information and booking travel-related services in India;

2)   to ascertain the willingness of Indian consumers to use the Internet to buy travel products; and,

3)   to identify the service dimensions relevant to actual and potential Internet users that would add value to travel agency products and services

3. Method

In order to achieve the objectives set for this exploratory study it was necessary to gain access to travel agency customer data so that how and why travel agency customers had used, do use and might use the Internet as a travel information or booking medium could be mapped. To this end TCIL fully supported the project by facilitating access to their customer database in order to identify appropriate respondents. In the context of the study an appropriate respondent constituted one who had previously purchased a TCIL product or availed themselves of the services of another Indian travel agency. In turn, these respondents were asked to provide referrals to other appropriate respondents. In an attempt to gauge whether there were any significant differences in Web-based travel information and booking expectations and behaviour on the part of different market segments the sample was broadly split between business and leisure travellers. In all, 109 business travellers responded and 81 responded from the leisure segment. In order to provide for an element of richness in the data and to avoid relying on the somewhat capricious Indian postal service all data were collected via face-to-face semi-structured interviews that lasted approximately 30 minutes. The interviews were conducted over a period of one month and were divided into four segments. Segment one dealt with general background and demographic information; segment two sought to map travel booking behaviour; segment three focussed on the use of the Internet to make travel arrangements and segment four set out to identify those service dimensions that were of importance to consumers when making travel arrangements.

4. Findings

4.1 Profile of respondents

Approximately 57% of respondents consisted of business travellers and 43% leisure travellers, and of all respondents four in ten were not TCIL customers. There was a wide age range although almost one-third of respondents fell into the 26-35 band. Using the Market Research Society of India socio-economic classification 95% of respondents came from the officers/junior executives category (educated to at least degree level) or above. The sample was predominantly male (82%). This profile is entirely consistent with countries in the Internet take-off stage. Almost two-thirds of respondents' trips are domestic and nine out of ten domestic trips involves a simple as opposed to complex travel itinerary. This proportion changes to five out of ten for international trips.

4.2 Current use of the Internet

Some 70% of all respondents have access to a computer at work with 40% having one at home and almost a third having access to a computer at home *and* at work. Over half of all respondents access the Internet on a daily basis but almost a quarter have never accessed it. The most common Internet activity is corresponding by e-mail with nine in ten respondents using e-mail on a regular basis. The next most common type of Internet activity is news and general information gathering, with just under half of all respondents using the Internet occasionally for travel information. Interestingly, almost a quarter of respondents have used Internet facilities for travel booking and on-line shopping, which is consistent with recent Project Atlas results from IDC [13]. Of those users who had never or very rarely made use of the Internet the majority stated that they would use it for e-mail and information gathering primarily, with only one-third of both business and leisure respondents considering using the Internet for travel booking. In this context it needs to be pointed out that almost a quarter of respondents were unaware that travel arrangements could be made on the Internet, but this is partly explained by the fact that nearly all of these respondents had never accessed the Internet. Nonetheless almost all have already gathered or would consider gathering travel information on the Internet and this has implications for the marketing communications functions of Indian ISPs and travel agencies.

Well over two thirds of respondents heard about the possibility of making travel arrangements or gathering travel information on the Internet from the Internet itself. Again this has implications for the marketing communications functions of Indian travel agencies and for consumer awareness initiatives. A substantial majority of respondents (85%) stated that they would be prepared to arrange their own travel itineraries via the Internet and this will undoubtedly have an impact on numbers who visit high street travel agents for the same purpose. Most respondents visit travel Web sites to gather information with only one-fifth visiting such sites *and* making a booking. It is unclear from the data whether this is due to a reluctance on the part of the consumer to buy over the Internet or an inability on the part of the tourism service provider to effect such a purchase as yet.

A number of advantages and disadvantages to the consumer making travel arrangements on the Internet was identified by respondents in the study. These are presented in Table 1.

Table 1. Advantages and disadvantages of booking travel via the Internet

ADVANTAGES	DISADVANTAGES
Speed	None identified (majority of responses)
Convenience	Accessibility and telecommunications infrastructure
Independent travel design with no human contact	Impersonal medium and loss of human contact
24-hour accessibility and service	Lack of credit card security
Amount of information	No physical or tangible confirmation
	Inaccurate or outdated information

Clearly, most respondents were positively disposed towards making travel arrangements via the Internet and the disadvantages mentioned may be resolved with time. Indeed, already the issue of accessibility and telecommunications infrastructure is being partly addressed through the recent deregulation of the ISP market. There is concern however that problems of accessibility and infrastructure will continue in the light of insufficient bandwidth, difficulties with securing phone lines from the telecommunications providers (VSNL and MNTL), high access charges, inflexible tariffs and access plans and a lack of PC penetration [14]. The Indian government is gradually relaxing its regulatory grip on the Internet and the situation is improving markedly. In some ways though a number of the perceived disadvantages of using the Internet can be addressed by the travel organisations themselves: the impersonality of the Internet medium can be offset through the use of interactive multimedia; improved encryption techniques already available can allay fears about the lack of credit card security; printed (or even posted) confirmations will provide some tangible evidence of purchase for the consumer; and sites can be updated regularly with timely and accurate information.

4.3 Preferred features on a travel web site

There was some agreement amongst respondents as to the features that they would prefer to see on a travel web site (see Table 2). Top features unsurprisingly were information (on services offered and information on prices and discounted fares) and booking (of accommodation and flights) with provision of e-mail contact addresses also preferred. Respondents also commented on the eight dimensions of service that were distilled as a result of the internal TCIL research workshops aimed at improving the organisation's customer-orientedness.

These eight dimensions represent those attributes that TCIL considered to be crucial to consumers when they make travel arrangements. Respondents were asked to rank the service dimensions in order of importance. Table 2 clearly shows that for both business and leisure travel consumers reliability and speed were ranked most highly and creativity and personal care least highly. It is evident that the Internet has the potential to satisfy the requirements for reliability and speed and is therefore in this context an appropriate medium for the fulfilment of these dimensions.

However, respondents were also asked to articulate independently of TCIL's service dimensions what they considered important to themselves when making travel arrangements. Here, there appears to be some disparity with the TCIL understanding of what consumers regard as important (see Table 2). Overall, reliability seems to constitute the most important dimension, as also identified by TCIL, followed by a professional service and flexibility. However, those factors identified by respondents do not always correspond neatly with the TCIL dimensions and there is in fact a compelling case for revisiting these dimensions. Respondent factors point to a marked difference between leisure and business priorities which is not readily discernible from the TCIL dimensions, and which has implications for Internet intermediaries. Whilst reliability is still seen as a key service consideration both leisure and business customers value the provision of a range of options to choose from, and they value the imparting of all travel-related information in good time. They also set store by the provision of cultural and general information that furnishes insights into the destination and it is indeed this cultural information that is most highly valued by business respondents. Perhaps unsurprisingly the most highly valued service feature for leisure respondents was the travel intermediary providing the customer with a variety of travel options that were also low-budget. The Internet is not the only travel intermediary that can fulfil these service dimensions but the Internet can provide a less costly, less labour and resource intensive and a more rapid means of satisfying customers' service demands, and above all it can add value to the travel agent's offerings rather than be seen as a substitute or a threat.

Table 2. The eight service dimensions and preferred travel web site features

Features	Market		Service dimension							
	Leisure	Business	Creative	Care	Reliability	Speed	Flexibility	Service	Proactiveness	Transparency
Rank										
Offer customer various travel options	1	3			✓		✓			
Provide low-budget options and accurate information	2	-			✓					
Inform the customer beforehand	3	4							✓	✓
Provide knowledgeable consultancy	4	2						✓		
Provide cultural background	5	1			✓			✓		
Loyalty schemes	6	7						✓		
Information on local transportation	7									
Ticketing for rail travel	8						✓			
Special requests on flights	9									
Flight and hotel confirmed all the way through	10	5			✓					
Local assistance for emergencies		6								
Personalised global account number		8								
24-hour accessibility		9				✓				
Representation on the Internet		10				✓				

5. Conclusion

It is appropriate to return to the stated research objectives and to assess the degree to which these have been fulfilled.

1) to investigate and identify current usage of the Internet in accessing travel information and booking travel-related services in India

The Internet is growing apace in India as in other developing countries and with the recent deregulation of the ISP market take-up is likely to accelerate. It has been posited that the Internet will not have the same impact in India that it has had in Western countries due to differentials in income distribution [15]. But in a country with a population that will shortly exceed that of China there is a good possibility of long-term growth in Internet access and usage, although it is likely that Internet travel sales in India, as in many other developing nations, will follow the pattern of travel agent sales in India in targetting and appealing to a relatively small, but growing, elite. The likely importance of the Internet in India is attested to by figures from this study showing that more than 90% of Indian travellers surveyed would consider gathering travel-related information via the Internet and over 80% would make their bookings via the Internet. It has been seen that in common with developed countries in the Internet take-off stage the Internet is a predominantly middle-class and professional activity that is set to grow further. E-mail is still the most common use of the Internet and although only one third of respondents at present would consider using the Internet for travel booking purposes and almost a third have already used it for on-line purchases this number is likely to increase rapidly with greater personal computer penetration, cheaper access charges, more competition and deregulation in the ISP market, greater credit card security and active awareness-raising on the part of travel intermediaries.

2)   to ascertain the willingness of Indian consumers to use the Internet to buy travel
       products

Indian travel consumers seem to be favourably disposed towards booking travel via the Internet as evidenced by the fact that a majority of surveyed respondents could not identify any major disadvantages of doing so, and indeed a third have already purchased on-line.

3)   to identify the service dimensions relevant to actual and potential Internet users
       that would add value to travel agency products and services

It has been shown that some of those service dimensions related to making travel arrangements identified by Thomas Cook India Limited were largely appropriate. And when respondents commented on those dimensions reliability and speed were ranked most highly. Whilst these are important dimensions to most Internet users their importance may perhaps be exaggerated in the Indian market as a result of high access charges, the frequency of down-times and broken connections and the inadequacy of bandwidth prevailing at the time of the study. It may be that, as these issues ameliorate, other, softer dimensions such as creativity and personal care will come to play a greater part. It is of interest that, when prompted to articulate those service dimensions important to them, respondents identified a set of dimensions that did not correspond neatly with TCIL's dimensions but which the Internet was well placed to fulfil.

There is also compelling evidence that in spite of sometimes marked differences in the service priorities between the travel intermediary and the customer and between the key business and leisure markets the Internet has the means and capability of playing a major role in satisfying these priorities. It is also clear from the study that service demands made of the Internet are broadly similar to service demands made of other travel intermediaries.

There is little doubt that the Internet will play a greater role in travel distribution and in adding value to travel offerings and will increasingly be embraced by travel agents and other intermediaries. The pace of change in Internet take-up by both consumer and travel agent is likely to be slower in developing countries such as India but is also likely to be no less impactful than in developed countries.

References

1   Zeithaml, V.A. and Bitner, M.J. (1996), *Services marketing*, London: McGraw-Hill p35.
2   Berry, L. (1995), *On great service*, New York: The Free Press, chapter 7, p149.
3   Inkpen, G. (1998), *Information Technology for Travel and Tourism*, Harlow: Addison Wesley Longman.
4   Kotler, P., Armstrong, G., Saunders, J. and Wong, V. (1996), *Principles of Marketing*, London: Prentice-Hall, p401
5   O'Connor, P. (1999), *Electronic information distribution in tourism and hospitality*, Wallingford: CABI publishing, p116.
6   Collier, D.A. (1989), Expansion and development of CRS, *Tourism Management*, June, pp86-88.
7   Walle, A.H. (1996), Tourism and the Internet: opportunities for direct marketing, *Journal of Travel Research*, Summer, pp72-77.
8   Dombey, A. (1998), Separating emotion from the fact – the effects of new intermediaries on electronic travel distribution, *Information and Communication Technologies in Tourism*, Proceedings of the International ENTER conference in Istanbul, Turkey, pp129-138.
9   Jeans, T. (1999) *Travel Trade Gazette*, 25/10/99, p8.
10 Bly, L. (1998), Travel agents take slow journey to service fees, *USA Today*, 04/10/1998, p05D.
11 Hamill, J. and Gregory, K. (1997), Internet marketing in the internationalisation of UK SMEs, *Journal of Marketing Management*, p13.
12 Internetnews.com (1999): Substantial demand for internet in India, May 21, IN: *http://www.nua.ie/surveys/*
13 IDC (1999), IDC releases results from the world's largest web survey, *http://www.idc.com/telb/112399pr.htm*
14 Internetnews.com (1999): 72 ISPs licensed to operate in India, Feb 24, IN: *http://www.nua.ie/surveys/*
15 Clemente, P. (1998), *The state of the Net – the new frontier*, New York: McGraw-Hill.

The Competitiveness Of Traditional Tourist Destinations In The Information Economy

M. A. Rastrollo and P. Alarcón
Department of Economy and Business Administration, University of Malaga
Malaga, Spain

1 Introduction

A new kind of economy has risen all over the world in the last twenty years, which is known by different names: post-fordism, digital, electronic, information, knowledge based and learning economy. Each of these terms reflects a different aspect of this modern economy, but the basic features behind each of them are the same: the importance of knowledge, and information and communication technology (ICT) in economic activity.

Owing to its very nature, tourism has been one of the first industries to fall under the influence of the changes in the newly emerging information economy. Information is a basic aspect of the product of the tourist industry, and the use of ICT has been at the core of the way it has been structured in the last few years. The changes that are having an impact on the development of the supply and demand of the tourist industry are a clear indication that ICT has a critical role to play in the processes of production, distribution and promotion of the tourist industry. These changes are altering the way the industry is structured, the aspects of tourism that affect competitiveness, the professional level required from its human resources (traditionally under qualified) and the strategies to be applied by tourist enterprises [24].

The first studies made about the influence of electronic commerce are identifying the special relevance of both transaction costs and how they affect intermediation [4, 22], and the opportunities that are available for the internationalisation and re-organisation of Small and Medium-Size Entreprises (SMEs).

Thus, traditional tourist destinations are finding that the electronic environment is giving them the opportunity to eliminate what have traditionally been their two weaknesses: their dependency on tour operators and the existence of a fragmented supply. This study specifically is concerned with this idea. We intend to evaluate the changes that have taken place in what the industry has to offer and what the tourist is demanding, so that tourist destinations are able to take full advantage of the opportunities made available by electronic commerce. In the first place, we try to identify what it is that the tourist is demanding and what is his behaviour during the purchasing process. Secondly, we determine which are the resources and features that are required to satisfy these behaviour profiles and concrete demands. Finally, we establish how the supply meets the demand, that is, bring some light to the debate on disintermediation, re-intermediation in electronic commerce.

2 The tourist and electronic commerce

If there are two main characteristics that describe the demand for tourism in the second half of the 20th Century, they are "continuous growth" and "heterogeneousness". Given that there are no specific studies available on the subject, we have to assume that heterogeneousness in tourist behaviour might be transferable to electronic commerce.

At the present time, however, this is not true, mainly because of two phenomena to be observed in electronic commerce:

1. The very precise profile of the typical Web user, which only finds its match in some specific travel segments.
2. The natural restrictions of an expanding market – lack of assurance and experience, limited availability of the appropriate offer, etc.

2.1 The profile of the tourist using the Internet

The newly emerging electronic commerce is being used mainly by young people, with a high financial standing, who are highly qualified and live in the most developed countries, above all in the United States and Northern Europe [1, 8]. Here, therefore, is the definition of the target market that should today be taken into account in Internet marketing strategies.

Studies carried out by the WTO (World Tourism Organisation) and the IET (Institute for Tourist Studies) [13, 14, 15, 28, 29, 30] lead us to identify in this social and demographic profile of the Internet user an active tourist, interested in sports, culture or the environment and, since many Internet users are executives, there is considerable demand for luxury products and the organisation of professional travel. To summarise, we have an expert tourist who demands new products and a new approach to traditional ones.

Nevertheless, in the long term we can describe other variables that will have an impact on tourist consumption and predict the rapid increase in those tourist profiles that will be affected by electronic commerce, such as the pulling-in effect, the consumption cycle of current Internet users or the future development of the Net itself. The electronic commerce of tourist products will itself create new profiles with new demands [25] (Figure 1).

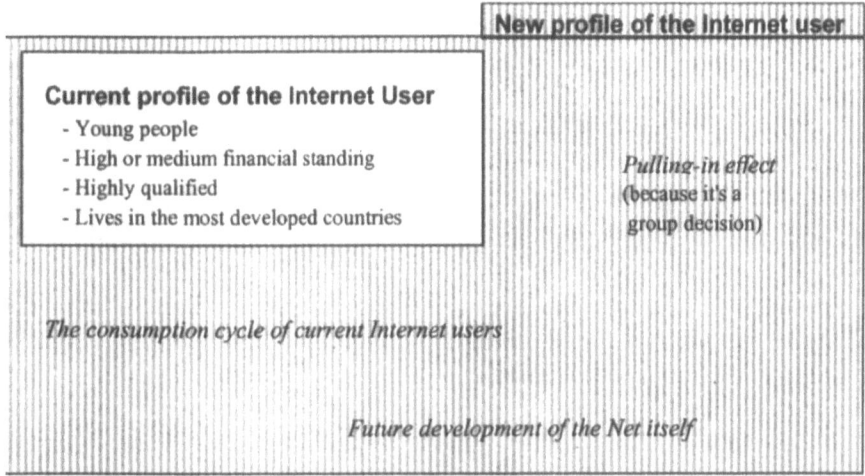

Fig. 1. Extension of the tourist user of electronic commerce's profile

There is one very interesting aspect of this tourist profile that allows us to evaluate the possibilities of electronic commerce for different destinations, and that is the way travel is organised. At the present time, there appears to be nearly an equal proportion of organised travel (21%), direct reservations (20%), reservations through travel agencies (26%) and even unplanned travel (33%) [5].

If we analyse the organisation of travel taking into account social and demographic profiles, this proportion is altered. There are no general studies available on the organisation of travel, but in the information supplied by the System for the Analysis and Statistics of Tourism in Andalusia, SAETA, which refers exclusively to Andalusia as a tourist destination, there is empirical evidence to support the idea that the Internet user is very active when it comes to his own travel plans [23].

When we refer to a more active and expert tourist, this does not necessarily mean that he makes direct reservations with suppliers but that he personally makes a greater contribution to the process of organising his own travel, obtaining a lot of additional information himself, even though eventually he relies on agents to contract the service.

2.2 The use of electronic commerce

The tourist could potentially use the Internet at all the different stages of the purchasing process. At the present time, however, it is being used specifically at the "search for information" and "choice of alternatives" stages [25]. Standard products, such as airline tickets, are being purchased electronically, but there are important difficulties involved in the purchase of other, more complex, tourist products [17].

The most important impediments to electronic commerce as an alternative way to purchase complex tourist products are: the difficulties in accessing electronic markets, legal barriers related to payment security, fraud, the privacy of personal information and the legal aspects of electronic contracts [19], a generalised lack of trust in the medium and a product mainly oriented to the Anglo-Saxon customer. The result of these difficulties is a decrease in the percentage of the population that is willing to pay for the right to access these services (9.5%) compared with those who are not willing to, but they make use of them in other stages of their travel plans (42,3%), according to the European Commission [6].

Therefore, the tourist consumer is attracted by the use of the Internet to organise travel for the following main reasons: a) he/she is able to establish an interactive relationship with the provider, without the influence of intermediary agents and receive information tailored to his own particular needs; b) better prices as a result of the more accurate and tight information provided by the customer, and c) he/she gets better service in terms of timing, available information, response times, the quality of the information received, etc.

On the other hand, we are dealing with a more experienced customer who has easy access to alternative suppliers, so, a priori, he tends to be less loyal and has greater negotiating power, which in turn is amplified by the creation of virtual communities and organised interest groups. The customer's increased power of negotiation means that tourist agents are obliged to invest in the development of intellectual assets to enrich their product and to increase the level of client participation [9, 21].

3 Resources and the capabilities for relationship marketing in tourist destinations

Recent changes in tourist behaviour are only one aspect of the new environment in which present day tourist enterprises must operate. With the help of ICT, but also for other reasons, the key to competitiveness is moving away from scale economies and towards information management carried out by the customer, for the customer and with the customer. In this new environment –greater and more varied supply, market fragmentation, globalisation, more experienced and demanding tourists- the customer has become the most scarce and most valued element in the system. For this reason, for a tourist business to be totally successful it needs to do more than attract the customer in the first place. It needs to assure his loyalty and consider him as a reference source for the industry. This new concept of exchange stress long-term relationships, rather than single transactions and suits the profile of the present day tourist as it considers him/her to be an active and familiar element in the process [2].

From this point of view, the strategy of tourist companies changes from specialising in the products they have to offer to become expert connoisseurs of "their customers". Indeed, success depends on offering a product that incorporate a greater level of knowledge of the customer and this obviously means including a relationship between the tourist business and the client. A priori, there appears to be less barriers to accessing electronic markets because the basic infrastructures needed for access have lessen and the investment required is also substantially lower [18]. In addition to this, the possibility of having direct contact with the customer could result in a greater level of control over the relationship.

On the other hand, because of their reduced size, the tourist companies associated with traditional destinations have less margin for covering the fixed costs related to the search and compiling of information and to the evaluation of risks, costs and profits associated with investment in new technology.

At the same time, they will need to be sufficiently endowed financially and with adequate human resources and capabilities for organisation if they are going to make a successful approach to the personal tailoring of their products in order to assure customer satisfaction, considering that they will be obliged to offer innovative products and processes, an absolute necessity in the new production and distribution model, and to negotiate on the global electronic marketplace taking into account that purchasing power has shifted to the individual customer [3]. The knowledge economy emphasises the importance of intangible resources as a source of competitiveness, and investment in these resources increases the minimum size of the companies that are going to be truly competitive [7].

At this point, however, we should stop to analyse to what extent suppliers in traditional tourist destinations can benefit from direct electronic links to the consumer, and whether intermediary agents will disappear from the process.

It has been suggested that tourist intermediaries are at risk because of new technologies that allow direct contact between the provider and the consumer. The main argument for the disappearance of intermediary agents is based on the analysis of the impact that data transmission networks have on transaction costs [16, 27]. However, this theory can also be used to argue the opposite, i.e. that new technologies can increase the functionality of intermediaries.

The fact is that information technologies not only reduce market costs compared with hierarchical forms of management, but they also increase economic operational efficiency, by adding flexibility to the development and modification of business relationships [12]. This also helps to maintain different markets and types of relationship at the same time, which is more in line with the heterogeneousness of the demand.

Another argument against the hypothesis of the disappearance of intermediary agents is related to the help that ICT can give to traditional agents to reduce transaction costs and achieve scale, scope and knowledge economies. Intermediary activities that are mainly associated with the availability of asymmetrical information (for example, travel agencies) or the sale of digital products that can be distributed on the Web will indeed be in danger [20]. But generally speaking, it does not seem probable that intermediation will disappear altogether. It seems more likely that there will be a change in its basic functions, which will be directed towards supplying advice and trust and reducing the risks involved in electronic commerce.

Recent experience indicates that we might possibly soon be hearing of *cybertraders* [26], new middlemen that, loyal to traditional marketing theory, will supply certain services to the customer (aid in searching and evaluating, risk reduction, product distribution, range of products and guarantee) and to the suppliers (their influence on the customer's final decision, customer information, reductions in distribution costs) thus increasing the efficiency of the entire process by adding transactions to create scale and scope economies.

In the case of the tourist industry we can identify a considerable number of agents from different areas of the activity, who are involved in the networks and adding value to the organisation of the consumer's travel plans. The tourist needs the support of intermediaries that will direct him to the different tourist destination business that offer the services that will make up the complete package. For example, the tourist needs Internet providers and telecommunication service suppliers. In order to locate the tourist offer, he/she will possibly rely on a search engine, a virtual community or a travel magazine, which will not only include advertising for different destinations but also other useful information such as other tourists' experience, etc. In order to complete the transaction, there will be a need for agents that guarantee the security of banking operations, travel insurance, etc. Finally, we have to make sure that all the aspects of any one travel plan are available on the Internet.

Consequently, electronic markets is creating a change in intermediary functions rather than the disappearance of the intermediation, and new agents are acting as intermediaries [11]. "Disintermediation" may well increase efficiency but at the same time it increases risks, for both the supplier and the customer. If intermediaries disappear some-one has to give the services that they are now giving to the tourist. At this point we should also consider the difficulties that suppliers of tourist products will have to overcome if they are to assemble their offers in such a way as to make the global products tourists want to purchase available through electronic commerce.

4 Conclusions and implications

The electronic marketplace, then, is both a threat and an opportunity for SMEs. It contributes to internal efficiency, gives access to precise and up-dated information and paves the way for internationalisation and access to specialised services. If the opportunities are to materialise complementary resources are required: to understand and apply complex technologies, to dedicate time and effort to the management of the new relationships by network organisation, and to negotiate with partners from other cultures [10].

Tourist behaviour has led us to identify two basic implications. First of all, the progressive use of the up to date and interactive information available from tourist product providers is forcing tourist supply to be responsible for customer contact. Secondly, the creation of a brand image that will convey assurance and security for complete electronic transactions. Even though it is true that there are less difficulties in gaining access to the electronic marketplace, the maintenance of this activity and in particular the development of *one-to-one* marketing strategies and the creation of a global brand image require distinct capabilities over and above the mere possession of financial and technological resources. It appears that we will not be witnesses to the disappearance of all intermediaries, because they will be using the Internet as a means to continue to offer services that are valued by the consumer.

It is evident that there will still be a need for travel agencies or other intermediaries to package the complete product, but the customer will indeed search for additional information, which he/she will expect to access directly. In any case, therefore, the development of electronic commerce has a considerable impact on the organisation of the industry. It not only has to take the of value system into account, but is also forced to progress towards the development of a common strategy. Otherwise, the increased difficulties in attracting the consumer's attention and consolidating a brand image could increase the risk of dependency on the new intermediary.

Undoubtedly the competitiveness of intangible resources means that the size factor is of greater significance, which limits the competitive capability of traditional destinations. The industry response to this seems to be alliances and partnerships with other companies, including suppliers and intermediaries.

Therefore, if tourist destination businesses are to take full advantage of ICT they need the support of the Public Administration in order to create e-commerce initiatives and consequently learn and develop greater capabilities.

References

1. A.U.I.: Resultados del Estudio General de Usuarios. Asociación de Usuarios de Internet. http://aui.es/estadi/egu/datos98 december 1998.
2. Barroso, C., Martín, E.: Marketing relacional. ESIC, Madrid (1999)
3. Beam, C., Segev, A.: The rise of electronic commerce: contributions from three factors. 96-WP-1015 University of California. http://haas.berkeley.edu. (1996)

4. Benjamin, R., Wigand, R.: Electronic Markets and virtual value chains on the information superhighway. Sloan Management Review, 2: 62-72 (1995).

5. ETM: Las vacaciones de los europeos. European Travel Monitor. (1997).

6. European Commision: Eurobarometre 50.1. Les Européens et la Société de L'Information. http://www.ispo.ce.be/polls/98 october 1999.

7. Fernández, E., Montes, J.M., Vázquez, C.J.: Factores de competitividad en la pequeña y mediana empresa. Inversión en activos intangibles, tamaño y límites al crecimiento. Economía Industrial 310: 141-148. (1996).

8. G.V.U.: 9th WWW user survey. Graphic, Visualization and Usability Center's. http://www.gvu.gatech.edu/user_surveys/survey-1998-04 december 1998.

9. Go, F.M., Pine, R.: Globalization Strategy in the Hotel Industry. Routlegde. London. (1995).

10. Gulbro R.D., Herbig P.: Can small firms compete internationally? A study of negotiating behavior. http://www.wasbec.uca.edu/docs/proceedings/95sbi221.txt (march 1996)

11. Hawkins, R.: Creating a positive environment for electronic commerce in Europe, FAIR Working Paper nº 36. SPRU, march (1998).

12. Holland C., Lockett A.G.: Mixed mode networks: a theory of electronic competition in business markets. http://www.wasbec.uca.edu/docs/proceedings/95sbi229.txt. (1995).

13. IET: Colección: Estudio de los mercados turísticos emisores, Polonia y Rusia (paper). Turespaña, Madrid. (1995).

14. IET: Colección: Estudio de los mercados turísticos emisores, Alemania, Holanda, Reino Unido, Francia, Canadá, Austria, Suiza. Turespaña, Madrid. (1997).

15. IET: El mercado turístico EEUU. Estudio Prizm (paper). Turespaña, Madrid. (1998).

16. Malone, T., Yates, J., Benjamin, R.: La lógica de los mercados electrónicos. Harvard-Deusto Business Review 41:107-112 (1990).

17. Margherio L.; Dave, H.; Cook, S.; Montes, S.: The emerging digital economy. U.S. Department of Commerce. http://www.ecommerce.gov. (1998).

18. OCM: El comercio electrónico y el papel de la OCM. OCM, Ginebra. (1998).

19. OECD: Electronic commerce: opportunities and challenges for government, the "Sacher report". http://www.ocde.org/dsti/it/ec/act/sacher.htm (1997).

20. OECD: The economic and social impacts of electronic commerce: preliminary findings and research agenda. http://www.ocde.org/ dsti/sti (1998).

21. Poon, A.: Tourism, technology and competitive strategies. CAB international. (1993).

22. Quelch, J.A., Klein, L.R.: The Internet and International Marketing. Sloan Management Review, spring: 60-75. (1996).

23. SAETA: Balance del año turístico en Andalucía - 1998. Junta de Andalucía. 1999.

24. Rastrollo, M.A.: El comercio electrónico: un nuevo entorno económico para la empresa turística. III Congreso Andaluz de Turismo de las Cámaras de Comercio, Málaga. (1999).

25. Rastrollo, M.A.; Alarcón, P.: El turista ante el comercio electrónico. Instituto de Estudios Turísticos (paper). (1999).

26. Sarkar, M.B.; Butler, B.; Steinfield, C.: Intermediaries and Cybermediaries: A Continuing Role for Mediating Players in the Electronic Marketplace. Journal of Computer Mediated Communication 1, 3. (1997).

27. Schmid, B.: Electronic markets in tourism. Revue de Tourisme, 2: 9-15 (1994).

28. WTO: El turismo hasta el año 2000. Aspectos cualitativos que afectan a su crecimiento mundial. OMT, Madrid. (1995).

29. WTO: Previsiones del turismo mundial hasta el año 2000 y después. OMT, Madrid. (1995).

30. WTO: Turismo: panorama 2020. Influencias, flujos direccionales y tendencias claves. Resumen ejecutivo. OMT, Madrid. (1997).

Industrial Mapping Of
Tourism Information Technologies

Pascal Tremblay
Northern Territory University
Darwin, Australia

Pauline J. Sheldon
School of Travel Industry Management
University of Hawaii, USA

1 Introduction

The impact of rapidly developing communication and information technologies (CITs) has been increasingly recognized in tourism and retailing circles and has led to alarming statements concerning the future of tourism [19]. But there have been few attempts to systematically predict the evolution of tourism marketing and production systems or even to model possible tourism futures. This is surely largely explained by the breadth and depth of the methodological challenges involved and the inextricable nature of tourism as an object of study. This paper explores first the methodological reasons behind the overwhelming difficulties associated with prophesying the future of tourism, emphasizing the relationships between technological considerations and other socio-economic variables shaping the tourism phenomenon. After examining the potential roles played by diverse stakeholders affecting the tourism system, the paper focuses on the specific role of CITs in shaping the production, distribution and consumption of tourism. The paper then explores a recently developed categorization of CITs and uses it to differentiate between types of technological innovations and ultimately distinguish between evolving techno-industrial domains on the basis of the most likely evolutionary drivers. The paper then suggests a primary mapping of various technological developments (CIT-related) identified as critical in the tourism literature and speculates about the main factors driving the changes in tourism technological and industrial organization.

2 The Determination of Tourism's Future

It is possible to illustrate the breadth of technology-related issues which have preoccupied tourism marketing and planning analysts with a very brief and admittedly simplistic summary of the evolution of concerns regarding the tourism-technology nexus. A cursory survey of the literature could distinguish changing concerns and identify the following four stages.

1) The early tourism literature embraced the future by identifying historical

developments which have led to tourism growth. In pre-electronic times, transport-related technological drives and eco-socio-political institutional changes (mainly linked with rising disposable income and institutionalised rights to "free time") constituted the most visible explanations for extensive tourism growth. The continued development of transport and communication technologies has sustained that growth. There is little precise information regarding the changing organizational structure of present and future tourism.

2) The U.S. airline deregulation led to the radical transformation of distribution through the development of Computer Reservation Systems (CRSs) which ultimately became the giant Global Distribution Systems (GDS). These early CIT developments raised unprecedented concerns: issues of fairness at the user level, potential dominance of direct sales of airlines services over traditional distribution channels and potential for excessive competitive advantage linked with CRS ownership capable of ultimately decreasing competition. In Europe, the development of early national all-purpose or dedicated electronic communication systems with great tourism potential such as Minitel (France) and Prestel (UK) were seen as possible alternatives and possibly competing trends.

3) Early CIT-related re-structuring of airlines, hospitality organizations, intermediaries and industrial organizations were observed. In most cases, the advantages of scale economies were presumed to explain structural transformations (in terms of firms boundaries, scale, degrees of concentration, extent of product differentiation and changing relative market shares). They were portrayed as forerunning signs of the global tourism corporate structures (not yet perceived as the information network it has become). This was accompanied by the growth of travel services and the emergence of transnational alliances based on telecommunications, banking transactions and new information services [5,11]. But the identification of new marketing tools, scale economies or sources of competitive advantages available to existing large tour operators supported concerns regarding scenarios of a rapid demise of conventional tourism intermediaries.

4) The more recent trends (typical of ENTER Conference proceedings) have shifted towards the globalization of distribution systems, electronic document interchange and inter-connectivity issues. This usually involves identifying potential winners and losers in the tourism system, comments about various degrees of adoption of technology in various sectors or by firms of various sizes. The strategic management literature has done much to attempt to identify the types of technological-marketing developments. This includes the use of databases, smart cards, forms of automation affecting producers, and intra- or extra- network alliances, all of which are capable of generating transaction or organizational economies eventually leading to competitive advantage. The increasingly pervasive but intricate role of the internet, in particular of its WWW component, in tourism and its relationship to existing global distribution systems remain the object of speculation.

5) Other developments have strong potential to transform tourism products and distribution channels even more radically. Examples of these are voice recognition systems, data warehousing and mining, artificial intelligence applications, virtual reality or geographical information systems, but the range of possibilities is extremely broad. Other overlapping discussions concern the creation of communication standards, the complementary and rival role of IT-based destination marketing -and planning- systems and the way that policy will coordinate all this so that it transforms the industry in the best way possible.

Despite the ability of the literature to identify critical and radical technological changes in the tourism system, there is very little analysis or even comprehensive speculation as to what the tourism organizational structures of the future might be like. There are too many interacting and relevant developments identified and very little lasting technological convergence.

There are many interesting avenues to envisioning the future of tourism. It is clear, however, that any avenue must encompass the indirect impacts on tourism via lifestyle changes which could be far greater in affecting the future of tourism than those directly associated with changing communications tools. The changing nature of consumption and work (household technology), the role of identity, heritage, environment, global and local cultures as well as transformations in the geo-political landscapes due to increasing trade, institutional and electronic interconnections are all relevant [6]. They constitute critical components of a broader analysis of the future of tourism. These components themselves interact closely with the CITs so often scrutinized in recent writings. Poon [12] touches on these interactions but anthropologists and sociologists have been far more forthcoming in attempting to tackle these issues; for instance Urry (1990) constitutes useful examples.

Even when restricted to conjectures about industrial matters, technology-tourism predictions hold potentially contradictory outcomes for the tourism system which make it risky for analysts to attempt generalizations. Sheldon [15] looks at the relationship between CIT developments and industrial structures to show that many CIT impacts hold both stabilizing and destabilizing potential and that this could lead to more or less concentrated travel and tourism industrial structures in different contexts.

Even in terms of the very near future of specific tourism stakeholders, it seems very difficult to find any convergence in the beliefs of commentators interested in the impacts of new CITs. The popular and controversial issue of disintermediation provides a telling example. Early alarming statements about the threat from GDSs have been replaced by even broader concerns for the role of internet-based distribution channels and the possible disappearance of traditional distribution channels. Yet the literature includes all possible scenarios for the future, ranging from that of very little change (only a redistribution of customers according to propensity to use that sort of technology) to the integration of the new channels by dominant and large agencies capable of capitalizing on the new possibilities and creating their own applications. This can extend even further to darker scenarios of completely redundant travel agents [9,4,2]. Others believe that agents will gain a privileged position as experts capable of handling the new networks and electronic engines. Predictions range therefore between the emergence of perhaps excessively fast-growing highly sophisticated complex technological networks to that of a new, democratic electronic market-place for travel services providing increasingly broad opportunities for individuals and probably small, innovative operators [10].

A thorough analysis of the above possibilities would require an investigation of a large number of issues.

- First, the extent to which various user market segments are becoming increasingly computer- and system- literate;
- Second, the extent to which agents hold an advantage over the public in finding, comprehending or processing information or in safely executing travel-related transactions;
- Third, assessing the extent to which the explosion of data is likely to become matched by intelligent software or expert systems with the ability to affect the usability of internet-based networks; and
- Fourth, the relative speeds at which various groups of stakeholders will be capable of learning and influencing the designs of those systems to circumvent technological disadvantages.

To progress in assessing such complex developments requires a more thoroughly dynamic analytical approach applicable to complex, evolutionary systems. Viewing CIT-related developments as either increasing, decreasing or shifting barriers to entry for existing industrial and corporate structures assumes peripheral technological impacts and does not adequately reflect the organic relationships between complex tourism motivations, evolving products and changing distribution methods. The first step in attempting to portray the shaping of technological and organizational futures of the broad tourism system lies in attempting to classify various technological trends and connect them with various (and possibly contradictory) components of the tourism system.

In fact, difficulties in constructing predictions about the future of tourism might be critically linked with deeply entrenched postulates regarding the convergence of technological systems and the usually hidden assumption that industries tend to become standardized. Recent work in the study of complex and rapidly changing technological systems such as tourism have shown that it would be erroneous to assume that these are compelled to converge towards ever stable technological standards and organizational structures [17]. Whether the industry is becoming bipolar [3,15] or simply more complex remains to be established. But it seems that a more realistic and valuable prognosis for the future of tourism needs to explicitly take into account, and eventually model, the role of systemic diversity and identify the seeds of novelty in the tourism system [16].

3 Tourism as an Innovation System: To Learn or not to Learn?

It is fortunate that calls for a greater focus on the conceptual role of "information" in the tourism system have been well received and noted [12,14]. But progress towards comprehending the evolution of tourism requires that the analysis move even further; towards comprehending how knowledge is divided among tourism-related stakeholders, how it leads to process and product innovations, and identifying institutions involved in its coordination [17].

Some older concerns have re-surfaced and a number of relatively recent contributions have moved towards addressing directly the nature of the innovation process in tourism. One such customary question is whether technological development in tourism is driven or shaped by organizations exogenous to the conventionally defined tourism system (often referred to as "technology-push") or whether it is mainly exhorted and articulated by tourism services producers and intermediaries. Our incomplete knowledge of the global impacts of CITs on tourism (and the wisdom from other areas of computer applications) suggest that it is wise to move away from pure technology-push and tourism demand-pull models. Recognizing that tourism is characterized by a great diversity of uses, users, market segments and producing sectors implies that little generalization can take place regarding the sources of technological change in the system and their likely directions. This explains why tourism-technology surveys are usually valid only in specific tourism contexts (market or destination) and that the extent of control, reliance or adoption of technology is different between sectors (transport firms, hospitality firms, tour operator or travel agents). Moreover the origins of technological progress and the extent of CIT impacts differ for firms of various sizes and can diverge as the new applications, products or modes of distribution develop [15].

Yet the literature includes representations of tourism firms ranging from that of rather passive (as individual firms but not necessarily sector-wide) with respect to the adoption of new technologies to that of tourism innovators often driven by IT-based product differentiation strategies [13,6]. Poon's analysis of tourism competitive strategies has played a significant role in challenging long held views about tourism services sectors being purely passive in incorporating new technologies. It promotes the notion that tourism firms would undertake product-market differentiation and keep on adjusting their positioning strategies through clever use of CITs. Poon's vision of flexible, segmented and diagonally integrated businesses replace those firms who in the past invested in the supply of mass, standardized and rigidly-packaged tourist products. Flexible tourism firms establish their competitive advantage by creating new products in the form of attractions, distribution channels or marketing concepts rather than simply appropriating economic rents from the large-scale coordination of complex tourism flows.

While central to the model, the role of information technology and the nature of its evolutionary drive remain in large part ambiguous. Poon divides the tourism system into information-processing components and basic services suppliers. Standardization in the sphere of activities dedicated to managing information channels is assumed to be complementary to the maintenance of variety in the area of service provision. If the former group of services provides a broad and commonly available information technology platform, small services suppliers do not suffer from scale economies in marketing disadvantages. Service suppliers in general can depend less on tour operators as packaging can be undertaken by retailers or tourists themselves with the help of these market-enhancing technologies [13]. Although Poon does not make such a clear-cut distinction, she presumably assumes that a large share of CIT infrastructure is essentially driven outside tourism organizations while tourism firms use available information flows (and potentially some applications and peripheral product innovations) to compete with each other, but without much of an impact on technology design. This seems to be the sense in which she argues that new tourism technologies are "integrating" the system, but this has little connection with corporate vertical integration or even standardization of the technological make-up of tourism firms. In fact, Poon does not attempt to make predictions about the impacts of CIT growth on market structures or on corporate boundaries. She even explicitly recognizes that the advent of flexible tourism firms does not equate with smaller size or even flatter structures. Integration apparently refers to the density of the information network in which the contemporary tourism firm operates. But tourism firms show very diverse propensities to integrate in that information network; they can well choose to ignore it and yet perform well. If Poon's theme of differentiation is developed further, it would support the view that competitive advantage arises from diversity in "information strategy", and such strategies can range from isolated, endogenous technological (process, product or market) adaptation to highly integrated leadership in the determination of technological standards. Perhaps it is necessary to move away from analyzing such issues as "disintermediation" and the role of technological networks in terms of information efficiency and move towards relative learning abilities [16,17]. The survival of various organizations will depend indeed on their ability to coordinate diverse and changing knowledge networks - networks about production technology, markets and emerging new products.

There have been few attempts to understand the technological innovation in tourism. Barras [1] was a precursor in attempting to show that traditional product lifecycles models of innovations applied mainly to conventional industries featuring the manufacturing of standard goods. In that case, radical innovations (establishing new products or standards, and possibly new industries) emerge unpredictably in a given industrial sector which are followed by technological competition in which a number of standards compete with each other. Eventually an industrial standard dominates and technological progress is mainly dominated by converging, incremental technical improvements. From a services perspective, Barras describes incremental improvements in services eventually followed by services differentiation and possibly new products.

When innovation and tourism are jointly examined, the situation portrayed is one in which very few clear patterns emerge. Hjalager examines and categorizes many sources of innovations but does not attempt to predict technological directions or draw policy implications. Ioannides and Debbage [8] notice the fact that technological developments ranging from CRS, GDS and Internet-WWW are continually shifting the relative advantages of large and/or big tourism operators. They refer to a "travel polyglot" to describe heterogeneous and evolving production and distribution systems whose course and boundaries are difficult to perceive. The overwhelming diversity and complexity of the tourism-technological nexus should not be attributed to simplistic adaptations on the lifecycle idea. For instance, it could be suggested that technological diversity in tourism is due to the fact that various markets or destinations are at different development stages in their adoption of relevant tourism-related CITs but will eventually follow similar patterns and produce similar industrial systems. This would be rejected by much of the recent tourism literature which instead associates the inherent nature of the tourism phenomenon with the unpredictable and volatile technological system it creates [8,17].

In recognizing the chaotic aspect of the tourism system and the technologies supporting it, an evolutionary methodology is proposed. This does not equate with suggestions that nothing useful can be learned about tourism development, which can be used for strategic management or policy. Rather it suggests that how the tourism system learns, by adopting and adapting exogenous CIT development, or by endogenously shaping new markets and products, ought to constitute the object of investigation in tourism research [17].

4 The Sources of Innovation in Tourism

This paper proposes a macro-exploration of the various technological developments shaping and influenced by tourism organizations. It constitutes only a first stage in analyzing the tourism-technology nexus and it is restricted to the direct connections between CITs and tourism production-distribution. The first step proposed is to categorize major technological drivers by building on recognized and meaningful dimensions of various CIT industries. This will lead to a mapping of various technologies encountered in tourism. It will be suggested that diverse mixes of industries within and outside tourism steer technological trajectories that ultimately affect tourism industrial organization. It will be followed by an attempt to link relevant CIT examples of such developments in the context of tourism (identified in the literature) with the various categories of tourism industrial sectors.

Fig. 1
Industrial Mapping of CIT Industry
(Source: Houghton,J.W., Pucar, M. and Knox, C., 1996)

SERVICES ↑

FORM → / CONDUIT			SUBSTANCE / CONTENT
BASIC TELEPHONY SERVICES Voice: local, STD, ISDN Mobile: Voice, Paging, Data Equip rental & Repairs, etc	**CALL/ TELEPHONY SERVICES** Resale/ Aggregation Callback Account mgmt Call completion Centrex Etc.	**HIGHER LEVEL & NETWORK** EFT & Transactions EDI, Voice/E-mail Video conference Video & Broadcast News & Directory Svcs. Etc	**PROFESSIONAL SERVICES** Consulting Systems Integration EDP account/audit Engineering services Education & Training etc.
COMMUNICATION	**SERVICES**	**INFORMATION**	**SERVICES**
BCS & TRANSMISSION Interconnect (ends) Transmission Services Etc.	**LEASED LINE & PSDN SERVICES** Leased lines Data network svc VANs, VPNs, IVANS Etc.	**NETWORK & SERVICES** ISP/IAP MSN, Compuserve, Etc. Pay-TV nets Etc.	**COMPUTER, COMMS & SOFTWARE SVS** Bureau/Data Proc FM Outsourcing Maintenance, Etc.
LINE, TRANSMISSION & B'CASTING EQUIP Cable and Wire Line, Cellular, Radio Microwave & Satellite transmission equip Etc.	**SWITCH,LAN, WAN & DATA EQUIP** COS Bridges, Routers, Hubs, Mux, Multiplexers Modems Etc.	**NETWORK SOFTWARE** Net Operating Systems Net mgmt/diagnostics Navigation tools OSS, Etc.	**PACKAGED SOFTWARE** Applications Tools Etc.
INFORMATION	**COMMS EQUI**	**INFORMATION**	**PRODUCTS**
TERMINAL & PERIPHERAL EQUIP CPE Mobile & Paging I/O Devices Components Office equipment Etc.	**COMPUTER EQUIPMENT** PCs Workstations Small-scale Mid-range Large-scale etc.	**SYSTEMS SOFTWARE** Systems Utilities Etc.	**NETWORKED CONTENT** Online publications News services content Database content Programming, Multimedia, Etc.

PRODUCTS ↓

We use the information technology mapping developed by Houghton, Pucar and Knox [7] to identify relevant dimensions for the categorization of CITs. This mapping is itself an adaptation of the older Harvard map which depicted IT-related industries in terms of the positioning of firms in the aggregate technological process i.e. whether the firm's product is closer to "form" - or hardware - or closer to "substance" - or software. The second dimension broadly distinguishes between services and products (or perhaps more adequately "goods"). Both dimensions incorporate useful attributes for the sake of identifying influences on technological developments and they constitute continuous scales.

The Houghton & al. map builds on the same dimensions and develops more precisely the types of product-technology categories that can be drawn from the broad CIT sector. The vertical dimension still differentiates between "services" and "products". Items placed closer to the services end are "closer to the network end users' use and to final consumption" while those closer to products constitute the building blocks or "elemental parts of the network" [7]. In terms of CITs, this means that items classified as closer to services tend to be more customized and necessarily more likely to be shaped by end users insofar as product differentiation is concerned. In other words, the ability to adapt the design and marketing of these products to suit the distinct needs of users (either customers or firms) is critical to competitive advantage for these CITs. At the product (lower) end of the vertical scale, competitiveness is driven by more traditional imperatives of standardization allowing scale economies and cost competition. The ability to design or adopt dominant standards applying across types of users, industrial sectors and firms promotes technological races supporting technology-push types of strategies.

The horizontal scale features the form (conduit) - substance (content) dimension. Conduit commodities involve communications and information infrastructure - related products and services. Again, contests and rivalries over dominant standards play a particularly important role and their success will depend on their acceptance by connected users (for instance tourism stakeholders or members of given tourism industrial networks). Rapid diffusion of given types of communication infrastructures within tourism would constitute a necessary condition for success. At the other end of the horizontal dimension, firms producing CIT commodities involving content will benefit if their products or services are both widely acceptable to user-customers and are sufficiently inimitable (in terms of design, marketing or distribution) to offer temporary relief from imitation. In this case competitive advantage involves retaining some advantage in proprietary production or distribution knowledge and often results in producing products and services bundles designed to meet the needs of the end-user customer and simultaneously prevent competitors to reverse-engineer the product.

Using the mapping of CITs developed by Houghton & al., it becomes possible to formulate a number of hypotheses as to the most important influences on various technologies. In the present exploratory paper, these categories are quite broad. It is useful to distinguish between:

[a]   tourists (as final consumer-users)
[b]   tourism production firms (direct services suppliers involved associated with passenger transportation, hospitality services, interpretation and attractions...)
[c]   tourism intermediaries (conventional tourism retailing and wholesaling...)
[d]   CIT organizations (including data and telecommunications infrastructure)
[e]   information-services firms (financial transactions, professional services and other information-processing firms)
[f]   governments and other organizations dealing with tourism policies
[g]   governments and other organizations dealing with CIT policies

This simple categorization allows us to differentiate between forces endogenous and exogenous to tourism. Defined in a conventional way, tourism includes categories a, b, c and f. A tentative connection is made between technological development and driving forces related to these sectors in the following way:

-       If a technological innovation or type is located closer to the "services" end, it is customized for specific users (in the present context more likely for tourism services providers) and is largely influenced by tourism firms using it. Alternatively, if it is closer to products, it is more standardized and "pushed" by technology developers.

-       If a technological innovation or type is closer to the content end of the horizontal dimension, it is more likely to be flexible and influenced by end-users (for a given choice or standard of conduit-form) while if it is located closer to the form-conduit end, it is more likely to be shaped by contests between organizations attempting to impose their standards.

This could usefully be summarized by a matrix depicting zones of greatest influence, and in theory overlapping with CIT technologies described in the table above. See Fig. 2 below.

When products related to form-conduit are developed, they are mainly influenced by CIT industries and other (non-tourism) industries adopting the same types of products [7]. When services connected with form-conduit evolve, they involve a certain degree of customization. Recent communication services, including telephony, have developed services and packages specifically used in tourism and sometimes specific to given organizations. Examples of these are the hand-held terminals used in restaurants and rental car check-ins. Also the telephone systems used by airlines for customers to check flight arrival and departures and frequent flyer status. These are voice recognition systems using the latest in that technology.

228

Fig. 2
Spheres of Influence in the Technology-Tourism Nexus

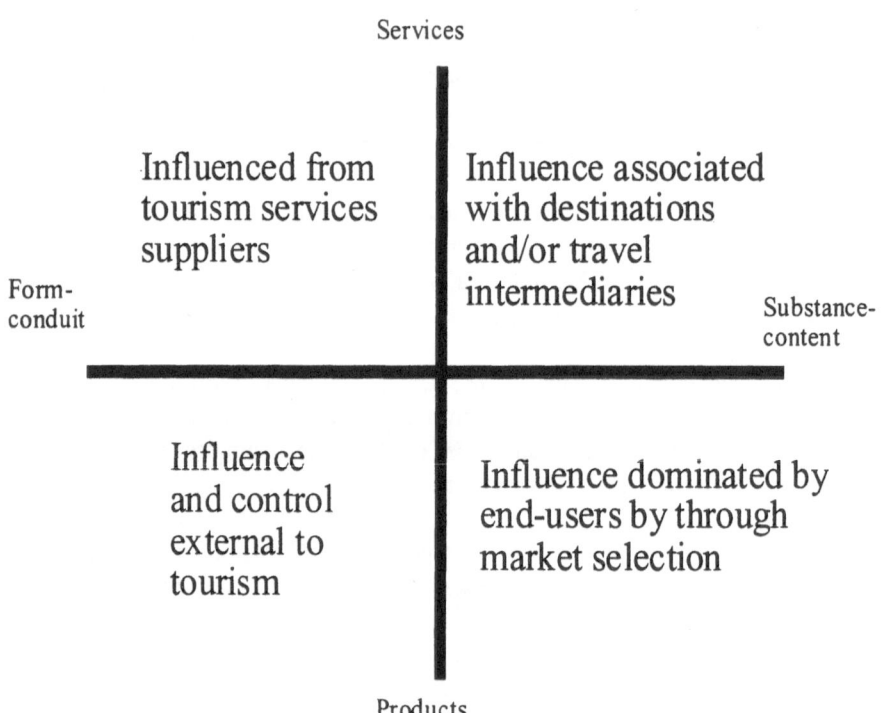

Services

Influenced from
tourism services
suppliers

Influence associated
with destinations
and/or travel
intermediaries

Form-
conduit

Substance-
content

Influence
and control
external to
tourism

Influence dominated by
end-users by through
market selection

Products

Services involving the design and creation of content involve customized content shaped in large part by local tourism systems. Such services are used by destination marketing organizations and localized groups of travel intermediaries. Products involving content (including multimedia applications, applications tools, on-line publications, database content etc.) involve the tourists as end-users directly and indirectly. Through market interactions, tourists shape the products that become successful and choose the marketing and distribution channels that come to dominate the tourism system.

In the tourism industry, there are examples of services and products with both form-conduit and substance-content. Fig. 3 shows how various tourism technologies fall into the four quadrants.

5 Implications for Tourism Industry Structure

The complexity of the industry and the speed of technological change make the mapping tentative at best. It does however allow an initial examination of the evolving technologies and their impacts on the various tourism sectors.

The influence of developments in the CIT industry is strongest in the lower left (technology-push) quadrant, where new products are not determined by the tourism industry directly, but by the new communication technologies being designed and marketed. New products arising from developments in data communication technology affecting air, car and hotel reservation systems are expected in this section. Developments in both left quadrants will be important as the inter-sectoral and international communication links become increasingly important to the growth of the tourism industry. The transportation service providers tend to be the drivers of the technologies in these quadrants. The progress in the upper left quadrant is impacted by, and has consequences for, the GDS as they redefine themselves in the light of new standards and Internet developments. Whatever changes ensue there will definitely affect the industry structure in yet unknown ways.

The technologies in the lower right quadrant are most affected by changes in the tourism market. End-consumers, with their increasing sophistication and expectation levels, drive new developments here and will pull the migration of technologies from other sectors. While the technologies are becoming more standardized, the service and value-added offered by firms will be important sources of product differentiation and competitive advantage. Competitive forces will be strong and firms are likely to remain lean and flexible, as they identify new markets for their products.

In the upper right quadrant, the role of public, private or quasi-public destination organizations and travel intermediaries will be paramount in the service development. The forces impacting the tourism distribution channel will play an important role as the battle to reach the consumer continues, and new services and new products are developed. Destinations that continuously scan the technological developments and integrate them into their destination's operations and create incentives or directions for the suppliers to use them will gain competitive advantages. The DMO's and other tourism-related organizations can have a strategic influence over the development of telecommunications and other technology policies to potentially strengthen the industry.

The impact of technologies on market concentration and firm size in tourism can be difficult to predict and fragmented. Mergers and acquisitions between tourism firms and CIT firms are likely to continue, particularly those related to the Internet, as technology continues to drive the industry. Mergers that permit firms to reach broader markets, both internationally and across sectors, are expected, mostly in the two services quadrants. Firms that are closer to the substance-content end of the continuum are likely to remain smaller, to face more direct competition, and will need to rely on intellectual capital more heavily. They will also need to be aggressive and creative in identifying new markets and working with customization and relationship marketing concepts.

230

Fig. 3
Mapping of Tourism Technologies

SERVICES

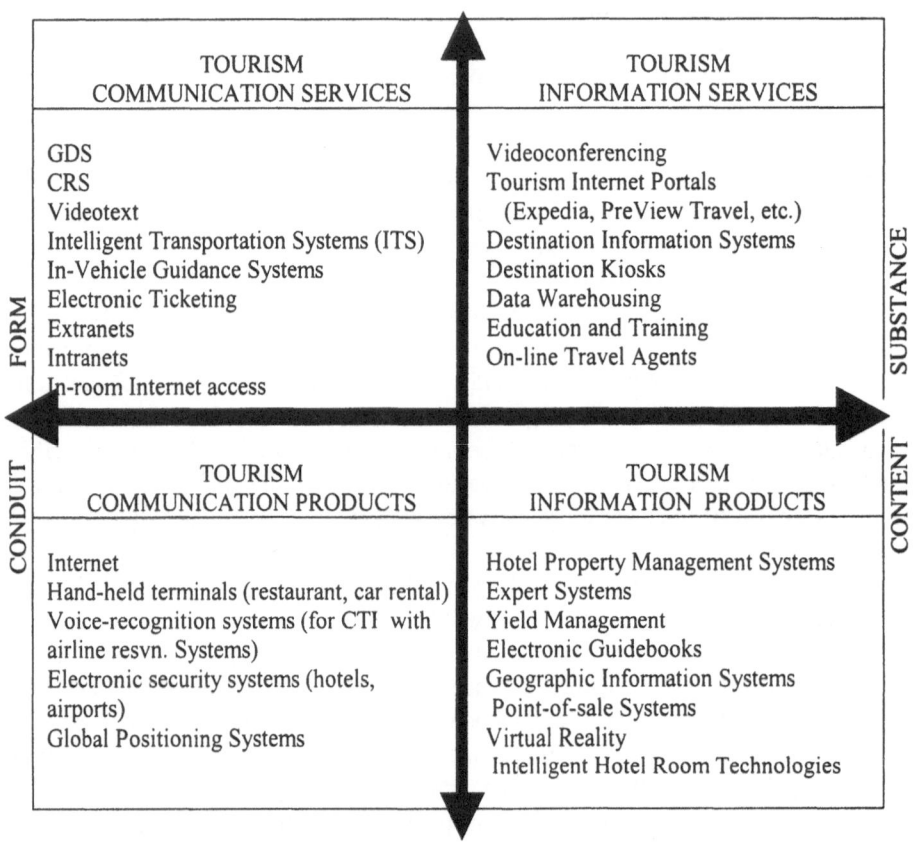

PRODUCTS

This tourism technology map is only a beginning to identify the impacts of CIT developments on the industry. Further research to examine the impacts of information technologies on tourism is needed.

References

1. Barras, R.: Towards a theory of innovation in services. Research Policy, 15, 161-73, (1986).

2. Boberg, K. and Fred Collison: Computer Reservation Systems and Airline Competition. Tourism Management, 174 -183, (1984).

3. Cazes, G.: Le tourisme international: mirage ou strategie d'avenir. Paris, Hatier, (1989).

4. Cottin, Denis: Rythmes du Monde Voyages une agence pionniere sur L'autoroute de L'information," Teoros, 14, 20-21 (1995).

5. Feldman, J.M.; The Growth of International Travel Service Companies, Travel and Tourism Analyst, 88(2): 56-69 (1989).

6. Hjalager, A.M.: Dynamic Innovation in the Tourism Industry. in Cooper (ed.) Progress in Tourism and Recreation and Hospitality Management, 6 197-224 (1994).

7. Houghton, J.W., Pucar, M., and Knox, C.: Mapping the Information Industries. Productivity Commission Staff Information Paper, Australian Government Publishing Service, Canberra 20 (1996).

8. Ioannides, D., and Keith Debbage: Post-Fordism and Flexibility: The Travel Industry Polyglot. Tourism Management, 18 229-241 (1997).

9. Le Roux, P. and Francois Bedard: Les Agences de Voyage vont-elles finir dans le Fosse des Inforoutes?. Teoros, 14 8-10 (1995).

10. Lin, Lily: Computer Based Information Technologies and Their Impact on the Marketing of International Tourism Industry in Proceedings of Information and Communications Technologies, Springer, 318-327 (1998).

11. Mowlana, H., and G. Smith: Tourism, Telecommunications and Transnational Banking: A Framework for Policy Analysis. Tourism Management 12.315-324. (1990).

12. Poon, Auliana: Tourism, CAB International Publishing, Oxford, England, (1995).

13. Poon, Auliana: Tourism and Information Technologies, Annals of Tourism Research. 15: (1988).

14. Sheldon, Pauline J.: Destination Information Systems. Annals of Tourism Research, 20, 633-49, (1993).

15. Sheldon, Pauline J.: Tourism Information Technology, CAB International Publishing, Oxford England (1997).

16. Tremblay, Pascal: The Economic Organization of Tourism, Annals of Tourism Research, 25 837-859 (1998).

17. Tremblay, Pascal: The Economic Organization of Tourism, PhD Dissertation, University of Melborne, (1997).

18. Urry, J.: The Sociology of Tourism. In Progress in Tourism, Recreation and Hospitality Management, C.P. Cooper (ed.), 3 48-57. London: Belhaven. (1990).

19. Werthner, Hannes and Klein, Stefan: Information Technology and Tourism - A Challenging Relationship. Springer, Vienna New York, (1999).

Developing Rural Tourism Destinations: Implications for, and of, Information Systems

G.A. Lyons
Wolverhampton Business School
University of Wolverhampton

1 Introduction

This paper emanated from an exploratory research project relating to the process of tourism development in a market town and surrounding rural area. Using a services marketing approach, samples were drawn from three categories of stakeholders - visitors, service providers and local government. Communication and knowledge requirements in product/service development and the potential role of information technology evolved as issues for further research.

The focus of the paper is to highlight certain aspects which arose as a consequence of data interpretation. It does not presume or pretend to provide definitive knowledge relative to information technology in tourism.

Tourism as a leisure pursuit has many facets, encompassing a wide variety of provision and degrees of sophistication. Technology has made the world more accessible, more frequently, necessitating up to date, timely and reliable information. This holds true not only for the consumer but also for those whose livelihood is perceived to be dependent upon tourism revenue and who need to ensure that they are meeting tourist needs and reaching relevant markets. Consumer knowledge, confidence and sophistication are generating an increasing number of independent travellers, many of whom are seeking respite from the stresses of modern life. Whilst they clearly require information, the mode by which it is given, and whether it is perceived as facilitative or core in relation to the experience, is largely under-researched. Implicit are issues of perceived quality and value.

Rural tourism is an international growth sector which has received comparatively little research attention to date. It is a sector characterised by small businesses, often at the level of single self-employment - one third of businesses in the UK are situated in the rural economy. Market towns, suffering from the effects of agricultural decline, seek ways of developing products and providing information to tourism segments as an alternative economic strategy. The geographical area within which the research project was undertaken, Middle England, benefited from 2.8mn bed nights with £85mn domestic spend and 0.6mn bed nights (£25mn) spend from overseas visitors(Tourism Facts 1997). Rural-Europe - European Commission (1997) expresses concern with regard to the relatively limited product range and lack of structured rural tourism visibility to the market, pointing out that an inadequacy of product precludes viable promotional campaigns. The organisation acknowledges an "unstructured pool" of tourists, tired of the mass experience, seeking opportunities for independence, cultural bonding and highly personalised intellectual discovery. Emotive experience, as opposed to consumption, evolves from a high element of human interaction. Service levels are critical and customer diversity indicates "kit" products for self-assembly, dictating a need for an appropriate and comprehensible data bank, enhanced by an interrogative facility.

2 Information and the product

Computer technology as part of an information infrastructure is an accepted tool of the tourism industry yielding two strands for information technology applications - demand side and supply side requirements. A third strand, information technology *as part of the tourism product,* (as opposed to facilitating specific development and access) is an area which deserves greater attention. Within the concept of the research this projected as *information regarding issues which furthered the self actualising process,* involving interaction, acquisition, evaluation and informing the next course of action. This is perceived as essentially different in type, purpose and value from information such as directions to the ancient burial site or the opening times of the museum.

It is appropriate to distinguish between "marketing", being the identification and servicing of tourists' needs and wants, and "promotion", which is primarily the advertising of tourism offerings to potential consumers. Early Internet applications tend towards "push" strategies, presumably due to the complexities of refinement towards a more personalised "pull" strategy, but there is evidence that this is changing (Inkpen 1998). There is a growing need for deeper understanding of tourist motivation and experiential requirements, which in the case of particular scenarios and segments, dictate both the role and place of information systems *within the tourism product,* as opposed to an important linked resource and facilitator. Success in both promotion and product development is contingent upon the understanding of the segments attracted, rather than the promotion of existing provision, on a relatively undifferentiated basis.

Cowell (1998) points to neglect in new product development in the service context as being contingent upon the skill base, (see also Pessenier 1966) limited resources and the lack of innovation found in public sector organisations. This is supported by Kosters (1988) who refers to passivity of government at all levels interested solely in promotion, ignoring innovation. Complexities, inter-relationships and historic experience of tourism as being " the attraction to attractions" combine to focus resources upon place promotion. Destination development often uses planning frameworks which do not encompass the marketers insight into creation of a product which serves more than one market, highly subjective, experiential, and personalised.

Current market trends necessitate an in-depth marketing approach. As Buhalis (1998) observes, strategically astute, creative and innovative suppliers employing the full scope of IT coupled with novel management methods, organisation and training will be best placed to benefit from a New Wave in tourism. There is an imperative to establish a knowledge base of product linkages and desired consumer benefits. The holistic product dimension of emerging markets and segments is exemplified in the Servicescape model of service delivery (Bitner 1990). This model indicates that everything which contributes to the consumer experience is a product attribute, not only in the "what" but also the "how". Discrete and personalised information which informs the day-to-day activities of the tourist (as opposed to choice of destination and the different services which contribute to the experience) has traditionally been supplied at destination level by a human rather than an electronic force. The introduction of local computerised linkages to tourism suppliers, theoretically operable on a 24hour basis, is gradually changing the nature of this interface. The physical environment plays a significant role and raises the question as to how feasible or appropriate is ye olde worlde computer terminal in a backwater of cobbled streets, horse troughs and a butter cross. Does information technology at destination level hold an overt place in this particular product at all?

From the supply side perspective, such a facility minimises resource input and potentially provides scale economies leading to long run cost effectiveness; the provision assumes that demand side (tourist) requirements for information will be met by this method. Whilst this might be true for many instances, it is important that the role, nature and methodology of information transfer are compatible with the tourist's perception of the product.

3 The Research project

The research forming the basis of this paper was essentially exploratory. The project attempted to discover and highlight aspects which might contribute to a new rural tourism development framework, and to point up issues for future research. Utilising primary research relating to the identification of tourists and their product requirements, the analysed data was mapped against the perceptions of the community, and the views and development processes of the policy and decision makers. Analysis revealed an information/perception mismatch in a number of areas. The project uncovered a common tourist typology across three related samples, which dictated the desired product, the service attributes, value and quality embedded in the product.

3.1 The identified tourist

A number of authors agree that rural tourism is known to be accessed largely by the middle - aged upwards, who demonstrate an increasing degree of discernment, high disposable income and a pre-disposition towards nostalgia, coupled with an independence which frequently eschews package holidays. Bramwell (1993) attests to the increased affluence, education, spending inclinations and quality requirements of rural tourists

The data identified a quiet, educated affluent tourist for whom aesthetic fulfilment and a sense of belonging and welcome were instrumental in a satisfactory experience. Largely professional and retired, they demonstrated that physical and experiential factors stimulated emotional responses, which influenced length of stay, spending level and propensity to revisit. As such, they provide evidence of the importance of the SOR model of Donovan & Rossiter (1982) in rural tourism development. Intangibles such as ambience and congruity play an important role in certain experiences.

3.2 The identified rural product

Academic authors Alexander & McKenna (1998) refer to the highly fragmented activity base, Wheeler (1995) cites changing social values as drivers of demand for authenticity and exclusivity. Proctor (1996) & Theobald (1998) highlight a need for quality and service excellence, with organisations offering core and augmented services in order to respond to changing requirements (Morash, Droge & Vickery, 1997). Hopkins (1998) cites Goss (1993) and Park & Coppack (1994) referring to rurality in tourism as being a mythical cultural landscape created by both organic and induced means. Page & Getz (1994) indicate that rural areas have unique attributes and it is important to recognize that access and development fundamentally change and eventually destroy the product. Information is therefore a critical management tool.

For the sample under study, one of the key product features was the interaction with the population, particularly in the context of historic information, places to visit and local knowledge. Data suggested that this was a preferred information source. Part of the attraction was that local people with special interests were perceived as a resource for tourist enjoyment. The "welcome factor" formed part of the core benefit; strong personal involvement indicated Maslovian elements of belongingness and self-actualisation. Nostalgic experiences, exploration and discovery, knowledge acquisition and exposure to traditional values were important. Whilst the actors were embedded as part of the product, the relationship was that of informer and adviser rather than of entertainer.

The segment was concerned with authenticity rather than the pastiche or parody of certain "modern" tourist heritage attractions. Authentic (that is to say standard verbal, as opposed to dramaturgical or technological) interaction with the community and culture appeared to be a value measure, adding another dimension to the school of thought which denotes value as being a price - quality relationship (Murphy, Pritchard

& Smith 1999). Information or lack of it at destination level appeared in this research to be a quality issue with no price application in terms of financial or time cost. However, such information and the culturally interactive means of accessing it were instrumental to enjoyment. Tourists were open to "experiential" costs. There are potential implications for host communities in terms of lost revenue from the "disappointment factor" which may prevent repeat or recommended visits.

3.3 The product-information interface

At the operational level, service provision breaks down broadly into front office and back office activities.

The front office application is appropriate for remote, i.e. destination removed information and booking systems which provide a broad destination outline with particular, discrete booking information. This promotes, facilitates or otherwise decides the pre-purchase knowledge base and is instrumental in the buying decision process. It is part of the sales promotion armoury. Another dimension is the (traditionally) destination located and personalised activity specific information which tourists such as those identified in the survey require. This is where the potential problems begin.

It may be prohibitive for a small Town Council in the early stages of tourism activity to provide and staff an information centre or service; a cost effective option is deemed to be a stand-alone interactive computer terminal, such as the UK Visitor Links. This may not always fit with the product concept, nor does it necessarily solve the problem.

For operational and security reasons, terminals may be sited in, say, public libraries where there is extremely limited access at weekends. This is precisely the time when there is likely to be a heavy demand for information. Where units are externally sited, they are vulnerable. How are destination image damaging issues such as malfunction, vandalism and the inevitable paper jam or run-out to be overcome? What lessons have been or need to be learned from the vending machine explosion of the 60s and 70s? Because that is exactly what is being advocated - an information vendor with the attendant problems of superglue in the keyboard and dents in the cabinet from a passing drunk. There is the issue of appropriateness alluded to earlier - does nostalgic authencity preclude modern technology in an accessible public place? Evidence from the research project showed clearly that in this market town, the attraction was that there was no attraction, in the sense of fee-based tourist "entertainment" or experiences such as castles or museums. "Untouched England" as a place of self generated discovery and a slower pace was the essence of the product. Time, whilst not quite standing still, had moved more slowly. There had been no tourism investment, and the very few shop fronts which had bowed to modernity were criticised as being incongruous and out of character.

There are scenarios, some of them rural, where taped commentaries, virtual reality and computer generated images provide links with the past, and in these cases overt information systems are not out of place. Where the concept of tourism differs to encompass a more relaxed way of life, a different set of values, classical interests and a retreat from the stresses of modernity then technological aids to tourism need to be very much of the back office variety. How then, in this most pertinent of situations might we ensure that technology will indeed be "transparent, invisible for the consumer"? (FITT White Paper, 1998).

3.4 The Technological /Tourist Interface

There is potential for enhanced creativity in the way technology is used. Page & Getz (1997) suggest that an in-car direct access information system might be appropriate where information centres are concentrated in towns. The suggestion linked to information relating to America which is geographically different from small English market towns, or those in Mediaeval France which themselves epitomise rurality. This distinguishing aspect emphasises that rural tourism is not a single entity and that product development has to reflect a number of differing characteristics, attitudes, and requirements. A single location does not have the capacity to be many things to many people in the way that urban areas might. It therefore follows that technology aids and inputs perhaps need a greater degree of specificity and customisation.

Linking Buhalis (1998) and Lue, Crompton & Fesenmaier (1993) with the independent tourist indicates that a facet of innovative management is the recognition that competitiveness stems from strategic alliances; in this instance trip chaining, a feature of packaged tours, might be utilised in rural tourism in order to enhance the benefit to the area. Such a feature enables a region to showcase synergistic products and facilitates a tourist's enjoyment of the different chosen facets of rurality. The independent traveller needs sufficient prior information to plan his/her linked destination experience, necessitating complementary, strategically interlinked (rather than competing) web pages. This then implies that a previously identified bundle of characteristics, which made up the single product has transformed into one containing multi elements. An extension of experiential location creates a requirement for a standardised continuity of   inputs such as information, access and quality of service, which stems from strategic development and interactive planning.

CD Rom, Internet, and e-mail facilities are capable, both jointly and independently, of providing the base and added value information *prior* to the tourism experience, thereby separating it from the point of consumption, detaching it from the product as experienced. Inkpen (1998) explains the Microsoft Expedia programme which offers chat lines with travel experts and a subsite where travellers are able to exchange experiences, This application might usefully be adapted for destination use, incorporated in a website, supplemented by a facility which utilises willing local specific expertise (historians, naturalists) as contributors and more particularly as human rather than technological contacts/advisers for visitors. This would provide the basis of a facility whereby the tourist elicits information, some of which may be too specialized or personalized to warrant general public availability. Obtaining this prior to the trip enables pre discussion and planning, facility to write down or print off details in advance, utilising technology "upfront" thereby minimising or negating the direct intrusion of technological modernity into a nostalgic experience. The self-actualising exploratory focus of a bygone age remains *image intacta,* and the opportunity to re-establish physical contact provides an introduction to local cultural interaction.

3.5 Sustainability and Ethics

Another facet to be considered is the extent to which IT is able to influence preservation or desecration. It is instrumental in increasing or decreasing volumes of tourists by selective imaging and messaging, but has the capacity to extend its role, promoting care in use by the tourist of the resources which are being consumed. Rural locations are inherently fragile with little commercial infrastructure and a heritage which needs to be preserved for future generations. There is a delicate balance between provision and destruction of the resource, needing special care in management (OECD 1994). Here, essentially, is an issue of ethics, relating to the moral obligation of the tourist to adhere to particular cultural codes of conduct in the destination choice. Information technology could provide support. Dress codes, differences in the interpretation of words, gestures and actions, which may provoke offence, might be conveyed; the international tourist is often ill prepared in such aspects. In this context, IT acts as not only an information provider, playing field leveller and cost reducer, but also has a potential role as guardian of resources and public relations officer.

4 The rural product development process

Research indicates that much of the activity which is described as marketing, is in fact promotion and that described as tourism development largely utilises planning frameworks to solve logistical problems. Development is also a descriptor for public/private sector initiatives to restore and promote some crumbling edifice, or to create a physical attraction which will increase tourist numbers. Bottom-up needs based approaches are more time consuming than top down planning, in part due to the process but also stemming from unfamiliarity with marketing techniques.

The public sector structure comprises a variety of organisations offering tourism promotion facilities at regional, county, and district levels (larger town councils holding umbrella responsibility for smaller market towns and rural areas). The project focused primarily at the district/ local interface of the decision making process with regard to the tourism offering. Under the guidance of a District - based tourism development unit, an active tourism association was in place; larger attractions were represented and the many small tourism operators were offered opportunities for joint promotion by inclusion within an internationally distributed brochure. The major remit of the unit was facilitation and promotion and local initiatives were required to fit within a regional strategy. Structured ideas for tourism initiatives requiring capital funding needed to be submitted from local level to district. Expertise in product development, both at individual provider and local government level was limited..

4.1 Expertise

Data revealed little evidence of local market knowledge and an absence of tourist data relative to typologies, behaviours and current growth trends in the general tourism market place. Each tier in the decision structure (provider, interest groups, tourism association, local and district councils) assumed that tourism innovation was the remit of the other. There was evidence of a shortfall in marketing expertise across the sample, most particularly related to new product development. Although party to a jointly commissioned consultancy report outlining key recommendations for economic regeneration (of which tourism formed a part) each market town appeared to operate independently of the others, with no strategic co-operation or appreciation of the benefits of destination branding, synergistic as opposed to duplicated development, and associated market rewards. Economic regeneration drivers conflicted also with the desire to remain true to heritage. Private sector investors were seen as the catalyst which would develop new tourism products. The issue of whether or not new investment should belong to the *enhancement* or the *development* regime, and the potential this would have in terms of changing the product and influencing the type and number of visitors to the area was not appreciated. There was scant appreciation of the importance, *as a development tool,* of data such as local, national and international intelligence relating to future tourism trends or tourist typologies.

4.2 Frameworks

The data indicated little knowledge of development processes. Much of the marketing and other tourism related literature exhibits a distinct lack of models and frameworks in the public sector, reinforced by Hall &Jenkins (1995) "......lack of definition, lack of data, lack of well defined analytical and theoretical frameworks".

Olsen, Cooper & Slater (1998) make reference to competencies, co-operation and relationships as being interdependent in new service development, echoing Palmer (1996) who calls for a seamless organisation, highlighting the importance of communication and training. Murphy (1985) stresses the need for community participation in concept design and development, whilst integration of cross-functional activities is advocated by Piercy & Cravens (1995) and Morash Droge & Vickery (1997). Gummesson (1994) refers to a stakeholder interface as being a social construct, similar to the "shamrock organisation" referred to by Handy (1990). In the study, the informal network appeared not so much shamrock as a couch grass network, some visible clumps hither and yon, with below ground activity, (often random and inappropriate) and some dormant nodes.

Development models utilised in public sector tourism incorporate role-play, scenario planning and spatial planning models. A number of authors such as Seaton (1994), Cooper (1994), Ashworth & Goodall (1990), identify various other useful models - situation analysis, benefits led service encounter frameworks and opportunity sets.

Where they are known, diverse constructs and methodologies potentially serve to confuse the disparate and inexpert elements which combine to offer the rural tourism experience.

4.3 Information, communication and training

The OECD in the paper Tourism Strategies and Rural Development (1994) highlights the paucity of training programmes in rural tourism with few formal qualifications available through an accreditation body, as a major stumbling block to development. Sporadic adaptations of business elements offered to small operators are deemed inappropriate for rural tourism planners and professionals. From a research perspective, it appears that provider and planner training requires some commonality in order to achieve consensus and commitment in development

An element highlighted by the study was the burden of competing business interests and personal commitments of the majority of the sample, and the consequent lack of time available to participate fully in idea generation and strategy formulation. Those in tourism provision work long hours; coupled with the lack of expertise in tourism development, it is no surprise that rural tourism does not always achieve full and equitable potential. Conversely, there is an inherent danger that local economic urgency may provoke "knee jerk" reactions. Initiatives undertaken without due regard for definition of core and peripheral products, corporate image, value versus volume, segment compatibility and community roles and attitudes to mention but a few will lead to problems.

Low entrepreneurial activity and little market expertise indicated that leadership and training was required. The combination of public and private sector activities complicates the formulation of coherent approaches. (TourISt Executive Summary, 2000). The public sector does not always provide the degree of co-operation and exchange of information, which may be necessary between the different levels and sectors. Lack of clarity in roles and responsibilities was highlighted by the research as a stumbling block., together with apparent communication deficiencies.

There is a need for communication which is timely and relevant and it is often the case that official paper based communications do not always fulfil this need. Lack of communication also leads to perceptions (sometimes erroneous) about the attributes and motivations of others. A perception gap can lead to the formation of attitudes and opinions, which do not aid the development process. It is not only the communication methodology that is an issue, but also frequency, nature and style are important. There is evidence that the perception gap existed also in relation to the supply side notion of what tourists wanted, and the product which they desired.

4.4 Potential role of Information Technology

Five years on from the call for an International Tourism Training Network (OECD 1994) there is a need for IT to provide networked training and a rural tourism product development template using a marketing perspective. This should be interactive and capable of integration with appropriate planning development frameworks. The package should be multilevel, correspond with role set definition, offer feedback, and an interrogative facility, reflecting the degree and direction of input, knowledge and expertise, familiarity and time available. Rural tourism encompasses mini and microbusiness as contributors to local decision-making forums, therefore simplicity of input and clarity of output is essential. Tourism is a constantly changing entity, and therefore such a system should encompass monitoring facilities enabling product adjustments to be determined over time.

Given the diversity of most public sector agencies involved with or holding responsibility for rural tourism, there is a need for an independent, unbiased overarching, centre of expertise to co-ordinate, monitor and advise. External consultants, international organisations and the increasing number of academic centres of excellence are contenders for the role.

From the communication perspective, an Intranet facility would enable relevant parties to disseminate information and ask questions with minimum interruption and inconvenience to their other commitments. The financial and time costs of equipment supply and training need to be overcome; costs could be minimised by the supply of a centralised allocation of hardware with open access. Training also relates to vocational aspects which small business find difficult to access. Standard skills materials linked to elements of customised application delivered electronically would enable flexible learning.

5 Conclusions

Rural destinations need to understand the commitment required to develop viable and equitable tourism, and the nature and extent of the associated costs and benefits. It is as important for the destination and the community to attract the "right" sort of tourist as it is for the tourist to access the "right" product. Sophisticated product development techniques can be facilitated by computer-based packages which encompass new thinking, state of the art databanks and scenario building, coupled with technical (soft and hardware) and procedural (marketing expertise) helpline.

The development and implementation of an on-line product development template package, or indeed communications networks and training packages, is subject to a number of constraints at the local level, two of which relate to incentives to become involved and funding for pump priming on going development and training. The former requires education as to the potential benefits for individuals, whilst the latter has a number of initiatives such as Leader 11, which applies in areas, which qualify under European Objectives 1. 5b and 6.

Research by other parties indicates that benefits are obtained from facilities to solicit the co-operation and experience of other initiative takers. The Website Inforurale-Rural Initiatives provides a number of headings under which information and contacts are listed, whilst the UK Rural Liaison Group comprises four country specific rural organisations co-operating in rural tourism knowledge and development. Expansion of this facility and a wider promulgation of the knowledge would assist in devolving necessary skills and expertise.

A key issue is to understand the precise role of different types of information *within* the rural tourism product. This ultimately means that for certain situations, knowledge has to be delivered at different times and in different ways by both human and technological processes. In the same way that prior warning will spoil a surprise, inappropriate information delivery can have adverse effects upon a tourism experience. As reach and capability become more advanced there is a need to re-examine not only what can be done, but also the reason it is being done, whether this is yesterday's, today's or tomorrow's reason, indeed for the benefit of whom. Just because we can, does not mean that we should. If a true market oriented approach is adopted, then the tourist comes first, with benefits accruing from satisfying needs. This, in the context of rural tourism, may invoke high short term costs but with long term benefits, economically, culturally and environmentally.

Information Technology has much to offer future tourism activities; it is envisaged that benefits to the industry and the tourist will accrue from the refinement of the "big" picture – the front office, and from added applications to the back office, particularly those involving the public sector and community involvement in planning.

References

Alexander, N. & Mckenna, A. (1998).: Rural Tourism in the Heart of England. International Journal of Contemporary Hospitality Management Vol 10 Issue 5

Ashworth, G.& Goodall, B. (eds) (1994).: Marketing Tourism Places based on 3rd International tourism conference workshop organised by Geographical Institute of the Universities of Groningen (Netherlands) & Reading (United Kingdom), 1988. Routledge, London.

Bitner, M.J. (1992).: Service scapes: the impact of physical surroundings on customers and employees. Journal of Marketing No 56 April pp57-71

Bramwell, B. (1998).: User satisfaction & product development in urban tourism. Tourism Management Vol 19 No.1 35-47

Buhalis, D. (1998).: Strategic use of Information Technologies in the Tourism industry. Tourism Management October 1998 vol 19 No 5 pp 409-421 (13)

Cooper, J. (1998). : Multidimensional approaches to the adoption of innovation Management Decision Vol 36, 8

Cowell, D. (1989).: The Marketing of Services. Heinneman Professional Publishing, Oxford.

Gummesson, E. (1994).: Making relationship marketing operational. International Journal of Services Management Vol 5 (5), 5-20

Hall, C.M. & Jenkins, J. M. (1995).: Tourism & Public Policy. Routledge, London & New York.

Handy, C. (1990).: The age of unreason, Harvard Business School, Boston. MA

Hopkins, J. (1998).: Signs of the postrural. Marketing myths of a symbolic countryside. Geografiiska Annaler; 80 (B): 65-81

http://tourist.madinfo.pt/exe.htm.: Tourism. Towards the Information Society. Executive summary.

http://www.ifitt.org/ifitt/inputs.htm.: IFITT White Paper - Inputs of the workshop.

http://www.nrec.org.uk/inforurale/inits/htm.

http://www.rural-europe.aeidl.be/rural-en/biblio/touris/art07.htm.: Marketing Quality Rural Tourism. Rural Tourism, the need for a product strategy. 1997

http:www.staruk.org.uk/tourpg2.htm.: Tourism Facts and Figures, 12.12.2000

Inkpen,G. (1998).: Information Technology for Travel & Tourism (2nd edn) Longman, Essex.

Kosters, M. J. (1988).: Changing tourism requires a different management approach, in Goodall, B. & Ashworth, G. (eds) (1988).: Marketing in the tourism industry: the promotion of destination regions. Croom Helm Limited, Beckenham.

Lue, C-M, Crompton J.I. & Fesenmaier, J. R. (1993).: Conceptualization of multi destination pleasure trips. Annals of Tourism Research 20(2) 289-301

Morash, E.A., Droge, C. & Vickery, S. (1997).: Boundary spanning interfaces between logistics, production, marketing and new product development. International Journal of Physical Distribution & logistics Management. 27 (5/6)

Murphy, P., Pritchard, M. & Brock, S. (1999).: The destination product and its impact on traveller perceptions. Tourism Management 21 (2000) 43-52

OECD/GSD (94) 48 (1994).: Tourism Strategies & Rural Development. OECD Paris

Olsen, E.M., Cooper, R. & Slater, S.F. (1998).: Design Strategy & Competitive Advantage Business Horizons, USA. Vol 41, 2

244

Page, S. & Getz, D. (1997) (eds).: The Business of Rural Tourism - International
    Perspectives, Thompson Business Research, London
Palmer, A. (1996).: Linking external & internal relationship building in networks of
    public & private sector organisations: a case study. International Journal of Public
    Sector Management. Vol 9 (3)
Pessenier, E.A. (1966).: New Product design – an analytical approach. McGraw Hill
    Book Co. New York.
Piercy, N. & Cravens, D. (1995).: The network paradigm & the marketing
    organisation. Developing a new management agenda. European Journal of
    Marketing 29 (3)
Proctor,T. (1996).: Marketing Management, integrating theory and practice,
    International Thompson Business Press, London.
Theobald, W. (1998).: Global Tourism (2nd edn}. Butterworth-Heinneman, Oxford
Wheeler, M. (1995).: Tourism Marketing Ethics: an introduction International
    Marketing Review Vol 12 Issue 4.

The Canadian Tourism Exchange: Content, Collaboration, and Commerce

René Waksberg, Blair Stevens and Guy Vales*
Canadian Tourism Commission, Canada
[waksberg.rene| stevens.blair]@ic.gc.ca
*Business Interactive, Canada
guy_vales@bi-corp.com

Abstract

The Canadian Tourism Commission (CTC) was created in 1995 to promote Canadian tourism in order to capitalize on one of the fastest-growing international industries. The CTC is a unique public/private sector partnership that provides an innovative approach to tourism: one that is industry led and market driven. In delivering its mandate to the industry, the CTC needs to be as efficient as possible in communicating with its partners in order to share information, create and manage the knowledge and wisdom to make the right business decisions to strengthening Canada's competitive advantage. The Canadian Tourism Exchange (CTX) is one such way, as a new communications, marketing and commercial tool, all in one. The CTX is a Web-based business-to-business Extranet for the Canadian tourism industry. It's purpose is to connect the tourism industry - to bring buyers and suppliers together, to disseminate information and knowledge quickly and extensively, to allow for collaborative marketing initiatives, and to enable business-to-business transactions; tools to help Canada gain a competitive advantage.

1 The origins of CTX in the Canadian Context

1.1 The creation of the CTC

The former solitudes of industry and government were thrown together by the formation of the Canadian Tourism Commission in 1995. Two completely different cultures were brought together; one corporate, the other governmental. Each with its set of attitudes, working styles, decision making processes, ways of determining effectiveness, and ways of determining results. One driven by business efficiencies and profits, the other driven by the impact of policies and programming on groups and individuals and how they respond to initiatives undertaken by governments whether in tourism markets at home or abroad, or whether in the context of federal-provincial relations, or relationships with other societal stakeholders.

The resulting Canadian Tourism Commission now serves as an organizational platform for the Canadian tourism industry. Industry-led, market-driven and research-

based. The synergy between government and industry helped propel Canada from being on the ropes as a tourism destination in 1994 to a top-ten destination in 1999.
But having the structure is not enough in today's marketplace, where competition is high, and new destinations are crowding the tourism landscape as never before. The processes and constraints of trying to continue business under the weight of the old systems have held the CTC back from competing as effectively as it can, given the right business climate. As a result, the CTC is moving from a government department, to a special operating agency, to a Crown corporation, a private corporation wholly owned by the government.

As a Crown corporation, the CTC will be able to allocate, or reallocate resources from non-starters to starters quickly, and be able to make instant business decisions in response to, or ahead of, rapidly changing market conditions.

1.2 Why an Industry Vision

The CTC recently led a tourism industry vision and mission exercise in order to a) provide a framework in which the industry could cooperate and b) give a focus to the actions taken by the many industry players. The vision is this:

"Canada will be the premier four-season destination to connect with nature and to experience diverse cultures and communities."

The mission says:

"Canada's tourism industry will deliver world-class cultural and leisure experiences, year round, while preserving and sharing Canada's clean, safe and natural environments. The industry will be guided by the values of respect, integrity and empathy."

1.3 What are the tools to attain that vision?

To actually carry the vision through to gain that competitive advantage requires tools. In delivering its mandate to the industry, the CTC needs to be as efficient as possible in communicating with its partners in order to pass information, create and manage knowledge to allow businesses to make the right business decisions and ultimately strengthening Canada's competitive advantage.

The CTC has taken the lead in developing and implementing a technology strategy to benefit the industry. From this initiative has emerged The Canadian Tourism Exchange (CTX). CTX grew out of a series of consultations between the CTC and tourism businesses to establish a private business-to-business network over the Internet that would give access to a series of useful applications. CTX has been purposely designed and built for the size of Canada, the diversity of the industry and the need to work together. CTX becomes the tourism industries' foundation for the knowledge-based economy. It will help fulfill the information mandate of the CTC, while enhancing the ability to build partnerships. Businesses within the tourism industry will use this network to access relevant information. Tourism industry members will have a tool to communicate with one another, exchange information, and conduct business, which in turn would enhance competitiveness and industry performance. The network is flexible, intuitive, affordable and designed to take advantage of leading edge technologies. It offers a level playing field to businesses of all types and sizes within the industry regardless of location.

In the simplest terms, CTX will help tourism operators --- large, medium and small – to communicate with each other to better package market and sell Canada and its tourism offerings in the international marketplace. Through links with its sister consumer travel Website, it allows consumers to have access to, and learn about Canada's tourism products through CTX members.

In the same way that the CTC has become the organizational platform to mobilize the Canadian tourism industry, the CTX, itself becomes the *technological* platform that will connect the members of industry, stimulating new demand as a competitive advantage. It is free to any business or organization that stands to improve Canada's competitive advantage in tourism. In addition to the obvious - hotels, car rental companies - this includes those who require information about starting a tourism business, those who sell commodities to tourism businesses, and those abroad who promote travel to Canada.

The aim is for CTX to become a portal for tourism organizations, where the CTC prepares the business rules of membership, the technology foundations and the programs to integrate other organizations functions into CTX, such as e-commerce. CTX will be used as an Internet-based teaching tool, allowing travel agents to be better informed about the country they are selling as well as allowing consumers to be better understand the country they will be visiting.

CTX is part of a national tourism knowledge network. It provides value-added tools to transform data and information to knowledge which, in turn, allows for better customization of the system, better means of responding to user needs, and greater efficiencies. It helps to bridge the knowledge gap between information producers and potential users, by providing a value-added product that is relevant to the users.

1.4 The CTX Vision

The vision for CTX is that of a tool for content and communication (sharing information and providing training), collaboration (helping the CTC do business and partner with industry), and commerce (facilitating business-to-consumer commerce and business-to-business commerce through procurement modules and other applications). The goal is to provide an online community that breaks down the perception of "us" (government) versus "them" (the industry).

Some of the specific CTX applications to be developed or refined over the coming year are: Taste of Nova Scotia regional cuisine procurement module, to be expanded to other provinces and other areas once the pilot project has been proved successful; Rendez-Vous Canada Marketplace allowing all buyers and sellers to peruse each others profiles in order to plan who to meet during the actual RVC meeting and continue such collaboration beyond the meeting; media center meetings & incentive travel module, Canada Specialist Program module and leveraging the CTX database for powering the consumer Website, all of which help the CTC facilitate program delivery; and further Intranet development (partner funding modules, master calendar, and CTC personnel directory), fulfilling the CTC's internal communication objectives. Several of these initiatives are discussed in this paper.

2 The Development of CTX

2.1 Target Market Description

As a membership-based Extranet, a description of the CTX's admissible members is in essence a description of its target market: any business or organization that stands to improve Canada's competitive advantage in tourism. In addition to the obvious - hotels, car rental companies - this includes those who require information about starting a tourism business, those who sell commodities to tourism businesses, and those abroad who promote travel to Canada.

According to a 1998 report prepared by Statistics Canada, the total number of tourism establishments in Canada is approximately 90 000. There are also several thousand businesses abroad which promote travel to Canada.

Many of these businesses are small-to-medium enterprises (SMEs). CTX provides them with "big business tools" and access to more information to help them make informed business decisions and provide exposure to their business to foreign tour operators.

2.2 A look at CTX

Registered members of CTX have access to the following features:

- *Tourism News*: Gives users daily news from newswires, magazines, newspapers, trade publications and clipping services allows members to post their own news, and allows news to be delivered to your email.

- *Business Connections:* Allows users to post messages to message boards, to join or create discussion forums, and to create mailing groups from search results.

- *Tourism Businesses:* Allows users to search through the ever-expanding database of industry products and services to reduce search time and improve business operations.

- *Research & Publications:* Gives users access to CTC publications, surveys, research studies, Canadian tourism, market profiles, statistics, sectoral analyses, and market intelligence and analyses

- *Intranet:* CTC staff members have access to an "Intranet" within CTX where they can make use of tools and exchange ideas on best practices.

The coming year will see new developments such as a marketplace, enabling business-to-business transactions, and an employment exchange, which will bring together employers and employees in the tourism sector.

2.3 Relationship between CTX and the consumer Website

The ability for other sites, including the CTC's consumer Website, to leverage CTX data provides users of CTX added value. Refer to Fig. 1.

All the information is stored in the "shared database" also known as the CTX database. Information in this database comes from a variety of sources, including CTX members, and the relevant information gets delivered to the appropriate site, whether that be the CTX business site, or the Travel Canada consumer site.

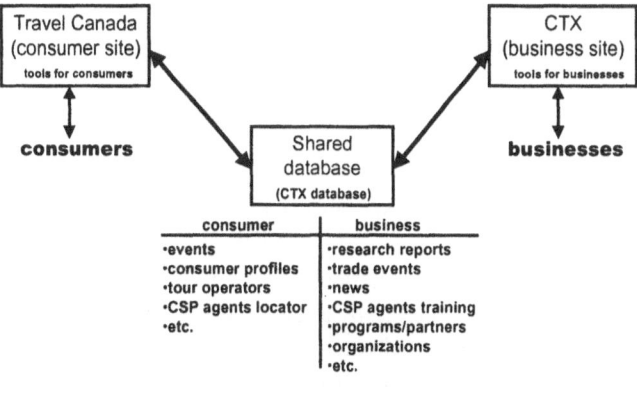

Fig. 1. Relationship between CTX and the consumer Website

Therefore, tourism organizations who register in CTX will have their full information available to businesses through CTX for other businesses to see, while their core information - address, phone number, Website etc - can be made accessible through the consumer site, depending on the appropriate business rules. In that vein, CTX members are encouraged to keep their information up-to-date.

2.4 The Real Value of CTX - Platform & Database

CTX's database is membership driven; the CTC provides the infrastructure that is complemented by industry content. Although CTX is a repository of information and derived knowledge, it is industry members who, by their presence as members within CTX, create value. Value, for example, through the increased news articles posted, through the participation and creation of additional discussion forums, and through an increasingly comprehensive database of tourism allowing for greater awareness of available tourism products and services.

The real value of CTX is in its flexibility to enable the 3 Cs: collaboration, content, and commerce. CTX allows the CTC to collaborate with industry on marketing initiatives and industry to create its own collaboration and community; allows 3rd parties to make use of CTX as a platform to introduce commerce applications; and most importantly allows CTX to provide richer content through content sourcing.

To achieve these 3 Cs requires the formation of partnerships. These partnerships can take many forms, from collaboration in ideas (i.e. willingness to work together), to sharing of the CTX database, to direct content sourcing, to an environment where all partners have direct access to each other's databases. These ideas are further explored in the coming pages.

The following three case studies highlight the 3 Cs of CTX, and the methods and partnerships used to implement each one.

2.5 Case study - Collaboration for marketing initiatives

The ability to leverage company profiles within CTX to appear on the consumer Website allows the marketing programs to use CTX as the place tourism businesses profile themselves to market to consumers, as well as a place where these businesses have access to useful business information. The CTX allows the CTC to go beyond the traditional limitations of marketing by allowing them to respond quickly to market conditions and to target specific clientele by mining organizational data through membership in CTX and consumer data from the consumer Website.

One case in point was the development of several adventure travel marketing initiatives.

The US Adventure Travel program was a print campaign and Web campaign, organized by the US Marketing group. All partner tour operators having bought into a print brochure of adventure packages geared to the US market, would have their package description also stored in the CTX database and made accessible to consumers on the consumer site. In that way, the result of a consumer search by province, package category or keyword on the consumer Website would extract the relevant packages from the CTX database.

The Canadian Adventure Travel initiative, organized by the Domestic Marketing group, was a straight-to-Web initiative, with no print brochure. The CTX database was mined to find adventure tour operators who were members of CTX (about 1600 at the time), and these were sent an offering, by email, to encourage them to join the campaign. Instructions were given to go to a special section of CTX, where they could register their package information, which they could, at any time, change. Tour operators selected an appropriate category for their package (the same categories were used as for the US program), the dates of their package availability, etc. See Figure 2.

In essence then, two parallel programs were launched for different geographic marketing areas. This caused great confusion and exposed the need for the various marketing programs to work together on Web initiatives.

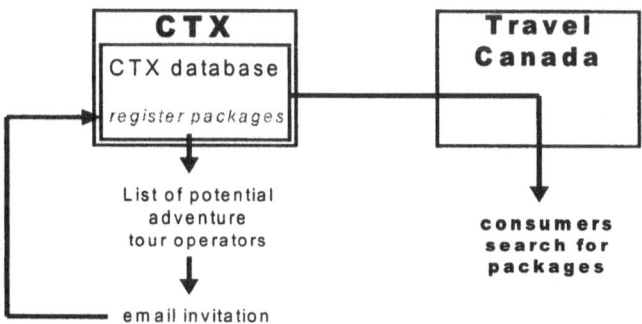

Fig. 2. CTX and the Domestic Marketing Program

Businesses that had bought in to the US program did not understand why they had to buy into the Canadian program too, given they were both on the same Website. There was confusion as to what the different buy-in levels for the program, each offering a different level of visibility and banner advertisements would produce in terms of a return-on-investment. On the other side of the equation, consumers were confused because their choice was limited to the US and Canada for adventure packages - what if they were from the UK?

The new consumer travel Website being developed will continue to leverage the CTX database in a similar manner, but there is now the greater understanding of the need for marketing groups to work together as a team.

2.6 Case study - Content through partnerships

The need to have richer content (new company profiles available to other CTX members, additional consumer events stored in the CTX database and made available to consumers through the consumer Website) led to the development of some strategic partnerships, described in this case study.

CTX enables other tourism Web sites to leverage the data and functions provided by CTX and vice-versa. The model of sharing data, or partnerships can include other partners, presumably each with an expertise in a relevant area of tourism. Through such initiatives as partnerships and affiliate programs, partners provide functions and information that are integrated with, or linked to, CTX.

The following models highlight some of the various partnership arrangements that can exist.

2.6.1 Sharing events with Festival Seeker

The Festival Seeker Website was undertaken to create a communication link between festival organizers across the country and to provide a central information source for all Canadian festivals. In order to reduce duplication and cost of creating its own listing of festivals, the Canadian Tourism Commission signed a Memorandum of Understanding with the creators of the Festival Seeker Website.

In this model, one database is shared between various sites. Event organizers will be able to add and edit their events to the database via either the Festival Seeker Website or through CTX so that a festival & event organizer sees his information exposed through a variety of sites to a variety of audiences. Festival Seeker will be responsible for administering this database (verifying that the festivals exist etc), while the festival information will be searchable and displayed in CTX, through Festival Seeker, and on the Travel Canada Website. See Figure 3.

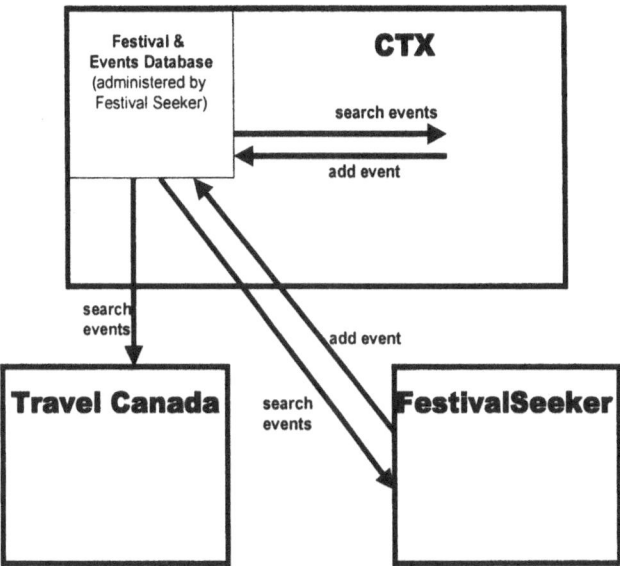

Fig. 3. Festival Seeker Partnership: Sharing one database

The sharing of the database is not limited only to CTX, TravelCanada, and FestivalSeeker. Events could be added or viewed from any variety of sources. The key is that administration of the events is the responsibility of one organization.

The responsibility for the data is quite clear and resides with the administrator, but this particular model brings up the question of ownership of data. If Festival Seeker decides that it would like to sell the data, is it entitled to ?

2.6.2 Sharing attractions databases with the Canadian Heritage Information Network

This model is slightly different than the first in that each database remains with its creators, the Canadian Heritage Information Network (CHIN) and CTX. Canadian Heritage has created a database of Canadian attractions, and, as they will keep this database up-to-date, it makes more sense to use this information rather than try and recreate it.

Currently, the data provided to CTX is limited to skeletal core information, allowing users in CTX, and perhaps, by extension the Travel Canada consumer Website, to search for attractions by category. Users are then guided by hyperlink to the CHIN Website for more detailed information. This was required to allow CHIN to retain its branding; a very important issue in creation of Web traffic and justification of Web initiatives.

Furthermore, given the limited technology resources of CHIN, the data exchange at this time is limited to data being copied from the CHIN database to the CTX, but as database structures, human resources, and technical expertise permits, each entity will be able to directly query the other's database. For example, the profile of a museum within the CHIN database could be complemented by a listing of accommodations and restaurants in the neighbourhood as supplemented by the CTX database.

Currently, profiles of CHIN attractions in CTX can be assumed by their owners (i.e. the attractions), allowing them to add any complementary information in CTX that isn't already asked for in CHIN.

This begs the issue of control of membership. Once a profile changes in CTX, ownership of the data is no longer the responsibility of CHIN, but of the attraction itself. Any new data coming from CHIN will not overwrite that which already exists in CTX.

Once again, many of these issues will be alleviated when standards are developed for sharing core data between databases, so that businesses will only have to enter their core information into a database once.

Future content partnership initiatives: The Tourism Exchange

Content partnerships will go much further. The concept of a "tourism exchange" will allow seamless exchange of data between various sites. This is more easily implemented in both government and non-profit organizations, where the content is often more important than commerce.

Each site retains its brand and provides basic information and specialized information relative to its area of expertise, while being able to access information from complementary sites. As previously stated, the profile of a museum within the CHIN database could be complemented by a listing of accommodation and restaurants in the neighbourhood as supplemented by the CTX database. This can be leveraged even further to include commerce, so that tickets and accommodation could all be booked online.

Such a scheme will also simplify matters for the business profiling itself. Any business will be able to profile itself with basic core information at any participating site with one username and password to access all sites, much like the Microsoft Passport initiative. All participating sites will share this core information. The business can choose to provide complementary information to any site particular to those sites that it deems appropriate to its target markets. See Fig. 4.

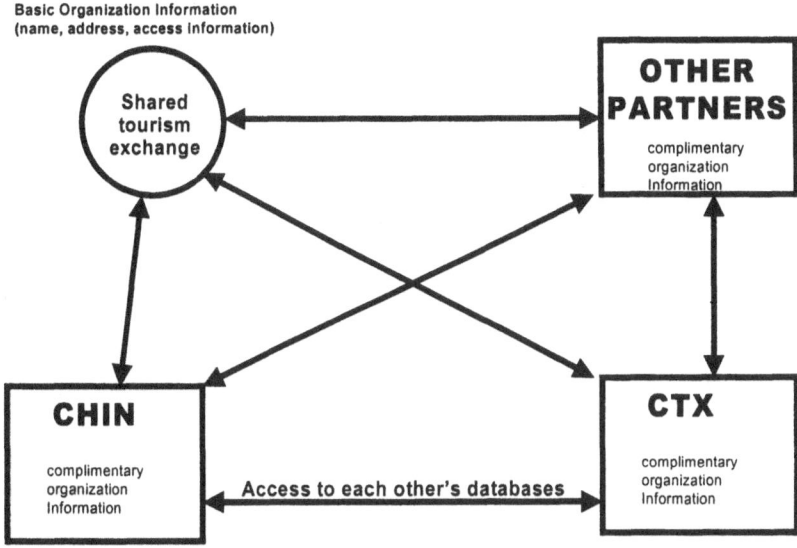

Fig. 4. The Future of Partnerships

It should be stressed that as partnerships become more and more prevalent, the issue of standardization of core information will become the main focus of cooperation in order to create efficiencies in sharing and exchanging information. At this time, this will likely mean the adoption of XML for marking up the data. Although creation of standard dictionaries and XML have been embraced by such organizations as the Open Travel Alliance on the hotel, car, airline, side of the tourism business, the content side has been slower to adapt.

2.6.3   Other Issues related to partnerships

Some of the other issues related to partnerships that have not already been mentioned include private sector vs. public sector, funding, resources, different missions, technical ability, use of advertisements, and the perception of exclusivity with certain partners.

2.7 Case Study - CTX Commerce Applications

2.7.1 Procurement

One of the applications the industry needs developed is a solution to procurement problems. Facilitating procurement would help both large and small operators. Small businesses able to buy collectively could save large amounts of money. Just- in-time delivery of goods, would reduce inventory costs considerably. Knowing where to obtain interesting high quality goods would be of significant benefit. Those tourism businesses providing for tourists' basic needs for food and shelter are competing in a global market. They realize that differentiation and high quality products are important ingredients to success. For example, hotels and restaurants want to offer high quality multi-season food services; however, many properties have difficulty obtaining supplies, in all seasons, which allow them to offer truly Canadian cuisine experiences. There may well be existing suppliers of such services but the tourism businesses don't know about them. There may also be suppliers to the industry who would be willing to offer such goods; but they don't know that there is a market for them.

Technology offers an opportunity to bridge the gap between buyers and suppliers. It offers possibilities for increased participation, cost reduction, greater effectiveness through higher inventory turnover, reduced cost of distribution, improved efficiencies from reducing paperwork and time spent searching, improved productivity of resources overall, leading to more competitive pricing. A small improvement in these areas will show significant benefits for business operators and for the industry as a whole. Altogether these benefits would offer the opportunity to improve competitiveness of the Canadian tourism industry in an increasingly competitive market.

2.7.2   Rendez-Vous Canada (RVC)

RVC is the annual meeting of Canadian travel sellers and foreign travel buyers. In the coming year, the organizers of RVC will work with the CTX team to include all buyers and sellers within CTX. This initiative was first suggested several years ago, but was never accepted due to fear that membership would be compromised.

A "marketplace" module will be conceived in CTX allowing all buyers and sellers to peruse each other's profiles in order to plan who to meet during the actual RVC meeting. This will also allow both buyers and sellers to update their profiles on a continual basis, and search out new buyers and sellers who might not be able to attend the actual RVC event.

One of the challenges is to ensure that no seller has access to another sellers profile, only a buyers, and vice versa. This will prevent unfair competition in the development of new products.

2.8 Other CTX Issues

2.8.1 Data quality

The value of data within CTX is only as good as the quality and reliability of the data. This is a major issue with which the CTC must continuously contend. As the CTC is not a membership-based organization but rather a partnership organization, the CTC does not profile all of Canada's tourism businesses. In any case, given resources, it would be impossible to profile 90 000. Additionally, many province and city tourism offices already have this information.

Because CTX is not a pay-service, and because individual company profiles are created by the companies themselves, there is a lack of consistency, and in some case quality, in the information contained in the database. This could have an adverse effect on the way CTX is perceived. As currently CTX members profile themselves, there is no validation of their profile beyond cursory verification that they are industry members. For example, some businesses profiled themselves as offering services in all categories (for example accommodation and cycling, for example), such that their profile would come up in all searches. To counteract this, the CTC is implementing within the CTX mechanisms which limit the number of categories a business can select, as well as a weighting when returning search results that displays a businesses' primary activities before its secondary.

Additionally, a notification service is being implemented which will automatically notify businesses if their profile has not been updated in some time in order to ensure its currency.

By partnering with other organizations that have databases of qualified businesses, there is less duplication of effort, and higher quality content, an advantage given the high cost of populating a database with "valid" members.

Building on the partnership concepts previously discussed, in the future, it will be possible to exchange data with the other organizations. So, for example, a partnership with Tourism Montreal would allow the CTX to share their database of 650 members, while giving Tourism Montreal members access to all the other features of CTX.

This sharing of data is somewhat more problematic with industry associations. On the one hand, they want to expose their members to the maximum number of other businesses, something they could achieve by making them a part of CTX, while on the other hand these associations sometimes derive revenue from selling their membership lists to others and may feel that by sharing their association membership information with CTX, it will allow users to bypass the association for listings of association members.

However, associations offer their members and the industry at large many services and information not provided by CTX (CTX, as an example, does not contain the size of any hotel room) and should not ignore new distribution channel possibilities for their members.

The issue of data quality extends to news and events. In both cases, these are administered by a central organization to ensure data quality and relevance. However, as more users begin posting news articles, it is conceivable that this will stretch verification resources to the limit.

2.8.2   Mass Customization

One of the strong points of CTX, and one of its biggest challenges, is mass customization. CTX already allows each user to select the frequency and type of news (i.e. category) he would like to receive. Canada's status as a bilingual nation adds a twist to the mix. Users can choose whether to receive only news posted in English, news posted in French, or all news.

As previously discussed, the database was mined to extract all CTX members who were adventure tour operators in order to notify them of a new adventure tourism campaign. This same mechanism is partly available to other CTX users, giving them the ability to create a "mailing list" of CTX members resulting from a search (say, of all hotels). Although this could lead to spamming, in the 2 years of operation of CTX, there have been only 3 cases of spamming. Mechanisms will be put in place to create "opt-in" mailing lists, whereby users can choose whether to allow others to include them in mailing lists.

Although untapped at the moment, the current CTX registration provides information about businesses' target markets, methods of advertisement etc. This information could be leveraged by marketing to determine likelihood of partners for a campaign using a particular medium, and targeting a particular geographical region. A mechanism to follow up on these leads and an understanding and willingness to do so will provide the CTC with new opportunities. The flexibility of the CTX database will allow just about any information and criteria to be used for data mining, data filtering, or notification.

2.8.3   Attracting new membership/Retaining existing membership

There is always a trade off to be made between trying to attract new users to the CTX, and increasing the value of the CTX for those who are already members. Better a small group of active users who contribute, than a large group of passive users who neither add nor extract value from CTX.

The CTC needs to continue to fulfill, and indeed try to get ahead of its users' expectations to maintain the value of membership in CTX. New policies and procedures must be implemented regarding what information should be made available online as well as a better definition of ownership and responsibility for the shared data. That involves content management -- who should update the data and information and how often.

And, particularly vital, is the need to select the appropriate knowledge tools and applications to provide value-added content for CTX members. These tools must be accompanied by the information required to make them applicable to users' needs.

Given the makeup of the tourism industry, comprising mostly small and medium size enterprises, many of whom may not be as familiar with the technologies and databases as the larger organizations might, ways must be found to make membership more inclusive, by making the technologies and content more user friendly and understandable to them.

Despite the prevalence of technology in our everyday lives, there is still reluctance among many individuals to embrace technology. Additionally, among those who have embraced technology, there is still a steep learning curve in making use of technology. Caution must be exercised in creating a CTX environment that is easily navigable and intuitive, with sufficient help

Another factor to be considered is the low penetration of PCs in SMEs or remote towns. CTX is a tool to level the playing field - to allow small business access to big business tools. Penetration of PCs in SMEs, or in remote areas of Canada is somewhat low, slowing adoption of CTX as a business tool by these potential target markets.

Finally, there is industry's and even internal marketing's lack of understanding of the potential of CTX. At present, most members of CTX use its daily tourism news delivery feature while not making much use of its other features. Awareness campaigns might shed light on use of existing value-added applications while additional industry feedback will be required to build required value-added tools. Particular attentions must also be paid to easy navigation within the CTX, to make relevant information easily accessible thus meeting user expectations:

That the information is comprehensive:
It must be clear to users that the information can never be exhaustive and that other sources must be considered. The issue of proprietary information limits the content that can be put online.

That all the information is accurate
However, the information will only be as accurate as the original source (and in the case of research, its methodology). Users have to be given some understanding of the limitations of the information. It is important to determine who is responsible for the data.

That all the information is current
Technology allows information to be distributed more quickly, but unless it is kept current it will quickly be out of date. People won't come back unless information is fresh.

That the information is relevant
As CTX reaches more users than ever before, so the information has to be organized such that users can quickly identify what is relevant to them. This requires listening to industry feedback.

Information must be controlled to some extent, for even if the CTC cannot assume the responsibility for all the content in CTX, poor information creates a poor perception of CTX, and by extension, the CTC.

It is interesting to note that none of these are technology issues.

2.9   Future Directions - Where we do we go from here ?

Complying with some of the current government regulations impacts the potential of CTX - no advertising, for example. The CTC's move to a Crown corporation might provide it and CTX with additional opportunities to develop revenue-generating schemes, perhaps from advertising, selling online, or creating cost-based modules.

The CTCs position makes it the natural leader to bring together the various levels of government and industry to lead in the application of these technology initiatives, while mitigating what could be perceived as competing initiatives from private sector: Some private sector initiatives may compete with the CTX.

But the success of CTX won't be measured only by its ability to move information quickly and to all points. It will be measured by its usefulness -- the *quality* of knowledge -- when it gets there.

In order to retain its first-entrant advantages, CTX must continuously reengineer itself and provide users with value-added tools and personalized business analysis tools to be used on a day-to-day basis.

3 The Technical Reality

3.1 Technical Architecture

CTX has adopted a flexible and scaleable technology architecture that allows it to grow both in web application functionality and in user load. The technology components are based on industry standards anticipated technology trends and were chosen to be easily replaceable with newer technology. Other important factors in the selection of the CTX technical architecture include security and low ownership costs.

CTX uses a three-tier architecture where a user (the first tier) equipped with any Web browser accesses one or more application servers (web, e-mail, proxy server etc.) through an initial firewall located in a DMZ a.k.a. a demilitarized zone. The application servers access other servers and software services such as relational database, collaboration and video streaming software. The application servers are arranged to allow fail-over and load balancing. The environment operates within a redundant high-speed network.

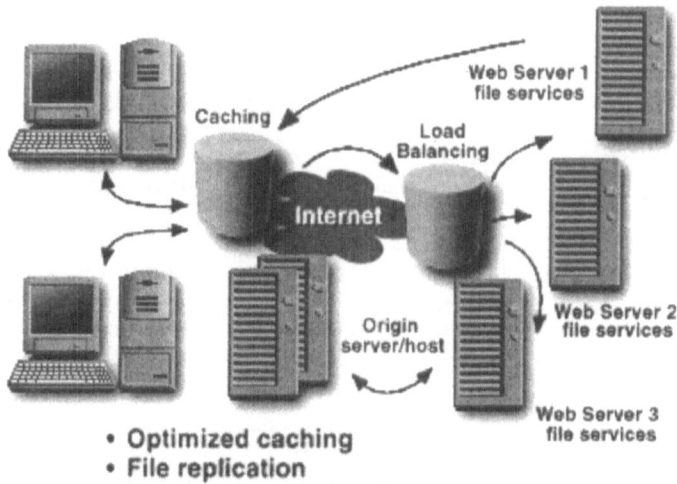

IBM WebSphere Performance Pack

- Optimized caching
- File replication
- Dynamic load balancing

3.2 Technology components and their functions

Here is a brief description of the functions of the various technology components of CTX.

Category	Technical Component	Comments
Web Application Server	- Netscape Web server - Cold Fusion for Web application server engine. - Servlet and Java execution environment	The Web application server processes users' requests. As necessary the request processor accesses other services (e.g. relational database), retrieves the information, and formats response in html and sends response to the user.
Web Application Development	- IBM Visual Age for Java development (e.g. serviettes and Java Server pages) - Cold Fusion Mark-up language for scripting environment	Tools for the development of web programs.
Data Storage	Oracle Relational Database	Stores data in a shared and integrated environment.
Media Streaming	RealServer	Allows the efficient delivery of streaming media. E.g. tourism educational video.
Data Exchange	- XML, Messaging, Java objects	Tools used to pass information between programs within the same environment and/or over the Internet.
Security	SSL with PKI experimentation	Tools for the protection of data during and after transmission.
System Management and Reporting	Tivoli and others	Tools to monitor and manage the different components of the technical environment.
Web usage Statistics, Business Intelligence, Data Mining	Web Trends and others	Tools to report on user activity and behavior. Allows the discovery of unsuspected patterns.
Load Balancing Software and Fail Over software	IBM Performance Pack	Provides ability to handle peak in user load. Prevents system outages.
Operating Systems	NT for application servers and UNIX for database servers	
Hardware	Intel and RISC	

3.3 Powered by CTX i.e. Leveraging the Internet to exchanging data and functions between sites

Rationale - Using Metcalfe's Law to leverage the Web and increase value

The CTC has expanded a great deal of time and effort into building a set of e-business web applications and in developing content (e.g. research and publications) for the tourism industry. The CTC wishes its web site to do much more and become what could be deemed a combination of a portal and a destination site.

To achieve its goals, the CTC intends to leverage the Web by moving from being a strictly end-use application to being a back-end services that custom business applications residing anywhere on the network can leverage. As well, the CTC intends to source and leverage content and services from other sites and sources. This idea of cooperating nodes forms the basis of "Powered by CTX".

Technical Implementation

Using tag based language (for ease of programming) and Java, web applications are developed in the form of well-defined modules. Individual programs or modules may be used by other web sites to perform specific services based on levels of access and parameters passed between the programs using different techniques for data exchange (e.g. XML, remote procedure calls or simple Web passing parameter techniques).

The data stored in a relational database (e.g. DB2, Oracle, and SQL Server) may be retrieved by calling existing CTX modules or by calling customized modules developed by and specifically for the needs of the accessing party a.k.a. the subscriber. A direct connection to the database may also be established between the subscriber's program and the relational database.

The consumer equivalent of the CTX site uses the Powered by CTX concept to deliver services and data to would be travelers. In a mirror agreement, CTX uses information gathered by the consumer site to add value to CTX members. (E.g. web marketing)

3.4 Leveraging pervasive computing, wireless technology, increase bandwidth to deliver data on any device and enhance user experience

Rationale – The number of non-PC computers (e.g. Palm Pilot) and users will greatly surpass that of traditional PCs

The CTC supports the idea of the dissemination of data and services to users of any device. The CTC sees great opportunity to leverage that trend to deliver services in a way that enhances the experience of would-be and in-country travelers.

As an example, it is possible to combine a "Places" database that contains information about the place and GPS location data to provide what could be termed a "mobile kiosk" or in context data.

With the right Internet appliance and computing capabilities embedded in devices ranging from cameras and palm pilots, the traveler standing in front of (for instance) the Canada parliament building would be able to hear or read information about the building, its history etc. In effect the traveler would get its personal travel guide.

The same concept may be used to deliver both information and transaction services to travelers during his/her trip.

Technical Implementation

Although the concept may sound futuristic for some, all the technical elements required to implement this idea are available today.

A prototype of the delivery system could be built using the current CTX Web site, wireless access, a Palm Pilot, a Web capable modem or other device supporting GPS and or the upcoming Bluetooth technology.

Using a customized web application, a user would request information on places of interest within a certain distance from a set location. The web applications communicate with the tourism places database and geographical mapping services to retrieve information on places of interests. Selection of a place would retrieve its related information.

The information can be delivered using text, voice and videos depending on the information appliance used by the traveler. Although such applications are being developed, the realization of the immense potential of the technology stills awaits some technological deployment and large-scale deployment. The CTC and CTX may act as a catalyst.

Reference Model Of An Electronic Tourism Market

Wolfram Höpken
START AMADEUS GmbH
Wolfram.Hoepken@start.de

Abstract

The distribution of tourism services from the supplier to the customer presently takes place via different distribution channels and service- and travel-type specific electronic markets (i.e. tourism information systems). This coexistence of heterogeneous electronic markets results in non-uniform information available about tourism services, non-uniform access to tourism services and a lack of interoperability between different tourism markets. The objective of the project presented in this paper to avoid these problems is the elaboration and implementation of a methodology for unifying different electronic tourism markets. In order to reach this objective, a framework for modelling electronic tourism markets, a *reference model*, has to be elaborated. Instead of a fix standard the reference model provides an open specification of electronic tourism markets based on a uniform language with standardized building blocks as vocabulary. The reference model presented in this paper focuses on the conceptual modelling of electronic tourism markets on an abstract, communication mechanism independent level, based on the *Unified Modeling Language* (UML). In this way, the reference model enables the description of specific models in a form understandable for all communication partners and supports the interoperability on different concrete communication levels.

1 Introduction

1.1 Motivation

The distribution of tourism services from the supplier to the customer presently takes place via different distribution channels and service- and travel-type specific electronic markets (i.e. tourism information systems) [10]. The following problems result from the coexistence of heterogeneous electronic markets:

- Nonuniformity of the access to tourism services in different markets
- Nonuniformity of the information, which is available or has to be provided for tourism services in different markets
- No interoperability between different electronic markets or systems
- Only specific services are available within each market (e.g. services of specific suppliers or specific service types); an all-embracing search or combination of services of different markets is not possible
- A service has to be provided within several different markets to reach all customers

266

The objective to avoid these problems is the unification of different electronic markets and the merging of existing markets into *one* open electronic tourism market (Fig. 1). Such a market enables the direct communication between all participants. The complete tourism value chain takes place within this market.

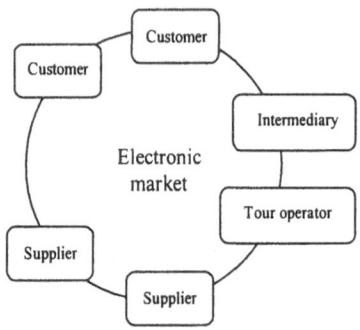

Fig. 1. Model of the tourism market

Within the field of tourism a lot of initiatives dealing with standardisation aspects have evolved in the past. Examples are UN/EDIFACT TT&L (United Nations rules for Electronic Data Interchange for Administration, Commerce and Transport – Travel Tourism & Leisure), HITIS (Hospitality Industry Technology Integration Standards), omnis-online, IATA (International Air Transport Association), TTI (Travel Technology Initiative) and ACRISS (Association of Car Rental Industry System Standards). However, a broad standardisation, enabling a global interoperability between tourism information systems has up to now not been reached due to the heterogeneity and diversity of tourism markets. A complete standardisation of electronic markets for tourism services is unlikely for the future as well and even not meaningful due to the following problems:

- One fix standard is not flexible enough to consider all specific details of different electronic markets
- One fix standard is not flexible enough to be adapted to occurring changes
- One fix standard offers no possibility for suppliers of tourism services to differentiate their offer

Therefore, instead of defining fix standards current efforts turn into the direction of open, more flexible specifications of tourism markets e.g. OTA (Open Travel Alliance) or XML/EDI. Based on XML (eXtensible Markup Language [4]) fix structured data are substituted by semi-structured data and a common vocabulary and a uniform syntax enable the flexible description of tourism services or markets.

However, a crucial drawback of XML-based models lies in an insufficient consideration of semantic aspects of the modelled problem domain. This restricts or prevents the interoperability of markets based on different models. Therefore, an utmost broad modelling of electronic markets, considering especially semantic aspects, is an important challenge for the tourism domain.

1.2 Objective

The objective of this project to avoid the above problems is the elaboration and implementation of a methodology for unifying electronic tourism markets, taking into consideration the following requirements:

- Interoperability of different electronic markets or systems (supply of mechanisms for translating between different models)
- Uniform access to different markets
- Flexibility and extendibility (to be adaptable to specific requirements or changes)

For this purpose, a framework for modelling electronic tourism markets, a *reference model*, has to be elaborated. Instead of a fix standard the reference model provides an open specification of electronic tourism markets based on a uniform language with a common vocabulary and serves as a foundation for building concrete models, tailored to specific requirements. The reference model has to enable a sufficiently expressive modelling, in order to describe all information, necessary for the interoperability of different markets or systems, especially information about semantic aspects. In this way, the reference model enables the uniform description or modelling of heterogeneous electronic markets and their interoperability. Presently existing electronic markets become components of one open electronic market ([7] p. 162).

2 The concept

The reference model presented in this paper focuses on the conceptual modelling of electronic tourism markets on an abstract, communication mechanism independent level. In this way, the reference model enables the description of specific models in a form understandable for all communication partners and supports the interoperability on different concrete communication levels, e.g. on the level of XML documents or distributed objects. The reference model uses the *Unified Modeling Language* (UML [9]) as language for describing or modelling electronic tourism markets. The UML enables a modelling sufficiently expressive for the interoperability and especially the consideration of semantic aspects. The UML is a universal, standardised modelling language and enables a modelling independent of the concrete communication level. In order to facilitate the interoperability on different communication levels, the necessary specifications are derived from the UML model.

As vocabulary for describing electronic tourism markets the reference model provides a modelling library in the form of standardised building blocks and in this way, enables the flexible construction of concrete models for components of the electronic markets. The provided building blocks can be derived and tailored to specific requirements as well as composed to new building blocks or specific models.
The reference model specifies in particular:

- *Open interface*: A uniform language with standardized building blocks as vocabulary enables the flexible description of interfaces for components of the electronic market. A supplier, who provides a component within the electronic market, can describe his specific interface in a form understandable for other market participants.
- *Building blocks*: Standardized building blocks are provided as a basis for constructing concrete models or systems – starting with elementary building blocks (e.g. date, time...) over more complex building blocks (e.g. tourism services) up to process building blocks, representing entire processes (e.g. booking process).
- *Classification of tourism services*: Tourism services (as central building blocks) have to be classified according to selection relevant characteristics. Considerable tourism services are all services relevant in the context of one of the following travel types: *business travel, holiday travel* and *excursion* [11].

Constructing concrete models for components of the electronic tourism market is done based on the following fundamental mechanisms:

- *Derivation*: The building blocks provided by the reference model are derived and tailored to meet specific requirements. The service *hotel* for example can be extended by the attribute *cure services* or the building block *customer data* by a supplier-specific *customer number*. Participants, who know the new building block, can use its specific characteristics. Participants, who do not know the new building block, can use it in the same way like the original one.
- *Composition*: The building blocks provided by the reference model are composed to new, more complex building blocks. A specific booking object for example can be composed of the given building blocks *customer data* and *tourism service* or a new tourism service can be composed of the elementary building blocks *date, time, location* or *meal plan*. The standardized building blocks, being part of the specific building blocks and the use of a language with a uniform syntax for describing the structure of building blocks enable the interoperability between different market components.

The following aspects will be considered within the reference model in order to support such mechanisms, especially concerning tourism services as central building blocks:

- *Selection hierarchies*: Providing selection hierarchies for characteristics (i.e. selection criteria) of tourism services supports the flexible derivation of tourism services. A selection hierarchy is built from the hierarchical arrangement of the values of a selection criterion on different levels of abstraction. Selection hierarchies enable the extension of the derivation mechanism and in this way support the flexible derivation of tourism services, which are nevertheless accessible uniformly. In addition, selection hierarchies enable the integration of fuzziness into the selection process by the definition of fuzzy requests and the search for similar results. In this way, selection hierarchies support a comfortable selection process ([7] chapter 4).

- *Composition of tourism services*: The flexible construction of tourism services is supported by a mechanism for composing tourism services. The composition mechanism enables the flexible construction of elementary services based on elementary building blocks (e.g. the tourism service *hotel* based on the building blocks *meal plan*, *room*...) as well as complex services based on elementary services (e.g. the complex service *journey* based on the elementary services *flight* and *hotel*). In addition, the composition mechanism enables customer-initiated compositions of elementary services to complex services during selection and in this way supports the comfortable selection of complex services, consisting of several services of different suppliers ([7] chapter 5).

3 Architecture of the reference model

3.1 3-tier architecture of the electronic tourism market

The architecture of the electronic tourism market is a three-tier distributed architecture, consisting of the following tiers ([7] chapter 3):
- User tier: The user tier contains the functionality concerning the interface to the user as well as the execution of requests from the user to the application tier.
- Application tier: The application tier contains the functionality needed within the electronic market to deal with the available services
- Data tier: The data tier provides the data on all available tourism services as well as elementary access mechanisms to this data.

The application tier is the central component of the three-tier architecture of the electronic tourism market. Each component of the application tier provides a definite set of services. These services are available to user components as well as other application components. This modelling concentrates on the examination of the processes and entities within the application tier as well as the common interface, which provides the services within the electronic market.

3.2 Communication levels and mechanisms

The communication between the participants of the electronic tourism market can be based on different communication levels and mechanisms.

Message level

The communication between two participants takes place via the exchange of messages. Using a service is carried out by the exchange of a series of messages following a committed protocol.

According to the type of exchanged messages it can be differentiated between:
- *Structured messages:* The communication between two participants takes place

via the exchange of fix-structured messages (e.g. EDIFACT). The message structure has to be committed between the participants before the communication starts.

- *Self-describing documents*: The communication between two participants takes place via the exchange of self-describing documents. Beside the exchanged data the documents contain information about their structure (metadata). Therefore, the structure of the documents is not completely fixed, but can vary. The recipient can determine the structure of a document from the metadata. Possible languages for self-describing documents are e.g. SGML or XML.

Distributed object level

The communication between two participants takes place based on distributed objects. Here, the fundamental communication mechanism is the remote method invocation (RMI). The services are provided as distributed objects. The market interface corresponds to the interfaces of the distributed objects, which are described by a special, programming language independent *interface definition language* (IDL). On the distributed object level the communication can be based on different concrete communication mechanisms:

- *CORBA*: The communication is based directly on the common object request broker architecture (CORBA).
- *JAVA-RMI*: The communication is based directly on the mechanism for remote method invocation provided by JAVA.
- *Proxy object architecture*: The communication is based on specific local proxy objects, i.e. for accessing a remote object is used a corresponding proxy object. The market interface corresponds to the interfaces of the proxy objects and is independent of the underlying communication mechanism.

Fig. 2 shows the different communication levels and mechanisms.

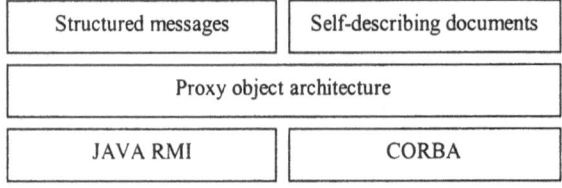

Fig. 2. Communication levels and mechanisms

Levels of the reference model

In the following the different communication levels and mechanisms will be discussed concerning their relevance for the reference model. The message level enables a looser coupling, offers more flexibility and an easier integration of existing applications. The distributed object level enables a tighter coupling, a more efficient communication, a higher semantic consistency and a better support of developing applications for market components (compare [6]). As both levels have advantages and disadvantages depending on the type of communicating market components, the interface has to be provided on both levels. In contrast to the document level, the distributed object level provides the link between the data and its processing. In this way, the distributed object level ensures the transferability of the document level into market applications.

Message level: As a prerequisite for the interoperability of different market components, the interfaces, i.e. the exchanged messages have to be committed dynamically between the participants. Structured messages have to be committed before the communication starts and therefore are inexpedient. Documents, describing their own content, fulfil this requirement because they enable the dynamic commitment of the communication interface between two participants. Due to the extendibility and flexibility with at the same time low complexity, on the message level the reference model makes use of XML documents.

Distributed object level: When the communication is directly based on JAVA RMI or CORBA, the market interface depends on the possibilities of the communication mechanism. The proxy object architecture encapsulates the communication mechanism. Dependencies on the possibilities of the communication mechanism as well as adoptions to changes are restricted to the internal structure of the proxy objects and have no consequences on the market interface. Therefore, on the distributed object level the reference model makes use of the proxy object architecture.

3.3 The model

Within the reference model the modelling of electronic tourism markets takes place on an abstract, communication mechanism independent level, based on the UML (*Unified Modeling Language*). The concrete models for the different communication levels and mechanisms, i.e. for the XML level and the distributed object level, are derived from this abstract level. In this way, the reference model supports the interoperability on different communication levels and is independent of the used communication mechanism.

The reference model enables a modelling sufficiently expressive for the interoperability of different market components, especially by considering semantic aspects, e.g. the relationships between the entities of the problem domain. In this way, the reference model enables the description of specific models in a form understandable for all communication partners.

On the XML level the descriptions of specific models (i.e. the metadata) are provided to the communication partners in the form of DTDs (Document Type Definition), on the distributed object level in the form of interface descriptions using the IDL (Interface Definition Language). However, XML DTDs as well as IDL-descriptions do not allow the representation of all information necessary for the interoperability of different market components. They both concentrate on structural information and lack in the ability of expressing semantic aspects of the model. XML tags certainly contain semantic information for a human observer (at least if they follow a common understanding of the problem domain or if they are defined within a common vocabulary) but not any machine-readable semantic information. Approaches to replace XML DTDs by more expressive metadata languages, e.g. XML Data [8]), SOX (Schema for Object-oriented XML [5]) or DDML (Document Definition Markup Language [3]), aim to eliminate this shortage.

The UML, used by the reference model as modelling language, allows the consideration of all information necessary for the interoperability between different market components, including the necessary semantic information. The exchange of the UML models between the communication partners takes place via XMI (XML Metadata Interchange), a standardized, XML-based language for serializing UML models. Here, XMI can replace or complement XML DTDs and IDL. In this way, the complete information of the UML models is available for the communication partners in machine-readable form. Using the UML and corresponding modelling tools enables a comfortable usage of the models of electronic tourism markets. Fig. 3 shows the different levels of the reference model.

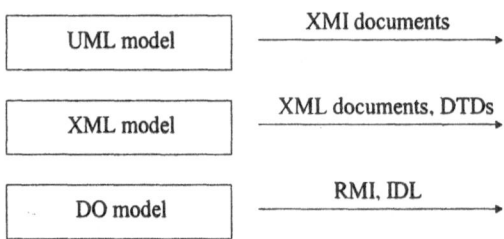

Fig. 3. Levels of the reference model

4 Implications on the tourism market

The reference model enables the uniform description of heterogeneous electronic markets and their interoperability. The use of the reference model has the following implications on the tourism market and its participants:

- The interoperability of different systems leads to one open electronic tourism market instead of the different existing markets. The complete value chain takes place within this open market.
- All participants of this open electronic market can communicate directly. Because of the possible direct communication between suppliers (tour operators) and customers, the intermediaries (as a link between customer and supplier) can be bypassed, especially in the case of experienced customers and elementary, not advice-intensive services. Therefore, the field of activity of the intermediary will shift to the supply of intermediary services *within* the electronic market.
- In an open market with a great amount of available services the need for intermediary services will increase. The supply of metadata, bundling of requests,

forwarding of requests to relevant suppliers and supply of additional information will be typical intermediary services within the open electronic market.

- Due to the easy access to all tourism services and the comparability of the services of different suppliers, the market transparency for the customer and the power of demand of the customer over the supplier will increase. The open market will become more customer-oriented than the existing markets and the customer will be increasingly integrated into the value chain.
- The access to the open electronic market is easier than to existing markets. Therefore, the number of participants will increase (especially small suppliers and tour operators) and industry newcomers will enter this open market, especially as intermediaries.
- Increasing competition between participants will lead to increasing consolidation. Consolidation will not only take place between participants on the same level of the value chain (e.g. suppliers of the same services or tour operators) but as well between participants on different levels of the value chain. Especially it has to be expected an increasing expansion of suppliers (particularly of several suppliers of different services) into the direction of the corresponding tour operators and vice versa.

5 Conclusion

Although standardisation initiatives have a long history in the field of tourism, a broad standardisation, enabling a global interoperability between tourism information systems has up to now not been reached due to a lack of flexibility and extendibility of those standards. Therefore, current efforts turn into the direction of open, more flexible specifications of tourism markets, mainly based on XML. In this paper has been presented an approach for unifying electronic tourism markets focusing on a conceptual modelling on an abstract, communication mechanism independent level, based on the *Unified Modeling Language* (UML). This reference model enables the flexible description of specific models in a form understandable for all communication partners and supports the interoperability on different concrete communication levels.

The process of elaborating a reference model of an electronic tourism market in cooperation with domain experts and participants of the tourism market (suppliers, tour operators, intermediaries, customers) has already been started. This process is executed by a series of workshops and an accompanying email discussion. An email forum (the Reference Model Special Interest Group – RMSIG, www.rmsig.de) has been established. The future task is to complete this process and commit an open specification for electronic tourism markets, approved by all participants.

References

1. Bohrer, K. et al.: Distributed Object Applications. Communications of the ACM, Vol. 41, No. 6, pp. 43-48 (1998).

2. Booch, G.: Objektorientierte Analyse und Design. Bonn, Addison-Wesley (1994).
3. Bourret, R. et al: Document Definition Markup Language (DDML) Specification, Version 1.0, W3C Note, http://www.w3.org/TR/NOTE-ddml (1999).
4. Bray, T. et al: Extensible Markup Language (XML) 1.0, W3C recommendation, http://www.w3.org/TR/REC-xml (1998).
5. Davidson, A. et al: Schema for Object-Oriented XML 2.0, W3C Note, http://www.w3.org/TR/NOTE-SOX (1999).
6. Glushko, R.J., Tenenbaum, J.M., Meltzer, B.: An XML framework for agent-based E-commerce. Communications of the ACM, Vol. 42, No. 3, pp. 106-114 (1999).
7. Höpken, W.: Modelling of an electronic tourism market. In: Buhalis, D., Schertler, W. (eds.): Information and Communication Technologies in Tourism, Innsbruck, Springer-Verlag, pp. 161-171 (1999).
8. Layman, A. et al: XML-Data, W3C note, http://www.w3.org/TR/1998/NOTE-XML-data-0105 (1998).
9. OMG Unified Modeling Language Specification, Version 1.3, OMG (1999).
10. Schmid, B.: Electronic Markets in Tourism. In: Schertler, W., Schmid, B., Tjoa, A.M., Werthner, H. (eds.): Information and Communications Technologies in Tourism, Innsbruck, Spinger-Verlag, pp. 1-8 (1994).
11. Schroeder, G.: Lexikon der Tourismuswirtschaft. Hamburg, TourCon Hannelore Niedecken GmbH (1995).
12. Tenenbaum, J.M., Chowdhry, T.S., Hughes, K.: Eco System: An Internet Commerce Architecture. IEEE Computer 30 (5), pp. 48-55 (1997).
13. Waldo, J.: The Jini architecture for network-centric computing. Communications of the ACM, Vol. 42, No. 7, pp 76-82 (1999).
14. Werthner, H., Klein, S.: Information technology and tourism: a challenging relationship. Springer-Verlag, Wien (1999).

Agents Solving Strategic Problems In Tourism

Josef Withalm
Siemens – PSE
Eibel Karl Sds-Hogatex

Michael Fasching
TU-Vienna-ICT

1 Introduction

One of the greatest obstacles in introducing reservation systems in tourism, and especially in SMTEs (Small and Medium-Sized Tourism Enterprises), has always been the allotment problem.

The smaller the business, the more mental reservations with regard to allotments because on the one hand the tour operator will charge a big commission, between 20% and 60% of the room price, and on the other hand there is no guarantee for the service provider (hotelkeeper) that his rooms will actually be sold. To use the sales channel of miscellaneous tour operators many different allotments are necessary.

1.1 Advantages of the current system

+ The allotments given to the *euro*START® franchisers offer the possibility to be booked in nearly all german travel agencies.
+ *Euro*START® has a powerful search engine that is offered to all START/Amadeus Terminals.
+ The *euro*START® system is working very well, offers transaction acidity and, due to the fast response time, is suitable for call centers, travel agencies and Internet..

1.2 Disadvantages of the current system

– The relevance of the allotment is unobtainable due to the manual entering of the data.
– From the franchiser's point of view there are also high marketing costs involved. The activities he has to perform include:
  • making contracts about allotments with service providers
  • presenting products and services in brochures
  • introducing products and services to the electronic system
  • marketing products and services at travel agents, call centers and internet
– High commissions

2 Theory

2.1 Description of the task – objective

Alternatives to allotments could be achieved by agent technology due to autonomous "looking and booking" of the Agents. This is the object of this project. The following provides a functional overview. The customer searches for a product/service by his preferred method. His requirements are passed on to the electronic booking system *euro*START® to find out if these requirements can be met. The reply is processed by the Agent Factory which sends out agents to all of the hotel's property management systems. A main function of property management systems is the administration of a service provider's resources, so this system knows which rooms are vacant on which days. The Agent gets this information, comes back to *euro*START® and sends it to the customer. In this case the service provider has no allotment problem: Whoever books first gets the product/service.

2.2 Why agent technology

- The hotel manager can control his hotel agent to offer his products at the electronic marketplace. Special offers can be presented this way very easy and fast.
- A new hotel property management system can be connected to the electronic marketplace like *euro*START® in establishing a new agent platform at the own property management system.
- Very important is the fact, that neither changes at *euro*START® nor at sds-hogatex Starlight® are necessary.
- *Agent technology is a mighty tool that suits the requirements.*

2.3 Definition

Software agent: *a computing entity that performs user developed tasks automatically*

Therefore we request the following attributes from a software agent:
- Delegation   (the user hands over the responsibility to the Agent)
- Ability to communicate (enhanced and more complex future tasks possible)
- Autonomy   (working in the background, authorization to negotiate)
- Monitoring   (ability to orientate in own neighborhood)
- Actuation   (neighborhood is changed by an action)
- Intelligence   (ability to interpret and make decisions)
- Mobility   (able to transport itself from one machine to another)
- Security   (in JAVA implemented, Sandbox)
- Personality   (encapsulation of the own identity)

The following skills of an agent model are distinguished:

- Task level skills: Typical tasks are information retrieval, information filtering and coaching
- Knowledge
- Communication skills

2.3.1 Knowledge

Two main categories are distinguished: A-priori knowledge: knowledge: which can be developer, user or system specified learning: can be dialogue or case based, or take place with the help of neural nets.

2.3.2 Agent communication

Here are two main categories as well:
- With the user: To offer the possibility to learn, the user has to communicate with the Agent. It can be with the help of an interface, with speech (Voice Agents [1]) or social interaction
- With other agents: Interagent communication language (XML, ACL)

XML. The XML (eXtensible Markup Language) uses markups to give text special attributes. The characteristic of XML is the independence/seperating of content and style. Word processing applications use visual markups for the form of text documents ("bold" or "Times New Roman"). Having the possibility of doing generic markup, which means giving semantic information to connected letters ("heading"), it is pssible to use semantic for searching the content and for exchange. [2]

ACL. The ACL (Agent Communication Language) is part of the FIPA specifications The Foundation for Intelligent Physical Agents (FIPA) [3] is an open international collaboration of member organisations and published the FIPA97 [4] specifications that maximise interoperability across agent-based applications. Syntax and semantics for many domains (tourism) is defined in that reference model..

This ACL, will soon make it possible, for service providers to create their individual Agents themselves or they have them created by someone else. Either way, the hotel can then offer ist services to the electronic market place via this agent. The ACL extends the electronic business possibilities by allowing the hotel's agent to sign contracts with booking Agents met at the electronic market place.

2.4 Involved Systems

This paper specializes on the SIEMENS *euro*START® system and the sds-hogatex Starlight® system used by a vast amount of hotel owners.

2.4.1 *euro*START®

*euro*START® handles the entire business process between the individual providers of tourism services and the tourist customers. It employs classic sales channels such as tourism associations, tour operators, the airline CRS/GDS (Computerised Reservation System/Global Distribution System) and travel agencies. *euro*START® covers the full spectrum of marketing techniques such as information, reservation and management information. About 95% of the German travel agencies are equiped with START/Amadeus terminals, that are operated via the "TOMA-Mask".

The use of state-of-the-art, object-oriented development technology means that the system can easily be adapted to the differing regional and national requirements (internationalisation) and guarantees that it can be expanded to accommodate modern technologies such as new methods of communication (Internet, integration in multimedia systems). Interprocess communication between client and server is handled by VisiBroker, that is based on the CORBA 2.0 standard (Common Object Request Broker Architecture). This standard was developed by the Open Management Group (OMG), which includes well-known manufacturers such as IBM, Siemens, Olivetti, Sun etc. VisiBroker is also used on the server. The *euro*START® application software was designed and programmed according to object oriented principles (with C++). *euro*START® servers can be run on all operating systems which conform to the UNIX standard (e.g. SUN, HB). As *euro*START® client a Windows 95 PC with a minimum of 16 MB main memory and a hard disk capacity of at least 340 MB is needed.

2.4.2 SDS-Hogatex Starlight®

The company sds-hogatex [5] develops and sells the hotel (property) managementsystems "SDS-Hotel®" and "HOGATEX-Starlight®" in over 1200 hotels in 30 countries. Depending on the size, the Starlight® System is put together using the modules Starlight® Front-Office System, Sales and Marketing, Conference and Banqueting, Starlight® Back Office, Telephone-Management system and Yield-Management-System.

Any number of clients (Cash register, PayTV, Telephonesystems, barequipment , PayTV, KeyCards, cash desks, and so on - also of different companies) can use the server via flexible Interfaces. There the Data is stored centrally on a Progress Database [6]. The Client uses a Windows 95/98 or NT Workstation PC. Windows NT Server, UNIX or NOVELL Netware is offered as serverplatform

2.4.3 Agent systems

Aglets. The mobile agents of IBM [7] are called Aglets, a mix of the words agents and applets. The agen tplatform is Tahiti. The Aglets work and the Documentation is sufficient [7,8]. They were choosed for this project. (see 4.1)

Java Seal / J-Seal2. The Agentplatform J-Seal2, that is currently developed by the company CoCo [9] originates in the JAVA-Seal Software developed by the University of Geneva. It offers an improved JAVA-Kernel, that supports mobile Agents. Due to the monitoring of safety relevant JAVA-Methods high secure Sandboxes are offered. The Software was not available at the time of decision.

MECCA. This "*M*ulti-Agent *E*nvironment for *C*onstructing *C*ooperative *A*pplications" (MECCA) Classlibrary is developed by SIEMENS [10] for a german research project. It pays attention to the FIPA 97 [4] standardisation, and supports all FIPA-Agents. It supports planning, where the Agents own generated plan can be shared with other Agents to receive a common/specific goal. It also supports communicative acts (*request, inform, handleRequests)*. It does neither support mobile Agents nor information retrieving/filtering. The Documentation was not available at the time of decision.

Voyager. The Produktline Voyager (current version 3.1) by ObjectSpace [11] includes the Voyager ORB Professional, Voyager Application Server and Voyager Security. It supports mobile Agents and CORBA, but the documentation was insufficient at the time of decision.

3 Methods

3.1 *euro*START® Client and Server

Vacancy queries are used to search for available products. In such queries the user can specify search criteria (locations, features) in accordance with customer requirements. These criteria are then used to select all relevant products. They are keyed in at a *euro*START®-Client. This generates an object at the *euro*START®-Server and a reference is sent back to the client. With those CORBA-references the client can access the objects located at the server.

3.2 CORBA-Filter

The filter is logically located between the *euro*START®-Client and the *euro*START®-Server, simulating a ferver for the *euro*START®-Client and offering itself as a client for the *euro*START®-Server. The *euro*START®-Client only binds to the "new" ORB ("Filter ORB" is only a new name!), the other functionality remains unchanged! In this ORB the Filter acts as the Server. On the other side the Filter binds to the original ORB and so to the *euro*START®-Server.

A mirrorobject is created by the Filter acting as a Server for the the *euro*START®-client. On the other side the filter acts as a client and forwards the vacancy query to the *euro*START®-Server. The result of the query are all Hotels that suite the search criteria. This result is forwarded by the Filter Client to the Agentfactory.

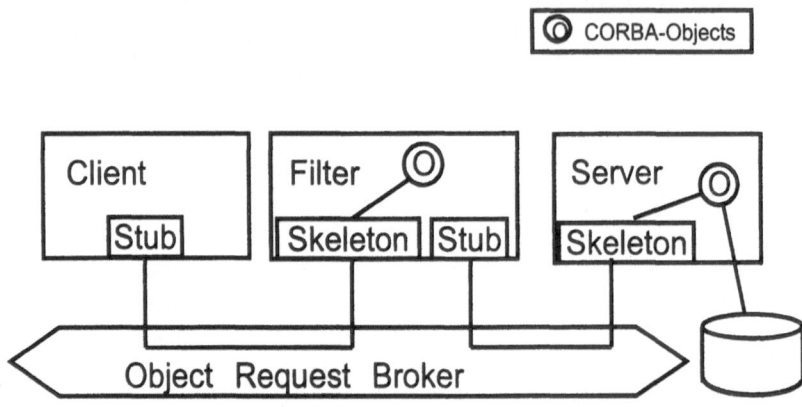

Fig. 1. Design of the CORBA-Filter

3.3 Agent system

Deriving from the vacancy query, the appropriate Agents are generated. The Agentsystem ("Agentfactory") converts the hotel names of the query result to Internet adresses (URL) and sends the agents to these locations with the orders to search there for vacant rooms..

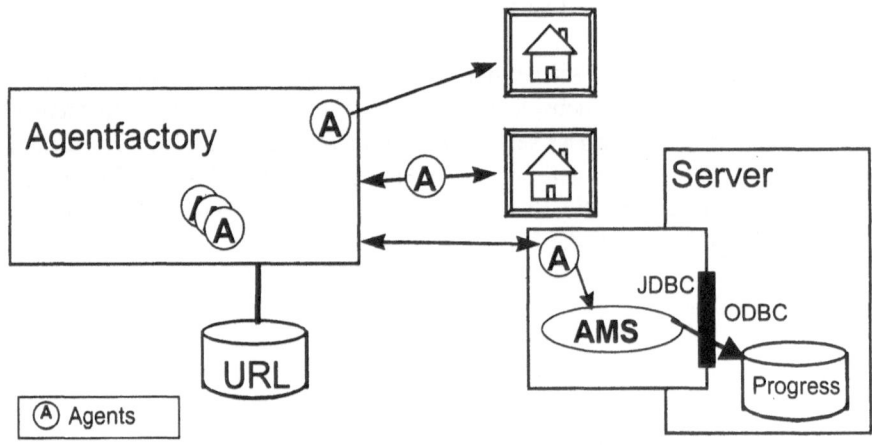

Fig. 2. Design of the Agentfactory and the Database access

3.4 Query of the Hotel Database

At the hotel the agent management system (AMS) is continous waiting for incomming

Agents. The mobile agent reaches the hotel and informs the AMS of his request. That connects via JDBC-ODBC bridge (JAVA Database Connectivity - Open Database Connectivity) to the Database of the property management system, and searches for vacant rooms. The result is passed to the mobile agent, that returns back to the agent factory.

3.5 Agent analysis

The positive answers (the Hotels with vacant rooms) are collected and passed on to the *euro*START®-Client by the Filter Server (see Illustration 4.1)

4 Results

To introduce an agent system, the following is necessary:
- The filter in the ORB of *euro*START®
- At the *euro*START® site an agent factory has to be established.
- At every sds-hogatex server an agent execution platform has to be installed.
- In a meta-database, the IP-address of every involved service provider is stored.
- No changes in the software at *euro*START® or at sds-hogatex Starlight® are necessary

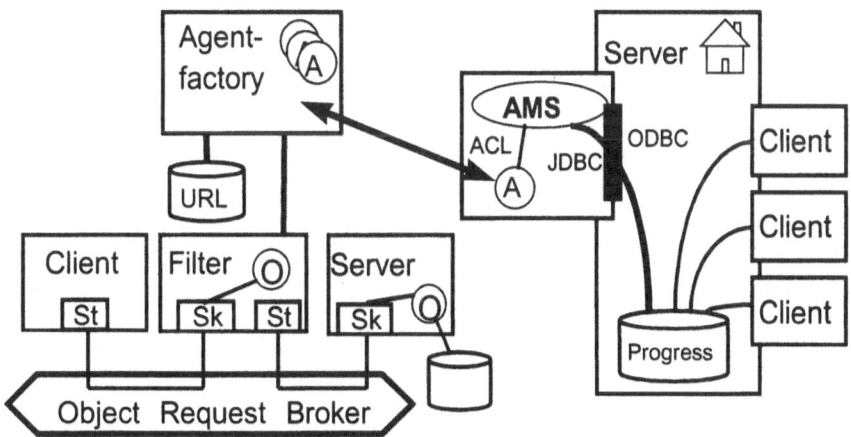

Fig.3. Communication design

In the course of this project, a trial application will be carried out, where products of some selected service providers who use the property management system Hogatex Starlight®, will be regarded. In the pilot phase, customers who access *euro*START® via internet will be specially supported because in this case the requirements in view of performance are not as relevant. However, performance and security are definitely the most difficult problems which have to be solved in the pilot phase.

4.1 Agenten platform

The version 1.0.3 of the Aglets Software Development Kit (ASDK) by IBM [7] is used in this project.

4.2 CORBA
At *euro*START® the Inprise VisiBroker 3.3 is used. [12]

4.3 Database access

The JDBC-ODBC Bridge that is used to access the Progress Database [6] of sds-hogatex Starlight® is the DataDirect SequeLink JAVA Edition Version 2.0 by Merant. [13]

5 Conclusions

The experiences of this trial application support the technical feasibility; now, the commercial aspects will be considered where the agents and the agent platforms will be implemented in the products (Applications) *euro*START® and Starlight®.

References

1. http://www.genmagic.com/asa/danny/
2. http://www.w3.org/XML/
3. http://www.fipa.org/
4. Foundation for Intelligent Physical Agents; Field Trial Specifications Version 1.0; Geneva, Switzerland (1997), http://www.fipa.org/spec/FIPA97.html
5. http://www.hogatex.de
6. http://www.progress.de or http://www.progress.com
7. http://www.trl.ibm.co.jp/aglets
8. Lange, D. B., Mitsuru Oshima: Programming and Deploying Java Mobile Agents with Aglets, Addison Wesely Inc., (1996)
9. http://www.coco.co.at/
10. http://w1.siemens.de/FuI/de/zeitschrift/archiv/Heft2_99/artikel03/index.html (German only)
11. http://www.Objectspace.com
12. http://www.visigenic.com/
13. http://www.merant.com/

Open Network for Tourism (OnTour): A Concept for Electronic Commerce in the Business Processes of the Tourism Industry

Jörg Zabel
Bremen Institute of Industrial Technology and Applied Work Science (BIBA)
P.O. Box 33 05 60, D-28335 Bremen, Germany
Email: zab@biba.uni-bremen.de

Dietmar Bönke
Fachhochschule Reutlingen
Alteburgstraße 150, D-72762 Reutlingen, Germany
Email:dietmar.boenke@fh-reutlingen.de

Penelope Constanta
Institute of Computer Science, FORTH
P.O. Box 1385, GR-71110 Heraklion, Greece
Email: penelope@ics.forth.gr

Abstract

The OnTour project aims to develop and validate new ways of workflow in the tourist market by implementing an open network of electronic commerce. This paper summarises the basic concept of the OnTour network including the server architecture, the integration of the OnTour smart card, the network functionality, and the technical concept. Furthermore, the approach and the expected benefits of the envisaged OnTour solution are briefly outlined.

1 Introduction

The tourist business is based on the co-operation of commercial organisations representing the tourist value chain. The economy of tourist services depends on the ability of the companies to adapt their offerings to market changes on extremely short notice.

The Open Network for Tourism (OnTour) project aims to develop and validate new ways of workflow in the business between suppliers, destination agencies, tour operators, and travel agencies. Therefore, an open network of electronic commerce in the tourist business will be developed offering new access to and distribution of information for the partners of the tourist value chain as well as the travellers.

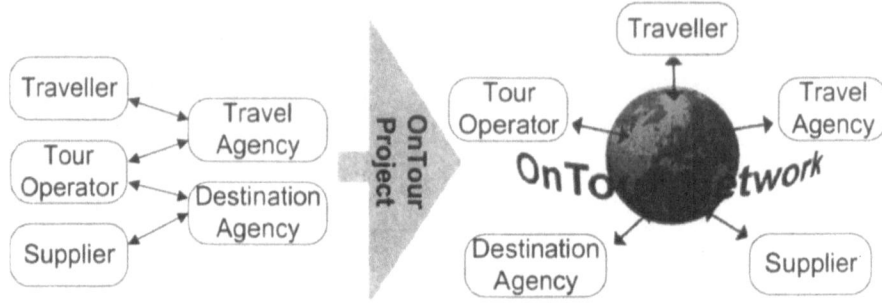

Fig. 1. Today's communication chain versus the OnTour communication network

OnTour is mainly focused on the business-to-business commerce, but addresses also the business-to-consumer market. Whilst existing solutions are of proprietary character or apply the Internet only as advertising medium, the objective of the envisaged OnTour solution is to establish an open platform enabling a continuous electronic information flow between all business partners based on only one medium – the Internet.

The project is funded by the Commission of the European Communities (CEC) under the ESPRIT programme (Project No. 26956) as well as by the participating partners. The OnTour consortium consists of six partners and 3 associated partners from 4 European countries. Each member is uniquely placed to exploit the results of the OnTour project to the overall extent from differing yet complementary perspective.

All OnTour industrial partners are actors in a highly dynamic travel market and faced with the current lack of integration. Moser Reisen is both a travel agency and a tour operator for special interest tours in Linz, Austria. Viajes Necan and Zeus of Crete represent the leading destination agencies on the Canary Islands respectively Crete. The three associated partners Autopapas, Istron Bay and Maris Hotels can be characterised as typical suppliers offering accommodation and car rental services.

The German software and consultancy company VSS is co-ordinator of the OnTour project and brings in their specific expertise in software development. They are assisted by the Bremen Institute of Industrial Technology and Applied Work Science (BIBA) and the Greek Institute of Computer Science (ICS-Forth) as research organisations with experiences in the field of Inter- and Intranet technologies.

The following chapter outlines the approach applied in the OnTour project. Chapter 3 summarises the OnTour server architecture, the functions of the OnTour smart card, the general network functionality and the technical concept. Before the paper is concluded, chapter 4 highlights the expected benefits of the OnTour system.

2 Approach

The conception of the OnTour solution has been carried out using a classical development approach. The following steps have been executed:

1. *Modelling of the as-is situation.*
   Firstly, the current business processes of the industrial OnTour partners have been captured and modelled in order to achieve a detailed mutual understanding about the business activities of the different actors in the tourist value chain.

2. *Drawback analysis*
   In step 2 the drawbacks of the current business processes have been identified.

3. *Definition of the to-be situation*
   Based on the drawbacks the specific and generic user requirements have been defined and structured. The generic requirements concern for example the
   - information flow and processing: e.g. continuous use of electronic media by performing availability requests or generating vouchers
   - information quality: e.g. the reliability of booking confirmations, the actuality of service offers, and the security of business transactions
   - information handling: e.g. smart cards instead of printed travel documents
   - information access: e.g. to objective assessments of suppliers
   - information distribution: e.g. to announce special offers at the target market

   An important result of the drawback and requirement analysis was that many similarities exist regarding the main business processes of the different actors in the value chain. Although the specific methods and tools may vary the general requirements and procedures for instance regarding a booking transaction are alike. Therefore, the roles of "buyers" and "sellers" have been introduced as an abstraction for tourists, travel agencies, tour operators, destination agencies, and suppliers to reduce the complexity of the value chain.
   Based on the requirements an optimised model of the to-be situation has been generated containing the main business processes for the buyers and sellers of tourist services. The definition of these reference processes was the basis for the network specification and a prerequisite to enable a direct mutual co-operation between all members in the value chain.

4. *Specification of the OnTour network*
   The specification of the envisaged OnTour solution has been the subject of the fourth step. The concept of the network architecture is content of this paper.

An important principle in the OnTour project is the use of iterative and participatory development approaches in all project phases. The as-is processes and their drawbacks have been captured by carrying out interviews with the OnTour industrial partners and distributing questionnaires. The generic models of the as-is and to-be situation have been defined using the IDEF0 approach. The OnTour network has been specified using the Unified Modelling Language (UML).

3 OnTour Network Architecture

The OnTour architecture represents a multi-layer client/server solution based on the Internet as communication medium. The network integrates different existing tools and technologies. By ensuring interoperability a continuous electronic information flow will be realised covering all business transactions in the tourism value chain.

3.1 Server Architecture

The OnTour architecture allows to connect different servers to a common service. In contrast to a monolithic approach the envisaged architecture is characterised by advanced flexibility and scalability. The server concept is based on the ISI standard (ISI - International Standard Interface developed by the DIRG - Deutschland Informations- und Reservierungsgesellschaft mbH, June 1999) [2], whereas the communication details are solved differently in OnTour compared to ISI.

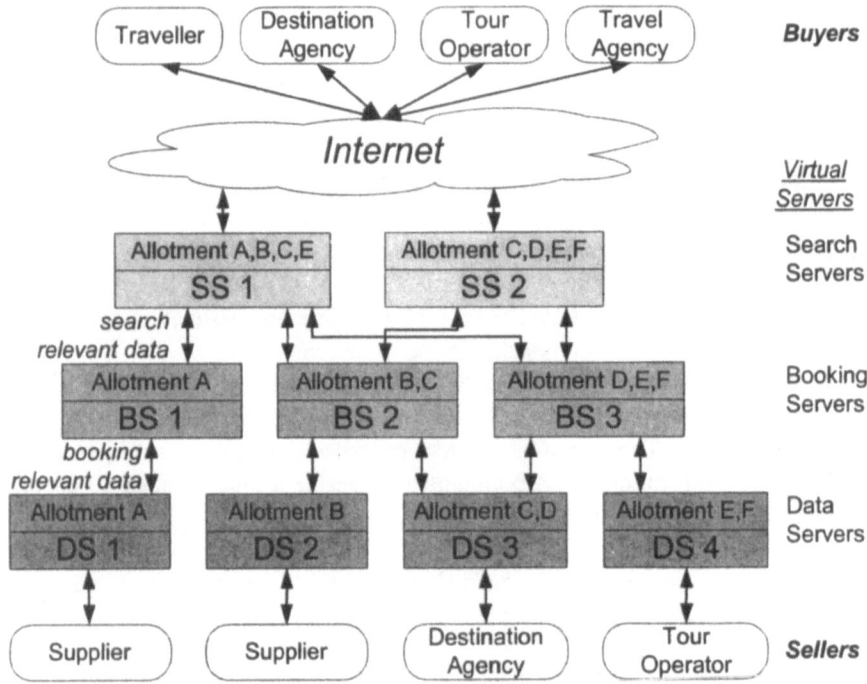

Fig. 2. Example of the OnTour Network Architecture

3.2 OnTour Card

In addition to the three server types the OnTour Card (OTC) represents an important element in the overall network concept. The OTC is a smart card for the traveller respectively consumer of tourist services and offers the following functionality:

- *Ticket replacement.* The OTC is used as substitute for printed travel documents, like tickets and vouchers. The Search Server allows the traveller to download "e-vouchers" onto his OTC respectively to remove cancelled services from the OTC. On the supplier's side the OnTour Standard Application (part of the Data Server) will mark the e-vouchers as consumed and collect them. A corresponding business scenario is depicted in Fig. 3.

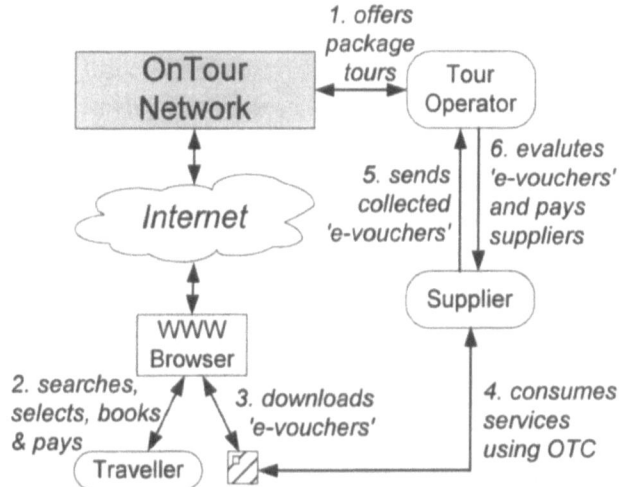

Fig. 3. Simplified OTC Scenario

Both the traveller as well as the seller/supplier benefits from the OTC. Since all travel documents are collected on a single card travellers do not need to manage several different tickets. The sellers and suppliers profit from the OTC by a more efficient and secure handling of vouchers. By using the OTC, the entire information flow concerning the generation, sending, capturing, collecting and evaluation of tickets can now be carried out fully digital without impeding media breaks.

- *Digital signature*: The OTC holds, PIN protected, the private key and its associated X.509 certificate (public key). The selected smart card is capable to perform the asymmetric algorithm for digital signatures on card, so that the private key never needs to exist anywhere other than on the smart card in secured storage.

If a user points his browser to a security relevant OnTour site (e.g. for a booking operation) the Web server will inform the browser that certificates are required on this page. By inserting the OTC into a smart card device the server can verify the certificate and establish a secure session. The further communication is carried out fully encrypted and mutually authenticated.

Furthermore, the digital signature function of the OTC is used for signing the consumed e-vouchers at the supplier's location. By signing the e-vouchers the tourist confirms the consumption of the services.

Therefore, the OTC helps to:
– Make the business transactions reliable through mutual authentication. Neither a buyer nor a seller can easily deny a business transaction.
– Facilitate the authentication process. The certificate and the private key are portable and easy to handle.
– Protect the user's private key. By generating the private key on the smart card it never exists in a computer memory, where it could be sniffed by a malicious program. Additionally, the users have more control when and where the private key is being used because they can carry the smart card with them.

- *Check-in support*. The OTC stores the basic personal data of the user. This information can be used to automate the check-in procedure at the supplier. Instead of filling in the registration form in a hotel or car rental company the tourist can put his OTC in the card device connected to the supplier's OnTour application.

3.3 Network Functionality

In addition to the above mentioned functions regarding the smart card the OnTour servers will provide the following functions for the sellers and buyers of tourist services:
- Management of service offers
  Including for example functions for pricing, splitting of allotments as well as for accessing the current booking status and the booking data. In order to reduce the system complexity the first prototypes will mainly be focused on accommodation and car rental services.
- Access to service information and assessments
  To assess the reliability of the sellers the OnTour system will offer the buyers the possibility to rate and comment consumed services.
- Functions for searching, selecting, and negotiating
  After the buyer has entered his search criteria the Search Server will provide a list of appropriate service offers. By selecting an offer, service details can be displayed and an availability check can be performed. Moreover, commercial buyers can negotiate the conditions of the service with the seller by exchanging

emails. During the negotiation the service is temporary looked for other buyers (booking option).

- Management of special service requests
  All buyers of tourist services can also 'push' service requests to a Search Server if they are looking for example for a very specific travel offer. These requests can be browsed and answered by sellers (especially interesting for travel agencies) able to make an appropriate offer.
- Functions for booking, rebooking, and cancelling
  The OnTour system provides the common booking functions. Since the integration of an electronic payment system is not subject of the OnTour project payment transactions have to be confined to the transfer of credit card information in the first OnTour prototype.
- Registration and authentication of buyers and sellers
- Graphical User Interface

Additional features, like for example advanced booking functions (e.g. booking on waiting list), e-payment, auction, integration of existing computerised reservation systems, and multi-lingual capabilities, are planned for the commercialisation of the OnTour system after the end of the OnTour project.

3.4 Technical Concept

The technical decisions with regard to the OnTour architecture are depicted in Fig. 4.

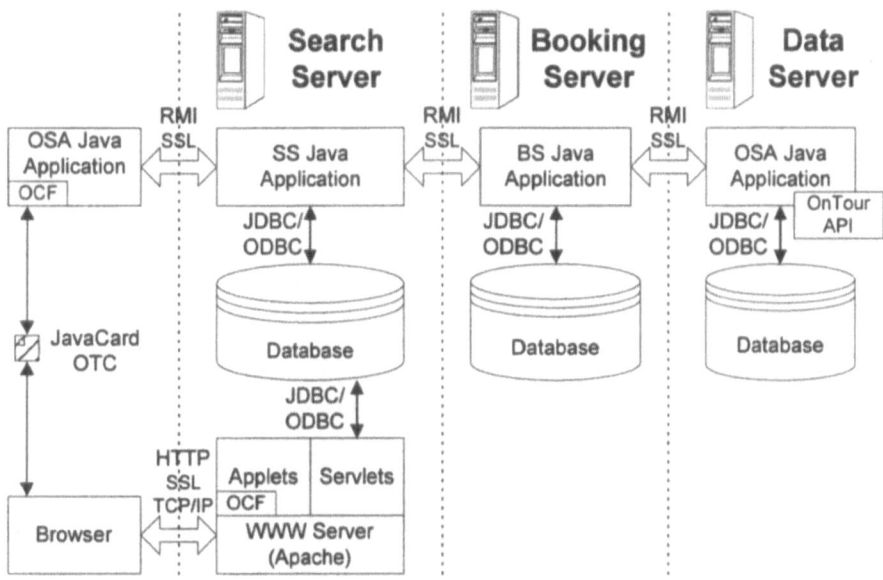

Fig. 4: Technical Concept

The Search Server provides two interfaces and can be accessed by using the OnTour Standard Application (OSA) or a standard browser. The main component of the Search Server represent the Java application. By using the OSA, buyers can directly access the Search Server. This is primarily interesting for commercial buyers who need to integrate OnTour in their existing back office systems. Alternatively, the buyers have the possibility to access the OnTour service by HTML pages. To generate dynamic HTML documents from the content of the database the Web interface of the Search Server is based on servlets. But also (certified) applets are needed to read and modify the content of the OnTour Card.

In order to allow the dynamic extension of the OTC functionality, by e.g. credit card or room key functions, a multi-application smart card was required. In OnTour the Java Card [3] has been selected as platform for the smart card application. For the integration of the OTC into the overall network the Open Card Framework (OCF) [9] is applied. The OCF is a Java based framework providing interoperability of smart cards and card devices.

The Booking Server and the Data Server consist each of a Java application and a database. The application of the Data Server is called OnTour Standard Application. The OSA is based on the OnTour API, a generic library and interface developed to integrate OnTour into commercial back office solutions.
The communication between the different servers as well as with the OSA is done by SSL (Secure Socket Layer) protected Remote Method Invocations (RMI) [11,12] and controlled by a so-called Administrator Module, which is integrated in each application. The OnTour servers will access their respective database using SQL ANSI compliant statements and the JDBC protocol. The Search Servers and the Booking Servers are protected by firewalls.

4 Expected Benefits

The OnTour network is an open and user-friendly platform based on the Internet. OnTour allows the commercial users to activate their global competence and expand their market by participating in the international e-market. The OnTour solution provides improvements regarding the
- accessibility, actuality and reliability of service information and booking data,
- ability to find relevant information and qualified business partners,
- promptness to react on market changes (market transparency),
- selection and individual combination of services,
- handling of travel documents,
- security of the business transactions, and thus the
- cost and time needed for the business processes.

5 Conclusion

The digitalisation of economic transactions has far reaching effects on the tourist market. Electronic commerce will not allow some classic business to act like before but will bring a lot of chances and new opportunities to companies and travellers. The concentration on special competencies and the widening of the distribution of tourist services will bring a globalisation of resourcing and distribution markets. In this sense, the OnTour project will not only help to design one part of the electronic commerce in tourism but also can be a basis of experience for other branches.

The envisaged OnTour solution represents the consequent implementation of electronic commerce addressing all actors in the tourist value chain and covering all business transactions. The OnTour network will allow all kinds of companies in the tourist business to offer and request services, enabling especially smaller and medium sized organisations to participate in the business as equal partners. By following a distributed approach with three different server types a flexible, open and extendible solution will be realised. The introduction of a smart card as replacement for printed travel documents is a promising approach to achieve a continuous electronic information flow in all business processes.

The pilot installation of the OnTour network will be established in June 2000. Within the pilot phase the OnTour industrial users as well as the OnTour User Interest Group will test the server prototypes to proof the adequacy of the implementation as well as to gain more feedback for the further refinement of the software.

References

1. Constanta, P., Marazakis, M., Papadakis, D., Nikolaou, C., Bönke, D.: Efforts Towards an Open Electronic Commerce Infrastructure for the Tourism Industry. In: Proceedings DEXA 98, Ninth International Workshop on Database and Expert Systems Applications, Vienna, Austria, pp. 633-637 (1998).

2. DIRG: ISI-Standard Version 1, Heft 2: Allgemeine Beschreibung und Regelwerk, 10.06.1999, http://www.dirg.de/ISI/index2.htm.

3. Java Card Forum, WWW-Page, September 1999, http://www.javacardforum.org/

4. Legal Framework for the development of Electronic Commerce, Proposal for a European Parliament and Council Directive on certain legal aspects of electronic commerce in the internal market: COM(98) 586 final, in Official Journal C 30, 05.02.1999.

5. Legislative resolution embodying Parliament's opinion on the proposal for a European Parliament and Council Directive on a common framework for electronic signatures (COM(98)0297 C4-0376/98 _ 98/0191(COD)), in Official Journal C 104 of 14.04.1999.

6. OnTour consortium: ESPRIT project No 26956, Deliverable 13: Definition of the To-be Situation, 1999.

7. OnTour consortium: ESPRIT project No 26956, Deliverable 21: OnTour Network Architecture, 1999.

8. OnTour consortium: ESPRIT project No 26956, Deliverable 23b: OnTour Smart Card Specification, 1999.

9. Open Card Framework - General Information Web Document, Second Edition, WWW Page, October 1998, http://www.opencard.org/docs/gim/ocfgim.html.

10. Papadakis, D., Marazakis, M., Nikolaou, C., Constanta, P.: An Infrastructure to Support Collaboration and Co-operation in Electronic Commerce. In: Proceedings Working Conference on Electronic Commerce, Metsovo, Greece (1997).

11. Sridharan, P.: Advanced Java Networking, Prentice Hall PTR, New Jersey, 1997.

12. Sun Microsystems Inc.: Remote Method Invocation Specification, WWW Page, 1997, http://java.ei.jrc.it/javadocs/guide/rmi/spec/rmiTOC.doc.html.

TOURISTS' VALUATION OF OTHER TOURISTS' CONTRIBUTIONS TO TRAVEL WEB SITES

Benedict G.C. Dellaert
Department of Marketing, Faculty of Economics, Tilburg University
PO Box 90153, 5000 LE Tilburg, The Netherlands
phone: +31 13 466 8224, fax: +31 13 466 3066, email: dellaert@kub.nl

1 Introduction

Virtual communities represent one of the most interesting phenomena in the recent growth of the World Wide Web (e.g., Armstrong and Hagel 1996, Hoffman and Novak 1996). An important characteristic of virtual communities is that they require contributions from their members; both active, e.g. by participating in discussions, or putting up web sites, and passive, e.g. by looking at other people's web sites, or placing requests. It is not surprising therefore, that firms operating on the Internet increasingly attempt to use virtual communities as instruments to compete for consumer attention, and that companies that are successful at attracting active contributors to their web sites have seen their stock market values go up dramatically (e.g., GeoCities, eBay).

In tourism also, it has been proposed that virtual communities may play a crucial role in marketing tourist destinations and services over the Internet (e.g., Dellaert 1999). Such communities could for example provide valuable information to tourists about travel destinations or about tourism service providers. However, despite high researcher and practitioner interest in this area and the fact that the view that tourist input constitutes a major part of the value of virtual tourism communities is widely supported, only little empirical research exists in this area, and few methods and models are available to determine the value that tourists attach to the contributions by other tourists to travel web sites. If such methods and research results were available they could increase our understanding of tourists' decision making when using the Internet and they also could provide tools for tourism service providers to increase the impact of their travel web sites.

Therefore, the central question in this study is how tourists' valuation of the availability of such contributions by other tourists to travel web sites can be modeled and measured, and, subsequently, to explore the relative importance of such contributions compared to other web site characteristics. To address these issues effectively, the paper is structured as follows. First, some micro-economic arguments why other tourists' contributions can be relevant to tourist travel decision making are reviewed and an econometric model of tourists' valuation of the availability of such contributions is introduced. Secondly, conjoint analysis is introduced as a suitable approach to measure the variables in the proposed model. Thirdly, the model and measurement technique are illustrated in an empirical study. In particular, results are presented from a conjoint analysis on Dutch tourists' preferences for Internet travel web sites with and without other tourists' contributions. Model estimates are presented and it is shown that tourists' valuation of other tourists' contributions to travel web sites is relatively high compared to some other important travel web site characteristics. The monetary equivalent of this value is calculated also. The paper concludes with a section discussing results and limitations and suggesting some opportunities for future research.

2 Theory

This study focuses on a micro-economic explanation of tourists' valuation of other tourists' contributions to travel web sites. Two main benefits of the availability of such contributions are discussed and an econometric model that captures the value that tourists attach to these benefits is introduced.

A first benefit tourists may derive from the availability of other tourists' contributions is that they may experience efficiency gains in their household production costs (e.g., Kooreman and Wunderink 1997). For example, virtual travel communities can allow tourists to benefit from scale advantages in going through their travel decision making. In particular, efficiency is increased if information on a certain topic (e.g., a specific attraction) can be collected by only one individual and then shared amongst others, compared to the case in which each individual collects his or her own information. Furthermore, sharing information between tourists may allow individuals to specialize in certain areas in which they are experts. For example, some tourists may be interested in museums, while others may be knowledgeable about restaurants. If their information is shared, both individuals benefit from higher quality information, while each can still focus on the topic that interests them most.

Secondly, the availability of other tourists' contributions on travel web sites may allow tourists to overcome some of the inherent information asymmetries that exist between tourism services suppliers and tourists (e.g., Rindfleish and Heide 1997). It is often difficult to evaluate the quality of tourism services and experiences before they are consumed. For example, hotel room quality, the attractiveness of a location, and the food quality in a restaurant, all are difficult to evaluate before they are experienced. Therefore, tourists may get 'trapped' in a certain activity if a tourism service doesn't meet the expectations the tourist had at the time of booking. The availability of evaluations of other tourists that have experienced these services before can help overcome such difficulties. In particular, other tourists' evaluations can provide valuable insights in matching tourism demand and supply and in facilitating reputation development.

Econometrically, tourists' preferences for the availability of other tourists' contributions on travel web sites can be modeled using a random utility model (e.g., Ben-Akiva and Lerman 1985). This type of model assumes that tourist choices can be represented as a process in which tourists evaluate the attributes of the alternatives relevant to a given choice are evaluated in terms of the utility they provide. The part-worth utilities associated with each of the attributes are assumed to be integrated cognitively into an overall utility for every alternative, after which the alternative with the highest overall utility is selected. The utility function in the model consists of two basic parts: i) a deterministic component that describes the structural utility that the tourist derives from the attributes that make up the alternative, and ii) a random error component that captures the errors in modeling this structural utility. Such errors can be due to various sources including measurement error, omitted explanatory variables, and unobserved variations in taste.

Depending on the assumptions one is willing to make with regard to the error component, the random utility model supports fairly straightforward estimation of coefficients that express the impact of each of the attributes on the total utility of an alternative. By applying the simple choice rule that the alternative with the highest utility is selected, it also allows one to express the choice probability of a given alternative. This probability is modeled as a function of the attributes of the alternative and the attributes of the other alternatives in the choice set. Effects due to characteristics of the individual and the choice situation can be included also. In formula, the random utility model is expressed as:

$$U_j = V_j + \varepsilon_j \qquad (1)$$
$$= \mathbf{X_j}'\beta + \varepsilon_j$$

where: U_j is the utility of alternative j, V_j is the structural utility of alternative j, $\mathbf{X_j}$ is the vector of attributes of alternative j, β is the vector of parameter values of the attributes, , ε_j is the random error component.

For the binomial case in which tourists choose whether or not to select a certain alternative over a generic 'other' option, the related choice probability is expressed as:

$$P(j) = P(U_j > U_{other}) \qquad (2)$$
$$= P(V_j + \varepsilon_j > V_{other} + \varepsilon_{other})$$
$$= P(\varepsilon_j - \varepsilon_{other} > V_{other} - V_j)$$

where, $P(j)$ is the probability that alternative j is chosen, U_{other} is the utility of the generic 'other' option, of which V_{other} and ε_{other} are the structural and the random error component respectively.

In most applications, random utility models are based on the assumption that the random error components in the utilities of the alternatives follow independently and identically distributed distributions, for example following a normal or Gumbel distribution in which case the well known probit and logit models arise respectively.

By expressing the coefficients of the non-price attributes of the utility function in terms of the respondents' equivalent responses to price changes, the economic value of non-price attributes can be determined (e.g., Lindberg et al. 1999). In this study, this technique is used to express tourists' monetary valuation of the absence or presence of other tourists' contributions to travel Web sites. Specifically, if the price attribute is expressed in dollar gains expected on the Internet, the monetary equivalent E of the availability of other tourists' contributions on a travel web site is equal to the ratio of the parameter for the availability of other tourists' contributions and the parameter for price:

$$E = \frac{\beta_{contr}}{\beta_{price}}$$
(3)

3 Measurement

Relatively few data are available on tourist preferences for travel web sites, and if such data are available it typically is difficult to single out separate effects of changes in web site characteristics such as the availability of other tourists contributions. The reason is that most web sites are updated by implementing multiple changes simultaneously. Therefore, the effects of these changes are confounded. Furthermore, tourists' contributions to travel web sites typically are not traded commercially, making the matter of determining the price equivalent of tourists' valuation of these contributions a non-trivial problem.

Conjoint analysis represents a way to overcome these difficulties by presenting individuals with hypothetical alternatives that are constructed by the researcher. Conjoint analysis is growing in popularity in tourism research, and is often used as a method to explore tourist choice (e.g., Louviere and Timmermans 1990, Dellaert et al. 1997). The method is most commonly used in marketing, for example in developing new product options (e.g., Moore et al. 1999), but also is applied in other areas such as environmental economics, where it is used to value non-market goods such as the availability of natural resources (e.g., Boxall et al 1996).

Parameter estimates in conjoint analysis are based on consumer responses to hypothetical alternatives or choice situations (Louviere 1988). The researcher creates these hypothetical situations (or conjoint profiles) on the basis of statistical experimental designs in which the levels of the attributes in the choice alternatives are varied systematically. Columns in the experimental design prescribe the variation in the different attributes and are (close to) orthogonal to support statistically efficient estimation of the model's coefficients. Sometimes, other criteria such as context specific limitations are taken into account also (e.g., Kuhfeld et al. 1994).

Response formats in conjoint analysis may differ between applications depending on research objectives and data collection limitations. Traditionally, the most popular approach has been to ask respondents to provide preference ratings for every alternative in the experimental design. For example, respondents are asked to rate how attractive they find the alternatives, or to rate the probability that they would buy each alternative. Recently, choice based response formats also have grown in popularity. In choice tasks, respondents are asked to choose between competing alternatives. For example, a choice task could consists of two travel options and a base option of not going. Ratings and choice responses have been compared in a number of theoretical analyses and empirical applications and in many cases it was justified to assume that the underlying utilities for both response formats were identical (e.g., Elrod et al. 1994).

Estimation techniques applied in conjoint analysis depend on the type of responses collected and the assumptions the researcher is willing to make with regard to data properties. For example, in some estimations corrections are made for correlations in taste between multiple responses of the same individual, or for correlations between responses to the same brands, travel modes or destinations.

In the case of preference rating responses, the researcher typically assumes that the responses are measures of the latent underlying utilities that the respondents attach to the different alternatives (eq. 1). Estimation of the appropriate utility function can be done using traditional OLS techniques if one is willing to assume that the scale properties of the preference responses are those of an interval scale. If one wishes to be more cautious and assumes that the response scale has ordinal scale properties, ordered response models are appropriate (e.g., ordered logit). In the latter case maximum likelihood algorithms are used.

In the case of choice responses, the choices observed represent the outcome of each individual's comparisons between the latent utilities of the alternatives in the different choice sets. These latent utilities can be derived and estimated from the choices by applying the choice rule and the appropriate assumptions with regard to the error term (eq. 2). Logit and probit are well known examples of models based on this type of responses. Estimation of such models is done using maximum likelihood algorithms.

4 Empirical exploration

This section explores empirically the value tourists attach to other tourists' contributions to travel web site by applying the proposed modeling and measurement approach in a survey of Dutch tourists' preferences for travel web sites. Data were gathered as part of a larger survey distributed in April 1998 to 2055 respondents who regularly participate in an ongoing consumer panel in the Netherlands. Of these respondents those that had traveled in the last two years and that were familiar with using the Internet were selected for the analysis. This group consisted of 351 people.

The conjoint profiles presented to respondents described different travel web sites in terms of four attributes. Three of these attributes were selected as relevant indicators of the quality of the information provided at travel web sites. Price was added as a fourth attribute to allow for monetarization of the other attributes in the analyses. Specifically, the attributes included in the study were: i) the type of organization providing the web site (ORG), described in four levels (independent travel agent, airline, hotel and Internet-based intermediary), and dummy coded in three columns in the analyses (100, 010, 001, and 000), ii) the level of information provided on the web site (INFO), described in two levels (comparable in level to a travel guide, and comparable in level to a travel brochure), and also dummy coded (1,0) in the analyses, iii) the availability on the web site of other tourists' contributions sharing their travel experiences (CONT), described in two levels (available, and not available), and dummy coded (1,0), and iv) the relative price of booking a trip through the web site (PRICE), described in two levels (25$ more expensive, and $25 cheaper than one's regular travel agent), and dummy coded (1,0).

A 2^3 fraction in eight profiles of a 4.2^3 full factorial experimental design with independent main effects was used to create the conjoint profiles presented to the respondents. Respondents were asked to rate their preference for each profile using a ten point response scale, ranging from 0 (*very unattractive*) to 9 (*very attractive*). Each respondent was presented with all eight profiles. An example of a conjoint profile from the study is presented in figure 1.

Scenario Y
Please rate your preference for the following travel web site on a ten point scale
Web site features
• The travel web site is run by an independent travel agent.
• The information provided on this web site is comparable in quality and detail to that of a travel brochure.
• Other tourists report their experiences on this web site.
• Travel bookings through this web site are $25 cheaper than through your usual agent.
Rating: ..... points   (0= *very unattractive*, 9 = *very attractive*)

Figure 1 Example of conjoint profile presented to the respondents.

Table 1 presents the OLS estimates of a regression model on the respondents' preference ratings for the different scenarios. The model was estimated including individual specific constants (α_n) to correct for unobserved heterogeneity between respondents in terms of their average taste across all eight profiles. Specifically, individual n's utility for alternative i was specified as follows:

$$U_{in} = \alpha_n + \beta_{ORG1}X_{ORG1} + \beta_{ORG2}X_{ORG2} + \beta_{ORG3}X_{ORG3} + \beta_{INFO}X_{INFO} + \qquad (4)$$
$$\beta_{CONT}X_{CONT} + \beta_{PRICE}X_{PRICE} + \varepsilon_{in}$$

where, α_n is the individual specific constant, the β's represent the parameters for each attribute and the X's represent the dummies for the attribute levels, and ε_{in} is the error term related to conjoint profile i and individual n.

The overall fit of the model was good ($R^2 = 0.662$) and parameters for all attributes were significant and had signs as expected. The strongest effect was observed for price, followed by (in order of strength of effect) the availability of contributions by other tourists, the type of organization providing the web site, and the level of information on the web site. With respect to type of organization, respondents had a strong preference for web sites by independent travel agents, while their preference for web sites by airlines, hotels and Internet-based intermediaries was low and did not differ between the three.

Table 1 The impact of the availability of other tourists' contributions and some other web site characteristics on tourists' preferences for travel web sites[*]

Attribute	Level	Coefficient	t-value
Type of organization providing web site	Independent travel agent	0.053	4.376**
(ORG)	Airline	0.014	1.169
	Hotel	0.001	0.093
	Internet-based intermediary (base)		
Level of information (INFO)	Extensive (travel guide) vs. Limited (travel brochure)	0.025	2.409**
Contributions by other tourists (CONT)	Available vs. Not available	0.120	11.360**
Price (PRICE)	$25 more expensive than regular agent vs. $25 reduced price	-0.324	30.697**

$* R^2 = 0.662$, *estimates are based on a model specification with individual specific constants to correct for unobserved heterogeneity, N=351.* ** *significant at 95% confidence level*

The results show that tourists value the availability of travel information from independent experts quite highly in their evaluation of travel web sites. Information provided by other tourists in particular is valued highly, but more extensive information from and information from independent travel agents is valued relatively positively also. The fact that Internet-based intermediaries are not valued very highly, indicates that independence of the information source is a necessary, but not sufficient condition for a high tourist valuation of a travel web site. Expertise acquired either through previous visits (other tourists) or through professional experience (travel agents) is a second requirement. The fact that other tourists' contributions had a higher impact than the services of a travel agent alone may indicate that tourists view other tourists' contributions as a more effective way to increase their search efficiency and/or to overcome information asymmetry than by using traditional travel intermediaries.

Finally, the monetary equivalent of the availability of other tourists' contributions to travel web sites can be calculated for the average respondent in this study (eq. 3). First, the equivalent of a one dollar gain is determined using the price parameter (-β_{PRICE} / \$50 = 0.00648). The parameter for the availability of other tourists' contributions (β_{CONT} = 0.120) is divided by this value to determine E. Thus, the value of E can be determined as \$18.52, which is the monetary equivalent for the average respondent in this study of adding other tourists' contributions to a travel web site. Similarly, the monetary equivalents of running a web site through an independent travel agent vs. running it through an airline, hotel or Internet-based intermediary (E_{ORG1}) and of adding more extensive travel information (E_{INFO})can be determined These values are \$8.18 and \$3.86 respectively. These values underline the validity of the believe that the availability of other tourists' contributions on travel web site is important in terms of creating consumer value, and that it may be more important also than some other key web site characteristics.

5 Discussion

This article discussed two micro-economic reasons why tourists can be expected to value other tourists' contributions to travel web sites: i) gains in search efficiency, and ii) overcoming information asymmetries with tourism service providers. A random utility model was proposed to model the value tourists attach to the availability of other tourists' contributions and allow one to express this value in monetary terms. Conjoint analysis was introduced as a method to overcome difficulties in measuring tourists' utility for travel web sites and other tourists' contributions to such web sites. The results of an empirical application of the proposed model and method were discussed. These results showed that Dutch tourists' valuation of the availability on travel web sites of other tourists' reports on their travel experiences was high and carried greater weight than some other important web site characteristics such as the type of organization providing the web site and the level of detail of the information provided. Thus the view that tourists' contributions to travel web sites can increase the value of such web sites considerably was supported.

Given the outcomes of this initial analysis of the value of tourists' contributions to travel web sites, various theoretical and methodological issues remain open for research. For example, a more detailed investigation of the content and type of information that tourists would like to exchange on travel web sites would be quite valuable. Some tourist travel information may be more relevant or suitable for exchanges on web sites than other information. Also, the costs of exchanging some tourist information may not outweigh the benefits, for example due to required level of detail. Likewise, some information provided by tourism service providers may be more detailed or credible than other information, and therefore the relative benefits of receiving the information from other tourists may be smaller. A classification of travel information along such lines would be useful in determining the optimal design features of travel web sites and virtual travel communities in terms of tourism service provider and tourist contributor responsibilities.

Extending this line of reasoning, it would be very relevant also to extend the currently proposed random utility model to a model including exchanges between multiple agents. Thus, a welfare function could be developed describing the value of a 'virtual travel community economy'. Such a function could be used to explore the welfare effects of different economic exchange mechanisms in virtual travel communities (e.g., sharing, bartering or auctioning) and of different community compositions in terms of participants (e.g., a community of tourists only vs. a joint community of tourists and tourism service providers). This type of analysis would support evaluation of the likely success of different virtual travel communities.

Acknowledgements

The author's research is funded by the Dutch Science Foundation (NWO). A CentERdata grant for data collection through the CentERdata-panel is gratefully acknowledged.

References

1. Armstrong, Arthur R. and John Hagel III (1996), 'The Real Value of On-Line Communities', *Harvard Business Review* 74, 134-141.
2. Ben-Akiva, Moshe and Steven R. Lerman (1985), *Discrete Choice Analysis: Theory and Application to Travel Demand*, Cambridge, MA: MIT Press.
3. Boxall, Peter C., Wiktor L. Adamowicz, Joffre Swait, Michael Williams and Jordan Louviere (1996), 'A Comparison of Stated Preference Methods for Environmental Valuation', *Ecological Economics* 18, 243-253.

302

4. Dellaert, Benedict G.C., Aloys W.J. Borgers and Harry J.P. Timmermans (1997), 'Conjoint Models of Tourist Portfolio Choice: Theory and Illustration', *Leisure Sciences* 19, 31-58.

5. Dellaert, Benedict G.C. (1999), 'The Tourist as Value Creator on the Internet', in D. Buhalis and W. Schertler eds., *Information and Communication Technologies in Tourism 1999,* Vienna: Springer-Verlag, 66-76.

6. Elrod, Terry, Jordan J. Louviere and Krishnakumar S. Davey (1992), 'An Empirical Comparison of Ratings-Based and Choice-Based Conjoint Models', *Journal of Marketing Research* 29, 358-370.

7. Hoffman, Donna L. and Thomas P. Novak (1996), 'Marketing in Hypermedia Computer-Mediated Environments: Conceptual Foundations', *Journal of Marketing* 60, 50-68.

8. Kooreman, Peter and Sophia Wunderink (1997), *The Economics of Household Behavior,* London: Macmillan Press.

9. Kuhfeld, Warren F., Randall D. Tobias and Mark Garrat (1994), 'Efficient Experimental Design with Marketing Research Applications', *Journal of Marketing Research* 31, 545-557.

10. Lindberg, Kreg, Benedict G.C. Dellaert and Charlotte Rømer Rassing (1999), 'Resident Tradeoffs: A Choice Modelling Approach', *Annals of Tourism Research* 26, 554-569.

11. Louviere, Jordan J. (1988), *Analyzing Decision Making: Metric Conjoint Analysis*, Sage University Papers Series No. 67, Newbury Park: Sage.

12. Louviere, Jordan J. and Harry J.P. Timmermans (1990), 'Stated Preference and Choice Models Applied to Recreation Research: A Review', *Leisure Sciences* 12, 9-32.

13. Moore, William L., Jordan J. Louviere and Rohit Verma (1999), 'Using Conjoint Analysis to Help Design Product Platforms', *Journal of Product Innovation Management* 1, 27-39.

14. Rindfleisch, Aric and Jan B. Heide (1997), 'Transaction Cost Analysis: Past, Present and Future Applications', *Journal of Marketing* 61, 30-54.

The Interplay Of Holiday-Related Travel Habits And The Use Of New Information And Communication Technologies[1]

Barbara Baier
Institute for Advanced Studies
Vienna, Austria

1. Introduction

Within the scope of my thesis one of the analyzed questions is whether a parallel process of development or interplay can be observed between the use of new information and communication technologies on the one hand and holiday-related travel habits and travel patterns on the other.

For the knowledge- and design-intensive tourism industry, the new information and communication technologies turn out to be a major challenge. In this context the Internet is a very interesting technology. The Internet represents the realization of a network of virtual places, which exists besides the world of real places and locations. Today, the Internet is already used in tourism in the areas of advertising, booking, and reservations. These applications of new technologies aim to increase tourism. But one is also able to make small, simple virtual trips to far away destinations on the Internet. This virtual experience can be used, for instance, to visit virtual cities, to stroll through virtual museums such as the Louvre, and so on.

Opposing assumptions about the connection between electronic communication as it takes place on the Internet and the physical mobility of people can be figured out [8]: On the one hand, there is the opportunity to handle a large portion of the arising communication by means of these new technologies. This would diminish the need for physical traffic to a large content. On the other hand, it is assumed that these new information and communication technologies expand the individual action radius, that people can interact and be in contact over large distances, and that electronic communication will soon be followed by the wish for face-to-face communication. This would mean that the use of new technologies would not decrease but increase mobility. The relationship between a trip to virtual places and the resulting desire to experience them in real life could be shaped in a similar way.

2. Research questions and research methods

I'm taking these assumptions about the connection of Internet use and mobility and

---

[1] This contribution to the conference discusses selected and preliminary research results from the empirical part of my thesis, which is a work in progress.

expose them to an empirical evaluation. In this special case the focus lies on holiday tourism. Business tourism and convalescence trips, which are covered by social security, are not included in the analysis.

The central question in this analysis is whether Internet users differ from the total population concerning the intensity and pattern of holiday-related tourism.

In order to answer that, I conducted an Internet survey asking Internet users living in Austria about their holiday-related travel habits[2]. As a comparison, data from a special micro-census program investigating the travel habits of the total Austrian population are used[3]. In both surveys all holiday-related travels within the time period from November 1st 1995 to October 31st 1996 were taken into consideration.

The second question deals with the methodological evaluation of the usability of Internet-surveys for the collection of data in tourism research.

A standardized questionnaire was developed for the WWW, which should serve as an instrument for the Internet survey. Since there are no reliable data about all the Internet users living in Austria the conducted survey presents a so-called survey from an unknown total population [1]. In this case the strategy is usually to reach the highest possible distribution level of the questionnaire in order to obtain the highest number of answers as well as the most heterogeneous answers. During the course of this Internet survey the interview partners were not contacted directly but the questionnaire was published throughout the Internet by different means of communication[4]. In this particular process the choice of people who were questioned is based on the method of self-selection. However, the fact that this selection method makes it impossible to control a certain systematic bias that might occur presents a problem. In this Internet survey about travel habits the people who are going away on vacation and therefore are more likely to respond to the announcement are possibly over-represented. On the other hand, the Internet users who rarely travel and for that reason may be less interested in vacation trips are probably under-represented.

---

[2] The Internet survey was conducted from June to November 1997. Altogether, a total of 175 usable questionnaires were returned for evaluation.
[3] Every three years, the micro-census of the Austrian Census Bureau contains a special program about the travel habits of the Austrian population. During the course of the micro-census 1996 about the travel habits the data of 57.000 people were collected by means of personal, oral questioning. Projected onto the total Austrian population, the micro-census counts 7979381 people.
[4] Publication on newsgroups, creating links to other sites, entering information in search engines, informal means of communication based on the snowball effect, etc.

3. Comparison of the social structure of Internet users with the total population

In comparison to the total Austrian population Internet users are a relatively young population group and distinguish themselves by an extremely high proportion of men. It has to be pointed out that Internet users have an exceptionally high educational level with a high share of university graduates and people with upper secondary education level. A relatively large portion of Internet users is gainfully employed, students and pupils are also highly represented. Compared to that, unemployed people, retired people, homemakers, and people who are temporarily away from their workplace are hardly present. The job situation of the Internet users is also very good: An exceptionally high portion of the gainfully employed Internet users is working in higher-qualified white-collar jobs and public service positions. The portion of self-employed people and freelances is also above average (see Table 1 and Table 2).

Table 1: Social structure of Internet users and the general population

		Internet survey		Micro-census	
		%	Total n	%	Total n
gender	male	68.0	175	48.5	7928396
	female	32.0		51.5	
marriage status	single	70.1	174	41.6	7928396
	married	27.0		46.7	
	divorced	0.6		7.2	
	widowed	2.3		4.5	
education level	compulsory schooling	1.1	175	34.8	6451987
	apprenticeship	7.4		44.9	
	upper secondary level	40.1		13.6	
	university level	51.4		6.7	
means of subsistence	employed	75.7	173	43.7	7928396
	students/pupils	19.7		15.5	
	others	4.6		40.8	
employment status	farmer	0.0	153	5.7	3886272
	self-employed/freelance	24.2		7.4	
	apprentice	0.0		3.1	
	worker/laborer	2.0		38.2	
	low/medium-level public service /white-collar jobs	25.4		28.9	
	higher-level/qualified public service/white-collar jobs	48.4		16.7	

Table 2: Average age of Internet users and the general population[5]

	Internet survey			Micro-census		
	$\bar{x}$	s	Total n	$\bar{x}$	s	Total n
Age	30.6	8.1	171	38.1	22.2	7928396

---

[5] $\bar{x}$ ...mean; s...standard deviation; total n...number of valid cases.

4. Comparison of the travel patterns of Internet users with the total population

One central question in this analysis is whether Internet users differ from the total population in terms of holiday-related travel intensity. An important criteria for a population's travel intensity is the proportion of regular travelers and of short-term travelers in a certain time period[6]. About half of the total Austrian population took one or more regular holiday trips in the period mentioned above. After all, among Internet users it was 90.3 %. However, the proportions of short-term travelers were quite similar in both examined groups (see Table 3).

Table 3: Indicator of travel intensity: Proportion of holiday-related travelers

	Internet survey		Micro-census	
	%	Total n	%	Total n
one ore more holiday-related regular trips	90,3	175	48,4	7888102
one or more holiday-related short-term trips	29,7	174	29,6	7979381

The amazingly high proportion of Internet users who had taken one or more regular journeys can be a result of the self-selection mechanism of the Internet survey. The Internet survey concentrated on the topic of holiday-related tourism. Therefore it may well be the case that only those answered who actually took a holiday-related travel during the aforesaid time period.

For a further analysis it makes sense to build comparable subgroups in both populations by focusing on those who actually took one or more holiday-related trips. This selection is based on the assumption that this will make it possible to successfully avoid the possible bias of this survey. The question is whether the travel intensity and travel patterns of the actual holiday-related travelers who are participating in the Internet survey differ from those of the total Austrian population.

Looking at the average number of holiday trips per year, one will observe, that compared to the actual holiday-related travelers of the total population, those of the Internet survey stand out for their particularly high travel enthusiasm (see Table 4 and Table 5). Not only do Internet users travel more frequently, their trips also take them to more distant destinations. The proportion of trips to countries outside of Europe is considerably higher for Internet users. Analyzing the average annual duration of holidays, Internet users again show a higher travel intensity whenever they are compared to the total population. Summing all this up, one may say that, compared to the holiday-related traveler of the total population, those of the Internet survey travel more frequently, further, and for longer periods of time.

---

[6] According to the micro-census, holiday-related regular travels are all journeys that cover at least four overnight stays. Holiday-related short-term travels are defined as journeys with at least one overnight stay and three at most. Research results concerning data about a one-year period are based on the period from November 1st 1995 to October 31st 1996.

Table 4: Average number and average duration of holiday-related trips

	Internet survey			Micro-census		
	$\bar{x}$	s	Total n	$\bar{x}$	s	Total n
number (per year)						
regular trips	2.5	1.4	156	1.5	0.9	3820528
short-term trips	4.5	4.2	118	2.7	3.3	2333301
duration (overnight stays)						
per regular trip	10.6	6.5	153	11.4	7.0	3786005
per year	24.3	16.6	158	16.8	11.8	3820528

Table 5: Destinations travelers choose for holiday-related trips

	Internet survey		Micro-census	
	%	Total n	%	Total n
one or more regular trips to Austria	54.1	157	43.4	3820528
Europe	73.2	157	66.3	3820528
outside of Europe	30.6	157	12.1	3820528
one or more short-term trips to Austria	73.9	119	72.4	3820528
foreign country	49.6	119	41.8	3820528

An especially plastic presentation of the more or less small one-dimensional differences of travel intensity can be obtained with a multiple indicator of travel intensity. This indicator combines the individual dimensions of travel intensity like number, duration, and traveled distance of all the trips in one characteristic value[7]. This indicator contributes to the fact that the comparative analysis gains in exactness. The more complex and multi-layered this indicator is constructed, the more obvious are the differences of travel intensity between the compared groups. In our research model the multiple indicator of travel intensity shows that compared to the total population the travel intensity of Internet users is especially high (see Table 6).

Table 6: Multiple indicator of travel intensity

	Internet survey		Micro-census	
	median	Total n	median	Total n
multiple indicator of travel intensity	28.3	168	15.5	4906622

Differences between Internet users and the total population do not just arise in terms of their travel intensity. There are also slight differences regarding the types of

---

[7] Calculation of the multiple indicator of travel intensity: average duration per regular holiday trip * number of regular holiday trips * indicator for traveled distance for these regular holiday trips + number of short-term holiday tips * indicator for traveled distance for these short-term holiday trips. Since this is a fictitious characteristic value, the absolute number of the multiple indicator for travel intensity is not very expressive. Due to the large dispersion the median is used for the comparative analysis.
Calculation of the indicator for traveled distance for holiday-related regular trips: 1.1 for trips to Austria, 1.2 for trips to a European country, 1.3 for trips to countries outside of Europe.
Calculation of the indicator for traveled distance for holiday related short-term trips: 1.1 for trips to Austria, 1.2 for trips to a foreign country.

holidays they choose for their regular holiday trips. The willingness to choose active holiday types is slightly stronger among Internet users (summer and winter sports, visiting cultural events, educational trips). The general population rather leans towards the classical passive holiday types like beach holidays, recreational holidays (see Table 7).

Table 7: Types of holidays of all regular holiday trips per year

	Internet survey		Micro-census	
	%	Total n	%	Total n
beach and bathing holidays	22.9	353	29.2	6212375
relaxation/recreation/health	23.5		31.1	
summer sports	16.2		12.7	
winter sports	12.7		9.2	
culture/studies/sightseeing	24.7		17.8	

A very surprising result was that the amount of people who book their vacations with a travel agency lies above average among Internet users (see Table 8). In current discussions about the use of new information and communication technologies in tourism some people fear that the possibility for a client to book and make reservations directly could result in losses for travel agencies. However, the fact that among Internet users the willingness to organize their vacations with the aid of a travel agent is quite high may very well be seen as an advantage for travel agencies.

Table 8: Type of organization of all regular holiday-related trips per year

	Internet survey		Micro-census	
	%	Total n	%	Total n
travel agency	25.9	220	10.9	4466126
travel agency and private	20.9		27.5	
Private	53.2		61.6	

5. Comparison of the travel patterns of Internet users with a population group that Internet users belong to due to their social status

The analysis whether Internet users differ from the total population concerning the intensity and pattern of holiday-related tourism has to pay attention to the fact that Internet users belong to a group with a high social status. After all, Internet users have a higher education level, better jobs, etc. And, as it is known from tourist research, the travel intensity increases as education, work position, and income improve [2,4,9].

For this detailed comparative analysis a population group was selected which on the one hand is to a large extent also part of the group of Internet users and on the other hand stands out for its exceptionally high travel intensity. The analysis included people who have upper secondary or university level education and work in a white-collar job, or are self-employed or freelances respectively.

The portion of travelers during the main holiday season and short-term travellers is relatively high in this particular population group. In terms of holiday mobility this population group is considered an élite (see Table 9).

Table 9: Indicator of travel intensity: proportion of holiday-related travelers

	Internet survey		Micro-census	
	%	Total n	%	Total n
one ore more holiday-related regular trips	90.4	138	70.2	833545
one or more holiday-related short-term trips	73.2	132	45.7	837335

Table 10: Multiple indicator of travel intensity

	Internet-Survey		Micro-census	
	median	Total n	median	Total n
multiple indicator of travel intensity	28.9	132	18.0	687848

However, even when compared to a group within the same social stratum that Internet users predominantly belong to, which is a group that can already be distinguished by an exceptionally high mobility, they still show a much higher level of travel intensity (see Table 10) and tend to choose more active holiday types than the rest of the people in this same group (see Table 11).

Table 11: Types of holidays of all regular holiday trips per year

	Internet survey		Micro-census	
	%	Total n	%	Total n
beach and bathing holidays	23.6	280	27.4	1080295
relaxation/recreation/health	23.2		26.4	
summer sports	16.4		12.8	
winter sports	12.1		11.8	
culture/studies/sightseeing	24.7		21.6	

6. Examination of the validity of the research results

The validity of the research results from the Internet survey and the differences in travel behavior between Internet users and the total population or a selected population group respectively were examined by means of a parallel evaluation of the Austrian-Life-Style survey which is representative for the total Austrian population[8]. The survey included questions about Internet use as well as travel behavior. The proportion of Internet users in the Austrian-Life-Style survey equals 13.5 %

---

[8] The market research institute Fessel-GfK conducts an annual Austrian-Life-Style survey. From June to August 1997 4500 people living in Austria were interviewed.

310

(n=4500)[9]. The questions about holiday-related trips are based on the year 1996. The questions in the Austrian-Life-Style survey were not worded exactly like those in the Internet survey and the micro-census. That's why this examination of the results can mainly compare the emerging trends and tendencies.

Although there are differences between the groups of the Internet users from the Austrian-Life-Style survey and the Internet survey, a very similar overall picture of the socio-economic structure of the Internet users who live in Austria may be generated: Compared to the general population Internet users are mainly male, younger on average, they tend to have a higher level of education, they are more likely to be gainfully employed or still studying, and they have good jobs (see Table 12 and Table 13).

Table 12: Social structure of Internet users und the general population

		Internet users		total population	
		%	Total n	%	Total n
gender	male	62.1	610	47.9	4500
	female	37.9		52.1	
marriage status	single	51.8	609	24.2	4494
	married	32.1		57.5	
	long-term relationship	10.6		6.2	
	divorced/separated	3.5		4.6	
	widowed	2.0		7.5	
education level	compulsory schooling	11.2	597	17.2	4448
	apprenticeship	28.2		53.1	
	upper secondary level	40.8		18.7	
	university	19.8		11.0	
means of subsistence	employed	62.4	610	53.2	4499
	students/pupils	25.0		7.5	
	others	12.6		39.3	
employment status	farmer	0.0	380	5.5	2391
	self-employed/freelance	16.4		7.9	
	higher-level/qualified public service/ white-collar jobs	61.1		45.3	
	low level public service/ white collar jobs	8.0		9.9	
	worker/laborer	14.5		31.4	

Table 13: Average age of Internet users and the general population

	Internet users			total population		
	$\bar{x}$	s	Total n	$\bar{x}$	s	Total n
age	32.5	13.3	610	44.1	17.6	4500

---

[9] The definition "Internet users" included all those people who stated that they used the Internet for personal reasons, for their job or studies.

The differences between the travel habits of Internet users who live in Austria and the total population could be confirmed in this comparative analysis. In the Austrian-Life-Style survey Internet users also stand out for the fact that compared to the total population they tend to travel more often, for a longer period of time and farther away (see Table 14, Table 15 and Table 16). However, the differences of travel intensity that were found in the examination were comparably less.

Table 14: Indicator of travel intensity: Proportion of holiday-related travelers

	Internet users		total population	
	%	Total n	%	Total n
one ore more holiday-related regular trips	71.8	610	57.9	4500
one or more holiday-related short-term trips	61.4	610	44.4	4500

Table 15: Number of regular holiday-related trips

	Internet users		total population	
	%	Total n	%	Total n
1 regular holiday-related trip	41.4	438	44.7	2606
2 regular holiday-related trips	30.6		33.2	
3-4 regular holiday-related trips	25.2		19.2	
5 and more regular holiday-related trips	2.8		2.9	

Table 16: Average duration of holiday-related trips

	Internet users		total population	
	median	Total n	median	Total n
duration per year (overnight stays)	20-21	438	15-19	2606

Within the selected group of people with a high travel intensity (high education level and higher-level/qualified white collar jobs or public service) the proportion of Internet users equals 27.0 % (n=1239). The differences between travel patterns of Internet users and non-Internet users are also less clear. There are hardly any differences between the number of trips that were made and the average annual duration of these holiday-related trips (see Table 17, Table 18 and Table 19). However, the portion of Internet users who traveled to far-away locations was clearly higher (see Table 20).

Table 17: Indicator of travel intensity: Proportion of holiday-related travelers

	Internet		non-Internet	
	%	Total n	%	Total n
one ore more holiday-related regular trips	76.1	335	72.7	904
one or more holiday-related short-term trips	62.4	335	47.1	904

Table 18: Number of regular holiday-related trips

	Internet		non-Internet	
	%	Total n	%	Total n
1 regular holiday-related trip	38.3	255	36.8	657
2 regular holiday-related trips	30.5		33.2	
3-4 regular holiday-related trips	28.6		25.1	
5 and more regular holiday-related trips	2.6		4.9	

Table 19: Average duration of holiday-related trips

	Internet		non-Internet	
	median	Total n	median	Total n
duration per year (overnight stays)	20-21	255	20-21	657

Table 20: Destinations travelers choose for holiday-related trips

	Internet		non-Internet	
	%	Total n	%	Total n
one or more regular trips to Austria	41.6	255	49.0	657
Europe	79.3	255	77.6	657
outside of Europe	22.0	255	11.6	657

7. Conclusion

As it is known form tourism research international tourism and communication technologies are the essential driving force of cultural globalization and are part of the border-crossing and accelerated lifestyle of modern times which stands out mainly for its principal spatial and mental mobility [2,5,7,9]. Entire socio-economically disadvantaged population groups are excluded from the possibility for holiday-related travel and even more are excluded from access to the new information and communication technologies [3,4,6,9]. This border-crossing and accelerated lifestyle is in a global view only accessible to a so called kinetic élite and Internet users belong to those privileged social groups.

One reason for the quantitative deviations of the research results may be the specific instrument – the Internet survey – which was used to select a group of Internet users living in Austria with an exceptionally high travel intensity. Thus, the evaluation of the usability of Internet surveys for tourism research shows, that Internet surveys can be a very useful tool for collecting data in tourism research – taking into account the specific problems concerning the process of conducting them. Nevertheless, the application of Internet surveys is restricted to specific research questions as well as to limited areas within tourism research, due to the exceptional travel habits of Internet users.

References

1. Batinic, B., Bosnjak, M.: Fragebogenuntersuchungen im Internet. In: Batinic, B. (ed.): Internet für Psychologen. Hogrefe Göttingen Bern Toronto Seattle, pp.221-243 (1997).

2 Bauman, Z.: Flaneure, Spieler und Touristen. Essays zu postmodernen Lebensformen. Hamburger Ed., Hamburg (1997).

3. Bühl, A.: Die virtuelle Gesellschaft. Ökonomie, Politik und Kultur im Zeichen des Cyberspace. In: Gräf, L., Krajewski, M. (eds.): Soziologie des Internet. Handeln im elektronischen Web–Werk. Campus, Frankfurt/M, pp. 39–59 (1997).

4. Grümer, K.W.: Gesellschaftiche Rahmenbedingungen für Mobilität/Tourismus/Reisen. In: Hahn, H., Kagelmann, H.J. (eds.): Tourismuspsychologie und Tourismussoziologie. Quintessenz, München, pp. 17–24 (1993).

5. Lash, S., Urry, J.: Economies of Signs and Space. Sage, London (1994).

6. Latzer, M.: Mediamatik - Die Konvergenz von Telekommunikation, Computer und Rundfunk. Westdeutscher Verlag, Opladen (1997).

7. Luger, K.: Kommunikation im Tourismus. Projektskizze für eine kommunikationswissenschaftliche Tourismusforschung. In: Medien Journal 4, pp. 2-19 (1994):

8. Sachs, W.: Geschwindigkeit und Ökologie. Eine Skizze. In: Prokla. Zeitschrift für kritische Sozialwissenschaft 2, pp. 181-194 (1997).

9. Urry, J: The tourist gaze. Leisure and travel in contemporary societies. Sage, London (1990).

A Conceptual Framework for Evaluating Effects of a Virtual Tour

Yong-Hyun Cho and Daniel R. Fesenmaier
National Laboratory for Tourism and eCommerce
University of Illinois at Urbana-Champaign
(ycho@uiuc.edu) (drfez@uiuc.edu)

Abstract

Tourism marketing has become increasingly segmmented and specialized with the development of new styles of travel. An important focus of of this effort is "experience-oriented tourism" which emphasizes activity, events, and fantastic or exotic experiences. However, it is hard for tourists to form a clear destination image without direct experiences. With the development of Internet, tourists have become able to access interactive multimedia easily. Interactivity and multimedia are key factors to create virtual environment and provide virtual experiences. With experiential information, a virtual tourist creates his/her own unique memory and personal story which in turn enables him/her to form a more vivid and clear destination image and to reduce the uncertainty about destination.

1. Introduction

Destination image has been considered an important facet of the travel decision making process [21, 23]. Researchers have investigated how destination image influence on the tourists' choice behavior and found that it is primarily based on the information that a person has about the destination. Tourists typically will use information obtained from the memory. . If the tourist has not been to the destination, he/she also will collect information using brochures, advertising, word of mouth and other sources for information

Socio-demographic changes such as active aging population and childless couples have led to substantial changes in travel and tourism demand. The result of these social changes has been a greater variety in tourism types, needs and patterns. Pearce [12] suggested 'The future trends for tourism seem to suggest that travelers will be especially concerned not with just being "there", but with participating, learning and experiencing the "there" they visit. According to Stebbins [16], leisure in post-industrial society is no longer seen as chiefly a means of recuperating from the travail of the job. Leisure has become a way of finding personal fulfillment, identity enhancement, self-expression, and the like. Therefore, the importance of experience in travel is increasing.

The virtual tour is emerging as an effective tool for destination marketing. Many well-known destinations offer virtual tours through the World Wide Web. Current virtual tour programs are typically created using slide shows or animation with sound. It appears that the richness of information provided by the web-based virtual tours is not high enough yet to attract the users to be immersed in the virtual destination. In spite of the current problems, the virtual tour appears to offer the potential to provide an extremely rich perceptual and cognitive environment. Virtual tours can afford potential tourists the opportunity to "preview" destinations which may remove elements of uncertainty and provides information so that visitor's destination image is more likely to match actual experience [1].

The purpose of this study was to investigate the following questions about virtual tour through the review of related literatures.

- Why virtual tour should be distinguished from other traditional media?
- Is WWW appropriate for the virtual tour?
- What is the impact of virtual tour on the destination image formation process?

Through the answers to these questions, the present study will suggest a framework of virtual tour itself and its impact on the tourism promotion. Furthermore, future studies related virtual tour will be suggested.

2. Virtual tour

Although the term of "virtual tour" is widely used on web sites for tourism destinations, it appears never to be defined by researchers. In spite of the little effort to define virtual tour, web users do not feel strange to this term due to the well-known concept of "virtual reality". Virtual reality is usually considered a complex mechanic system for training or games. However, researchers have proposed definitions of virtual tour within the context of experience.

2.1. Virtual tour through 'telepresence'

Virtual tour can be defined as a tour through a virtual environment where one experiences "telepresence". Csikszentmihalyi's [2] concept of "flow" explains the concept of telepresence within the context of personal psychology. The flow experience is a state in which one concentrates so much on some activity that he/she becomes unconscious of stimuli outside of the activity, including even awareness of self and the passage of time. Flow and telepresence are similar in that the most singular characteristic of each is a high degree of involvement in a task or activity. In both, the impact of concentration excludes distracting stimuli to the point of loss of awareness of self as separate from the task.

Steuer [18] defined telepresence as "the sense of being" in an environment by means of communication medium. He suggested that vividness and interactivity determines the level of telepresence. Vividness refers to the level of sensorial richness of mediated environment and is mainly influenced by sensory breadth (number of sensory dimensions simultaneously presented) and sensory depth (resolution of each perceptual channel). He defined interactivity as the degree to which users can participate in modifying the form and content of a mediated environment in real time. Three factors that contribute to interactivity include speed (the rate at which input can be assimilated into the mediated environment), range(the number of possibilities for action at any given time), and mapping (the ability of a system to map its controls to changes in the mediated environment in a natural and predictable manner). Sheridan [14] defined telepresence as the phenomenon in which a media user loses awareness of the physical environment, convincing that he/she stays within the virtual environment. The important aspect of this definition is that telepresence is experience. He also suggested three determinants of experience level. These are the fidelity and richness of sensory information, the dexterity of sensor control, and the ability to affect the remote environment. Slater and Usoh [15] also indicated display quality, consistency of presentation across displays, ability to interact with environment as internal determinants of the sense of telepresence. Through the review of these studies, two main factors that influence on the level of telepresence were found. The factors include the richness of sensory information and the interactivity between human and virtual environment.

2.2 Performance of virtual tour

Although multi-sensory environment and interactivity have been considered the primary determinants in creating virtual environment for telepresence, the effects of telepresence is not determined only by these factors. As mentioned in the concept of flow telepresence is a psychological concept. Even when using virtual reality system and other advanced communication system, people are still people and the effect of telepresence is finally dependent on the human-computer interface. Therefore, individual differences may play an important part in determining the level of experience [4]

Among the studies on the telepresence, Slater and Usoh [15] indentified two personal determinants of telepresence. They indicated that personal information precessing and involvement are the factors using the terms of representation system and perceptual position. They suggested the effects of personal memory and prior image as the first factor and the second factor was individual's point of view such as a participants, an observer, or a stranger. In another study, Csikszentmihalyi and LeFerve [3] found that people report flow occurring when they perceived task-related requirements were high but in balance with their perceived skills. This implies a task-related focus. Draper, Kaber, and Usher [4] found that attentional resource is related with task performance. They also suggested 'attentional model for synthetic environments' and interpreted telepresence as a state arising from commitment of attentional resources to the virtual environment. They proposed that the more attentional resources that a user devotes to the virtual environment, the greater the identification with virtual environment and the stronger the sense of telepresence. Figure 1 outlines the determinants of the level of virtual experience.

The importance of personal factors on the level of telepresence has been supported by a number of the studies examining the effects of multimedia. Although several studies have been conducted to examine the effect of multi-sensory media, divergent results have been found. Leigh [10] has suggested that procedural or contextual differences can explain the variation in findings; Smith and Buchholz [17] suggested that the effects of multimedia vary based on the involvement level of people and the congruency between different types of sensory information. They both agree that a number of psychological factors influence the effects of multimedia. That is, richness of sensory information has potential to help users to be immersed to the virtual environment. However, this potential does not always result in individuals gaining telepresence; it partly depends on the psychological factors such as involvement or congruency between information.

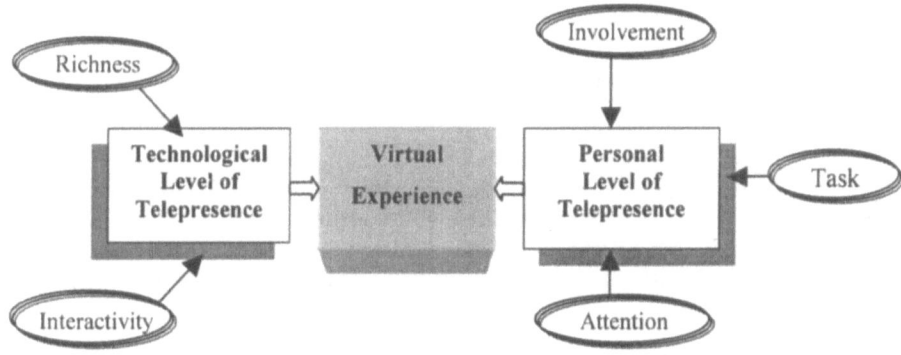

Fig. 1. The framework of virtual experience

3. Media for Virtual Tour

By employing the concept of telepresence, the virtual tour can now be defined based on the context of personal experience. According to this definition, virtual tour is theoretically available through every type of media. Even through the printed media such as a brochure tourists can imagine the situation that he is in the destination and forget where he is physically. However, a number of researchers have argued that multimedia and interactivity have a greater capability to enable users to experience telepresence. Thus, new high technology based media have advantages over traditional media in creating virtual environment for virtual tour.

The WWW is one of the most powerful media in both multimedia and interactivity. Every type of traditional media from simple text to streaming multimedia such as video can be represented on the web sites. That is, it appears the WWW has huge a potential in terms of offering richness of sensory information including multi-sensory information. Hoffman and Novak [9] indicate that the various uses of the WWW through the evaluation of 35 types of media with 7 objective characteristics related with the interactivity or the types of information that the media can deliver. They suggested "web plus video" as the most typical media sharing characteristics with a wide variety of other media types. Although the WWW has potential to provide very rich sensory information, it currently has a disadvantage in delivery speed. Thus, information providers have to reduce data size to reach more users. However, the development of technology will broaden the bandwidth and solve the problem. Figure 2 shows the effects of technological development on the richness and penetration on the web.

Interactivity is the most critical advantage of WWW over other traditional streaming multimedia such as TV and video. Interactive search is available in the non-linear information source and nonlinear system is based on hypertext technology, where information can be accessed and presented in a non-sequential order. Through this type of interactive media, users are able to actively participate in the information search process and collect the information that they need. Studies about interactive information search have been done in several fields such as psychology and education. Ramarapu et al. [20] found that the association provided by links in a hypertext (nonlinear) database should facilitate remembering, concept formulation, understanding and superior problem solving which, in turn, facilitates higher levels of user satisfaction. The WWW also has potential to support diversity in forms of interactivity. It can be used as an impersonal mass media such as TV and as a media for personal communication (e.g., face-to-face meeting). The diversity of interactivity of WWW enables the user of virtual tour create his/her own virtual experience.

4. Effects of virtual tour

According to Stigler [19], the information search process is a trade-off between the perceived costs of additional search and the expected benefits of that search. That is, consumers continue the information search only when the expected benefit is greater than the perceived cost. The use of the virtual tour will influence individual's direct and indirect (perceived) costs of search. The amount of impact of virtual tour will be influenced by the amount of experiential information of the destination. In case of experience-oriented destination, virtual tour may provide the greatest value of "virtual experience".

4.1 Experiential Information

Nelson [11] indicated the role of "experiential information" in the decision-making process through the concept of 'search goods' and 'experience goods'. Search goods are defined as those dominated by product attributes for which full information can be acquired prior to purchase. Experience goods are dominated by attributes that cannot be known until the product is purchased and used. Zeithaml [24] suggested similar concepts by the terms of 'extrinsic attributes' and 'intrinsic attributes'. Extrinsic attributes are those which are observable "outside of the product" such as price and brand. Intrinsic attributes are often unobservable prior to purchase and include kindness, taste, and texture. She also indicated that most service buyers, as like tourists, relied more on extrinsic attributes due to the high cost and evaluation barriers in assessing intrinsic attributes prior to product purchase. With reference to this research, "experiential information" can be defined as information that the customer wants and needs, but can be acquired only through actual use.

The tourism destination is clearly a typical 'experience good' due to the intangible nature of tourism. Its most important attributes include activities, events, atmosphere, and quality of service. Thus, tourists have had to make destination decisions without important information about destination. Research about tourists' information needs also supported the importance of experiential information for the tourists. Vogt and Fesenmaier [22] suggested a model of tourists' information needs and search. They found that tourism information seekers need rich sensory and emotional information for their hedonic and aesthetic needs. However, the information channels without actual experience usually cannot satisfy their needs because some types of information cannot be acquired without experience.

The development of web-based technology reduces the cost for experiential information and removes other difficulties. Through this virtual experience, the tourists can acquire experiential information. That is, by allowing the tourists to experience destination prior actual visit, tourists will be able to search information though experience. If experiential information were available via the information search process (i.e., a virtual tour) and the costs to obtain them were reduced via WWW, we might expect an increased reliance on those "intrinsic" attributes. It appears the virtual tour is one of the media that can change the travel experience from experience goods to search goods in tourism field.

4.2 Destination Image

Although the concept of image appears to have diverse definitions and no well-established and precise definition exists, numerous studies on destination image have been conducted due to the importance of destination image in the tourists' decision making. Woodside and Lyonski [23] proposed a general model of traveler destination choice. According to the model, marketing variables and travelers experience influence on the destination awareness and destination preference. Um and Crompton [21] also conceptualized a model of pleasure travel destination choices with regard to images and attitudes toward destination. These models suggest that destination image is formed based on the all information, knowledge, impressions, prejudices and emotional thoughts individual has of a particular place. In addition, research indicates that personal characteristics such as value, socio-economic status, and personal experience influence on the formation of destination image. The created or changed destination image is composed of cognitive and affective components. The cognitive component is the sum of beliefs and attitudes of a place. Affective component refers to the feelings about the place [7]. Researchers agree that the affective component can be distinguished from the cognitive component, but it is formed based as a function of cognitive component [7][13]. This suggests that, in large part, destination image is formed based on the information that was personalized by tourist. Thus, Gartner [7] suggested the sources for information as the agents of image formation.

Figure 2 is a simplified model of destination image change process. Tourists use various types of sources for information before the actual trip to the destination. Then, destination image is changed when the tourists acquire new information about destination. Fakeye and Crompton [6] conceptualized a model of a tourist's image change process based on Gunn's [8] seven phases of a travel experience. According to the model, individuals have a certain image (naïve image) about a place even before one considers the place as travel destination. They develop the image with gathered information (induced image) about a destination through various channels to decide their destination. Prior to actual travel, tourists search information from advertising, word-of-mouth, and other types of public information and form their expectation. Then, they have experiential information and new information by actual experience and compare the experience with the expectation (re-evaluated image). They found that tourists, through experience, acquire some information that cannot be delivered by other sources for information and their destination image tend to be more realistic, complex and differentiated.

Fig. 2. Simplified model of destination image formation

4.3 Experiential information and image formation

Virtual tour users will have more information than non-users about the selected destination because they have not only traditionally searchable information but also experiential information. Therefore they can create more detailed, clear expectation about the travel and they can develop more vivid destination image. As mentioned, tourists can acquire information through a virtual experience in an efficient and effective way. Through the virtual experience, tourists establish a context within which to create personal stories and to personal evaluate the destination. Thus, the image after the virtual experience could be named as evaluative image.

The change of image will finally influence on the decision making process. Through the experience of virtual tour, the user would be in a better position to make an informed decision and initiate travel arrangements. Even though the alternative destination have not been selected, images from the virtual experience still linger in the user's mind and these could create a desire and induce the user to visit those places in the future. Therefore, it seems that virtual tour marketing of travel destinations has an advantage over other traditional media. Traditional media offer only short and rather limited glimpses of a destination's attractions. At times, the accompanying destination information may be inadequate for marketers and tourists alike to make travel decision. Travelers who possess insufficient knowledge of the destination being visited might find that the trip fails to meet expectations, resulting in an unsatisfactory vacation. The virtual tour, in comparison, permits users the opportunity to explore each destination in great depth. Virtual tour strives to dispel elements of uncertainty and ensures that visitors' expectations of their future visit are equitable to the subsequent actual experience [1].

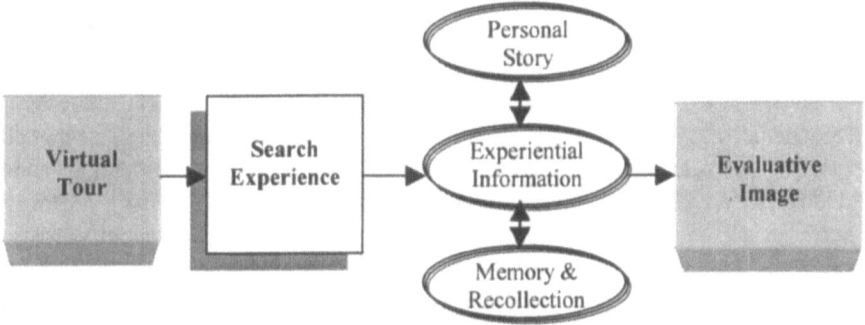

Figure 3. Effects of Virtual Tour

5. Conclusion

This study approached the virtual tour from both technological and personal factors and defined it as an experience of telepresence in a virtually created environment using multimedia technology. The WWW is a new media which offers great potential as a marketing tool for the following reasons:

- WWW has great diversity in both terms of richness and interactivity. It delivers a variety of data ranging from text to streaming multimedia and the level of interactivity is defined by the user.
- WWW could be an impersonal mass media or very personal media enabling the tourist to have his/her own virtual experience.

Thus, it is argued that through the virtual tour users can gain experiential information that has been available only through actual experience. However, research suggests that virtual tours may impact a number of aspects related to travel behavior. The primary effects of the virtual tour are hypothesized as the following:

H_1: Information search behavior will be changed because tourists can get great benefit will less cost.

H_2: Tourists can enhance the memory of destination and create a personal story of the destination. Then they form more vivid and clear destination image.

H_3: Tourists would be in a better position to choose destination because the uncertainty from experiential information will be removed.

Because the WWW is a new media and the virtual tour is a newly emerging concept it is critical that research on evaluating the impact of such technologies as well as the factors which moderate these impacts. In addition, there are many interesting topics for future studies. One of the most interesting contributions of the virtual tour for the tourism industry is its ability to affect the implementation of sustainable tourism. As mentioned above, the virtual may enable tourism marketers to avoid unnecessary development of environmentally or culturally important resources. Sustainable tourism is a typical type of experience-oriented tourism and the destination usually provides very unique and exotic experiences; thus, it is especially difficult for tourists to form an accurate destination image. Virtual tours can help potential tourists to develop expectations about what they can experience at the destination. Importantly, tourists can learn about the uniqueness of destination and appropriate behavior through virtual tour in a natural way.

References

1. Cheong, R., 'The Virtual Threat to Travel and Tourism', *Tourism Management*, 6, 1995, 417-422
2. Csikszentmihalyi, M., *Beyond Boredom and Anxiety*, San Francisco, CA:Jossey-Bass, 1975
3. Csikszentmihalyi, M. & LeFevre, J., 'Optimal Experience in Work and Leisure', *Journal of Personality and Social Psychology*, 1989, 815-822
4. Draper, J. V., Kaber, D. B. & Usher, J. M., 'Telepresence', *Human Factors*, 1998, 354-375

5. Echtner, C. M. & Ritchie, J. R. B., 'The Meaning and Measurement of Destination Image', *The Journal of Tourism Studies*, 2, 1991, 2-12

6. Fakeye, P. C. & Crompton, J. L., 'Image Difference between Perspective, First-time and Repeat visitors to the Lower Rio Grande Valley', *Journal of Travel Research*, 2, 1991, 10-16

7. Gartner, W. C., 'Image Formation Process', *Journal of Travel and Tourism Marketing*, 2/3, 1993, 191-215

8. Gunn, C. A., *Vacationscape: Designing Tourist Regions*, Austin:Bureau of Business Research, University of Texas, 1972

9. Hoffman, D. L. & Novak, T. P., 'Marketing in Hypermedia Computer-Mediated Environments: Conceptual Foundations', *Journal of Marketing*, July, 1996, 50-68

10. Leigh, J. H., 'Information Processing Differences among Broadcast Media: Review and Suggestions for Research', *Journal of Advertising*, June, 1991, 71-75

11. Nelson, P. J., 'Information and Consumer Behavior', *Journal of Political Economy*, 2, 1970, 311-329

12. Pearce, P. L., *The Ulysses Factor: Evaluating visitors in tourist settings*, Springer-Verlag, New York, 1988.

13. Russell, J. A. & Pratt, G., 'A Description of Affective Quality Attributed to Environment', *Journal of Personality and Social Psychology*, 2, 1980, 311-322

14. Sheridan, T. B., 'Musings on Telepresence and Virtual Presence', *Presence*, 1992, 120-126

15. Slater, M. & Usoh, M., 'Representation Systems, Perceptual Position, and Presence in Immersive Virtual Environments', *Presence*, 1993, 221-233

16. Stebbins, R. A., Serious Leisure: A Conceptual Statement, *Pacific Sociology Review*, 1982, 251-272

17. Smith, R. E. & Buchholz, L. M., 'Multiple Resource Theory and Consumer Processing of Broadcast Advertisements: An Involvement Perspective', *Journal of Advertising*, September, 1991, 1-7

18. Steuer, J., 'Defining Virtual Reality: Dimensions Determining Telepresence', *Journal of Communications*, 1992, 73-93

19. Stigler, G. J., 'The Economics of Information', *Journal of Political Economics*, June, 1961, 213-225

20. Ramarapu, N. K., Frolick, M. N., Wilkes, R. B., & Wetherbe. J. C., 'The Emergence of Hypertext and Problem Solving: an Experimental Investigation of Accessing and Using Information from Linear versus Nonlinear Systems', *Decision Sciences*, Fall, 1997, 825-849

21. Um, S. & Crompton, J., 'Attitudes Determinants in Tourism Destination Choice', *Annals of Tourism Research*, 1990, 432-448

22. Vogt, C. A. & Fesenmaier, D. R., 'Expanding the Functional Information Search Model', *Annals of Tourism Research*, 3, 1998, 551-578

23. Woodside, A. G. & Lysonski, S. 'A General Model of Traveller Destination Choice', *Journal of Travel Research*, 4, 1989, 8-14

24. Zeithaml, V. A., 'Consumer Perception of Price', *Journal of Marketing*, July, 1988, 2-22

Evaluating Electronic Channels of Distribution in the Hotel Sector

Peter O'Connor
IMHI, Group ESSEC, Paris
oconnor@essec.fr

Andrew J. Frew
Napier University, Edinburgh
a.frew@napier.ac.uk

Abstract

The paper is based on the findings of the initial round of a Delphi study, and is the first step towards identifying a range of methods that could be used to help hotels select and evaluate electronic channels of distribution. A review of the background to both electronic distribution in the industry and hotel distribution in particular is provided showing the key issues for hoteliers The lack of a currently accepted evaluation tool is highlighted and potential utility of a channel evaluation methodology brought out. Construction of the Delphi and the selection process for participants is described along with preliminary findings – the identification of some key evaluation factors - and interim conclusions.

1 Introduction

In any consideration of interactive marketing the points made by Deighton [1] relating to the adoption of new technologies, are especially relevant. This is particularly true today in the hotel sector where one of its most powerful facets, electronic distribution, is rapidly evolving. Despite being relatively conservative and not renowned for its prompt embrace of new technology, the concepts (and practice) of electronic marketing and product distribution have nevertheless quickly gained acceptance. In fact several authors, most notably Poon [2] and Buhalis [3] specifically identify electronic distribution as a means of enabling tourism enterprises to improve their competitiveness and performance. The number and diversity of electronic channels available has grown significantly in recent years so how best may hotel managers differentiate and evaluate the appropriateness of each potential channel?

2 Electronic Distribution

Electronic distribution systems have their origins in the inventory systems installed by airlines at the end of the 1950s and originally developed as internal control systems. Their scope was expanded in the mid-1970s by installing terminals in travel agency operations which gave access to real-time availability, pricing information and booking capability, thus improving the quality of service to their customers. Deregulation of the airline sector triggered an absolute increase in the number of flights and the number of fare options , while at the same time producing significant difficulties for travel agents through increased competition and reduced airfares. As a result, use of computerised systems became essential in untangling the complex information [4]. However developing and operating such systems was expensive, and there were insufficient airline bookings being processed to provide adequate return on investment. To counteract this, most systems began cross-selling complementary travel products [5] and reservations system operators used spare capacity to distribute these products over their systems [6]. This approach has continued to develop and now includes scheduled and charter airline flights, hotels and other forms of accommodation, car rental, package holidays, ferry, rail and bus tickets, cruise packages, yachting, excursions, theatre tickets and even flowers and champagne. In effect, the GDS have become a one-stop-shop for all an agent's travel information and reservations needs.

3 Distributing the Hotel Product

One of the first complementary products distributed through GDS was hotel accommodation. Initially hotels loaded their various room types, descriptions and price categories into spare capacity on the GDS database and benefited by having their product distributed to a wider audience, while travel agents benefited by being able to book a wider range of products through their computer systems. The GDS also benefited as a result of increased booking volumes that helped offset their operating costs [7]. However, using the GDS to distribute hotel products was problematic. Three factors in particular (the limited number of rates allowed by the database architecture, the abbreviated and truncated descriptions and the unacceptable amount of time that it took to update data) meant that travel agents were not completely confident in the hotel information provided by their systems. As a result, the effectiveness of the GDS as a hotel distribution channel was questionable. Many subsequently developed their own computerised or centralised reservation systems (CRS), with database structures more appropriate to the hotel product and in so doing were able to benefit from the experience gained by the airline companies. Initial systems helped to manage inventory for an entire group at central telesales offices, and were subsequently forwardly integrated into travel agencies through electronic connections with the GDS. However, as each GDS serviced different geographical markets, hotels needed to be represented on each of them in order to gain maximum benefit. This involved developing multiple interfaces, as each was different in terms of its technical requirements and methods of operation. As developing such links was both technical and expensive, several of the leading players in the sector combined to develop the concept of a "universal switch" [8]. Such switches act as a bi-directional translator, connecting the hotel CRS to the entire GDS marketplace.

As the cost of developing and maintaining a CRS was substantial, many hotel companies chose to out-source instead of creating their own systems. According to HEDNA [9], over one fifth of the major international hotel companies outsource some aspect of their reservations function. Different levels of reservation service are available. Fees are normally based on transaction volumes plus a fixed monthly fee, but the hotel company has no capital costs and is freed from maintenance and upgrade costs [10]. The downside is that in both cases a transaction cost has to be paid on each booking, which increases the variable cost of processing reservations.

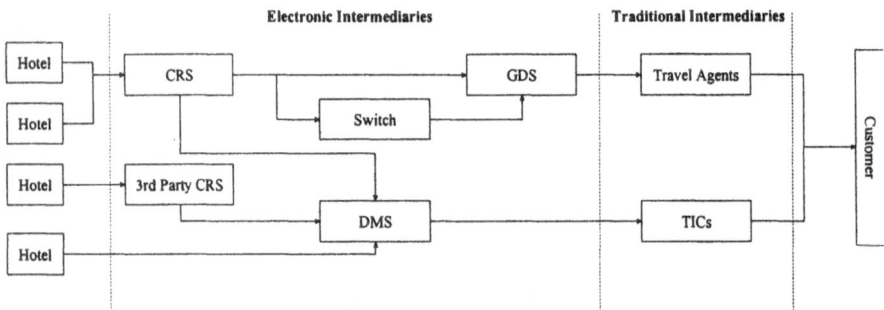

Fig. 1. The propriety electronic distribution channels

4 Confusion in the Marketplace

Until the early 1990s, the electronic channels of distribution that serviced the hotel industry were as described in Figure 1 – a status quo with more co-operation than competition. Relationships were linear and each participant within the chain had a mutually beneficial role to play [11]. The systems were in effect a closed user group, as the information they contained was distributed over proprietary networks and was not available to the general public [12]. Between 1993 and 1997, commissions and other reservation costs (measured on a per available rooms basis) grew from US$429 to US$930 – an increase of 117% in four years [13]. This increase in costs, together with the growth in the use of direct marketing, convinced many hotels of the need to find alternative and cheaper ways to distribute their product [14].

In 1994, the arrival of the Web as a potential mainstream communications medium provided just such an opportunity [15]. Widely promoted as a medium for electronic commerce, opportunities on the Web have been quickly exploited by tourism actors, in part because of the existing high level of computerisation in airlines and travel agencies [16]. Suppliers can achieve a lower booking cost by selling over the Web, as the distribution cost of voice calls and commission levels are eliminated [17]. In addition, the Web gives direct access to customers with a high propensity to travel with few barriers to entry, and provides companies with substantial opportunities to communicate directly with their customers [18]. As a result, many tourism suppliers have begun distributing over the medium [19] and it is having a profound effect on the way in which travel products are being marketed, distributed, sold and delivered [20]. This is also reinforced by Jung [21], who found that the majority of marketing and general managers in the chain hotels now regard the Internet as a "mainstream marketing medium", and who consider that Internet marketing will become even more important over the next two years.

Perhaps the most significant effect of the arrival of the Web in the tourism arena has been a shake up in distribution channels. In addition to their historical co-operation, most tourism actors have started to compete and the situation is summarised by Dombey, who describes the situation as "little short of a technological stampede. Up and down the traditional distribution chain, ... providers are working feverishly to re-engineer their travel systems ... to bypass both the GDS and the travel agent to create a direct link with the customer" [14]. As in the past, the airline sector seems to be leading the trend. For example, [22] points out that most airlines are encouraging their best customers to book online at their Web sites. United, Northwest and Delta have all introduced incentives to book via this rather than any other route. This is placing pressure on many of the "traditional" intermediaries, with as many as 20% of travel agents forecast to go out of business within the next three to four years [23]. Similarly the Switch companies have created their own form of onward distribution, from being behind the GDS within the traditional arena to being a direct route to the customer over the Web. In essence, the level of mutual dependence between participants within the arena has decreased and each intermediary now has the potential to distribute directly to the end consumer [9]. In addition, new entrants have also identified the potential of tourism within e-commerce and are moving in [24]. Such companies have no pre-existing relationships with other players, which permits them to position themselves advantageously by ignoring conventional methods of operation. Such disruption is only the beginning, with further change forecast from the potential widespread diffusion of interactive television, giving consumers the potential to book directly from their living room using their television sets and remote controls [25]

Paradoxically, in addition to increasing competition between the distribution players, there is also more co-operation, for example, the GDS, in addition to attempting to distribute directly over the Web, are also servicing the reservation requirements of a variety of new players such as travel agency Web sites and corporate booking sites [14]. Non-exclusive virtual alliances are also being formed, with companies combining to form new synergistic relationships. An example of such alliances is demonstrated by Pegasus Systems, where in addition to distributing its hotel products directly to the consumer through its TravelWeb product (www.travelweb.com) Pegasus also provides the engine behind other Web based travel services such as Expedia and Preview Travel, services that many might see as the company's competitors. However each partner benefits – Pegasus by leveraging its investment in developing and maintaining its hotel reservation system and its allies by having access to an efficient and effective service without having to develop one for themselves. Such developments, with suppliers using multiple simultaneous distribution channels, and the coexistence of competition and co-operation has given rise to a phenomenon which Werthner and Klein have dubbed "coopetition" [8]!

Individual hotel companies are clearly taking advantage of the opportunities presented by the Web. In a survey of the top fifty hotel companies (ranked by number of rooms) carried out in 1999, over 90% of the those examined had a chain Web site, with nearly 80% of these providing reservation facilities to allow the customer to book directly [7]. The advantages of having a site are clear – lower distribution costs, increased sales as a result of specific promotions and increased customer loyalty [12]. Hotel chain sites appear to be highly effective, with the vast majority of Internet bookings (over 80%) flowing from these sites rather than from the Web intermediaries discussed above [26]. The attraction of Internet based channels for hotels is easy to understand. If they select the service(s) carefully, they have few up-front costs and no initiation or periodic fees, which gives a risk-free supplemental source of confirmed reservations, and allows them to take advantage of free marketing opportunities [27]. Furthermore, these new systems make global distribution possible for many smaller establishments that could never have afforded the traditional GDS / CRS channel [14].

In addition to the rapidly expanding number of channels available, most of the channels are becoming interconnected, with each system offering multiple routes to the customer. Which channel is likely to dominate in the future? In all probability, it is likely that dissimilar distribution channels will be targeted at different market segments at different times [3]. Research among members of HEDNA (the Hotel Electronic Distribution Network Association, which represents the majority of the larger hotel companies) shows that, in addition to the CRS / GDS route, over 98% of members utilise at least one other form of electronic distribution [28]. However, from the hoteliers' point of view, such a situation has made it difficult to establish firstly which channels they should be using to distribute their product, and secondly, the implication of using each channel. In short, the arrival of the Web has upset the distribution apple cart and this challenge leads directly to the purpose of this research.

5 Evaluating Hotel Electronic Channels of Distribution

Simply because new technology is involved does not necessarily mean that normal business principles change, as Connolly explains, "Selecting an appropriate distribution channel is paramount to success and important if hotel firms are to grow top line revenues and control overhead, yet the number of choices facing hospitality executives is overwhelming" [29]. Like any other asset, the use of a particular distribution channel must be justified [30] and in fact, Lewis claims that such channel management is the whole backbone of distribution and that every organisation must take the time to evaluate their current systems and organise a cohesive plan for improvements [31]. Similarly Andersen Consulting maintain that hotel companies urgently "need to get better at managing their channels, understanding the profitability of each and developing levers to divert traffic through one channel or another. Success in the future will accrue to those who are able to best manage their channels as profit centres" [11]. Hence arises the question of how to evaluate a channel of distribution.

Unfortunately answering this question is not easy. A review of the literature available on both tourism electronic distribution and ecommerce failed to reveal any generally accepted techniques that could be used to assess / evaluate the electronic channels of distribution being used or considered by the hotel sector. In addition, informal discussions with distribution service providers, academics and hoteliers also failed to identify any commonly accepted techniques. Given the demonstrable importance of electronic distribution and the growing level of booking volumes currently being experienced, appropriate evaluation tools, techniques or approaches would clearly benefit many.

6 Research Methodology

After consideration of alternative approaches, the Delphi technique was adopted as a means to assist identification of the range of evaluation techniques available to the hotel sector. This research method is particularly useful where the problem "does not lend itself to precise analytical techniques but can benefit from subjective judgements on a collective basis", where "time and cost make frequent group meetings infeasible" and where "disagreements among individuals are so severe that anonymity must be assured" [32]. In addition, research about complex problems and future developments is better studied through methods using experts [33].

One of the major criticisms of the Delphi method is the validity of the criteria used to identify participants in the panel of "experts". Previous research in the subject area [9] used a quasi-Delphi technique, involving iterative personal interviews with "recognised experts" in the field. These were chosen on the basis of "industry knowledge and experience and were recognised as being authoritative industry leaders, key influencers and decision makers at senior management level". However such an approach was felt to be too subjective and a more empirical method was thought to be more appropriate for the purposes of this study.

The potential Delphi participants were tentatively identified as those who had given presentations on technology related subjects at major international hospitality and tourism conferences. A list of tourism and hospitality conferences held in the 30 months prior to the start of the study was drawn up - a total of 139 conferences identified on a worldwide basis. However, from their titles and themes it was clear that certain of these events were not relevant to the subject of this study and those dealing exclusively with subject matter such as geography, ecology, education, heritage and anthropology were eliminated from further consideration, leaving a total of 105 candidate conferences. Of these, 50 were able to furnish speaker lists and a database of participants who spoke on technology related subjects was thus compiled. Over 600 speakers at thirty different events gave over 800 presentations and those who made three or more presentations at different events were selected, giving a subset of 48. Six presenters could not be traced, and two subsequently declined to participate in the study, giving a usable panel of forty experts.

A combination of literature-derived issues and information gleaned from informal interviews with industry practitioners provided the basis for the design of the initial questionnaire. However, following the suggestions of Gordon and Helmer [34], this was purposely kept general to avoid influencing the respondents. Efforts were made to make the questionnaire as "blank" as possible – thus helping to minimise variations in interpretation or difficulties in assimilation until the common vocabulary of the group could be established. The first round commenced by asking very general open questions on the respondent's understanding of the term "electronic distribution"; on the range of electronic distribution channels currently available to the hotel industry; and on how such channels should be evaluated. A total of 25 experts replied within the time-frame and a brief analysis of their views is presented in the next section.

7 Summary of Findings

7.1 What is hotel electronic distribution?

The first item on the questionnaire presented panel members with a broad definition of electronic distribution and asked them to comment on its appropriateness: *"Electronic distribution systems are those which use electronic media to provide relevant information to the customer to allow a purchase decision, and subsequently allow the transaction to be completed by facilitating the ordering and purchase of the product".* Comments showed that there was broad general agreement on this definition, only one participant fundamentally disagreed with its scope. Otherwise comments were in agreement, with "accurate, comprehensive and succinct", "accurate and concise" and "appropriate to the hotel product" being among the most favourable.

Suggestions for improvement focused on four main issues. Firstly, several respondents felt that clarification was needed as to the meaning of the term "electronic media". Confusion was expressed as to whether this was limited solely to channels that use the Internet as their communications media, or if the meaning was broader than this. Furthermore, should only electronic media that facilitate two way communications be included? If not, where do broadcast media such as radio and television, fit into the framework? Suggestions for improvement focused on including the terms "information and communications technology" in the definition to help clarify the issue. The second group of comments focused on the use of the word "allow" in the definition. Many respondents felt that this term was too passive to describe the role of electronic distribution in the hotel sales process. Two alternatives suggested were "enable" or "facilitate" the purchase process. The third issue concentrated on exactly which point the electronic distribution process finishes. Is the process completed once the customer "orders" the product by making a booking, or does it continue until the "purchase" is complete? With the hotel product, electronic fulfilment is clearly not possible, but further transactions (such as confirmation, modifications to the booking or outright cancellation are possible). What should be included in the definition is unclear and thus merits further investigation.

The fourth issue identified by panel members is related to the above and focuses on whether the definition should include *payment*. Several panel members suggested that the definition as presented be extended to specifically include payment, using phrases such as "enabling payment to be made", "allowing secure payment to be made" or "facilitating a financial transaction resulting in the completion of the purchase process". Others specifically mentioned that payment should not be included in the definition. This point also reflects another issue highlighted by one panel member. Does a system that solely distributes information, with no expectation or facility for completing the transaction, comply with the definition of an electronic distribution system?

7.2 Electronic distribution systems available to hotels

Panel members were then asked to identify the electronic distribution channels currently available to hotels in an attempt to develop a typography of the systems being used. Twenty-five different routes to the customer were identified, with each panel member, on average, highlighting five different alternatives. The most common routes identified (>15% of respondents) are shown in table one. Most respondents focused on four major routes to the marketplace (GDS, CRS, direct sales over the Internet and via an Internet Travel site). However the large number of other channels also identified reflects the variety of channels available and confirms the complexity of the choice facing the hotelier in relation to the distribution arena.

7.3 Evaluation Factors

The third part of the questionnaire focused on identifying the range of factors that need to be taken into consideration when evaluating an electronic channel of distribution for use with the hotel product. A large amount of qualitative data was collected in response to this question and a content analysis was performed on the

Table 1 – Electronic distribution systems available to hotels today

Electronic distribution channel	Total
Direct sales over the Internet	20
Global Distribution Systems	16
Hotel Central Reservation System	13
Internet via Travel Intermediary	13
Destination Management System	8
Internet via switch company site	7
Internet via hotel chain Web site	6
3rd party representative company	5
Teletext systems	5
Auction Web Sites	5
Interactive Digital TV	4

replies, with a total of 54 different evaluation factors being derived. For current purposes these factors have been clustered into the six categories below:

- Financial
- Market
- Operational
- System Provider
- Strategic/Tactical
- Technical

Most commonly cited were *financial factors*, related to the potential financial performance of the proposed channel (35) and eleven respondents pointed out that the overall cost of using the system needed to be taken into consideration. Five respondents mentioned transaction costs, with set-up costs being mentioned by a further three. On the opposite side of the equation, six panellists stressed the importance of assessing the potential volume of transactions that use of the channel might bring as well as (2) the amount of revenue that would potentially be generated. Only eight respondents explicitly combined these factors together by mentioning that the hotel should balance costs against benefits or examine the possible effect of using the channel on profitability.

Market factors were also mentioned frequently (33). Foremost among the suggestions in this category was the potential to service existing target markets (21), both in terms of market segment and geographical spread, while the channel's ability to address new customers was mentioned far less often (7). *Operational factors* and issues related to the day-to-day running of the system were also mentioned often (20). Primary among these was that the system should be easy to work with from a technical perspective (8), and that the number of databases used to support all electronic distribution channels should be minimised – preferably to just a single one (6). Less frequently cited suggestions focused on back office issues, such as the overall level of automation of the process, control issues and reporting issues. There were also a variety of comments focusing on the *system provider* of the electronic distribution channel (15) and on the technology behind its operation (15). In the former case, the reputation or brand image of the system supplier was the most commonly cited factor, while their independence (3) and level of understanding of the hotel sector (2) were also mentioned. A wide variety of *technical factors* that should be taken into account were also suggested, including security (3), speed of operation (4), data quality (4), multimedia capability (2) as well as many others. Finally, several *strategic / tactical factors* were also suggested by the panel (30). Eight respondents felt that electronic distribution channels needed to be evaluated in terms of how they affect the hotel's "brand image". Competitive positioning was also cited (4), as was the effect that using the channel would have on existing business relationships (6).

8 Conclusion

The approach discussed above has helped to clarify both what is meant by electronic distribution in the hotel sector, the range of channels available and how such channels might potentially be evaluated. The paper has not attempted to show the relative importance or effectiveness of each of these evaluation techniques, it has helped to clarify the range of techniques available and clearly the evaluation process is multifaceted. While cost and market factors are important, a much wider range of criteria also needs to be taken into account. Further research will now concentrate on the attempt to prioritise these factors and assess their importance specifically in relation to the hotel product.

References

1.   Deighton, J., *The Future of Interactive Marketing.* Harvard Business Review, 1996. November-December: p. 151-162.
2.   Poon, A., *Tourism, Technologies and Competitive Strategies.* 1st ed. 1993, Oxford: CAB International. 370.
3.   Buhalis, D., *Strategic Use of Information Technologies in the Tourism Industry.* Tourism Management, 1998. 19(3): p. 409-423.
4.   Hitchins, F., *The Influence of Technology on UK Travel Agents.* Travel & Tourism Analyst, 1991. No 3: p. 88-105.
5.   Knowles, T. and M. Garland, *The Strategic Importance of CRSs in the Airline Industry.* EIU Travel and Tourism Analyst, 1994. 4: p. 4-16.
6.   Coyne, R., *The Reservations Revolution.* Hotel and Motel Management, 1995(July 24th): p. 54-57.
7.   O'Connor, P., *Electronic Information Distribution in Tourism and Hospitality.* 1999: CAB International.

334

8.   Werthner, H. and S. Klein, *Information Technology and Tourism - A Challenging Relationship.* 1st ed. 1999, Vienna, Austria: Springer-Verlag. 323.

9.   HEDNA, *Onward Distribution of Hotel Information via the Global Distribution Systems,* . 1997, Partners-in-Marketing.: London.

10.   Burns, J., *Electronic GDS Distribution - What Are Your Options?,* in *Hospitality and Automation.* 1995. p. 1,3,11.

11.   Anderson Consulting, *The Future of Travel Distribution: Securing Loyalty in an Efficient Travel Market,* . 1998: New York.

12.   Wade, P., *L'impact des nouvelles technologies sur les systems d'information et de reservation,* . 1998, Conseil Nationale de Tourisme.: Paris.

13.   Waller, F., *The Distribution Revolution,* in *Hotels.* 1999. p. 103.

14.   Dombey, A., *Separating the Emotion from the Fact - the Effects of New Intermediaries on Electronic Travel Distribution,* in *Information and Communications Technologies in Tourism,* D. Buhalis, A.M. Tjoa, and J. Jafari, Editors. 1998, Springer-Verlag: Vienna, Austria. p. 129-138.

15.   Smith, C. and P. Jenner, *Tourism and the Internet.* Travel & Tourism Intelligence, 1998. 1: p. 62-81.

16.   Web-Week, *Travel Industry Embraces Web,* in *Web-Week.* 1997.

17.   ByLine Research, *Going Nowhere Fast: Ecommerce in the Travel Industry,* . 1999, ByLine Research: London.

18.   Jeong, M. and C. Lambert, *Measuring the Information Quality of Lodging Web Sites.* International Journal of Hospitality Information Technology, 1999. 1(1): p. 63-75.

19.   Pusateri, M. and J. Manno, *Travelers take to the 'Net.* Lodging, 1998. June: p. 23-24.

20.   Williams, A. and A. Palmer, *Tourism destination brands and electronic commerce: Towards synergy?* Journal of Vacation Marketing, 1999. 5(3): p. 263-275.

21.   Jung, H.-S. and R. Butler, *The Perception of the Internet as a Marketing Tool by Representatives of the Hotel Industry,* in *Hospitality Information Technology,* A.J. Frew, Editor. 1999, HITA: Edinburgh. p. 105-120.

22.   Stoltz, C., *The E-travel Revolution is Over,* in *Washington Post.* 1998.

23.   Reinders, J. and M. Baker, *The Future for Direct Retailing of Travel and Tourism Products: The Influence of Information Technology,* in *Information and Communications Technologies in Tourism,* A.M. Tjoa, Editor. 1997, Springer-Verlag: Vienna, Austria. p. 119-128.

24.   Nealon, T., *New Age Travellers,* in *Revolution.* 1998. p. 42-44.

25.   Reynolds, I., *The Changing Face of the Travel Industry.,* in *Distribution Channels in the Changing Travel Industry.* 1998, Distribution Channels in the Changing Travel Industry: London.

26.   HSMAI, *Interview with Phillip C Wolf, President and CEO of PhoCusWright Ltd.,* in *HSMAI Gazette.* 1999.

27.   Chervenak, L., *CRS Today and Tomorrow,* in *Lodging.* 1999. p. 75-77.

28.   HEDNA, *Electronic Distribution Trends Survey - Executive Summary*, . 1999, HEDNA.

29.   Connolly, D., *Understanding Information Technology Investment Decision Making in the Context of Hotel Global Distribution Systems: A Multiple-Case Study*, in <u>*Hotel and Tourism Management*</u>. 1999: Blacksburg, Virginia.

30.   Griffin, R., *Evaluating the Success of Lodging Yield Management Systems*. FIU Hospitality Review, 1997. Spring: p. 57-71.

31.   Lewis, R. and R. Chambers, *Marketing Leadership in Hospitality*. 1995, New York: van nostrand Reinhold.

32.   Linstone, H. and M. Turoff, eds. *The Delphi Technique*. . 1975, Addison-Wesley: Reading MA, Addison Wesley.

33.   Welters, K., *Delphi-Technik*, in *Enzyklopadie der Betriebswirtschaftslehre-Handworterbuch der Planung*. 1989: Stuttgart.

34.   Gordon, T. and O. Hemler, *Probing the Future*, in *News Front Magazine*. 1965.

Tomorrow's Travel Agency: A Survey of Adaptation And Positioning Strategies to New Technologies in Services

François Bédard
Department of Urban Studies and Tourism
School of Management, Université du Québec à Montréal
Email : bedard.francois@uqam.ca

1. Introduction and purpose

The tourism industry faces several major challenges in the new millenium. Sweeping changes in the technologies of services, changes in consumers demographics and sophistication, rapid developments in information technologies all combine to challenge the traditional approaches of travel agencies to the industry. Although the challenges are similar worlwide, several adaptation / positioning strategies may be available to various key players. Although there is no research data available yet, major thinkers of the industry, like Eastman (1997), Loverseed (1999), Oppermann (1999), Poon (1993), Sheldon (1994), Skapinker (1999), Van Rekom and Teunissen (1999) and Vellas and Bécherel (1999) have predicted that survival of travel agencies in the near future will be predicated on evolving from a generalist to a specialized approach.

The purpose of our study was to survey Quebec travel agencies and document their favored adaptation / positioning strategies in the wake of recent technological changes in tourism services. We hypothesized that travel agencies, before year 2002 :

a) would favor evolving from generalist entities to specialized entities, in order to respond to the challenges related to the introduction of new technologies in services;
b) would favor regrouping and networking to increase access to up-to-date technology;
c) would favor developing exclusive goods and services, tailored to their target market demographics, rather than basic wholesalers packages.

2. Defining potential adaptation / positioning strategies

In order to identify the emerging challenges facing travel agencies, in depth interviews were conducted with 15 experts in the industry. These experts were selected from areas such as travel agencies networks, tours operators, airlines and travel journalism. A focus group was also held with twelve travel agencies' customers who already use the Internet. We specifically explored their views on how they see the role of travel agents in the future given the growing offer of travel services on the

Internet. The existing literature on electronic commerce and its impact on travel agencies and on adaptation strategies was reviewed extensively.

From this preliminary research, four potential adaptation / positioning strategies were defined :

a) A *generalist approach*: The generalist travel ˙agency in not dedicated to a specific market (either client or product) or a specific supplier. It sells « everything to everyone », and acts as an intermediary between clients and suppliers. Its revenues stem from commissions, which are dictated by suppliers; the suppliers clearly dominate the financial relationship with the generalist travel agency. The agency may charge a service fee to its clients. Its technology abilities are limited. This agency is usually independant or belongs to a small loose network with no or little integration.

b) A *specialized approach with emphasis on suppliers:* This type of travel agency specializes in goods and or services offered by one or more dedicated suppliers. The agency is a *dealer* for the suppliers; if more than one supplier is involved, there is no competition and the relationship between suppliers and the agency is based on cooperation. Technology support is provided by the suppliers. Revenues stem from commissions from the suppliers; a bonus is garanteed to secure exclusivity from the agency. The agency is either independant or belongs to a group centered on the main supplier.

c) A *specialized approach with emphasis on customers and products*: This type of travel agency specializes in a market share. It negociates with various suppliers on its clients' behalf. Its products are made to order for its clients needs and demographics. Revenues may stem from several sources; the agency may charge service fees to its clients while receiving a commission from suppliers; or it may negociate a package deal with suppliers and sell it for profit to its clients. Clients are the main beneficiaries of this approach. This type of travel agency relies moderately on technology, particularly with regards to clients' loyalty. The agency is usually independent, or belongs to a small loose network with little integration.

d) A *mixed specialized approach, regrouping (b) and (c)*: This type of travel agency meshes characteristics of the suppliers and customers and products approach. The agency is usually independent, but may belong to a well-integrated network. It relies heavily on technology support. Revenues stem from commissions or from charging suppliers a transaction fee to distribute their products, and from selling for profit to its clients. The distribution of power is balanced between suppliers, clients, and the agency.

3. Survey of Quebec travel agencies

3.1 Materials and methods

A 143 questions survey was developed and piloted in 15 travel agencies. The survey covered 5 main topics, i.e. tomorrow's travel agencies, travel agents' education and training, technology equipment, individual travel agencies strategies, and participants demographics.

During Summer 1998, the survey was mailed to all 958 Quebec travel agencies permit holders. One hundred and ninety surveys were returned (19,8 % response rate for a margin error of 7 %, 19 out 20 times). The responders were a representative sample of the total population of Quebec travel agencies (Table 1).

Table 1
Comparaison between responders and
all Quebec travel agencies permit holders

Description	Responders (n = 190)	All Quebec travel agencies permit holders (n = 958)
Member of Quebec Association of Travel Agencies (ACTA-Quebec)	54,3 %	52,6 %
Annual revenues	1,8 M $	1,6 M $

Statistical analysis of survey responses was done using SPSS and STATA.

3.2 Results

At the time of the survey, 80 % of travel agencies considered themselves « generalists » and 20 % « specialists ». When surveyed on their perception of tomorrow's typical travel agency in year 2002, travel agencies favored a diversity of adaptation / positioning strategies rather than a single approach to the new technologies in tourism services :

- 30 % of agencies favored a *generalist approach*;
- 20 % of agencies favored a *specialized approach with emphasis on suppliers*;
- 30 % of travel agencies favored a *specialized approach with emphasis on customers / products*;
- and 20 % of agencies favored a *mixed specialized approach, focusing both on suppliers and customers / products*.

The were significant differences in overall perception of tomorrow's typical travel agency between the four favored approaches. Travel agencies faovring a *generalist approach* were the most different from the surveyed group. Almost 95 % of the agencies favoring a *generalist approach* already considered themselves generalists. They were most likely to predict status quo for year 2002. They foresaw tomorrow's typical travel agency as small (4 agents or less). They were least likely to think that the number of agencies would decrease over the next few years; that groups / networks would have more power and individual agencies less power, that travel agencies would have to regroup in order to survive, and that travel agents would need better training in sales and marketing in the future. Their level of technology competence and development was lower that the average for the entire group surveyed. Their approach was more conservative, as their owners mostly belonged to the age group 55 and over. Since these owners are close to retirement, these agencies are least likely to consider major changes to their current modus operandi.

Travel agencies favoring a *specialized approach with emphasis on suppliers* were most likely to predict that tomorrow's typical travel agency would have more than 4 agents, that groups / networks would be powerful, and most likely to rely on basic technology services more easily available through a network of agencies. Although 81,1 % of these travel agencies considered themselves generalists at the time of the survey, only 36,1 % considered that status quo could be maintained until year 2002. They felt that survival was linked to adherence to a network. The majority of these agencies' owners belonged to the age group 45-54 years old, belying experience and contacts with suppliers of travel services.

Travel agencies favoring a *specialized approach with emphasis on customers / products* were most likely to find that individual agencies had little power; their drive for specialization may be perceived as self-preservation. All these agencies felt that travel agents would need better training in sales and marketing to succeed, and that survival would directly be linked to joining a group or network. These agencies were most technologically adept compared to the entire surveyed group. The majority of these agencies' owners were in the 35-44 year old age group, thus most likely to consider major changes in order to compete and survive.

Travel agencies favoring a *mixed specialized approach regrouping emphasis on suppliers and customers / products* scored slightly above average of respondents regarding the lack of power of individual agencies and the strength of groups / networks. The majority of these agencies' owners belonged to the 25-34 year old group, and did not have a defined strategic plan for the future of their agencies.

Irregardless of the adaptation / positioning strategy favored by the travel agencies, the data reduction analysis on SPSS identified 8 indicators for enabling strategies, regrouped in three categories (Table 2):

Table 2
Categories and indicators for enabling strategies in the travel sector

Category 1 : Improving client services through technology
         a)   Developing clientele loyalty programs
         b)   Increasing data gathering on clientele
         c)   Increasing training and knowledge of travel agents
         d)   Increasing use of technology
         e)   Creating networks / groups sharing technologic tools

Category 2 : Transforming the structure of travel agency
         f)   Acquiring the dual role of intermediary and producer of their own travel products or tours
         g)   Finding new financial partners

Category 3 : Withdrawing from the market
         h)   Selling of closing the agency

The first category deals with improving client services through technology. One-on-one marketing will directly benefit from information technology, ensuring client loyalty through an up-to-date database. Travel agents encreasing their training and knowledge of new technologies will increase their use and mastery of this powerful instrument, and participate in networks and groups, providing worldwide access to tourism goods and services.

The second category relates to structural transformations of tomorrow's travel agency. Their traditional role as an intermediary will be expanded into producing exclusive tours and product for their clients. Financial stability will be ensured by funding new financial partners.

Confronted with the changes heralded by new information technologies, 20,1 % of agencies surveyed indicated that they would consider selling or closing the agency, if the previous enabling strategies fail to secure financial success in year 2000.

4. Conclusion and future works

This survey identified a diversity of adaptation / positioning strategies rather than a single approach to the new technologies in travel agency sector. Differences in adaptation / positioning and enabling strategies were based, amongst other factors, on the age and flexibility of the respondents. Choosing a strategy will directly impact on the agencies organizational structure and relationships with suppliers and customers alike. Several areas of research remain open; the nature of groups, whether partnership, alliances, consortia, a franchise will likely determine the structure of individual agencies; the nature of revenue sources will need also to be redefined; finally the core role of travel agencies will be redefined by external market forces brought on by technology. Individualization of approaches will ensure seamless delivery of services in the new millenium.

References

BEIRNE Elizabeth, CURRY Philip. *The Impact of the Internet on the Information Search Process and Tourism Decision Making.* In : *Information and Communication Technologies in Tourism.* Ed. par BUHALIS Dimitrios, SCHERTLER Walter. Vienna: Springer. 1999. – p. 88-97.

BJÔRK Peter, GUSS Thomas. *The Internet as a Marketspace - The Perception of the Consumers.* In : *Information and Communication Technologies in Tourism.* Ed. par BUHALIS Dimitrios, SCHERTLER Walter. Vienna: Springer. 1999. – p. 54-65.

EASTMAN Richard. « Future of Travel Agents? ». Web site of *Travel Technology Association.* December 1995. – 2 p.

EASTMAN Richard. « Travel Marketing and Technology ». Web site of *Travel Technology Association.* 1997. – 2 p.

GATES Bill, MYHRVOLD Nathan, RINEARSON Peter. *The Road Ahead.* New York: Vicking Penguin. 1995. – 286 p.

GODART Jean-Marc. *Combinatorial Optimisation Based Decision Support System for Trip Planning.* In : *Information and Communication Technologies in Tourism.* Ed. par BUHALIS Dimitrios, WALTER Schertler. Vienna: Springer-Verlag. 1999. – p. 318-327.

LOVERSEED Helga. « Travel Agents in Canada ». *Travel & Tourism Intelligence.* 1999, 1, p. 71-86.

OPPERMANN Martin. « Databased Marketing by Travel Agencies ». *Journal of Travel Research.* Boulder. February 1999, 37, 3, p. 231-237.

PODMOLIK Mary Ellen. « Travel Agents' Focus Shifts ». *Chicago Sun – Times.* 5XS Edition. 7 April 1999, p. 56.

POON Auliana. *Tourism, Technology and Competitive Strategies.* Oxon (U.K.): CAB International. 1993. – 360 p.

SCHERTLER Walter, BERGER-KOCH Claudia. *Tourism as an Information Business: The Strategic Consequences of E-Commerce for Business Travel.* In : *Information and Communication Technologies in Tourism.* Ed. par BUHALIS Dimitrios, SCHERTLER Walter. Vienna: Springer. 1999. - p. 25-35.

SHELDON Pauline J. *Tourism Information Technology.* New York: CAB International. 1997. – 224 p.

SKAPINKER Michael. « Roles Redefined in a Changing World: Agents Can no Longer Afford to Be Just Ticket Vendors; To Survive They Must Deliver a Range of Services, Writes Michael Skapinker ». *Financial Times.* Surveys Edition. 6 May 1999, p. 1.

342

TRAVEL TRADE GAZETTE ASIA. « Special Report: Technology: New-Age Agencies in the Making ». *Travel Trade Gazette Asia.* 23 April 1999, p. 1.

VAN REKOM Johan, TEUNISSEN Wim, GO Frank. « Improving the Position of Business Travel Agencies: Coping With the Information Challenge ». *Information Technology & Tourism.* 1999, 2, 1, p. 15-29.

VELLAS François, BÉCHEREL Lionel. *The International Marketing of Travel and Tourism - A Strategic Approach.* Great Britain: MacMillan Press Ltd. 1999. – 329 p.

WADE Philip, FALCAND Didier. *Cyberplanète.* Paris: Editions Autrement. Collection Mutations. No 176. 1998. – 349 p.

The Application Of E-Commerce To Enhance The Competitive Advantages Of Hotels In Hong Kong

[1]Allen K.L. Yu and [2]Rob Law
[1]Department of Management
The Hong Kong Polytechnic University, Hung Hom, Kowloon, Hong Kong
[2]Department of Hotel & Tourism Management
The Hong Kong Polytechnic University, Hung Hom, Kowloon, Hong Kong

1 Introduction

Enterprises around the world recognize that the Internet has enabled a new economic era – the networked economy (Oracle Corporation, 1998). This has considerable implications on the business environment. To remain competitive, business and technology strategies have to be re-defined. It is therefore not surprising that with the rapid development of Internet technologies and its applications, E-commerce, which bases mainly on the Internet, has changed the ways business is done globally. While E-commerce is a hot topic, its definition can be different in literature. In this paper, E-commerce is defined as *the use of computer networks to conduct business electronically between the buyers and the sellers*. Internet commerce is considered as a kind of E-commerce.

1.1 Problem Definitions

Many firms are providing hardware, software, information content or services for realizing E-commerce systems with the support of reputable computer vendors in market. For example, Lotus Domino Application supports the vision of Cascading Commerce (Lotus Development Corporation, 1999) while Compaq and Microsoft, working in tandem with Intel, have created Complete Commerce for medium to large-sized enterprise businesses (Compaq Corporation, 1999). Another example is from Microsoft, which formed the Microsoft E-commerce Alliance, consisting of Commerce One, Great Plains, Compaq and Ernst & Young. This alliance supports E-commerce through the delivery of a one-stop-shopping solution to business users (Microsoft Corporation, 1999). While the functional capabilities of the technologies employed are evolving rapidly, E-commerce solutions are applicable to many businesses and realized with little investment. Accordingly, many E-commerce establishments can be found in overseas hotel industry. Whereas in Hong Kong, the hotel practitioners have failed to take a pro-active role in making use of the benefits of E-commerce solutions as the use of IT has concentrated mainly in the support of the internal hotel operations. Also, many hotel managers do not seem to realize the essence of IT in the business strategy (Law and Au, 1997). When comparing with hotels in overseas countries, the hotels in Hong Kong could lose their competitive power derivable from E-commerce.

1.2 Objectives

In order for the hotel practitioners in Hong Kong to enhance their competitive advantages, it is necessary that these practitioners begin to take actions in evaluating what E-commerce products and services are available in the market. Then they have to explore the possible benefits offered to them by these products and services and how the competitive advantages can be enhanced through their employment. Finally, for realizing the E-commerce solutions, they have to devise a systematic approach for facilitating the planning and implementation processes. In view of these, the objectives of this study are derived as follows:

-   to explore the ways that the competitive advantages of the hotels in Hong Kong can be enhanced,
-   to consolidate the business values of E-commerce to the hotel industry in Hong Kong and
-   to devise a framework through which the competitive advantages can be derived from E-commerce solutions for the hotels in Hong Kong.

2   Literature Review

E-commerce can be used in all phases of the business transaction life cycle which begins well before the transaction occurs and continues after the sales has been made. In general, E-commerce solutions deal with the exchange of *information, influence* as well as *money and goods* between buyers and sellers. This affects the operations across the functional groups of an organization. Typical functional groups affected include: marketing (Arrange to Provide), sales (Find Customer and Arrange Terms), production (Fulfill Order), inventory control (Fulfill Order), accounting (Fulfill Order), technical support (Support Customer) and servicing (Support Customer). Though this new strategy of business is effort demanding, the rewards can be tremendous as relevant deployment of E-commerce solutions can add values to the operations and enhance the competitive advantages of an organization.

According to Porter (1980), the operations of any enterprise could be divided into a series of activities, such as, salespeople making sales calls, service technicians performing repairs, scientists in the laboratory designing products or processes etc. By coordinating linked activities, an enterprise could reduce transaction costs, gather better information for control purposes, and substitute less costly operations in one activity for more costly ones elsewhere. When competitive advantages are considered in the context of an industry, Porter (1980) proposed to use the Five Forces model as shown in *Figure 1*.

Fig. 1 : Porter's Five Forces Model

Fig. 1 : Porter's Five Forces Model

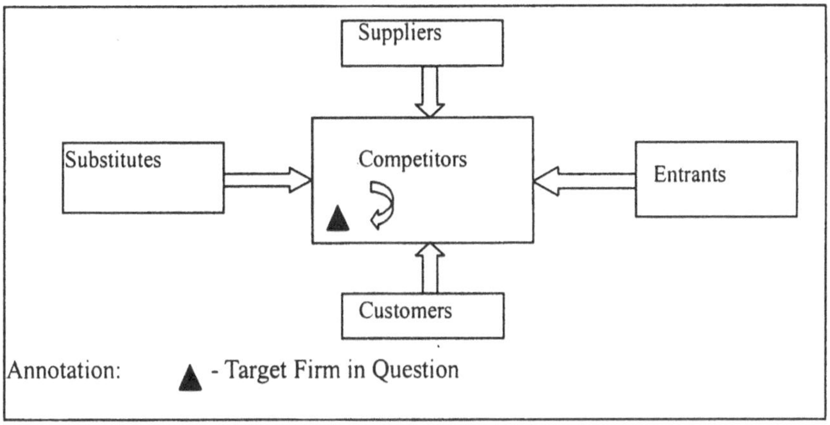

To gain competitive advantages in the industry, a firm can use the generic strategies as shown in *Table 1*.

Table 1 : Porter's (1980) Generic Strategies

	Competitive Advantages	
Competitive Scope	Lower Cost	Differentiation
Broad Target	Cost Leadership	Differentiation
Narrow Target	Cost Focus	Focused Differentiation

In Porter's (1980) views, the relevant use of the above strategy could help attain the desirable competitive position for enhancing the firm's competitive advantages.

In this article, the business values as found in the literature are firstly considered as business functions. These *business functions* will become *business values* if they can add values to the hotels' operations. As a reference, examples of the business functions of E-commerce identified in the research include:

- Communicating with suppliers and customers
- Evaluating products
- Evaluating suppliers
- Collecting products / services information
- Enhancing sales channels
- Enhancing customer services
- Enhancing customer relationships
- Adding values to products / services

Information technology is critical to the implementation of an organization's strategy. As proposed by Porter (1980), competitive advantages in either cost or product differentiation is a function of the value chain of an enterprise. IT is spreading through the value chain, transforming the way value activities are performed and the nature of the linkages among them. As the value chain links the internal activities with those of the external ones, the industry structure and the organizational goals have implications on the choice of relevant IT strategies. Porter and Millar (1985) proposed the use of an information intensity matrix to assess IT's role. The matrix evaluates the information intensity of the value chain against that of the product. They suggest that IT plays a strategic role in an industry that is characterized by high information intensity in both the value chain and the product. As E-commerce solutions affect the business processes across the functional groups and deal with lots of information content, the realization of E-commerce endeavors requires the presence of relevant IT strategies.

Another view that shows the critical role of IT in E-commerce relates to transaction costs. Transaction costs are the costs of administering an exchange relationship. These include the costs of negotiating, drafting and monitoring contracts; the costs of settling disputes and enforcing settlements; and the opportunity costs associated with administering a contract inefficiently until a new agreement is recognized as necessary and then reached (Quartz and Graff, 1995). These costs can be predicted in the typical E-commerce model. It can be seen in the model that the organization involved is in effect administering an exchange relationship for realizing E-commerce solutions. For the model to function effectively, the transaction costs involved have to be addressed well. IT can play a key role in reducing these costs. As mentioned by Kraut et al. (1998), greater use of electronic networks, which are supported by IT, would be associated with fewer errors in orders, greater efficiency in orders and more satisfaction with the suppliers.

It can be concluded from the above that IT is the enabling tools of E-commerce. From Porter's (1980) views, IT not only affected how individual activities are performed but also greatly enhanced a company's ability to exploit linkages between activities. Companies can coordinate their actions more closely with those of their buyers and suppliers, thus creating many new interrelationships among businesses and expanding the scope of industries in which a company must compete to achieve competitive advantages. While facilitating organizations in streamlining internal activities and connecting with outsiders, IT strategies have to cater for the needs of the internal as well as external environments of an organization.

3 Methodology

In this research, Porter's Five Forces Model is used for deriving a favorable hospitality environment through which the competitive advantages of hotels can be enhanced. In this approach, the hotels would in effect be taking a series of actions with respect to five areas of concern, namely, suppliers, customers, entrants, substitutes and competitors. The research method involved is to generate a number of questions corresponding to the actions for deriving the favorable hospitality environment and to measure how likely hotel practitioners would react through conducting a survey. By relating the functions of E-commerce to these actions, the likeliness of taking actions would become a factor for determining whether E-commerce can be of business values to the hotels. This is shown in *Figure 2*.

Fig. 2. Design Logic of Questions

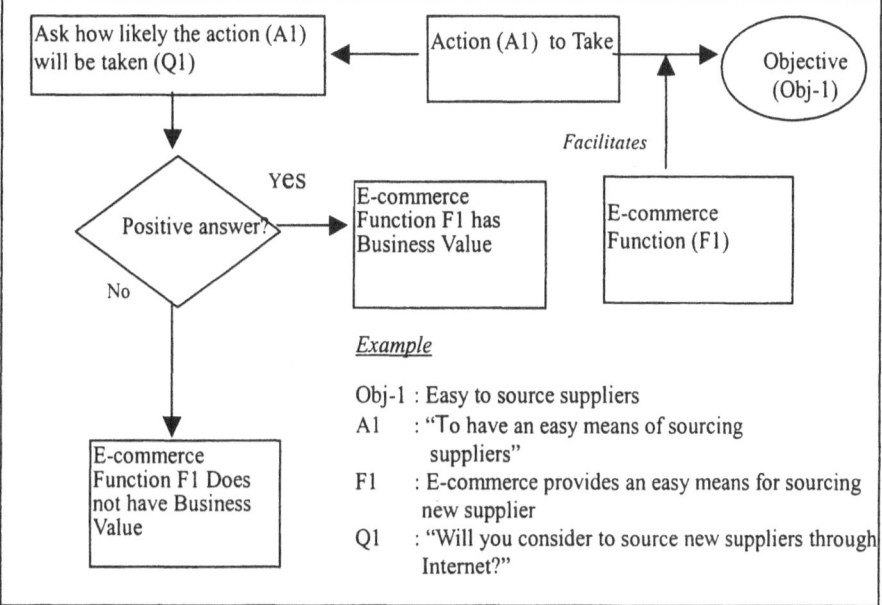

In the survey, the 77 members currently in the Hong Kong Hotels Association were used as the population. Typical IT applications can be found in nine functional groups of a hotel. These are Accounting, Purchasing, Front Office, Information Systems, Food & Beverage, Housekeeping, HR & Training, Engineering, and Sales & Marketing. As E-commerce is related to IT strategies, it was logical to select these departments as the target functional groups of the survey. Accordingly, questionnaires are sent to the department heads of these nine functional groups in Hong Kong's hotels.

4   Findings And Analysis

The typical functional departments in the hotel industry were firstly categorized into three groups, namely, Front Office (FO), Sales & Marketing (SM) and Back Office (BO). The Front Office Group consisted of the Front Office Department. This group is customer-oriented and service-oriented. The front office personnel have many chances to deal with customers directly. They have frequent needs to communicate with customers, establish good relationships with the customers and strive for enhancing company loyalty through the provision of professional services. Many primary functions of front office overlap with the strengths of E-commerce. As such, E-commerce solution is well suited to the operations in front office. Hence, the analysis on the views of the Front Office Department is important for devising relevant E-commerce strategies. As for the formation of the Sales & Marketing Group, it relates to the special role of E-commerce on marketing. E-commerce has already re-defined the rules for carrying out sales and marketing activities to a great extent. The marketing impact of the Internet is further concluded by Dietrick (1996) who stated that the Internet would bring about a new trend of marketing that comes with numerous opportunities for marketers. In other words, E-commerce has affected the marketing concepts and practices considerably. The understanding of the views of the Sales & Marketing Department is therefore important for any kind of E-commerce endeavors. Lastly, in this research, other than the Front Office Department and the Sales & Marketing Department, all other departments were classified under the group of Back Office. When comparing with the Front Office Group and the Sales & Marketing Group, the Back Office Group focuses more on the internal operations of the hotel. It should be noted that the Food & Beverages Department is customer-oriented as well as service-oriented. This seems to be in contrast to the internal nature of the group at first glance. The "internal" nature of the Food & Beverages Department is derived from the fact that quite a lot of its target customers are within the hotel, rather than outside the hotel.

The analysis of data was divided into two parts. The first part focused on the views of the hotel industry as a whole and corresponded to the research objectives directly. The second part compared the views of the three groups of departments BO, SM and FO and enabled useful conclusions to be drawn on the similarities and differences of the departmental views. In this paper, Mann-Whitney Test was used for comparing the views of the BO, SM and FO groups on a pair-by-pair basis.

The results obtained in the research support the achieving of the target objectives. In general, the hotel managers are likely to take the actions in the question which correspond to the business functions of E-commerce. Also, they believed that upon taking the actions, they would likely obtain benefits deriving from cost and product differentiation. This implies that E-commerce can add values to the operations of the hotels as E-commerce can facilitate the completion of the actions. In other words, E-commerce can enhance the competitive advantages of hotels in Hong Kong. This is a remarkable result for this research. On comparing the views of the BO, SM and FO groups, the Mann-Whitney Test results are shown in *Table 2*.

The favorable hospitality environment is made up of five areas of concern – suppliers, customers, entrants, substitutes and competitors. The analysis of questions in these five areas of concern has implications on the main interests of the groups and can facilitate the meeting of departmental needs during the implementation of E-commerce solutions in hotels. *Table 3* summarizes the smallest and largest medians in the five areas of concern.

Table 2: Comparisons of Mann-Whitney Test Results for BO, SM and FO Groups
(Note: Null Hypothesis is "Samples come from populations of same median")

	Areas of Concern	BO versus SM	BO versus FO	SM versus FO
1	Likeliness of Taking Actions for Procuring the Favorable Hospitality Environment (E-commerce functions can facilitate completing these actions)	Null hypothesis not rejected at $\alpha = 0.20$, 0.10, 0.05 and 0.01	Null hypothesis not rejected at $\alpha = 0.20$, 0.10, 0.05 and 0.01	Null hypothesis not rejected at $\alpha = 0.20$, 0.10, 0.05 and 0.01
2	Likeliness to Have Cost Advantages when Taking Actions	Null hypothesis not rejected at $\alpha = 0.20$, 0.10, 0.05 and 0.01	Null hypothesis rejected at $\alpha = 0.20$, but not at other values	Null hypothesis rejected at $\alpha = 0.20$ and 0.10, but not at other values
3	Likeliness to Have Benefits from Differentiation when Taking Actions	Null hypothesis not rejected at $\alpha = 0.20$, 0.10, 0.05 and 0.01	Null hypothesis rejected at $\alpha = 0.20$, but not at other values	Null hypothesis rejected at $\alpha = 0.20$, but not at other values
4	Likeliness to Have Benefits from Focus when Taking Actions	Null hypothesis not rejected at $\alpha = 0.20$, 0.10, 0.05 and 0.01	Null hypothesis rejected at $\alpha = 0.20$, 0.10 and 0.05, but not at 0.01	Null hypothesis not rejected at $\alpha = 0.20$, 0.10, 0.05 and 0.01

Table 3: Smallest and Largest Medians of Areas of Concern for Procuring the Favorable
Hospitality Environment
(Notes: the smaller the median total, the more positive the view)

	Areas of Concern	Smallest Median Total	Largest Median Total
1	Suppliers	BO	FO
2	Customers	FO	BO
3	Entrants	FO	SM
4	Substitutes	FO	SM
5	Competitors	FO	BO

In general, there is no major difference in the views of BO, SM and FO. However, one interesting point to note is that the unexpected high median value of SM in the Entrants and Substitutes areas. This indicates that the SM group is less sensitive to the emergence of new market players and any possible products and services replacements in the markets than the BO group.

5   Conclusions And Implications

The research results indicate that E-commerce can enhance the competitive advantages of hotels in Hong Kong. This can be achieved by adding values to the operations of hotels. The business values of E-commerce derived from this research are in the following areas:

- Communicating with suppliers and customers
- Evaluating products
- Evaluating suppliers
- Collecting products / services information
- Enhancing sales channels
- Enhancing customer services
- Enhancing customer relationships
- Adding values to products / services
- Enhancing company / brand loyalty
- Analyzing market and customer needs
- Introducing products / services to overseas customers

The research results have implications on practical E-commerce endeavors. The hotel managers are already aware of the business values of E-commerce. At the same time, E-commerce solutions are available with the support of major computer vendors in Hong Kong. As such, it is time to promote E-commerce solutions to the hotel industry at this stage. E-commerce affects business strategies. Accordingly, the organizational goals of hotels may have to change for deploying E-commerce solutions. This requires the top management of the hotels to review the organizational particulars in details, as changes at lower levels are also foreseeable. Since state-of-the-art software systems are seldom used in local hotels and that many staff in the hotels do not seem to understand clearly the linkage of adopting the latest IT and business advantages (Law, Au and Cho, 1996), there is a need to educate the top management in this aspect.

At the departmental levels, different primary functions of departments imply the different values of E-commerce to them. Departments have to review individual departmental operations and evaluate the possible functional areas that E-commerce can add value to. Also, the departments have to get prepared to adapt to the new demands arising from the support of E-commerce operations in the long-term considerations. The Front Office Department and Sales & Marketing Department have to evaluate their situations with particular care as E-commerce can be of high business values to them. The research results indicate that the Sales & Marketing Department has failed to understand clearly or has got wrong understanding on the values of E-commerce to them, hence, additional efforts may be required to educate the department in this regard.

With respect to implementing customer-oriented or service-oriented E-commerce applications, the research results show that the Front Office Department is the most relevant department to start with. As analyzed in the section, the Front Office Department has got the smallest median total for four of the industrial areas of concern, that is, *Customers, Entrants, Substitutes* and *Competitors*. Moreover, special attention has to be paid to the structure and capabilities of the computer department, as E-commerce endeavors would bring about new technologies that may impact the existing computing environment considerably. Also, the implementation of E-commerce solutions would demand special skills that the existing computing department may be in lack of.

Recently, the Hong Kong government has been active in promoting E-commerce to the business sector, however, not much has been done to cope with the specific requirements of the hotel industry. In this regard, industry authorities like the Hong Kong Hotels Association and the Hong Kong Tourists Association should take a leading role in the related E-commerce endeavors. For example, they can begin to arrange to provide E-commerce education to the hotel practitioners and organize E-commerce activities to arouse the interests of the hotel practitioners on the topic.

The research is conducted in the context of the hotel industry of Hong Kong, whether the same results are applicable to overseas countries have to be confirmed with other empirical results. Also, the research results are derived from all hotels in Hong Kong, disregarding of whether there are any E-commerce solutions in the hotels or not. The limitations of research reveal some of the future research directions. Similar empirical analysis being conducted in other countries as well as in hotels with E-commerce setup are useful for validating the model in the corresponding aspects. Also, it is desirable that the following aspects can be addressed in future research initiatives for the successful implementation of E-commerce solutions:

- the views of the top management of hotels on E-commerce endeavors,
- the difficulties of implementation of E-commerce solutions in hotels and how to overcome these difficulties, and
- the views of the computer department on the sufficiency of IT resources and capabilities for E-commerce endeavors in hotels.

References

Compaq Corporation. Electronic Commerce. http://www.compaq.com/solutions/ecommerce/index.html. (1999).
Dietrich, K. The Emerging Importance of the Internet and Online Services as a Marketing Tool. European Management Academy, Vienna. (May 1996).
Kraut, R., Steinfield, C., Chan, A., Butler, B. and Hoag, A. Coordination and Virtualization: The Role of Electronic Networks and Personal Relationships. JCMC 3 (4). http://www.ascusc.org/jcmc/vol3/issue4/kraut.html. (June 1998)
Law, R. and Au, N. Hong Kong Hospitality Industry: The Application of Information Technology to Achieve Competitive Advantages. Proceedings of the Hong Kong International Computer Conference 97, Hong Kong. 52-56 (October 1997).

352

Law, R., Au, N. and Cho, V. Bridging the Gap between Non-technical Managers and Technical Computing Experts in Hong Kongì¼ Hotels. Proceedings of the Hong Kong International Computer Conference '96, Hong Kong, Day 1. 57-61 (September 1996).

Lotus Development Corporation. Lotus E-business Solutions for Commerce: White Paper. (1999).

Microsoft Corporation. Microsoft Launches New Alliance to Simplify E-commerce for Customers. http://www.microsoft.com/presspass/features/1999/04-27iec.htm. (1999).

Oracle Corporation. Capturing Electronic Commerce Opportunities – An Oracle Business White Paper. (November 1998).

Porter, M. E. Competitive Strategy – Techniques for Analyzing Industries and Competitors. New York: Free Press (1980).

Porter, M. E. and Millar, V. E. How Information Gives you Competitive Advantage. Harvard Business Review. (1985).

Quartz and Graff, J. An Introduction to the Work of Oliver Eaton Williamson (1932-Pres.) http://www.iems.nwu.edu/~jamison/quartz/will-wp.html. (1995)

Partnership Australia's National Tourism Data Warehouse: Preliminary Assessment Of A Destination Marketing System

Roberto Daniele
Lecturer, Department of Hospitality, Tourism and Leisure
RMIT University
roberto.daniele@rmit.edu.au

Nina Mistilis
Centre For Tourism & Hospitality Research
Faculty of Business
University of Western Sydney Macarthur
n.mistilis@uws.edu.au

Liz Ward
Manager, Online Distribution Services
Tourism Queensland
wardl@tq.com.au

1. Background

Much has been written since the early 1980's about Destination Marketing Systems (DMSs), particularly in the form of case studies most of which seem to reflect a high degree of system failure (eg BRAVO, Hi-Line, ETNA and earlier versions of the Gulliver system). Indeed Archdale has characterised this field as follows:

> "the overall pattern of systems development in the field has been diverse, geographically disparate and generally reactive. This has led to a confused pattern of business objectives, a marked absence of technical, commercial or data definition standards, a plethora of often conflicting developments within individual countries and little evidence of inter-NTO cooperation or even formal discussion on the issue" (Archdale et al: 1992).

Whilst some of such shortcomings have been addressed during the intervening years by new developments, the Australian situation has been similarly characterised by a multiplicity of websites and/or destination marketing systems displaying information at varying levels of quality, content and format.

The issue of systems development is made more complex in Australia by its political structure - a federation consisting of a national government and seven states and territories. Each has its own tourism commission responsible for tourism marketing and characterised by the varying stages of technological development of its DMS. Although the Australian Tourist Commission has the main responsibility for marketing Australia overseas, each State and Territory tourism authority also engages in inbound tourism marketing.

The National Tourism Data Warehouse is an initiative of Partnership Australia, a strategic alliance between the State and Territory tourism authorities and the Australian Tourist Commission (ATC) developed to better market Australia overseas through a cooperative marketing agreement that delivers tactical marketing campaigns, help-lines and fulfilment services for product internationally.

Whilst the project is still in its early stages of development, it is envisaged that the NTDW will combine all the information from the States and Territories destination databases into a common format in a centralised location where distributors (ie. inbound operators, wholesalers, retailers online agents etc) will access it for distribution through their channels (ie CRS, GDS and websites).

The objectives of the NTDW are twofold:
a) to allow (through a series of web based interfaces to the NTDW) domestic and international trade partners and consumers to search for consistent and reliable product and destination information in Australia across all state and territory boundaries;

b) to maximise distribution by making the NTDW accessible by both the ATC web site (to become the main portal for Australian tourism) and the Partnership Australia Domestic Limited (PADL) website (to become a main portal for Australian domestic tourism clients) and by other distributors such as inbound tour operators, wholesalers, retailers, online retailers (eg Expedia, travel.com.au etc), consumer portals (Yahoo, Excite etc) and existing GDSs.

2. Methodology

This paper aims to identify some of the possible key issues relating to the proposed development of the NTDW in Australia.

As the Partnership Australia NTDW is still in the project development stage, only little public literature and some internal documentation and preliminary reports are available. The paper takes the form of a case study based mainly on the review of these documents and contributions by one of the authors of this paper who is involved in the project on behalf of Partnership Australia.

A literature review was undertaken to examine similar developments elsewhere: in particular the case study uses earlier work by Frew and O'Connor (1999) by adopting, some of their key system attributes as a framework for analysis of the proposed NTDW project.

It is important to note that because of the project's timeframe (1999/2001 development and implementation phase, 2001/2002 operational phase) several issues are yet to be addressed or resolved. In such cases the range of options being considered are presented.

3. Current ATC and State tourism authorities' systems

In order to understand many of the issues behind the proposed NTDW project, it is important to provide an overview of some of the key characteristics of a selection of existing State and Federal DMS.

3.1 Australian Tourist Commission

The Australian Tourist Commission (ATC) currently operates a suite of tourism applications known as Marketing Information Database (MID).

3.1.1 Technical specifications

ATC uses an Oracle V8 database running on a Sun UltraSPARC hardware platform and under a Sun Solaris V2.6 operating system (Interim Technologies:1999a:31).

3.1.2 Data collection policy

Once a year the ATC mails out a questionnaire to all of its industry contacts. Operators who respond are listed in the database free of charge. There is currently no capability for direct contribution of information by the source (Interim Technologies:1999a:34).

3.1.3 Quality assurance

Operators responsible for data entry have also the responsibility to check the consistency and accuracy of the information being entered into the database (Interim Technologies:1999a:34).

3.1.4 Web publishing

Tourism products can elect to have their product represented on the ATC Website at no cost (Interim Technologies:1999a:34).

3.1.5 Booking and reservations

The ability to offer bookings services is not consistent with ATC's charter (Interim Technologies:1999a:34).

3.2 Western Australia Tourism Commission

The Western Australia Tourism Commission (WATC) operate the PowerTOUR V2 Tourism Information Data Warehouse.

3.2.1 Technical specifications

WATC uses a Sybase Adaptive Server Enterprise V11.5.1 database system running on a Sun ULTRA Enterprise 250 hardware platform and under Solaris V2.6 operating system (Interim Technologies:1999a:47).

3.2.2 Data collection policy

The WATC Electronic Distribution Unit (EDU) manages the PowerTOUR Database the team has a workforce of three people. The EDU is responsible for the collection and quality assurance of all Perth (Capital of WA) product. regional product is quality assured by the respective Regional Tourist Authorities. Importantly operators are able to perform their own data entry within the PowerTOUR Data Warehouse (Interim Technologies:1999a:53).

The WATC provides operators with a number of distribution options including representation on the Western Australia Tourism website, ATC website and in WA Travel Centre booking bureau "Travwest".

3.2.3 Quality assurance

The quality assurance process enables the EDU or the delegated Regional Tourism association to verify the consistency, accuracy and format of the data. Once the information is approved it is applied to the product database and queued for replication to the Travwest booking bureau (Interim Technologies:1999a:54).

3.2.4 Web publishing

It is the desire of the WATC to operate their website on a cost recovery basis. This involves the charging of fee for public website membership (Interim Technologies:1999a:54). At the time of writing, approximately 5% of tourism operators in WA have taken up a paid listing on the WATC Website.

3.2.5 Booking and reservations

The WATC operates a retail travel centre and plans to facilitate the online booking of product in conjunction with providers of commercial booking engines. (Interim Technologies:1999a:56).

3.3 Tourism Queensland

Tourism Queensland (TQ) operate the ATLAS2000 Reservations System as their core tourism information management system. Internally the ATLAS suite provides application areas including Tourism Product Management, Reservations, Wholesaling and End User Reporting. Externally Tourism Queensland provides a website with full booking and reservations capability (at the moment only made available to travel agents through a dedicated trade Intranet)

3.3.1 Technical specifications

TQ does not operate a consolidated central Data Warehouse. Information is managed by a variety of operational databases, which in turn are used by the relevant business units within TQ (Interim Technologies:1999a:64).

3.3.2 Data collection policy

Tourism Queensland collect their information centrally where team of consultants enter information directly into the ATLAS database. This information covers areas such as Attractions, Events, Town Information, Miscellaneous Information and Purveyors. The Purveyor Information is only entered for those purveyors who are members of the Sunlover Holiday Program, or who offer a booking commission. There is currently no capability for external parties to contribute to the data entry process (Interim Technologies:1999a:70).

3.3.3 Quality assurance

The data collection exercise has a manual system of quality assurance. Information entered into the ATLAS database must be manually reviewed by Tourism Queensland staff (Interim Technologies:1999a:70).

3.3.4 Web publishing

It is the desire of Tourism Queensland to have as much information as possible on their public Website. In order to achieve this, each informational items needs to have a "Website" created. This is a manual process in which the baseline ATLAS data is value added with additional items and texts. The value adding process takes time and resources, which means that not all items are allocated web pages (Interim Technologies:1999a:70).

358

3.3.5 Bookings and reservations

Tourism Queensland currently operate a number of retail travel centres and a wholesale division (Sunlover Holidays). Tourism Queensland are committed to operating a comprehensive electronic distribution strategy, which includes the transacting of business (Interim Technologies:1999a:71).

4. The proposed National Tourism Data Warehouse

The blueprint for the NTDW was developed through the identified need to market Australia's tourist product in a unified, consistent and customer friendly manner. The disparate nature of the State Tourism systems and their limitations in terms of state geographic boundaries are a barrier to Australia achieving its greatest potential competitive position in the online tourism environment.

The main aim of the NTDW is that of standardising the destination and product information held on the ATC and individual State databases into one common format so that all information can be housed and distributed from a central data warehouse.

The information included in the NTDW will then be distributed mainly through the ATC's and PADL's official websites, but also through other websites and CRSs. A schematic representation of the NTDW is shown in Figure 1 below.

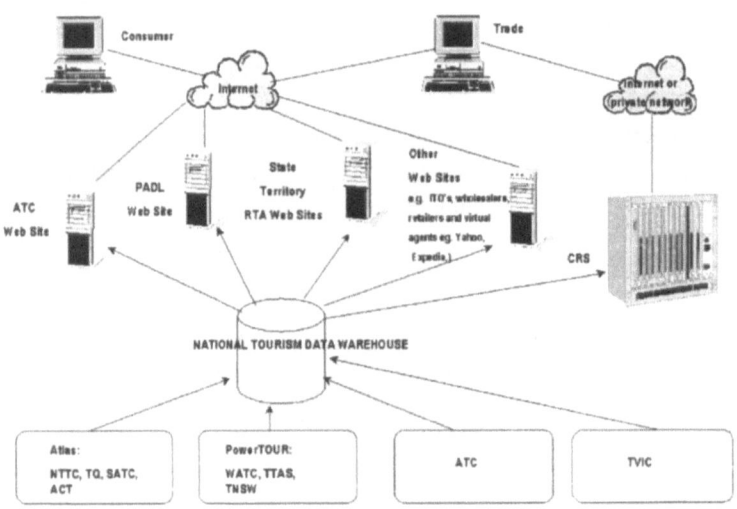

Fig. 1: NTDW infrastructure model (Partnership Australia:1999b:4)

The primary objectives of the project are to:

o establish the most comprehensive warehouse of Australian tourism information comprising extensive, consistent and current product, motivational information and images;
o enable State Tourism Organisations to easily contribute their destination and product information;
o provide a powerful searching capability across all information without the limitations of state geography;
o enable rationalised and standardised classification and categorisation of products;
o provide access to and contribution of information by authorised tourism industry trade users;
o provide for immediate and future distribution mechanisms to trade and consumers;

and in the longer term,

o provide an itinerary planner module, which can be accessed from distributors, web sites to interrogate the NTDW data and develop online itineraries;
o provide access to airline and wholesaler systems;
o upgrade/replace existing services and products such as Aussie Helplines (ATC's network of phone information for tourists).

As mentioned earlier the NTDW is in its early stages of development with a launch of the fully functional system expected by April 2001.

The following is an attempt by the authors to assess some of the key critical success factors for this project. Following Frew and O'Connor (1999b) methodology, they are grouped into three areas of interrelated issues associated with Database, Distribution and Management factors. Given the early stage of the project it was not possible to analyse any of the Operational factors considered in Frew and O'Connor's paper.

4.1 Database issues

4.1.1 Database comprehensiveness

According to most literature on the topic (Frew and O'Connor:1999a; Buhalis: 1995; Archdale et al: 1992; Sussmann and Baker:1996) one of the critical success factors for any DMS development is the level of comprehensiveness of its database of tourism products.

Whilst it is expected that the NTDW will host a higher number of products than the current ATC MID system, there are substantial differences between the states regarding the selection of which products to replicate to the NTDW. Generally the States fall in two camps, either contributing all products without restriction, or a designated subset of products determined by specific business decisions related to their distribution strategies: Tourism Queensland for example mainly list in their database products which are included in their Sunlover Holidays wholesale program, complemented by a small number of products which are commissionable. Both Tourism New South Wales and Western Australia Tourism Commission charge operators to be listed in their Websites which currently hold only 2% and 5% respectively of the total available tourist products in each state.

Partnership Australia has not yet issued a statement as to weather they are expecting to create a database of all tourism products, or weather they wish to accept a designated subset of information. The potential risk is that the NTDW could contain an uneven and far from complete product listing thus reducing the potential appeal of the system to consumers. Indeed the current estimates are that the NTDW will contain between 5,000 and 7,500 listings (not including events nor attractions) out of an estimated total population of 30,000 products nationally.

Options being considered include a limited free information listing of all State products. The commercial sustainability of the project could easily be impacted by a decision to allow free entry by industry to the NTDW, therefore encouraging 100% take up, as the present revenue model for the NTDW relies on a per product fee.

4.1.2 Product classification standards

One of the major achievements for this project so far has been the creation of a clear national standard classification scheme for tourism products particularly considering that of all the States and Territories only two were able to contribute a well documented and comprehensive classification scheme to the project (Interim Technologies: 1999a:25). Integrating information from disparate sources while classifying and standardising the product information is always a considerable challenge: while the States have expressed the desire to move towards a consistent standard, there is also the need to limit the impact on their systems, people and procedures.

The proposed system enables the warehouse to implement a standard classification scheme to which the States can move progressively. It will enable the States to retain and contribute their existing data classifications and map these to agreed national naming standards. Over time they can gradually reclassify their source information to bring it in line with the national scheme, or maintain all or part of their own schemes if preferred. The scheme enables information to be managed and distributed in a consistent manner while minimising the impact on the States' human and financial resources, information management procedures and computer systems (Interim Technology:1999b:10).

4.1.3 Quality Assurance

As outlined in section 3 of this paper, all State DMSs have already in place a series of quality assurance provisions to guarantee that the data contained in their databases is relatively accurate and up to date. There are however some differences: State Tourism Authorities which run a wholesaler program (eg Tourism Queensland and Tourism Tasmania) tend to have more detailed and frequent contact with tourism operators which in some instances provides more accurate and up to date data.

The NTDW also provides for a further level of quality control by ensuring that all data loaded from the States' DMS is double checked by its system administrator. The need for consistent data to be imported in the NTDW is also encouraging some states to improve their data collection methods and data quality: the South Australia Tourist Commission for example did not use to collect images of its tourist products but is now starting to address this shortcoming.

4.2 Distribution issues

It is envisaged at this stage that the information contained in the NTDW will be made available to a variety of distribution channels. ATC and State marketers who deal with distributors will promote the system as a benefit to those distributors. A dedicated marketing effort will also exist in the NTDW resources.

By using the ATC's Internet address *www.australia.com*, the Website, linked to the NTDW will become the major portal for Australian Tourism and as such will be featured on all ATC's international television and print advertising. In addition, it will be promoted through the ATC's Public Relations representatives to the media and trade events such as the Australian Tourism Exchange (ATE), Travel Australia Business Seminar (TABS), Internationale Tourismus Borse (ITB) and World Travel Market.

The NTDW business plan envisages distribution via third party online retailers such as Travelocity or the domestic travel.com.au and via consumer portals such as Yahoo, Altavista and Excite. The achievement of this objective seems, at least for the time being, unrealistic particularly in consideration of the relatively limited budget for the project (see section 4.3.2 below) and the extremely high costs involved to establish long term partnerships with such organisations.

Another area of concern for the project is the lack of online booking facilities. Whilst the original NTDW project brief included a booking component which was most likely to be managed by one or more private sector operators, strong opposition from some private sectors of the travel and tourism industry has meant that this component of the project has been shelved.

It is the intention of the NTDW business plan to make the comprehensive data set available to private sector businesses with online booking capabilities, therefore taking advantage of their distribution facilities and alleviating their efforts to collect the data.

It must be noted however that whilst the availability of comprehensive online information on tourism destinations and products is definitely a welcome development, consumers, are increasingly demanding a "one stop shop" solution where they can get information on and book tourism products. This facility would also make the NTDW much more marketable to third party distributors, online retailers and consumer portals for whom this level of functionality is often crucial.

4.3 Management issues

4.3.1 Management structure

Whilst the initial phases of the NTDW were conducted by a Partnership Australia steering committee made up of those officers responsible for the online marketing and distribution of State Tourism Products, the necessity to establish a specific entity to manage the finished NTDW product was made early in the project.

The NTWD will operate as a Pty. Ltd. Company. Its partners will be all the State and Territories Tourism Authorities and the Australian Tourist Commission. Direction for the company will be set by a Board of Directors which, whilst not yet finalised at the time of writing, will be most likely composed by ATC's CEO some of the State Tourism Authorities' CEOs (some of the State's legislation does not allow the CEO of partner organisations to be on the Board of Directors of a private company) and relevant industry representatives (Partnership Australia:1999c:1).

The initial NTDW steering committee will also have an ongoing role to ensure that the strategic and business objectives of partners are achieved and to act as an intermediary for escalation of issues to the Board of Directors. The Steering Committee will also ensure that modifications or enhancements to the NTDW or its associated applications are approved and that any potential impact on the State tourism authorities' systems is appropriately evaluated (Partnership Australia:1999c:3).

4.3.2 Project funding

Funding for the project has been secured for the first three years of operations through contributions from the ATC and each of the state tourism commissions for a total of approx $AUS 1.5 million per year. One mandatory requirement however is that the project must be self-sustaining by year 3 of operation. This is to ensure the ongoing effectiveness of the NTDW without having to rely on funding from partner organisations. To achieve this goal the decision has been made to sell entry into the data warehouse at an agreed national rate per product.

4.3.3 Intellectual property issues

With regards to intellectual property issues there are two areas of concern for any DMS development: a) ownership of the data in the system and b) ownership of the intellectual property of the system. With regards to ownership of the data, the approach taken by the NTDW is that ownership of the data lies with the tourism operators who provide it; the operator in effect "licenses" both the State tourism authority DMS and the NTDW to use it for the purpose of promoting the destination and the individual tourism product.

With regards to the intellectual property on the system, Partnership Australia has built into the tender process the requirement that ownership of intellectual property will rest entirely with NTDW Pty Ltd. Initial responses from tendering companies however seem to indicate that whilst they are prepared to comply with the request where a totally new system is envisaged, they are understandably not prepared to hand over intellectual ownership of existing DMS systems (or components of them) which might be part of the NTDW.

5. Conclusion

The paper has analysed many of the key critical success factors for this project. Many of the issues relate to the disparate nature of the states. The issue of systems development is made more complex in Australia by the reality that each State and Territory tourism authority has its own DMS at varying stages of technological development. Considering these circumstances this project has been so far significantly successful in terms of addressing technical issues of data classification and integration. It has also encouraged the states to work together to provide consumers with a DMS which is truly national and independent from State borders which are of little or no significance particularly for international tourists.

There are however some significant issues that are yet to be addressed or resolved. Indeed it appears that the earlier stages of this project have focused on technical issues, whilst delaying grappling with other important concerns which ultimately will determine the success of the project in the market place.

Of particular concern are the potential lack of comprehensiveness of the database, the lack of a direct booking facility and a yet relatively undefined distribution strategy.(at least with regards to third party distributors). Interestingly most of these weaknesses fall in the management/policy area rather than the technological one.

In conclusion whilst this project seems to have several key success factors in place or in the process of being effectively addressed, as Frew and O'Connor (1999a:4) also found in their analysis of DMS in Scotland and Ireland: "its biggest challenge lies in addressing the various stakeholders issues explicitly, effectively and, most importantly, in advance of implementation plans".

References

Archdale, G., Stanton, R.M., and Jones, C.B. (1992) Destination Databases: Issues and Priorities, a paper prepared for the Pacific Asia Travel Association, PATA Intelligence Centre, San Francisco, Harvard Business School Press, Boston.

Buhalis, D. (1995) Regional Integrated Computer Information Reservation Management Systems and tourism distribution channels. Schertler, W., Schmid, B., Tjoa, A., Werthner, H., (Eds), Information and Communication Technology in Tourism, ENTER '95 Springer-Verlag, Wien-New York, pp.53-64.

Frew, A.J. and O'Connor, P. (1999a) Destination Marketing Strategies in Scotland and Ireland: an Approach to Assessment, Information Technology an Tourism Vol 2, #1, pp3-13

Frew, A.J. and O'Connor, P. (1999b) Destination Marketing Refining and Extending an Assessment Framework, Buhalis, D., Schertler, W., (Eds), Information and Communication Technologies in Tourism, ENTER '99 Springer-Verlag, Wien-New York, pp.398-407.

Interim Technologies (1999a) Report #1 Summary of Australian Tourist Commission and State Tourism Organisation Databases, unpublished document prepared for Partnership Australia.

Interim Technologies (1999b) Report #2 Design Options and Impact, unpublished document prepared for Partnership Australia.

Partnership Australia (1999a) Position Paper - Partnership Australia National Data Warehouse Project, unpublished document.

Partnership Australia (1999b) Information Technologies Online Program, unpublished document

Partnership Australia (1999c) National Tourism Data Warehouse Management and Resource Plan, unpublished document.

S. Sussmann and M. Baker (1996) Responding to the electronic marketplace: Lessons from Destination Management Systems, International Journal of Hospitality Management Vol. 15, N0. 2, pp 99-112.

Supplements in Airline Cabin Service

J. König[1]and C. Strauss[2]
[1] AITC Aviation-Information-Technology-Consulting
Kaltenleutgebnerstr. 9a/2/8, A – 1230 Vienna, Austria
email: jokoe@ibm.net
[2] Department of Management Science
University of Vienna, Brünner Strasse 72, A – 1210 Vienna, Austria
email: christine.strauss@univie.ac.at

Abstract

Airlines and their services are very often part of the supply chain in tourism. Therefore, the quality of on-board service contributes to the passengers' overall satisfaction with the entire journey. Given that the cost of personnel is the second highest component of direct operational costs next to fuel, airlines are more inclined to reduce the level of their workforces rather than to invest in additional services. Our paper presents how the quality level of services can be raised by ensuring that appropriate steps are taken during the operational planning phase in which crews are assigned to certain flights. A basic crew rostering model is extended by introducing constraints that produce a schedule that raises a flight's service quality without causing additional costs. The ideas presented in this paper are also applicable to cruise lines, international hotel chains, and railway companies.

1 Introduction

Airlines are essential suppliers in the tourism sector. A tourism consumer's core activity (i.e., travelling) often starts or ends by means of a plane trip. As a result, plane travel is an important factor in determining the consumer's overall satisfaction and his view on the quality of tourism products and services. The relative importance of this consumer-based evaluation of airline services will continue to grow, as a rapidly increasing number of consumers become frequent flyers. Airlines can directly improve the quality of their services and indirectly contribute to a trip's overall quality by providing their passengers with a variety of supplementary services. Because crew costs are the second highest component of direct operational costs next to fuel, the main developments in airlines' attempts at lowering costs will have to focus on gradual reductions in personnel-intensive services and result in the introduction of additional charges (e.g., for movies, newspapers or beverages). This article will not only present several strategies by which airlines can mobilize existing capabilities and make the skills of their work forces more readily available, and it will propose three specific supplementary services that raise the level of consumers' satisfaction while not directly impacting costs. In principle, our suggestions for and ideas on airline service improvements are independent of the underlying planning tool; however, we will use a very efficient rostering algorithm - namely, SWIFTROSTER - to discuss the following enhancements. We will emphasize three beneficial service offerings: (1) language, (2) gender and special skills, and (3) the concept of downgrading. At least one of the flight attendants on each flight should speak the language of the flight's destination, so as to better service those passengers who speak only their own language. Another free supplementary service could be offered by providing mixed-sex cabin crews on flights to and from those Islamic countries in which crews consisting solely of female flight attendants are considered unacceptable due to the passengers' cultural background. A third optional measure involves the temporary downgrading of some crew members, thereby making use of the skills hierarchy for cabin crew. Temporarily downgrading crew members from a higher to a lower rank has a beneficial effect in that the service quality of a cabin crew containing one or more downgraded flight attendants is usually higher than that of a cabin crew with a conventional assignment of crew members.

The remainder of the paper is structured as follows: Section 2 describes the basic crew rostering approach. The core ideas of this paper are presented in Section 3, which demonstrates how three measures for raising the quality level of services (language, gender, downgrading) can be integrated. Exemplary numerical results are presented in Section 4, while Section 5 provides some concluding remarks.

2 The Basic Rostering Approach

All of the supplementary services described above do not require additional personnel (and, in some cases, not even any specific training for the existing work force), but rather, imply some extensions to the traditional crew rostering procedure. Widespread in Europe, "rostering" takes into account pre-assignments (e.g., observer flights and training) and crew requests (e.g., for specific flights and days off) when constructing individualized schedules for each crew member. (The other widespread approach is the "bidline" method, in which schedules are generated anonymously and employees choose their preferred schedules sequentially according to their seniority. "Preferential bidding" represents a compromise between bidline and rostering in that it generates personalized schedules that also take into account a set of bids that have been weighted to reflect the employees' preferences.) Rostering's primary goal is to provide a fair-and-even distribution of the workload among all crew members and to maximize the crew members' aggregated satisfaction with their individual schedules. An enhanced crew rostering model that exploits problem-specific knowledge provides the basis for SWIFTROSTER, a branch-and-bound-like procedure that implements an algorithm in order to efficiently generate airline crew rosters [4]. This paper discusses and formally presents those modifications that are necessary for implementing the supplementary services.

Figure 1 depicts a segment of the graphic representation of a sample roster. Each crew member has a line of work that contains several duties (called "pairings"), which are represented by a bar whose length is determined by the start and ending times, as well as by an arrow that represents minimum rest times. For example, Catherine's duties start on Monday evening with pairing 311 (together with Barbara and Dominique) and continue on with pairing 703 (together with Suzie and Natja).

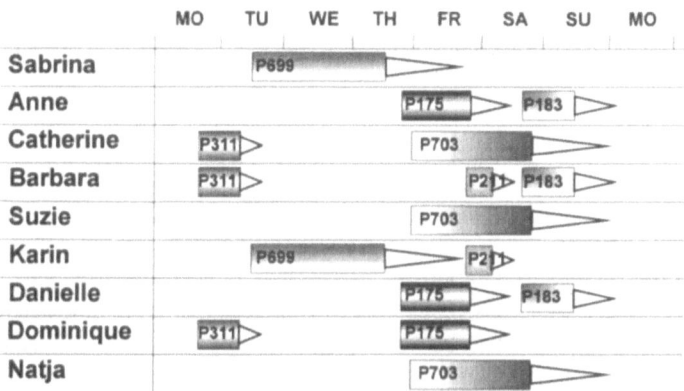

Fig. 1. A sample crew roster

To generate a roster automatically, we must map the problem into an adequate formalized model. The input data to our model is a set W containing a large number of a-priori generated valid lines of work, a set of given crew members M, and a set of given pairings P, whereas each pairing j requires a certain number d_j of crew members.

We define a line of work L as a subset of non-overlapping pairings $j \in P$, subject to constraints given by regulative requirements. Modeling the non-overlapping property, we denote P_t as the set of pairings that cover a certain time t, therefore $|P_t| \le 1$ has to hold for all t within each line of work L. Furthermore, we define $W_k \subseteq W$ as the set of all lines of work that are possible for crew member k. All W_k are disjoint, formally $W_{k1} \cup W_{k2} = \{\}$ for all $k1 \ne k2$. Moreover, we define $W_j = \{L|\, j \in L\}$ as the set of all lines of work L containing pairing j.

We introduce a binary variable $x_i \in \{0,1\}$ for each line of work in W. If the *i-th* line of work appears in the solution, then $x_i = 1$ otherwise 0. A utility value u_i can be associated with each line of work, aiming at maximizing the total utility value of the solution.

$$\max \sum_{i=1}^{n} u_i x_i \qquad (1)$$

where n is the number of lines of work in set W.

For each crew member k we have generated a set W_k of lines of work. Out of that set W_k there must be exactly one schedule assigned to each crew member k.

$$\sum_{i \in W_k} x_i = 1 \qquad\qquad k = 1, ..., m \qquad\qquad (2)$$

where m is the number of employees in set M.
The demand d_j of crew members for pairing j has to be fulfilled for every pairing.

$$\sum_{i \in W_j} x_i = d_j \qquad\qquad j = 1, ..., q \qquad\qquad (3)$$

where q is the number of pairings in set P.

Only limited work has been published so far on the topic of modeling the crew-rostering problem for airline applications [1, 2]. The need for efficient methods for generating computerized crew rosters is growing because the complexity involved in this issue is too large for it to be managed manually. Also, more efficient methods would allow airlines to apply their personnel resources closer to the regulative limits.

As this model is typically applied to large sets of data, we place our emphasis on finding a feasible solution rather than maximizing any utility function. Ryan [8], who uses a comparable model, solves this issue by applying linear programming techniques, although other approaches might prove more efficient if no objective function is maximized.

Although Gamache et al. ([5] p. 148) use a similar model, they focus on optimization by means of column generation and analyze the effects of pre-assignments using rather small problem instances involving 22 employees. Even recent approaches [6, 7] focus mainly on finding feasible solutions, while only optimizing the line of work for a single crew member. This kind of local optimization strategy must find a feasible solution at least m times (m corresponds to the number of crew members) and therefore relies heavily on a fast method for obtaining such feasible solutions, even for medium-sized problems. Other related approaches to rostering can be found for such cases as the scheduling of mass transit drivers (cf. [3, 9]). However, these models are not applicable to airline crew rostering, because airline crew rostering is more restrictive and complex and the lines of work generated must be tailored for each and every individual crew member.

3 New Concepts in the Crew Planning Process

Besides pricing strategy, the level of service is an essential factor in airlines' efforts to differentiate themselves from their competitors. Airlines try to stand out among their competitors by providing superior cabin service and by offering a product with a unique selling point (USP) – this is especially true for the business class segment, which is largely free of price competition. This marketing strategy also has a striking effect on the process of crew assignment, particularly for cabin crews.

The following chapters show how marketing decisions influence the construction of crew duty rosters, as well as how these requirements can be introduced into the mathematical crew assignment model presented above.

3.1 Language

One of the results of the boom in the tourism industry is that more people are travelling to a larger number of foreign destinations without speaking any language other than their own. At least one crew member should have a good command of a passenger's mother tongue in order to assure that monolingual passengers are also provided with optimal comfort (and security) on their journey. The polyglot nature of our global society will clearly make it impossible to always fully realize this aim. Therefore, this supplementary service should be confined to flights where communication problems arise regularly; such destinations include not only Japan (Japanese) and Africa (French), but also for example South and Central America (Spanish and Portuguese). As a consequence, at least one of the flight attendants on each flight should speak the language spoken at the flight's destination. Some steps to providing passengers with such language services can already be seen as side-effects of airline alliances. In some cases, codeshare flights have crews that have been provided jointly by the participating airlines; for example, during Austrian Airlines' cooperation with All Nippon Airways (ANA), Japanese native speakers were on board flights from and to Japanese destinations because part of the crew came from ANA. Making such an offering part of the planning process and integrating it into the rostering procedure will help to anchor this service as part of an airline's marketing policies.

However, such an approach requires long-term and short-term decisions: First, the planners must consider language knowledge in their crew capacity planning so as to ensure to have a sufficient number of crew members with the required language qualification are available. If necessary, this potential can be improved over the medium term by offering language courses; however, an adequate hiring strategy that takes language requirements into account is even more important in this context.

The short-term problem in crew planning is of greater relevance for this paper. The challenge that this problem poses lies in optimally assigning the scarce resource of qualified crew members to important flights. There are several ways for solving the language problem in crew planning. Because crew assignment is increasingly being handled by automated planning systems, the requirements must be implemented into a mathematical crew assignment model. For this reason, the basic crew assignment model introduced earlier is extended with additional constraints that ensure that the demand for foreign language-skilled crews is fulfilled, and the model is altered respectively. It may well happen that not all flights can be staffed with language-skilled crews in the event that crew resources are tight. To nevertheless obtain a crew schedule, such language restrictions are not modeled as hard rules, but rather as soft rules. The goal function is used to drive the model towards a solution that assigns the highest possible number of flights with the crews that they require.

Formally, we introduce a subset $M_l \subseteq M$ as the crew members that possess the language qualification l. Furthermore $d_{l(j)}$ denotes the number of crew members of pairing j that are required to possess language qualification g. Moreoever, for those pairings that require a crew with special language qualifications, we introduce an additional pairing constraint:

$$\sum_{\substack{i \in l_j' \\ i \in M_l}} x_i + y_{lj} \geq d_{l(j)} \qquad j = 1, ..., q \qquad (4)$$

The integer variable y_{lj} is an artificial variable used to calculate a negative penalty for unmatched language requirements in the goal function. The goal function therefore becomes:

$$\max \sum_{i=1}^{n} u_i x_i - \sum_{\forall (l.j)} v_l y_{lj} \qquad (5)$$

where v_l is the penalty for having no employee with the required language on board.

3.2 Gender and Special Skills

To emphasize the individual service characteristics of an airline, crew members are sent to training sessions and seminars aimed at providing them with additional qualifications. For example, crew members can be trained to serve as *sommeliers*, advising passengers about the high-quality wines offered on-board. If such a service should be offered on all flights, then at least one crew member with such a qualification would need to be on each and every flight. At the same time, economic reasons and/or the lacking individual prerequisites make it impossible to provide such training to all crew members. Therefore, the problem is shifted towards the crew-planning department, which must ensure that such a marketing measure can actually be realized.

Another free supplementary service could be offered on flights from and to those Islamic countries in which cabin crew consisting solely of female flight attendants are considered unacceptable due to the passengers' cultural background: these states include Saudi Arabia, Kuwait, Qatar, United Arab Emirates, Iran, Iraq, Pakistan, Algeria, and Morocco. There should be a certain ratio of male flight attendants on each flight, not least due to the fact that the flights' passengers are more likely to follow instructions given by a male flight attendant in the event of an emergency. Taking these cultural factors into account during the operational crew planning phase might ensure that at least one male crew member is on-board of all flights to the Middle East.

Both optional requirements can be implemented into the crew assignment model through additional constraints.

We introduce a subset $M_g \subseteq M$ to represent the crew-members that possess the special qualification g. Furthermore, $d_{g(j)}$ denotes the number of crew members of pairing j that are required to possess special qualification g. Additionally, for those pairings that require a special regulation we introduce an additional pairing constraint:

$$\sum_{\substack{i \in W_j \\ i \in M_g}} x_i + y_{gj} \geq d_{g(j)} \qquad j = 1, ..., q \qquad (6)$$

The integer variable y_{gj} is an artificial variable used to calculate a negative penalty for unmatched qualification requirements in the goal function. The goal function therefore becomes:

$$\max \sum_{i=1}^{n} u_i x_i - \sum_{\forall (g, j)} v_g y_{gj} \qquad (7)$$

where v_g is the penalty for having no employee with the required special regulation on board.

3.3 Downgrading

It is common practice in the airline industry that jobs on a flight are performed by crew members according to their rank in the organizational hierarchy. Generally, the purser represents the top rank among the cabin crew, while the senior flight attendant holds the second rank and the junior flight attendant represents lowest rank. Temporarily downgrading crew members from a higher rank to a lower rank has a beneficial effect in that the service quality of a cabin crew containing one or more downgraded flight attendants is usually higher than that of a cabin crew with a conventional assignment of crew members. Additional benefits of the downgrading concept include the higher likelihood of finding feasible solutions for tight scheduling problems and the stabilization of the level of employment over time.

In his paper on crew rostering, Ryan states that the "full Rostering problem can usually be broken into smaller independent subproblems corresponding to groups of crew members of same rank" ([8] p. 460). In principle, this statement is correct: the crew assignment problem can be divided into subproblems according to the categories, and the subproblems can then be solved within these strictly separated categories. However, Ryan's suggested approach is not always applicable to real world problems and can actually reduce the likelihood of finding any feasible solution.

In the following subsection, we will introduce a new approach for handling tight problems by means of temporarily downgrading crew members from a higher rank to a lower rank in one step. As a positive side effect, this approach also helps to stabilize the level of employment over time.

Consider the case of an airline that has an abundance of senior flight attendants, but suffers from a shortage of junior flight attendants. Due to the shortage of lower-ranking employees, a feasible solution for this situation might not be found if conventional models (i.e., those without downgrading) are applied. Only the option of downgrading permits a temporary levelling among adjacent ranks and can possibly lead to a solution. This downgrading-based levelling of human resources makes an essential contribution to the concept of a fair and even workload distribution. A numerical example for such a situation is presented in Section 4.

We introduce two new sets to account for downgrading in certain pairings: let $W_{jH}^P \subseteq W_j^P$ denote the set of lines of work for pairing j for employees with higher rank and $W_{jL}^P \subseteq W_j^P$ the set for employees with lower rank; both sets are disjoint $W_{jH}^P \cap W_{jL}^P = \{ \}$. As a consequence d_{jH} is the demand that pairing j creates for higher-ranked employees and d_{jL} is that for lower-ranked employees.

Without restriction to generality, we now replace restriction (3) with two new restrictions (8) and (9), which are:

$$\sum_{i \in W_{jH}^{P}} x_i \geq d_{jH} \qquad\qquad j = 1, ..., q \qquad\qquad (8)$$

$$\sum_{i \in W_{jH}^{P}} x_i + \sum_{i \in W_{jL}^{P}} x_i = d_{jH} + d_{jL} \quad j = 1, ..., q \qquad\qquad (9)$$

Constraint (8) allows overcoverage of higher-ranked employees, whereas (9) ensures that the total demand is covered exactly. In the event that downgrading is regarded as undesirable and is consequently desired to remain low, a penalty can be applied to downgrading by assigning a negative objective value to the slack variable of restriction (8). Generalizing the above for r ranks, one can observe that the set of constraints generally becomes more complicated if downgrading is allowed.

4 Results

The application of the extended model to a numerical example is provided to substantiate the utility of the downgrading concept. Using an adapted version of the SWIFTROSTER algorithm and real data from a medium-sized European airline, we present numerical results in Table 1.

Table 1. An example of downgrading

	# crew	# pairings	# LoWs	CPU-time	solution
higher ranked	25	280	25,000	1.22	found
lower ranked	30	280	30,000	n/a	not found
high & low	55	280	55,000	5.18	found

Table 1 provides an example with 55 crew members, of which 25 are high-ranked and 30 members are lower-ranked. These crew members have to perform 280 pairings, each requiring one higher- and one lower-ranked crew member. Without downgrading, no solution can be found for the lower rank subproblem, whereas the higher rank problem can be solved easily. Introducing the downgrading concept and concatenating these two problems into one extends the problem to 55,000 columns (lines of work) and 560 rows for the pairing constraints and another 55 rows for crew constraints. We can now find a solution within a few seconds: the solution generated contains 65 pairings in which someone is downgraded to a lower position. This value can be used to quantify the increase of the service quality level provided to passengers.

5 Conclusions

The product "flight" is an important item in the supply chain of tourism. Although the general development in the airline business suggests a reduction of free on-board services, this article demonstrates that there are "hidden" potentials for service quality improvements. Services such as providing at least one flight attendant speaking the language of the origin and/or destination of the flight leg, or having one or several male attendants on board of airplanes flying to/from the Middle East are explicit services which will raise the consumers content. In contrast, downgrading is an implicit measure which cannot be directly observed by the passenger, but which nevertheless provides another means of improving the quality of service. The ideas presented in this paper are also applicable to cruise lines, international hotel chains, and railway companies.

References

1. Barnhart, C., Talluri, K.T.: Airlines Operations Research. In: McGarity, A., Revelle, C. (eds.): Design and Operation of Civil and Environmental Engineering Systems. Wiley, New York, pp. 435-469 (1997).
2. Barnhart, C., Johnson, E.L., Nemhauser, G.L., Vance, P.H.: Airline Crew Scheduling. In: Hall, R.W. (ed.): Handbook of Transportation. Kluwer, Boston, to appear.
3. Bianco, L., Bielli, M., Mingozzi, A., Ricciardelli, S., Spadoni, M. A heuristic procedure for the crew rostering problem. European Journal of Operational Research 58:272-283 (1992).

4. Dawid, H., Koenig, J., Strauss, C. An Enhanced Rostering Model for Airline Crews. POM-Working Paper 2-99, University of Vienna (1999).

5. Gamache, M., Soumis, F. A method for optimally solving the rostering problem. In: Yu, G. (ed): Operations Research in the Airline Industry, Kluwer, Boston, pp. 124-157 (1998).

6. Gamache, M., Soumis, F., Villeneuve, D. The Preferential Bidding System at Air Canada. Transportation Science 32:246-255 (1998).

7. Gamache, M., Soumis, F., Marquis, G., Desrosiers, J. A column generation approach for large-scale aircrew rostering problems. Operations Research 47:247-263 (1999).

8. Ryan, D.M. The Solution of Massive Generalized Set Partitioning Problems in Aircrew Rostering. Journal of the Operational Research Society 43:459-467 (1992).

9. Wren, A. Scheduling, Timetabling and Rostering – A Special Relationship? In: Goos, G., Hartmanis, J., van Leeuven, J. (eds.): Practice and Theory of Automated Timetabling. Springer, Berlin, pp. 46-75 (1996).

Involving The DMO's In A Larger Part Of
The Value Chain

Michael Borge
Managing Director
Tellus IT-solutions AS, Norway
michael@tellus.no, http://www.tellus.no

"As we move into the Information Age, consumers' expectations are being radically altered. The Internet, more than any other technology, is teaching people that they can go online and quickly find out about any subject that is currently holding their interest. Not only can they obtain a substantial depth of information, they can do this instantaneously. Consumers in the Information Age are no longer satisfied with requesting information and then awaiting its arrival. They are expecting instant information gratification." (WTO, Marketing Tourism Destinations Online - Strategies for the Information Age, 1999, pp3).

Who will be the content provider in the Information Age as described above?

1. Introduction

There is a great paradox in the international tourism industry today: When you and I decide to visit a certain destination, it is 9 times out of 10 due to the marketing efforts of the DMOs. Despite this fact, it is the accommodation-, transport- and car rental companies together with the CRS' and the travel agencies that pocket most of the profit. See Fig. 1.

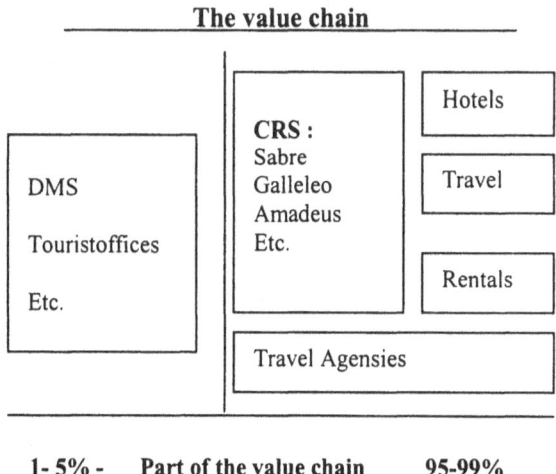

Fig 1. The Value Chain

How can the DMO's take a larger part of this value chain? Many resourceful people in the tourist industry is convinced that the DMO's must become professional content providers in order to survive, and make their profit in the realm between the product owners and the international distributors (internet and wap portals).

If the DMO's do not become a content provider, others will take over this task and thus leaving the destination without a purpose!

2. DMO's as professional content providers in the national tourist portal in Norway.

2.1 Norwegian Tourist Board (NT):

NT has a national portal for toursim in Norway. One of the most important elements on this web site is a searchable database. One should be able to search for hotels, activities, attractions, events, and other products. One should also be able to search for å specific product i.e. a specific hotel or a specific place i.e. Oslo or one should be able to search geographically by clicking an interactive map and then search the database for that specific region. Such a database should contain large quantities of information and should be of high quality. Most important of all, the information should be updated on a regular basis. This is a problem known to many, but few has found a solution

2.2 How to keep the information current

There are basically three ways to address this problem.

1. The product owners update their own information through a web interface. There are two major problems attached to this alternative. **First**, there are many interesting travel products that are not on the Internet such as small one man businesses like fishing boats, canoe rentals, bike hire, guest harbours, etc. In addition, non-profit organisations that offer products like hiking trips, churches, parks and other places of interest are examples of products that would not be included in such a system. **Second**, commercial companies as hotel chains, will not take the time to update such a system through a web interface before this channel generate enough business. This alternative is therefore not viable.

2. A central organisation updates the database. There is evidence that one organisation on a national level would not be able to keep the amount of information required in a tourist database current on a day to day basis. Telenor, Norway's largest telephone company has more than 6.000 corrections in their database each day. The corrections include only phone numbers, fax numbers, company names and personal names and addresses. A tourist database must also include information such as opening hours, prices, events, and seasonal changes

to mention a few. Keeping these elements current alone will dwarf the amount of corrections that is being done today by Telenor. Thus, an organisation such as Norwegian Tourist Board will not be able to perform this task successfully.

3. Destinations and tourist offices update their local information. The local information is aggregated to a national level. The advantages with such a system are that the DMO's are much closer to the travel products and are thus better qualified for updating them. In addition, they perform this task anyway with regards to their brochures and Internet presentations. However, there is a problem with this alternative as well. The DMO's do not have the resources or the technical ability to supply NT with the information they want. In Norway, as in most other countries, the DMO's are often under-staffed and under-funded. They have an array of different tasks to solve on a day-to-day basis. In addition to administrative tasks, these tasks include; production of brochures; handling ad-hoc questions by phone or at the tourist information centers; gathering, registration, updating, quality controlling and distributing information, updating their web site, etc.

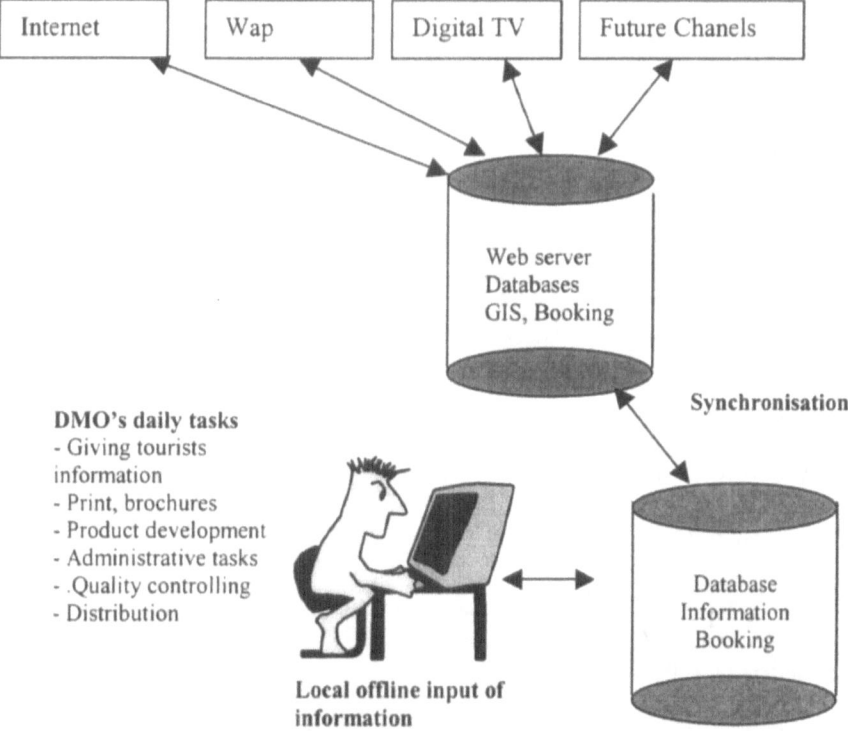

Fig. 2. DMO Inquiry

2.3 Conclusion

If a national web site with a searchable and updated database is to be updated by the local DMO's, they would need to have a system that make them more efficient in their day to day work and simultaneously supplied the national database with the information required. In other words, what was needed was a system that killed two birds with one stone.

3. The solution

Since the heart of the problem is making the DMO's more efficient, the solution must include a system tailor made for the DMO's needs. These needs include:
- An efficient system for handling large quantities of information and of many different types.
- An effective way of updating and quality controlling the information.
- An effective system for producing brochures and printed matters
- Efficient distribution to:
- Internet
- Local web site.
- Themed based web sites such as golf, fishing, etc.
- Regional or national web sites.
- WAP, smartphone, palm tops.
- Digital TV, etc.
- It is important that the chosen platform easily can adapt to new media such as WAP represents today.
- It is also important that information should be recorded only once, but utilised in many ways. The database must therefore be thoroughly structured.

The system should facilitate reduction in operating costs for the DMO's. Reduction in producing brochures, internetpages and the manpower needed are examples.

The system should also improve the DMO's income. By implementing such a system, the DMO's will be able to have the best information and a good distribution and at the same time keeping the cost down. This will position the DMO as a professional content provider and thus enabling them to charge for this service.

Tellus has developed a destination management system that includes the above mentioned needs and thus supplies Norwegian Tourist Board with a national database that are updated locally by the DMO's.

4. The future is here now – WAP, GIS, Online Booking

The Destination Management System, must include gateways to booking, e-commerce, GIS (geographical information system) and WAP. In addition we are enabling the system to incorporate standards of information exchange and standards in categorising tourist information in Europe.

The destination management system should be able to distribute information to digital tv, WAP in addition to internet, brochures and other printed matters. Also, the system must be able to deliver data on the format required by these media. This includes exchanging information on any standard i.e. XML that looks like a standard that will become universally accepted.

Navigation and searching a database must constantly be improved. We believe that dynamic and intelligent maps are important to achieve easy search and presentation of information. TellMap (Tellus IT-solution's Map Information System) is an R&D-project, financed by the Research Council of Norway, and will last for 2 years, from mid 1999 to mid 2001. TellMap ties all available travel information in the Tellus database to electronic maps. Based on state of the art technology, we are further developing intelligent maps as a tool for printed and electronic media.

As many products as possible must be done bookable through the Internet and WAP. The system must be open and adaptable to different local, regional, national and international booking systems. This can be achieved by using a standardised exchange format, which the different booking systems can relate to. Tellus has an open interface and can thus utilise such channels.

In order to achieve our goals Tellus has establish partnership with IT companies and organisations that excel in fields as e-commerce, GIS and information exchange

5. Conclusion

If the DMO's do not become a content provider, others will take over this task and thus leaving the destination without a job to do!

Since the heart of the problem is making the DMO's more efficient, the solution must include a system tailor made for the DMO's needs.

The system should also improve the DMO's income. By implementing such a system, the DMO's will be able to have the best information and a very good distribution and at the same time keeping the cost down. This will position the DMO as a professional content provider and thus enabling them to charge for this service.

Garry McGovern from "Local Ireland" has published the statement:

"The information value formula = Content – Structure – Publication."
- Content must be excellent and up to date.
- The information must be thoroughly structured.

- The information must be published in the right channels.

Full utilisation of a destination management system as described in this paper will enable the DMO's to position themselves as professional content providers, reducing their operating costs and improve their income.

A Typology of Tourism Related Web Sites: Its Theoretical Background and Implications

Bing Pan and Daniel R. Fesenmaier
National Laboratory for Tourism and eCommerce
University of Illinois at Urbana-Champaign, USA
bingpan@uiuc.edu, drfez@uiuc.edu

Abstract

The application of thriving information technology, especially the World Wide Web, is changing our way of life and doing business. In the tourism area, a well-defined typology is necessary to facilitate the information search process and therefore provide guidance to the building of web sites. A typology of tourism-related web sites should be based on both the analysis of the nature of information provided by web sites and the channels of information flows the web sites created. The implications of this typology for website design is discussed as well.

1 Introduction

Undoubtedly, we are witnessing an information revolution in which the information technology, especially the Internet, *has* changed and continues to change our way of life. According to Forrester Research, 17 million US households were shopping online during 1999, and by 2004, the retail sales will reach $184 billion [1]; compared with other industries, travel related transactions have become the number one in terms of sales [2]. This implies that the web as a communication channel has been become an important part of our daily life. Also, more and more researchers are using the Internet as a source for information and a way to communicate among each other.

The extraordinary effects of the Internet rely on the power of its networking. In the business area, information technology, especially the development of electronic commerce, has changed the paradigm of doing business from the one-to-many communication process of traditional mass media (e.g., newspaper) into a many-to-many communication model. Because of the interaction and navigation capabilities hypertext can provide, the Internet is not only a medium for t he market, but also a market by itself [3, 4]. Tourism, as an "extremely information-intensive" industry [5], has been greatly affected and mostly benefited by this information revolution.

The web interface has a very important role in this arena. Since there is a trend toward integration of technologies (for example, newsgroups, email and ftp all can be implemented through web browser in this virtual market of Internet [6], web sites are gaining more and more popularity and weight in the business world. As the single identity in the computer-mediated environment, web sites will be the most important and probably the only one communication channel between corporations and their customers. Thus, the importance of domain names cannot be overemphasized (a company just bought the domain name business.com with $7.5 million USD, New York Times, 1999).

Most major tourism organizations have already gained Internet-presence, including commercial organizations (destination web sites, airline companies, hotels and restaurants, cruise, travel agencies, newly emerged virtual online portals) and non-commercial organizations (like researching organizations TTRA, IFFIT and industrial organization like Cruise & Freighter Travel Association and American Society of Travel Agents). These web sites provide the potential traveler with relevant information or offer tourism professionals and researchers with tourism related information. Some web sites also provide real-time electronic transactions.

Behind this optimistic view of the use of web sites in tourism area, there are still many problems need to be clarified, including:

Poor Usability

According to J. Nielsen [7], about 90% of commercial websites have poor usability. In tourism, lots of people get easily frustrated when trying to book online, even including those CEOs of online travel portal companies [8]. One reason for it is that the virtual market of Internet can be seen as mostly technology-driven and the research of electronic commerce and Internet can hardly keep up with the development of new technology. Sometimes research published one or two year ago has already been outdated. On the other hand, the design of web sites needs multi-disciplinary research in a number of areas including psychology, advertising, marketing, computer science and others. Especially in tourism area, the information needs and the process of information search by travelers are even more complex.

Overwhelming Quantity of Tourism Related Web Sites

A search of Yahoo! using the keyword "travel" yields 285 categories and about 17,000 web sites (accessed Nov 11, 1999). The extreme variability and complexity of tourism related web sites causes confusion not only for customers but also for tourism professionals and researchers. The phenomenal number of tourism related web sites provide overwhelming information with lots of redundancy.

From the above analysis, we can see the importance of a typology of tourism related web sites. According to the Merriam-Webster Dictionary, typology is the "study of or analysis or classification based on types or categories". The building of a typology can be seen as the examination of the hidden structure in accordance with certain attribute of the interested objects. From the view of information inundation in cyberspace, a typology or taxonomy can reveal the structure of online tourism and travel related community and facilitate the use of web regarding either customers' or tourism professionals' information searching process. More importantly, a typology of travel and tourism related web sites can illustrate the difference between them and establish a basis for guiding the design and maintenance of different web sites.

In order to build a typology for tourism related web sites, this paper begins with a review of existing perspectives on the structure and characteristics of cyberspace. The investigation of the nature of web sites using an information exchange perspective is then conducted. Last, a typology of tourism related web sites is proposed.

2 Literature Review

It's not a surprise that the Internet and the World Wide Web has attracted lots of attention from various research areas. A number of studies have been conducted regarding the functions, characteristics, structure and uses of the Internet and the web in different fields. The following provides a brief review of the major ideas on this topic.

2.1 Definition of Web Sites

In order to establish a typology of travel and tourism related web sites, a clear definition of the concept of web sites is necessary. Unfortunately, many terms related with the Internet, including the definition of web sites, are ambiguous and ill - defined. In an attempt to clarify the terminology, O'Niell and Lavoie defined web site as "a cluster of pages" which is composed of "a unique node on the web" and always associated with one domain name. Web site can be seen as an information concept instead of physical and tangible entity, since one logical web site can have multiple mirrored sites. Most of the time, the logical web site is the main interest when analyzing the content of web sites [9]. The URL is the global address of documents and other resources on the World Wide Web [10], which is the most important access information for an organization in the virtual market place.

2.2 Existing Web Typologies

The typology or taxonomy of web sites depends on one's view of the whole cyberspace. From the date of birth of the Internet, cyberspace has been viewed as an advertising media, a marketing tool, a mass communication channel [11], and recently as a computer-mediated environment (CME) [4]. The WWW, as "the first and current networked global implementation [4], is becoming more and more ubiquitously used for travel planning and purchasing of travel-related products. Numerous researches have tried to categorize different web sites from a variety of perspectives. The following are some major concepts and models (see Table 1).

Table 1 Existing web typologies

Name	Users or Authors	Classification Scheme	Limitations
Technical Classification	O'Neill and Lavoie (1998)	Classify web sites according to their accessibility	Content is not addressed.
Dewey Decimal Classification system	Yahoo! and other online portals	Hierarchical structure, mostly used in library material classification	Multi-faceted, cannot be easily applied to large quantity of web sites
North American Industrial Classification System	O'Neill and Lavoie (1998)	Economic activity of a web site is the only criteria.	Excluding those sites including more than one industrial area and those non-commercial web sites
Functional Classification	Hoger, Cappel and Myerscough (1998)	Classify corporate uses of web sites according to their functions in the corporate operation	Excluding those non-commercial web sites
Value Chain	Ho (1997)	Classify the different values created on the web sites	Targeting at commercial web sites

2.2.1 Technical Classification

O'Neill and Lavoie discussed three types of web sites from a technological perspective [9]:

1. Public web sites: Those web sites have at least one portion of the web site open to the public;
2. Private web sites: Those web sites intend to be accessed by specific customers or only homepage can be accessed by the public, and prohibit other parts of web sites unless password or IP address is recognized;
3. Provisional sites: Those web sites serve meaningless content, such as: server-templates, web page re-directing or under construction and not ready for access.

2.2.2 Dewey Decimal Classification System and Industrial System

The Dewey Decimal Classification system (DDC) conceived by Melvil Dewey in 1873 is "a general knowledge organization tool that is continuously revised to keep pace with knowledge", which is the most widely used library classification system in the world [12]. The DCC system follows a hierarchical structure in which the world of knowledge is divided into ten main classes where each class is divided into ten divisions and in turn, each division is divided into ten sections. Many online portals follow a similar structure as the DCC system. Take Yahoo! as an example, its highest level includes 14 broad areas which is similar to DCC system (Table 2). Another important characteristic of Yahoo! is that one entry (web site) can appear in more than one directory, which is also similar to the DCC system.

O'Niell suggested that just because of the "multi-faceted" characteristics of the DCC system, it cannot be easily applied to the largest proportion of public web sites. Instead, he proposed to use the North American Industrial Classification System as a taxonomy of web sites; it is "single-faceted" and the economic activity of a web site is the only criteria for classification [9].

Table 2. Highest level of Yahoo! classification system

| Arts & Humanities |
| Business & Economy |
| Computers & Internet |
| Education |
| Entertainment |
| Government |
| Health |
| News & Media |
| Recreation & Sports |
| Reference |
| Regional |
| Science |
| Social Science |
| Society & Culture |

2.2.3 Functional Classification

Hoger and his colleagues [13] discussed a typology of corporate uses of web sites. He pointed out that corporations may use webs for promotion, advertising and communication tools. Five categories of corporate use of web sites were identified:

1. Promoting awareness;

2. Providing customer support;
3. Selling products or service;
4. Selling advertising space on web sites;
5. Offering electronic information services.

2.2.4 Value Chain

Another schema uses value chain analysis to evaluate web sites [14]. Ho argued that since technical issues regarding bandwidth and security can be resolved eventually along with the technological development, the more important question to ask is what "value" can be created on the web. Based on his evaluation of 1000 commercial web sites, he classified commercial web sites into three categories:

      I.   Promotion of product and services;
      II.   Provision of data and information;
      III.   Processing of business transactions.

Four types of value creation are identified: 1. Timely; 2. Custom; 3.Logical; 4. Sensational. Based on this analysis, Ho built a framework in the form of a three by four matrix (Table 3):

Table 3. Value matrix (Ho, 1998)

Value\Purpose	Promotion	Provision	Processing
Timely			
Custom			
Logistic			
Sensational			

2.3 Limitations of Above Frameworks

The frameworks discussed above provide different perspectives on cyberspace. However, the limitations in these views cannot be ignored. The technical classification of public, private and provisional web sites clarified the technological aspect of web sites in terms of accessibility. Nevertheless, it does not differentiate web sites according to their contents; thus, it does not provide insights into strategies for the design and management of web sites. Classifying web sites through their economic activities basically exclude the web sites that are either too comprehensive to summarize using one or two economic activities or non-commercial web sites which intend to provide free online communities. The frameworks focusing on functionality of web sites and particularly on the commercial use of web sites also ignore the fact that the WWW is more than a virtual market that provides product information and electronic exchange functions. It also offers the ability to create a virtual community, a "global village" whereby we as villagers can share our experiences, emotions and thoughts.

3 A Typology For Tourism Related Web Sites

3.1 Broad View of Web Sites from Information Perspective

Beyond the view of merely comparing the functions and the usage in a marketing environment, web sites can be seen as a tool for the exchange of information. Therefore, a typology should be based on the analysis of the nature of information and information exchange. According to Shannon [15] information is something that reduces uncertainty. Wiio [16] argued that this definition can be hardly applied to human interaction and human-computer interaction, since the meaning of *uncertainty* varies drastically across different individuals and contexts (for example, the information about a certain car model can only reduce uncertainty to a specific buyer in a specific context), and its use is mainly in electronic communication. Either in psychology or in information science, information is understood more as information *per se*. In psychology, information is "anything that produces changes in consciousness" of the human being [17]. In information science, Saracevic differentiates three levels of information: information as messages, information as cognitively processed and information as being in a context (situation, task, and the like) [18]. Using the third level of the concept of information, different web sites can be seen as different *channels* to facilitate the exchange of information among different users. In other words, web sites should be analyzed through the interaction between the user and the web; more specifically, between the information users and the information itself the site intends to provide. The proposed typology is based on the analysis of the information flows between information users and the information richness of tourism related web sites.

3.2 Analysis of the Typology

In order to define a typology of tourism related web sites, we need to first inspect both the information flow of these web sites and the attributes of information these travel related web sites contain.

3.2.1 Analysis of Information Flows

Information Flows in Tourism

The scope of the concept *"tourism"* has been greatly extended in the cyberspace. Since cyberspace includes every aspect of our life, it breaks the barriers between different disciplines when we use the term *tourism*. For example, in ordinary life, when we are trying to find the web site for a specific destination, we call it tourism web site. When we try to find tourism statistics for a place (i.e., city, state etc.) in United States, we still refer it as tourism web site. All these web sites are also categorized as tourism web sites in most online portals. Therefore, the term *"tourism"* in cyberspace is more than an industry or a research area; it has been referred to every aspect related to tourism. Using this broad sense of tourism, all information users related to tourism area can be divided into three groups: travelers, tourism industry professionals and tourism researchers. Travelers are the central character of the whole arena; tourism professionals serve travelers at the frontline; tourism researchers study the relationship, activities of travelers and tourism professionals. A basic typology of the information flow between these groups of travel-related information in computer-mediated environment can be illustrated as follows (Fig. 1).

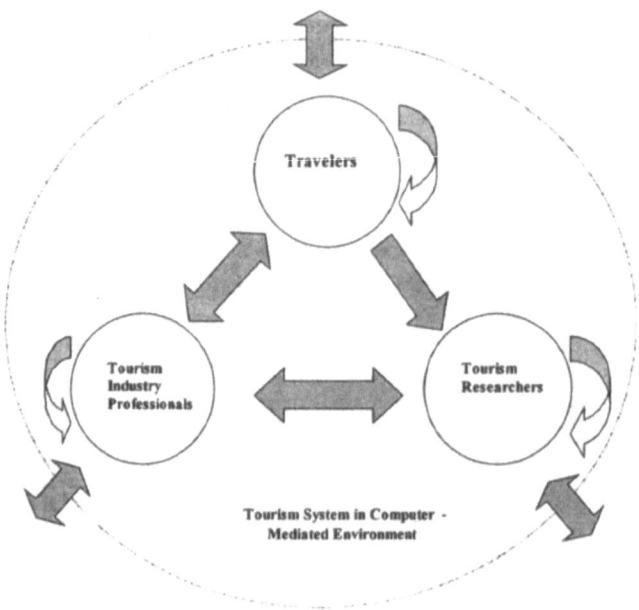

Fig. 1. Information Flow of Tourism in computer-mediated environment

In the tourism system in the computer-mediated environment, information flows occur: (1) between the three parts in tourism system; and, (2) between one of these three parts and the outside of the tourism system. Tourism related web sites can be seen as those sites designed for facilitating the information flow inside the tourism system, since the information flows link outside parts with inside parts are too general to define as tourism web sites (for example, those industry web sites which provide hotel equipment can hardly be defined as tourism related web sites).

An analysis of information users combined with a common sense of the words *travel* and *tourism* web sites can be categorized into travel web sites and tourism web sites.

Travel Web Sites

Travel web sites focus on travelers as their target audience, and their main objective is to satisfy the information needs of travelers. Corporations, non-profit organizations, and personal web sites that provide information and electronic transactions or facilitate communication and information exchange among travelers can be categorized into travel web sites.

Tourism Web Sites

Tourism web sites have the tourism professionals or tourism researchers as their target audience. These web sites include tourism organizations that aim at facilitating communication and information exchange between or within tourism professionals and tourism researchers (Table 4).

Table 4. Classification of Travel and Tourism Web Sites According to Information Uses

	Information Flow	Explanation	Web Site Examples
Travel Web Sites	Traveler -- traveler	Facilitate information exchange between travelers	Online traveler communities: www.lonelyplanet.com
	Traveler -- professional	Facilitate information exchange between travelers and different tourism professionals	Provide online information to travelers: www.enjoyillinois.com
Tourism Web Sites	Professional -- professional	Business to business communication, web sites of tourism professional associations	International Association of Convention & Visitor Bureaus: www.iacvb.org4
	Professional -- researcher	Web sites to enhance communication between professionals and researchers (e.g., online - consulting and knowledge base)	National Laboratory for Tourism and eCommerce: www.tourism.uiuc.edu
	Researcher -- researcher	Communication between researchers	Tourism Research Webring: www.waksberg.com/webring/
	Traveler -- researcher	Online traveler survey to gather information from travelers	NYC 20000 Traveler Survey: nyctourist.com/survey_recent4.htm

Different Information Flows

Traveler – traveler: The web sites used among the travelers for the exchange of personalized, non-commercial information can be fit in this type.

Traveler - professionals: These web sites are created by tourism industries to facilitate the information flow between travelers and tourism industry professionals in order to satisfy the information needs of travelers.

Professional – professional: These web sites focus on communication and business information exchange between partners in tourism industry.

Professional – researcher: These web sites are used by researchers to provide tourism industry professionals with industrial knowledge and consulting services, and also by professionals to provide sufficient and real-life research topics for the tourism researchers.

Researcher- researcher: Web sites devoted to researchers' based communities focus on the exchange of ideas and academic materials between researchers.

Researcher – travelers: This relationship is not so common and usually is uni-directional. Researchers may use online tools to investigate the traveler's behavior. Using fill-out forms, the method of online survey has been relatively widely used.

3.2.2 Analysis of Information Richness

Information Richness

Evans and Wurther [19] used the concept of richness (this concept was firstly devised by Daft and Lengel [20]) and reach to describe the effects of information exchange in the cyberspace. Information richness refers to the "quality of information" in the view of the users: accuracy, bandwidth, currency, customization, interactivity, relevance, security and others. Reach means the number of the audience who can exchange information. Actually, the analysis of information users and different information flows discussed previously can be seen as a classification scheme of information reach. The concept of information richness can be used to describe the nature of information and taken as another decisive factor for the typology of tourism related web sites, since tourism web sites vary tremendously regarding their information richness, and accordingly the design and use of these web sites differ significantly.

Research done by Palmer and Griffith [18] supports this perspective concerning the information intensity-richness, even though their definition of information intensity is slightly different. Since the web site is used for the exchange of information, the concept of "information intensity" can be used to analyze and understand the difference between web sites and to guide the design of web sites. According to Porter and Millar [19], information intensity refers to "the proportion of an organization's market offering and/or value chain that is information-based". Different companies with different information intensity should use different marketing and communication strategies. For example, information intensified companies should increase their competitiveness by providing product online or offering online product-related information. Information intensity-richness theory has surpassed the view of insignificant functional difference between web sites and provides an in-depth perspective in viewing a variety of web sites. Thus, tourism related web sites can be categorized into three levels of information richness: low richness, moderate richness and high richness (Table 5).

Table 5. Levels of Information Richness in Tourism System

Levels	Characteristics of Information	Web Site Examples
High Richness	Customization, High bandwidth, Currency, Interactivity, Security transaction	www.expedia.com
Moderate Richness	Moderate bandwidth, Interactivity, Updated periodically	www.enjoyillinois.com
Low Richness	Static web pages with low bandwidth	www.cupartnership.org/cvb/main.htm

Different Information Richness

Low Richness: Provides static web pages, has a lot of links to other pages and may have fill-out forms for suggestions and comments.
Moderate Richness: Provides some degree of interactivity like basic search engines for this web site and the content of its web pages may be updated periodically.
High Richness: These web sites can provide web user with customized, up-to-date, interactive information and real-time, secure electronic transactions.

Discussions on the Determinants of Information Richness

Different features of web sites may determine the information richness of a web site. For tourism related web sites, two important attributes are prominent: the operation scope and different types of information it may provide. For example, www.enjoyillinois.cm provide statewide traveler information (operation scope) and it can provide information on accommodations, attractions, and transportation (types of information). Naturally we can hypothesize that the scope of operation and types of information may determine the information richness of a web site, since the more types of information it can provide and the more broad the operational level (it lead to more users of information, in other word, wider reach), the more information it needs to provide and the more customization the information needs to be, since it will have large quantity and more diversified audience.

3.2.3 The Typology based on Information Flows and Information Richness

Based on the above analysis about information users and the essence of information itself, a basic typology can be proposed (Table 6). There are 18 types in which tourism related web sites can be categorized using the nature of information flows and levels of information richness. For example, www.expedia.com facilitates information flow between travelers and tourism industry professionals, and because of the customized, secure, current, and high bandwidth information it provides, it can be categorized into traveler-professional type with a high level of information richness. On the other hand, the web site of National Laboratory for Tourism and eCommerce in Univesity of Illnois at Urbana-Champaign (www.tourism.uiuc.edu) intends to serve professionals with tourism information for the State of Illinois and other consulting service. This type of web page can be described as researcher-professional with a low level of information richness.

Table 6. Typology Based on Information Flows and Information Richness

		Information Richness		
		Low Richness	Moderate Richness	High Richness
Information Flows	Traveler – traveler			
	Traveler – professional			
	Professional – professional			
	Professional – researcher			
	Researcher – researcher			
	Traveler – researcher			

One phenomenon is that not all these 18 types of tourism related web sites do not have the same quantity of web sites. For example, most travel web sites tend to have middle or high level of information richness (like most online travel portals and online traveler communities like www.lonlyplanet.com), while tourism web sites tend to have low to middle level of information richness (most tourism professional organizations like www.ttra.com and most research institutions). One possible reason for that may be an implicit lack of awareness of the value of tourism related information for researchers and business-to-business information exchange.

3.2.4 Design Implications for the Typology

Different types of web sites should use different design strategies, since different types of web sites has different information user groups, who have different information needs and at the same time the contents of different web sites differ greatly in terms of information richness.

From the Perceptive of Information Flows

Traveler - traveler: Because of its commercial-free attribute, these web sites should focus on how to facilitate the sharing of experience among travelers. Accordingly, suitable tools for this purpose include bulletin board, e-mail list and other tools that are focusing on the sharing of personal experience.

Traveler – professional: The function of real-time transaction should be provided in order to let the tourists to book online. In order to attract more tourists, experiential aspect of web site should be emphasized. It means all kind of image and interactive tools can be used, such as, Java applet, Shockwave, and 3D imaging tools.

Professional-professional: Real-time and secure information exchange is needed. Accordingly, Electronic Data Interchange (EDI) is indispensable.

Professional - researcher: These sites should focus on the organization and representation of knowledge. Different tools should be provided to facilitate the knowledge search and representation, like search engine, text mining and others.

Researcher - researcher: Time issue is not so important as in professional-professional relation, nor is the experiential aspect compared with traveler-professional relationship. Instead, research tools include links to online references, libraries and search engines.

Traveler - researcher: Implicit methods of investigating web users' information search behavior, like Java applet and cookies, have started to be employed in those traveler-researcher web sites. Along with the demographic data and travel preference from traditional survey methods, valuable information about travelers' information search behavior can be obtained. However, since this is a new area for online research, many issues like privacy should be taken into account and need to be studied.

From the Perceptive of Information Richness

The design of the <u>low information richness</u> web sites should focus on its idiosyncratic style to attract more web visitors; the focus of the design of <u>moderate information richness</u> web sites should be on the concise, easy-to-navigate, and elegant layout and structure; for those <u>high information richness</u> web sites, the designing should focus on how to allow the visitor access and exchange the relevant information at the shortest time instead of confusing visitors with fancy Java applet and tools, and thorough knowledge about the target audience should be obtained and careful planning should be carried out before the real designing process.

4 Further Research

The proposed typology requires careful investigation along with the development of information technology, since the cyberspace is changing so rapidly that any predictions are problematic. Contractor and Wasserman stated that the development of technology will not only improve and facilitate traditional marketing and transaction activities, but also "re-configurate" the corporations and the industry [21]. In tourism the development of information technology may lead to the integration and re-configuration of online travel and tourism; consequently, in-depth and repeated investigations of the nature of web sites are necessary.

References

1. Forrester Research: Online retail to reach $184 billion by 2004 as post-Web retail era unfolds. http://www.forrester.com/ER/Press/Release/0,1769,164,FF.html (1999).
2. Werthner, H., Klein, S.: Information Technology and Tourism – A Challenging Relationship. Wien: SpringerWienNewYork (1999)
3. Hoffman, D.L., Novak, T.: A new marketing paradigm for electronic commerce. Information Society 13: 43-54 (1996).
4. Hoffman, D.L., Novak, T.: Marketing in hypermedia computer-mediated environments: conceptual foundations. Journal of Marketing, 60: 50-68 (1996).
Maddox, Lynda M, Mehta, Darshan, Daubek, Hugh G (1997), The role and effect of web addresses in advertising, Journal of Advertising Research, 37: 47-59
5. Poon, A.: Tourism, technology and competitive strategies. Oxon: CAB International (1993).
6. Sterne, J.: World Wide Web: integrating the Web into your marketing strategy. New York: John Wiley & Sons (1999).
7. Nilsen, J.: When bad design elements become the standard. http://www.useit.com/alertbox/991114.html (1999).
8. Stoltz, C.: Each year, a bit less. Washington Post (1999, Nov 11)
9. O'Neill, E.T., Lavoie, B.F., and etc.: Web characterization using sampling methods. http://www.w3.org/1998/11/05/WC-workshop/Presentations/oneill/sld001.htm (1998)
10. Webopedia. http://webopedia.internet.com/TERM/U/URL.html (1999, accessed Nov 20, 1999)
11. Kaye, B., Medoff, N.J.: World Wide Web: a mass communication perspective. Mountain View: Mayfield Publishing Company (1999)
12. OCLC: A Brief Introduction to the Dewey Decimal Classification. http://www.oclc.org/oclc/fp/about/brief.htm.
13. Hoger, E.A, Cappel, J.J., Myerscough, M.: Navigating the Web with a typology of corporate uses. Business Communication Quarterly, 61(2): 39-47 (1998).
14. Ho, J.: Evaluating the World Wide Web: a global study of commercial sites. Journal of Computer Mediated Communication. 1 3(1). http://www.ascusc.org/jcmc/vol3/issue1/ho.html (1997, June).
15. Shannon, C., Weaver, W.: The mathematical theory of communication. Champaign: University of Illinois Press (1948).
16. Wiio, O. A.: Information and communication: a conceptual analysis. (Unpublished monograph) (1981).

17. Kubey, R., Csikszentmihalyi, M.: Television and the quality of life: how viewing shapes everyday experience. Mahwah: Lawrence Erlbaum Assoc. (1990).

18. Saracevic, T.: Information science, Journal of the American Society for Information Science, 50(12): 1051-106 (1999).

19. Evans, P.B., Wurster, T.S.: Strategy and the new economics of information. Harvard Business Review, 75(5): 70-82 (1997).

20. Daft, R.L., Lengel, R.H.: Information richness: a new approach to managerial behavior and organization design. in Staw, B.M., Cummings, L.L. (eds.), Research in Organizational Behavior, 6:191-233. Greenwich, Conn.: JAI Press (1984).

21. Contractor, N.S, Wasserman, S. Testing multi-level, multi-theoretical hypotheses about networks in 21st century organizational forms: An analytic framework and empirical example http://www.spcomm.uiuc.edu:1000/contractor/pstarpaper.html (1999).

The Diffusion And Application Of Multimedia Technologies In The Tourism And Hospitality Industries

Marianna Sigala, David Airey, Peter Jones and Andrew Lockwood
School of Management Studies of the Service Sector
University of Surrey
{M.Sigala, D.Airey, P.Jones, A. Lockwood} @surrey.ac.uk

1 Introduction

The tourism and hospitality sectors have a number of characteristics, which mean that the development of information and communication technologies (ICT) as well as multimedia present some major opportunities yet at the same time bring some important challenges. There are great, even worldwide, space and time differences between the demand and the supply, the supply is highly perishable since lost sales are lost for ever, the supply consists of a great variety of products that cannot normally be inspected, seen or felt prior to purchase. All these mean that advanced reservations and the availability of up-to-date, accurate and accessible information as well as planned co-operation and collaboration between the different suppliers are indispensable operational activities for tourism businesses. As Buhalis (1997) has suggested: *"information technology will be instrumental in the industries' ability to enhance their future efficiency and strategic competitiveness"*.

On the other hand, the structure of the tourism industry, with many small operators, some not trading on a strictly commercial or professional basis has meant that access to and take-up of technologies has been slow. Multimedia are expected to affect large areas of the operations of large multinational companies whereas operators of small outlets may not even have heard of multimedia. However, developments in this field can bring them major opportunities.

This paper is based on a study carried out for the DIME (Defining Multimedia for Employment) project, a programme funded under the ADAPT initiative. The study investigated the diffusion and application of several multimedia technologies by a great variety of operators within the UK tourism and hospitality industries. By conducting a questionnaire-based mail survey and personal interviews, data were gathered regarding the current and projected availability and use of multimedia by three star hotels, Bed and Breakfasts (B&Bs), travel agencies, Tourism Information Centres (TICs) and the visitors attraction sector. The study also looked at whether or not these operators provide any training in multimedia as well as the content and the effectiveness of the training methods that are being used.

The paper reports on the results and analysis of findings of this survey, highlighting the key issues arising. A large majority of players from all sectors uses multimedia PC and the Internet for advertising, promotion and reservation purposes, while it is projected that operators will adopt and make wider application of more multimedia technologies in the future. However, it was found that training in multimedia is provided by a small percentage of respondents including those that are currently using multimedia technologies.

2 Multimedia and tourism

2.1 Multimedia technologies

Multimedia is an all-embracing term that cuts across a wide variety of technologies. However, based on the DIME working definition of multimedia, i.e. *"the seamless integration of data, text, sound and images of all kinds within a single, interactive digital environment"*, the study included the following multimedia technologies: internet, (WWW, e-mail), multimedia PC, interactive CDs, information/sales kiosks and digital TV, videoconferencing systems, intranets/extranets, CD-I devices, virtual reality and Personal Digital Assistants (PDA).

Multimedia is being referred to as the technological wave of the future, which promises to have tremendous influence in tourism and hospitality. This is because of the large volume of information that multimedia carries and disseminates over great distances and speed and in varied ways all over the globe, as well as because of multimedia's user friendly and interactive interface. Developments in multimedia systems have substantially improved the effectiveness and efficiency of information presentation and dissemination through electronic channels. Pollock (1995) argued the suitability, appropriateness and the opportunities that the new media offer to tourism by analysing the enhanced features of the electronic over the conventional analogue channels.

2.2 The adoption of multimedia technologies in tourism and hospitality

The study aims to examine rates and patterns of adoption of different multimedia technologies over time and among varied operators within the tourism and hospitality industry. Thus, a theoretical basis for the study is found in the organisational innovation literature. Innovation theory applies to the study of the adoption (the decision to use) and the diffusion (the extent of implementation) of innovations within organisations.

Factors found to influence diffusion can be generalised in the following categories: a) adopter characteristics; b) the social network to which the adopters belong; c) innovation attributes; d) environmental characteristics; e) the process by which an innovation is communicated; f) the characteristics of those who are promoting an innovation; g) the type of the innovation; h) the level at which innovations are adopted and diffused, i.e. organisation, work group, individual; i) the scope of innovation (Rogers, 1983, Wolfe, 1994).

In addition, expansions of innovation theory have included an additional factor namely, absorptive capacity. According to Cohen and Levinthal, (1990) the adoption and diffusion are limited by a firm's ability to "recognise the value of new information, assimilate it and apply it to commercial ends". Buhalis, (1997) argued that education and training is the most crucial factor enabling managers effectively and strategically apply ICT in their organisations and highlighted the need of a well-trained *"humanware"*. Daniele et al (1999) looked at the skills and qualities required in graduates in the Australian tourism industry due to the wide diffusion of ICT.

There have been several studies examining the take up of ICT by tourism businesses. For example, Mutch (1998) investigated the investment and use of IT in holiday cottages in UK. Main (1994) examined the application of IT in independently owned hotels. Whitaker (1985) conducted research on the usage and types of IT applications across firms within the hotel and catering industry. Buhalis (1997) examined the use of IT in hospitality businesses in La Plagne France and he also applied a push-pull model type of innovations' adoption in the tourism industry. Evans et al (1999) used a questionnaire-based survey of a cross-section of 500 Small and Medium Tourism Enterprises (SMTEs) in the UK in order to measure usage, range and awareness of various IT applications and their development potential and training needs, including barriers to ICT development. Marcussen (1999) investigated the use of Internet by Danish holiday cottages for distribution purposes. Finally, Buhalis (1999a and b) developed a cost-benefit analysis of the Internet, He gave an example of how a small guest house managed to develop and maintain its web site using a PC running Windows 95 Office software and he examined the use of Internet for the distribution of B&B accommodation in York, UK.

Factors mentioned in the previously mentioned studies that can inhibit the diffusion of ICT in tourism industries are: high proportion of small independent firms; high degree of organisational inertia; general lack of awareness and confusion about IT equipment and application; piecemeal approach to purchasing (which usually leads to legacy systems and integration problems); low level of technical expertise and lack of training; inability to attract specialist personnel; poor relationship with systems suppliers; lack of involvement in systems design and specification; lack of project management; weak systems and information management skills; misconceptions that ICT are not consistent with the high service standards and quality customer experience (illustrated in the debate between high tech versus high touch). As the size of the firms was claimed to be a major factor, Buhalis (1997) in his study claimed that: *"small properties have consistently failed to incorporate IT in their operational and strategic management as a result of their deficient economic resources in order to invest in essential hardware, software and humanware required, lack of expertise, functional disadvantages and management structure ... internal constraints, attitudes and misconceptions".*

2.3 The application of multimedia in tourism and hospitality

It has been widely argued that ICT and nowadays multimedia are an essential and indispensable partner of the tourism industry that increasingly play a more important role in tourism marketing, distribution and co-ordination (Poon, 1988). Vlitos-Rowe (1995) explains that ICT are *"having a dramatic impact on the travel industry because they force this sector as a whole to rethink the way in which it organises its business, its values or norms of behaviour and the way in which it educates its workforce".*

A number of models have been developed that provide a conceptual synthesis of the usage of ICT in business strategy, and in tourism demand and supply in particular; e.g. the early *"value chain"* model by Porter and Millar (1985), to the *dual production system* by Poon (1988) and recently the framework regarding the strategic use of ICT that incorporate the re-engineering processes that reshape the tourism industry by Buhalis (1998). However, Poon (1988) argued that ICT will have their greatest impact on the information-intensive areas of tourism production and lesser impact on the service and labour intensive areas while *"...the imperatives of distribution of travel and tourism services will dictate the pace of technology adoption".*

Jupiter Communications (1999) reported that tourism products are the second most heavily sold commodities online, whereas Baker et al (1999) predicted that *"... around a half of business travel and up to a third of single component leisure travel will be booked online by 2005".* The increasing use of ICT and particularly multimedia technologies for E-commerce and/or E-business practices on the one hand and the lower emphasis on the use of multimedia for computer based training (CBT) on the other illustrates the above.

3 Methodology

The selection of the methods as well as the sample of the study had to take into consideration two characteristics of the tourism industry. First, its complexity since it includes a great variety of companies, and secondly, its fragmentation between many small players and just few large operators.

The sample of the study included both large and small operators drawn from four major components of the tourism industry, namely three star hotels and Bed & Breakfasts (B&Bs), travel agents, Tourism Information Centres (TICs) and visitor attractions. These also represent some different dimensions of the industry. For example, TICs are typically in the public sector, travel agencies are primarily concerned with distribution issues while hotels and B&Bs focuses on the provision of food and accommodation. Different methods for collecting data from small and big operators were used. A mail survey targeted small operators whereas more in-depth data were gathered by conducting personal interviews with large operators, where multimedia were expected to have a more profound effect in several areas of their work. Personal interviews were conducted with two visitor attractions and one major travel agency company. A breakdown of the research structure is given in Table 1.

Table 1. Structure of the research

Sector	Sample Size	Response rate	Method
Travel agents-chain/independent	200/200	3.0%	Postal questionnaire
Travel agents-large	1		Interview
Hotels 3***	300	13.3%	Postal questionnaire
B&Bs	300	14.0%	Postal questionnaire
TICs	476	31.7%	Postal questionnaire
Visitor attractions	2	n.a.	Interviews

4 Major results of the study

4.1 Response rates

The response rates (Table 1) did not allow any correlation studies to be carried out to give any reliable results regarding the factors (e.g. size/ownership of company, education/age of respondent etc) that could have affected the take up and use of multimedia within each sector. Moreover, because of the very limited representation of the travel agent sector, the analysis of the findings from the mail survey did not include any data from travel agents. However, the findings provided a good insight into the major factors that may have influenced the different adoption rates of the multimedia technologies by the four sectors as well as the pattern of their application.

4.2 Current and projected multimedia availability

The research findings regarding the current and projected availability of multimedia are illustrated in Table 2. Multimedia PC and Internet were found to be the most popular multimedia technologies within all sectors, they attracted 53.2% and 63% of the total respondents respectively. Their easy, flexible and varied use, their relatively low cost as well as the "cyberintermediaries' push", mainly explain their heavy adoption. Adoption levels of other technologies were substantially lower and depended on the operational context within which they were applied. So, videoconferencing systems were heavily adopted by 3 star hotels (17.5%), while TICs accounted for the greatest adoption of interactive kiosks (15.2%).

The research showed that the majority of operators have only heavily adopted multimedia during the last five years. However, 3 star hotels were found to be the early adopters followed by B&Bs while TICs were characterised as laggards. These findings are not surprising given that the tourism industry has usually been a late-come in the adoption of new technologies, TICs are mainly public funded and that about 70% of 3 star hotels were part of a hotel chain or consortium. The latter is important since access and availability of funds as well as membership in associations and/or consortia can in a great extent affect IT adoption.

It was surprising that B&Bs accounted for the greatest adoption of Internet (66.7%). However, as B&Bs availability of multimedia PC (64.3%) was lower than the Internet adoption figure, it is evident that the former is mainly attributed to the push from the Internet service providers and other "cyberintermediaries". On the other hand, from responses gathered from the mail survey and from the personal interviews, it seemed that the travel agent sector lagged well behind in the adoption of multimedia technologies mainly because of its heavy investments in its major suppliers' systems, i.e. the viewdata of tour operators. Thus, it is very likely that the adoption of new media by the travel agency sector is influenced by the existence of such legacy systems as well as the need to retrain personnel on new technologies.

All sectors reported plans for future investment in multimedia technologies. This is expected to decrease the number of respondents without any multimedia technologies at all and to increase the average number of multimedia technologies per respondent. Because the currently most popular technologies, i.e. Internet and multimedia PC, attracted the greatest percentages of future investors, the adoption pattern among the different multimedia technologies is not expected to change. However, Intranets/Extranets, interactive kiosks and TV and videoconferencing systems seem to

Table 2. Current and projected availability of multimedia by mail respondents,

% of respondents	TICs (139)		Three star hotels (40)		B&Bs (39)		Total (218)	
	Now	Future	Now	Future	Now	Future	Now	Future
Multimedia PC	55.6	78.81	90.0	95.00	64.3	80.95	53.2	81.97
Internet	47.0	86.09	62.5	85.00	66.7	92.86	63.0	87.12
Intranet/extranet	15.2	32.45	2.5	12.50	2.4	2.38	9.8	29.61
(Touch)screen kiosks	11.3	37.09	15.0	30.00	0.0	2.38	10.7	23.61
Interactive CDs, Videos	5.3	10.60	10.0	27.50	7.1	14.29	6.4	14.16
Videoconferencing systems	4.0	7.28	17.5	50.00	0.0	0.00	5.6	13.30
Interactive TV	0.0	11.00	5.0	3.00	2.4	7.14	3.4	9.44
CD-Interactive device	0.7	3.31	5.0	22.50	0.0	2.38	1.3	6.44
PDA	1.3	1.99	10.0	22.50	4.8	4.76	0.4	6.01
Virtual Reality	0.7	3.31	0.0	12.50	0.0	0.00	0.4	4.29
Voice recognition systems	0.7	0.66	0.0	0.00	0.0	0.00	1.3	0.43

be emerging technologies. On the other hand, the pattern of multimedia adoption among sectors is expected to change. Although, all sectors claimed that they had planned to make substantially greater future investments in multimedia technologies, B&Bs will continue to have only Internet and multimedia PC.

As concerns the visitor attraction sector, the two interviewed companies also reported availability of the most popular technologies previously mentioned and claim plans for further investments in the future. This indicates that multimedia technologies significantly affect the operations of this sector as well.

4.3 Multimedia application

Table 3 shows that fewer differences are found among sectors regarding their current and future use of multimedia technologies. Generally, current applications of multimedia focus on operational and marketing activities. Very limited use of multimedia was found for training and other human resource management activities. Thus, great percentages of total respondents claimed to use multimedia for the following activities: "advertising", 60%; "information provision", 56.6%; "reservations/bookings", 50.9%; "other financial activities", 42.9%; "billing and invoicing", 41.7%. Sectors did not differ in their pattern of multimedia use across activities but they did differ in their degree/level of multimedia use. Based on the respondents' percentages from each sector reporting use of multimedia for each of the provided activities, three star hotels accounted for the heaviest use, TICs followed while B&Bs focused their multimedia use on advertising and reservations only.

Sectors also differ in terms of their top multimedia activities. However, this is not surprising when taking into consideration that the three sectors differ in their operations and technological needs. Thus, the biggest in size, three star hotels, place more emphasis on the automation and so, streamlining of their transactions, i.e. reservations, billing, invoicing, stock control, other financial activities than on advertising and promotion which is the major concern of B&Bs operators. The latter heavily depend on the Internet for the distribution and promotion of their product, since they do not usually have access to corporate reservation systems and have limited resources for advertising and promotion. On the other hand, since the primary role of TICs is the provision of information, the considerable use of multimedia for "information provision", "customer service" and "communications" activities was expected. Another important activity of TICs is "inventory control" either in terms of brochure stocks or in terms of managing the product capacity of their tourism suppliers, e.g. B&Bs, attractions.

As concerns the projected application of multimedia technologies, respondents from all sectors reported plans to use multimedia for more activities in the future. However,

Table 3. Current and projected application of multimedia by mail respondents with at least one type of multimedia technologies

	TICs (139) %		3 star hotels (40) %		B&Bs (39) %		Total (218) %	
	Now	Future	Now	Future	Now	Future	Now	Future
Marketing activities								
Market research	32.7	46.1	66.7	70.0	31.3	38.5	40.0	49.08
Competitors research	7.7	9.4	38.5	50.0	18.5	25.6	16.6	19.72
Advertising, promotion, Public relations	44.2	59.0	77.0	85.0	90.6	92.3	60.0	69.72
Trade shows & Business presentations	16.4	24.5	15.4	35.0	9.4	10.3	14.9	23.85
Building communications & relationships with the customers	27.9	39.6	30.8	42.5	31.3	33.3	29.1	38.99
Operational activities								
Reservations/ bookings	35.6	74.1	79.5	92.5	65.7	79.5	50.9	78.44
Measuring customers satisfaction	11.5	31.7	30.8	62.5	28.1	30.8	18.9	37.16
Procurement & purchases	19.2	26.6	33.3	57.5	21.9	33.3	22.9	33.49
Stock & inventory control	41.4	59.7	48.7	70.0	15.6	18,0	38.3	54.13
Safety & security provision	1.9	3.6	12.8	25.0	15.6	12.8	6.9	9.17
Customer services	39.4	54.7	35.9	57.5	21.9	20.5	35.4	49.08
Customer management	17.3	28.1	30.8	50.0	12.5	12.8	19.4	29.36
Customer entertainment	15.4	23.7	15.4	40.0	6.2	7.7	13.7	23.85
Enhancement of customers' experience	12.5	31.6	23.1	35.0	12.5	12.8	14.9	28.90
Information provision	60.6	79.1	53.9	65.0	46.9	48.7	56.6	71.10
Billing and invoices	27.9	37.4	76.9	90.0	43.7	48.7	41.7	49.08
Other financial operations	31.7	42.4	69.2	70.0	46.9	43.6	42.9	47.71
HRM activities								
Human resource recruitment	6.7	9.4	28.2	45.0	3.1	7.7	10.9	15.60
Human resource selection	2.9	5.8	15.4	37.5	3.1	7.7	5.7	11.93
Human resource training	6.7	12.2	30.8	47.5	6.2	10.3	12.0	18.35
Other activities								
Communicating within the organisation or the company group	45.2	60.4	53.8	67.5	6.3	7.7	40.0	52.29
Creating networks and collaborating with others	25.0	51.1	41.0	60.0	9.9	12.8	25.7	45.87
Environmental management	0.0	1.4	5.1	25.0	0.0	0.0	1.1	5.50

because the greatest percentage of future users of multimedia concentrated their interest on the currently top multimedia applications, the level of multimedia use is expected to increase but its pattern of application between the different activities will remain the same. The latter is clearer for B&B respondents who are expected to be focused only on "advertising" and "reservations" in the future as at present. On the other hand, other activities such as "collaborating/networking", "communications" were found to be emerging as significant multimedia applications.

Findings from the travel agency sector and the two interviewed visitor attraction companies illustrate a high current as well as projected level of multimedia use in terms of the range of activities performed. However, multimedia applications by these sectors cluster around marketing and operations activities as well.

4.4 Training in multimedia technologies

Despite the high levels of multimedia adoption and application, it was found that a large proportion of tourism operators which also had multimedia (32%) did not provide any training at all. This is not surprising since small-sized tourism operators provide very limited training in general. The B&B sector provided the least training (12.2% of total respondents and 15.6% of current multimedia users), which is expected as B&Bs only use Internet and multimedia PC for advertising and reservations. The TIC sector provided the most training (63.2% and 82.7% respectively), which is mainly attributed to their respondents' profile, i.e. relatively old with no up-to-date and professional education. Regarding the three star hotels the percentages were 70% and 71.8% respectively.

Table 4. Training methods and their evaluation by mail respondents

	TICs (84)	3 star hotels (28)	B&Bs (5)	Total (116)	Evaluation
In-house training	91.6	75.0	50.0	86.2	2.3
On-the-job training	85.7	92.9	25.0	85.3	2.2
Manuals and other literature	64.3	64.3	100.0	65.5	2.2
Self learning	64.3	60.7	5.00	52.9	2.2
Training centres	52.4	35.7	75.0	49.1	2.0
Suppliers' training	42.9	39.3	0.0	40.5	1.9
Specialist lectures/workshops	36.9	35.7	50.0	37.1	1.9
On line/distance learning	13.1	21.4	50.0	16.4	1.6
Exhibitions, trade shows	15.5	14.3	25.0	15.5	1.6

1=Not highly effective, 2=Effective and 3=Highly effective

Training was mainly provided in-house (86.2%) and/or on-the-job (85.3%), which was also evaluated as effective (Table 4). The fact that training provided by third parties was evaluated as equally effective as that provided in-house suggests that the popularity of in-house training can be attributed to the specific features of the tourism industry, i.e. high levels of labour turnover and part-time staff.

The content of training basically focused on operating multimedia technologies (89.1%) and databases (79%). See Table 5. Very limited interest was shown for training in technical skills such as development and maintenance of multimedia as well as in learning about new technologies. This is a significant indicator of the skills that tourism operators currently require from their staff. However, the TIC sector provided training in a greater variety of competencies than the other sectors.

Findings from the travel agency and visitor attractions sectors did not differ from the pattern mentioned above. The patterns regarding the provision of training, its methods and evaluation as well as its content was similar to those reported above.

Table 5. Content of training

	TICs (86)	3 star hotels (28)	B&Bs (5)	Total (119)
Operation of multimedia	89.5	89.3	80.0	89.1
Database management and use	87.2	60.7	40.0	79.0
Learning of new technologies	40.7	17.9	0.0	33.6
Security/protection of information	27.9	21.4	0.0	25.2
Development of multimedia	25.6	14.3	20.0	22.7
Maintenance of multimedia	20.9	21.4	0.0	20.1

5 Conclusion

A whole system of multimedia technologies is heavily being adopted and used for reservations and advertising purposes by all segments of the tourism and hospitality industries. As Poon claimed (1988) "no player in the travel and tourism industry will escape the impacts of information technologies". The diffusion of multimedia in the tourism and hospitality industries are system-wide. Multimedia is not adopted only by travel agents or hotels or TICs, but by all of them, and it is so not only because of competitive reasons but also because operators within the tourism industry are interdependent. However, some sectors were found to be leaders in terms of their adoption of and use of multimedia. It is clear that multimedia technologies have become instrumental in the development and prosperity of companies' competitiveness by permeating all functions of strategic and operation management. Hence, tourism operators have to realise that failure to adopt and utilise them will lead to competitive disadvantages. This in turn can jeopardise the prosperity of destinations.

References

Baker M., Cossey A. and Sussmann S. (1999), *"The WWW and the Hotel: On-line or off course?"*, Proceedings of the 8th Annual CHME Hospitality Research Conference, 7-9 April , University of Surrey, UK, p. 330-345

Buhalis D. (1999a), *"The costs and the benefits of Information Technology and the Internet for small and medium sized tourism enterprises"*, and Buhalis D. and Keeling S. (1999b), *"Distributing accommodation in York, UK; advantages and developments emerging through the Internet"*, ICT in tourism 1999, Proceedings of the International Conference in Innsbruck, ENTER, Buhalis D. and Schelter W. (eds)

Buhalis D. (1998b), "Strategic use of information technologies in the tourism industry", Tourism Management, Vol. 19, No. 5, pp.409-421

Buhalis D. (1997), *"Information technologies as a strategic tool for economic, social, cultural and environmental benefits enhancement of tourism at destination regions"*, Progress in tourism and hospitality research, Vol. 3, p. 71-93

Cohen W. and Levinthal D.A. (1990), *"Absorptive Capacity: a new perspective on learning and innovation"*, Administrative Science Quarterly, 35, pp.128-152

Daniele R. and Mistilis N. (1999), *"Information Technology and Tourism Education in Australia: an industry view of skills and qualities required in graduates"*, ICT in tourism 1999, Proceedings of the International Conference in Innsbruck, Buhalis D. and Schelter W. (eds), p. 140-149

Evans, G. and Peacock M. (1999), *"A comparative study of ICT, Tourism and Hospitality SMEs in Europe"*, ICT in tourism 1999, Proceedings of the International Conference in Innsbruck, Austria, Buhalis D. and Schelter W. (eds), p. 247- 258

Vlitos-Rowe, (1995) in Kettinger W. and Hackbarth G. (1997), *"Selling in the era of the "Net": integration of electronic commerce in small firms"*, ICIS, 1997, p.249-262

Horner T. (1998), *"In-room technology; Where is it headed? Guests access to the world through your technology"*, Lodging, November 1998, p. 163-164

Main H.C. (1994), *"The application of IT in independently owned hotels"*, Mphil Thesis, University of Wales

Marcussen C. (1999), *"Distribution of Danish Holiday Cottages via the Internet/WWW"*, ICT in tourism 1999, Proceedings of the International Conference in Innsbruck, Buhalis D. and Schelter W. (eds), p. 259-269

Mutch A. (1998), *"Using IT"*, in *"The management of small tourism and hospitality firms"*, Rhodri Thomas (ed), (1998), Cassell, London

Pollock A. (1995), "The impact of information technology on destination marketing", EIU Travel and Tourism Analyst, No.3, 1995, pp. 66-83

Poon A. (1988), *"Tourism, technology and competitive strategies"*, Wallingford C. A.

Porter M. and Millar V. (1985), *"How information gives you competitive advantage"*, Harvard Business Review, July-August, p. 149-160

Rogers, E. (1975), *"Diffusion of innovations "*, New York, Free Press

Whitaker M. (1987), "Overcoming the barriers to successful implementation of Information Technology in the U.K. hotel industry", International Journal of Hospitality Management", Vol. 6, No. 4, pp. 229-235

Wolfe R.D. (1994), *"Organisational innovation: review, critique and suggested research directions",* Journal of Management Sciences, 31:1, May 1994, pp.405-431

www.jupiter.com, Jupiter communications website

Usability of Information and Reservations Systems: Theory or Practice?

Elaine Crichton
Napier University, Edinburgh
e.crichton@napier.ac.uk

Andrew J. Frew
Napier University, Edinburgh
a.frew@napier.ac.uk

Abstract

Computer-mediated information and reservations systems have become widespread, yet their interface approaches are often anything but user-friendly. This paper describes an attempt to add a little to the extremely limited applied research work in the area and outlines the methodology and findings of survey and interviews work with system suppliers. The research sought to elicit their practice and views regarding system 'usability' issues. Findings indicate that general user interface standards and guidelines are not perceived as meeting the needs of the hospitality and tourism industry and are, therefore, not being adopted. Consequently information and reservations systems in the marketplace display significant user interface differences.

1 Introduction

This paper discusses the further development of previously reported work by the authors [1] as part of a research programme investigating the usability of information and reservations systems within the hospitality and tourism industry. The central hypothesis is that the information and reservations systems used across this industry are poorly designed and present significant barriers to effective access and use. There is much anecdotal evidence to support the notion that these widely used systems, generally present rather user-*un*friendly interface configurations. However, published research work in the area has been sparse. The hospitality and tourism industry as a whole has benefited significantly from information and communications technology developments [2] as can be seen in exceptional growth and diversity of electronic distribution channels such as Global Distribution Systems (GDS), Central Reservations Systems (CRS), Property Management Systems (PMS), Destination Management System (DMS), etc. Barriers to access to such systems are falling and the march of the Web is catalysing and transforming their use (witness the growth of the Alternative Distribution Systems such as WorldRes.com). Thus, the field of *systems*, *users* and *user interfaces* is expanding apace and any contribution to the development of a solid foundation and consistent approach to considering usability issues should be useful.

1.1 Literature Search (HCI)

The research programme commenced with a *general* literature search (i.e. *not* hospitality and tourism specific) of the main computer science databases. The term user interface derives from the broader area of human computer interaction (HCI), a comparatively new multi-disciplinary field which has been described [3] as *"...the design of computer systems that are safe, efficient, easy and enoyable to use as well as functional"* and it, therefore, seemed reasonable to set the context within which user interfaces as well as usability issues in hospitality and tourism could be examined. A wealth of generic literature exists and the importance of user interfaces is emphasised in mainstream HCI research [4],[5]. As Myers [6] points out, "even the remarkable growth of the World Wide Web is a direct result of HCI research...More than anything else, improvements to interfaces have triggered this explosive growth."

Fig. 1. Cumulative User Interface Output

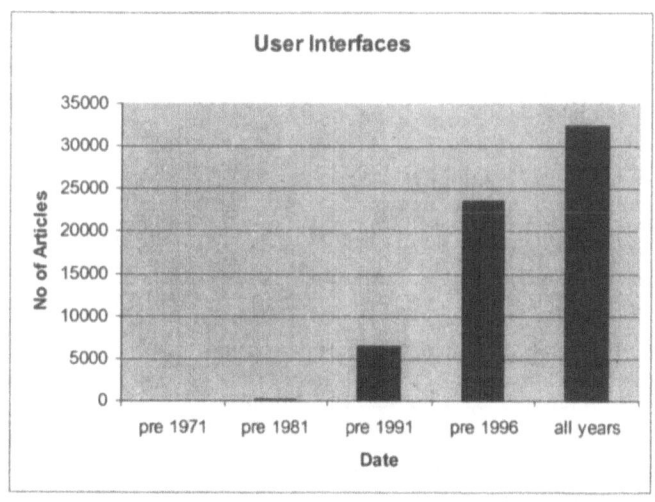

1.2 Importance of User Interface Design

To illustrate the growing importance of user interface design the scale of the research field was explored using key term (user interface) online searches. The major computer science databases were 'trawled' for specific time periods, and the results, as Figure 1 illustrates, show a sudden and dramatic rise for this specialist user interface field. Before 1980 only a handful of articles in this field were recorded. The picture started to change in the 1980's with over 6,000 articles in total recorded by 1990. However, by the summer of 1999 this had increase to over 35,000 with the notion of "usability" beginning to emerge as a significant area of study within this. As can be seen, the rate of increase has slowed in the second half of the 1990's.

1.3 Literature Search (Hospitality and Tourism)

However, despite considerable mainstream generic research, there has been very little applied hospitality and tourism research in this field, notable exceptions including [7-11]. Werthner, for example, discusses several design issues of tourist information systems, whilst Loban explores cognitive and usability issues related to the design of online documents such as those used in these systems. Some further work has been carried out on the development of a Web-oriented end-user interface on distributed tourism information systems [12]. However, apart from these examples of usability specifics in the tourism sector there has been little primary research reported in the area.

1.4 Systems, Users and User Interfaces

The three key dimensions to the work are clearly systems, users and user interfaces, and considerable time and effort was spent on definition and classification of these dimensions. Classification of information and reservations systems and their users was elusive; classification of user interfaces even more problematic. Definitions of the user interface have evolved and changed over time – one reason perhaps for the difficulties in the classification task.

For the purposes of this research, users have been classified as suppliers of hospitality or tourism products or services; intermediaries in the distribution chain or consumers of the product or service, with an additional category of "secondary users" – namely those who use the systems during development, sales, installation, training, support, etc. Each of these aspects may be further divided for example by role, function or skill level, etc.

Given that it is relatively easy to identify the principal system types that address information and reservations tasks, it was decided that, for the purposes of this research, that systems would be classified by their application (for example, the SABRE system can be classified as a GDS). As with "users", systems may be further divided – in this case by contextual dimensions such as location, ownership, scale and scope and so forth.

With regard to the user interface, no obvious classification approach has emerged from the literature. What is needed is a means of classifying any particular user interface by its key attributes and which can be readily employed when investigating users. A tentative approach which seemed to best embrace the key issues was, therefore, adapted from Crerar [13], who identified 4 dimensions as follows:

- *Interaction devices*
- *Interaction styles*
- *Screen design*
- *Modelling the users tasks*

The research approach (bringing user interface dimensions to bear on users and systems) that emerged from the classification work is represented diagrammatically in Figure 2 and it is anticipated that this model will prove to be a useful tool in examining specific systems in the latter stage of the overall research programme.

Fig. 2. Usability Evaluation

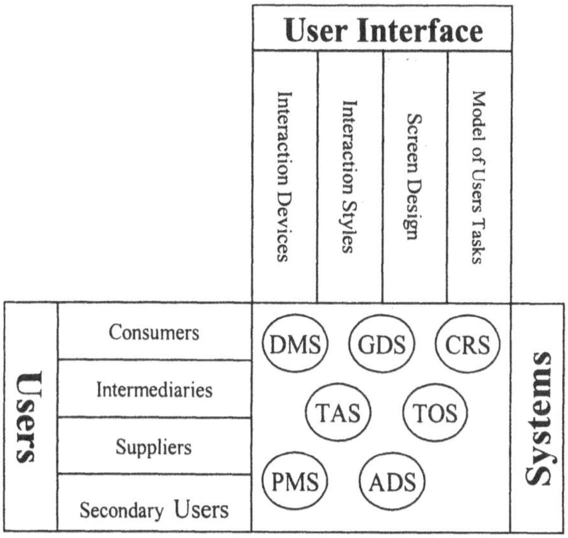

2 Methodology

Because of the dearth of applied research in the area, some primary research was necessary to explore the various approaches to usability in information and reservations systems. To that end, a postal survey of suppliers of information and reservations systems to the UK hospitality and tourism market was selected as the most appropriate method of primary research given the large (and geographically disparate) population of suppliers.

2.1 Population/Sample Size

Defining the supplier population proved no easy task as for many suppliers our industry may be a secondary or peripheral market. The authors were afforded access to a number of conference and exhibition exhibitor and attendee lists and employed a number of sources of hospitality and tourism system suppliers, for example, the World Travel Market Official Catalogues, the 1999 Hospitality & Travel Technology Source Book (5th edition), websites such as Hospitality Net (http://www.hospitalitynet.org), Genesys Consulting (http://www.genesys-consulting.com), Hospitality Solutions (http://www.hosp-solutions.co.uk), HITA (http://www.hita.co.uk), the general trade press as well as the authors own knowledge of the marketplace. This generated over 1,200 potential suppliers of such systems. The emphasis is on 'potential' as in the majority of cases it was difficult to elicit qualifying information and the numbers were at odds with the authors' experience of the marketplace, the true population was believed to be around 200.

To establish a more accurate and thus more appropriately qualified population, three basic criteria were used;

- The company must supply to the UK market
- The company must be based in Europe or the UK, and
- Must be established by the authors as supplying hospitality & tourism systems

Inappropriate companies were, therefore, deleted from the database of potential suppliers and the size of the population was reduced to **214** appropriately qualified companies.

2.2 Questionnaire Design

The Questionnaire was deliberately kept brief (10 questions) to encourage response, and comprised a mixture of open and closed questions. A cover letter outlining the importance of usability in the software/system development process was also included. Not all suppliers develop their own systems. Therefore, a distinction was drawn between suppliers who develop AND distribute their own systems and suppliers who simply distribute systems for another company that develops the software. Those in the latter category were only required to answer the first 4 questions and to provide company details. These companies were, therefore, unable to provide information on usability issues

3 Results

The questionnaire, together with cover letter was distributed to the 214 suppliers in August 1999 and a 3-week turnaround time allowed to complete and return the questionnaire either by mail or fax. A total of 41 companies completed and returned the questionnaires – 19.2%. The first four questions are general in nature and all respondents were required to answer these.

Question 1 was designed to elicit the number/percentage of companies that develop their own software/systems in-house and it was discovered that 80.5% of all respondents develop their own software/systems in-house while the remainder are suppliers of products developed by other companies. This is very helpful in identifying the scale of in-house development and the potential control over usability issues.

Question 2 invited respondents to provide a broad indication of their total business conducted in the UK and this varied from less than 10% to 100%. The responses here will prove useful in further qualifying subsequent research samples and subjects.

Question 3 asked respondents to indicate the percentage breakdown of total UK business that is carried out within a) hospitality; b) tourism; and c) "other" market sectors. The responses showed 88% of respondents supply systems to the hospitality market and 36.6% to the tourism market with a further 36.6% involved in supplying systems to other market sectors (as well as to either the hospitality and/or travel and tourism markets). Again this will prove valuable in refining further investigation.

Question 4 sought to identify the type(s) of software/systems that are supplied by the respondents. The majority of the sample companies supply Central Reservations Systems 39%; Restaurant Management Systems 29.3% and Conference and Banqueting Systems 24.4% with the remaining companies supplying a wide range of niche information and reservations systems.

Questions <u>five to ten</u> are specifically about usability issues and were only to be answered by respondents who develop their own software/systems in-house.

Question 5 addressed the issue of user skill level and explored whether suppliers took account of varying user skill level in their approach and two-thirds of all companies replied in the affirmative. This is a fairly positive response but leads one to consider the precise nature of this.

Question 6 asked respondents to indicate whether users are involved in the development process of their product(s) and all respondents claimed to involve users in the development process at some stage. More specifically 54.5% of suppliers involve users during the pre-design phase, 63.6% during the design phase, and 63.6% during the post-design phase. As with question 5, this raises questions regarding the extent, nature and impact of involvement

Question 7 looked at the type of user that suppliers claimed to involve in their development processes and although management and front office staff constituted the main category there was a wide range of other user types including guests/clients.

Questions 8 and 9 refer specifically to user interface development guidelines. 84.8% of respondents are "aware of generally accepted User Interface principles, standards, and guidelines" (such as Microsoft Windows Style Guide), although only 39.4% respondents "follow formal user interface development guidelines".

Of the respondents who specified which 'guidelines' they are aware of, 42.4% were aware of "Microsoft Windows" guidelines with one or two companies mentioning "HCI" guidelines; "HEDNA"; and "Hotel Standards."(?)

Reasons given for **not following** formal guidelines include:

"we have developed our own constantly improving standards based on Microsoft's development software"

"the development guidelines do not address all the operational dynamics : we find that operators at the sharp end can cope with concentrated and sophisticated layouts"

"there has not been a need to at the time. But as the system gets bigger the process will be formalized"

"I have been in industry 30 years and do what I have always done/learnt from experience"

"there are no standards so far!"

"we use interfaces that are plain and simple for the user, we tend not to use menus"

"sometimes exact guidelines do not always promote ease of use for operators, extra pop-up windows, etc. may be required to comply with formal development guidelines"

"we understand the principles of GUI design but we do not employ any specific design as ours is a web based product"

Finally, *Question 10* was intended to elicit how suppliers monitor and evaluate the usability of their systems. "Feedback from users" was the most popular answer then "Beta testing" was cited, other responses included "trial and error" and "monitor help desk".

4 One-to-One Interviews

World Travel Market (WTM) held in London in November 1999 provided an opportunity to interview suppliers of information and reservations systems on a one-to-one basis.

The questionnaire used in the postal survey formed the basis of the structured interviews carried out at WTM. The selection of suppliers to be interviewed was straightforward - any appropriately qualified supplier prepared to spend the time required to answer the questions was interviewed. Six successful interviews were carried out with tourism system suppliers.

4.1 Results

Responses from the six companies interviewed were similar to the responses to the postal survey, although it was obviously possible to explore answers to the questions in more depth. All six companies develop their own software/systems in-house and were, therefore, able to give responses to the questions relating to usability.

In *Question 5* where interviewees were asked if they take into consideration the different skill levels of users, only four of the six suppliers responded in the affirmative. However, when asked whether users are involved in the development process of their product(s), *Question 6*, all interviewees responded in the affirmative.

When asked to specify the types of users involved in the development process (*Question 7*), responses were similar to those of the postal survey respondents, with a wide range of staff mentioned - from senior management to junior operational staff.

All companies interviewed were **aware of** generally accepted User Interface principles; standards; and guidelines (*Question 8*). and five of the six companies **follow** such guidelines (*Question 9*). Of the five companies that follow guidelines, however, two of them stated that they could only do so "up to a point" and a further company stated that they "try to - but it is not always possible."

Assessment of the usability of their systems (*Question 10*) was carried out by listening to feedback (3 interviewees) and by performance measurement (2 interviewees).

5 Conclusions

Analysis of the findings highlights the following points:

- Most suppliers are aware of general user interface standards and guidelines.
- Suppliers who are aware of these standards and guidelines are not necessarily following them.
- Suppliers who do not follow general user interface standards and guidelines cite a wide range of reasons for this but the main theme is a belief that general guidelines need to be tailored to meet the needs of the hospitality and tourism industry.

At best the inference from the above is that most suppliers treat usability in a rather haphazard and unstructured way with there being no real evidence of an formal systems in place throughout the development process and little to challenge the contention that most information and reservations systems offer poor usability. There is much to suggest that there is a requirement for a specific set of user interface guidelines for the hospitality and tourism industry.

Suppliers in the main claim to be aware of general user interface standards and guidelines but are not adopting general standards; or indeed are modifying existing guidelines to meet the needs of their particular clients. It follows that all information and reservations systems in the marketplace will display significant user interface differences. The software industry in general appears to adopt accepted user interface standards and guidelines, but within the hospitality and tourism sector, these guidelines are by no means universally applied. It would seem, therefore, that there is a gulf between "theory" and "practice".

Future work will incorporate further in-depth postal and telephone survey, exploration of approaches to usability, and their consequences, and subsequently, the intention is to study user interface aspects of one specific type of information and reservations system - the Destination Marketing System (DMS) by carrying out ethnographic/observational studies on one or two specific systems. Thus, the research aims to progress from an exploration of general user interface issues prevalent in the hospitality and tourism industry to the highly specific usability issues displayed in the DMS sector in the UK and to do so by mapping supplier-side research onto user-side research.

References

1. Frew, A.J. and E. Crichton, *User Interfaces in Information and Reservation Systems: Classification and Development Issues*, in *Information and Communications Technologies in Tourism*, D. Buhalis and W. Schertler, Editors. 1999, Springer-Verlag: Vienna, Austria. p. 328-336.
2. O'Connor, P., *Electronic Information Distribution in Tourism and Hospitality*. 1999: CAB International.
3. Preece, J.et.al., *Human Computer Interaction*. 1994, London: Addison Wesley.
4. Chi, H.U., *Formal Specification of User Interfaces: A Comparison and Evaluation of Four Axiomatic Approaches*. IEEE Transactions on Software Engineering, 1985. 11(8): p. 671-685.
5. Johnson, P., *Task Analysis and Software Engineering*. 1992: McGraw-Hill.
6. Myers, B., *A Brief History of Human Computer Interaction Technology*. Interactions, 1998(March and April).
7. Garzotto, F., L. Mainetti, and P. Paolini, *Using and Developing Hypermedia Points of Information: Lessons Learned*, in *Information and Communications Technologies in Tourism*, W. Schertler, *et al.*, Editors. 1994, Springer-Verlag: Vienna, Austria. p. 102-109.
8. Werthner, H., *Design Principles of Tourist Information Systems*, in *Information and Communication Technologies in Tourism*, S. Klein, *et al.*, Editors. 1996, Springer-Verlag: Vienna, Austria. p. 70-77.
9. Dunzendorfer, A., J. Kung, and R.R. Wagner, *Heterogeneous Tourism Information Systems*, in *Information and Communications Technologies in Tourism*, D. Buhalis, A.M. Tjoa, and J. Jafari, Editors. 1998, Springer-Verlag: Vienna, Austria. p. 46-54.
10. Loban, S.R., *Designing Effective Documents for Destination Information Systems*, in *Information and Communications Technologies in Tourism*, D. Buhalis, A.M. Tjoa, and J. Jafari, Editors. 1998, Springer-Verlag: Vienna, Austria. p. 73-83.

11.   Cettolo, M., *et al.*, *A Speech-to-Speech Translation Based Interface for Tourism*, in *Information and Communications Technologies in Tourism*, D. Buhalis and W. Schertler, Editors. 1999, Springer-Verlag: Vienna, Austria. p. 191-200.
12.   Tjoa, A.M. and H. Werthner, *Interfacing WWW with Distributed Database Applications in the Field of Tourism*, in *Information and Communications Technologies in Tourism*, S. Klein, *et al.*, Editors. 1996, Springer-Verlag: Vienna, Austria. p. 78-85.
13.   Crerar, A. and D. Benyon, *Integrating Usability into Systems Development*, in *The Politics of Usability*, L. Tanner and J. Bawa, Editors. 1998, Springer.

Destination Management Systems and Small Accommodation Establishments: The Irish Experience

Deborah Blank and Silvia Sussmann
University of Surrey, UK

Abstract

This paper describes an empirical study which attempted to identify the perceptions of small and medium accommodation establishments in South West Ireland with respect to the potential benefits of being represented on the Irish destination management system known as Gulliver. In the course of the research, a thorough review of both the current structure of Gulliver and of the previous literature on the subject was undertaken. Following from this research, a mail questionnaire was designed and distributed to establishments represented on the system which had been identified using probability sampling methods. The responses from this questionnaire were analysed using an appropriate set of statistical techniques using SPSS software. Conclusions and recommendations for further research have been formulated.

1 Introduction - Destination Management Systems (DMSs)

A review of the literature referring to the use of information and communications technologies within the tourism and travel industry in the 1990s highlights the emphasis that has been placed on the development and implementation of what are often referred to as Destination Management Systems.

The literature referring to destination oriented systems highlights a variety of important issues regarding DMS development. The literature regarding DMSs in the early 1990s considered the possibilities that DMS afforded destinations, expounded the necessity of their development in light of moves by airline CRS into the leisure market, concentrated on the benefits that stakeholders could achieve and considered the qualities that DMS needed to be successful (Baker et al, 1996). More recently, however, the literature has been more critical and skeptical about some of the assumptions made about DMS (Sussmann and Baker, 1996:110 and Frew and O'Connor, 1998:266) as these types of systems have become more common.

This skepticism could be explained in light of the many failures of DMS, including projects in England (Beaver, 1995), Scotland (Pringle, 1994, Frew and O'Connor, 1998) and Switzerland, all of which failed in the early 1990s. Many reasons are given for these failures, and appear to arise from a combination of *lack of funding, inappropriate technology, insufficient distribution networks, lack of political support, lack of marketing to stakeholders*, and *lack of industry support*.

In the research on the failure of various DMS, some interesting issues have emerged regarding DMS and SMTE relationships. One of the major justifications given for investment in DMS is to support SMTEs at the destination level. However, through the investigation of DMS failure, some authors have discovered that some of the assumptions made about SMTE support for these systems may not have accounted for the complexity involved in their operations nor considered the dynamics of these organisations and the characteristics of their owner/managers (Pringle, 1994, Sussmann and Baker, 1996, Frew and O'Connor, 1998).

Recent literature has pointed to the possibility that the assumptions made regarding the benefits accruing to SMTEs from DMS representation could be incorrect. The research in this paper has attempted to examine SMTE attitudes in a destination where there has been successful implementation of a fully functional DMS in order to identify whether these organisations are, in reality, achieving the benefits that are promoted by academics and industry supporters.

The rationale for this particular study lies in the fact that many destinations are investigating DMS implementation and investing enormous amounts of resources in the process. While the research on DMS failures has to some extent highlighted inconsistencies in the theoretical versus the actual benefits accruing to SMTEs from DMS representation the authors felt that it would be appropriate to examine SMTE representation on a fully functional DMS to obtain a more accurate understanding.

2 Gulliver – Irish Tourism's Information and Reservation System

A prominent system which is often referred to within tourism literature on the subject of DMS is the Irish DMS otherwise known as Gulliver. As explained by the following quote from Bord Fáilte (the Republic of Ireland's Tourist Board):

> "Gulliver is Ireland's national tourism information database which is used by the tourism industry and by visitors to learn all there is to know about Ireland and its services".
>
> (Bord Fáilte Gulliver Information Pack)

Unlike many DMS projects in the 1990s, Gulliver has survived through its developmental and pilot stages, in spite of a process of reengineering which became necessary due to the initial use of inappropriate technology, and through its change in status from a solely public venture into a commercially viable public/private operation. It has been held up for a long time as a relatively successfully implemented DMS. Authors such as Archdale et. al. (1992: Appendix II) have described Gulliver as "one of the best examples of a true Destination Database currently operational. It has been set up with a clear strategic purpose and is being developed as an integrated part of the overall Irish tourism marketing effort." While this comment was made before subsequent changes were made to the technology architecture and configuration, it has been mirrored in recent literature comparing Gulliver with other systems (Frew and O'Connor, 1998; Inkpen, 1998).

2.1 Gulliver's Current Structure and Function

At the core of Gulliver is the central "product" database which stores a wealth of information about the Irish tourism industry including transportation information, historical and political information, specialist activities and services, leisure facilities, a calendar of events and accommodation information. On the supply side, currently, accommodation suppliers are the only tourism suppliers that are electronically linked to the system via *Faxlink*, a fax-based solution designed to link small suppliers with the system and *GullNet*, an extranet which uses standard internet technology to provide a method of electronic allocation and reservations to a closed group of users. On the demand side, there are currently four main distribution channels that link potential visitors to the information provided on Gulliver:

Ireland Reservations Direct: Gulliver drives Ireland Reservations Direct, an accommodation booking service devised and operated by Gulliver InfoRes Services Ltd, the joint venture company that now operates and develops Gulliver. A freephone service is provided from selected international tourism generating countries which routes calls to the International Call Centre in Killorglin, County Kerry.

Bord Fáilte – Freephone Number on International Promotional Material: Promotional material features a localised freephone number which also routes calls to the call centre in Killorglin. BFE outsourses its tourism information provision function to GISL.

Bord Fáilte – Ireland Website (www.ireland.travel.ie): The website is developed and operated by BFE but is powered by Gulliver. At the time of this study there was no capacity for on-line accommodation booking, Those visitors who wish to book accommodation from the site must either call the premises direct or call the freephone number that routes their calls to Ireland Reservations Direct.

Bord Fáilte – Tourist Information Offices (TIOs) and Tourist Information Centres (TICs): Accommodation can be booked once visitors are actually in Ireland at TIOs and TICs which use Gulliver as the backbone of their information provision and accommodation booking services. These offices are electronically linked to the system.

2.2 Gulliver Membership

Accommodation is the only bookable service through Gulliver and as such it is these tourism suppliers that are charged an annual fee to cover administrative costs. In order to ensure a comprehensive listing of premises, Gulliver lists all approved properties in

Ireland and Northern Ireland for information purposes (over 11,000). However, not all of these premises are members of Gulliver and therefore available for bookings through Gulliver. To become a member of Gulliver, suppliers must pay a fee to GISL that is calculated depending on the size and type of each establishment. Aside from the annual membership fee, Gulliver charges a commission for each booking based on whether the booking is for serviced or self-catering accommodation. The two types of memberships are based on a "tier" type of system designed to encourage room allocation and electronic connection to the system. *Allocation* members regularly provide a specific number and type of rooms to Gulliver which are available for reservations. Only allocated rooms can be booked automatically through the system and are therefore given priority. *Request* members do not allocate rooms to the system and therefore need to be contacted via fax, phone or post to ascertain whether a member has availability. These members are given less priority and are only contacted if no allocation properties are available.

3   Methodology

The primary purpose of this research was to examine the attitudes of owners/managers of small accommodation establishments in South West Ireland towards a selection of possible benefits they were receiving from membership on Gulliver and the differences in these attitudes dependent on a variety of variables.

The variables chosen were:
♦   Type and rating of accommodation establishment
♦   Size of accommodation establishment
♦   Owner/Manager characteristics
♦   Type and Length of Gulliver membership
♦   ICT experience of owner/managers

A set of hypotheses were formulated with respect to these attitudes and a questionnaire was carefully designed to test these hypotheses and submitted to pre-testing by a small subset of the final sample. As a result of this, some statements were modified and the final questionnaire was administered to a probability sample of the chosen population.

The population chosen for the study was defined as:
> *All small serviced accommodation establishments who were members of Gulliver and categorised as being located in South West Ireland.*

The sample was chosen using stratified random sampling. The population was stratified first by the two counties within the South West region (County Kerry and County Cork) and then by accommodation category with a sample randomly generated based on the total number of elements in each strata as a proportion of the total.

422

Premises were randomly selected using random number generation in an Excel spreadsheet.

The questionnaire was mailed to 300 premises out of a population frame of 1,089 in the hope of a response rate of at least 20%. The response rate was 18%, providing a valid sample size for the subsequent statistical analysis, carried out using SPSS software (Statistical Package for the Social Sciences).

4 Results

The questionnaire identified sixteeen benefits that could be derived from Gulliver membership. These were subdivided into five categories, as shown in Figure 4.1.

4.1 Business Performance

As Figure 4.1 illustrates, of the valid responses received for the statements regarding their business performance, the majority of respondents disagreed that Gulliver membership *had contributed towards increased profitability* or *had improved their occupancy figures*. Of interest is the *extent* to which respondents disagreed with these two statements. In the case of profitability, 53 per cent of all respondents *strongly disagreed* that their membership had contributed towards profitability while 44 per cent *strongly disagreed* that membership had improved occupancy.

Fig. 4.1 – Perceived Benefits of Gulliver Membership - Level of Agreement With Each Statement

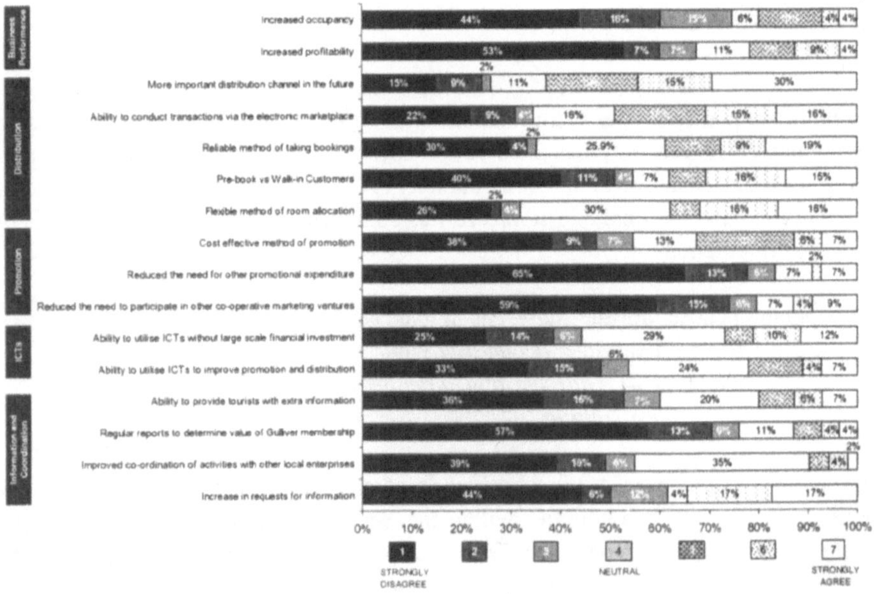

Further analysis of the data revealed that of the 18 premises that had experienced an increase in profitability in the last twelve months, only 4 premises agreed that Gulliver had been beneficial in improving their profitability. Of the other 14 respondents, 4 were neutral and the remaining 14 (61%) did not believe that Gulliver had contributed to improved profitability. This indicates that these owners perceived other factors as contributing to this increase. With respect to occupancy, of the 16 premises that had experienced an increase in occupancy in the last 12 months, an overwhelming 13 respondents (81%) disagreed that this increase was attributable to their Gulliver membership. Only two respondents (13%) agreed that Gulliver membership had contributed to this, with one respondent indicating that they neither agreed nor disagreed.

4.2 Distribution

The findings for the five statements regarding distribution emphasize several important points. First, a limitation of the questionnaire was highlighted through the large percentage (30%) of respondents that were neutral about whether Gulliver allows a *flexible method of room allocation..*

It was thought that perhaps a reason for this neutrality was the fact that this particular statement was only applicable to allocation members since respondents were asked to rate each statement based on their own experiences and not on their general view of Gulliver. In this case, request members could not reliably answer this question based on their own experiences, unless of course, they had previously been an allocation member but were now currently a request member. Further analysis of responses broken down by membership type (as shown in Table 4.1) shows that the majority of

Table 4.1: Responses to Whether Gulliver Provides a Flexible Method of Allocation by Membership Type

| | | Type of Gulliver Member | | | | Group Total | |
| | | 1 Allocation | | 2 Request | | | |
		Count	Col %	Count	Col %	Count	Col %
Flexibile method of	1	5	17.9%	9	40.9%	14	28.0%
room allocation	2			1	4.5%	1	2.0%
	3	1	3.6%	1	4.5%	2	4.0%
	4	8	28.6%	7	31.8%	15	30.0%
	5	3	10.7%			3	6.0%
	6	8	28.6%			8	16.0%
	7	3	10.7%	4	18.2%	7	14.0%
Group Total							
		28	100.0%	22	100.0%	50	100.0%

request members did answer this question, with approximately 50 per cent disagreeing that Gulliver provided a flexible method of room allocation. The results for this question should therefore be taken with some caution because it cannot be determined whether they were in fact answering with respect to previous experience or answering based on their overall perception of the system rather than on their own experiences.

Looking specifically at responses from allocation members, 50 per cent agreed that Gulliver provides a flexible method of allocation. However, there were still a large number (29%) who neither agreed nor disagreed with this statement, with 21 per cent disagreeing that the system provides a flexible method of room allocation.

With respect to perceptions regarding whether Gulliver has contributed to *an increase in pre-book as opposed to walk-in customers*, 56 per cent disagreed, the majority of them strongly, that Gulliver membership has led to an increase in pre-booking customers. As with the statement regarding flexibility of room allocation, a high percentage (26%) of respondents were neutral about whether Gulliver provides a *reliable method of booking*. This could be due to the low percentage of bookings that many respondents have received, therefore feeling that they cannot evaluate this particular benefit. Overall, 35 per cent agreed that it provided a reliable method of taking bookings and the remaining 39 per cent disagreed.

The responses to the two other statements in this category were more positive, with almost 50 per cent of respondents agreeing that Gulliver provided them with a means of conducting transactions via the electronic market place and an encouraging 63 per cent of respondents stating that they thought Gulliver would be a more important distribution channel in the future. This has important implications for the future of Gulliver and the willingness of this sector to support the system. It is also positive given respondents' overall perceptions of Gulliver's contribution to their businesses to date and their overall satisfaction with the system.

4.3 Promotion

There was very strong disagreement amongst respondents that Gulliver membership has resulted in promotional benefits. An overwhelming 80 per cent of respondents disagreed that their membership had *reduced the need to participate in other co-operative marketing ventures* and 84 per cent stated that they disagreed that it had *reduced the need for other promotional expenditure*. This indicates that these premises are certainly not relying on Gulliver as their main method of promoting themselves, although this is not surprising in a sector in which organisations have traditionally used a variety of methods to promote and distribute themselves to their markets. With respect to whether Gulliver provides a *cost effective method of promotion*, the level of disagreement is not so severe but 38 per cent of respondents still *strongly disagreed* that Gulliver was a cost effective means of promoting their establishment.

4.4 Information and Communications Technology (ICT)

For the two questions regarding the use of information and communications technologies, there were a large number of respondents who neither agreed nor disagreed that their Gulliver membership had either enabled them to *use ICTs to improve their promotion and distribution* or enabled them to *use ICTs without large scale financial investment*. This response has highlighted what could be another problem with the structure of the questionnaire in that these questions did not apply to those premises which did not use ICTs which could explain the large neutral response. Further analysis showed that a large percentage of premises which had indicated utilisation of the fax or the Internet in their daily operations also neither agreed nor disagreed with these two statements.

4.5 Information and Co-ordination

Over half of the respondents disagreed that they were receiving any of the four benefits classified under information and co-ordination. The majority of respondents disagreed with each statement, with 62% per cent disagreeing *that requests for information about their organisation had risen*, 55 per cent disagreeing that membership with Gulliver *had improved co-ordination of activities with other local businesses*, an overwhelming 72 per cent disagreeing that they *regularly received reports from Gulliver* and 58% disagreeing that membership with the system enabled them to *provide more information to tourists*.

The large number of neutral responses to the statement regarding the improvement of activities with other local enterprises indicated that perhaps this question was unsuitable when examining a national system such as Gulliver because it is very centralised and therefore individual premises do not become as involved in it as they might a local or regional system. The strong response to the statement regarding information sent from Gulliver regarding booking information indicates that premises don't perceive that there is very good communication between themselves and GISL. The strength of feeling to this comment was interesting because premises can actually call Gulliver at any time to request booking statistics for their premises. However, it seems that many of the respondents did not know this and, as a result, they have a negative perception of the system.

4.6 Results of Statistical Tests

In order to make inferences about small accommodation establishments in South West Ireland based upon this study, statistical tests were carried out to test a series of stated null hypotheses. The original intention was to examine the differences in attitudes based on a variety of demographic and organisational variables, however in the case of the variables such as ownership, size and number of employees, the responses were such that it was not possible to discriminate between the categories due to the small sample size and therefore there has been no attempt to draw any conclusions about the population based on these variables.

◆ **Hypothesis 1: H₀ - Type of membership does not affect owner attitudes towards each of the sixteen selected benefits**

It was hypothesised that owner attitudes towards the selected benefits would differ depending on the type of membership the premises had. In order to test the significance of any differences between the means of each statement by allocation and request members, a *t* test was performed. It was found that five out of the sixteen benefits were rated differently by these two groups, thus rejecting the null hypothesis and accepting the alternative hypothesis, at p=0.05 level of significance, that type of membership does affect owner attitudes towards the following five benefits: *flexible method of room allocation, reduced the need for other promotional expenditure, positive change in pre-book as opposed to walk-in customers, cost effective method of promotion and ability to utilise ICTs without large scale financial investment.* For all five statements, allocation members tended to have a more positive attitude, although it should be noted that for several of the statements, such as *cost effective method of promotion* and *reduced the need for other promotional expenditure,* the mean rating for allocation members is still in the zone of disagreement. The significance in these cases merely means that while allocation members in the South West disagree with the statement, the extent of their disagreement is significantly less than that of request members.

The significant differences between attitudes of allocation and request member regarding whether Gulliver had led to an *increase in pre-booking customers, has reduced the need for other promotional expenditure* and is a *cost effective method of promotion* is probably a reflection of the fact that as request members they get less priority when bookings come through the call centre in Killorglin. It is likely therefore that allocation members would be more inclined to agree or have a more positive perception with these statements because these properties get higher priority for bookings and thus achieve a higher level of bookings. With respect to the statements regarding *flexible method of room allocation* and *the ability to utilise ICTs without large scale investment,* the results of these questions should be taken with caution. However, the significant difference could be explained by the fact that the allocation members are familiar with the system and know how it works and therefore have a more positive attitude. This is contrasted with request members who have either never allocated rooms and therefore can not reliably evaluate this statement, or were once allocation members who have changed their membership and, quite possibly, have a negative view of the method of allocation.

◆ **Hypothesis 2: H₀ - Method of allocation does not affect owner attitudes towards each of the sixteen selected benefits**

Hypothesis 2 stated that there would be significant differences between owner attitudes towards each of the sixteen benefits depending on their method of allocating rooms. An analysis of variance (ANOVA) was used to test this because it involved testing three groups against the dependent variable, that is, the use of *GullNet, FaxLink* or *Phone/Post*.

The null hypothesis was accepted for all sixteen statements. At the $p = 0.05$ level of significance the result was that method of allocation does not affect owner attitudes towards the benefits that they think Gulliver membership is bringing to their organisation.

♦ **Hypothesis 3: H_0 - Length of membership does not affect owner attitudes towards each of the sixteen selected benefits**

The null hypothesis for Hypothesis 3 stated that attitudes towards the benefits they received would not be affected by the length of their membership with Gulliver. The statistical test used was the ANOVA and it was found that there were significant differences at the $p = 0.05$ level for three of the benefits: *flexible method of room allocation, cost effective method of promotion, reliable method of taking bookings*, rejecting the null hypothesis. An examination of the post-hoc tests indicated that there were significant differences between owners of serviced accommodation in South West Ireland who began their membership in 1992-93 and those who joined after the privatisation in 1998-1999, and also between those who began their membership in 1994-1997 and those who joined after the privatisation. There was no significant difference in attitudes towards these three benefits between South West establishments who became members in 1992-93 and those who joined between 1994-97. This significant difference in attitudes between the most recent members and the other two groups could be due to several factors. First, it may be that these owners have a more positive attitude about Gulliver in general because they have not experienced the previous problems with the system. Older members may be more cynical about Gulliver and its contribution to their businesses because it has taken so many years to develop and many problems have been encountered. It may also be due to the fact that newer members are less experienced and therefore they have different expectations.

♦ **Hypothesis 4: H_0 - Accommodation category does not affect owner attitudes towards each of the sixteen selected benefits.**

ANOVA was used to test this hypothesis, with a significant difference in attitudes towards two of the sixteen benefits being found, thus rejecting the null hypothesis for the following two benefits: *cost effective method of promotion* and *ability to provide tourists with extra information*. For the statement regarding Gulliver providing a cost effective method of promotion there was a significant difference between two sets of pairs at the $p = 0.05$ level of significance: Country Homes and Farmhouses and Country Homes and Townhouses. A possible reason for the difference in attitudes between Country Homes and Townhouse owners could be the locational aspects of their businesses. Townhouses are generally located in more urban or town centres whereas Country Homes tend to be in more rural areas and therefore may not benefit as much from tourist office bookings and bookings from GISL. The differences in agreement about the statement regarding the ability to provide tourists with extra information were significant between Country Homes and Townhouses and Country Homes and Guesthouses. Once again, it could be the urban location that could explain these differences in attitude, with Country Homes owners in the South West in more peripheral areas having a more negative attitude.

5 Conclusions

A variety of recommendations emerge from the findings of this research. Whereas the overall indication is that the majority of the respondents do not seem to perceive any benefits from Gulliver, their perception is also that Gulliver will become a more important distribution channel in the future. This has implications for the cooperation of this sector and the willingness of the small accommodation provider to continue participating in the future.

Moreover, since this research was carried out only after serious changes were being introduced to Gulliver as a result of privatisation, it points to a very important area of future research, to test the hypothesis advanced by some researchers and practitioners in the field, that destination management systems should be developed initially by the public sector and then privatised to operate as commercial ventures.

Finally, Connor and Cronin (1993) stated that there are many gaps within tourism academic research about Ireland. It is hoped that this study will assist in contributing to the body of knowledge about tourism in Ireland and SMTEs' place within the industry.

References

Archdale, G., Stanton, R., and Jones, C., 1992, **Destination Databases: Issues and Priorities**. A Paper Prepared for the Pacific Asia Travel Association.
Baker, M., Hayzelden, C. and Sussmann, S., 1996, Can Destination Management Systems Provide Competitive Advantage? Discussion of the Factors Affecting the Survival and Success of Destination Management Systems, **Progress in Tourism and Hospitality Research**, 2, 1-13.
Beaver, A., 1995, Lack of CRS Accessibility May Be Strangling Small Hoteliers, The Lifeblood of European Tourism, **Tourism Economics**, 1(4), 341-355.
Blank, D., 1999, **Destination Management Systems and Small Accommodation Establishments: The Irish Experience**. M.Sc. Thesis, University of Surrey.
Bord Fáilte, Gulliver: Ireland's Tourism Information and Reservations Network. Information Pack.

Connor, B. and Cronin, M., 1993, Tourism in Ireland: A Critical Analysis. Cork: Cork University Press.

Frew, A.J., O'Connor, P., 1998, A Comparative Examination of the Implementation of Destination Marketing System Strategies: Scotland and Ireland. In: Buhalis, D. et. al., eds., **Information and Communication Technologies in Tourism 1998: Proceedings of the International Conference in Istanbul, Turkey, 1998**. Wien, New York: Springer, 258-267.

Inkpen, G., 1998, **Information Technology for Travel and Tourism**, 2nd ed. Essex: Longman.

Pringle, S.M., 1994, Destined to fail? An investigation of the Hi-Line destination management system. In: Seaton, A., ed., **Tourism State of the Art**. Chichester: Wiley, 500-509.

Sussmann, S.M., Baker, M., 1996, Responding to the Electronic Marketplace: Lessons from Destination Management Systems, **International Journal of Hospitality Management**, 15(2), 99-112.

The Use Of Internet Sites By Smaller Travel Agencies In The Netherlands

G.J. van der Pijl
Erasmus University, Tilburg University,
The Netherlands
e-mail: vdrpijl@tref.nl

1 Introduction

Internet seems to open up new marketing possibilities for smaller companies in the tourism sector. Therefore, it is interesting to now how these smaller companies make use of the possibilities of the World Wide Web. Much of the literature, however, focuses on Internet use by larger companies. Thus, it seems worthwhile to focus some empirical research on the smaller companies in the trade. Such a research effort is reported on in this paper. It is based on empirical research carried out by masters students of the IS department of Tilburg University. They studied the websites of 30 smaller travel agencies in the Netherlands and conducted interviews with their owners. Although the number of observations in the research is too small too draw statistically reliable general conclusions the results seem interesting enough to share with a broader public. In this paper we first focus on the research methodology, then provide the description of the websites and next report the outcomes of the interviews. In the final paragraph some conclusions are drawn.

2 Research methodology

Small travel agencies were randomly selected from the Internet. In total we included 29 sites in the survey. A group of students judged each site, using a set of criteria derived from literature. After that, each of the travel agencies was visited and, where possible, the owner was interviewed. In a few instances another person, responsible for the site did the interview. Table 1 gives the distribution of the sample in terms of the number of branch offices. The conclusion is that we really are considering very small travel agencies with mostly only one office.

Table 1: Number of branch offices

No of branches	Frequency	Valid Percent
1	19	70
2	5	18
3	1	4
5	1	4
6	1	4
Total	27	100
Missing	2	
	29	

Not all companies were willing to reveal their turnover. For those who did, turnover varied between 30 thousand and 30 million Dutch Guilders. The mean was 6 million Dutch Guilders

3 Description and rating of the sites

Each of the sites in our research was described in two ways. First the global classification as suggested by Angehrn (1997) was used. Angehrn recognizes that sites normally develop from purely information oriented to transaction oriented presence on the web. The classification contains four categories:

1. Sites serving as information channels
2. Sites serving as communication channels
3. Sites serving as distribution channels
4. Sites serving as transaction channels

It will be clear that a particular site can fall in more than one category.

Fig. 1: Types of sites

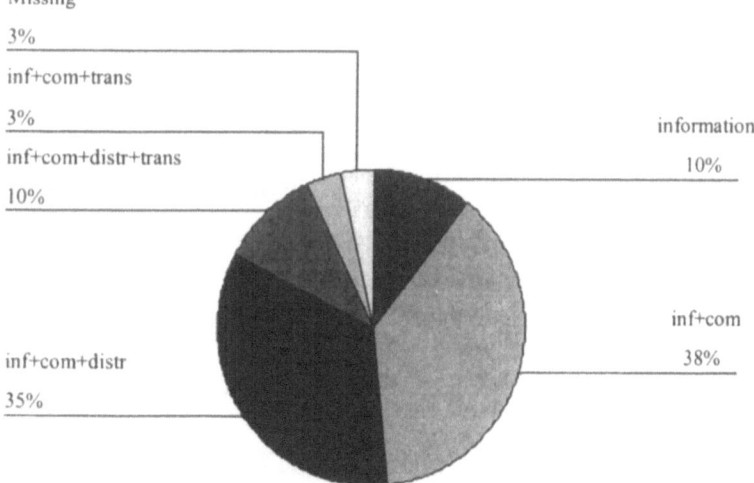

Fig. 1 gives the percentages of sites in the different categories. We can conclude that most sites are in the stages 2 and 3 of Angehrn. That means that they offer some communication facilities like e-mail or request for information forms and that they are used to distribute the information that formerly was distributed by way of brochures to the consumer. Only a minority of sites (10%) makes it possible to process transactions on line by means of the site and thus belong to the most highly developed type of sites as distinguished by Angehrn..

Next we looked at the context of the site in somewhat more detail. From Table 2 it is clear that almost all sites offer the basic information that can be expected from travel agencies. There are, however, only a few sites that offer more than the basic information. Only eleven out of the 29 inform the consumer on the terms of delivery. No more than 6 out of the 29 sites offers experiences of former clients. Only 3 sites offer their visitors a search engine. Although the importance of the use of virtual reality on the web is growing, none of the sites we surveyed made use of virtual reality.

Table 2: Information and communication properties

	yes	no
Summary of products offered	26	3
	90%	10%
Experiences of former clients	6	22
	21%	76%
Terms of delivery	11	18
	38%	62%
Links to related sites	14	14
	50%	50%
Virtual reality		28
		97%
Email?	29	
	100%	
Email form	18	11
	62%	38%
Postal address	29	
	100%	
Telephone number	29	
	100%	
Location	25	4
	86%	14%
Form for brochure or other information	18	8
	69,2%	30,8%

Some recent authors (Creemers 1999) argue that the best internet sites offer a lot of value before the moment of sails by providing as much information related to the decision the client has to make as possible. On tourism sites one of the best sources of information would be links to other sites, describing destinations or destination alternatives, travel possibilities etc. We found that about 50% of the sites provided this type of facilities be it mostly in a very modest way.

As for the communication aspect of the sites we note that all of them enable e-mail communication. Only 18 out of the 29 facilitate e-mail by providing a standard e-mail form. Almost 70% of the sites support communication by providing a form for requesting a brochure or for asking information.

Table 3: Transaction services

	yes	no
Booking by e-mail	5	24
Boking by form	11	18
online booking	3	25
Travel insurance	12	17
Reservations possible?	9	19
Payments possible	1	28
Form for complaintsr	2	27
after sales service	3	26
Search engine	3	26

Table 3 gives an overview of the results relating to the transaction oriented aspects of the sites. Slightly less than half of the sites allow booking by e-mail or by providing a standard booking form. Online booking with immediate response is possible with only 3 sites. Preliminary reservations are possible for 9 sites. There are twelve sites that offer possibilities for arranging for travel insurance, sometimes through their own site, sometimes through the site of one of the larger travel insurance companies in the Netherlands. Only one side allows for paying electronically. This, however, for very specific reasons that are not valid for other travel agencies. After sales services are provided by only a few sites. 2 sites offer forms to send in complaints, 3 sites provide other forms of after sales services.

Table 4: Quality of the sites

Score	2	3	4	5	6	7	8	9	10
Userfriendlyness	1	1	1		4	6	9	5	2
quality of the information	1	1	1	3	4	7	6	3	3
"fun" level	1	1	3	5	6	6	4	3	
Clearness	1	1		2	5	6	8	3	3
esthetical quality	1	1	1	2	5	8	7	1	3

In Table 4 the ratings the students gave for the sites are summarized. For the rating process we used quality aspects similar to those presented by Werthner and Klein (1999). The numbers in the table indicate the number of times a particular score was given for a particular quality aspect. The table shows that in general the students found the sites quite satisfactory and awarded relatively high scores. Only the "fun" level of the sites was rated somewhat lower although even here the average scores are higher than 6.

4 Interview results

Students did not only look at the sites, they also visited the companies involved and interviewed the owners. In this paragraph we summarize the results of the interviews. To start with, in Fig. 2 the number of years the companies have been active on the Internet is indicated. 70% of the companies are in the game for three years or less.

Fig. 2: No of years on internet

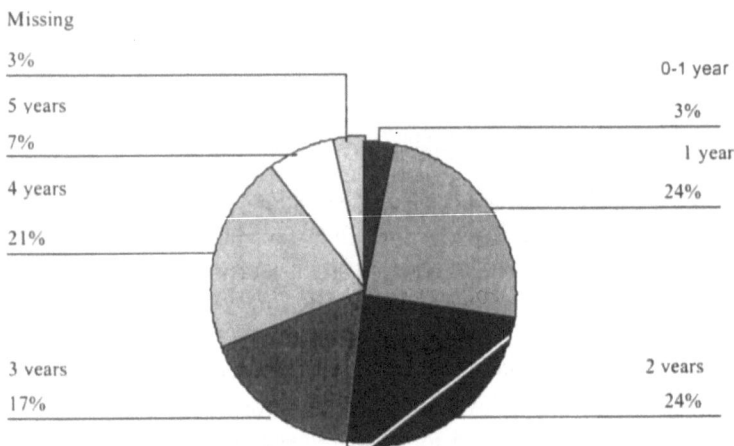

The reasons why companies are present at the Internet are summarized in table 5. The main reasons prove to be the fact that respondents believe that the nature of the product they are selling and the nature of the clients they are serving are good reasons

Table 5: Why an Internet site?

	yes	no
Everybody has one	10	16
Nature of the product	23	3
Nature of the client	23	3
Competitor does it too	13	13
hotels do it too	7	19
Airlines do it took	8	18
To reduce costs	12	14

to maintain a site. Especially companies that offered adventure holidays or other types of holidays felt that they could reach their type of clients through the web. Some companies serving older groups of consumers felt that for those the Internet was irrelevant.Less than half of the respondents give the presence of competitors, or of hotels and airlines, on the web as a reason for being there themselves.

Once we have seen that there seems to be some general believe that "you have to be there", it is interesting to see how important one thinks the presence on the Internet is (van der Pijl 1993). Table 6 shows that 44 percent of our respondents thought the Internet to be important for their business. Explaining their viewpoints to the students, many respondents indicate that they think that the importance of the www is still growing.

Table 6: Importance of the site

		Frequency	Percent
Valid	Very important	9	36
	important	11	44
	Somewhat important	5	20
	Total	25	100
Missing		4	
Total		29	

Next we asked whether our respondents had an idea about benefits and costs of their Internet activities. The results are presented in table 7. As indicators for benefits we asked about their knowledge on number of hits, number of requests for information and number of bookings. The number of hits is known by 16 of the 29 respondents. 17 of them know the number of requests for information. The number of bookings as a result of the site is said to be known by 6 respondents. Others say that it is hard to know this because you are never sure whether a booking is a result of the site or of something else.

The majority of the companies that have a site with booking facilities (8 out of 12) know the number of bookings directly through the site. Amazingly, four respondents indicate that they do not know this number.

Asking site owners for their insight in the costs of their sites gives a less clear picture. We presented them with a number of cost categories asking them whether they knew the cost figure for each category. Many respondents answered "yes we know the costs: they are 0 " to several questions. These are shown separately in table 7. In many cases we doubt whether the idea of 0 costs our respondents is correct. In some cases the argument is that the computers one needs were already there. Replacement needs are often left out of consideration. Also one often forgets to calculate the time spent by the owner of the business or by his employees. In our view, therefore, knowledge of the costs of the sites is even less than is suggested by table 7. It is also worth noticing that most respondents do not know the costs of handling transactions and requirements. This is important because, if Internet trade has to grow to a considerable part of total turnover, the handling of inquiries and transactions is very important.

Table 7: Knowing the costs and benefits

	?	0	yes	no
HITS			16	10
Requests for information, absolute			17	9
Requests for information, relative			11	11
Bookings because of site, absolute			6	15
Bookings because of site, relative			4	16
Bookings via site, absolute			7	4
Bookings via sit, relative			5	4
Payments via site			1	
Costs of development, externally	4	7	13	5
Costs of development, externally	4	5	14	6
Costs of equipment	4	15	4	6
Hardware costs	5	14	6	4
Maintenance costs, externally	3	7	11	8
Maintenance costs, internally	5	5	10	9
Costs of use of hard and software	6	13	1	9
Handling of inquiries and transactions	5	1	7	16
Other costs	10		7	12

The next item we were interested in was the organization of the sites. Therefore, we first asked who was doing the work in the design, technical maintenance and content maintenance of the sites. The results are summarized in table 8. It shows that in most cases design and technical maintenance was outsourced to a third party or done in cooperation with a third party. Even then, a considerable percentage of the site owners design and technically maintained the site themselves (7 and 9 respectively). This gives an indication of the fact that for quit a lot of small companies in tourism in the Netherlands the Internet activities are not yet seen as a business activity that needs professional attention.

Table 8: Who does the work?

	?	owner	employee	external	combination
design	3	7		15	4
Technical maintenance	3	9	1	14	2
Content maintenance	3	19	2	1	4

5 Discussion

From the above it is clear that many small Dutch travel agencies are active in the Internet. Looking at the type of sites they present and the organization behind it there is an enormous variety. We found a couple of sites that are in the forefront of transaction handling Internet sites. But on the other hand we must conclude that it is still a minority that makes on line transactions possible. Looking at the fast rate of development of transaction oriented sites of larger travel agencies there seems to be some urgency to move to the transaction-oriented side of the market. In contrast to this many owners of small travel agencies still do not think of competition as the main reason for being on the Internet. Saving costs is an important driver for quite a number of companies. In itself it seems to be true that using internet as a means of distributing product information can save a lot of costs of expensive brochures. Focussing on cost savings alone however can divert the attention from the real threat of fierce product competition through the Internet. On top of that the cost-benefit analysis does not seem to be done as carefully as needed in all cases. Cost of hardware and software and above all handling costs seem to be underestimated in many cases. This might steer strategic decision making on this type of issues in the wrong direction.

Although almost all site owners acknowledge the importance of Internet, the actual behavior does not always illustrate a real sense of urgency. Quite often business owners build their sites in their spare time or outsource it to the whiz kid next door. Although this can be considered as a good and cheep way of experimenting with new technology, in the long term one has to change to a more professional form of organization. Much attention will also have to be paid to embedding the handling of Internet generated transactions in the back office. Good Internet trade requires very quick and very effective response to clients requests. Small businesses have to think well about how to organize business procedures in order to respond well to the growing expectations of clients in this domain.

References

Angehrn, A., Designing mature Internet business strategies: the ICDT model, European Management Journal, 1997, vol.15 nr.4, p.361-369;
Creemers, M.R., In de electronische boekhandel is informatie belangrijker dan prijs (In electronic bookstores information is more important than price), Holland management review, 1999, nr. 6.
Pijl, G.J. van der, Quality of information in theory and practice, PHD thesis in Dutch, Tilburg University May 1993, summarized in Enter proceedings 1994
Pijl, G. J. van der and Zee, H. van der, Measuring the value of IT, Enter proceedings 1997
Werthner and Klein, 1999, Information technology and Tourism, a challenging relationship, Springer, Wien, new York, 1999;

Internet As A Destination Marketing Tool: A Case Study (Spanish National Tourism Organisation)

Castelltort, M.

Jefe del Area de Información. SubBureau de Medios de Promoción.
Instituto de Turismo de España, TURESPAÑA (Spain)
Magi.Castelltort@tourspain.es

Mora, J. I.; Navarro, G.; Pernas, J. I.; Zapata, M. J.
Research scholars in the SubBureau de Medios de Promoción de TURESPAÑA
Infotur.spain@tourspain.es

Abstract

This paper aims to illustrate the relevant role that the Internet plays as a tool for marketing tourism destinations online by focusing on a study of the web site of Spain's National Tourism Organisation, TURESPAÑA. The research covers three main areas, firstly, the collaborative model of TURESPAÑA in promoting Spain through its own network of web sites coupled with those of the Spanish Tourist Offices abroad. Secondly, by means of a case-study, the paper sets out the need to combine different sources of information to research web-user's profiles in order to prevent misleading conclusions. Finally, the study ends with a report on current and future developments to improve the efficiency of the TURESPAÑA web site with the hope this experience could guide further improvements in the sector of Information Technology and Tourism.

1 The role of the Internet for marketing in National Tourism Organisations (NTO)

Information and communication systems constitute key elements in increasing the competitiveness of the tourist sector, a sector which is not only extremely fragmented and heterogeneous, (e.g. travel agents, tour-operators, hotel chains, ski resorts, theme parks, etc.) but also often features large geographical distances between supplier and consumer. As a result, there is a vital need to establish information flows between the different stakeholders concerned, (tourism public administration, tourist industry, local communities and tourists) in order to create the travel experience and make it mutually profitable for all involved.

Tourism marketing systems (TMS), electronic commerce, and computer reservation systems (CRS) are some of the technological developments of the Information Age already incorporated in the industry. Their application has facilitated the discovery of new dimensions and opportunities, e.g. the empowerment of SMTE, the rapid analysis of changes in consumer behaviour, the emergence of new niches in the market, the direct link between suppliers and consumers with its serious repercussions for traditional travel distributors, the implications inherent in the adoption of IT within the organisational structure, the change in the inter-organisational relationships and management strategies of tourist organisations, and the large variety of new means for promotion and marketing.

One of the most relevant applications of Information Technology is the use of the Internet as a marketing tool for tourism. Indeed, during the last few years a proliferation of local, regional and national tourism web sites for promotional purposes have been observed together with an increasing use of the Internet by consumers. The success of the Internet rests on its advantages compared to traditional information channels: customisation of the message, its interactive and real-time nature, low cost of communication, and the world wide scope of the information it provides.

The need for a unique and comprehensive 'voice' promoting any tourism destination, made up of diverse and numerous suppliers and institutions, has driven many tourism public organisations to integrate the Internet as a relevant tool within their marketing strategy plan. Indeed, most NTO's have significantly adopted the Internet as a tool for marketing their national destinations by providing information on accommodation, transportation or attractions. These web sites range from information providers only to complete on-line reservation services, although the latter are still rare.

With the growth in the use of Internet by tourist boards, the tourist industry and tourists alike, there is a need to stop and reflect on the existing experience and the Internet contribution to the objective of marketing tourism destinations, especially when considering the role that these information-providers increasingly play as a 'direct bridge' between the tourist and the final service.

This paper sets out the means to identify the steps and methods for improving the efficacy of the Internet as a tool for marketing tourism destinations, employing the experience gained from the web site of the National Tourism Organisation of Spain, (TURESPAÑA) and its Tourist Offices abroad.

The research adopts a case-study approach and combines quantitative and qualitative techniques to gather the necessary data for the analysis. Primary and secondary sources of data have been used in order to ensure the reliability of the results. The research techniques consist of a survey of the web sites of the Spanish Tourist Offices, a content analysis of the information requests to the web site, a statistical analysis of the use of the web site by consumers, and the analysis of figures on visits to the web sites through different information channels.

The results of this research have been structured into three main areas. The first section introduces the TURESPAÑA web site, launched in 1998, the characteristics of the web sites and those of the Tourist Offices abroad linked to www.tourspain.es. Available resources, information and services provided and the statistics on the use of these web sites are assessed by means of both a survey and the observation of each web site. The second section offers an interesting case-study based on the experience of TURESPAÑA on the need to combine different sources of information to establish web-user profiles. A third section details the steps recently undertaken or planned for the near future by TURESPAÑA to ensure the optimisation of the Internet as a tool for marketing tourism destinations which include improving the Feed-back Travel Advice Service, quality audits of the web site and the Feed-back Travel Advice Service, the commercial and promotional use of the data provided by site users, (surveys and content analysis of information requests), the refining of the existing Tourist Information System (SIT) and new services such as supplier advertising and the implementation of an Indirect Booking System (IBS).

Finally, the paper concludes with a discussion of the methods and steps undertaken by TURESPAÑA from the point of view of a cumulative experience and is offered as assistance in the marketing of tourism destinations through the Internet.

2   The web site of TURESPAÑA and the associated web sites of the Spanish Tourist Offices abroad

2.1 The web site of TURESPAÑA: www.tourspain.es

The web site of the Spanish National Tourism Organisation (TURESPAÑA) was launched on January 1998. One of the main reasons to establish www.tourspain.es was to facilitate the cost-effective distribution of a large amount of specific, destination-related information to a world-wide audience. Market research including general travel and tourism statistics was undertaken to develop the design and content of the site. This research was conducted over a period of 3 years and the cost to establish the site was approximately $150.000.

The web site of TURESPAÑA is a comprehensive tourist guide offering general knowledge about Spain whilst at the same time providing the user with a powerful tool to obtain the most accurate information on-line about the country. Visitors can access the available information in any one of four languages: Spanish, English, French and German, and can navigate through the 7 000 HTML pages, 13.000 photos and images, 40 tables containing 22 810 files. As a result, the web site of TURESPAÑA has become the most important computer-based channel for the distribution of Spanish tourist information. Currently it occupies 410 MBytes and its usefulness has been established with an average of over 4000 visits and 100 enquiries per day arriving from all over the world.

Information is accessed through an index with generic options that permits the user to select different types of travel, e.g. leisure, business, adventure travel and learning Spanish. These general options are complemented with practical information on other global aspects about the country such as climate, population, political structure, passports and visas, currency, customs regulations, etc. The information is structured into twenty eight chapters with headings such as "Events", "Accommodation", "Cities and Islands", "Art and Culture", "Tour-operators and Travel Agents", "Active Tourism", "Transport", "Gastronomy", and the like. It also provides a link to 15 different Spanish news sources and Spanish news published in newspapers from around the world as well as a current list of domestic and International Spanish Tourist Offices.

An interactive map of Spain offers information at city and island level including local services and infrastructure, accommodation, transport, etc. Furthermore, an active index allows the visitor to consult each content site in turn or return to the home page or to any other site directly which makes www.tourspain.es very easy to navigate. There are also links to the most important external web sites containing other useful information. Similarly, there is a check-list which is made available to the traveller which is very useful for organising their travel arrangements. The site also contains a powerful search engine which makes it easy to locate specific information along the site.

The web site of TURESPAÑA is gradually increasing its links to other prestigious and popular web sites so that www.tourspain.es is becoming the accepted Internet portal for tourism information on Spain.

2.2 TURESPAÑA and the web sites of the Spanish Tourist Offices abroad

Evaluation of the web sites

Among its many functions TURESPAÑA is also responsible for supporting the marketing of Spanish tourism in foreign markets as well as defining general marketing directives in collaboration with Spanish Tourist Offices abroad who in turn, maintain direct contact with their local markets. As a result, it is not surprising that TURESPAÑA has decided to create a web site for every market (Japan, USA, Canada, Italy...), managed by the leading Office in every country in co-ordination with the one of TURESPAÑA.

This collaborative model is continued through the main web site of TURESPAÑA and the associated web sites of the Spanish Tourist Offices as shown.

Table 1. Assessment of the web sites of TURESPAÑA and the Spanish Tourist Offices abroad

	Spain	U.K.	Canada	U.S.A.	Japan	Denmark	Italy	Belgium Luxemburg	France	Holland
ORIGIN										
Year of creation	1998	1998	1999	1997	1995	1997	1999	1999	1999	1998
Previous research	✓	✓	✓	✓					✓	
Frequency of maintenance	Daily	Monthly	Monthly	Twice a week	Once a year	Monthly	Monthly			
Webmaster	Internal	Internal	External	External	Internal	External	External			
FEATURES										
Country/ies	General	UK and Ireland	Canada	USA	Japan, Korea, China, Taiwan, Hong-Kong	Scandinavian Countries	Italy	Belgium, Luxemburg	France and French-speaker countries	Holland
Languages	Spanish, English, French and German	English	English	English	English, Japanese, Korean and Chinese	Spanish, English and Danish	Italian	French and Dutch	French	Dutch
Interactive database & search	Accommodation, Sports, Active Tourism, Fiestas	Tour-operator							Fiestas	
List of external links	✓								✓	
Direct links to the site of Turespaña in the home page	Links with the Tourist Offices	Icon in main frame	Two icons in main frame		Link by hypertext	Link by hypertext		Icon in main frame		Link by hypertext
Other sites with link to tourspain es	Links with the Tourist Offices	Accommodation, Museums	Accommodation, Active Holiday, Gastronomy	Accommodation, Tour-operator	Accommodation, Tour-operator		Accommodation, Cultural Holiday, Feed-back site		Regions, Transport, Accommodation	
Services provided										
Feed-back service	✓	✓	✓	✓	✓	✓	✓	✓		✓
Brochures	✓	✓	✓	✓	✓	✓	✓	✓		✓
Advertising										
Indirect on-line Booking System	✓	✓		✓						
Online booking							✓			
Information										
Climate	✓	✓	✓	✓	✓	✓	✓	✓	✓	✓
Food & Drink	✓	✓	✓	✓	✓	✓	✓	✓	✓	✓
Visa & Customs	✓	✓	✓	✓	✓	✓	✓			
Currency	✓	✓	✓	✓						
Travel Agents & Tour-operators	✓	✓	✓	✓	✓	✓	✓	✓	✓	✓
How to get to the destination	✓	✓	✓	✓	✓	✓	✓	✓	✓	
Public transport	✓	✓	✓	✓	✓	✓	✓	✓	✓	✓
Telecommunications	✓	✓		✓	✓	✓				
Information on cities & regions	✓	✓	✓	✓	✓	✓	✓	✓	✓	✓
Culture & Customs	✓	✓	✓	✓	✓	✓	✓		✓	
Suggested itineraries	✓	✓	✓	✓	✓	✓	✓		✓	
Events & Attractions	✓	✓	✓	✓	✓	✓	✓	✓		✓
Accommodation	✓	✓	✓	✓	✓	✓	✓			
STATISTICS (1999)										
Average time of connection	12'13"	9'25"	Unknown yet	9'15"	8'20"	9'50"	Unknown yet	9'02"	8'05"	
Average visits per day	4.120	425		606	1.000			250	300	
Average enquiries per day	100			20	10					
Most visited sites	Accommodation, Art & Culture	Tour-operator, Accommodation, Useful information	Unknown yet	Accommodation, Tour-operator	Accommodation, Tour-operator	Accommodation, General links	Unknown yet	Useful addresses, General links, survey, Tour-operators	Accommodation, General links	Tour-operator, General links
Origin of users	U.S., Spain, U.K., Germany, France	U.K., U.S., Spain, Ireland						Belgium, Spain, U.S., Germany, U.K., Austria		
DESIGN										
Index seen on every page	✓	✓	✓	✓	✓	✓	✓	✓	✓	✓
Logo of Spain at home-page	✓	✓	✓	✓	✓	✓	✓	✓	✓	✓
Photographic Images	✓	✓	✓	✓	✓	✓	✓	✓	✓	

Source: TURESPAÑA

Why are the associated web sites necessary for TURESPAÑA?

As the table above shows, some of the web sites of the Spanish Tourist Offices were launched prior to the web site of TURESPAÑA. That was certainly the case for www.okspain.org, the web site for the United States market, and www.spaintour.com, the web site for Japan, Korea and China. The rapid and widespread use of PCs and the Internet in these countries prompted these Tourist Offices to use this information channel for promotional purposes at an early stage. Indeed, both examples confirmed the potential need to develop a new communication channel with high cost-effective capability to reach potential visitors in their markets of origin.

After the creation of www.tourspain.es, the web site of TURESPAÑA in 1998, the earlier web sites continued operating and new web sites were developed by some of the other Spanish Tourist Offices abroad. Despite the fact that this would appear to hinder an integrated and co-ordinated tourist information system, the existence of these associated web sites permits decentralisation of resources, rationalisation of the infrastructure of the Spanish Tourist Offices abroad with their ability to customise the promotional actions of TURESPAÑA by means of the direct knowledge that these tourist offices hold, both of the local language (when it is not covered by the TURESPAÑA web site, as the case of the web site for Japan, Korea, China, Italy, and so) and the culture and customs of their particular markets.

The web site of TURESPAÑA is translated into the languages of its three main tourist markets: Germany, England and France, thus providing a language base that covers other countries such as the United States, Canada, South America, Switzerland, Austria, India, Pakistan, Australia, New Zealand and South Africa. Other markets that TURESPAÑA cannot reach can be covered by the web sites of some of these Tourist Offices translated into the local languages e.g. Japan, Netherlands or Russia.

Similarly, the increasing development of the promotional functions of these web sites will allow Tourist Offices in the near future to concentrate resources on marketing activities which require active personnel involvement.

At the same time, integration of the associated web sites in the marketing actions of TURESPAÑA, together with the centralisation of the services of www.tourspain.es rationalises existing resources such as the Tourist Information System, the commercialisation of the web sites, the provision of Internet connections to some of the Tourist Offices or direct links to the accommodation database of the web site of TURESPAÑA.

Finally, with regard to the co-ordination of associated web sites with www.tourspain.es, although a degree of autonomy is allowed, minimum standards for the establishment of the contents of the web sites are required. As illustrated in Table 1, the web sites show some common design features such as the logo of TURESPAÑA, direct links and calls to www.tourspain.es or the existence of a contents index which shows current information on attractions, accommodation, visas and customs regulation, transport and the like.

3. The need to triangulate the sources of information in researching web-user profile.

Information on the profile, preferences and interests of the visitors to the web site has become indispensable for the operation of TURESPAÑA website since its functions and design and those of the web sites of the other Tourist Offices abroad are modified according to the changing requirements and characteristics of the users. For instance, special promotional actions focused on cultural events can be mounted by a particular Spanish Tourist Office abroad when a significant percentage of visitors of that nationality are observed to be specially interested in these events on our web site.

Nonetheless, as the following experience of TURESPAÑA will illustrate, in order to gather such data it is necessary, possibly vital, to employ different sources of information to identify users. The following shows that statistics obtained by some of the existing special software for analysing web site data is not sophisticated enough and may even lead to serious misunderstandings.

Should we trust our computers?

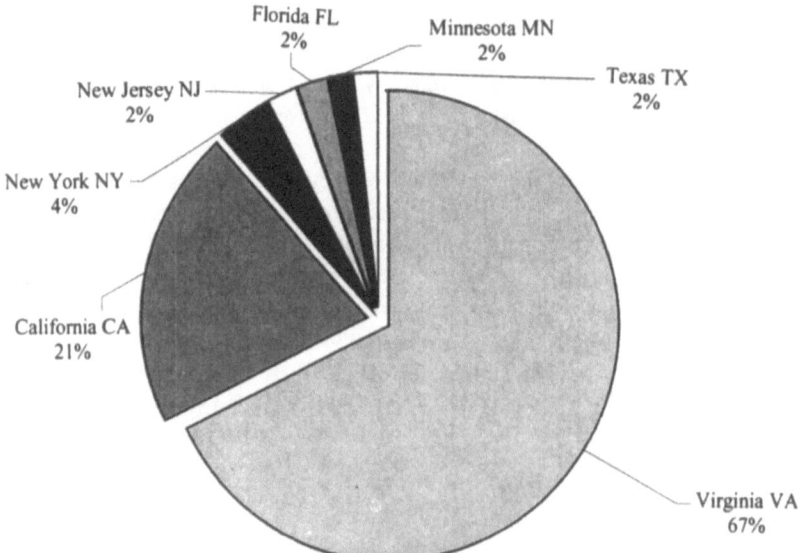

Fig. 1. Percentage of visits to www.tourspain.es
by states of US - APRIL 1999

Results shown in Fig. 1 employing web site data demonstrate that US residents of Virginia are, by a large margin, our most popular fans, accounting for 67% of our traffic on the Internet. According to cybermarketers and other experts in advertising, we should focus our campaigns on Virginia, even establish a new branch of the Spanish Tourism Office in order to deal with such a huge demand for information about Spain. Even though none of our market studies showed any particular preference by the people of Virginia for Spain as a tourist destination, should we not trust our Internet statistics? Is really cybermarketing more reliable than traditional methods? In order to elucidate this matter we used a huge variety of sources, either traditional or newer methods but here we will only introduce a few.

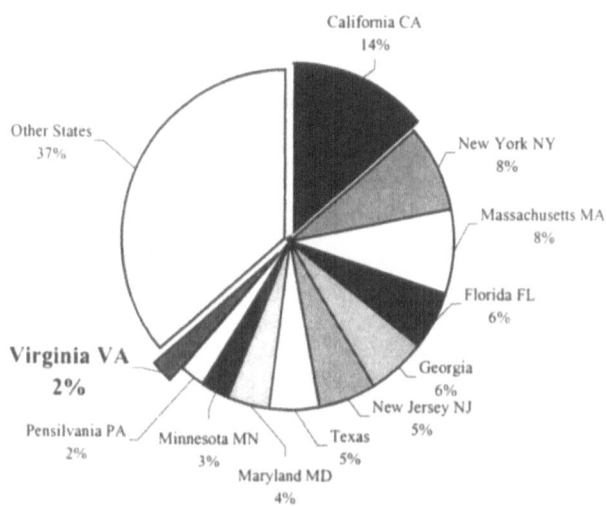

Fig. 2. Percentage of enquiries to www.tourspain.es
by states of US - ARIL 1999

For cybermarketing tools we had two main sources: our information request form and our statistics. We use the first in order to obtain information from our internauts so that we can help them to know our country better and to assist them in planning a future visit to Spain. As can be seen from comparing Fig. 1 and Fig 2, the difference between these two sources raised the dilemma and we had to use a third source: our US market studies. Although California has always shown a clear preference for us, with close links, both cultural and climatic (the Spanish population is one of the largest in the US and both enjoy the same Mediterranean-type weather), this was not the case for Virginia. Therefore the answer was technical rather than commercial and thus we focused on network matters where we found the solution: Proxy servers and the shortage of IP numbers. Currently there is a severe shortage of available IP numbers and ranges which obliges Internet Service Providers (ISP) to handle this issue by routing their users through proxy servers. In our case, visitors to the web site are coming in with the IP of their proxy server which relates directly to its physical location. The following shows this process.

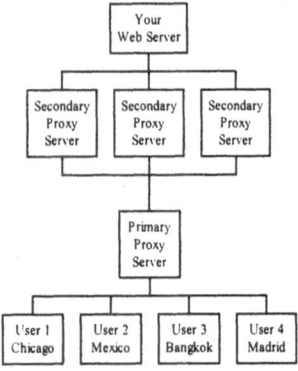

Fig. 3. Proxy servers and IP

As we can see in the figure above, each user of a particular organisation is dialling into a local city number in their area be it Chicago or Madrid or any other city. Their connection is routed by the ISP to a group of proxy servers, say the Federal Government of the US in Virginia which now becomes their ISP. This topology means that when a user is routed through the Federal Government of the US connects to our web site, our server logs the IP number of this proxy server on the log file. Therefore, any statistics analysis software relates the IP to the Federal Government, which is registered in Virginia even though most of our visitors might be located somewhere else. But even worse, for the time being there is no way to overcome this problem; even Cookies, which are frequently used by most of the web servers will not be of any help because they do not store demographic information. Thus the only thing certain about this data is that Spain appears to be very popular among US civil servants.

4. Current and future changes in the web site of TURESPAÑA

In this section we show the steps recently undertaken or planned for the near future to ensure the optimisation of the Internet as a tool for marketing tourism destinations which include improvements to the Feed-back Travel Advice Service, the quality audit of the web site and the Feed-back Travel Advice Service, the commercial and promotional use of the data provided by site users, (surveys and content analysis of information requests), the refining of the existing Tourist Information System (SIT) and new services such as supplier advertising and the implementation of an Indirect Booking System (IBS).

Feed-back service

Recent changes in the Feed-back Travel Advice Service of www.tourspain.es have been introduced in order to improve the speed of information flow, the quality of the data provided and to rationalise the human resource that supports the web site. Much of the information requested referred to data already available on the web site. Therefore, this mechanism has helped to channel information requests to the right site by highlighting the most often requested information. Even though, FAQs should be combined with the feed-back service in order to monitor any single change in the needs of tourists.

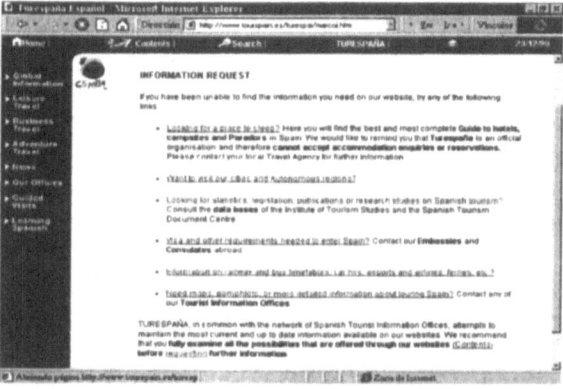

Fig. 4. Feed-back travel advise service

Commercial and promotional use of the data provided by the users of the web site

The users of the web site provide very diverse and interesting information which is extremely helpful to support decision-making processes in marketing and promotional matters as the experience of TURESPAÑA has already shown.

Firstly, this information has been very useful as market research necessary to identify new market niches and to support decision-making in the marketing plans of this institution. Data such as the socio-demographic profile of the tourist, (e.g. nationality, gender, seasonality), destination preferences, travel behaviour (e.g. time of year when trip planning, preferred accommodation and means of transport, average expenditure), the profile of the web-surfer tourist (e.g. method of Internet access, experience on-line, number of hours/week connected, on-line purchases) and intention to travel, just to mention a few, have been drawn out from the analysis of the information requests or, alternatively, from other more complete web surveys of users.

Secondly, there is promotional use of this information by means of the creation of a data-base of both the consumers who have requested information from the Feed-back Service and users who answer TURESPAÑA web site questionnaires. This data-base has already been employed for promotional purposes, for instance, by mailing information on cultural events to visitors who manifested their interest in this type of tourist product through their information requests to the Feed-back Service of our web site.

Finally, this data collection has become a useful tool to improve customer service through surveys to assess the quality of the Feed-back Service, the quality of the information provided by the web site as well as the degree of satisfaction with the tourist's trip to Spain.

Therefore, as the experience gained by the web site of TURESPAÑA shows, it is useful to research the data coming from cyber visitors through these three major sources: user enquiries, statistics on the use of the web site and information provided by e-mail and web surveys.

The Tourist Information System, Indirect Booking System and Advertisement services on the web site of TURESPAÑA

Another interesting improvement in the web site of TURESPAÑA is the refining of the Tourist Information System that supports the web site. In the near future, an extranet will be implemented whereby external companies, such as hotels or tour-operators, can update the information presented in this data base.

Similarly, it is intended to run an Indirect Booking Service by establishing links with the web sites and e-mail addresses of useful tourist companies as hotels, transport companies, travel agents or tour-operators. By adopting an Indirect Booking System instead of a direct booking service, political and legal responsibilities are avoided, economic burdens are not placed on public funds and a greater equity is achieved by allowing small, medium and large companies to directly market their products, while additional fees will be collected by returns and used to self-fund, at least partially, the costs of the web site.

5. Conclusions

By focusing on a study of the web site of TURESPAÑA this paper has demonstrated the valuable role that the Internet plays as a tool for marketing tourism destinations online.

Through the experience gained by TURESPAÑA, a collaborative model used to promote Spain through the Internet utilising and linking the associated web sites of the Spanish Tourist Offices abroad with the main web site of TURESPAÑA is demonstrated.The characteristics, co-ordination, means and justification of the need to maintain independant sites are discussed and positive results offered to support the model.

In researching web site user profiles the need to combine different sources of information in order to prevent misleading conclusions is shown by a case-study of misleading IP numbers from the state of Virginia.

Finally, current and future developments of the TURESPAÑA web site, introduced as a result of our experience to improve efficiency are discussed to provide a posible source of assistance to others in this field.

References

World Tourism Organisation: Marketing tourism Destinations Online. WTO (1999).
H.-S. Jung: The Analysis of Demographic Profiles and Prospects of Internet Users in National Tourism Organisations: Case Study (Korean National Tourism Organisation). In: Buhalis, D., Shertler, W. (eds.): Information Technology and Tourism. A Challenging Relationship Springer, Wien New York, pp. 98-107 (1999).
J.-S. Jung, A. Twigeri: The Use of the Internet as a New Marketing Tool to Promote New Tourist Destinations in Asia: Case Study (Korean National Tourism Organisation). In: Buhalis, D., Shertler, W. (eds.): Information Technology and Tourism. A Challenging Relationship Springer, Wien New York, pp. 119-129 (1999).
Frew, A.J., J. O'Connor, P.: Destination Marketing System Strategies in Scotland and Ireland: An Approach to Assessment. Information Technology & Tourism (2) 1: 3-14 (1999).
Spanish National Tourist Organisation (TURESPAÑA) http://www.tourspain.es
Tourist Office of Spain in Japan http://www.spaintour.com
Tourist Office of Spain in the United Kingdom http://www.uk.tourspain.es
Tourist Office of Spain in Canada http://www.tourspain.toronto.on.ca
Tourist Office of Spain in the US http://www.okspain.org
Tourist Office of Spain in Belgium http://www.tourspain.be
Tourist Office of Spain in Luxemburgo http://www.tourspain.lu
Tourist Office of Spain in France http://www.espagne.infoturisme.com
Tourist Office of Spain in Germany http://www.spaansverkeersbureau.nl
Tourist Office of Spain in Italy http://www.turismospagnolo.it
Tourist Office of Spain in Denmark http://www.spanien-turist.dk
TURESPAÑA: Plan de Apoyo a la Comercialización Turística. Turespaña, Madrid (1999).

Efficiency Measures in Benchmarking Decision Support Systems: A Hotel Industry Application

Karl W. Wöber
Institute for Tourism and Leisure Studies
Vienna University of Economics and Business Administration, Austria
Augasse 2-6, 1090 Vienna, Austria
karl.woeber@wu-wien.ac.at

Abstract

The purpose of this paper is to present the applicability of Data Envelopment Analysis in an interactive benchmarking system. The decision support system which is used for this experimental study is accessible on the World Wide Web and based on data obtained from Austrian small and medium sized hotel enterprises. The system was developed with financial support of the Austrian Chamber of Commerce and is operated by the Austrian Society for Applied Research in Tourism (ASART) at the Vienna University of Economics. It enables Austrian entrepreneurs as well as consultancy companies specialising in tourism to compare the performance of hotel and restaurant enterprises with others of a similar nature. In the present paper the author gives a comprehensive description of the conceptual approach, the technical realisation and experiences and implications with the prototype version of the system.

1 Introduction

The phenomenon of benchmarking has been discussed by many authors primarily in form of management handbooks [1, 2]. Effective benchmarking allows comparisons among similar business units to discover best practises and incorporate process and product improvements into ongoing operations. There exists a vast literature on operational requirements and managerial implications, however, very little attention is paid on methodological aspects in conjunction with benchmarking, especially on the right selection of benchmarking partners and the identification of 'who is best?'.

According to Bell and Morey [3] the identification of leadership companies in benchmarking studies is more art than science. Also benchmarking efforts regularly ignore for the larger part differences in operating environments, service levels, and rely on simple engineering ratios. As a solution for this problems Bell and Morey suggest the application of Data Envelopment Analysis (DEA) for the identification of benchmarking partners and they illustrate their proposal on a data set of corporate travel departments. Recently there have been several authors who have recognized the potential of DEA for the selection of benchmarking partners [4, 5, 6]. However, several important issues remain to be addressed when it comes to implement this methodology in an interactive Decision Support System (DSS).

This paper introduces this powerful tool for evaluating the performance of hotels and discusses conceptual problems which occur when this technique is integrated in an interactive DSS.

2 Data Envelopment Analysis

DEA is a mathematical model which originally has been used to measure the relative efficiency of operating units with the same goals and objectives. Organizations, similar to operating units, have multiple inputs, such as staff size, salaries, hours of operation, and advertising budget, as well as multiple outputs, such as profit, market share, and growth rate. In these situations, it is often difficult to determine which organizations/firms are inefficient in converting their multiple inputs into multiple outputs. DEA can separate the efficient firms from the inefficient on the basis of whether they lie on the efficient frontier which is spanned by the best companies in the data set.

The simple DEA program is formulated as a fractional programming problem and is then reduced to a linear programming problem that is easy to compute. DEA starts by building a relative ratio consisting of total weighted outputs to total weighted inputs for each institution in a given data set. The best organizations in the data set form a 'efficient frontier', and the degree of the inefficiencies of the other units relative to the efficient frontier are then determined using a linear programming algorithm. An advantage of DEA is that it needs no *a priori* information regarding which inputs and outputs are most important in the evaluation procedure.

Methodologically, the DEA algorithm can be best described through the original model developed by Charnes, Cooper and Rhodes [7], which is more comprehensively discussed in [8] and [9]. Consider N units that convert I inputs into J outputs. To measure the efficiency of this converting process for an organization, Charnes et al. propose the use of the maximum of a ratio of weighted outputs to weighted inputs for that unit, subject to the condition that the similar ratios for all other organizations be less than or equal to one. That is,

(1)
$$\max \frac{\sum_{j=1}^{J} u_j^o y_j^o}{\sum_{i=1}^{I} v_i^o x_i^o}$$

Subject to

$$\frac{\sum_{j=1}^{J} u_j^o v_j^n}{\sum_{i=1}^{I} v_i^o x_i^n} \leq 1; \quad n = 1, ..., N,$$

$$v_i^o, u_j^o \geq 0; \quad i = 1, ..., I; \quad j = 1, \cdots, J.$$

where y_j^n, x_i^n are positive known outputs and inputs of the nth organization and v_i^o, u_j^o are the variable weights to be determined by solving problem (1). The organization being measured is indicated by the index 0. The maximum of the objective function given by problem (1) is the DEA efficiency score assigned to the organization under evaluation. If the efficiency score is 1, the organization under evaluation satisfies the necessary condition to be DEA efficient; otherwise, it is DEA inefficient.

It is difficult to solve problem (1) as stated, because the objective function is nonlinear and fractional. However, Charnes et al. [7] transformed the above programming problem into a linear one as follows,

(2)
$$\max \sum_{j=1}^{J} u_j^o y_j^o$$

subject to

$$\sum_{i=1}^{I} v_i^o x_j^o = 1,$$

$$\sum_{j=1}^{J} u_j^o y_j^n - \sum_{i=1}^{I} v_i^o x_j^n \leq 0; \quad n = 1, ..., N,$$

$$v_i^o \geq \varepsilon, u_j^o \geq \varepsilon; \quad i = 1, ..., I; \quad j = 1, ..., J.$$

To ensure that all of the known inputs and outputs have positive weight values and that the optimal objective function of the dual problem to problem (2) is not affected by the values assigned to the dual slack variables in computing the DEA efficiency score for each organization, an arbitrarily small positive number, ε, is introduced in the model. The objective value is interpreted in the same way as in (1).

A complete DEA model involves the solution of N such problems, each for a base organization, yielding in N different weight sets. In each program, the constraints are held constant while the ratio to be maximized is changed. The DEA problem described in this article were solved using the computer software LINDO Rel. 6.1 [10].

3 Case Example

In the late 60s the Austrian Professional Hotel and Restaurant Associations, situated within the Federal Chamber of Commerce, had realized that Austrian small and medium sized enterprises cannot cope with this information deficit on their own. Therefore they decided to fund a research project to establish a company panel which allows the industry to exchange data on business operations on a global basis in order to benchmark individual performances. The project is carried out by the Austrian Society for Applied Tourism Research (ASART).

Financial information is collected annually on a confidential basis from approximately 1,300 hotels and restaurants. The data is provided by interested companies on a voluntary basis and by cooperating industry related organizations (Österreichische Hotel- und Tourismusbank, BÜRGES Förderungsbank des BmwA).

The data comprises information from the balance sheet, the profit and loss statement and information obtained from an additional questionnaire. The accounting part of the database is following the most common arrangements of Austrian hotel and restaurant businesses. A comprehensive list of all definitions is given in the regular report published by the author [11].

The case example presented here is based on a sub-set of the panel database. 61 hotels with similar business characteristics have been selected for the DEA. The operating data entered in the analysis are based on financial information from 1997.

Morey and Dittman's model was partially adopted to develop the input and output variables for the DEA test [4]. Hotel outputs used in the current study are: (1) total accommodation revenue; (2) total F&B revenue; (3) average annual bed occupancy adjusted by the number of opening days. Factors determined by the market and therefore uncontrollable to the hotel management are: (1) number of beds; (2) number of seats (in the F&B section of the hotel); (3) number of opening days (for the DEA to distinguish between annual and seasonal accommodation providers). Factors controllable by the general manager are: (1) Total payroll and related; (2) Material-type expenditures; (3) Energy costs; (4) Cleaning costs; (5) Maintenance costs; (6) Communication costs; (7) Marketing costs; (8) Administration costs.

The payroll costs include costs for social insurance contributions, personnel expenses for F&B and housing, seminars, employees' travel expenses etc. Costs for cleaning captures costs for cleaning materials and rental laundry. The administration costs include office utilities, insurance costs, consultancy costs, and travel expenses of the manager. The complete data description is summarized in Table 1.

Table 1. Data description for 61 Austrian hotels

	Mean	Min	Max	Stdev	in %
Number of beds	109	28	398	61.2	
Number of seats	212	27	630	110.1	
Number of opening days	296	152	365	61.4	
Total F&B revenue (€)	728,590	88,720	2,976,870	514,300	
Total room revenue (€)	495,950	1,460	1,931,640	387,060	
Occupancy[1] (%)	54.9	19.5	83.5	15.5	
Total expenditures (€)	1,016,987	77,340	4,503,940	765,190	100.0
- Payroll and related (€)	506,828	28,970	1,944,620	387,760	49.8
- Material-type exp. (€)	213,270	14,880	907,490	151,770	21.0
- Energy costs (€)	67,973	5,180	223,840	48,230	6.7
- Cleaning costs (€)	23,984	3,280	124,690	25,690	2.4
- Maintenance costs (€)	84,578	5,910	688,970	93,170	8.3
- Communication costs (€)	12,577	880	61,720	11,300	1.2
- Marketing costs (€)	40,296	800	234,860	45,060	4.0
- Administration costs (€)	67,481	8,460	402,890	69,960	6.6
Gross profit (€)	207,553	-436,670	546,040	196,220	

Notes: [1] per opening days.

4 Analysis and Results

Figure 1 shows the operating profit plotted against the DEA efficiency score for each of the 61 hotels. The hotels which were deemed efficient and received a score of 1 are plotted along the right border. Although the relationship between profitability and efficiency is obvious, the plot clearly shows that not all hotels who have been classified as efficient are necessarily also profitable. There are some low-profitability hotels that are run efficiently, and some high-profitability hotels that are run inefficiently. The DEA solution plotted in Figure 1 illustrates that by the use of this methodology, unanticipated insights may be obtained and may thus redirect managerial action. In a broader sense, the DEA framework creates an approach for learning from outliers and for inducing new theories of best practice.

Hotel #38, which is a 89-beds property, was selected for more detailed analysis and interpretation in the present text. In the year under consideration hotel #38 achieved € 819,600 in total F&B revenue, € 394,200 in total room revenue and spent € 968.800 for operating expenses. The gross profit was € 245,000, or 20 percent of the total revenue. The occupancy rate was 67 percent. That compares favorably with the average set's occupancy rate of 54.9 percent, total F&B revenue of € 728,590, and total room revenue of € 495,950. Hence hotel #38 exceeded the average output measures of all hotels in the data set on all three of the performance measures (see Table 1 and 2). A ranking of the hotels solely on the basis of gross profit would have ranked hotel #38 above average compared to the other hotels in the data set.

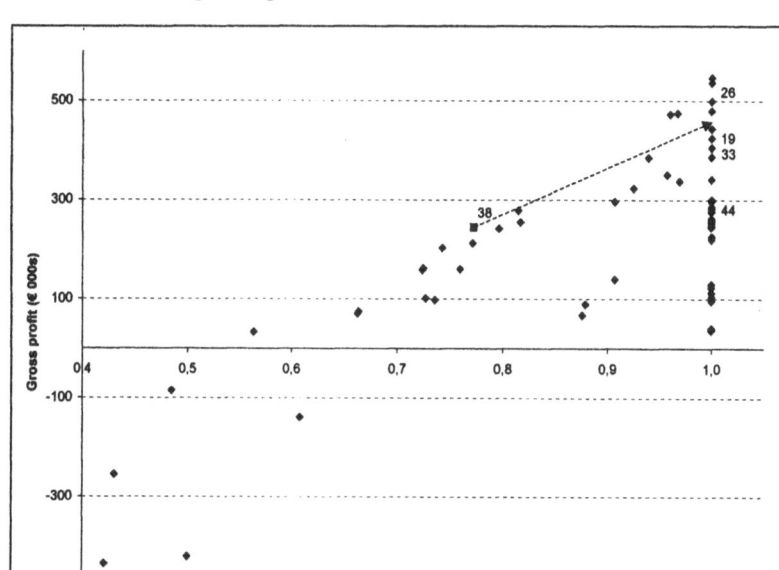

Fig. 1. Profitability versus DEA efficiency scores for 61 Austrian hotels

Using allocative DEA we find that three of the remaining 60 hotels constitute a peer group for company #38. However, as is typically the case, the characteristics of the peer-group members do not perfectly match those of the unit being evaluated.

To account for the difficulty in comparing actual property-operation characteristics, the linear program builds a weighted composite of the three identified, efficient peer-group members that perfectly matches the levels of outputs and the operating environment of the unit being evaluated. Thus a composite, efficient benchmark general manager is derived to develop a scorecard. It shows the resource-expenditure targets for hotel #38 based on the management's achieving at least the same total room revenue and service levels in the same or more difficult environment.

With the benchmarking figures listed in Table 2, it is possible to calculate the efficiency score for hotel #38. Dividing the total expenditures of the composite benchmarking partners by hotel #38's expenditures results in the efficiency score of .773. As it turns out, hotel #38 ranks only 46th out of the 61 hotels in efficiency, notwithstanding the fact that the hotel's occupancy rate and revenue figures all exceed those of the average set.

Table 2. Benchmarking example for hotel #38

	# 38	# 19	# 26	# 33	# 44	BM^2
Number of beds	89	80	96	65	55	89
Number of seats	200	120	210	450	100	197
Number of opening days	365	350	310	360	300	311
Total F&B revenue (€)	819,600	254,000	957,700	1,072,500	139,800	819,600
Total room revenue (€)	394,200	1,261,300	347,400	214,800	445,300	394,200
Occupancy^1 (%)	67.0	78.6	73.0	39.6	67.1	71.6
Total expenditures (€)	968,800	1092,000	806,300	901,100	288,200	748,400
- Payroll and related (€)	484,000	645,800	434,000	535,600	140,600	404,400
- Material-type exp. (€)	234,400	197,400	186,200	174,100	61,700	169,200
- Energy costs (€)	28,000	41,500	67,900	79,700	33,800	62,400
- Cleaning costs (€)	25,200	28,200	17,600	11,700	9,000	16,700
- Maintenance costs (€)	119,000	70,000	45,500	64,400	7,000	41,600
- Communication costs (€)	8,600	6,400	12,000	14,000	5,600	10,900
- Marketing costs (€)	34,200	34,600	4,200	9,300	6,300	5,800
- Administration costs (€)	35,300	68,100	39,000	12,300	24,200	37,500
Gross profit (€)	245,000	423,400	498,800	386,200	296,900	465,400

Notes: ^{1} per opening days; ^{2} Benchmark (composite group) based on LP solution with $\lambda_{19}{}^* = 0.04$, $\lambda_{26}{}^* = 0.799$, $\lambda_{33}{}^* = 0.023$, and $\lambda_{44}{}^* = 0.138$; $e_{38}{}^* = 0.773$.

The peer group is matched to hotel #38 based both on the non-controllable factors as well as on the levels of all outputs as so far as the environmental factors in the benchmarking group are either equal or less favorable compared to the one of hotel #38. In the case of the output factors the virtual benchmarking company either performs equal or even better than the hotel under evaluation. The benchmark revenue figures are the same as hotel's #38 revenues, and the benchmark for the annual occupancy rate shows a higher level compared to hotel #38.

The benchmarks that are most interesting are those for the eight resource expenditures. They constitute a set of guidelines for hotel #38 to work toward. If hotel #38 utilizes the resources more efficiently, it should be able to achieve the same output with lower expenditures. The DEA analysis indicate that hotel #38 has the potential to improve its output by € 220,400 (improvement of about 90 percent), when it reduces it expenditures to € 748,400 (a decrease of 22.7 percent).

Fig. 1 depicts the ideal direction for hotel #38 to move regarding efficiency and profit, as well as the position of the three benchmarking partners. The identification of the three peer properties can be made available to hotel #38 so that the management can ascertain from them (perhaps through site visits) the details of the processes, cultures, and practices that enable them to perform better.

Fig. 2. Selecting a Competitive Group from the Database

5 Strength and Weaknesses of DEA in a DSS Environment

Managerial Decision Support Systems (DSS) in tourism are relatively rare (exceptions are [12, 13, 14, 15]). This is especially true in the hotel operation segment, where most of the applications can be found in the yield management or F&B operations area (e.g., [16, 17, 18]). Traditional forms of benchmark publications do not allow the flexibility and interactivity which is necessary to build a system which adapts to individually varying information needs. Therefore, a procedure for interactive performance benchmarking, would extend the performance measurement technique available in DEA. An example of such an interactive decision support instrument is available within the tourism marketing information system TourMIS displayed in Figure 2 (http://tourmis.wu-wien.ac.at/db-bench/bv).

Several advantages result when DEA is incorporated in an interactive environment. For example, in DEA, the input and output variables must be carefully selected to make the analysis useful for the manager. Although DEA has fewer limitations than other econometric approaches in the choice of input and output variables, the efficiency measure obtained by DEA is very sensitive to the combination of inputs and outputs. The advantage of an interactive system is that the user can go back and forth and learn from the output. The manager can change the selected variables and he is not bound to a strict classification as is usual in ordinary printed publications of panel studies. Hence he will realize soon that results may vary significantly, sometimes even through minor changes in the preliminary assumptions. Therefore the manager can gain more insights and a better understanding how to interpret benchmarking results and how to use them for managerial purposes.

Another opportunity for a more intensive use of DEA applications occurs in an multi user environment like the Internet offers to SME hotel managers. Extranet applications of an on-line database of financial hotel data offer the adequate platform for competitive analysis similar to DEA, especially for SME which are less organized in the exchange of business data than international (multiple unit) hotel chains. Finally, the advantage of a real time application is that additional insights can be gained by multi-period analysis and extrapolations of business data time series. A database system can therefore easily convert the DEA model from a *ex post* evaluation instrument to a prospective oriented instrument which might support budgeting tasks in SME companies.

There are several research problems which have been experienced during the development phase of the hospitality benchmarking program and which have to be discussed in the future.

For example, the standard DEA model is a static, one-period evaluation and difficult to integrate in an interactive environment. When a new company's data is added to the database, all efficiency runs for all other firms have to be repeated as the effect on the efficiency frontier is unclear. In response, panel data and window analysis have been adapted to minimize the distortions in isolated cross sections (e.g., [19]). The resulting efficiency scores are thought to give a better assessment of underlying performance. However the repeated application of DEA through a panel data set produces little more than a continuum of 'static' results, when a static perspective may be inappropriate. In reality the behavior underlying the production process is likely to be dynamic because hotels may take more than one time period to adjust their choice variables to desired levels. Furthermore, capital inputs have a multi-period dimension since they generate outputs in future periods. It would clearly be appropriate to move towards some more general dynamic DEA modeling. This would have to deal with the problems of trended data in growing organizations and inflationary environments. In addition it would need to provide an explicit partial adjustment mechanism, which is more efficient than the replication of linear programming runs.

References

1. Camp, R.C.: Benchmarking: The Search for Industry Best Practices that Lead to Superior Performance, Milwaukee: Quality Press (1989).

2. Spendolini, M.J.: The benchmarking book. New York: Amacom (1992).

3. Bell, R.A., Morey, R.C.: The search for appropriate benchmarking partners: A macro approach and application to corporate travel management. Omega, International Journal of Management Science, 22(5), 477-490 (1994).

4. Morey, R.C., Dittman, D.A.: Evaluating a hotel GM's performance. A case study in benchmarking. Cornell Hotel and Administration Quarterly, 36(5), 30-35 (1995).

5. Morey, M.R., Morey, R.C.: Mutual fund performance appraisals: A multi-horizon perspective with endogenous benchmarking. Omega, International Journal of Management Science, 27, 241-258 (1999).

6. Siems, T.F., Barr, R.S.: Benchmarking the productive efficiency of U.S. banks. Financial Industry Studies, December 1998, 11-24 (1998).

7. Charnes, A.C., Cooper, W.W. Rhodes, E.: Measuring the efficiency of decision making units. European Journal of Operational Research, 2(6), 429-444 (1978).

8. Charnes, A.C., Cooper, W.W., Lewin, A.Y., Seiford, L.M. (Eds.): Data Envelopment Analysis: Theory, methodology, and application, Boston: Kluwer (1994).

9. Norman, M., Stoker, B.: Data Envelopment Analysis. The assessment of performance, Chichester: J. Wiley & Sons (1991).

10. Schrage, L.E.: Optimization modeling with LINDO, 5th edition, Duxbury Pr. (1997).

11. Wöber, K.W.: Betriebskennzahlen des österreichischen Gastgewerbes. Bilanzjahr 1997, Wien: Österreichischer Wirtschaftsverlag (1999).

12. Mazanec, J.A.: A decision support system for optimizing advertising policy of a national tourist office. Model outline and case study. International Journal of Research in Marketing, 3, 63-77 (1986).

13. Moutinho, L., Rita, P., Curry, B.: Expert systems in tourism marketing. London: Routledge (1996).

14. Walker, P.A., Greiner, R., McDonald, D., Lyne V.: The tourism futures simulator: A systems thinking approach. Environmental Modelling & Software, 14, 59-67 (1999).

15. Wöber, K.W.: TourMIS: An adaptive distributed marketing information system for strategic decision support in national, regional, or city tourist offices. Pacific Tourism Review, 2(3/4), 273-286 (1998).

16. Yeoman, I., Ingold, A. (Eds.): Yield Management. Strategies for the service industries. London: Cassell (1997).

17. Kirk, D.: Catering technology – development of equipment and processes to increase productivity. In: Cooper, C. (Ed.): Progress in Tourism, Recreation and Hospitality Management, London: Belhaven Press, 232-241 (1989).

18. Wöber, K.W.: Comparing operating ratios for small and medium hotel and restaurant businesses. A decision support system using Internet technology. In: Buhalis, D., Schertler, W. (Eds.): Information and Communication Technologies in Tourism (1999). ENTER 99, Proceedings of the International Conference in Innsbruck, Austria 1999, Springer: Wien – New York 1999, 238-246.

19. Charnes, A.C., Clark, T., Cooper, W.W., Golany, B.: A developmental study of Data Envelopment Analysis in measuring the efficiency of maintenance units in the U.S. Air Force. In R. Thompson and R.M. Thrall (eds.) Annals of Operations Research, 2, 95-112 (1985).

The Measurement of the Marketing Effectiveness of the Internet in the Tourism and Hospitality Industry

Timothy H Jung
School of Management Studies for the Service Sector
University of Surrey
H.Jung@surrey.ac.uk

Richard Butler
School of Management Studies for the Service Sector
University of Surrey
R.Butler@surrey.ac.uk

Introduction

The subject of the use of Information Technology (IT) in the tourism industry has become increasingly important in recent years and Information Technology (IT) has already begun to have a great influence on the tourism industry. In its various forms, the advent of the Internet and its remarkable growth has enabled tourism organisations to reach customers worldwide with both ease and cost effectiveness. As the number of Internet users increases and the size of the electronic market grows, tourism organisations, such as National Tourism Organisations (NTOs), Hotels, Airlines, and Travel Agencies are developing an Internet presence and adopting the Internet as a mainstream marketing strategy. It is meaningful, therefore, to investigate the perception by marketing managers of the Internet as a marketing tool and to identify how they measure the success rate of any websites they have established in the tourism and hospitality industry.

As many tourism organisations are putting increasing resources into their websites, the issue of the effectiveness of these resources becomes of increasing importance. This gives rise to the need to examine issues such as the effectiveness of the Internet as a marketing medium, the characteristics of a successful website, the key factors of website design, and the methods of measuring the efficacy of websites of each tourism organisation. In order to explore these issues, the Modified Technology Acceptance Model (MTAP) is introduced. Many researchers have attempted to investigate the factors affecting the take-up of IT. Of particular interest has been the attitude of managers to IT because this has an important influence on both diffusion rates and in what way, and how successfully, IT is used once adopted (Baker *et al*, 1997). Therefore, the rate of adoption and diffusion of the Internet as a marketing tool by managers of tourism/hospitality organisations is examined by applying the Modified Technology Acceptance Model through this study.

The paper begins by presenting a review of literature on the Technology Acceptance

Model and conceptual framework for the research. The second part of the paper discusses the main measurements of marketing effectiveness of the Internet. The final part of the paper provides the results of the perceptions of the Internet as a marketing tool and the measurement of the success of websites by marketing managers of a sample of tourism organisations.

Technology Acceptance Model

The Technology Acceptance Model (TAM) is based on principles adopted from Fishbein and Ajzen's (1975) attitude paradigm from psychology, which (1) specifies how to measure the behavior-relevant components of attitudes, (2) distinguishes between beliefs and attitudes and (3) specifies how external stimuli, such as the objective features of an attitude object, are causally linked to beliefs, attitudes and behavior. From the previous research, two specific beliefs, perceived usefulness and perceived ease of use, have been identified as important user acceptance criteria (Davis, 1989; Goodwin, 1987; Gould et al., 1991; Hill, Smith & Mann, 1987). Perceived usefulness is defined as the degree to which an individual believes that using a particular system would enhance his or her job performance. Perceived ease of use is defined as the degree to which an individual believes that using a particular system would be free of physical and mental effort. Two factor analyses reported by Davis (1989) suggest that perceived ease of use and perceived usefulness are statistically distinct constructs.

A marketing study by Hauser and Simmie (1981) concerning use perceptions of alternative communication technologies similarly derived two underlying dimensions: ease of use and effectiveness, the latter being similar to perceived usefulness. Both ease of use and effectiveness were influential in the formation of user preferences regarding a set of alternative communication technologies. The human computer interaction (HCI) research community has heavily emphasized ease of use in design (Branscombe and Thomas, 1984; Card, et al., 1983; Gould and Lewis, 1985).

Conceptual Framework

This research attempts to study the acceptance of the Internet from the industry's points of view. This will have implications for the eventual adoption and deployment of the Internet as a tourism distribution channel. A conceptual model adapted from Loh and Ong (1998) is introduced based on the notion that perception is a critical determinant of individual behaviour, which, in turn, leads to a certain outcome and performance. The eventual outcome, which in this case is the user acceptance of Internet technology, is dependent on user perceptions of system evaluation and concerns, and attitude, as well as usage behaviour. These will influence user satisfaction, which will also affect future perceptions and behaviour.

In the previous Technology Acceptance Models (TAMs), two main factors, perceived usefulness and perceived ease of use, were used in the user evaluation stage. The model suggested by Loh and Ong (1998) also introduced those two main factors and in the issues and concerns stage, payment, privacy, and other factors were introduced. However, the literature review on the market effectiveness of the Internet suggested that more factors are necessary to research effectively the perceptions of Internet Technology. The additional variables, perceived effectiveness and perceived success, as well as measurement issues are derived from the literature review and research undertaken.

This research specifically focuses on the perception stage including user evaluation and issues, and the concern substage. In this research, two additional variables, the perceived success of a website and the perceived effectiveness of a website, which are supported by Hauser and Simmie (1981), were introduced in the user evaluation stage, and the measurement issues (web design, success of website) were imported into the issues and concerns stage.

Fig. 1. The Modified Technology Acceptance Model (adapted from Loh and Ong (1998))

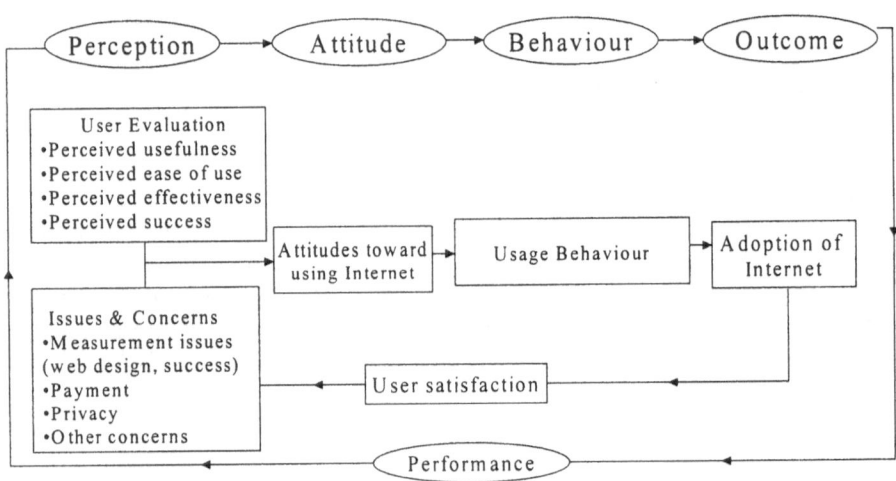

Measurement of Marketing Effectiveness of the Internet

Web Design

As the Internet grows and expands, the question for marketers is not only how to get potential consumers to visit their Web site, but how to keep them involved. Good Web design is one of the most important factors of a successful website. There are number of issues raised in the literature, and some of the key references are summarised here. Wilson (1997) suggested 12 key ingredients of web page design, purpose, index page and site organisation, site and domain names, main graphic to highlight site, background color or texture, basic page elements, finishing touches, photos and graphics, forms to get customer response, uploading and testing pages, registering and advertising web site, and maintaining web site. Sickle (1996) suggested five steps to get results from website; finding a good Internet service provider, getting interactive, not overdoing graphics, keeping it simple, and making ordering easy.

Narayan (1997) pointed out a checklist for finding the right design firm: define your goals; reconcile internal strengths and weaknesses; draw up a request for proposals; set up a budget to prevent creeping expansion; establish a retainer relationship instead of specific prices; include members from several departments to ensure different perspectives; don't get carried away by the bells and whistles; set clear milestones and make sure design firms deliver to those milestones; request co-operation from the entire organisation. The research by Loban (1998) focuses on cognitive and usability issues related to the design of online documents and suggest several important topics, such as expectations, metaphors, consistency and coherence, performance, context, feedback, and controls.

Sullivan (1997) suggested seven guidelines in order to get maximum impact and user friendliness on the World Wide Web including; loading time; browser friendliness; organised message; meta statements; frequent updating; giving something back; and asking for feedback. IFITT (1997) evaluated the innovative design of Web pages in the area of tourism. Invited categories of web page sites were regional sites operated by regional tourist boards, sites of tourist principals, and products and services. The evaluation criteria include ease of use, joy of use (entertainment), content (information, education etc.), design & creativity (innovative, graphical presentation, media adequacy), interactively, transaction support (reservation billing etc.), and added value.

According to Sumser (1996), there are ten basic requirements for a successful recruiting website: clearly identify the clients and candidates; envision it as an Enterprise, not a website; provide security for clients and candidates alike; develop irresistible content; encourage on-line resume submittal and job applications; on the first visit, give something of value to each visitor; use automation to make exquisite customer service easy; build relationships with candidate pool by delivering a stream of value; integrate existing business systems into the enterprise; reduce customer's transaction costs using the website. Table 1 shows important factors of Web design as identified by these authors. Added value, content, and transaction support were regarded important factors by both IFITT (1997) and Sumser (1996).

Table 1. Summary of Important Factors of Web design

• Added Value	• Feedback	• Meta statement
• Browser friendliness	• Frequent updating	• Organised message
• Content	• Integration	• Relationship with customers
• Design & creativity	• Joy of use	• Security
• Ease of use	• Loading time	• Transaction support

Measurements Methods of Success

Despite the fact that the popularity of the World Wide Web among the business community has grown rapidly, how companies rate the effectiveness of the web for various purposes is not generally known. (Ng *et al*, 1998). As web based models are still in a relatively early stage, there are no obvious criteria against which to evaluate the effectiveness of commercial websites. The earliest attempts were purely subjective forms of individual preferences, and are recorded as pages of "Cool links", "Top Lists", and "Hot Sites" (USA Today, 1996). Nielson Media Research (1996) suggested two measurement approaches: site based and outsourcing. The site-based approach is to buy and install software on one's own premises to run reports and is suitable for small sites with no advertising. The outsourcing approach is to have log files transferred to another location for processing and is suitable for large site and sites requiring audits. According to Nielsen Media Research (1996), site auditing has two elements: planning stage-evaluation of multiple sites for link placement; and post analysis-proof of performance. The planned stage can be measured by number of visitors, time spent, section popularity, and the traffic source by domain, country and organisation. The proof of performance is to track specific ads by the number of views, number of clicks, benchmark with other advertising on site, banner position's exposure and response rate. These are extremely difficult to measure due to complex rotations at sites.

In the academic area, an evaluation of the generic functions of commercial sites has been suggested by Hoffman, Novak, and Chatterjee (1995). Hoffman and Novak (1996) proposed a terminology for Web advertising measurement. There are three distinct levels of analysis for Web advertising measurement: vehicle level; page level; and advertisement level. For each level of analysis, there are exposure metrics and interactivity metrics. The exposure metrics are based on the one-to-many communication model underlying traditional media, and indicates that a visitor has been exposed to a web site, a web page, or an advertisement. However, interactivity metrics is based upon the many-to-many communication model underlying the Web, and indicates the extent to which the visitor actively engages with the Web content or advertisement.

Murphy et al (1996) explored the analysis of sites and features in hotel industries, and Ho (1997) went a stage further in proposing a general framework for evaluating a website from a customer's perspective of the value added. Pollock (1997) suggested that the measurements of success should include the number of hits recorded; the number of browsers who register and provide information about themselves, the ability to convert first-time browsers into regular, repeat visitors, bookability, the ability to persuade browsers to replace traditional and expensive print forms of information with this electronic source, and the amount of positive publicity about the site generated in traditional print media. In addition, Jung and Baker (1998) reported the results of research on which measurements of success rate are used by National Tourism Organisations (NTOs), and Jeong (1998) proposed a conceptual framework for measuring the overall effectiveness of hospitality websites. Morrison (1999) via his website has provided some general guidelines on creating effective tourism websites for destinations. Countryman (2000) also suggests general criteria for evaluating website effectiveness.

Table 2. Summary of Measurement Methods

• Number of Hits	• Repeat visit
• Time Spent	• Feedback
• No of Browsers	• Regular updating
• Booking Rate	• Forming partnership or marketing consortia to promote a major
• Interactivity	gateway

Successful Website

Hamill and Gregory (1997) suggested successful business web sites have a number of common characteristics including being information-rich and featuring regular updating to encourage repeat visits, having clear navigation paths to allow smooth movement around the site, providing value-added to the user in the form of real information and services rather than just a place for marketing and sales, including interactivity and responsiveness to user feedback. Such a site should be designed to allow the gathering of information by users and the integration of the site with other marketing channels used by the company to insure institutional support.

In addition, the site needs to be marketed properly in order to ensure high access. This can be done in various ways including registering the site with all of the on-line search engines; establishing reciprocal cross-linkages to other sites; and ensuring that the URL address is used in all company correspondence. Bredenberg (1995) suggests eight ways to get results from website: make your World-Wide Web effort part of an overall marketing plan; do not abandon conventional advertising; do not build your website in a vacuum; provide useful content; get help if you need it; make sure your Web Site's design fits the marketing purpose; promote visibility through off-line channels; devote on-line time to building a community. According to Pollock (1997), the key ingredients to success are effective promotion, forming strategic partnerships/alliances or marketing consortia to promote a major gateway, appearance, content, good navigating tools, interactivity, repeat visits, and develop a relationship and build loyalty.

Table 3. Summary of Important Factors of A Successful Website.

• Appearance	• Information	• Relationship
• Clear Navigation Paths	• Institutional Support	• Repeat Visits
• Design	• Interactivity	• Updating
• Forming Strategic Partners	• Promotion	• Value-Added

Issues and Problems of EC

The problem of barriers to business use of the web has been discussed by many writers. Nath *et al* (1998) report the results of a survey on the benefits of the Internet for electronic commerce. These include ease of access and global reach, low-cost advertising medium, low barriers to entry, and perceived image enhancement. Nath *et al* (1998) assert that six major impediments of the Internet for electronic commerce are security, start-up cost, legal issues, training and maintenance, lack of skilled personnel, and uncertainty and lack of information. Hoffman (1997) concluded that accumulated industrial experience and evidence strongly support the contention that the primary barrier to consumer adoption of the web as a commercial medium is ease of access. Even when access is gained, some users worry about information overload. According to Tesco, a United Kingdom supermarket chain, even if the technology was adequate, some failures might be caused by a lack of support infrastructure, such as having enough people to deliver on-line shopping (Monles, 1997).

A study by Newdom (1997) indicated that one of the main barriers to use of the web is consumer fear of unknown retailers: on the web, an unknown retailer can appear as a well-established retailer with a stylish design of his website. Newdom (1997) also pointed out that although web users represent an above average income group, they do not match the majority of people in retailers' target markets. Also, there is a great deal of concern regarding the security of financial information transmitted over the Internet and its impact on consumer willingness to buy or sell products (Information Infrastructure Technology and Application Task Group, 1994).

Table 4. Summary of Potential Barriers

• Security	• Difficulty navigating the web
• Privacy	• Maintaining/updating websites
• Access, Availability to all customers	• Executives' fear of technology
• Computer capability	• Lack of knowledge among consumers
• Measuring Effectiveness	• Consumer reluctance of purchase on the Web
• Difficult to reach/find target market	
• Overload of information	• Costs of reaching consumers
	• Other barriers

According to Meroz (1997), consumers still prefer to see and feel a product before they buy it. Moreover, real shopping is more of a leisure activity that fulfills many needs, while virtual shopping is not. Bjork and Guss (1999) also report barriers for not using the Internet as a marketplace, and these include perceived uncertainty, personal service, sceptism of the system, and security.

Methodology

The paper reports the results of a survey by e-mail of those responsible for websites at tourism organisations, generally marketing directors. The websites were obtained from the main tourism/hospitality related websites, including the Tourism Offices World Directory, International Air Transport Association (IATA), Hospitality Net, Hotel Travel, and Yahoo. The survey procedure included three main stages. The first stage was to select a sample from the Internet and to compile the lists of the e-mail addresses of the webmaster of each tourism organisation. The second stage was to send a request to each of these for the name and e-mail address of their marketing managers. The final stage was to send the e-mail questionnaire to these people who had been identified. The sample size in this study consisted of 33 marketing managers in NTOs, 33 in International chain hotels, 16 in airlines, and 33 in travel agencies. The period of the research was four months from September 1997 (NTOs) to November 1998 (Hotels), November 1999 (Travel Agencies), and December 1999 (Airlines).

The questionnaire sought respondents' views on the effectiveness and importance of the Internet as a marketing medium, how the success of their website is measured and what they regard as important factors in website design and what the potential barriers. It consisted of four main sections. The first section contained questions on the marketing director's view of the Internet, including its effectiveness, the importance of the Internet as a marketing strategy, and any change in views on the Internet within certain periods. The second section examined the success of the website and the methods which each tourism organisation used to determine its effectiveness. The third section was concerned with identifying the important elements of successful websites and successful web design. The fourth section investigated the factors of potential barriers when doing business on the Internet.

Results

This study provides general views about the Internet as a marketing tool and the key factors of a successful website, and whether and how the effectiveness of the website is measured by marketing managers of each tourism organisation. In relation to this, a comparative analysis is undertaken on the views of the Internet by marketing managers among different tourism organisations. Table 5 shows the views about the Internet's value as a strategic marketing tool. Most marketing managers regard the Internet as an effective marketing tool and promotional tool. However, as the reservation tool, the mean values were relatively lower than as a marketing and promotion tool. The majority of marketing managers in the tourism and hospitality industry, have changed their views about the importance of the Internet marketing and, furthermore, they considered that Internet marketing will become even more important in the near future.

Table 5. Views about the Internet (Mean value, 1-5)

Effectiveness	NTOs	Hotels	Travel Agencies	Airlines
Marketing tool	4.12	4.18	4.61	4.50
Reservation tool	-	3.86	3.73	3.93
Promotional tool	3.93	4.12	4.48	4.18
Overall MKT Strategy	-	3.76	4.55	4.37
Changed View	3.37	4.03	4.55	4.31
Future View	-	4.42	4.79	4.40

The next section is related to the measurement of the success rate of the website. The questions asked respondents if they measured the success rate of their website and if so, what methods were used for measuring the success of the website. Table 6 shows the different methods used by the respondents who did measure the rate of success in anyway. The number of hits is the most popular method used. The feedback (80%) was the second most widely used method in NTOs. Interestingly, booking rate was the second most widely used method in hotels (65%) and travel agencies (69.7%) and airlines (53.5%).

Table 6. Measuring Methods (Proportion of Sample Using Method)

Methods	NTOs	Hotels	Travel Agencies	Airlines
Booking Rate	24%	65%	69.7%	53.3%
No of Hits	92%	80%	84.8%	68.8%
No of Browsers	28%	25%	21.2%	31.3%
Interactivity	24%	30%	51.5%	18.8%
Regular updating	32%	45%	57.6%	43.8%
Feedback	80%	30%	36.4%	50.0%
Time spent	20%	50%	15.2%	25.0%
Repeat visit	16%	25%	33.3%	6.30%
Forming Partnership	32%	20%	36.4%	18.8%

The next section contained twelve statements concerning potentially important elements of successful websites. Respondents were asked to express their level of agreement with each statement representing the importance of those key factors of successful websites. Table 7 shows the rating of factors of a successful website. Respondents in hotels (mean: 4.67) and travel agencies (mean 4.90) regarded useful information as the most important factors of successful website. However, marketing managers in the airline industry (mean 4.86) regarded regular updating as the most important factor and useful information (mean 4.73) as the second.

Table 7. Factors of Successful Website (Mean Value, 1-5)

	NTOs	Hotels	Travel Agencies	Airlines
Regular updating	-	4.42	4.73	4.86
Repeat visits	-	4.00	4.60	4.46
Appearance	-	4.55	3.76	4.46
Useful Information	-	4.67	4.90	4.73
Interactivity	-	4.12	4.58	4.20
Web Design	-	4.39	4.15	4.26
Promotion(off-line)	-	4.03	3.97	4.40
Forming partners	-	3.79	3.79	4.30
Value-added Info	-	3.81	4.09	4.20
Institutional support	-	4.25	4.03	4.26
Building a royalty	-	4.39	4.19	4.60
Clear navigation paths	-	4.58	4.52	4.56

The next section deals with the factors of successful web design. The questions asked respondents what were the most important factors of successful web design. Table 8 shows that the content (information) was regarded as the most important factor of successful web design in NTOs (mean: 4.66) and travel agencies (mean: 4.84). However, the ease of use (mean: 4.87) was regarded as more important factor rather than content (mean: 4.87) in the airline industry.

Table 8. Factors of Successful Web Design (Mean Value, 1-5)

	NTOs	Hotels	Travel Agencies	Airlines
Added value	2.20	-	4.03	4.32
Appearance	3.16	-	3.51	4.25
Content	4.66	-	4.84	4.81
Design & Creativity	-	-	-	4.31
Ease of Use	4.2	-	4.39	4.87
Joy of use	2.3	-	4.21	3.81
Relationship with Customers	2.73	-	4.54	4.37
Security	-	-	-	4.62
Transaction support	1.96	-	4.30	4.31

The questions concerning potential barriers to doing Internet based business were asked in the latest survey, to marketing managers in the airline industry. Respondents identified several potential barriers including security, rapid growth vs limited time, being lost in the crowd, no clear strategy, forgetting visitors' needs, co-ordination with classical marketing, costs of connecting and listing in search engine, reluctance from certain popular group, low penetration on Internet, customer perception, slow reacting time.

Limitation

There are several limitations to this research. Firstly, even though the duration of the research effort time is similar, approximately one month, the time which the 4 surveys were conducted was different (NTOs: September 1997, Hotels: November 1998, Travel Agencies: November 1999, Airlines: December 1999). Therefore, the research did not show the results about perceptions on the Internet by 4 different tourism/hospitality organisations for the same time. Although four months is short period, developments in e-commerce and IT are very rapid and opinions can change quickly. Secondly, a larger sample size would preferable, especially, travel agencies and hotels, in order to have more reliability and representativeness. Finally, the questionnaire for this research has evolved and improved from a basic questionnaire to a more sophisticated one, therefore, there are some differences in number of criteria which were tested in each survey.

Conclusions/implications

The principal objectives of this paper were to investigate the perceptions of the Internet as a marketing tool by marketing managers of tourism organisations and to identify if and how they measure the effectiveness of their websites. Despite being somewhat constrained by the research methodology (an e-mail survey using a fairly simple questionnaire with potential but unknown bias in responses), it is felt that useful insights have been gained in the way this set of users regard the Internet.

Firstly, the marketing managers of tourism and hospitality organisations who responded to the survey are rapidly becoming converted to the idea of the Internet as a marketing medium. Secondly, most marketing managers regard the Internet as a very effective marketing, reservation, and promotional tool. They also have changed their view on the effectiveness of the Internet as a marketing tool over the last few years and they expect that the importance of Internet as a marketing tool and marketing strategy will become even greater. Thirdly, with regard to factors that mark a successful website, most respondents regarded useful information as one of the most important factors, while respondents in airlines regarded regular updating as the most important one. Fourthly, concerning measurement issues, marketing managers are at a fairly early stage in measuring how successful their websites are, and the most common method of measuring the website's success rate is "number of hits". Finally, with regard to the factors of successful web design, content (information) was regarded as one of the most important factors and the other factors such as ease of use and security were regarded as significant ones.

In conclusion, this research suggests that if the results are representative, that marketing managers of tourism and hospitality organisations now perceive the Internet as a mainstream marketing tool. This relatively recent view (given the proportion of respondents who had changed their opinions in the last few years) suggests that the tourism industry will remain enthusiastic about this new innovation for some time to come and continue to modify and improve their websites to attract an ever greater segment of the market.

References

Baker, M., Sussmann, S., and Welch, S. (1997). Information Technology Management, Univeristy of Surrey.

Branscomb, L.M., and Thomas, J.C. (1984). Ease of Use: A System Design Challenge, IBM Systems Journal, pp. 224-235.

Brendenberg, A. (1995). 8 Ways to Get Results from Your Web Site, Web Markting Today, Issue 1, November 6.

Card, S.K., Moran, T.P, and Newell, A. (1984). The Psychology of Human-Computer Interaction, Erlbaum, Hillsdale, NJ.

Countryman, C (2000) Designing Effective Bed and Breakfast Websites, Proceedings of 5th Annual Graduate Education and Graduate Students Research Conference in Hospitality and Tourism, Jan 2000, University of Houston.

Davis, F. D. (1989). Perceived Usefulness, Perceived Ease of Use, and User Acceptance of Information Technology, MIS Quarterly, 13, 319-340.

Fishbein, M. J., and Ajzen, I. (1975). Belief, Attitude, Intention and Behavior: An Introduction to Theory and Research, Addison-Wesley, Reading, MA.

Goodwin, N.C. (1987). Functionality and Usability, Communication of the ACM, 30, 229-233.

Gould, J. D., Boies, S. J., and Lewis, C. (1991). Making Usable, Useful, Productivity-enhancing Computer Applications, Communications of the ACM, 34, 74-85.

Hamil, J., and Gregory, K. (1997). Internet Marketing in the Internatioanalisation of UK SMEs, Journal of Marketing Management, 13, pp 9-28.

Hauser, J.R., and Simmie, P. (1981). Profit Maximizing Perceptual Positions: An Integrated Theory for the Selection of Product Features and Price, Management Science (27:1), January, pp. 33-56.

Hill, T., Smith, N. D., and Mann, M. F. (1987). Role of Efficacy Expectations in Predicting the Decision to Use Advanced Technologies: The Case of Computers, Journal of Applied Psychology, 72, 307-313.

Ho, J. (1997). Evaluating the World Wide Web: A Global Study of Commercial Sites, Journal of Computer-Mediated Communications 3 (1). http://www.ascusc.org/jcmc/vol3/issue1/ho.html.

Hoffman, D. L., and Novak, T. P. (1996). New Metrics for New Media: Toward the Development of Web Measurement Standards, Project 2000 White Paper, Vanderbilt University, draft September 26, 1996.

Hoffman, D.L., Novak, T. P., and Chatterjee, P. (1995). Commercial Scenarios for the Web: Opportunities and Challenges, Journal of Computer-Mediated Communication. 1.

IFITT. http://www.ifitt.org

Information Infrastructure Technology and Application Task Group. (1994). Electronic Commerce and VII. Washington DC: National Coordination Office for High Performance Computing and Comminication.

Jeong, M. (1998). A Conceptual Freamework for Measuring Effectiveness of the Web, Proceedings of 3rd Annual Graduate Education and Graduate Students Research Conference in Hospitality and Tourism, January, University of Houston.

Jung, H., and Baker, M. (1998). Assessing the Market Effectiveness of the World Wide Web in National Tourism Offices, Proceedings of ENTER'98, January, Istanbul, Turkey.

Loban, S, R. (1998). Designing Effective Documents for Destination Information Systems, *Proceedings of ENTER'98 Conference*, Istanbul, Turkey

Loh, L and Ong, Y. (1998). The Adoption of Internet-based Stock Trading: A Conceptual Framework and Empirical Results, Journal of Information Technology 13, pp 81-94.

Monles, J.(1997). Brand Warfare, Information Strategy http://www.info-strategy.com/branding.html

Morrison, A (1999) WWW Design in Destination Marketing, http://omni.cc.purdue.edu/~alltson/wwwdesign.htm

Murphy, J., Forrest, E.J., Wotting, C.E., and Brymer, R.A. (1996). Hotel Management and Marketing on the Internet, Cornell Hotel and Restaurant Administration Quarterly, pp 70-82.

Narayan, S. (1997). Choosing a Design Firm Requires Clear Assessment of Goals, Strengths, Web Week, June 2, 1997.

Nath, R., Akamanligil, M., Hjelm, K., Sakaguchi, T., and Schultz, M. (1998). Electronic Commerce and the Internet: Issues, Problems, and Perspectives, International Journal of Information Management, 18 (2), pp 91-101.

Ng, H., Pan, Y.J., and Wilson, T.D. (1998). Business Use of the World Wide Web: A Report on Further Investigations, Intrernational Journal of Information Management, Vol 18. No.5 pp.291-314.

Nielson Media Research. (1997). Web Audience Measurement Issues, Challenges and Solutions, http://www.nielsonmedia.com.

Pollock, A. (1997). Creating Intelligent Destinations for Wired Consumers: A Conceptual Framework and Its Scottish Application, ENTER 97 Conference, Edinburgh, January Scotland.

Pollock, A. (1997). Marketing Destination on the Internet Why and How?, ENTER 97 Conference, Edinburgh, January Scotland

Sullivan, R. (1997). Design Tips for Your Webpage. http:// frontpage.inet-images.com/progressive/authors/sullivan/designtips.htm

Sumser, J. (1996). Characteristics of a Great Website, Electronic Recruiting Index.

USA Today. (1996). Hot Sites, June 11, http://www.usatoday.com/life/cyber/ch0611.htm.

Wilson, R. F. (1997). How to Attract Visitors to Your Website, Web Marketing Today, Issue 2, November 20.

Destination Management Systems:
Criteria for Success - An Exploratory Research

Dimitrios Buhalis and Antonella Spada
Dept of Tourism, University of Westminster
London, NW1 5LS, UK
Tel: + 44 207 9115000x3112   Fax: + 44 207 9115171
Email: buhalid@wmin.ac.uk http://www.wmin.ac.uk/tourism/staff/buhalis/buhalis.htm

Abstract

Destinations become brand names for tourism regions incorporating the entire range of attractions and enterprises locally. Information technology developments propel the tourism industry to the digital economy and develop an e-commerce applications. The emergence of Destination Management Systems (DMSs) as "info-structures" enables destinations to disseminate comprehensive information about resources and services of destinations and local tourism products as well as facilitate the planning, management and marketing of regions as tourism entities or brands.

This paper explores success criteria for DMSs for six key tourism destination stakeholders. The paper analyses the needs and wants of stakeholders and thus provides guidance for the development and assessment of DMSs. The research is based on qualitative and quantitative research with leading authorities on the field. Attention is drawn to the role played by the public and private sectors, and the need for partnership to ensure successful application of DMSs in the future.

1. Introduction and the research rationale

Destinations increasingly attract tourists from distant or long haul markets and thus the need to disseminate information globally will continue to increase. Tourism destinations must compete in an increasingly fiercely competitive marketplace. Domestic markets are usually characterised by short get-away-breaks, with trip decisions made on impulse, previous experience and shortly before departure. Tourists request a wide variety of information on areas, facilities, attractions and activities at destinations before departure and once at the destination. The emphasis is on speed and on the ability of destinations to satisfy the needs of buyers by providing appropriate and accurate information as well as by facilitating reservations efficiently.

The radical developments of IT in tourism also reflect the change in demand patterns of the contemporary "sophisticated and wired traveller", who is increasingly seeking new experiences and destinations and innovative tools to access information. Destinations that provide timely, appropriate and accurate information to consumers and the travel trade have a better chance of being selected, achieve more benefits from tourism and strengthen their competitiveness [4,14,21,22,26,27]. In addition, destinations are increasingly regarded as amalgams of Small and Medium Sized Tourism Enterprises (SMTEs) and as a result they need not only to enhance the individual competitiveness of each single enterprise locally but also to co-ordinate all individually produced and delivered services offered in their region [4,9,10,12,18].

Information technologies (ITs) have tremendous implications for tourism [24,28,19,30]. ITs change the "best operation practices and provides opportunities for business expansion in the geographical, marketing and operational sense" [8]. ITs have therefore become a critical factor in determining future success or failure, as well as tourism impacts at destinations. It is a combination of both technological enablers and demand drivers that have propelled the realisation of Destination Management Systems (DMSs). These systems should not only satisfy demand therefore, but also contribute to the enhancement of the long-term competitiveness of destinations [5,25]. DMSs are usually managed by Destination Management Organisations (DMOs) which may be private or public organisations, or a combination of both [2,3,4,6,7,13,15,16,17,20,22,23,24 27,29,31,32].

However, the majority of DMSs have been implemented at local level and operate on a limited basis or collapsed few years after their initial development. They are often limited in their scope and ambition either by their organisational structure or by their technology. Hence, nearly one decade after the conceptualisation of DMSs and the development of more than 200 systems around the world few systems have yet been established as a major distributor of all products at destinations [1,25,7,2,15]. DMSs' underdevelopment hitherto, therefore, has prompted the need for a deeper examination of those success criteria that need to be taken into consideration when developing or evaluating DMSs. Results from this research are set out to develop a list of success criteria by establishing and evaluating the needs of key stakeholders for destinations and DMSs.

2. Research Methodology

Both secondary and primary research was undertaken in order to collect information of sufficient quality and quantity. Secondary research focused on a comprehensive literature review with the intent to identify existing research and aimed to explore both the technological enablers and demand drivers that have paved the way for the DMSs evolution. Secondary research was conducted by means of reviewing publications from a wide range of sources. Existing research frameworks were used to design the primary research [5,6,16,17]. Both quantitative and qualitative data was collected to enable the in-depth exploration of this fairly new research area and also to allow the initial quantification of concepts in order to provide a more accurate analysis as well as to assist in the interpretation of the results. The primary research was divided into three parts. Firstly, an exploratory research of the successful criteria for DMSs was developed. A judgmental sample of 5 experts was selected to provide their opinion on the most important criteria. Following this stage, a comprehensive list of relevant criteria was developed. Secondly, a quantitative research was undertaken, whereby the criteria selected from the exploratory stage were incorporated into a questionnaire.

This study entailed the selection of a sample of 265 experts on the subject, who were approached to rate the importance of the criteria listed. The panel of experts that was assembled included experts on the DMSs field. Their involvement in researching and operating DMS projects was a critical criterion for their selection and involvement. A total of 18 experts returned the questionnaire. Thirdly, results obtained from the survey were analysed and discussed in-depth with 6 selected experts. This qualitative exercise aimed at testing the importance and validity of the list of criteria obtained from the research and to justify the emerging results. Experts were encouraged to provide insightful examples of successful systems and to highlight factors that have stimulated or impeded their development.

Extensive literature review illustrated that DMSs have to satisfy the needs of the 6 main stakeholders of both destinations [11], namely Consumers/Tourists, Tourism Suppliers, the Public Sector, Investors, Tour Operators and Travel Agents. An average of 10-12 success criteria per stakeholder were developed through consultation of the literature the experts in the first phase of the research. These criteria included an appreciation of all the importance issues from the viewpoint of each stakeholder. A questionnaire was developed to incorporate the 68 criteria established in the exploratory research and required experts to rate them from very unimportant to very important. The aim of the survey was not only to develop a comprehensive list of all issues raised on DMSs' success factors in previous literature, but also to assist their assessment. Although the issues raised in the survey are far from exhaustive, they constitute an extensive list of criteria that are set to aid future research in this field area.

A 6.8% response rate was achieved and it was also complemented by a rich qualitative survey to enhance the interpretation of the results. The findings obtained from the quantitative exercise were used to conduct in-depth, structured interviews with six selected experts on the third stage. This enabled the analysis and interpretation of the main findings of the questionnaire. The analysis and discussion of the research findings integrate results from both quantitative and qualitative research. Combining the two research approaches provides the paper with a better understanding and interpretation of the criteria. The complementary contributions of both quantitative and qualitative research, provided the opportunity to challenge some issues with experts in these field areas.

3. Research Findings

The success criteria analysed in this paper are simplified and the list obtained cannot be exhaustive. However, they comprise a comprehensive framework reflecting human/visitor aspects, the challenging technical, commercial and political environment, as well as the industry structure within which DMSs operate and compete.

3.1 Success criteria from the Customer's/Visitor's point of view

The provision of tourist information is of paramount importance, as illustrated in Table 1. User-friendliness and easiness of understanding was rated as very important with limited variation as illustrated by the fairly small value of the standard deviation (STD). Accurate and comprehensive destination information should be supplied before and during the trip. Equally, secure payment methods, speedy transactions and ability to book from a variety of distribution channels attracted high ratings. Interestingly the "after-visit" information was rated as unimportant, although opinions varied as illustrated in the STD. This illustrates that experts failed to identify the opportunity for DMSs to develop relationships with consumers.

Table 1. Success criteria for the Consumer/Visitor

The Consumer	1	2	3	4	5	Mean	STD
What do consumers want out of a DMS?	%	%	%	%	%		
1 User-friendly and easy-to-understand system				16.6	77.7	4.82	0.39
2 Comprehensive destination information before their trip		5.5		22.2	72.2	4.61	0.78
3 Comprehensive destination information during their trip			11.1	33.3	55.5	4.44	0.71
4 On-line booking confirmation			11.1	33.3	50.0	4.41	0.71
5 Speed of transactions			11.1	38.8	50.0	4.39	0.69
6 Range of prices available to accommodate different budget needs			16.6	27.7	50.0	4.35	0.79
7 Late-availability information		5.5	11.1	27.7	50.0	4.29	0.92
8 Secure payment methods			16.6	50.0	33.3	4.17	0.71
9 Option to conduct virtual tours and view pictures of a destination			16.6	55.5	33.3	4.16	0.69
10 Book products from a variety of distribution channels, such as via computer, Travel agency, TIC, etc.			27.7	38.8	38.8	4.11	0.81
11 On-line bookings through DMSs		5.5	22.2	38.8	38.8	4.05	0.91
12 Availability of help function such as a toll-free telephone, intuitive on-line help			22.2	16.6	16.6	3.90	0.88
13 Obtain comprehensive destination information after the trip	5.5	27.7	44.4	11.1	11.1	2.94	1.06

Notes: 1=Very Unimportant 5=Very Important

3.2 Success criteria from the tourism suppliers' point of view

The management, marketing and planning functions of DMSs were considered to be very important attributes of these systems for tourism suppliers, as can be seen in Table 2. The reliability, accuracy of information and services as well as the user

friendliness were rated highly. However, experts emphasised that from the suppliers'
point of view, DMSs should play a key role in marketing the destination. This can be
achieved through increasing awareness and visitor levels due to the ability of DMSs'
to distribute information and services globally. DMSs can support SMTEs to develop
their distribution mechanisms and to reach wider markets. Tourism suppliers are likely
to attach great importance to the cost of membership fees, commissions and
technology. The ability of DMSs to aid the reduction of seasonality peaks as well as
the importance of sharing information locally were rated as important to tourism
suppliers, whilst DMSs are not regarded as capable to reduce labour costs.

Table 2. Success criteria for Tourism Suppliers

	The Tourism Supplier	1	2	3	4	5	Mean	STD
	What do suppliers want out of a DMS?	%	%	%	%	%		
1	Reliability and accuracy of services provided by a DMS				22.2	77.7	4.78	0.43
2	User-friendly and easy-to-understand system				44.4	61.1	4.58	0.51
3	Distribution of information globally			11.1	44.4	44.4	4.33	0.69
4	Collection and compilation of market information			5.5	5.5	55.5	4.17	0.79
5	DMSs' commission fees		5.5	22.2	27.7	38.8	4.06	0.97
6	The role of a DMS be in increasing awareness and visitor levels for a destination		5.5	22.2	33.3	33.3	4.00	0.94
7	Impact of cost of membership of tourism organisations on tourism suppliers		5.5	22.2	27.7	33.3	4.00	0.97
8	Reduction in cost of computer equipment and telecommunications	5.5		22.2	38.8	27.7	3.88	1.05
9	Need to receive guaranteed bookings	5.5		33.3	33.3	22.2	3.71	1.05
10	Interface and share information with other trade suppliers	5.5	5.5	38.8	38.8	5.5	3.35	0.93
11	The role of a DMS be in reducing seasonality peaks and troughs for a destination		16.6	22.2	50.0	11.1	3.56	0.92
12	Role of DMSs in minimising labour costs	16.6	27.7	33.3	5.5	16.6	2.78	1.31

Notes: 1=Very Unimportant 5=Very Important

3.3 Success criteria from the Public Sector's point of view

The public sector traditionally has overall responsibility for planning, management
and marketing of destinations. Survey findings in Table 3 revealed that the public
sector is likely to attach great importance to the marketing functions of DMOs. The
public sector should consider DMSs as a very important promotional tool, which can
enable destinations to increase their market awareness, and thus rated these criteria

very highly. Similarly, the management and planning functions of DMSs emerged to be critical attributes. The public sector should regard DMSs as tools for the planning, management and marketing of destinations, which can offer reliable information and promote the region and its enterprises. The strategic role of DMSs on supporting strategic alliances or reducing seasonality was debated though.

Table 3. Success criteria for the Public Sector

Public Sector	1	2	3	4	5	Mean	STD
What does the public sector want out of a DMS?	%	%	%	%	%		
1	Reliability and accuracy of a DMS for overall destination credibility			38.8	44.4	16.6	4.61	0.73
2	Promotional tool			5.5	38.8	50.0	4.47	0.62
3	Support of SMTEs			16.6	38.8	44.4	4.28	0.75
4	Increasing awareness and visitor levels for a destination		5.5	11.1	44.4	33.3	4.12	0.86
5	DMS as a management and planning tool, for the compilation of tourism statistics, etc.		11.1	5.5	50.0	33.3	4.06	0.94
6	Reduction in cost of computer equipment and telecommunications	5.5		27.7	27.7	44.4	4.00	1.11
7	Increase the competitiveness of SMTEs in the marketplace		11.1	27.7	16.6	38.8	3.88	1.11
8	Redistribution of benefits to local or regional economies		5.5	38.8	27.7	27.7	3.78	0.94
9	Display of unbiased supplier information		16.6	33.3	27.7	16.6	3.78	0.73
10	Promote strategic alliances with other destinations	5.5	11.1	16.6	38.8	27.7	3.72	1.18
11	Reduce seasonality peaks and troughs		16.6	27.7	27.7	16.6	3.47	1.01

Notes: 1=Very Unimportant 5=Very Important

3.4 Success criteria from the investors' point of view

As shown in Table 4, investors' criteria for success mainly lie in the commercial attributes of these systems and their ability to generate profitability. Many DMSs have either been privatised or sold to attract private sector capital and to develop partnerships with the private sector. Experts were asked to rate the criteria of success for DMSs from the private or public investors' point of view. Apart from the reliability and efficiency of the system, investors consider DMSs' ability to develop a successful revenue model, which will enable them to create adequate return on investment. Not surprisingly, the survey also revealed that it is important to investors to operate profitable DMSs whilst other strategic issues such as co-operate with other destinations were rated of lesser importance.

Table 4. Success criteria for Investors

Investors	1 %	2 %	3 %	4 %	5 %	Mean	STD
What do Investors want out of a DMS?							
1 Operating reliability and efficiency			11.1	22.2	66.6	4.56	0.70
2 Public-private sectors partnerships relevance on the DMS revenue model				44.4	44.4	4.50	0.52
3 Ability for a DMS to interface with a multiple distribution channel in the placement of investments, such as CRS, GDS, and Digital TV			16.6	22.2	61.1	4.44	0.78
4 DMSs' ability to embrace new technology such as open platforms and scaleability		5.5	11.1	22.2	61.1	4.39	0.92
5 Impact of pressure to make a profit on the development of DMSs			11.1	44.4	38.8	4.29	0.69
6 Ability of a DMSs to make a profit			5.5	38.8	44.4	4.21	0.79
7 Need to boost membership		5.5	16.6	27.7	44.4	4.18	0.95
8 Role of type of visitors attracted to a destination play in the placement of investment decisions			22.2	50.0	22.2	4.00	0.71
9 Reduction in cost of computer equipment and telecommunications	5.5	5.5	27.7	33.3	27.7	3.72	1.13
10 Use of a DMS for strategic alliances with other destinations	5.5	22.2	27.7	16.6	27.7	3.39	1.29

Notes: 1=Very Unimportant 5=Very Important

3.5 Success criteria from the Tour Operators' point of view

Table 5 illustrates that many criteria raised in relation to Tour Operators (TOs) were rated by experts of average importance or unimportant. The ratings are consistently lower than other stakeholders and a higher STD illustrates that experts are less

Table 5. Success criteria for Tour Operators

Tour Operators (TOs)	1 %	2 %	3 %	4 %	5 %	Mean	STD
What do Tour Operators want out of a DMS?							
1 User-friendly and easy- to-understand system	5.5		5.5	33.3	50.0	4.29	1.05
2 Provision of unbiased service	11.1	16.6	11.1	22.2	33.3	3.53	1.46
3 Access a range of market information	11.1	11.1	33.3	22.2	27.7	3.42	1.30
4 Use of DMSs as a marketing tool?	16.6	22.2	16.6	16.6	27.7	3.17	1.50
5 Manage product inventory	16.6	22.2	16.6	16.6	27.7	3.17	1.50
6 DMSs ability to reduce seasonality	11.1	22.2	33.3	22.2	16.6	3.11	1.24
7 Minimum membership charges	11.1	22.2	16.6	16.6	11.1	2.93	1.33
8 Minimise trading communication costs for tour operators	16.6	22.2.	27.7	27.7	5.5	2.83	1.20
9 Role of DMSs in supporting the bulk-buy process of tour operators	22.2	22.2	27.7	16.6	11.1	2.72	1.32
10 Role of DMSs in the cost of distribution for tour operators	16.6	27.7	22.2	16.6.	5.5	2.63	1.20

Notes: 1=Very Unimportant 5=Very Important

confident about the ways DMSs can assist the needs and wants of TOs. This is consistent with trends for disintermediation as well as the strategic role of DMSs to reduce dependency on existing distribution channels and support the bridging of destinations with their markets. The only criteria which were rated on the important range were the user-friendliness and unbiased service of the system. Surprisingly, the ability of DMSs to provide TOs with access to market information was underrated although smaller tour operators can use this facility for their research and development function without having to travel to the destination.

3.6 Success criteria from the Travel Agents' (TAs) point of view

Travel agencies attach great importance to criteria relating to the accuracy and functionality of DMSs as illustrated in Table 6. DMSs' information accuracy and their ability to provide expeditious and reliable responses to queries were rated highly as they enable TAs to answer specific requests and provide specialised content to their clients. Guaranteed bookings are also rated highly as travel agencies would like to provide confirmed bookings on the spot to their clients. However, experts rated the unbiased information criterion as less important, illustrating that as long as a booking is easy to make, secured and guaranteed it may be based on biased information. Travel agents' global survival is contingent upon their ability to add value and therefore DMSs can assist them to develop products and offer improved service. All criteria are rated higher than TOs and there is higher consistency throughout.

Table 6. Success criteria for Travel Agents

Travel Agents		1 %	2 %	3 %	4 %	5 %	Mean	STD
What do Travel Agents want out of a DMS?								
1	Accurate and reliable information				16.6	83.3	4.83	0.38
2	Quick and reliable responses				22.2	77.7	4.78	0.43
3	Instant on-line reservations				38.8	61.1	4.61	0.50
4	User-friendly and easy-to-understand system			5.5	33.3	61.1	4.56	0.62
5	Depth of information and product range			5.5	33.3	55.5	4.53	0.62
6	Guaranteed bookings			16.6	11.1	66.6	4.53	0.80
7	Real-time availability of information			11.1	22.2	55.5	4.50	0.73
8	Booking commissions from a DMS on the travel agency business		5.5	16.6	33.3	44.4	4.17	0.92
9	Unbiased destination information		16.6	16.6	5.5	38.8	3.86	1.29
10	Compete alongside tour operators in terms of commission revenues	11.1	16.6	5.5	50.0	11.1	3.53	1.27
11	Reduction in cost of computer equipment and telecommunications	5.5	5.5	38.8	38.8	11.1	3.44	0.98
12	Compete alongside airlines in terms of commission revenues	16.6	11.1	11.1	38.8	5.5	3.07	1.33

Notes: 1=Very Unimportant 5=Very Important

4. Conclusion

Technological developments revolutionise business processes and re-engineer the business model in most industries. In tourism, IT provides new opportunities and challenges for all players. In particular at the destination level IT enables organisations to collaborate locally and use DMSs to represent their entity to the global markets. The importance of co-operation stems from the fragmented nature of the tourism product and from the mutual interdependencies within the industry for the development, sale and delivery of travel and tourism services. Few practitioners in the various sectors of the tourism industry understand that their participation in a co-operative network can enable the creation of a value-chain that strengthens the performance of all actors in a synergetic manner. On the contrary, conflicts created by the dissimilar objectives and interests of the various stakeholders often represent obstacles to the development and implementation of DMSs. It is increasingly becoming evident that instead of competition, local co-operation will need to drive the competitiveness of both independent enterprises and destinations as a whole.

Research on the criteria that determine the success of DMSs indicates that unless the requirements of all stakeholders are satisfied, the effective deployment of these systems will find difficult to develop viable solutions. It also demonstrates that some stakeholders exercise a more influential role in the application of the identified criteria and in satisfying all other stakeholders' requirements, particularly the public sector and private investors. The intervention and active involvement of the public sector emerges as an essential catalyst in balancing the needs and wants of the various stakeholders, as well as in ensuring their satisfaction from DMSs. The considerable degree of influence that the public sector can have through planning, legislation and incentives, represents a unique tool for fostering cooperativeness amongst the various stakeholders at the destination region. Equally, the participation and investment of private sectors in DMSs appears to play a significant role in contributing essential capital, know how and industry drive and thus determine the future profitability and viability of these systems.

The expertise and financial resources that the private investors bring to DMOs for the development of DMSs is essential in ensuring that these systems deploy state of the art technology and operate in a cost efficient manner. The formulation of destination networks in turn, will represent a unique competitive advantage that will make some DMSs stand out from others. The criteria and values illustrated can only be achieved with the co-ordination and co-operation amongst the various stakeholders at the destination region towards enhancing their collective competitiveness and long term sustainable prosperity.

Acknowledgements

This research has benefited from the expertise, knowledge and precious time of

Alyson and Olivier Dombey (Partners in Marketing). We also wish to thank all experts who have contributed to this study, and especially Dr. Andrew Frew (Napier University) and Peter O'Connor (IMHI) for sharing their expertise with us.

References

1. Archdale, G., (1994), "Destination Databases: issues and priorities", in Seaton, A V., et al (eds), Tourism - The state of the Art, John Wiley and Sons, Chichester, 246-253.
2. Archdale, G., Jones C., Stanton, R., (1992), "Destination Databases: Issues and Priorities", Pacific Asia Association (PATA), San Francisco 1992.
3. Buhalis, D., (1993), "Regional Integrated Computer Information Reservation Management Systems as a strategic tool for tourism", Tourism Management, Vol.14(5), 366-376.
4. Buhalis, D., (1994a), "Information and Telecommunications Technologies as a strategic tool for small and medium tourism enterprises in the contemporary business environment," in Seaton, A., et al (eds), Tourism: The State of the Art, John Wiley and Sons, Chichester, 254-275.
5. Buhalis, D., (1994b), "Regional Integrated Computer Information Reservation Management Systems and tourism distribution channels", in Schertler, W., Schmid, B., Tjoa, A., Werthner, H., (eds), Information and Communication Technologies in Tourism, ENTER '94, Conference Proceedings, Springer-Verlag, Wien-New York, 56-72.
6. Buhalis, D., (1995), "The impact of information and Communication Technologies on tourism distribution channels: implications for the small and medium tourism enterprises' strategic management and marketing", University of Surrey PhD Thesis, Department of Management Studies, Guildford.
7. Buhalis, D., (1997), "Information Technologies as a strategic tool for economic, cultural and environmental benefits enhancement of tourism at destination regions", Progress in Tourism and Hospitality Research, Vol.3(1), 71-93.
8. Buhalis, D., (1998), "Strategic use of Information Technologies in the tourism industry", Tourism Management, Vol.19(5), 409-421.
9. Buhalis, D., (2000), Marketing the competitive destination of the future, Tourism Management, Vol.21(1).
10. Buhalis, D., and Cooper, C., (1998), Competition or co-operation: The needs of Small and Medium sized Tourism Enterprises at a destination level, in E., Laws, Faulkner, B., and Moscardo, G., (ed.), Embracing and managing change in Tourism, Routledge, London. 324-346
11. Buhalis, D., and J. Fletcher, (1995), Environmental impacts on tourism destinations: An economic analysis, in Coccosis, H., and Nijkamp, P., (eds), Sustainable Tourism Development, Avebury, England, 3-24.

12. Buhalis, D., and Main, H., (1998),"Information technology in peripheral and small and medium enterprises: strategic analysis and critical factors", in International Journal of Contemporary Hospitality Management, Vol.10(5), 198-202.

13. Cano, V., Prentice, R., (1998) "Opportunities for endearment to place through electronic visiting: WWW homepages and the tourism promotion of Scotland", Tourism Management, Vol.19(1), 67-73.

14. Fesenmaier, D., Vogt, C., (1993) Evaluating the economic impact of travel information provided at Indiana welcome centres, Journal of Travel Research, Vol.31(3), 33-39.

15. Frew, A. J., and O'Connor, P., (1998), "A Comparative Examination of the Implementation of Destination Marketing System Strategy: Scotland and Ireland", in Buhalis, D., Tjoa, A. M., Jafari, J., (eds), Information and Communication Technology in Tourism, ENTER '98, Conference Proceedings, Springer-Verlag, Wien-New York, 460-475.

16. Frew, A. J., and O'Connor, P., (1999a), "Destination Marketing System Strategies: Refining and Extending an Assessment Framework", in Buhalis, D., Tjoa, A. M., Jafari, J., (eds), Information and Communication Technology in Tourism, ENTER '99, Conference Proceedings, Springer-Verlag, Wien-New York, 439-407.

17. Frew, A. J., and O'Connor, P., (1999b), "Destination Marketing System Strategies: Refining and Extending an Assessment Framework", Information Technology and Tourism, Vol.2(1), 3-15.

18. Go, F. M., (1992), " The role of Computerised Reservation Systems in the hospitality industry", Tourism Management, Vol.3(3), 22-76.

19. O'Connor, P., (1999) Electronic Information Distribution in Tourism & Hospitality, CAB, Oxford.

20. O'Connor, P., and Rafferty, J., (1997), "Gulliver:-Distributing Irish Tourism Electronically", in Electronic Markets, Vol.7(2), 40-45.

21. Pollock, A., (1998a), "Creating Intelligent Destinations For Wired Customers", in Buhalis, D., Tjoa, A. M., Jafari, J., (eds), Information and Communication Technology in Tourism, ENTER '98, Conference Proceedings, Springer-Verlag, Wien-New York, 235-247.

22. Pollock, A., (1998b), "New Technologies as help for Integrated Quality Management", in European Tourism Forum, Conference Proceedings, Vienna , Austria 1-3 July, 78-87.

23. Pollock, A., (1999), Marketing destinations in a digital world, Insights, May, A149-158.

24. Poon, A., (1993), Tourism, Technology and Competitive Strategies, Oxford: CAB.

25. Pringle, S., (1994), "Destined to Fail? An introduction of the Hi-Line Destination Marketing System", in Seaton, A., et al (eds), Tourism: The State of the Art, Wiley, 500-509.

26. Roehl, W., Fesenmaier, D., (1995) Modelling the influence of information obtained at state welcome centres on visitor expenditures, Journal of Travel & Tourism Marketing, Vol.4(3), 19-28.

27. Sheldon, P., (1993), "Destination Information", Annals of Tourism Research, Vol.20(4), 156-212.

28. Sheldon, P., (1997), Tourism Information Technology, CAB International, Oxford.

29. Vlitos-Rowe, I., (1992),"Destination Databases and Management Systems", Travel and Tourism Analyst, Vol. 5, 84-108.

30. Werthner, H., and Klein, S., (1999) Information Technology and tourism: A challenging relationship, Springer-Verlag, Wien.

31. Wöber, K. W., (1998), "Improving the efficiency of marketing information access and use by tourist organisations", Information Technology and Tourism, Vol.1, 23-30.

32. WTO, (1999), Marketing Tourism Destinations On-line, World Tourism Organisation, Madrid.

Mentoring Small Destinations into Destination Management towards Electronic Marketing

U. Martini, G. Jacucci, C. Cattani and D. Calzà
University of Trento (Italy)
Information Engineering Laboratory
Department of Computer and Management Sciences
e-mail: martini@cs.unitn.it, gianni@lii.unitn.it

Abstract

The paper reports on fieldwork concerning destination management: the build up of a virtual organisation for a tourist destination, the choice of a destination marketing strategy, the creation of a destination management system. The work belongs to the research domain on Information Systems, involving IT aspects as well as aspects of people development, organisation and management, and of marketing and business. The solid structure of an enterprise organisation is here replaced by the weak-link structure of a local community. The character of the present work is that of a case study, and the research methodology employed follows the guidelines of Action Research [1] [7]. In some respects, it is akin to Participatory Design in the field of software development. The present work builds up on earlier research work on destination management and destination management systems in the ICT community [3] [4] [11] [18] [20]. The point of view here focuses on tourist destinations (TDs), intended as homogeneous territorial domains, identifiable each with its own name, personality, and offer of a tourist product. We have helped a small TD to get started in adapting to the new situation and to induce change, and we trained ourselves on how to help to induce change successfully.

1 Introduction and theoretical hypothesis

The nature of tourism is changing and TDs must learn to adapt to new situations. Successful destinations should become able to read the emerging demands of customers for specialized leisure opportunities and adapt to meet these needs. Prevailing market dynamics dictate that this adaptive review of opportunities must become an ongoing part of the operation. This is due to some ongoing phenomena inside tourist sector, such as:
- the evolution of tourist behavior, habits and expectations;
- the increase of international competition among destinations, related to the reduction of air-travelling costs;
- the growing dimensions of tourist intermediaries (tour operators and travel agencies);
- the impressive opportunities offered by the Internet to promote, sell and re-organize a tourist destination.

In this dynamic market situation, a TD can no longer afford to respond as a collection of individual entrepreneurs sharing a common location, that sometimes (but not always) becomes - from a marketing point of view - a recognized *brand*. A TD needs to act *as an organization* in order to spot and exploit emerging opportunities.

A TD requires a change of perspective, i.e. to choose a targeted market and be able to offer what the selected clients want. The new and dramatic fact is, those who do not shift from push to pull, risk to be out of market: a TD can no more offer a standard and fragmentized product, but has to define a *specific offering system*, containing both symbolic elements (destination image, brand value), and organizational elements (division of labour among economic operators, creation of a Destination Management), in order to develop a complete and integrated tourist product. These activities are the first step of destination marketing: a tourist product has to be promoted and sold in a specific way, using all the tools that permit to reach the desired consumers. But these activities cannot be done if an integrated tourist product does not exist, and the destination is only a place, with an own name and a geographical location, in which several organizations (private and public) do offer different tourist-related services competing - instead co-operating - among them.

In other words, we consider destination marketing not only as the promotional activities as a whole, but as the entire process of product creation, promotion and selling, including goal setting, market targeting, quality policies. So the implementation of a Destination Marketing Strategy requires the creation of a *Destination Management Board*, which has the task to follow all the marketing process:
- strategic market analysis (demand, competition, market position);
- strategic goals setting;
- planning and budgeting;
- implementation (product definition, promotion, selling, pricing);
- control and results measurement.

The real problem is: all these activities are relevant and necessary, but *who* can do them inside a TD? Is it possible to create a board, which operate just like inside a business organization?

In a TD, we think that the best solution could be the creation of a virtual organization (VO), i.e. a group of people representing all the local operators, connected by ICTs, which allow to work together and stimulate co-operative attitudes. Building a VO is a socio-technical undertaking, *which requires both technology and working relationships among trusted actors with a shared strategic objective.* In fact, the creation process of a TD-VO is based on two considerations:
1. the existence of shared goals about the growth and the development of the TD;
2. the existence of a minimum degree of co-operative orientation among the local operators (public and private) based on mutual trust.

Inside the organizational science, these aspects have been well studied in several works, which defined both the problem of task inconsistency among different decision-makers [9], and the decisional interdependency in strategy formulation among actors which share common resources [6]. In general, an interdependency problem arises when different actors have to take decisions affecting variables under their control, and the final result depends on each decision. If the decisional problem is well structured, and the degree of task sharing among the actors is high, it is defined as a problem of *coordination*. Our idea is that inside a TD the decision making processes relative to the creation, the promotion and the selling of an integrate offering system, represents a typical coordination problem: in fact, in a TD different operators control specific resources (accommodation services, food & beverage, transportation services, sport activities, cultural attractions, entertainment activities, information and tourist welcome), which must be combined in a single product, defined by the tourist depending on his/her needs, preferences and habits.

The first coordination problem is about the best combination of each resource, in order to create a competitive and effective tourist product; the second (and more relevant) problem, is that, in many cases, the aims, the tasks and the long term strategies of each actor can be inconsistent. In this case, the destination management board has to find a *political solution* to define a common strategy, or the arising conflict could stop every TD developmental project: the main resource-holders should find a compromise, giving a partial solution to their specific needs, in order to reach a global optimization.

The formation of a shared strategic objective for the community and the will to carry it out are essential elements in the creation of a VO. But which role can be plaid by the ICTs inside this process? From the beginning of the Eighties, the economic literature explored this phenomenon, posing some milestones about the impact of the new ICTs on business organization. In particular, two results have been achieved:
a) the ICTs can improve business competitiveness, offering new exploitable opportunities to the most innovative firms [10] [13];
b) the ICTs can re-define business organization and scope, both inside and outside the firm, enabling to create an electronic network which stimulate external partnerships and the division of labour among different organization in the value chain [16] [19].

Several studies have demonstrated that the same effects can be found inside tourist sector [ENTER Conferences Proceedings] [2] [3] [21]: tourist organizations can really benefit by the use of ICTs, especially with the aim to reach organizing and marketing goals. In the last five years, the diffusion of the Internet allowed SMEs and TDs to define *electronic marketing strategies*, in order to promote and sell tourist products aside from the intermediation industry. Moreover, the Intranet and Extranet applications enabled to re-define the organizational design of the firms, facilitating data exchange and information sharing among the connected actors.

If the power of ICTs is indisputable, the real problem is represented by the relational framework in which they are used: to create an effective Destination Management

System, able to provide promotional and commercial services for the destination as a whole [12], *the obstacle is not the technology, but the will to co-operate of all the actors involved*. In other words, the creation both of a Destination Management Board, and of a Destination Management System, is based on *mutual trust* among the actors [8] [11]: in the lack of trust, they will remain unrealized projects, and the TD will continue to offer its services as the sum of independent tourist products, without a long term strategy able to modify its developmental horizon.

2   An Action Research project to build a DMS in a mountain tourist destination of Northern Italy: The case of Folgaria

Starting from these theoretical assumptions, we worked in a mountain TD of Northern Italy to establish a steering committee of local operators, which serves as a sounding board for opportunities for technology introduction and a gateway into the community. We have also worked to establish a technological infrastructure and the expertise to make use of it. Our work draws upon our previous work on adult learning, our experience with organizational training by training a key individual, our ongoing work in the development of adaptive multi-media distance learning tools, and our previous work building client-databases for TDs.

We started with methodological hypothesis and used Action Research to produce theory through practice. Action research simultaneously assists in practical problem-solving and expands scientific knowledge as well as enhances the competence of the respective actors, being performed collaboratively in an immediate situation, using data feedback in a cyclical process. It aims at an increased understanding of the totality of a given social situation, primarily applicable for the understanding of change processes in social systems undertaken within a mutually acceptable ethical framework [1] [7] [17]. In action research, methods and procedures enabling change are investigated through iteration of the following phases:
a)   *conceptual analysis*, to define the problem, consider alternative solutions, identify the best candidate to introduce change in social life units;
b)   *field action*, to introduce sought change;
c)   *evaluation* of obtained change, identification of general findings.
Our starting hypothesis included the following general points:
a)   socio-economic development of a local community cannot be achieved through development in isolation of each single actor and enterprise;
b)   learning and change should originate inside the community, i.e., be endogenous, conscious, integrated, and locality- specific;
c)   knowledge management should not involve only transmission of codified knowledge, but development of tacit, context specific, social knowledge as well, or "milieu" knowledge.

The project on which the present research is based, is intended to make a specific intervention in Folgaria, a small mountain TD of Trentino (Northern Italy), with both winter and summer tourist seasons. We organized an introductory session of seminars during fall, to engage all available operators on tourism management, tourism marketing, service quality, technology applications, and stimulate their will to participate in the project; then, 15 operators spontaneously took part in the following sessions, on specific marketing activities supported by ICTs. The research team worked on data gathering and contextual analysis, involving the local representatives of public boards, professional categories (tradesmen, hotelkeepers) and economic actors, with the aim to share the formative needs of the tourist operators and the strategic vision of a possible tourist project. Thanks to this initial analysis, we have been able to define the main characteristics of the local operators:

- organizational backwardness, especially in comparison with other international mountain TDs;
- presence of small dimension units, based on owners management;
- lack of cooperative work attitude;
- lack of marketing activities planning attitude;
- presence of three significative tourist organizations: the local tourist board; an hotelkeepers consortium, controlled by the town council; a lift-plant company, which manages all the ski-runs, the artificial snowing system and the chair-lifts installations;
- besides the presence of these organizations, lack of a real TD management, promotion and selling in the past;
- lack of confidence with technological instruments and ICTs.

To maximize the participation to the project of the local actors, we adopted an involvement strategy, based on the following steps:
a) frequent and systematical group meetings;
b) application of group-building techniques to maximize interaction and discussion among the participants;
c) continuos interaction with the local public boards;
d) creation and recurrent meeting of a Policy Board, composed by the main representatives of the local economic and tourist activities, private and public;
e) direct involvement of the local citizens, during evening public meetings and common activities (for example, common definition of a questionnaire to submit to summer and winter tourists, direct involvement in its distribution, presentation of the final results).

In all these activities, the research group worked as a *group facilitator*, stimulating the discussion of problems, ideas and developmental projects: we were there to hear and to understand, not to propose generic solutions. The idea of "destination" and the opportunity to create a real "destination management and marketing system" should have arisen as the natural consequence of this analysis.

During this activity, which lasted for three months, we selected a small group of 15 persons, to participate to a 6 months formative course, in which we organized:
a) *group lessons* about the learning needs arisen in the initial analysis; these lessons

have been organized following adult learning methods [4] [14] [15], trying to combine general arguments with the specific individual working experience;

b) *individual support*, defining individual learning courses inside the participant's firm.

The group lessons and the individual support put right in the center two main arguments:

a) tourist marketing, management and tourist services quality;

b) ICTs applications to the tourist sector, to facilitate daily work inside the firm and to create an electronic network.

In this way, we created a group, composed by different operators, which began to work together both to define common marketing projects (such as the creation of a Locality Card to promote selling during the low season, or the creation of a promotional folder to be placed in all the hotels, containing information about the available tourist services), and to experiment with new technological application, first of all the creation of Internet Web Pages and of a local Destination Management System, collaborating with the local tourist board and the hotelkeepers consortium. This group was recognizable inside the local community, and the results of its work were periodically discussed inside the Policy Board.

This working method, despite its difficulties, allowed to reach some considerable effects:

− spread specific knowledge and skills inside the community;

− teach a method for cooperative working and decision-making;

− pose the basis for long-term cooperation inside the locality, demonstrating the added value of cooperative work;

− promote the diffusion of the ICTs inside the community.

In particular, the introduction of new technologies and training can be disruptive and requires motivation to succeed. We brought to Folgaria database and communication tools, proven beneficial to other TDs, dealing with the construction, maintenance and targeted use of client information databases. The combination of access to proven tools and emerging technologies, and the explanation of the links between management and technology, provided the required motivation.

At the beginning of our experience in Folgaria, we were convinced that the future of tourism was in the Internet, due to its capability to give access to all the information regarding a TD, to stimulate electronic commerce (on-line booking) and to facilitate the creation of group co-operating systems, thanks to information sharing and gathering to promote the TD as a whole. To drive the transition process of a TD towards a Destination Management System (DMS) is a very complex challenge. "The ways in which ICTs can be applied to the work of destination marketing organizations, must be sensitive to the characteristics of these organizations" [12]. In fact, ICTs introduction requires:

− *goals sharing*: the local community must share the objectives of the Action

Research, e.i. it must be convinced that the new technologies allow to reach incomparable results;

- *consensus*: the community must agree to implement and to set up all the technologies;
- *participation*: the community must decide to be the first protagonist of the transformation.

A second question refers to the relation between the local DMS and the other existing structures (local and regional tourist boards, hotelkeepers consortium, category associations): a DMS should integrate different kinds of data, and should be connected with several external links.

From a technological point of view, the goal of the Action Research in Folgaria was to start up a DMS building project able to involve the local community (endogenous development), not to install an existing one (exogenous development). This meant to create a local working group, which, after a formation period, could share with the research group the goals and the implementation steps of the DMS. In particular, the working group, assisted by a technical staff, learnt to use workgroup applications, electronic information gathering and database systems, Internet surfing engines, on-line promotion and selling tools (e-commerce and Internet marketing applications). At the same time, each member of the group experimented the use of PC and of Internet services inside his firm, developing personal Web Pages and individual database systems to be connected to the DMS.

The DMS developed in Folgaria, which is still under construction, provides for three kinds of services (see Fig. 1):
1) Destination Management Services (internal):
    - Extranet to share local tourist information (restaurants, hotels, events, packages, sport attractions, ...);
    - Office Automation Applications (database, word processing, invoicing, ...);
2) Promotional and Commercial Services to reach directly tourists:
    - Web Pages creation for hotels, shops, ski schools, local tourist board, hotelkeepers consortium;
3) External Suppliers Management Services:
    - Extranet access to on-line purchase groups;
    - Extranet access to a consultant remote staff (Expert on-line);
    - Extranet access to central system for long-distance training.

Fig. 1: The structure of the DMS designed for Folgaria.

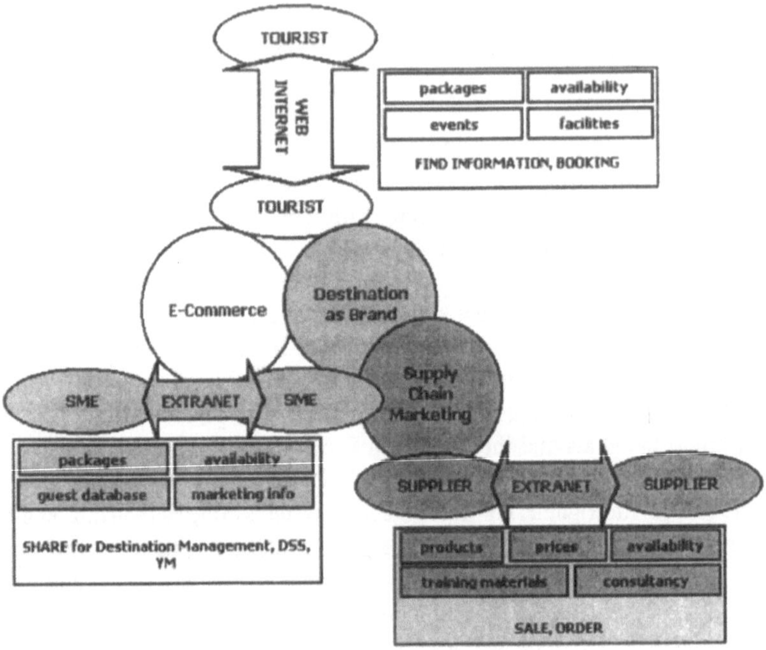

The Extranet, which implements internal services, contains the following database, built to manage all the information about the locality:
- hotel rooms availability database;
- restaurants database;
- client database;
- events database;
- tourist packages database.
-

The design of the entire database was carried out in collaboration with the Regional Tourist Board of Trentino. The joined study favored the identification of two main information categories, useful for destination management (Fig. 2):
a) *promotional information*, to be distributed by the Internet with the aim to maximize visibility and to reach a wide number of tourists;
b) *organizational information*, to be distributed by the Extranet for local operators exclusive use.

The design of the system, based on exhaustive analysis of the available data, has the aim to reduce redundant information, and to define single operator's role and responsibility in its management. At the same time, it is projected to contain all the data about the destination, and to be connected to the regional website of Trentino.

Fig. 2: The structure of the network for an optimized information management.

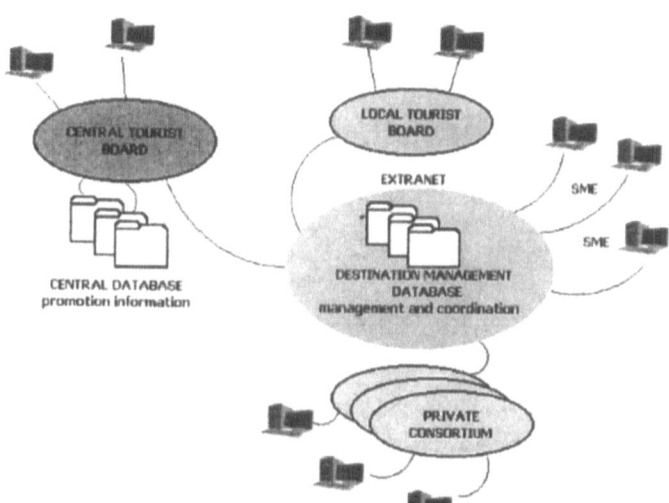

3 Conclusions and learning from the Action Research

The Action Research cycle - diagnose, plan, implement, evaluate and learn - took place many times as: project design and redesign together with actors; monitoring and adjustment of training activities employing "active" methodologies; co-construction of technology applications (participatory design and realization). Our field study proceeded towards organizational change and innovation along the following guidelines: create awareness, organize the community, choose a project, create management (pilot group), granting social and institutional consensus, implement the project by training people and introducing required technologies. Focus all along was on TD picking up its own destiny and performing participatory design and product realization in co-operation with a selected, involved client set.

At the end of the process, we can confirm the crucial role of the Big Four - Business, Organization, Training, Technology - and identify their features here:

1. *Business*: start from existing assets, exploit towards a client-driven product (interactive client);
2. *Organization*: VO enabled by technology; independent actors develop social commitment to the common goal;
3. *Training* of four kinds: on destination organization and management, on business content (destination marketing), on technical aspects (stand alone, networking and group-ware, Internet), on cooperation (group-work, communication and knowledge sharing, coordination);

4. *Technology* applied in different ways, all requiring motivation:
   - to improve efficacy of small businesses (individual business motivation);
   - to create the VO (social motivation);
   - to promote the growth of the VO through distribution of services on Extranet to individual small businesses (system advantages);
   - to avail distance training services (personal motivation);
   - to enable the electronic marketing channel (commercial motivation).

Thanks to the action research, we have found some critical issues and related enabling factors, which can be summarized as in Table 1, and that we think could easily be extended to other similar experiences.

Table 1: Critical issues and enabling factors of the AR project.

Critical issues	Enabling factors
Acceptance, social recognition and respect of project pilot group	Meeting place, management structure, consensus creating strategy, involving of stakeholders, interest conflict management
Learning role of project group	Creation of a learning center for knowledge sharing, community of practice, needs-based training
Focus and agglutination of knowledge creation effort	Implementation of well defined and feasible executive projects, demonstration of the ICTs real advantages for SMEs

From a theoretical point of view, we have reached three outcomes, partially contradicting the general hypothesis from which we started:

a) *a project of DM/DMS creation inside a tourist locality is deeply influenced by the relationships existing before its start among the actors*: a thorough analysis both of all actors, and of the past relationships among each other, allows to predict arising conflicts and antagonist behaviors;

b) *the creation of a DMS does not modify the relationships' structure inside the locality*: the design and the implementation of an effective DMS are like a veil or a superstructure, that covers the relationships among the actors, but it is not able to re-define actors' role inside the community or to re-distribute power among them;

c) *the creation of a DMS, and the use of the ICTs, do not stimulate collaboration, but strengthen competition*: the actors consider the power of ICTs like an instrument to increase their competitiveness, rather than an instrument to maximize the destination competitiveness. This means that they perceived more the individual than the collective benefits which could be drawn by the ICTs.

Perhaps these results are due to path-dependency, and this would mean that the most important learning for us is point *a*). Now we are trying to apply the same AR method inside other similar tourist destinations, to verify point *b*) and *c*). Anyway, we achieved two significant results:

1) from an organizational point of view, for the first time in the history of the locality, the main actors were sat around at table, to discuss about developmental tourist project and to promote the destination as a whole;

2) from a technological point of view, at the beginning of the project the operators did not use any ICT tool, and considered Internet as an "unknown technology"; at its end, more than 20 small operators were on-line and used PC for managerial purposes; the local Tourist Board and the hotelkeepers consortium had a website design and initial implementation; all the community realized the opportunities to be on-line, and considered the Internet as a precious allied to compete.

References

1. Argyris C., Putnam R., Smith D.M.: Action Science, Jossey-Bass, San Francisco (1987).
2. Buhalis D.: Strategic Use of Information Technologies in the Tourist Industry, Tourism Management, 19, 5 (1998).
3. Buhalis D.: Information and Telecommunication Technologies as a Strategic Tool for Tourism Enhancement at Destination Regions, Enter Conference Proceedings, Springer (1996).
4. Bruscaglioni M.: La gestione dei processi nella formazione degli adulti, Milano, Angeli (1997).
5. CISET International Conference: From Destination to Destination Marketing and Management, Venice (Italy), 15th-16th March (1999).
6. Freeman H.E.: Strategic Management: A Stakeholder Approach, Boston, Pitman (1984).
7. Hult M., Lennong A.: Towards a Definition of Action Research: A Note and Bibliography, Journal of Management Studies, 17, 4 (1980).
8. Laubenheimer M.C., Carlsson T.: From Intra-Regional Competition towards Intra-Regional Cooperation in Tourism: The Concept of Telecooperation and Virtual Enterprises in the Regional Tourism Business, TourIST European Project Paper (1998).
9. March J.G.: The Business Firm as a Political Coalition, Journal of Politics, 24, (1962).
10. McFarlan F.W.: Information Technology Changes the Way You Compete, Harvard Business Review, May-June (1984).
11. Morgan R.M., Hunt S.D.: The Commitment-Trust Theory of Relationship Marketing, Journal of Marketing, 58, July (1994).
12. Pollock A.: Creating Intelligent Destinations for Wired Consumers, Enter Conference Proceedings, Springer (1998).
13. Porter M.E., Millar V.E.: How Information gives you Competitive Advantage, Harvard Business Review, 63, 4, July/August (1985).

496

14. Quaglino G.P., Carrozzi G.P.: Il processo di formazione, Milano, Angeli (1996).
15. Quaglino G.P.: Scritti di formazione 1978-1998, Milano, Angeli (1999).
16. Scott Morton M. (Editor): The Corporation of the 1990s, Oxford, Oxford University Press (1991).
17. Susman G.I., Evered R.D.: An Assessment of the Scientific Merits of Action Reserch, Administrative Science Quarterly, 23 (-1978).
18. TourIST Seminar: Destination Management Systems, Madeira (Portugal), Madeira Tecnopolo, 26th-27th November (1998).
19. Venkatraman N.: IT-Enabled Business Transformation: From Automation to Business Scope Redefinition, Sloan Management Review, Winter (1994).
20. Werthner H., Carter R.: IFITT White Paper. Result of IFITT Workshop on Open Issues and Challenges in IT and Tourism, Innsbruck, September 21st-22nd (1998)
21. Werthner H., Klein S.: Information Technology and Tourism. A Challenging Relationship, Wien, SpringerComputerScience (1999).

Small is Beautiful? ICT and Tourism SMEs: a Comparative European Survey

Graeme Evans and Martin Peacock
Centre for Leisure and Tourism Studies, University of North London, UK;

Greg Richards
Tilburg University, The Netherlands

1. Introduction

This paper presents the results of a two year research project - *TOURIT* - which has investigated the extent to which ICT applications have been taken up by small tourism firms in three European regions; the possible barriers to participation in ICT and their related enterprise support needs. This survey project forms part of a European Union LEONARDO DA VINCI study (UK/97/1/39005/EA/III.2.a/CONT) which focuses on the vocational training needs and business development opportunities that might be offered to small and medium-sized enterprises (SMEs) in the tourism and hospitality sector. The survey compares three region-types and scales of tourism activity - the *World City-state* of Greater London, UK; The Netherlands, and the Aragon province, comprising three districts in north-east Spain. The study therefore provides a contrast between capital city and national tourism system in northern Europe and rural/mountain-based tourism in a lesser-developed region of Spain. The research has also been conducted in the context of both national and European (EU) tourism and related policy regimes, and the global ICT and CRS tourism systems within which small tourism enterprises operate. Initial research findings based on the pilot survey in London, together with a review of literature and European policy interventions, were presented at the previous ENTER conference (Evans and Peacock 1999) - this paper therefore presents the final results of this comparative survey, including an assessment of the findings and implications for tourism SMEs.

2. Context – *Small is Beautiful?*

Whilst the rapid growth of ICT usage and ownership and online travel and reservations systems dominate the field of *IT in Tourism,* the tourism "industry" (sic) in practice is both fragmented and represented by, on the one hand, a large number of small enterprises and on the other, a small but powerful number of global and national operators (Evans and Peacock 1999, Buhalis 1994, 1999). Small firms are key aspects of economic development and employment growth within European and local economies, and policies to support and enhance SMEs are evident at European (EU) and national levels. However whilst occupying the largest number (93% of all firms in the EU), SMEs represent a tiny proportion of total turnover and have below-average 'value added per employee', when compared with medium and larger firms (EC 1997) and despite their growth potential, small entrepreneurs are seldom regarded as serious partners in community development through tourism (Dahles 1997). The other side of the latest technological revolution and accompanying 'determinism', also sees a growing divide between those with full access and skills in *Information Society Technology* (IST), and those lacking such access, control and ownership - a form of social exclusion creating a group of disempowered consumers, employees and disadvantaged, non-competitive businesses, as Downey predicts writing on Europe: *"While it is likely that the greater use of ICT will have significant benefits in terms of productivity, GDP growth and employment, it is also probable that these benefits will not be equally distributed. Inequalities between core and peripheral regions will grow as core regions increase their grip on the global economy; inequalities within cities will widen..."* (1999: 137), a scenario also presented by Castells (1996) and Wanhill (1997). In practice, small firms may traditionally lack both capital and research and development resources and capability, and the scale of operation required to justify investment in ICT – a Catch-22 situation, as Werthner and Klein note: *"their size is their main disadvantage. Small suppliers have normally little know how about marketing and technology...and limited access to distribution channels"* (1999: 44), citing the fact that over 85% of European accommodation suppliers are not listed on airline CRS that serve travel agents worldwide (Werthner *et al* 1997). Another indication of this lack of awareness is in the preparation for the 'Millennium Bug' – in the UK nearly half of all small firms had done nothing towards Y2K, with SMEs employing under-10 staff and hotels and restaurants the worst culprits. Other barriers may include an antithesis to IT itself where 'personal service' and contact is a key comparative advantage of the owner-operator and niche supplier (Evans 1999).

The labour markets and training needs, and the management and marketing of small enterprises, have also been under-studied generally, due to the heterogenous nature of SMEs and the practical difficulties in conducting empirical research. Initial studies of the impact and awareness of ICT within small tourism and hospitality firms also do not present a consistent picture, with variations between activity type and location/country (Evans and Peacock 1999). Within SMTEs in particular, this is therefore exacerbated by the fragmented range of activities which make up the supply chain from the customer's perspective, but not necessarily from the viewpoint of the small firms themselves, who tend to identify with their core activity or trade (i.e. hotel, restaurant, museum, travel agent) rather than the 'visitor market' and economy itself. SMTEs also lack the integration and strategic alliances now common amongst transnational operators, and which have underwritten ICT development, notably CRS, online sales and joint-marketing schemes. Attention to SMTEs and *e-commerce* has however been devoted in recent studies, ENTER proceedings, and initiatives around Destination Marketing/Management Systems (DMS) at a local area level (Frew and O'Connor 1999, Evans 1999, Buhalis and Cooper 1998), as well as in training and research development (*cf.* IFITT, KNITE, TourISt), and policy intervention (*viz* EU

Fifth Framework Werthner *et al* 1997, *Philoxenia* CEC 1996b, 1997). The need for a greater understanding of SMTEs and ICT across the full range of tourism services, rather than studies of isolated sub-sectors such as hotels, travel and transport or single destinations, is therefore a particular aspect which this study explores, highlighting divergence in approaches to and usage of ICT within hospitality, visitor attractions and travel and tour operator sectors, which suggests that a more integrated destination area ICT strategy should be adopted by SMTEs.

3. Methods

In order to provide a robust comparative framework across the three European regions and between sectors, a common research instrument was designed. This was achieved by a standard questionnaire which as well as profiling the SMTE - by main activity, status (public, private, not-for-profit), service provided and number of employees - detailed their current and planned ICT usage; training expertise held in each ICT application; current online reservation/booking and payment facilities; and details of any presence on a web site, whether 'owned' or 'rented' (via server, DMS, TIC). The questionnaire was coded and translated into Dutch and Spanish for initial piloting to a small sample in each area after which some refinement to the questionnaire was made (mainly around technological terms and accommodation type and measurement) and the final coded questionnaires were circulated to a total of 4,500 SMTEs. Details of tourism firms were developed into an extensive database which each research team compiled from directory, local area networks (e.g. trade, chamber of commerce, tourist board/TIC), mailing lists and existing SME databases held from previous sectoral studies. Tourism and hospitality listings were surveyed in order to separate SMEs from larger firms and operators. In some cases firms were included where they were linked to a larger organisations but effectively autonomous (e.g. a local authority TIC-tourist information centre, or museum), but 'chains' were excluded from the SMTE databases even if stand alone they qualified as SMEs by employee size, since they potentially benefit from larger parent company network/IT systems. Data from the respondent questionnaires was coded and input via SPSS and the three-country data sets were merged to enable cross-tabulation. Within each data set, analysis by activity sub-sector and size of firm (numbers of staff) and some geographical analysis, enabled highlights to be made of the key factors which appear to influence the variation in ICT usage, skills/training and planned development.

4. Survey and Results

Nearly 900 completed questionnaires were received in addition to 100 telephone interviews, a net response rate of c.20% in each of the three regions. In order to determine reasons for non-response, telephone follow-up of 10% of firms was undertaken, with the common reply that they were "not interested in ICT", it was "not for them", or they had "no time to reply". Non-respondents therefore include a large proportion of 'non-ICT-aware' or disinterested firms which is in itself significant (given the industry predictions of ICT take-up) and suggests a further avenue for research (below). Responses to the questionnaire reflected the profile of SMTEs within each region, with notably higher return rates from accommodation and activity/tour providers in Aragon, Spain and The Netherlands, but lower responses from these sectors in London, where travel agents, cultural and visitor attractions were above-average respondents. Between 55% and 67% of respondents were micro-enterprises, employing less than 10 staff and a further 20% between 11 and 25 staff, confirming the credibility of the data base and sample, and reflecting the European tourism economy itself, with over 90% of enterprises being categorised as "small" or "micro".

Respondent activity types (sub-sectors) revealed the differing destination profiles between the urban/cultural tourism bias of London; the mixed urban and outdoor recreation in The Netherlands (a north-south divide, but more evenly spread); and the rural/historic towns and mountain resorts of the Aragon region. Whilst there was convergence over the level of penetration of ICT, Spain had the lowest usage (33% versus over 55% in London and Netherlands). Credit card acceptance (a key CRS requirement) was surprisingly low in The Netherlands (40%), and highest in Aragon (80%). Given the differing supply types, London exhibited greater ICT usage in the visitor attraction/cultural facility area than in the hotel/bed and breakfast (b&b) sector, but this was the reverse in Aragon and The Netherlands. The following tables present the main comparative survey results and these are then summarised, followed by a discussion of these, and the implications and issues arising for the development of ICT within small tourism enterprises. Quantitative data is shown in terms of the number or frequency against each category and/or in percentage terms (i.e. the proportion of the whole sample for each region) – for example in London 17 out of 190 SMEs responding classified themselves as Visitor Attractions, which represented 9.2% of the total survey sample for London.

4.1 Status of organisation

The status of SME distinguishes those that are public or private organisations or companies, from sole traders or those with other legal or corporate structures. These include not-for-profit or charitable organisations, trusts and foundations, trade associations, co-operatives, religious organisations and amenities (e.g. parks, markets). Company status differs between the three countries, despite European harmonisation, with various company-types operating and differing usage of organisational structures (e.g. use of charitable trust for museums in UK; private foundations in Spain, Tourist Information public in the UK and Netherlands; private in Spain). For the purpose of the survey, "status" has been grouped by main type, distinguishing between private, public, sole trader and other/not-for-profit enterprise.

Table 1 Status/Type of Organisation

	London, UK %	Aragon, Spain %	The Netherlands %
Private Company	31.8	76.4	1.6
Public/Limited Company	12.3	6.1	37.6
Sole Trader	2.8	15.7	23.9
Other	53.1	1.7	36.9

Variances between the proportion of status-types in each country also reflects the balance of activity, for instance a high proportion of cultural organisations explaining the high "Other" percentage in London compared with a high private and sole trader percentage in Aragon where small hotels and tour guides predominate. In The Netherlands a high proportion of sole traders in travel and tour activity, as well as small owner-occupied accommodation providers and a small number of private companies, reflects the higher public sector provision in travel and tour information, local tourist services and not-for-profit providers. The latter group is significant since ICT training and support will need to consider the needs and financial resource base of these semi- and non-commercial SMTEs.

4.2 Main SMTE activity (sub-sector)

The type of service provided by firms is obviously key since this sector is not homogenous and SMTEs seldom consider themselves as part of the 'tourist' industry, even if many of their customers are tourists or visitors. They are therefore primarily activity/trade, not customer-led, with insufficient understanding of the tourism production chain and joint marketing and product development. Translation of activity types varied in both Spain and Netherlands, with greater differentiation in The Netherlands in accommodation provision (caravans, camping, bungalow parks, hotels etc). The size of accommodation providers varied between the regions with the largest average in London (86 rooms), followed by Aragon (69 rooms) and The Netherlands with 43 rooms which is closer to the European average of 45 bedrooms. Again the profile of respondents reflected the tourism economy and geography of each region with the highest hotel and catering element in rural Aragon; the highest travel/booking agencies in The Netherlands and the highest cultural attractions in London (and lowest in The Netherlands). Outdoor activity and tour operators were also highly represented in Aragon, but also a significant group in (northern) Netherlands.

502

Table 2 Main SMTE Activity or Service

	London		Aragon		Netherlands	
	n= 190	%	n=229	%	n=455	%
Travel/bookings agency	7	3.8	24	10.5	61	13.6
Visitor attraction	17	9.2	3	11.4	2	0.4
Museum, gallery or heritage site	52	28.1	2	12.2	13	2.9
Arts/Entertainment venue	33	17.8	-	0	5	1.1
Tourist information/TIC	12	6.5	12	5.2	27	6.0
Tour guide	2	1.1	1	1.3	4	0.9
Café or Restaurant	5	2.7	47	20.5	53	11.8
Activity/Ttour organiser	5	2.7	18	7.9	73	16.3
Hotel/Accommodation	27	14.6	106	46.3	138	30.7
Other	25	13.5	17	7	73	16.3

4.3 Size of organisation by employees

The other key indicator of SMTEs is their size measured by the number of employees (full time equivalent-FTE). In all three regions SMTEs make up over 75% of tourism firms (80% of hospitality in London, 95% of SMTEs in The Netherlands), whilst in Europe as a whole this accounts for 95.5% of the hotel and catering ("HoReCa") sector, or 1.3 million enterprises which employ less than 10 people (Werthner *et al* 1997). As anticipated - and this validates the value of the database analysis and filtering exercise carried out prior to conducting the surveys - the majority of respondents were small businesses; between 75% and 88% with under-26 employees, and over 50% were micro-enterprises (under-10 staff). This is critical in developing training and ICT development approaches within this sector, since barriers to participation and support strategies will be specific to the small firm. The small to medium-sized respondent firms tended to be public sector such as tourist information centres, museums/attractions and small, independent hotel and travel agency chains.

Table 3 Size of Enterprise by the Number of Employees

Number of employees	London		Aragon		Netherlands	
	n=190	%	n=229	%	n=455	%
0-10	99	54.4	152	66.7	297	65.6
11-25	36	19.8	51	22.4	93	20.5
26-50	20	11	15	6.6	34	7.5
51-100	14	7.7	6	2.6	20	4.4
101-200	7	3.8	3	1.3	3	0.7
Over 200	6	3.3	1	0.4	6	1.3

4.4 ICT currently used or planned

The extent to which SMTEs currently used and planned to use ICT in the future was the key measure of ICT penetration and interest in this sector. In the prime area of *e-*

commerce over 50% of London and Netherlands firms currently use Email and (slightly less) the Internet/Web, but only 33% in Aragon. Intranet was, interestingly, used by a small proportion in each country, whilst CD-ROM was used by a lower but similar proportion between the three areas surveyed. Online reservation capability is obviously important in maintaining and enhancing market share, and the lower usage here than of the Net indicates that SMTEs may have secondary <u>access</u> to *e-commerce* facilities outside of their operation, but not full <u>ownership</u> of their own web-site (6. below). This will be an important area for further investigation and development, particularly since 8% to 15% of responding SMTEs planned to develop this facility in the near future. Some firms consulted also indicated greater use and access to email than internet/web, particularly for inter-personnel communication and external networking, with the web site either located/controlled externally or by one 'web master'. Larger SMTEs also tended to have an imposed ICT regime and restricted access by staff within more hierarchical organisational structures, and interestingly, a greater suspicion of the inter-active customer potential and staff 'democratisation' that this new communications technology offered. ICT is therefore seen as either an opportunity or threat depending on the degree of ownership, transparency and access staff have, with the micro-enterprise adopting a more flexible approach in contrast to the larger firm who adopted a more bureaucratic and controlling attitude to ICT.

Table 4 ICT Applications Used and Planned

Application	London		Aragon		Netherlands	
Used:	Currently %	Planned %	Currently %	Planned %	Currently %	Planned %
Teletext	7.9	0.5	13.1	4.8	23.7	5.7
E-mail	58.4	22.1	33.6	22.7	55.4	20.4
Internet/www	51.1	26.3	33.2	29.3	51.6	27.0
Intranet	12.1	10	3.5	5.2	7.9	10.3
CD ROM	41.1	11.1	26.2	11.4	47.3	9.0
CRS/Online	12.6	7.9	8.3	10.9	21.5	14.5
Virtual Reality	-	3.7	1.3	3.1	1.5	4.8

Variations between tourism activity sectors and within each region revealed wide differences in ICT usage however – for instance in Aragon over 70% of activity/tour organisers were on the Net compared with only 34% of hotels and 38% of travel agents; in The Netherlands this proportion was only 46% in hotels compared with 80% in arts venues and 100% of travel agents, whilst in London only 42% of tourist information/TICs used the Net compared with 63% of hotels and 71% of travel firms.

A follow-up of web sites cited by respondents in London also revealed that a third of the URL addresses given were no longer 'live' a year later, with no link to any new site. A recent survey of hotels in London (Buhalis) also found that they were neither using sites for discounting nor updating room availability, rendering web sites ineffective. This suggests maintenance/ continuation problems; rapid change in web technology/systems and perhaps a lack of robustness in ICT involvement at this stage.

Virtual Reality, which is increasingly being used as a 'walk through' and visualisation tool for sites, venues (hotels, museums) and destination areas, is showing a small interest amongst SMTEs. Despite the growth in ICT usage and planned usage, a significant proportion of respondents did not have access to *e-commerce* facilities and this group will need to be studied further in terms of barriers to ICT and possible support mechanisms both at a local area and sectoral (e.g. small hotels) level.

4.5 Methods to take reservations and payment

Booking systems need to integrate between information/promotion, reservation and actual payment stages, and the extent to which firms used automated payment was therefore assessed. Whilst the telephone and fax were the favourite method of taking bookings and receiving payment, a significant minority used Email for reservations – 33% in London, 46% in The Netherlands but only 24% in Aragon. Much lower numbers actually used the Net to receive payments even where email was used for the booking in the first place. Again this indicates that SMTEs have only partial access to the internet (e.g. shared or networked system, local area web site or destination marketing system), but no reliable payment/credit card facility. This is a lost opportunity for marketing and reservations (including pre-payment facilities), and a potential loss of income where commission payments are made by SMTEs to intermediaries.

A majority accept credit cards but not as many as one might expect in this sector, particularly in The Netherlands where less than 50% accepted cards, whilst in the more rural Aragon area the highest percentage accept cards. This reflects national systems and cultures and the extent of a residual cash economy (e.g. smaller payment areas such as visitor attraction, museum entry), as well as locational factors such as availability of bank/ATMs in remoter areas. Automated reservation and payment systems, including integrated and networked ticketing and booking will be an important aspect of ICT development and training. "Chip" credit cards which are now taking over the traditional swipe-card may start to replace small payment transactions, and therefore services which limited credit/debit card usage for small payments, may require online facilities for the first time, or risk the loss of custom.

Table 5 Reservation/Booking and Payment Systems Accepted

Application /System	London		Aragon		Netherlands	
	Reservation / Booking	Payment	Reservation / Booking	Payment	Reservation / Booking	Payment
Teletext	2.1%	1.6%	2.2%	1.3%	2.9%	0.2%
Telephone	77.4%	32.1%	79.9%	11.4%	88.1%	21.3%
Fax	66.8%	24.7%	62.4%	9.6%	82.4%	10.8%
E-mail	32.6%	11.1%	24%	3.5%	46.2%	5.5%
Internet	18.9%	5.3%	17.5%	2.6%	31.4%	4.4%
Accept Credit Card?	66.3%		84.8%		47.2%	

4.6 Expertise held or training provided in IT

The extent to which firms judged that their staff had expertise in the various IT applications was 'self-assessed', and also whether training was provided. In all cases firms has less expertise and training provision than actual usage of ICT (Table 4), suggesting that there may be a skills gap and under-utilisation of both ICT and staff capability. The relationship between SMTE end-users and ICT systems also affected the degree of training and perceived IT skill needs. If web/home pages were held on external or DMS sites, including TIC central reservation agencies, and the degree to which off-the-shelf programs and standard web-page design were used – this reduced the concern for in-house expertise and specialist training. Where more customised applications were used, including own web-site and design, and more extensive use of eMail for both internal and external communication, ICT capability and training development was higher. Firms more involved in ICT and customised design also expressed greater motivation in learning and satisfaction from the outcome of their work, however take up of external training was not considered a priority or an effective means of developing ICT skills by the SMTEs consulted.

Table 6 Expertise and Training in ICT

Application	London		Aragon		Netherlands	
	Expertise	Training	Expertise	Training	Expertise	Training
Teletext	3.2%	3.7%	6.6%	3.9%	7.0%	0.7%
E-mail	40%	20.5%	27.1%	9.6%	30.1%	13.4%
World Wide Web	33.7%	17.9%	27.9%	10.9%	29.0%	15.2%
Intranet	10%	6.3%	5.7%	2.6%	7.0%	4.8%
CD ROM	22.1%	13.2%	14.8%	2.6%	20.0%	5.1%
Online reservations	7.9%	6.3%	8.7%	4.4%	15.8%	8.1%
Virtual Reality	0.5%	1.1%	1.3%	1.3%	0.9%	0.9%

5. Summary

The above survey findings present a profile of the penetration and distribution of ICT applications amongst a range of SMTEs in the three selected European regions. This has also provided an insight to the extent of ICT application and development within three contrasting destination types, and has particularly highlighted the position of small tourism enterprises in *e-commerce*. With two thirds of all SMTEs surveyed indicating usage of one or more ICT application, and half already using email, internet and CD-ROM, this shows the rapid uptake of ICT within this sector, although the position of non-respondents must caution against any over-optimism over ICT adoption by SMTEs. This expansion is however also confirmed by surveys into IT penetration generally – and in The Netherlands for example, RECRON the trade association for 1,300 accommodation and recreation companies saw the number of its members with an Email address double from 8% to 18% between 1998 and 1999, and those with a home page rise from only 14 to 110 over the same period (Richards

1999). In Teruel, one of the least developed of the three districts of Aragon, of 40 villages (150 to 2,000 inhabitants) surveyed, 25% operated computerised networks to promote local area tourism (Molina 1998) – although not online/networked, this suggests that even at the very local level, this IT infrastructure may form the basis for ICT and related DMS development, linking small accommodation providers in this rural area.

The results have provided a useful comparison between supply-types and sub-sectors of tourism activity, with notable differences in ICT usage, plans, capability and attitude towards the benefits of ICT development as a marketing/communication and management tool. The relationship that SMTEs have with their own trade sectors and within both local areas/destinations and national/regional tourism systems, is varied, with clear opportunities for the development of networking, joint-marketing and collaboration between and across activity sectors, and in customer relationships generally, as Smeral points out: *"the support for building highly integrated destinations with flexible operating network alliances is an important measure to help SMEs compete with global players and restore their capabilities to deliver contributions to income and employment creation"* (1998: 380). The role of DMS and intranet systems is still undeveloped, with insufficient appreciation of, or means of evaluating the costs and benefits to SMTEs by firms themselves, or by service providers, and there is little evidence of DMS and joint web-based reservation systems being sustained beyond the set-up stage. The practical problems of web-site design, maintenance/updating, staff training and access to online information and booking systems are, from this survey, still fundamental barriers to SMTE involvement in ICT. Moreover, the lack of access/skills (design, operation and maintenance of site, management and IT supplier control), rather than capital equipment and finance; a lack of information on the quantitative benefits of ICT compared with the hype, global growth trends and pressure from commercial suppliers/servers currently experienced by SMTEs, are persistent concerns revealed in the survey. A case for customised advice (less so "training"), good practice guides and independent business support in ICT applications and greater attention to destination marketing and the design and maintenance of web sites are key requisites cited by SMTEs, echoed Europe-wide: *"The Commission should support the development and widespread dissemination of digital information, awareness raising and training tools and materials directly applicable to the business processes undertaken by SMEs"* (Werthner et al 1997: 26).

A major risk is that many SMTEs remain marginalised in *e-commerce*, or receive inappropriate advice and 'support' for applications which they are not able to fully exploit and derive sustained benefit from. Policy implications are therefore raised which may inform EU, national and regional initiatives, and which in part explain the limited success and impact of previous programmes in his field (CEC 1996a, Wanhill 1997, Evans and Peacock 1999) – as the Strategic Advisory Group on IST for Tourism concluded: *"SMEs may be lost in the electronic marketplace unless they are shown how and assisted in the usage of the tools and in learning skills necessary to participate in the Digital Economy"* (Werthner *et al* 1997: 27). The need for further research points to a greater understanding of non-ICT users (non-respondents, above) and the profiling of SMTEs within the tourism system, both public and private sectors. Finally the study concludes that there is a particular need for empirical research at the destination level to explore in greater detail the local tourism economy and ICT impacts - supply chain links, training and related organisation development needs, as well as the wider market and 'local-global' relationships, particularly between SMTEs and larger operators.

References

Buhalis, D.: *ICT as a Strategic Tool for Small and Medium Tourism Enterprises'*, in A.V.Seaton *et al*, *Tourism: The State of the Art*, West Sussex: Wiley: 254-274 (1994)

Buhalis, D.: IT as a Strategic Tool for Economic, Social, Cultural and Environmental Benefits Enhancement of Tourism Destination Regions, *Progress in Tourism and Hospitality Research* 3: 71-93 (1997)

Buhalis, D. and Cooper, C.: *Competition or Co-operation? Small and medium-sized tourism enterprises at the destination*, in *Embracing and Managing Change in Tourism'* (Laws, E. et al, eds.), London: Routledge (1998)

Castells, M.: *The Rise of the Network Society*, Ma., USA: Blackwell (1996)

CEC: *Report on the Evaluation of the Community Action Plan to Assist Tourism 1993-95*, 92/421 EC, Brussels: European Commission (1996a)

CEC: *First Multiannual programme to Assist European Tourism "PHILOXENIA" (1997-2000)*, Brussels: European Commission (1996b)

Dahles, H.: *Tourism, small entrepreneurs, and sustainable development: Cases from developing countries*, ATLAS, Tilburg University (1997)

EC: *The European Observatory for SMEs*, 5th Annual Report, Brussels (1997)

Evans, G.L.: *Networking for Growth and Digital Business*, Schertler W., *et al* (eds.), ENTER'99 *ICT in Tourism*, Springer-Verlag, Wein: 376-387 (1999)

Evans, G.L. and Peacock, M.: *ICT in Tourism: A Comparative European Survey*, Schertler, W., *et al* (eds.), ENTER'99 *ICT in Tourism*, Springer-Verlag, Wein: 247-258 (1999)

Molina, P.: *Rural Tourism in the Province of Teruel: Contribution to the stabilisation of its population and sustainable development*, MA dissertation, University of North London (1998)

Richards, G.: *ICT use by SMEs*, ATLAS Asia Conference, *Entrepreneurship and Education in Tourism*, Bandung (1999)

Werthner, H., Nachira, F., Orests, S., Pollock, A.: *Information Society Technology for Tourism. Report of the Strategic Advisory Group on the 5th Framework Program on Information Society*, 8 December (1997)

Smeral, E.: The impact of globalization on small and medium enterprises: new challenges for tourism policies in European countries, *Tourism Management* 19: 371-380 (1998)

Wanhill, S.: Peripheral Area Tourism: A European Perspective, *Progress in Tourism and Hospitality Research* 3: 47-70 (1997)

Werthner, H. and Klein, S.: *Information technology and tourism – A Challenging Relationship*, Springer-Verlag, Wien (1999)

Capacity to Change and Its Influence on Effective IT Use

U. Gretzel

National Laboratory for Tourism and eCommerce,
University of Illinois at Urbana Champaign
Champaign, IL 61820, U.S.A.
gretzel@staff.uiuc.edu

Abstract

Successful technology adoption requires a reconfiguration of organizational structures and mind-sets. Tourism organizations with a high capacity to change are more likely to benefit from the opportunities offered by new information technologies because of their ability to immediately integrate IT into the organizational fabric. This paper analyzes the factors that supposedly determine this organizational capacity to adapt to technological innovations and highly volatile environments. In addition, the paper proposes a theoretical model that illustrates the relationships among the factors and is intended to serve as a basis for future empirical studies in the field.

1 Introduction

With the emergence of the Internet various Web-based applications, and the affordability and accessibility of these technologies, a fundamental change in the "organizational world" seems to be more imminent than ever before. Consequently, the mere use of technology can no longer lead to comparative advantages; new competitive strategies should, therefore, focus on intelligent and innovative ways to use technology. Most tourism organizations have yet to grasp the full potential of information technologies. They need to see that their actual value lies in making the implementation of new business strategies possible, and not in facilitating the old, established ways of doing business. Other organizations have already realized that effective technology adoption can only be achieved if it is embedded in an organization-wide change concept and combined with the introduction of new informational strategies. Understanding the factors that determine the organizational capacity to change is a prerequisite for successful and quick technology adoption.

2 Trends in the Tourism Industry

Over the last two decades, the tourism industry has experienced rapid technological development that brought along: 1) increasing globalization and growing competition due to lower transportation and information costs, 2) fundamental changes in the industry structure through the emergence of new players like Expedia.com and Travelocity.com that led to industry disintermediation and re-intermediation at the same time, 3) more bargaining power for consumers and suppliers of tourism products and services, resulting in a power shift toward both ends of the supply chain [1], and 4) higher demands on the tourism work-force which has to be increasingly knowledgeable. Tremendous changes have also occurred regarding consumer behavior. The customers of tourism information, services and products get more and more accustomed to the use of new technologies. Serving these customers with up-to-date online information requires considerable investments, widespread knowledge sharing, and extensive collaboration on the industry side. New technologies can greatly support tourism organizations in addressing these challenges. There has always been a long-standing relationship between information technology and tourism; this interrelationship of IT and tourism is becoming increasingly intense and will probably reach a point where IT will be the strongest driving force for changes within the tourism industry [2]. Today, tourism is one of the most important users of the World Wide Web. Between 33 to 50 percent of Internet transactions are tourism based [2]. The emergence of the World Wide Web and Internet technologies opens up completely new perspectives for the tourism industry; yet, their potential remains largely untapped [1]. Most tourism organizations see a need for investments in new technologies but usually only use IT to substitute old ways of doing business. Small Convention and Visitor Bureaus are active IT users, for example, but they apply the technologies in a very basic and simplistic way and, thus, are not able to gain the full benefits [3]. It is the lack of expertise and the lack of information about the benefits of IT that make organizations less likely to effectively use information technology [4]. Another negative influence on effective IT use is the fact that the introduction of IT is hardly ever accompanied by profound organizational changes. Today's technologies cannot lead to future competitive advantages if they are applied within yesterday's organizational structures.

The changes in the tourism industry call for new organizational concepts. The key strategic variables that will drive successful tourism organizations in the future are [5]:

- Direction – Organizations must have a picture of where they are heading to in the longer term but must also be flexible enough to modify they way in the short term.
- Form – Organizations can be distinguished by the way plans are translated into action.
- Communication – Success depends on the nature and extent of communication within the organization and with its environment.
- Adaptation – The organization's approach to learning and change determines its long-term chances for survival.

Huffington, Cole and Brunning [6] formulate it in a slightly different and more specific way (see Table 1). Traditional structures and processes will soon become obsolete and a barrier to success. Successful organizations of the future will be characterized by learning, collaboration, flexibility, proactive change, and communication.

Table 1. Future Strategic Orientation (adapted from Huffington, et. al.)

Strategic Emphasis and Orientation	
Presence	Future
Structure / Form	Virtual Organization
Expert / Facilitator	Learner / Developer
Emphasis on People	Emphasis on All
Long-term Change	On-going Change
Remedial	Preventative
Hierarchical Structure	Networks
Discontinuous	Continuous
Linear	Cyclical
Planning	Alignment
Start / Step	Flow
Communication	Dialogue
Values	Meaning
Existing	Being

Information regard and knowledge management have to become a business imperative for tourism organizations, because organizations that stop processing information and neglect the creation, dissemination, and use of knowledge cease to change and ultimately die [7].

3 Organizational Capacity to Change

Information systems are valuable tools for managing knowledge within and across organizations, but achieving a competitive advantage through knowledge management takes more than sophisticated and leading-edge technologies [8]. Rather, it demands the change of organizational structures and cultures and a more comprehensive approach that combines the implementation of an information system with the adoption of new informational strategies, like information sharing, task sharing, virtual communities and learning organizations. These are profound change tasks that cannot be accomplished easily. Organizations differ considerably in terms of their ability and willingness to change, evolve, and adapt to the need for continuous change better than the competition [9]. They also differ regarding their understanding of the importance of such change efforts for their survival in a global and increasingly dynamic marketplace.

Capacity to change or organizational adaptability, respectively, comprises three different aspects that have an influence on an organization's effectiveness [10]:

1. Its ability to perceive and respond to the external environment
2. Its ability to respond to internal divisions and departments
3. Its ability to implement an adaptive response through restructuring and reinstitutionalizing a set of behaviors and processes.

An organization's capacity to change is an indicator of its ability to compete and, thus, the relationship between information technology and organizational change has become a vital concern for most organizations [11]. Change is the talk of the moment but the concept of capacity to change has not yet been comprehensively analyzed and explained. Looking at the significance of change and the numerous factors that influence the organizational capacity to cope with change will help to understand why differences among organizations in terms of their IT and informational strategies adoption exist and how laggards could improve their situation. Traditional literature on change and change management deals with general issues encountered in this field but usually does not refer to specific change initiatives related to the use of information technology. If it does, it focuses mainly on changes induced by the implementation of technology but not on change efforts that precede technology adoption. Therefore, it is necessary to combine several theoretical concepts from different areas including technology adoption/diffusion, information dissemination, organizational communication, intellectual capital, knowledge management, network organization, learning organization, change management, leadership theory, and corporate culture in order to gain a comprehensive theoretical understanding.

4 Methodology

The theoretical framework on which this paper is based has been derived from an in-depth study of tourism and general management literature. More than one hundred articles and books have been studied in order to find variables that supposedly influence an organization's capacity to change and, therefore, its willingness and ability to adopt information technologies and informational strategies. Various factors that could affect an organization's capacity to change have been identified through this procedure. The variables were then summarized into different constructs (see Figure 1).

The constructs are heavily intertwined which can be seen from the complex relationships in the model. Capacity to Change (CTC) is the central construct of the model. It has an influence on the adoption of informational strategies as well as the use of information technology. Whatever influences CTC has at the same time an indirect effect on IT Use and Development of Informational Strategies (DIS) as well as Integration. The different model constructs will be further explained in the following section.

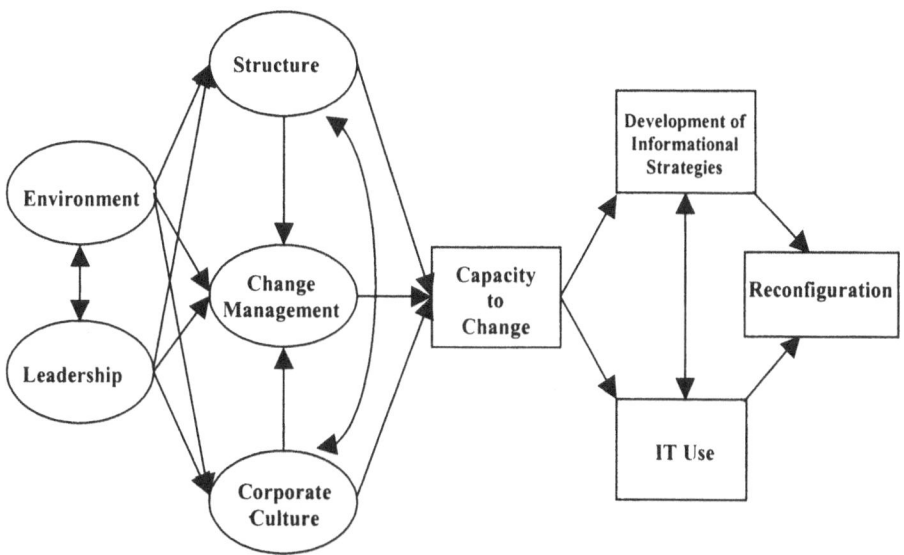

Fig. 1. Influences on the Organizational Capacity to Change

5 Description of the Model Constructs and their Interrelationships

Five distinct independent constructs were identified as factors that have a theoretical impact on an organization's capacity to change: *Environment, Leadership, Organizational Structure, Change Management,* and *Corporate Culture. CTC* in turn, affects *DIS, IT Use* and, consequently, *Reconfiguration. CTC* refers to the ability of organizations to successfully alter their structures, systems, values, beliefs, goals, and strategies. *IT Use* analyzes the extent to which technology is used in the individual organization, and the sophistication of those technologies. *DIS* describes the informational strategies already implemented. Variables included in this construct are if team work approaches have been established, if and what knowledge management strategies have been realized, if the organizations actively exchange information, and if the concept of learning organizations has been adopted. The model suggests that a high capacity to change facilitates the adoption of technology and informational strategies, and, in addition, that there is a strong relationship between the latter two constructs. The trial of IT leads to the development of new informational strategies and vice versa. What technologies and informational strategies are used and how they are integrated finally fosters or limits a possible reconfiguration of the organization.

5.1 Environment

The conditions prevailing in the technological, economical, political, and legal environment of an organization have a strong influence on an organization's capacity to change. These environmental factors are diverse and difficult to capture. The change equation proposed by Huffington, et. al. [6] can serve as a basic framework for explaining why environmental conditions have an influence on the number and extent of change projects accomplished by organizations. According to their findings, change efforts are only undertaken if the following equation holds true,

$$A \times B \times C > D$$

where A refers to the dissatisfaction with the status quo, B is the shared vision of a better future, C is the knowledge of the first practical steps, and D is the (psychological, financial, etc.) cost of making the change. Environmental conditions shape the status quo of a firm. Companies that belong to a stable industry where high profits are realized and high entry barriers exist are probably very satisfied with the status quo and are less likely to see a need for change. Believing in a better future gives incentives for change. Sharing this belief with other industry players increases the probability that change will be initiated because of group pressure. Knowing how to initiate change makes the whole change process a lot easier and, thus, more likely to occur. There are various costs, not to forget opportunity costs, involved in the decision whether to implement change or not. The higher the cost of change and the lower the cost of not changing, the higher the risk of change, and, as a consequence, the smaller the likelihood that a need for change will be perceived and translated into change action. Organizations in a highly competitive industry are forced to continuously adapt to new situations, thus, see a greater need for change, and, as a consequence, have probably already achieved a higher flexibility and greater capacity to change than companies in stable, less competitive environments.

Information relevant to a market can be expected to spread across all players in this market, but diffusion will occur more quickly for certain organizations [12]. It is the industry structure that determines how information circulates within and between industry groups and individual companies. Depending on the relationships with other industry players, a company will be more or less likely to change. For example, if one of the major partners uses a certain technology, the company will be very likely to get to know about the technology, will have an incentive to implement it, too, and may even get assistance from the partner in the adoption and implementation process.

The technological, economical and legal environment an organization has to face does not only depend on the industry it is part of, but also on what stage of the value chain it belongs to, and what markets it deals with. Different types of businesses typically face different business cycles. It is important to look at global and national economic trends in the context of these differences among organizations. Organizations also have a distinct history of technology use and act within discrete legal frameworks. It is necessary to include the markets a company deals with and its level of international business involvement in a model describing the influences on organizational capacity to change. The type of market, the political, legal and economic situation in the various countries and their technology status influence an organization's need to implement information technology and change.

5.2 Leadership

Leadership defines what succeeds and thus determines to a great extent the culture and structure of an organization as well as its approach towards change management. Leadership refers to the leader's attitude towards change, his/her power and respect and entrepreneurial spirit, especially in terms of technology adoption. In addition to its influence on organizational variables, leadership also has an influence on the organization's position within the industry. It is often the leader's network of personal contacts that shapes the organization's interaction with other organizations within or across industries. Variables measuring leadership in this context include the leaders' personal commitment, that is their feeling of being personally responsible for the execution and the outcome of change efforts. Furthermore, it is crucial to look at the leaders' vision regarding technological change and the leaders' perception of how effectively they can sell this vision throughout the organization and to external stakeholders. Another variable to be studied within the 'Leadership' construct is the leaders' attitude towards risk (i.e., financial risk, potential loss of power, etc.) because change always implies considerable amounts of risk.

5.3 Organizational Structure

Size (number of employees), organizational form (hierarchical versus network, number of organizational layers, broadly defined versus narrow job descriptions), communication structures and decision-making channels (long or short, formal or informal), determine the flexibility of an organization and, therefore, its ability to change. Organizational structure can be characterized by how rigid or flexible and how adaptive or non-adaptive an organization is, and how it deals with uncertainty and risk [13]. Rossetti and DeZoort [11] mention the shape, composition, and degree of decentralization as an important structural factor that influences an organization's capacity to change. The old command-and-control model of organizational structure will not be suitable for the environment organizations are going to face in the 21st century. Informational strategies like knowledge management are a direct threat to the hierarchical nature of most organizations [14]. Top-down management reinforces fear, distrust and internal competition and reduces collaboration and cooperation. It leads to compliance, but a high capacity to change requires commitment [15]. Rapid change per se is not a problem. The real issue is the organizations' inability to deal with change. This inability stems from the belief that change can be managed using a traditional, bureaucratic management approach. Bureaucracy, however, has been designed to resist change [16]. It is necessary for establishing consistency and stability in an organization, but hierarchies make the free exchange of knowledge more difficult and, thus, limit the organizational capacity to change. Flat organizations, on the other hand, have a built-in flexibility. They have a less rigid division of work, a constant search for innovative solutions, participation in decision-making, a free flow of communication in all directions, very general job descriptions, a delegation of authority, and a greater sensitivity to environmental changes [13].

Organizational structure also refers to the communication infrastructure. The more comprehensive and flexible the corporate communication network is, the more likely employees know where the organization wants to go. This is an important factor for reducing employee resistance and for initiating and sustaining change because change tends to ignore the proper channels and established bureaucratic lines [16].

5.4 Change Management

Change management can be divided into two sub-concepts: 1) Change Management Approach, and 2) Management of Resistance to Change. Change management approach refers to the change management procedures established within organizations. The questions to be addressed in this context deal with whether there are formal change strategies or not, if bureaucratic barriers have to be overcome, who usually initiates and sponsors changes (top-down or bottom-up changes), and if change is typically managed internally or if external help in the form of consultants is obtained (internal versus external change agents). In addition, organizations may differ in their change management approaches as regards how actively and continuously they seek change. A pro-active approach reduces the time gap between the occurrence of an event and the company's respective reaction, which leads to a higher capacity to change. On the other hand, a remedial, discontinuous change approach decreases the organization's flexibility and, therefore, makes a fast adoption of technological innovations a lot harder.

Employee resistance is still the biggest barrier to successful change. Successfully addressing resistance means ensuring the existence of incentives for employees to learn and change and the establishment of well-structured plans that embrace employee participation throughout all stages of a change process.

The ultimate goal of change management is to incorporate organizational learning into the corporate culture in order to increase an organization's capacity for continuous change. Having a capacity for continuous change means seeing change as a stimulus rather than a threat [17]. Openness to change and anticipating change are vital characteristics of an innovative organization. Since change is taking place with increased speed, new change management techniques are required to achieve such a proactive change approach. Unfortunately, most organizations still change only as little as they must rather than as much as they could and/or should. Research shows that a good change management concept can substantially increase the likelihood of successful IT adoption [18, 1].

5.5 Corporate Culture

DeLisi [19] identifies culture as the primary driver of strategic organizational change. Being aware of an organization's culture is already a big step towards a higher capacity to change (Hassard and Sharifi, 1989). An organization's culture should be adaptive, yet consistent in pursuing its long-term goals, and responsive to individuals, but within the context of a strong, shared mission. Organizational cultures have enormous inertia and change very slowly, and the larger an organization is, the greater is this inertia [10]. Corporate culture determines how organizations process information [20]. Knowledge cannot be shared without trust, honesty, and openness. Maintaining this culture of trust may be difficult when things are constantly changing, but it is crucial for establishing a capacity of continuous change because people change for emotional reason far more than for rational reasons [16]. Another very important aspect of corporate culture is an organization's attitude toward risk. This attitude has a direct influence on capacity to change and on technology management. A culture that tolerates high risks and the possible failures that are connected with it, makes it easier for organizations to pursue a proactive change approach and, thus, get less frustrated by volatile environments [21]. To develop a culture that thrives on continuous change is extremely important. Without it, single change projects may succeed, but will make the next change harder [22]. Success has a vaccinating effect against change and makes an organization resistant to future changes [23].

6 Conclusions and Implications

The relationships between the model constructs are based on theoretical considerations and have not yet been tested empirically. Future research has to focus on the actual testing of the model. Empirical studies will help to identify the most important variables within the constructs and will, therefore, further enhance the model. This theoretical framework will help tourism organizations to understand the necessity for organizational changes if they want to achieve effectiveness in the adoption and use of innovative information technologies. In addition, the practical implications that can be derived from the model will indicate possible strategies for increasing an organization's capacity to change. Only organizations with a high capacity to change will be able to successfully integrate IT and informational strategies and accomplish reconfiguration. Since traditional business models and organizational approaches have become increasingly outdated, reconfiguration will be the prerequisite for establishing competitive advantages in a new economy.

References

1. Baker, M., Sussmann, S., Welch, S.: Information Technology management. In: Brotherton, B. (ed.): The Handbook of Contemporary Hospitality Management Research. John Wiley & Sons, New York, pp. 397-413 (1999).

2. Werthner, H., Klein, S.: Information Technology and Tourism – A Challenging Relationship. Springer Verlag, Wien (1999).
3. Yuan, Y. Y., Fesenmaier, D. R., Xia, L., Gratzer, M.: The Use of Internet and Intranet In American Convention and Visitors Bureaus. In: Buhalis, D., Schertler, W. (eds.): Information and Communication Technologies in Tourism 1999. Springer, Wien, pp. 365-375 (1999).
4. Sheldon, P.: Tourism Information Technology. CAB In., New York (1997).
5. Finerty, T.: Evolutionary thinking about business change. People Management 3 (20): 60 (1997).
6. Huffington, C., Cole, C. F., Brunning, H.: A manual of organizational development: The psychology of change. Psychological Press/International Universities Press, Madison, CT (1997).
7. Adams, C., Adams, B.: The birth of transformation. Executive Excellence 12 (12): 15 (1995).
8. Greengard, S.: Will your culture support KM? Workforce 77 (10): 93-94 (1998).
9. Mariotti, J. L.: Continuous change. Executive Excellence 14 (10): 8 (1997).
10. Denison, D. R.: Corporate Culture and Organizational Effectiveness. John Wiley & Sons, New York (1990).
11. Rossetti, D. K., DeZoort, F. A.: Organizational Adaptation to Technology Innovation. Advanced Management Journal 54 (4): 29-33 (1989).
12. Burt, R. S.: The Network Structure of Social Capital. University of Chicago. Unpublished paper (1998).
13. Zeira, Y., Avedisian, J.: Organizational Planned Change: Assessing the Chances for Success. Organizational Dynamics 17 (4): 31-45 (1989).
14. Steck, R.. N.: Don't Automate – Informate. D&B Reports 42 (4): 42-43 (1993).
15. Drucker, P. F., Dyson, E., Handy, C., Saffo, P., Senge, P. M.: Looking Ahead: Implications of the Present. Harvard Business Review September – Oktober: 18-32 (1997).
16. Waterman, R. H.: Adhocracy: The Power to Change. Whittle Direct Books (1990).
17. Breuer, J. E.: Orchestrating Culture Shock: What Happens When Companies Must Change. Inform 3 (4): 11, 46 (1989).
18. Markus, M. L., Benjamin, R. I.: Are you gambling on a magic bullet? Computerworld 32 (42): C1-C11 (1997).
19. DeLisi, P. S.: Lessons from the Steel Axe: Culture, Technology, and Organizational Change. Sloan Management Review 32 (1): 83-93 (1990).
20. Linder, J. C.: Computers, Corporate Culture and Change. Personnel Journal 64 (9): 49-55(1985).
21. Watkins, W. M.: Technology and Business Strategy: Getting the Most Out of Technological Assets. Greenwood Publishing Group, Inc., Connecticut (1998).
22. Lewis, B.: Managing change is not enough: You must create a culture that embraces it. InfoWorld 20 (45): 105 (1998).
23. Mackiewicz, A.: The successful corporation of the year 2000. The Economist Intelligence Unit, New York (1994).

SpringerComputerScience

H. Werthner, S. Klein

Information Technology and Tourism –
A Challenging Relationship

1999. XX, 323 pages. 134 figures.
Softcover DM 85,–, öS 595,–
(recommended retail price)
ISBN 3-211-83274-2

Information systems in tourism, such as computer reservation systems, yield management systems, and tourism-marketing systems, have been among the pioneers of leading-edge technology applications and have driven the dynamics of development in tourism services. Tourism is regarded as one of the most successful applications of electronic commerce.

The book is synthesizing and analyzing the current situation, trying to set the stage and to show ways of future research. A common methodological approach and framework enables the analysis of the ongoing processes and the underlying trends. From both a technological and a management point of view, the work is focusing on interorganizational processes and information systems, it takes a network-oriented approach, corresponding with the fact that travel and tourism is an interorganizational business. In order to provide a coherent picture, the work is located within a triangle of tourism research, information technology and computer science, and management science.

 **Springer**WienNewYork

A-1201 Wien, Sachsenplatz 4–6, P.O.Box 89, Fax +43.1.330 24 26, e-mail: books@springer.at, Internet: **www.springer.at**
D-69126 Heidelberg, Haberstraße 7, Fax +49.6221.345-229, e-mail: orders@springer.de
USA, Secaucus, NJ 07096-2485, P.O. Box 2485, Fax +1.201.348-4505, e-mail: orders@springer-ny.com
Eastern Book Service, Japan, Tokyo 113, 3–13, Hongo 3-chome, Bunkyo-ku, Fax +81.3.38 18 08 64, e-mail: orders@svt-ebs.co.jp

SpringerComputerScience

D. Buhalis, W. Schertler (eds.)

Information and Communication Technologies in Tourism 1999

Proceedings of the International Conference in Innsbruck,
Austria, 1999

1999. XII, 407 pages. 66 figures.
Softcover DM 118,–, öS 826,–
(recommended retail price)
ISBN 3-211-83258-0

Within the last six years the conference ENTER (International
Conference on Information and Communication Technologies in
Tourism) united various experts – practitioners as well as researchers –
to exchange their experiences, ideas and visions in the sector of tourism and information technology (IT). The proceedings of the conference provide an international platform to discuss the topical situation
and future trends, and the possibilities to shape the own strategies.
The following topics are treated in this year's volume:
• knowledge management in tourism
• changing consumer behaviour through information technology
• using IT to support consumer choice and skills
• engineering tourism applications
• the empowerment of small and medium-sized enterprises through IT
• using IT for hospitality management
• using IT to redesign travel distributions and destination marketing
  systems and IT developments
The emphasis of this year's contributions lies on the strategic components more than on the technical issues.

 SpringerWienNewYork

A-1201 Wien, Sachsenplatz 4–6, P.O.Box 89, Fax +43.1.330 24 26, e-mail: books@springer.at, Internet: www.springer.at
D-69126 Heidelberg, Haberstraße 7, Fax +49.6221.345-229, e-mail: orders@springer.de
USA, Secaucus, NJ 07096-2485, P.O. Box 2485, Fax +1.201.348-4505, e-mail: orders@springer-ny.com
Eastern Book Service, Japan, Tokyo 113, 3–13, Hongo 3-chome, Bunkyo-ku, Fax +81.3.38 18 08 64, e-mail: orders@svt-ebs.co.jp

SpringerEurographics

N. Magnenat-Thalmann,
D. Thalmann (eds.)

Computer Animation and Simulation '99

Proceedings of the Eurographics
Workshop in Milano, Italy,
September 7–8, 1999

1999. X, 230 pages. 148 partly coloured figures.
Softcover DM 89,–, öS 625,–. ISBN 3-211-83392-7

E. Gröller, H. Löffelmann,
W. Ribarsky (eds.)

Data Visualization '99

Proceedings of the Joint EURO-
GRAPHICS and IEEE TCVG Symposium
on Visualization in Vienna, Austria,
May 26–28, 1999

1999. XII, 340 pages. 230 partly coloured figures.
Softcover DM 118,–. öS 826,–. ISBN 3-211-83344-7

D. J. Duke, A. Puerta (eds.)

Design, Specification and Verification of Interactive Systems '99

Proceedings of the Eurographics Workshop in Braga, Portugal, June 2–4, 1999

1999. IX, 280 pages. 89 figures.
Softcover DM 118,–, öS 826,–. ISBN 3-211-83405-2

D. Lischinski, W. Larson (eds.)

Rendering Techniques '99

Proceedings of the Eurographics
Workshop in Granada, Spain,
June 21–23, 1999

1999. XI, 382 pages. 212 partly coloured figures.
Softcover DM 118,–. öS 826,–. ISBN 3-211-83382-X

M. Gervautz, A. Hildebrand,
D. Schmalstieg (eds.)

Virtual Environments '99

Proceedings of the Eurographics
Workshop in Vienna, Austria,
May 31–June 1, 1999

1999. X, 191 pages. 78 figures.
Softcover DM 85,–, öS 595,–. ISBN 3-211-83347-1

B. Arnaldi, G. Hégron (eds.)

Computer Animation and Simulation '98

Proceedings of the Eurographics
Workshop in Lisbon, Portugal,
August 31–September 1, 1998

1999. VII, 126 pages. 82 figures.
Softcover DM 85,–, öS 595,–. ISBN 3-211-83257-2

All prices are recommended retail prices.

 SpringerWienNewYork

A-1201 Wien, Sachsenplatz 4–6, P.O.Box 89, Fax +43.1.330 24 26, e-mail: books@springer.at, Internet: www.springer.at
D-69126 Heidelberg, Haberstraße 7, Fax +49.6221.345-229, e-mail: orders@springer.de
USA, Secaucus, NJ 07096-2485, P.O. Box 2485, Fax +1.201.348-4505, e-mail: orders@springer-ny.com
Eastern Book Service, Japan, Tokyo 113, 3–13, Hongo 3-chome, Bunkyo-ku, Fax +81.3.38 18 08 64, e-mail: orders@svt-ebs.co.jp